Reader's Digest
GREAT
BIOGRAPHIES

Reader's
Digest

GREAT BIOGRAPHIES

selected
and
condensed by
the editors
of
Reader's
Digest

The Reader's Digest Association, Inc.
Pleasantville, New York
Cape Town, Hong Kong, London, Montreal, Sydney

READER'S DIGEST CONDENSED BOOKS
Editor-in-Chief: John S. Zinsser, Jr.
Executive Editor: Barbara J. Morgan
Managing Editors: Anne H. Atwater, Ann Berryman, Tanis H. Erdmann,
Thomas Froncek, Marjorie Palmer
Senior Staff Editors: Jean E. Aptakin, Virginia Rice (Rights), Ray Sipherd, Angela Weldon
Senior Editors: M. Tracy Brigden, Linn Carl, Joseph P. McGrath,
James J. Menick, Margery D. Thorndike
Associate Editors: Thomas S. Clemmons, Alice Jones-Miller, Maureen A. Mackey
Senior Copy Editors: Claire A. Bedolis, Jeane Garment, Jane F. Neighbors
Associate Copy Editors: Maxine Bartow, Rosalind H. Campbell, Jean S. Friedman
Assistant Copy Editors: Ainslie Gilligan, Jeanette Gingold, Marilyn J. Knowlton
Art Director: William Gregory
Executive Art Editors: Soren Noring, Angelo Perrone
Associate Art Editors, Research: George Calas, Jr., Katherine Kelleher

CB PROJECTS
Executive Editor: Herbert H. Lieberman
Senior Editors: Dana Adkins, Catherine T. Brown, John R. Roberson

CB INTERNATIONAL EDITIONS
Executive Editor: Francis Schell
Senior Editor: Gary Q. Arpin

Library of Congress Cataloging-in-Publication Data
Reader's digest great biographies.
Contents: v. 1. The Spirit of St. Louis/by Charles A. Lindbergh.
Florence Nightingale/by Cecil Woodham-Smith.
Edison/by Matthew Josephson.
Hans Christian Andersen/by Rumer Godden—[etc.]
1. Biography—Collected works. I. Reader's Digest Association.
II. Reader's digest. III. Title: Great biographies.
CT101.R42 1987 920'.02 86-29816 ISBN 0-89577-260-4 (v.2)

Printed in the United States of America

Contents

A CONDENSATION OF

ABRAHAM
LINCOLN

The
Prairie
Years

by
CARL SANDBURG

ILLUSTRATED BY
JOHN FALTER

On February 12, 1959, the one hundred and fiftieth anniversary of the birth of Abraham Lincoln, America's great—many say greatest—President, the poet Carl Sandburg addressed a hushed United States Congress:

"Not often in the story of mankind does a man arrive on earth who is both steel and velvet, who is as hard as rock and soft as drifting fog, who holds in his heart and mind the paradox of terrible storm and peace unspeakable and perfect."

No one could more eloquently have evoked the essence of Abraham Lincoln's tragic yet triumphant spirit. For Carl Sandburg, in one of history's monumental labors of love and writing, had spent more than half his life assembling a massive, six-volume, Pulitzer Prize-winning Lincoln biography. Like Lincoln, Sandburg had grown up on the Illinois prairies. As a boy, he had known men and women who remembered Abe Lincoln firsthand. And in trying, with a scholar's dedication and a poet's vision, to understand and explain Lincoln, Carl Sandburg was also struggling to understand and define America itself.

How well he succeeded in this struggle is glowingly evident in *The Prairie Years*, which tells of the boy and the man on his way to becoming the beloved, brooding figure we all remember.

Chapter 1

IN THE YEAR 1776, when the thirteen American colonies of England gave to the world that famous piece of paper known as the Declaration of Independence, there was a captain of Virginia militia living in Rockingham County, named Abraham Lincoln.

He was a farmer with a 210-acre farm deeded to him by his father, John Lincoln, one of the many settlers who were taking the green hills and slopes of the Shenandoah Valley and putting their plows to ground never touched with farming tools by the red men, the Indians, who had held it for thousands of years.

The work of driving out the red men so that the white men could farm in peace was not yet finished. In that same year of 1776, Captain Abraham Lincoln's company marched against Cherokee tribes to the south and west. It was a time of much fighting. Virginia was sending young men to the north and east to join the colonial soldiers under General George Washington. Amos Lincoln, a kinsman of Abraham, up in Massachusetts, was one of the white men who, the story ran, rigged out as Indians, went on board a British ship and dumped a cargo of tea overboard. There was a Hananiah Lincoln, a first cousin of

Abraham, who fought at Brandywine under Washington; and Jacob Lincoln, a brother of Abraham, was at Yorktown, a captain under Washington at the finish of the Revolutionary War. These Lincolns in Virginia came from Berks County in Pennsylvania and traced back to Lincolns in New England and Old England. Though they were fighting men, there was a strain of Quaker blood in them; they came from people who kept silence or spoke "as the spirit of the heart moved"; they were a serene, peaceable, obstinate people.

Now Abraham Lincoln had taken for a wife a woman named Bathsheba Herring. And she bore him three sons, Mordecai, Josiah, and Thomas, and two daughters, Mary and Nancy.

This family of a wife and five children Abraham Lincoln took on horses in the year 1782 and moved to Kentucky. For years his friend, Daniel Boone, had been coming back from trips to Kentucky, telling of valleys rich with black land and blue grass. So, while Bathsheba was still carrying in her arms the baby, Thomas, it happened that Abraham Lincoln sold his farm; they packed their belongings, especially the rifle, ax, and plow; they mounted horses and joined a party which headed down the Shenandoah Valley, around through Cumberland Gap, and up into Kentucky. This was the trail worn by Boone and his friends following an old buffalo path. Now it was more than a trail. It was called the Wilderness Road.

Tall mountains loomed about them with long blue shadows at sunup and sundown as they traveled, camped, broke camp, and traveled again. And as they rode they watched the mountains with keen eyes for any moving patch of shrub or tree—the red men who ambushed enemies might be there.

Coming through safe to Kentucky, Abraham Lincoln located on the Green River, where he filed claims for more than two thousand acres. He had been there three or four years when, one day, as he was working in a field, the rifle shot of an Indian killed him. After that, his children and his children's children scattered across Kentucky, Tennessee, Indiana, and Illinois.

Tom Lincoln, growing up, lived in different places in Kentucky, sometimes with his kith and kin, sometimes hiring out to farmers, and somehow betweenwhiles managing to learn the carpenter's trade and cabinetmaking. He bought a horse—and paid taxes on it. He put in a year on the farm of his uncle, Isaac Lincoln, in east Tennessee. He moved to Hardin County in Kentucky while still a young bachelor, and bought a farm on Mill Creek, where it was still wilderness, and once he bought a pair of silk suspenders for a dollar and a half at a time when most men were using homemade hickory-bark galluses. As he came to his full growth he was about five feet, nine inches tall, weighing about 185 pounds, with dark hazel eyes, a round face, and coarse black hair. A slow man with quiet manners, he still knew yarns, could crack jokes, and had a reputation as a story-teller. He never had much time for the alphabet, but could read some, and could sign his name.

When Tom Lincoln was getting along in his twenties, he looked for a woman to travel through life with, for better or worse. For a time he gave his best jokes to Sarah Bush, the daughter of a hardworking farmer of German descent, a young woman with a shining face and steady eyes. But it happened that Sarah Bush wanted Daniel Johnston for a husband and he wanted her.

Another young woman Tom's eyes fell on was a brunette sometimes called Nancy Hanks because she was a daughter of Lucy Hanks, and sometimes called Nancy Sparrow because she was an adopted daughter of Thomas and Elizabeth Sparrow and lived with the Sparrow family.

Lucy Hanks had welcomed her child Nancy into life in Virginia about 1784 and had traveled the Wilderness Road carrying what was to her a precious bundle through the Cumberland Gap and on into Kentucky. She was nineteen when she made this trip with her family. The name of her baby's father is unknown, vanished from any documents or letters that may have existed. In any case, Lucy and her child had to get along without him, even though Lucy might croon in the evening twilight to the little face in the sweet bundle, "Hush thee, hush thee, thy father's a gentleman."

While Nancy was still learning to walk and talk, her mother Lucy seems to have been talked about as too free and easy in her behavior, too wild in her ways. But in time she proved herself a woman of strengths and vitality, of passion for life and brave living. In 1791 she married Henry Sparrow, a Virginia-born Revolutionary War veteran, and the talk about her running wild let down. Eight children came, and in those days of little schooling she taught them all to read and write, Lucy Hanks being one of the few women of that time and locality who could herself read and write.

After she had married Henry Sparrow her daughter Nancy had gone under the roof of Thomas Sparrow, a brother of Henry, and Elizabeth Hanks Sparrow, a sister of Lucy. Under the same roof was an adopted boy named Dennis Hanks, a son of a Nancy Hanks who was one of three sisters of Lucy. There were still other Nancy Hankses in Hardin County and those who spoke of any Nancy Hanks often had to mention which one they meant.

Tom Lincoln had seen this particular Nancy Hanks living with the Sparrows and noticed that she was shrewd and dark and lonesome. He had heard her tremulous voice in church camp meetings; he had seen her at preachings in cabins when her face stood out against the firelights of the burning logs. She could read the Bible, and had read in other books.

Her dark skin, dark brown hair, keen gray eyes, slender build—these formed the outward shape of a woman carrying something strange and cherished along her ways of life. She was sad with sorrows like dark stars in blue mist. But hope was burned deep in her that beyond the harsh clay paths of today, the everyday scrubbing, washing, fixing, there are pastures and purple valleys of song. She believed in God, in the Bible, in mankind, in the past and future, in babies, people, animals, flowers, in time and the eternities outside of time. She knew . . . but so much of what she believed was yonder—always yonder; and there was so little time to think or sing about the glory she believed in.

On June 12, 1806, at Richard Berry's place, Beechland, Thomas Lincoln, twenty-eight years old, and Nancy Hanks, twenty-three years old, came before the Reverend Jesse Head to be joined together in the holy estate of matrimony "agreeable to the rites and ceremonies of the Methodist Episcopal Church."

After the wedding came "the infare," the Kentucky-style wedding celebration. One guest who was there said, "We had bear meat, venison, wild turkey and ducks, eggs wild and tame, maple sugar lumps tied on a string to bite off for coffee or whisky, syrup in big gourds, peach and honey; a sheep that two families barbecued whole over coals of wood burned in a pit, and covered with green boughs to keep the juices in; and a race for the whisky bottle."

The new husband put his June bride on his horse and they rode away on the red clay road along the timber trails to Elizabethtown. Their new home was in a cabin close to the courthouse. Tom worked at the carpenter's trade, made cabinets, doorframes, window sash, and coffins. A daughter was born and they named her Sarah. Tom's reputation as a solid, reliable man was growing.

In May and the blossom time of the year 1808, Tom and Nancy with little Sarah moved out from Elizabethtown to the farm of George Brownfield, where Tom did carpenter work and helped farm. The Lincolns had a cabin of their own to live in. It stood among wild crab-apple trees.

And the smell of wild crab-apple blossoms, and the low crying of all wild things, came keen that summer to the nostrils of Nancy Hanks.

The summer stars that year shook out pain and warning, strange laughters, for Nancy Hanks.

THE SAME YEAR SAW the Lincolns moved to a place on the South Fork of Nolin Creek, about two and a half miles from Hodgenville. They were trying to farm a little piece of ground and make a home. They lived in a cabin of logs cut from the timber nearby. The floor was packed-down dirt. One door, swung on leather hinges, let them in and out. One small window gave a lookout on the weather, rain or snow, sun and trees.

One morning in February of the year 1809, Tom Lincoln came out of his cabin to the road, stopped a neighbor and asked him to tell "the granny woman," Aunt Peggy Walters, that Nancy would need help soon.

On the morning of February 12, a Sunday, the granny

woman was there at the cabin. And she and Tom Lincoln and the moaning Nancy Hanks welcomed into a world of battle and blood, of whispering dreams and wistful dust, a new child, a boy.

A little later that morning Tom Lincoln threw some extra wood on the fire, went out of the cabin, and walked two miles up the road to where the Sparrows, Tom and Betsy, lived. Dennis Hanks, the nine-year-old boy adopted by the Sparrows, met Tom at the door. In his slow way of talking Tom Lincoln told them, "Nancy's got a boy baby." A half-sheepish look was in his eyes, as though maybe more babies were not wanted in Kentucky just then.

Dennis Hanks took to his feet down the road to the Lincoln cabin. There he saw Nancy Hanks on a bed of poles cleated to a corner of the cabin, under warm bearskins. She turned her dark head from looking at the baby to look at Dennis and smile. He stood by the bed, his eyes wide open, watching the even, quiet breaths of this fresh, soft red baby.

"What you goin' to name him, Nancy?" the boy asked.

"Abraham," was the answer, "after his grandfather."

Soon came Betsy Sparrow. She washed the baby, put a yellow petticoat and a linsey shirt on him, cooked dried berries with honey for Nancy, put the cabin in better order, kissed Nancy and comforted her, saying she would come again in the morning, and went home.

Little Dennis rolled up in a bearskin and slept by the fireplace that night. He heard the crying of the newborn child once in the night and the feet of the father moving on the dirt floor to help the mother and the little one. In the morning he took a long look at the baby and said to himself, "Its skin looks just like red cherry pulp." He asked if he could hold it. Nancy, as she passed the little one into Dennis's arms, said, "Be keerful, Dennis, fur you air the fust boy he's ever seen."

Dennis swung the baby back and forth, chattering about how tickled he was to have a new cousin to play with. The baby screwed up its face and began crying with no letup. Dennis turned to Betsy Sparrow, handed her the baby, and said to her, "Aunt, take him! He'll never come to much."

So came the birth of Abraham Lincoln that twelfth of February in the year 1809—in silence and pain from a wilderness mother on a bed of cornhusks and bearskins in a one-room cabin —with an early laughing child prophecy he would "never come to much."

Chapter 2

THE LINCOLN FAMILY lived three crop years on the farm where baby Abraham was born. It was discouraging land, with stony soils and thick underbrush. It was called the Rock Spring farm because at the foot of one of its sloping hills, where mossy rocks curved in like the beginning of a cave, there was a never-ending flow of clear, cool water.

With the baby she called Abe in her arms, Nancy Hanks sometimes came to this Rock Spring if she had an hour free from cooking, washing, sewing, spinning, weaving. She would sit with her child and her thoughts, look at running water and green moss. The secrets of the mingled drone and hush of the place gave her reminders of Bible language, *Be ye comforted,* or *Peace, be still.*

The baby grew, learning to sit up, to crawl over the dirt floor of the cabin; the gristle became bone; the father joked about the long legs getting longer; the mother joked about how quick he grew out of one shirt into another.

Sparrows and Hankses who came visiting said, "He's solemn as a papoose." An easy and a light bundle he was to carry when the family moved ten miles northeast to a farm on Knob Creek, near the main pike from Louisville to Nashville.

On the Knob Creek farm the child Abraham Lincoln learned to talk, to form words with the tongue and the roof of the mouth and the force of breath. "Pappy" and "Mammy," the words of his people meaning father and mother, were among the first syllables. He learned what the word "name" meant; his name was Abraham, the same as Abraham in the Bible, the same as his grandfather Abraham. It was "Abe" for short; if his mother called in the dark, "Is that you, Abe?" he answered,

"Yes, Mammy, it's me." The name of the family he belonged to was "Lincoln" or "Linkun," though most people called it "Linkern" and it was sometimes spelled "Linkhorn."

The family lived there on Knob Creek farm from the time Abe was three till he was past seven. Here he was told "Kaintucky" meant the state he was living in; Knob Creek farm, Hodgenville, the land he walked on, were all part of Kentucky. Yet they were also part of something bigger, "our country," the "United States." One summer morning his father started the day by stepping out of the door and shooting a rifle into the sky; and his father explained it was the day to make a big noise because it was the "Fourth of July," the day the United States first called itself a "free and independent" nation.

His folks talked like other folks in the neighborhood. They called themselves "pore" people. A man learned in books was "eddicated." What was certain was "sartin." A man silent was a "say-nothin'." They asked, "Have ye et?" There were dialogues, "Kin ye?" "No, I cain't." And if a woman had an idea of doing something she said, "I had a idy to."

Words like "independent" bothered the boy. So did others, such as "predestination." He was hungry to understand the meanings of words. He would ask what "independent" meant, or "predestination," and when he was told the meaning he lay awake nights thinking about the meaning of the meaning.

AGAIN, IN 1812, neighbor helpers had come and Nancy had given birth to her third child. They named him Thomas but he died a few days after and Sarah and Abe saw, in a coffin their father made, the little cold still face. They made their first acquaintance with the look of death in their own one-room cabin.

When Abe was seven, he and Sarah walked four miles a day going to the Knob Creek school to learn to read and write. Zachariah Riney and Caleb Hazel were the teachers who brought him along from A B C to where he could write the name "A-b-r-a-h-a-m L-i-n-c-o-l-n" and count numbers beginning with one, two, three, and so on. He heard twice two is four.

The schoolhouse was built of logs, with a dirt floor, no window, one door. The scholars learned their lessons by saying them to themselves out loud till it was time to recite; alphabets, multiplication tables, and the letters of spelled words were all in the air at once. It was a "blab school"; so they called it. Attending it, young Abe learned to form letters and shape words. He scrawled words with charcoal, he shaped them in the dust, in sand, in snow. Writing had a fascination for him.

Abe was also the chore boy of the Knob Creek farm as soon as he grew big enough to run errands, to hold a pine knot at night lighting his father at a job, or to carry water, fill the woodbox, clean ashes from the fireplace, hoe weeds, pick berries, grapes, persimmons. He hunted the timbers and came back with walnuts, hickory and hazelnuts. His hands knew the stinging blisters from using a hoe handle back and forth a summer afternoon, and in autumn the mash of walnut stain that wouldn't wash off, with all the rinsing and scrubbing of Nancy Hanks's homemade soap. He went swimming with Austin Gollaher; they got their backs sunburnt so the skin peeled off.

Wearing only a shirt—no hat nor pants—Abe rode a horse hitched to a bull-tongue plow. He helped his father with seed corn, beans, onions, potatoes. He ducked out of the way of the heels of the stallion and brood mares his father kept and paid taxes on.

One year Tom Lincoln was appointed a "road surveyor." That the county was beginning to think about good roads showed that civilization was breaking through on the wilderness. And that Tom Lincoln was named as road surveyor showed he was held in respect as a citizen and taxpayer.

Though Tom Lincoln was paying taxes on his farm, he was suspicious that even if he did get it cleared and paid for, the land might be taken away from him. This was happening to others; they had the wrong kind of papers. Knob Creek settlers talked a good deal about land titles.

Meanwhile, Hardin County had been filling up with Negroes, slave black men, bought and sold among the well-to-do. More than half the population of Hardin County were colored. And it seemed that as more slave black men were brought in, a poor white man had a harder time to get along.

While these changes were coming in Kentucky, the territory

of Indiana, just across the Ohio River, came into the Union as a state whose law declared "the holding any part of the human creation in slavery, or involuntary servitude, can only originate in tyranny." Here were two shores, two soils: one where the buying and selling of black slaves went on, the other where the Negro was held to be "part of the human creation" and not property for buying and selling. But both soils were part of the Union of states.

Letters and reports reaching Hardin County about this time told of rich, black lands in Indiana, with more bushels of corn to the acre than in Kentucky, government land with clear title, the right kind of papers, for two dollars an acre. This helped Tom Lincoln to decide in the year 1816 to move to Indiana.

That fall, Abe watched his father cut down trees, cut out logs, and fasten those logs into a flatboat on Knob Creek. And he had his thoughts, some running ahead wondering how Indiana would look, some going back to his seven little years in Kentucky. Here he had curled around his mother's apron, watched her face and listened to her reading the Bible at the cabin log fire, her fingers rambling through his hair, the hands patting him on the cheek and under the chin. God was real to his mother; he tried to make pictures in his head of the face of God far off and away in the sky, watching Kentucky, Hodgenville, Knob Creek, and all the rest of the world He had made. His thoughts could go back to the first time on a winter night around the fire when he lay flat on his stomach listening to his father as he told about his brothers, Mordecai and Josiah, and their father, Abraham Lincoln, who had staked out claims for more than two thousand acres of land on the Green River. One day Abraham Lincoln and his three boys were working in a field; all of a sudden the father doubled up with a groan of pain and crumpled to the ground, just after the boys had heard a rifle shot and the whining of a bullet. "Indians," the boys yelled to each other.

And Mordecai ran to a cabin, Josiah started across the fields to a fort to bring help, while Tom Lincoln—little knee-high Tom—stooped over his father's bleeding body and wondered what he could do. He looked up to see an Indian standing over

him, and a shining bangle hanging down over the Indian's shoulder close to the heart.

The Indian clutched upward with his hands, doubled with a groan, and crumpled to the ground; Mordecai with a rifle at a peephole in the cabin had aimed his rifle at the shining bangle, and Tom was so near he heard the bullet plug its hole into the red man. Tom; that was his father.

And there was his mother, his "mammy," the woman other people called Nancy or Nancy Hanks. . . . It was so dark and strange about her. There was such sweetness. Yet there used to be a fresher sweetness. There had been one baby they buried. Then there was Sally—and him, little Abe. Did the children cost her something? Did they pull her down? . . . The baby that came and was laid away so soon, only three days after it came, in so little a grave: that hurt his mother; she was sick and tired more often after that. . . . There were such lights and shadows back in her eyes. She wanted—what did she want?

Well—a boy seven years old isn't supposed to know much; he goes along and tries to do what the big people tell him to do. . . . They have been young and seen trouble: maybe they know.

All that fall of 1816, Abe ran after tools his father called for, a hammer, a saw, a knife. If his father said, "Fetch me a drink of water," the boy fetched; his legs belonged to his father. And he helped carry chairs, tables, household goods, and carpenter's tools, loading them onto the flatboat.

Nancy Hanks and Sarah and Abe stayed on the farm while the husband and father floated down Knob Creek to Salt River and into the Ohio River according to plan. Landing on the Indiana side, Tom left his household goods at the house of a man called Posey. He decided to live and to farm on a quarter section of land on Little Pigeon Creek; he notched the trees with his ax, cleared away brush and piled it, as the government land laws required. His Indiana homestead was now ready for a cabin and a family; he went back to the Knob Creek home in Kentucky and told the family he reckoned they'd all put in the winter up in "Indianny."

Pots, pans, kettles, blankets, the family Bible, and other things were put into bags and loaded on horses. Nancy and Sarah climbed on one horse, Tom and Abe on another. They had about a hundred miles to go, what with all the curves around hills, timbers, and rivers. When it was hard going for the horses, the father and mother walked. That hundred-mile ride made little Abe's eyes open. They were going deeper into the wilderness, and Abe saw miles and miles of wild raw country, rolling land with trees everywhere, tall oaks and elms, maples, birches, dogwood, underbrush tied down by ever-winding grapevines. Then they came to the Ohio River, and it was the biggest stretch of shining water his eyes had ever seen. And Abe thought how different it was from Knob Creek, which he could walk across on a log—if he didn't let his feet slip from under.

They crossed the river at Thompson's Ferry, where they reclaimed the household goods which Tom had left with Posey. They got a wagon, loaded the goods, and drove sixteen miles to their claim. The trail was so narrow that a few times Tom Lincoln got off the wagon with an ax and cut brush and trees so the wagon could pass through. It was a hired wagon and horses they came with, and the wagon and horse team were taken back to Posey.

So they arrived at Little Pigeon Creek, without a horse or a cow, without a house, with a little piece of land under their feet and the wintry sky high over. Naked they had come into the world; almost naked they came to Little Pigeon Creek, Indiana.

The whole family pitched in and built a pole shed or "half-faced camp." Two trees about fourteen feet apart formed corner posts of a sort of cabin with three sides, the fourth side open, facing south. The sides and roof were covered with poles, branches, brush, and mud. At the open side, a log fire was kept burning night and day. When Tom built this cabin he didn't own the land it stood on. He was a "squatter." Not until October 1817 did he file his claim at the land office in Vincennes, to be paid for at two dollars an acre.

Here they lived a year, while Tom chopped logs for a new cabin to be built forty yards away. In fair weather, the pole shed was snug enough. When rainstorms or wind and snow broke through and drenched the place, it was a rough life.

Abe did the best he could helping Nancy and Sarah trim

branches off logs, cut brush, clear ground for planting, hoe weeds, tend the log fire. The heaviest regular chore of the children was walking a mile away to a spring and carrying a bucket of water back home. Their food was mostly game shot in the woods; they went barefoot most of the year; in the winter their shoes were homemade moccasins; they were up with the sun in the morning; their lighting at night was fire logs. In summer and early fall the flies and mosquitoes swarmed.

They were part of the American Frontier. That year of 1816 sixteen thousand wagons had come along one turnpike in Pennsylvania, heading west, with people hungry for new land, a new home, just like Tom Lincoln. The Great Plains beckoned them—that vast area between the Mississippi River and the Rocky Mountains which Napoleon Bonaparte had sold to President Jefferson only six years before Abe Lincoln was born. And the eight million people in the United States, white men who had pushed the Indians over the eastern mountains, were now fighting to clear the Great Plains and the southern valleys of the red men, and were swarming westward. Many of these eight million were children and grandchildren of men who had come from the old countries of Europe. And they were coming still, out of war-taxed and war-crippled Europe, steady lines of ships were taking people across the water to America. And lines of ships sailing to Africa with whisky, calico, and silk, were coming back to America loaded with Negroes.

Now, as the wagons, by thousands a year, were slipping through the Allegheny Mountains, heading west for the two-dollar-an-acre government land, many steered clear of the South; they couldn't buy slaves; and they were suspicious of slavery; it was safer to go farming where white men did all the work.

At first the stream of wagons and settlers moving west had kept close to the Ohio River. Then it began spreading in a fan shape up north and west.

Sometimes along the pikes, roads, and trails, broken wagon wheels were left behind and prairie grass would grow up over the spokes and hubs. And nearby, sometimes, there would be a rusty skillet, empty moccasins, and the bones of horses and men.

In the dog days, in the long rains, in the casual blizzards, some had stuck it out—and lost. There came a saying, a pithy, brutal folk proverb: "The cowards never started and the weak ones died by the way."

Little Abe Lincoln, nearly eight years old, living in a pole shed there on Little Pigeon Creek in Indiana in that winter of 1816, was of the blood and breath of many of these things, and would know them better in the years to come.

DURING THE YEAR 1817, Abe Lincoln, now going on nine, had an ax put in his hands and began helping his father cut down trees and notch logs for the corners of the new cabin.

Once during that year Abe took a gun as a flock of wild turkeys came toward the unfinished log cabin and, standing inside, shot through a crack and killed one of the big birds; and after that, somehow, he never felt like pulling the trigger on game birds. Nor would he shoot at deer. His father did the shooting; the deer gave them meat for Nancy's skillet; and the skins were tanned, cut, and stitched into shirts, trousers, moccasins.

A few days of this year in which the cabin was building, Nancy told Abe to wash his face and hands extra clean; she combed his hair, kissed him, and sent him to school—nine miles and back—Abe and Sally hand in hand hiking through timberland where bear, coon, and wildcats ran wild. Tom Lincoln used to say Abe was going to have "a real eddication," explaining, "You air a-goin' to larn readin', writin', and cipherin'." But now he complained it was a waste of time to send the children nine miles just to sit with other children and read out loud.

At last after months the cabin stood up, four walls fitted together with a roof, a one-room house eighteen feet square. The floor was packed dirt. A log fire lighted the inside; no windows were cut in the walls. Pegs stuck in the side of a wall made a ladder for young Abe to climb up to a loft to sleep on a hump of dry leaves; rain came through chinks of the roof onto his bearskin cover. A table and three-legged stools had the top sides smoothed with an ax, and the bark side under, in the style called puncheon.

Fall time came and they were moved into the new cabin, when one day horses and a wagon came breaking into the clearing. It was Tom and Betsy Sparrow and their seventeen-year-old boy, Dennis Hanks, who had come from Hodgenville, Kentucky, to cook and sleep in the pole shed of the Lincoln family till they could locate land and settle. Hardly a year had passed, however, when both Tom and Betsy Sparrow were taken down with the "milksick," beginning with a whitish coat on the tongue. Both died and were buried in September on a little hill in a clearing in the timbers nearby.

Soon after, there came to Nancy Hanks Lincoln that white coating of the tongue; her vitals burned; the tongue turned brownish; her feet and hands grew cold and colder, her pulse slow and slower. She knew she was dying, called for her children and spoke to them her last choking words. Sarah and Abe leaned over the bed. A bony hand of the struggling mother went out, putting its fingers into the boy's sandy black hair; her fluttering guttural words seemed to say he must grow up and be good to his sister and father.

So, on October 5, 1818, on a bed of poles in a corner of the cabin, the body of Nancy Hanks Lincoln lay, looking tired . . . tired . . . with a peace settling in the pinched corners of the sweet, weary mouth, and silence slowly etching away the lines of pain and hunger drawn around the closed eyes. To the children who tiptoed in, stood still, cried their tears of want and longing, whispered "Mammy, Mammy," and heard only their own whispers answering, she looked as though new secrets had come to her in place of the old secrets given up with the breath of life.

Tom Lincoln took a log left over from the building of the cabin, and he and Dennis Hanks whipsawed the log into planks, planed the planks smooth, and made them of a measure for a box to bury the dead wife and mother in. Little Abe, with a jackknife, whittled pinewood pegs. And then, while Dennis and Abe held the planks, Tom bored holes and stuck the pegs through the holes. This was the coffin, and they carried it the next day to the same little timber clearing nearby, where a few weeks before they had buried Tom and Betsy Sparrow. It was in the way of a deer run leading to saltish water; light feet and shy hoofs ran over those early winter graves.

So the woman, Nancy Hanks Lincoln, died, thirty-four years old, a pioneer sacrifice, with memories of monotonous, endless everyday chores, of mystic Bible verses read over and over for their promises, and with memories of blue wistful hills and a summer when the crab-apple blossoms flamed white and she carried a boy-child into the world.

THE MILKSICK took more people in the neighborhood the same year, and Tom Lincoln whipsawed planks for more coffins. One settler lost four milch cows and eleven calves. The nearest doctor for people or cattle was thirty-five miles away.

Lonesome and dark months came for Abe and Sarah. Twelve-year-old Sarah acted as housekeeper and cook, and Tom Lincoln with the help of Dennis and Abe tried to clear more land and make the farm go. But worst of all for Abe and Sarah in that dark time were the weeks when their father went away.

Elizabethtown, Kentucky, was the place Tom Lincoln headed for. As he footed it through the woods he was saying over to himself a speech—the words he would say to Sarah Bush Johnston. He had once almost courted her, but she had married Daniel Johnston. Her husband had died a few years before, and she was now in Tom's thoughts.

He went straight to her house in Elizabethtown. "I have no wife and you no husband," he argued. "I came a-purpose to marry you. I knowed you from a gal and you knowed me from a boy. I've no time to lose; and if you're willin' let it be done straight off."

Her answer was, "I got debts." He paid the debts; a license was issued; and they were married on December 2, 1819.

Trying to explain why the two of them took up with each other so quickly, Dennis Hanks later said, "Tom had a kind o' way with women, an' maybe it was somethin' she took comfort in to have a man that didn't drink an' cuss none."

Little Abe and Sarah, living in the lonesome cabin on Little Pigeon Creek, Indiana, got a nice surprise one morning when four horses and a wagon came into their clearing, and their father jumped off, then Sarah Bush Lincoln, the new wife and mother, then John, Sarah, and Matilda Johnston, her three children by her first husband. Next off the wagon came a feather mattress, feather pillows, a black-walnut bureau, a large clothes chest, a table, chairs, pots and skillets, knives, forks, spoons. Abe ran his fingers over the slick wood of the bureau; this was the first time he had touched such fine things.

"Here's your new mammy," his father told Abe as the boy looked up at a strong, large-boned, rosy woman with a kindly face and eyes, with a steady voice, steady ways. Right from the beginning she was warm and friendly for Abe's hands to touch. She took the corn husks Abe had been sleeping on and piled them in the yard; and Abe sunk his head and bones that night in a feather pillow and a feather mattress.

Chapter 3

THE ONE-ROOM CABIN now sheltered eight people. At bedtime the men and boys undressed first, the women and girls following. Dennis and Abe climbed to the loft to sleep and liked it when later the logs were chinked against rain or snow coming in on them.

When he was eleven Abe went to school again. School kept at Pigeon Creek when a schoolmaster happened to drift in, and school was out when he drifted away. Andrew Crawford taught Abe in 1820. He had the barefoot boys in butternut jeans learning "manners" and how to open a door, walk in, and say, "Howdy do?" Two years later James Swaney was Abe's teacher, and then Azel Dorsey. With a turkey-buzzard quill Abe learned to write his name in ink made of blackberry briarroot and copperas; then he would say to his cousin, "Denny, look at that. *Abraham Lincoln!* That stands fur me. Don't look a blamed bit like me!" And Dennis Hanks said later, "He'd stand and study it a spell. 'Peared to mean a heap to Abe."

Abe went to three different schools in Indiana besides two in Kentucky; he later said, however, that all his schooling "did not amount to one year."

What he got in the schools didn't satisfy him. A taste of books only made him hungry with a wanting of more and more of what was hidden between their covers. Starting along in his eleventh year came spells of abstraction. When Abe was spoken to, no answer came from him. "He might be a thousand miles away," they said. The roaming, fathoming, searching, questioning operations of the minds and hearts of poets, inventors, beginners who take facts stark, these were at work in him.

Other forces were at work also. When he was eleven years old, Abe's young body began to change. The juices and glands began to make a long, tall boy out of him. As the months and years went by, he noticed his lean wrists getting longer, his legs too, and he was now looking over the heads of other boys. Men said, "Land o' Goshen, that boy air a-growin'!" When he reached seventeen years, and they measured him, he was nearly six feet, four inches high, from the bottoms of his moccasins to the top of his skull.

These were years he was handling the ax. Except in spring plowing time and the fall fodder pulling, he was handling the ax nearly all the time. The insides of his hands took on callus thick as leather. He cleared openings in the timber, cut logs and puncheons, split firewood, built pigpens. He learned how to measure with his eye the half-circle swing of the ax so as to nick out the deepest possible chip from off a tree trunk. The trick of swaying his body easily on the hips so as to throw the heaviest possible weight into the blow of the ax—he learned that.

On winter mornings he wiped the frost from the ax handle, sniffed sparkles of air into his lungs, and beat a steady cleaving of blows into a big tree—till it fell—and he sat on the main log and ate his noon corn bread and fried salt pork—and joked with the squirrels that frisked and peeped at him from nearby trees.

He learned how to make his ax flash and bite into a sugar maple or a sycamore. The outside and the inside look of hickory and jack oak, elm and white oak, sassafras, dogwood, sumac—he came on their secrets. He could guess close to the time of the year, to the week of the month, by the way the leaves and branches of trees looked. He sniffed the seasons.

Often he worked alone in the timbers all day long with only

the sound of his own ax, or his own voice speaking to himself, or the crackling and swaying of branches in the wind, and the cries and whirs of animals and birds.

So he grew, to become hard, tough, wiry. The muscle on his bones and the cords and tendons and nerve centers became instruments to obey his wishes. He found with other men he could lift his own end of a log—and more too. One of the neighbors said he was strong as three men. Another said, "He can sink an ax deeper into wood than any man I ever saw."

He put his shoulders under a new-built corncrib one day and walked away with it to where the farmer wanted it. Four men, ready with poles to put under it and carry it, didn't need their poles.

One night after Abe had been helping thresh wheat on a neighbor's place, he went with Dennis Hanks, his stepbrother John Johnston, and some other boys to Gentryville, where a blacksmith shop and a store had started up. There the farmhands sat around, and while Jones, the storekeeper, passed the whisky jug, they told stories and gossiped. Going home late that night, the boys saw something in a mud puddle alongside the road. They stepped over to see whether it was a man or a hog. It was a man—drunk—snoring—and on a frosty, windy night. They shook him by the shoulders, but he went on sleeping, snoring. The cold wind was getting colder. The other boys said they were going home, and they left Abe alone with the sleeper. Abe stepped into the mud puddle, slung the man over his shoulders, carried him to Dennis Hanks's cabin, built a fire, rubbed him warm and left him sleeping off the whisky. And the man afterward said Abe saved his life.

He found he was fast, strong, and keen when he went against other boys in sports. On farms where he worked, he held his own at scuffling, wrestling. The time came when around Gentryville and Spencer County he was known as the best "rassler" of all, the champion. In jumping, footracing, pitching the crowbar, he won against the lads of his own age always, and usually won against those older than himself.

A misunderstanding came up one time between Abe Lincoln and William Grigsby. It ended with Grigsby so mad he chal-

lenged Abe to a fight. Abe looked down at Grigsby, smiled, and said the fight ought to be with John D. Johnston, Abe's step-brother. The day was set. Grigsby and Johnston, stripped to the waist, mauled at each other with bare knuckles.

A crowd stood around, forming a ring, cheering, yelling, till after a while they saw Johnston getting the worst of it. Then Abe Lincoln shouldered his way through the crowd, took hold of Grigsby, and threw him out of the center of the fight ring. And Abe called out, "I'm the big buck of this lick," and his eyes sweeping the circle of the crowd, he challenged, "If any of you want to try it, come on and whet your horns." A riot of wild fistfighting came then between the two gangs and for months around the Jones grocery store there was talk about which gang whipped the other.

Abe was earning his board, clothes, and lodgings, sometimes working for a neighbor farmer. He understood firsthand the scythe and the cradle for cutting hay and grain. Farmers called him to butcher for them at thirty-one cents a day, this when he was sixteen and seventeen years old. He could lift the slippery two-hundred-pound hog carcass, holding the hind hocks up while others hooked and swung the animal clear of the ground. When he was eighteen years old, he could take an ax at the end of the handle and hold it out in a steady horizontal line. He could tell his body to do almost impossible things, and the body obeyed.

Growing from boy to man, he was alone a good deal. In some years more of his time was spent in loneliness than in the company of other people. It happened, too, that this loneliness he knew was not like that of people in cities. It was the wilderness loneliness he became acquainted with, solved, filtered through body, eye, and brain. He lived with trees, with the bush wet with shining raindrops, with the burning bush of autumn, with the lone wild duck riding a north wind, and with the ax which is a one-man instrument. And he rested between spells of work in the springtime when the upward push of the new grass can be heard, and in autumn weeks when the rustle of a falling leaf lets go a whisper that a listening ear can catch.

He found his life thrown in ways where there was a certain

chance for a certain growth. And so he grew. Silence found him; he met silence. In the making of him as he was, the element of silence was immense.

WHEN JOHN HANKS, a cousin of Nancy Hanks, came to live with the Lincolns about 1823, there were nine persons sleeping, eating, washing, and dressing in the one-room cabin. In all the country round about, families were living in one-room cabins. Dennis Hanks said at a later time, "We lived the same as the Indians, 'ceptin' we took an interest in politics and religion."

Cash was scarce; venison hams, bacon slabs, and barrels of whisky served as money; there were seasons when storekeepers asked customers, "What kind of money have you today?" because so many sorts of wildcat dollar bills were passing around.

Farmers lost thirty and forty sheep in a single wolf raid. Toward the end of June came "fly time," when cows lost weight and gave less milk because they had to fight flies. For two or three months at the end of summer, horses weakened, unless covered with blankets, under the attacks of horseflies.

Men and women went barefoot except in the colder weather; women carried their shoes in their hands and put them on just before arrival at church meetings or at social parties.

Rains came, loosening the topsoil of the land where it was not held by grass roots; it was a yellow clay that softened to slush; in this yellow slush many a time Abe Lincoln walked ankle-deep; he was at home in clay. During six and seven months each year in the twelve fiercest formative years of his life, Abraham Lincoln had the pads of his foot soles bare against clay of the earth. It may be the earth told him in her own tough gypsy slang one or two knacks of living worth keeping.

So he took shape in a tall, long-armed cornhusker. When rain came in at the chinks of the cabin loft where he slept, soaking through the book Josiah Crawford loaned him, he pulled fodder two days to pay for the book, made a clean sweep, till there wasn't a blade left on a cornstalk in the field of Josiah Crawford.

His father was saying the big boy looked as if he had been roughhewn with an ax and needed smoothing with a jack plane. His stepmother told him she didn't mind his bringing dirt into the house on his feet; she could scour the floor; but she asked him to keep his head washed or he'd be rubbing the dirt on her nice whitewashed rafters. He put barefoot boys to wading in a mud puddle, picked them up one by one, carried them to the house upside down, and walked their muddy feet across the ceiling. The mother came in, laughed an hour at the foot tracks, told Abe he ought to be spanked—and he cleaned the ceiling so it looked new.

The mother said, "Abe never spoke a cross word to me in his life since we lived together." And she said Abe was truthful. As time went by, this stepmother of Abe became one of the rich, silent forces in his life. Besides keeping the floors, pots, pans, kettles, and milk crocks spick-and-span, weaving, sewing, mending, and managing with sagacity, she had a massive, bony, human strength backed with an elemental faith that the foundations of the world were mortised by God with unspeakable goodness of heart toward the human family. Hard as life was, she was thankful to be alive.

Sally Bush, the stepmother, was all of a good mother to Abe. If he broke out laughing when others saw nothing to laugh at, she let it pass as a sign of his thoughts working their own way. So far as she was concerned he had a right to do unaccountable things; since he never lied to her, why not? So she justified him. When Abe's sister, Sarah, married Aaron Grigsby and a year after died with her newborn child, it was Sally Bush who spoke comfort to the eighteen-year-old boy of Nancy Hanks burying his sister and the wraith of a child.

A neighbor woman sized him up by saying, "He could work when he wanted to, but he was no hand to pitch in like killing snakes." John Romine remarked: "Abe Lincoln worked for me, but was always reading and thinking. I used to get mad at him for it. I say he was awful lazy. He said to me one day that his father taught him to work, but he never taught him to love it."

After a fox chase with horses, Uncle Jimmy Larkin was telling how his horse won the race, was the best horse in the world, and never drew a long breath; Abe didn't listen; Uncle Jimmy told it again, and Abe said, "Why don't you tell us how many short breaths he drew?"

Abe had the pride of youth that resents the slur, the snub, besides the riotous blood that has always led youth in reckless exploits. When he was cutting up one day at the Crawford farmhouse, Mrs. Crawford asked, "What's going to become of you, Abe?" And with mockery of swagger, he answered, "Me? I'm going to be President of the United States."

He drew a red ear at a husking bee, kissed Green Taylor's girl, and in a fight the next day hit Green Taylor with an ear of corn, making a gash and a scar for life. For the day of the marriage of his sister Sarah to Aaron Grigsby, he wrote "Adam and Eve's Wedding Song," telling in doggerel how the Lord made woman from a rib taken from Adam's side. The three final verses read:

> *The woman was not taken*
> *From Adam's feet, we see,*
> *So he must not abuse her,*
> *The meaning seems to be.*
>
> *The woman was not taken*
> *From Adam's head, we know,*
> *To show she must not rule him—*
> *'Tis evidently so.*
>
> *The woman she was taken*
> *From under Adam's arm,*
> *So she must be protected*
> *From injuries and harm.*

Visitors to the Lincoln house were shown in a copybook the scribbling:

> *Abraham Lincoln*
> *his hand and pen.*
> *he will be good but*
> *god knows When.*

He grew as hickory grows, the torso lengthening and toughening. The sap mounted, the branches spread, leaves came with wind clamor in them. Growing up, he heard his father and his cousins John and Dennis Hanks tell neighbors this and that about

their families, what kind of men and women they had for kins-
folk, blood connections. And young Abe learned there were
things the Lincolns and Hankses didn't care to tell the neighbors
concerning Abe's mother Nancy and his grandmother Lucy.

Back in the shadows of the years had lived the dark, strange
woman, Lucy Hanks, with flame streaks in her. And the years
had beaten on her head, and circumstance had squeezed at her
heart and tried to smother her hopes. And she had lived to pick
a man she wanted to marry and borne him eight children and
brought them up to read and write in a time when few could
read and still fewer could write so much as their own names.

Young Abe Lincoln was free to have his thoughts about this
mother of his mother. He could ask himself about what is called
good and what is called bad and how they are crisscrossed in
the human mesh. He could ask whether sinners are always as
crooked as painted; whether people who call themselves good
are half the time as straight as the way they tell it.

Maybe he ought to go slow in any deep or fixed judgments
about people. Did the ghost of his lovable mother or the
phantom of his lovely grandmother seem to whisper something like that?

A mile across the fields from the Lincoln home was the
Pigeon Creek Baptist Church, a log-built meetinghouse put up
in 1822. Most of the church people could read only the shortest
words in the Bible, or none at all. They sat in the log meetinghouse on the split-log benches their own axes had shaped,
listening to the preacher reading from the Bible by the light
of fire logs. There was a consolation in the Beatitudes: *Blessed
are the meek: for they shall inherit the earth. . . . Blessed are the pure
in heart: for they shall see God.* And there was exquisite fore-
tokening: *In my Father's house are many mansions: if it were not so,
I would have told you.*

Beyond Indiana was something else; beyond the timber and
underbrush, the malaria, milksick, blood, sweat, tears, there
must be something else.

Young Abraham Lincoln saw certain of these Christians
with a clean burning fire, with inner reckonings that prompted
them to silence or action or speech, and they could justify them-

selves with a simple and final explanation that all things should be done decently and in order.

They met understanding from the solemn young Lincoln who had refused to join his schoolmates in torturing a live mud turtle, and had written a paper arguing against cruelty to animals; who once had taken his father's rifle and shot a prairie turkey and had never since shot any game at all; who could butcher a beef or hog for food but didn't like to see rabbit blood; who as a nine-year-old boy had stood over the winter grave of Nancy Hanks Lincoln; who would bother to lug on his shoulders and save from freezing the body of a man overloaded with whisky; who had seen one of his companions go insane and who used to get up before daylight and cross the fields to listen to the crooning, falsetto cackling and disconnected babbling of one whose brain had suddenly lost control of things done decently and in order.

The footsteps of death, silent as the moving sundial of a tall sycamore, were a presence. Time and death, the partners who operate leaving no more track than mist, had to be reckoned in the scheme of life. A day is a shooting star. The young Lincoln had copied a rhyme:

> Time! what an empty vapor 'tis!
> And days how swift they are:
> Swift as an Indian arrow—
> Fly on like a shooting star,
> The present moment just is here,
> Then slides away in haste,
> That we can never say they're ours,
> But only say they're past.

His mother Nancy Hanks and her baby that didn't live, his sister Sarah and her baby that didn't live—time and the empty vapor had taken them; the rain and the snow beat on their graves. The young man Matthew Gentry, son of the richest man in that part of Indiana, was in his right mind and then began babbling week in and week out the droolings of a disordered brain—time had done it without warning. On both man and the animals, time and death had their way. In a single week, the milksick had taken four milch cows and eleven calves of Dennis Hanks, while Dennis too had nearly gone under with a hard week of it.

At the Pigeon Creek settlement, while the structure of his bones, the build and hang of his torso and limbs, took shape, other elements, invisible, yet permanent, traced their lines in the tissues of his head and heart.

And the farm boys in their evenings at Jones's store in Gentryville talked about how Abe Lincoln was always reading, digging into books, stretching out flat on his stomach in front of the fireplace, studying till midnight and past midnight.

Once, trying to speak a last word, Dennis Hanks said, "There's suthin' peculiarsome about Abe."

Maybe in books he would find the answers to dark questions pushing around in the pools of his thoughts and the drifts of his mind. He told Dennis and other people, "The things I want to know are in books; my best friend is the man who'll git me a book I ain't read." And sometimes friends answered, "Well, books ain't as plenty as wildcats in these parts o' Indianny."

This was one thing meant by Dennis when he said there was "suthin' peculiarsome" about Abe. It seemed that Abe made the books tell him more than they told other people. All the other farm boys had gone to school and read *The Kentucky Preceptor*, but Abe picked out questions from it, such as: "Who has the most right to complain, the Indian or the Negro?" and Abe would talk about it, up one way and down the other, while they were in the cornfield pulling fodder for the winter. He liked to explain to other people what he was getting from books; explaining an idea to someone else made it clearer to him. The habit was growing on him of reading out loud; words came more real if picked from the silent page of the book and pronounced on the tongue. When writing letters for his father or the neighbors, he read the words out loud as they got written. Before writing a letter he asked questions such as: "What do you want to say in the letter? How do you want to say it?"

As he studied his books his lower lip stuck out; Josiah Crawford noticed it was a habit and joked Abe about the "stuck-out lip." This habit too stayed with him.

Besides reading the family Bible and figuring his way all through the old arithmetic they had at home, he got hold of *Aesop's Fables, Pilgrim's Progress, Robinson Crusoe,* and Weems's *The Life of Francis Marion.* The book of fables, written or collected thousands of years ago by the Greek slave Aesop, sank deep in his mind. As he read the book, he had a feeling there were fables all around him, that everything he touched and handled, everything he saw and learned had a fable wrapped in it somewhere.

A book like that was a comfort against the same thing over again, day after day, so many mornings the same kind of water from the same spring, the same fried pork and cornmeal to eat, the same drizzles of rain, spring plowing, summer weeds, fall fodder pulling, each coming every year, with the same tired feeling at the end of the day. Books lighted lamps in the dark rooms of his gloomy hours. . . . Well—he would live on; maybe the time would come when he would be free from work for a few weeks, or a few months, with books, and then he would read. . . . God, then he would read. . . . Then he would go and get at the proud secrets of his books.

His father—would he be like his father when he grew up? He hoped not. Once his father had knocked him off a fence rail when he was asking a neighbor, passing by, a question, and why had he done that? Even if it was a smart question, too pert and too quick, it was no way to handle a boy in front of a neighbor.

In growing up from boyhood to young manhood, he had survived against lonesome, gnawing monotony and against floods, forest fires, snakebites, horse kicks, ague, chills, fever, malaria, milksick.

A comic outline against the sky he was, hiking along the roads in southern Indiana in those years when he read all the books within a fifty-mile circuit of his home. Stretching up on the long legs that ran from his moccasins to the body frame with its long, gangling arms, covered with linsey-woolsey, then the lean neck that carried the head with its surmounting coonskin cap or straw hat—it was, again, a comic outline—yet with a portent in its shadow.

Chapter 4

WHEN HE WAS SIXTEEN Abe had worked as a farmhand and ferry helper for James Taylor, who lived at the mouth of Anderson Creek and operated a ferry across the Ohio River. Two travelers wanted to get on a steamboat one day, and after Abe sculled them to it and lifted their trunks on board they threw him a half-dollar apiece; it gave him a new feeling; the most he had ever earned before was at butchering for thirty-one cents a day.

At Anderson Creek ferry, he saw and talked with settlers, land buyers and sellers, traders, hunters, peddlers, preachers, gamblers, politicians, teachers, and men shut-mouthed about their business. The ferry boy watched and listened.

Steamboats came past in slow, proud pageantry making their fourteen- to twenty-day passage from New Orleans to Pittsburgh; geography became fact to the boy looking on. Strings of flatboats passed, loaded with pork, flour, whisky; this was farm produce for trading at river ports to merchants or to plantation owners for feeding slaves. Other trading boats carried furniture, clothes, kitchenware, plows. Houseboats, sleds, flatboats with small cabins in which families lived and kept house, floated toward their new homesteads; on these the women were washing, the children playing. The life-flow of a main artery of American civilization, at a vivid time of growth, was a piece of pageantry there at Anderson Creek.

Within a couple of years, young Abe was out with ax, saw, and drawknife building himself a light flatboat of his own. He built it at Bates Landing, a mile and a half down the river from Anderson Creek. He was eighteen years old, a designer, builder, navigator; he cut down trees and hewed out planks for the bottoms and sides of his boat.

Pieces of money jingled in his pockets. Passengers paid him for sculling them from Bates Landing out to steamboats in the middle of the Ohio River. He studied words and figurations on the pieces of money. Thirteen stars circling the head of a woman called Liberty stood for the first thirteen states of the Union. The silver print of an eagle was on the half-dollar, and above its beak was inscribed *E Pluribus Unum;* this meant the many states should be One. Waiting for passengers and looking out across the Ohio to the drooping trees on the Kentucky shore, young Abe could think about money and women and eagles.

A signal came from that opposite shore one day and Lincoln rowed across. As he stepped out of his boat two men jumped out of the brush and said they were going to duck him in the river. They were John and Lin Dill, brothers who operated a ferry and claimed Abe had been transporting passengers for hire contrary to the law of Kentucky.

As they sized up Abe's husky arms they decided not to throw him in the river. He might be too tough a customer. Then all three went to Squire Samuel Pate, justice of the peace, near Lewisport. A warrant for the arrest of Abraham Lincoln was sworn out by John T. Dill. And the trial began of the case of "The Commonwealth of Kentucky versus Abraham Lincoln," charged with the violation of "An Act Respecting the Establishment of Ferries."

Lincoln testified he had carried passengers from the Indiana shore only to the middle of the river, never taking them to the Kentucky shore. And the Dill brothers, though claiming Lincoln had wronged them, did not testify he had "for reward set any person over a river," in the words of the Kentucky statute. Squire Pate dismissed the warrant against Lincoln.

The disappointed Dills put on their hats and left. But Lincoln sat with Squire Pate for a long talk. If a man knows the law about a business he is in, it is a help to him, the squire told young Abe. Afterward on days when no passengers were in sight and it was "law day" at Squire Pate's down the river, Abe would scull over and watch the witnesses, the constables, the squire, the machinery of justice. The state of Indiana, he learned, was one thing, and the state of Kentucky, something else. A water line in the middle of a river ran between them. He could ask, "Who makes state lines? What *are* state lines?"

THE BOY HAD GROWN longer of leg and arm, tougher of bone and sinew, with harder knuckles and joints. James Gentry, with the largest farms in the Pigeon Creek clearings, and a landing on the

Ohio River, looked the big boy over. He believed Abe could take his pork, flour, potatoes, and produce down the Mississippi River, to trade for cotton, tobacco, and sugar. Young Abe was set to work building a flatboat with a deck shelter, and two pairs of long oars at bow and stern.

As the snow and ice began to melt, a little before the first frogs started shrilling, in the year of 1828, two young men loaded the boat and pushed off. In charge of the boat Mr. Gentry had placed his son Allen, and in charge of Allen he had placed Abe Lincoln, to hold his own against any bushwhackers who might try to take the boat or loot it. There was many a spot along the shore where the skeletons of flatboatmen had been found years after the looters sold the cargo down the river. The honesty of Abe, of course, had been the first point Mr. Gentry considered; and the next point had been whether he could handle the boat in the snags and sandbars.

It was a thousand-mile trip to New Orleans, on a wide, winding waterway, where the flatboats were tied up at night to the riverbank, and floated and poled by day amid changing currents. The nineteen-year-old husky from Indiana found the Mississippi River tricky, with sandbars, shoals, islands, sudden rains, and shifting winds. Strong winds could crook the course of the boat, sometimes blowing it ashore. Warning signals must be given at night, by waving lantern or firewood, to other craft.

So the flatboat, the broadhorn, went down the Father of Waters, four to six miles an hour, the crew frying their own pork and cornmeal cakes and washing their own shirts.

Below Baton Rouge, on the Sugar Coast, they tied up at a plantation one evening and dropped off to sleep. They woke to find seven Negroes on board their boat trying to steal the cargo and kill the crew; the long-armed Lincoln swung a crab-tree club, knocked them galley-west, chased them into the woods, and came back to the boat and laid a bandanna on a gash over the right eye that left a scar for life as it healed. Then they cut loose the boat and moved down the river.

At New Orleans they sold their cargo of potatoes, bacon, hams, flour, apples, jeans, in exchange for cotton, tobacco, and sugar, and sold the flatboat. And they lingered a few days, seeing New Orleans, before taking steamer north.

On the streets of that town, which had floated French, British, and American flags, young Abraham Lincoln felt the pulses of a living humanity with far heartbeats in wide, alien circles over the earth: Dutchmen and French in jabber and exclamative; Swedes, Norwegians, and Russians with blond and reddish whiskers; Spaniards and Italians with knives and red silk handkerchiefs; New York, Philadelphia, Rome, Amsterdam, become human facts; it was London those men came from, ejaculating, " 'Ow can ye blime me?" And women wearing slippers and boots; Creoles with dusks of eyes; quadroons and octoroons with elusive soft voices; streets lined with saloons where men drank with men or chose from the women sipping their French wine or Jamaica rum at tables. Bets were laid on steamboat races; talk ran fast about the construction, then going on, of the New Orleans & Pontchartrain Railroad; slaves passed handcuffed in gangs; and everywhere was talk about niggers, good and bad niggers, how to rawhide the bad ones with mule whips, how you could trust your own children with a good nigger. And everywhere there was talk, too, about Andrew Jackson, running for President. Andrew Jackson, with the mud of all America's great rivers on his boots; Andrew Jackson, the Indian fighter, who had little grammar and many scars; for it was 1828, the year when Jackson was to ride to the election on a landslide of ballots.

As young Abe Lincoln and Allen Gentry made their way back home, riding a steamboat up the Mississippi, the tall boy had his thoughts. He had crossed half the United States, it seemed, and was back home after three months with what was left of eight-dollars-a-month pay in his pocket and a scar over the right eye.

That year Indiana University was to print its first catalogue, but Abe Lincoln wasn't among the students who registered. He was back again on his father's farm working, pulling fodder or sinking the ax in trees, and reading betweentimes a history of the United States, the life of Ben Franklin, and "The Revised Laws of Indiana."

IN THE FALL OF 1829, Abraham Lincoln's father made new plans; and the obedient Abe was put to work sawing trees big enough around to make wagon wheels, and hickories tough enough for axles and poles on an ox wagon.

The new plans were that the Lincoln family and the families of Dennis Hanks and Levi Hall, who had married Abe's step-sisters, thirteen people in all, were going to move to Macon County over in Illinois. John Hanks had gone there, and he was writing letters about rich land and better crops. A new outbreak of milksick had brought a neighborhood scare; and also Tom's farm wasn't paying well. After buying eighty acres for two dollars an acre and improving it for fourteen years, Tom Lincoln sold the land to Charles Grigsby for $125 cash. He and his wife also sold, for $123, a lot in Elizabethtown, Kentucky, which Mrs. Lincoln had inherited from her first husband. With the cash from both sales, Tom Lincoln was buying oxen and young steers. Moving was natural to his blood; he came from a long line of movers; he could tell about the family that had moved so often that their chickens knew the signs of another moving; and the chickens would walk up to the mover, stretch flat on the ground, and put up their feet to be tied for the next wagon trip.

The menfolks that winter used their broadaxes and draw-knives on solid blocks of wood, shaping wagon wheels. The three wagons they made were wood all through, pegs, cleats, hickory withes, though the wheel rims were iron. Bedclothes, skillets, and a few pieces of furniture were tied onto the wagons; early one morning the last of the packing was done. It was March 1, 1830; Abraham Lincoln had been for some days a full-grown man, a citizen who "had reached his majority"; he could vote at elections from now on; he was lawfully free from his father's commands; he was footloose.

At Jones's store he had laid in a little stock of pins, needles, tinware, and knickknacks, to peddle on the way to Illinois. And he had gone for a final look at the winter-dry grass over the grave of Nancy Hanks. He and his father were leaving their Indiana home that day; almost naked they had come, stayed fourteen years, toiled, buried their dead, and toiled on; and now they were leaving, almost naked.

Now, with the women and children lifted on top of the wagon loads, the men walked alongside, with a goad coaxing or prodding the animals and bawling at them to get along. They crossed the Wabash River, the state line of Illinois, and the Sangamon River, on a two-week trip with the ground freezing at night and thawing during the day, the oxen and horses slipping and tugging, the wagon axles groaning. A dog was left behind one morning as the wagons crossed a stream; it whined, ran back and forth, but wouldn't swim across; young Lincoln took off his boots, waded into the icy water, gathered the hound in his arms, and carried it over.

At the first stretch of the Grand Prairie they saw long levels of land, running without hollows, straight to the horizon.Grass stood up six, eight feet; men and horses and cattle were lost to sight in it; so tough were the grass roots that timber could not get rootholds in it. And they met settlers telling how the tough sod had broken many a plow; but after the first year of sod corn, the yield would run fifty bushels to the acre; and wheat would average twenty-five to thirty bushels.

The outfit from Indiana raised a laugh as they drove their wagons into the main street of Decatur, in Macon County, Illinois. To the question, "Kin ye tell us where John Hanks's place is?" the Decatur citizens told them how to drive four miles, where they found John, talked over old Indiana and Kentucky times, but more about Illinois. After the night stay, John took the Lincoln family six miles down the Sangamon River, where he had cut the logs for their cabin.

There young Lincoln helped raise the cabin, put in the crops, split rails for fences. He hired out to William Warnick nearby, read the few books in the house, and passed such pleasant talk and smiles with William's daughter, Mary, and with another girl, Jemima Hill, that at a later time neighbors said he carried on courtships, even though both girls married inside of a year after young Lincoln kept company in those parts.

He wrote back to Jones at Gentryville that he doubled his money on the peddler's stock he sold; and he earned a pair of brown jean trousers by splitting four hundred rails for each yard of the cloth. With new outlooks came new thoughts; at

Vincennes, on the way to Illinois, he had seen a printing press for the first time. John Hanks put him on a box to answer the speech of a man who was against improvements of the Sangamon River; and John told neighbors, "Abe beat him to death." More and more he was delivering speeches, to trees, stumps, potato rows, just practicing, by himself.

Fall came and brought chills, fever, and ague to most of the Lincoln family; Tom and Sarah used many doses of a quinine-and-whisky tonic mixture from a Decatur store. Then came December, Christmas week, and a snowstorm.

For forty-eight hours, with no letup, the battalions of a blizzard filled the sky, and piled a cover two and a half feet on the ground. Another drive of snow made it four feet. Rain followed, froze, and more snow covered the icy crust. Wolves took their way with deer and cattle who broke through the crust and stood helpless. Fodder crops went to ruin; cows, hogs, and horses died in the fields. Connections between houses and settlements broke down; for days in twelve-below-zero weather, families were cut off. Some died of cold, lacking wood to burn; some died of hunger. Those who came through alive, in the years after, called themselves Snowbirds.

The Lincoln family had hard days. Families like theirs, new settlers, had little of meat and corn laid by. Young Abraham in February made a try at reaching the William Warnick house, four miles off, got his feet wet and nearly froze them. Mrs. Warnick put his feet in snow to take out the frostbite, then rubbed them with grease.

For nine weeks that snow cover held the ground. When the winter at last eased off, the Lincoln family moved southeast a hundred miles to Goose Nest Prairie, in the southern part of Coles County. Abraham had other plans and didn't go with them. He had "come of age."

IN FEBRUARY 1831 there had come to the neighborhood of John Hanks, when Abraham Lincoln was lingering there, a man named Denton Offutt, a hard drinker, a frontier hustler, and a believer in pots of gold at the rainbow end, who was easy with promises. Hanks, Abe Lincoln, and John D. Johnston had made an agreement with him; they would take a flatboat of cargo to New Orleans for Offutt. Offutt was to have the flatboat and cargo ready on the Sangamon River near the village of Springfield as soon as the snow melted, and they were to meet him there. In order to travel to Springfield they bought a large canoe. And so, in the spring of 1831, with John Hanks, his mother's cousin, and John D. Johnston, his stepbrother, Abraham Lincoln, twenty-two years old, floated down the Sangamon River.

Leaving their canoe at the appointed meeting place, Judy's Ferry, and not finding Denton Offutt there, they walked to Springfield and at the Buckhorn Tavern found Offutt lush with liquor and promises and no flatboat. He hired them at $12 a month and sent them to government timberland, where they cut down trees and got logs for making planks and gunwales. They started building the flatboat near their camp on the Sangamon River.

In about four weeks they launched the boat, eighty feet long and eighteen feet wide, loaded the cargo of barreled pork, corn, and live hogs, and moved downstream, steering away from snags and low water. Lincoln was on deck in blue homespun jeans, jacket, vest, rawhide boots with pantaloons stuffed in, and a felt hat once black but now, as the owner said, "sunburned till it was a combine of colors."

On April 19, rounding the curve of the Sangamon at the village of New Salem, the boat stuck on the Camron milldam, and hung with one-third of her slanted downward over the edge of the dam and filling slowly with water, while the cargo of pork barrels was sliding slowly so as to overweight one end. She hung there a day while all the people of New Salem came down to look at the river disaster. They saw Lincoln get part of the cargo unloaded to the riverbank; they saw him bore a hole in the flatboat end as it hung over the dam, to let the water out; then they saw him plug the hole, drop the boat over the dam, and reload the cargo. As the flatboat headed off again toward the Mississippi, New Salem talked about the cool head and ready wit of the long-shanked young man.

Again Lincoln floated down the Mississippi River meeting other flatboats, keelboats, and proud white steamboats. At New

Orleans, he saw stacks of pork and flour from the West, and piles of cotton bales from the South, standing on the wharves. He could read the advertisements of slave traders. One trader gave notice: "I will at all times pay the highest cash prices for Negroes of every description, and will also attend to the sale of Negroes on commission, having a jail and yard fitted up expressly for boarding them." And he saw one auction where an octoroon girl was sold, after being pinched, trotted up and down, and handled so the buyer could be satisfied she was sound of wind and limb.

Again he could see on the narrow cobblestoned streets of this old strange city a dazzling, mingling parade of the humanly ugly and lovely—and what his eyes met had him thoughtful and brooding.

After a month's stay he worked his passage, firing a steamboat furnace, up the Mississippi River, stayed a few weeks on his father's farm in Coles County, Illinois, and then spoke the long good-by to home and the family roof. Saying good-by to his father was easy, but it was not so easy to hug the mother, Sally Bush, and lay his cheek next to hers and say he was going out into the big world to make a place for himself.

The father laughed his good-by, and not so long after told a visitor, "I s'pose Abe is still fooling hisself with eddication. I tried to stop it, but he has got that fool idea in his head, and it can't be got out. Now I hain't got no eddication, but I get along far better'n ef I had."

With his few belongings wrapped in a handkerchief bundle tied to a stick over his shoulder, Abraham was on his way to New Salem.

Chapter 5

ABRAHAM LINCOLN, in that spring of 1831, spent a night at the cabin of John Hanks, planning his canoe trip down the Sangamon River to New Salem, where he was going to work on a new job in a new store belonging to Denton Offutt.

Spring breezes moved in the oaks and poplars. The branches

of the trees registered their forks and angles in flat black shadows over the white flat spread of moon-silver on the ground.

For a moment there may have flitted through his head the memory of the face of an auburn-haired girl, a head with corn-silk hair; he had seen her at New Salem when his flatboat had stuck on the dam; he would see her again there.

For a moment, too, he may have stepped out of the cabin door of the Hanks home that night and he might have looked up and asked the moon to tell him what it saw. He might have asked the moon to tell him about the comings and goings of men and machines, guns and tools, events and enterprises, the drift of human struggle and history, over and around the earth.

And the moon might have told him many things that spring night in the year 1831.

The ships and guns of the white men of western Europe were beginning to travel world routes. A vast interwoven fabric of international selling, buying, manufacturing, merchandising was starting to develop. For, step by step, in America and around the earth, an industrial revolution was making itself felt in the lives and work of millions of people. A new form of world civilization was shaping, founded on the production of merchandise by power-driven machinery and the selling and trading of that merchandise in markets as far off as cargoes could be carried by sailing vessels—and by the new incoming steamboats and railroads.

The moon, looking down, could see that there were now about 10,000,000 white people in the United States, and about 2,300,000 colored slaves. The people lived in three sections or regions, each section with a character of its own in products, land, and people. There was the industrial North with its factories, shops, and mills; there was the plantation South with its cotton, tobacco, rice, and slaves; and there was the pioneer West with its corn, wheat, pork, furs. In some respects these regions were three separate countries, with different ways of looking at life. Time and events were operating, however, to shape intertwined lines of destiny for all three.

The South, in the early 1830's, was an empire of cotton blossoms, where the dominant interest each year was the quick rich returns brought by the cotton crop. The industrial and commercial fact of cotton had moved into world history as a reckonable factor. Every year Massachusetts, Connecticut, New York, Great Britain, France sent more and more ships for this cotton crop. And to produce it, the exploitation was decisive, blind, relentless. Land wore out as the soil was mined without care or manure, and the big planters went farther inland to Alabama and Mississippi in search of fresh and virgin soils. And fresh labor supplies were called for as imperative requisites toward larger cotton crops. New England shipowners in the African slave trade could double their money in six months, hauling cargoes of slaves packed "spoon fashion" in chains, between decks, in a space less than four feet high.

The North, at that time, was a section groping toward control of waterpower, iron, steel, canals, railways, oceangoing boats; and by one route and another, the money of American regions was streaming toward banks in New York, Philadelphia, and Boston. Here, cotton mills were the industrial phenomenon; and each year the mills called for increasing tens of millions of pounds of cotton from the South. One girl, operating a single spinning machine, spun as much cotton cloth as three thousand girls working by hand on the old-fashioned spinning wheel. Thread, sheeting, print cloth, gingham, and bags were leaving North Atlantic states for all parts of the world; the South itself was buying back in finished cloth part of the cotton it raised.

The West was a stretch of country with the Great Lakes at the north, the Gulf of Mexico to the south, the Allegheny Mountains to the east, and a ragged-edged, shifty frontier moving farther west every year out into the Great Plains toward the Rocky Mountains. Pioneers in waves were crossing this stretch of country. They were locating on prairie land, intermingling with the Indians, killing buffalo, learning to farm. Each wave of settlers made it easier for more to come. By the early 1830's, one-third of the population of the United States was in the West. The West had become a granary sending food supplies to the factory and textile-mill towns of New England and the Middle States, to Great Britain and France, as well as corn, horses, and mules to the big cotton planters of the South.

Such were a few of the things the white moon in its high riding over the sky might have told Abraham Lincoln that spring night in 1831. He would have listened, with understanding, because he was blood and bone of North, South, and West, because there were in him the branched veins of New England emigrant, Middle State Quaker, Virginia planter, and Kentucky pioneer. As the regions of America grew and struggled, he might understand their growth and struggle.

IN THE SUMMER of the year 1831, Abraham Lincoln, twenty-two years old, floated a canoe down the Sangamon River, going to a new home, laughter and youth in his bones, in his heart a few pennies of dreams, in his head a ragbag of thoughts he could never expect to sell.

New Salem, the town on a hill, to which Abraham Lincoln was shunting his canoe, was a place of promise, just as all towns in Illinois then were places of promise. New Salem then had a dozen families as its population, just as Chicago in the same year reckoned a dozen families. Both had water transportation, outlets, tributary territory, yet one was to be only a phantom hamlet of memories and ghosts, a windswept hilltop kept as cherished haunts are kept.

New Salem stood on a hill, a wrinkle of earth crust, a convulsive knob of rock and sod. The Sangamon River takes a curve as it comes to the foot of that bluff and looks up. There a thousand wagonloads of gravel had been hauled and packed into the river to make a power dam and mill grind. The Rutledges and Camrons, who had started the mill, had bought the ridge of land on the bluff above and in 1829 had laid out a town, sold lots, put up a log tavern with four rooms, and named the place New Salem.

Farmers came there from fifty miles away to have their grain turned into flour and to buy salt, sugar, hardware, and calico. And Denton Offutt had rented the Rutledge and Camron gristmill and had ordered a stock of goods and was going to open a new store. Lincoln was to be clerk in charge of the store and mill at $15 a month, with a back room to sleep in once the store was built.

He arrived in the hilltop village in late July, walked the village street, looked over its dozen or more cabins, searched faces he expected to see many times for many months. He arranged to board temporarily at the home of John Camron and got acquainted with Camron's eleven daughters, who teased him about his long legs and arms and heard him admit he wasn't "much to look at."

Election Day in New Salem came a few days later, and the polls were in John Camron's home. Voting was by word of mouth. Each voter spoke his choices to the election judges, who called out the names to clerks recording them "on poll sheets." Here Abraham Lincoln, twenty-two years old, cast his first ballot, voting for a Henry Clay Whig for Congress. He then stayed around the polls most of the day talking, telling stories, making friends, and getting to know nearly all the men in the New Salem neighborhood.

Offutt's stock for the new store had not come as yet, so when a Dr. Nelson said he wanted a pilot to take his flatboat through the channels of the Sangamon to Beardstown on the Illinois River, Lincoln was willing. When he came back, he said there were times he ran the flatboat three miles off onto the prairies, but always got back to the main channel of the Sangamon. A genius of drollery was recognized by the New Salem folks as having come among them to live. They were already passing along the lizard story, a yarn spun by the newcomer almost the first day he arrived.

He had said it happened in Indiana. There in a meetinghouse a preacher was delivering a sermon, wearing old-fashioned baggy pantaloons fastened with one button and no suspenders, while his shirt was fastened at the collar with one button. He announced his text: "I am the Christ, whom I shall represent today." And about that time a little blue lizard ran up under one of the baggy pantaloons. The preacher went ahead with his sermon, slapping his legs. After a while the lizard came so high that the preacher was desperate, and, going on with his sermon, unbuttoned the one button that held his pantaloons; they dropped down and with a kick were off. By this time the lizard had changed his route and circled around under the shirt at the

51

back, and the preacher, repeating his text, "I am the Christ, whom I shall represent today," loosened his one collar button and with one sweeping movement off came the shirt. The congregation sat in the pews dazed and dazzled; everything was still for a minute; then a dignified elderly lady stood up slowly and, pointing a finger toward the pulpit, called out at the top of her voice, "I just want to say that if you represent Jesus Christ, sir, then I'm done with the Bible."

At last Offutt bought a lot for ten dollars, and he and Lincoln built a cabin of logs; this was to be the new store. When Offutt's goods arrived, Lincoln stacked shelves and corners with salt, sugar, groceries, whisky, tobacco, hardware, dishes, calico prints, hats, gloves, socks, and shoes. Eighteen-year-old Bill Greene was put in as a helper for Lincoln. The two, Lincoln and young Bill, slept together on a narrow cot in the back of the store; "when one turned over, the other had to."

Denton Offutt's enthusiasm about his new clerk ran high; he told people, "He knows more than any man in the United States. Someday he will be President." And, "He can outrun, outlift, outwrestle, and throw down any man in Sangamon County."

And the Clary's Grove boys, just four miles away, began talking about these claims. What they said mostly was, "Is that so?" Bill Clary, who ran a saloon thirty steps north of the Offutt store, put up a bet of ten dollars with Offutt that Lincoln couldn't throw Jack Armstrong, the Clary's Grove champion.

Sports from fifty miles around came to a square next to Offutt's store to see the match; bets of money, knives, tobacco, drinks were put up. Armstrong, short and powerful, aimed from the first to get in close to his man and use his thick muscular strength. But Lincoln held him off with long arms, wore down his strength, got him out of breath and "rattled," and finally threw him to a hard fall, flat on his back.

As Armstrong lay on the ground, a champion in the dust of defeat, his gang from Clary's Grove started to swarm toward Lincoln, with cries and threats. Lincoln stepped to where his back was against a wall of Offutt's store, braced himself, and told the gang he was ready for 'em.

Then Jack Armstrong broke through the front line, told the gang Lincoln was "fair," had won the match, and "he's the best feller that ever broke into this settlement."

Armstrong gave Lincoln a warm handshake and they were close friends ever after. And the Clary's Grove boys decided he was one of them, even though he didn't drink whisky nor play cards. From then on they called on him to judge their horse races and chicken fights, umpire their matches, and settle disputes. Their homes were open to him. He was adopted.

STORIES WERE soon beginning to be told about Lincoln and what manner of man he was. They told about his honesty. Counting the money a woman paid for dry goods one day, Lincoln found she had paid a few cents more than her bill; that night he walked six miles to pay it back. Once, finding he weighed tea with a four-ounce weight instead of an eight, he took a long walk and delivered to the woman the full order of tea she had paid for.

A loafer used the wrong kind of language when women customers were in the store one day; Lincoln warned him to stop; he talked back. Lincoln took him in front of the store, threw him on the ground, and rubbed smartweed in his face.

When a small gambler tricked young Bill Greene, Lincoln told Bill to bet him the best fur hat in the store that he (Lincoln) could lift a barrel of whisky from the floor and hold it while he took a drink from the bunghole. Bill hunted up the gambler, made the bet, and won it; Lincoln lifted the barrel off the floor, sat squatting on the floor, rolled the barrel on his knees till the bunghole reached his mouth, drank a mouthful, let the barrel down—and stood up and spat out the whisky.

Betweentimes, in spare hours, and in watches of the night, Lincoln toiled and quested for the inner lights of what was known as education and knowledge. South of New Salem stood a log schoolhouse, and Lincoln occasionally dropped in there to sit on a bench and listen to the children reciting their lessons. He wanted to find out how much he already knew of what they were teaching in the schools. And he spent hours with Mentor Graham, the tall, slant-jawed schoolteacher, going over points in mathematics, geography, and correct language. When Graham told him there was a grammar at John C. Vance's house, six miles off, he walked the six miles, brought back the book, and burned pine shavings in the blacksmith shop at night to light the book so he could read it. As he got further into the book, he had Bill Greene at the store hold it and ask him questions. When Bill asked, "What do adverbs qualify?" Lincoln would reply, "Adverbs qualify verbs, adjectives, and other adverbs."

A literary and debating society was formed in New Salem. Lincoln stood up for his first speech one evening. And there was close attention. He opened in a tone of apology, as though he wasn't sure he could put on the end of his tongue the ideas operating in his head. He went on with facts, wove them into an argument, and said he hoped the argument would stand on its own legs and command respect.

Later, it came to him through friends that James Rutledge, the president of the society, was saying there was "more than wit and fun" in Abe's head; that a "high destiny" might be in store for him. This had a double interest for the young clerk, because he had spent afternoons and evenings in the Rutledge tavern, and he had looked wholly and surely into the face of a slim girl with corn-silk hair, a girl he had first glimpsed when his flatboat hung over the dam at New Salem—Ann Rutledge, the eighteen-year-old daughter of James Rutledge.

DURING THE WINTER OF 1832, Abe Lincoln had warnings that the business of Denton Offutt in New Salem was going to pieces. Offutt was often filling his personal pocket flask at his own barrels of pure and unsurpassed Kentucky rye whisky; and as his cash dwindled and his face became more bleary it was harder for his tongue to persuade men of the rainbow empires he saw beyond the horizon; it was said, "Offutt is petering out." And in another few months he would quietly leave New Salem, not to be heard from again for years.

In March 1832, therefore, Lincoln, who had just passed his twenty-third birthday, found himself, for all practical purposes, out of a job. Except for a few months as a grocery clerk, he still classified as a propertyless manual laborer. Yet he launched forth into an action that took as much nerve as wrestling Jack Armstrong the year before. He announced that he was going to run for the office of member of the legislature of the state of Illinois, to represent the people of Sangamon County.

He told friends he didn't expect to be elected; it was understood that James Rutledge and others had told him to make the run; it would bring him before the people, and in time would do him good. So he took his first big plunge into politics. In a long speech, later printed as a handbill, he expressed his views about navigation on the Sangamon River, pledging himself to support all measures for improving the river. Next, he called for a strong law to stop "the practice of loaning money at exorbitant rates of interest"; and then he spoke some of the wishes of his heart on the subject of education: "I view it as the most important subject which we as a people can be engaged in. That every man may receive at least a moderate education . . . appears to be an object of vital importance."

He closed in a manner having the gray glint of his eyes and the loose hang of his long arms: "If the good people in their wisdom shall see fit to keep me in the background, I have been too familiar with disappointments to be very much chagrined."

His campaign was interrupted. One morning in April, a few weeks later, a rider on a muddy, sweating horse stopped in New Salem and gave out handbills signed by the governor calling for volunteer soldiers to fight Indians.

The famous old red man, Black Hawk, had crossed the Mississippi River with the best fighters in the Sac tribe, to have a look at land where, for hundreds of years, they and theirs had planted corn, hunted, and fished. In the year 1804, they had sold this land of theirs in northwestern Illinois, the rich prairie valley of the Rock River, to the United States government, with the promise on paper saying that they could hunt and could plant corn in Illinois till the lands were surveyed and opened up for settlers. Then they had taken their horses, women, children, and dogs across the Mississippi. Now they were saying the white men had broken the promises; white squatters had come past the line of settlement; and more than that, the United States government could not buy land because "land cannot be sold." "My reason teaches me," wrote Black Hawk, "that land cannot be sold. The Great Spirit gave it to his children to live upon. . . . Nothing can be sold but such things as can be carried away."

Black Hawk was now sixty-seven years old and could look back on forty years as a chief of the Sac tribe. He had seen the red man drink the firewater of the white man and then sign papers selling land. Now he felt the Great Spirit, Man-ee-do, telling him to cross the Mississippi River, scare and scatter the squatters and settlers, and then ambush and kill off all the pale-faced soldiers who came against him. Already his young men on fast ponies had circled among settlers along the Rock River, leaving cabins in ashes and white men and women with their scalps torn out. Copper-faced men had tumbled off their horses with the rifle bullets of white men in their vitals; white men had wakened in their cabins at night to hear yells, to see fire and knives and war axes burn and butcher.

The white settlers had asked the governor at Springfield for help. And the Washington government, a thousand miles away, was sending the pick of its regulars, led by such young commanders as Albert Sidney Johnston, Zachary Taylor, and Winfield Scott, to handle the revolt of the Indian chief.

Abraham Lincoln had two reasons, if no more, for going into the Black Hawk War as a volunteer soldier. His job as a clerk was gone, with no Offutt store to clerk in. And he was running for the legislature; a war record, in any kind of war, would count in politics.

Lincoln borrowed a horse and rode nine miles to Richland Creek to join a company of friends and neighbors, mostly Clary's Grove boys, who were also enlisting. Jack Armstrong and the Clary's Grove boys said they were going to elect Lincoln captain of the company. They ran him against the sawmill owner William Kirkpatrick. When the two candidates, Lincoln and Kirkpatrick, stood facing the recruited soldiers, and each soldier walked out and stood behind the man he wanted for captain, Lincoln's line was twice as long as Kirkpatrick's.

He was now Captain Lincoln, and made a speech thanking the men for the unexpected honor; he would do his best to merit the confidence placed in him. After that he appointed Jack Armstrong first sergeant, with plenty of other sergeants and corporals from among the Clary's Grove boys. Their military unit was officially designated as Captain Abraham Lincoln's Company of the First Regiment of the Brigade of Mounted Volunteers, though they had no mounts as yet. All were afoot, including Captain Lincoln.

He knew his company could fight like wildcats but would never understand so-called discipline. The first military order he gave got the reply, "Go to hell." He himself was a beginner in drill regulations, and once couldn't think of the order that would get two platoons endwise, two by two, for passing through a gate. So he commanded, "This company is dismissed for two minutes, when it will fall in again on the other side of the gate." One time, against orders, somebody shot off a pistol inside the camp; the authorities found it was Captain Lincoln; his sword was taken away, and he was held under arrest for one day. Another time his men opened officers' supplies and found a lot of whisky; on the morning after, some were dead drunk, others straggled on the march. A court-martial ordered Captain Lincoln to carry a wooden sword two days.

An old Indian rambled into camp one day. The men rushed at him; they were out in an Indian war, to kill Indians. Lincoln jumped to his side, showed the men that the old copper-face had a military pass, and said with a hard gleam, "Men, this must not be done; he must not be shot and killed by us." One of the men called Lincoln a coward. His eyes blazed as he stood by the old Indian and quietly told the mob, "If any man thinks I am a coward, let him test it." And the hot tempers cooled down.

The Sangamon County volunteers became part of an army of 1600 soldiers mobilized at Beardstown. They were marched in cold and drizzly weather to Yellow Banks on the Mississippi, then marched to Dixon on the Rock River, while the U.S. regular army troops moved on boats. Sometimes the company cooks had nothing to cook and there was growling from the volunteers. Captain Lincoln went to the regular army officers of his brigade and told them that, representing his men, he had to say that there would be trouble if his men didn't get the same rations and treatment as the regulars. Bill Greene remembered Lincoln saying to a regular army officer, "Sir, my men must be equal in all particulars—in rations, arms, camps—to the regular army" and "Resistance will hereafter be made to unjust orders." This threat of mutiny, voiced by the leader of the Clary's Grove boys, resulted in better treatment, so that no mutiny followed.

Very little fighting followed, either. The Indians shaped and reshaped their army as a shadow, came and faded as a phantom, spread out false trails, mocked their enemy with being gone from horizons they had just filled. An ambush was their hope. They tried for it and couldn't get it. The white men had fought Indians before and had solved the theory of warfare by ambush.

By zigzag and crisscross paths Black Hawk was driven north out of Illinois and, in swamp and island battles on Wisconsin rivers, his armies were beaten and his last chance taken.

Black Hawk did not know then that the white men had ambushed him by a white man's way of ambush, that Sioux and Winnebago Indians acting as guides for his army were in the pay of the whites and had led his army on wrong roads. It was these same red men who were paid by the whites to bring him in as a prisoner after he escaped from a battle on the Bad Axe. And Black Hawk was taken a thousand miles to Washington, where at the White House he met President Andrew Jackson. They faced each other a white chief and red chief; both had killed men and known terrible angers, hard griefs, high dangers, and scars; each was nearly seventy years old; and Black Hawk said to Jackson, "I—am—a man—and you—are—another. . . . I took up the hatchet to avenge injuries which could no longer be borne. . . . I say no more of it; all is known to you."

Near Kellogg's Grove Lincoln had helped bury five men killed in a skirmish the day before. This was the nearest to actual war combat that he came. He and his men rode up a little hill as the red light of the morning sun streamed over the five corpses. Telling about it afterward, he said each of the dead men "had a round spot on the top of his head about as big as a dollar, where the redskins had taken his scalp." He said it was frightful, grotesque, "and the red sunlight seemed to paint everything all over."

When Abraham Lincoln, discharged at last, was mustered out at Whitewater, Wisconsin, his horse was stolen. So he walked two hundred miles to Peoria, Illinois. There with other returning soldiers he bought a canoe and paddled the Illinois River to Havana, sold the canoe, and set out on foot again to get back to good old New Salem.

He had been through an Indian war without killing an Indian, and having saved the life of one Indian. He had seen deep into the heart of the American volunteer soldier; he had fathomed a thousand reasons why men go to war, march in the mud, sleep in cold rain, and kill when the killing is good. In the depths of his own heart there were slow changes at work; a slant of light had opened when he was elected captain; it had made him glad; it had softened and lit up shadows that floated around him. If men chose him for captain as they were going to war, he might perhaps have other hopes. He had spent long hours talking with a volunteer from Springfield, Major John T. Stuart, who was a lawyer and had told him he could be a lawyer. Reading a tough grammar through hadn't stumped him; maybe reading law would be the same.

Meanwhile, Election Day was to be August 6, and, after reaching New Salem and washing the mud from his rawhide boots, Lincoln started electioneering.

He kept it up till the ballots were counted, traveling all over Sangamon County. To the reading and educated public, a small fraction, he gave the printed handbills of his address, written in the spring, on Sangamon River navigation, a usury law, and education. Mixing with other voters, especially those known as "the butcher-knife boys," who carried long knives in their belts, he had the lizard story and other stories to tell, besides all the fresh jokes and horsy adventures in the Black Hawk War. His first stump speech was at Pappsville, where some auctioneers called Poog & Knap were selling hogs, bulls, and steers. Lincoln stepped on a box and made a speech, which Bill Greene recalled afterward in these words:

"Gentlemen and fellow citizens: I presume you all know who I am. I am humble Abraham Lincoln. I have been solicited by many friends to become a candidate for the legislature. My politics are short and sweet, like the old woman's dance. I am in favor of a national bank. I am in favor of the internal-improvements system and a high protective tariff. These are my sentiments and political principles. If elected, I shall be thankful; if not, it will be all the same."

This was speech as plain and straight as if he were telling a horse-race or chicken-fight crowd which way to play their bets. In standing for a national bank, high tariff, and internal improvements, he was lining up with the Henry Clay crowd rather than the Jackson men. At that hour in Illinois politics, however, the large majority of voters were Jackson men.

In campaigning among farmers, Lincoln pitched hay at the barns and cradled wheat in the fields to show the gang he was one of 'em; at various crossroads he threw the crowbar and let the local wrestlers try to get the crotch hoist on him. At one town a doctor, who had heard about Lincoln, asked, "Can't the party raise no better material than that?" But after hearing a stump speech from the young candidate, he said, "He is a take-in, knows more than all of them put together."

On Election Day Lincoln lost, standing eighth in a field of thirteen candidates.

But in his own neighborhood, the New Salem precinct, where the pollbooks showed 300 votes cast, he got 277 of those votes.

Chapter 6

LINCOLN WAS NOW out of a job and had his choice of learning the blacksmith trade or going into business. He drifted into business; friends took his promissory notes.

Five stores were running in New Salem, and somehow, after a time, three of the stores, or the wrecks and debts of them, passed into Lincoln's hands. He bought Rowan Herndon's interest in the partnership of Herndon and William F. Berry, and they hung up the sign Berry & Lincoln. Also they bought the stock of Reuben Radford's store when it was wrecked in a brawl. On top of that they bought out the little grocery of James Rutledge.

Early harvest days came; the oat straw ripened to cream and

gold; the farmers bundled grain in the russet fields. From the Salem hilltop, the valley of the Sangamon River loitered off in a long stretch of lazy, dreamy haze. For Abraham Lincoln the days went by with few customers to bother him. He had never in his life sat so free with uninterrupted thoughts, so footloose day after day to turn and look into himself and find the measure of his personal horizons. He was growing as inevitably as summer corn in Illinois loam. Leaning at the doorpost of a store to which fewer customers were coming, he was growing, in silence, as corn grows.

As the store of Berry & Lincoln ran on through the fall and winter, business didn't pick up much, and nobody cared much. Berry was drinking and playing poker; Lincoln was reading law, dreaming, and learning Shakespeare and Burns.

At an auction in Springfield he had bought a copy of Blackstone's *Commentaries on the Laws of England*. He remembered that his Springfield lawyer friend, John T. Stuart, had said the law student should read Blackstone first. He remembered, too, how he had once walked barefoot to the courthouse at Booneville down in Indiana and heard a lawyer make a speech to a jury, and wished he might someday be a lawyer. So he read Blackstone, on the flat of his back on the grocery-store counter, or under the shade of a tree with his feet up the side of the tree. One morning he sat barefoot on a woodpile. "What are you reading?" asked Squire Godbey. "I ain't reading; I'm studying." "Studying what?" "Law." "Good God Almighty!"

By spring the store was almost a goner, as business continued to drop off. Berry & Lincoln took out a license in March 1833 to keep a tavern and sell retail liquors. But a few weeks later, in a deal of some kind, Lincoln turned his interest in the store over to Berry.

On May 7, 1833, he was appointed postmaster at New Salem. No Democrat wanted the job, and Lincoln wanted to read the newspapers. He himself said the office was too insignificant to make his politics an objection. The pay would run about $50 a year, in commissions on receipts. He had to be in the office at Hill's store only long enough to receive and receipt for the mail which came twice a week, by postrider at first and later by stage.

Letters arrived written on sheets of paper folded and waxed, envelopes not yet being in use. The postage was paid not by the sender but by the addressee, and for a one-sheet letter the cost started at six cents for the first thirty miles, up to twenty-five cents for more than four hundred miles. Two sheets cost twice as much, three sheets three times as much, and with every letter Lincoln had to figure how many sheets, how far it had come, then mark the postage in the upper right corner of the outside sheet. If the receiver didn't like Lincoln's figuring as to the number of sheets, he could open the letter before the postmaster and settle the question.

Lincoln was free to read newspapers before delivering them, and the habit deepened in him of watching "the public prints" for political trends. He kept in touch with events in St. Louis and Louisville and Cincinnati. And he could find excitement at times in reading the speeches made in Congress at Washington as reported in full in the *Congressional Globe* subscribed for by John C. Vance. It was no pleasure for him to write later to the publishers, "Your subscriber at this place *John C. Vance*, is dead; and no person takes the paper from the office."

It seemed he wasn't strict about regulations. At times the post office was left unlocked for hours while citizens who called for mail helped themselves. And he either was too careless or didn't have the heart to force newspaper subscribers to pay postage in advance, as required by law. When George Spears sent postage money to Lincoln by a messenger with a note telling Lincoln he wanted a receipt, Lincoln replied he was "surprised" at the request. "The law requires News paper postage to be paid in advance and now that I have waited a full year you choose to wound my feelings by intimating that unless you get a receipt I will probably make you pay again."

IN ADDITION to working as postmaster, to earn a living and pay his debts Lincoln took jobs splitting fence rails, worked at the sawmill, harvested hay and oats, and helped out at the Hill store. He was also reading books—Gibbon's *The Decline and Fall of the Roman Empire*, Thomas Paine's *The Age of Reason*. But always his debts haunted him. Misery and melancholy he had learned to chase away with a few comic stories told to the boys. But debts—they wouldn't laugh away. They were little rats, a rat for every dollar, and he could hear them gnawing in the night when he wanted to sleep.

Then, in the fall of 1833, the surveyor of Sangamon County, a man named John Calhoun, who had heard of Lincoln from a New Salem farmer, sent word he would like to appoint him his deputy. Lincoln walked eighteen miles to Springfield and arranged to take the job. Mrs. Calhoun, after he left, told her husband she had never seen such an ungodly looking gawk. To which he replied, "For all that, he is no common man."

As Lincoln walked back to New Salem, hiking along the low hills of prairie, he saw ahead of him a tough piece of work; he had to transform his blank ignorance of the science and art of surveying into a thorough working knowledge and skill.

With a copy of *The Theory and Practice of Surveying* by Robert Gibson, published in 1814, Lincoln hunted up Mentor Graham, the schoolmaster, and settled down to study. Many nights during the next six weeks Graham's daughter woke up at midnight, she told friends, and saw Lincoln and her father by the fire, figuring and explaining. On some nights Lincoln worked alone till daylight. From decimal fractions the book ran on into logarithms, the use of mathematical instruments, trigonometry, surveying by intersections. Lincoln grew fagged, with sunken cheeks and bleary, red eyes. Friends said, "You're killing yourself." And among themselves they whispered he would break under the load. In six weeks' time, however, Lincoln had mastered his studies, and Calhoun put him to work on the north end of Sangamon County.

The taste of open air and sun healed him as he worked in field and timberland with compass and measurements. He surveyed roads, school sections, pieces of farmland from four-acre plots to 160-acre farms. He surveyed the towns of Petersburg, Bath, New Boston, Albany, Huron, and others. His surveys became known for their accuracy and he was called on to settle boundary disputes. In Petersburg, however, he laid out one street crooked. Running it straight and regular, it would have put the house of Jemima Elmore and her family into the street, and Jemima was the widow of Private Travice Elmore, a member of Lincoln's company in the Black Hawk War.

For his surveying Lincoln was paid three dollars a day—when he worked. Yet he saw that even with the best of luck it would be a long time before he could pay all the money he owed. He could go away from New Salem by night, leaving no future address, as Offutt had done, as many others did on the frontier. Or he could stay and stick it out.

He had bought a horse for his surveying trips. Now he was sued for the balance he still owed; and his horse, saddle, bridle, and surveying instruments were to be sold at auction. James Short, a Sand Ridge farmer, heard about it; he liked Lincoln; he had told people, when Lincoln worked for him, "he husks two loads of corn to my one." Short went to the auction, bought in the horse and outfit, and gave them back to Lincoln, who had stayed away, too sad to show up.

It hit him as another of those surprises which kept coming regularly into his young life. It was a surprise when Gentry asked him to take a flatboat down the Mississippi River, when Offutt picked him to clerk in a new store, when the Sangamon River boys elected him captain for the Black Hawk War, when James Rutledge and others told him he ought to run for the legislature. Now Uncle Jimmy Short, without saying anything about it beforehand, came in at the last dark moment with his horse and surveying outfit.

His debts totaled $1100 when his former partner, Berry, died on short notice in January 1835. His estate amounted to practically nothing, and so Lincoln at almost twenty-six years of age was held responsible for their joint obligations and the debts of their bankrupt store.

LINCOLN'S DAYS were filled with many occupations besides surveying, politics, and being postmaster. He was at the barbecue pit when there were roastings; he was at the horse races on the main street; he took a hand often at pitching big round flat stones in a game played like horseshoes. He liked wrestling and crowbar throwing, and playing marbles with boys. He didn't fish or shoot, though some days he went down to the river with

Jack Kelso, the blacksmith. While Kelso fished he liked to talk and recite from the works of Shakespeare and Burns, and Lincoln listened. Lincoln could learn from Kelso. He sometimes joined in the discussion, but not in the fishing nor in the bottle which Kelso always had handy.

One of Lincoln's best friends was the justice of the peace, Bowling Green. Squire Green carried a little round paunch of a stomach in front of him, and was nicknamed "Pot." He knew his law, and he had been helping Lincoln edge into the law, helping him learn to write the simpler documents—deeds, bonds, bills of sale. Lincoln spent hours in the Green home talking about Illinois statutes while Nancy Green, the squire's wife, cooked hot biscuit smothered in butter and honey, doughnuts, and cookies, to eat with buttermilk and sweet cider.

Squire Green sometimes allowed Lincoln without fee to try small cases, examine witnesses, and make arguments. One afternoon a case came up before Squire Berry which Lincoln heard about, so that he left his surveying and acted as lawyer for a girl. It was a bastardy case. In his address to the court, Lincoln's speech likened a man's character in such a case to a piece of white cloth, which, though soiled, yet could be washed and hung out in the sun and become white again; whereas the character of the girl, who was no more to blame, was like a broken and shattered glass vase, which could not be made whole again.

In those New Salem days of Abraham Lincoln there were some who said he would be a great man, maybe governor of the state, anyhow a great lawyer. And there were others who looked on him as an athlete, an ordinary man, and a homely joker who felt sad sometimes and showed it.

In former days in Indiana he had hunted company, hungry for human talk of any kind; now he found himself drifting away from people; days came oftener when he wanted hours alone to think. He was seen walking the main street of New Salem reading a book, and, if attracted by a page or paragraph, shuffling to a standstill, pausing for contemplation. It was noticed that he had two shifting moods, the one of the rollicking, droll story and the one when he lapsed into a gravity beyond any bystander to penetrate.

He boarded round here and there in New Salem, his home first one place, then another. At one time, while storekeeping, he slept on the counter of the store. He wore flax and tow-linen pantaloons, no vest, no coat, and one suspender, a calico shirt, tan brogans, blue yarn socks, and a straw hat bound round with no string or band.

After the founders of New Salem, James Rutledge and John Camron, failed in business and moved their families to a house near Sand Ridge, Henry Onstott, who took over the Rutledge tavern, had Lincoln for a boarder a year or two.

Lincoln's old friend, Jack Armstrong, and his wife, Hannah, out at Clary's Grove, took him in two and three weeks at a time when he needed a place to sleep. Lincoln and Hannah sort of adopted each other; he was one of her boys; she talked to him with snapping lights in her eyes; she reminded him of Sally Bush. While Lincoln told the Armstrong children stories to chuckle over, Hannah sewed buckskins on the inner, lower part of his trousers, "foxed his pants," as the saying was, to protect his legs in briers and brush.

Hannah later said, "Abe would come out to our house, drink milk, eat mush, corn bread and butter, bring the children candy, and rock the cradle while I got him something to eat. I foxed his pants, made his shirts. He would tell stories, joke people, boys and girls at parties. He would nurse babies—do anything to accommodate anybody."

But Lincoln was not so at ease with all women. A. Y. Ellis, who kept a store where Lincoln helped out on busy days, later recalled: "He always disliked to wait on the ladies. He preferred trading with the men and boys, as he used to say. He was a very shy man of ladies."

On April 19, 1834, Lincoln's name ran again in the *Sangamo Journal* as a candidate for the state legislature. He had begun now to attend all sorts of political powwows, large and small; and those for whom he surveyed, and those he delivered letters to, did not fail to hear he was in the running. Backed by John T. Stuart, he had become a regular wheelhorse of the Whig party. Stuart was the Springfield lawyer who had been major of Lincoln's battalion in the Black Hawk War, who had encouraged his law studies and loaned him lawbooks. He was now the Sangamon County Whig leader.

This time Lincoln gave out no long address on issues as two years before. With no presidential ticket in the field, voters were freer in personal choice. Bowling Green was the local Democratic leader, and out of his liking for and belief in Lincoln, he offered him the support of fellow Democrats. Lincoln hesitated, talked it over with Stuart, then accepted.

All that late summer and early fall of 1834, even as he worked his hardest at electioneering, Lincoln must, in his own way, have been concerned about Ann Rutledge. Days were going hard for Ann; whisperers in New Salem were talking. Two years before, just after Lincoln's return from the Black Hawk War, she and a man named John McNeil had become engaged. McNeil, a storekeeper and farmer, had come to New Salem soon after its founding and had in a few years acquired property worth $12,000. In money and looks McNeil was considered a "good catch." Then McNeil had started on a trip east. As soon as he could visit his father and relatives in New York, he said, he would come back and claim his bride.

This was the promise and understanding, But after the first months away he had sent few letters to Ann, writing from Ohio that he was delayed by an attack of fever, writing again from New York that his father had died and he must settle his estate. Thus letters came, with excuses, from far off. And it was known to Lincoln, who had helped McNeil on deeds to land holdings, that McNeil's real name was McNamar. This was the name he had put in the deeds. He said he had come west taking another name in order that he might make his fortune without interference from his family back east. Whisperers talked about it in New Salem. Had his love died down? Or could a truthful love be expected from a man who would live under a false name?

Lincoln could hardly have been unaware of what Ann was going through; and he must have had his thoughts. Did Ann talk over with Lincoln the questions, bitter and haunting, that harassed her? Had death taken her betrothed? Would she see him, any day, riding into New Salem to claim her? Or, shifting to another awful possibility, would he come back to his land and properties, perhaps bringing a wife with him?

Possibly she kept silence and so did Lincoln, and there was some kind of understanding beneath their joined silence.

Lincoln was often away, sometimes for months, on his duties, writing her no letters that she kept and saved, she writing him no letters that he laid by as keepsakes. He was no man of property like McNamar. He had arrived in New Salem, "a piece of floating driftwood," as he later wrote; he was haunted by debts. Did he tell Ann of any dream or reverie that came to him about love in general or a particular love for her? Or did he shrink from such talk because she might be clinging to some last desperate hope that McNamar would return?

Two years of silence could be heavy and wearing. She was twenty-one and Lincoln twenty-five and in the few visits he had time for in this year of 1834 when surveying and politics pressed him hard, he may have gone no further than to be a comforter. He may have touched and stroked her auburn hair once or more as he looked into her blue eyes and said no word as to what hopes lay deep in his heart. Her mother could remember Ann's singing a hymn Lincoln liked, with a line, *"Vain man, thy fond pursuits forbear."*

Both were figures of fate—he caught with debts, with surveying, as he later wrote, "to keep body and soul together," while flinging himself into intense political activities; she the victim of a betrothal that had become a mysterious scandal.

But both were young, with hope endless, and it could have been he had moments when the sky was to him a sheaf of blue dreams and the rise of the blood-gold red of a full moon in the evening was almost too much to see and to remember.

Chapter 7

WHEN THE ILLINOIS LEGISLATURE met at Vandalia in December 1834, one of the sitting members was Abraham Lincoln. He had run second among thirteen candidates and so had won one of the four seats assigned to Sangamon County. He was twenty-five years old, holding his first elective office, and drawing three dollars a day pay, with privileges of ink, quills, and stationery. On being elected, he had gone to a friend, Coleman Smoot, who was farming near New Salem, and asked, "Did you vote for me?" and on Smoot answering, "Yes," he said, "I want to buy some clothes and fix up a little, and I want you to loan me two hundred dollars." So he sat at his desk in the state capital wearing a new suit, and having paid off one or two of his small but pressing debts. He had won his first important political office, and he was about to begin his training in the tangled and, to him, fascinating games of lawmaking and parliamentary management amid political labyrinths.

In Vandalia he roomed with John T. Stuart, also elected from Sangamon County, and Stuart's leadership made their room a Whig center. Here and in the legislature Lincoln was to meet men, most of them young, who would become governors, congressmen, United States senators, men of portent. Here he would meet a short, almost dwarfish man, a little giant, thick of body with a massive head, twenty-one years old and absolutely confident of himself—Stephen A. Douglas lobbying for his selection as state's attorney of the First Circuit. Many members had their wives and daughters along and there was a social life new to Lincoln—parties, cotillions, music, elegant food and liquor, silk gowns, and talk that ranged from idle gabble to profound conversation about the nation.

Among the fifty-four representatives Lincoln was one of thirty-five first-termers. Three-fourths of the members were southern-born; more than half were farmers. Lincoln's votes generally ran with those of Stuart and the Whig minority. He worked and voted for incorporation of a new state bank in Springfield. He introduced a bill limiting the jurisdiction of justices of the peace. His motion that it should not be in order "to offer amendments to any bill after its third reading" was tabled. Better luck came with passage of his bill to authorize his friend Samuel Musick to build a toll bridge across Salt Creek in Sangamon County. Several times other members put in bills that were in Lincoln's handwriting and it seemed his hand was in more affairs than he openly showed.

One lobbyist noted Lincoln in this legislature as "raw-boned, angular, features deeply furrowed, ungraceful, almost uncouth . . . and yet there was a magnetism and dash about the man that made him a universal favorite."

Once he had the House laughing. It had nominated a new surveyor of Schuyler County, and then word came there was no vacancy; the former surveyor still lived. On a motion that the nomination "be vacated" Lincoln stood up, unfolded to his full height, and remarked that the new surveyor could not legally oust the old one so long as the incumbent persisted in not dying. Let the matter be, he suggested, "so that if the old surveyor should hereafter conclude to die, there would be a new one ready without troubling the legislature." In the end the matter was tabled, as Lincoln had suggested.

Before midnight of February 13, 1835, the last batch of hacked and amended bills was passed and Lincoln in two days of below-zero weather rode the stage back to New Salem. Home again after the smoke-filled rooms and hullabaloo of Vandalia, he walked in open winter air over fields doing surveying, completing several surveys "to pay board and clothing bills." He also took up his lawbooks again, hoping and expecting the next year to be admitted to the bar. During that year, of whatever letters he wrote only three were saved, and they were perfunctory, shedding no light on his personal life or love or growth.

It was certain that Ann Rutledge and Lincoln knew each other and he took an interest in her. Probably they formed some mutual attachment. Possibly they loved each other and her hand went into his long fingers whose bones told her of refuge and security. But, if so, they were the only two persons who could tell what secret they shared.

Summer of 1835 came and in September it would be three years since McNamar had gone, more than two years since any letter had come from him. Probably Ann had, by now, written him that she expected release from her pledge.

Lincoln's resolution to study law drove him hard; friends worried about his health; he couldn't call on Ann often or for long. It was a seven-mile ride or walk when he called on her and her family at Sand Ridge, or at the nearby farm of Uncle Jimmy Short, where Ann worked for a time. She was saving money to go toward expenses at Jacksonville Female Academy twenty-five miles away, which she "had a notion" to enter in the fall term.

There seems to have been an understanding between Ann and Lincoln, with no pledges, that they would take what luck might hand them while they advanced their education. Lincoln had his debts, his law studies, his political ambitions, while she had her quandaries related to John McNamar. They would see what time might bring.

August of that summer came. Corn and grass, fed by rich rains in May and June, stood up stunted of growth, for want of more rain. To the homes of the settlers came chills and fever of malaria. Lincoln had been down, and up, and down again with aching bones, taking large spoonfuls of Peruvian bark, boneset tea, jalap, and calomel. One and another of his friends died; for some, he had helped nail together the burial boxes.

Ann Rutledge lay fever-burned. Days passed; help arrived and was helpless; her malady baffled the doctors. Her cousin, McGrady Rutledge, rode to New Salem and told Lincoln of her sickness growing worse. Lincoln rode out to the Sand Ridge farm. They let him in; they left the two together and alone for a last hour in the log house, with slants of light on her face from an open clapboard door. He saw her pale face and wasted body, the blue eyes and auburn hair perhaps the same as always. He may have let his bony right hand lie softly on her small white one while he tried for a few monosyllables of hope.

A few days later, on August 25, 1835, death came. Burial was in nearby Concord cemetery. Whether Lincoln went to Ann's funeral, whether he wept in grief with others at the sight of her face in the burial box, no one seemed to know; nor can we know his inner feelings. Later when Lincoln was the center of incalculable death and agony and a friend rebuked him for telling funny stories, he cried back, "Don't you see that if I didn't laugh I would have to weep?"

It was to come to pass that thirty years later New Salem villagers soberly spoke and wrote that Lincoln at the time of

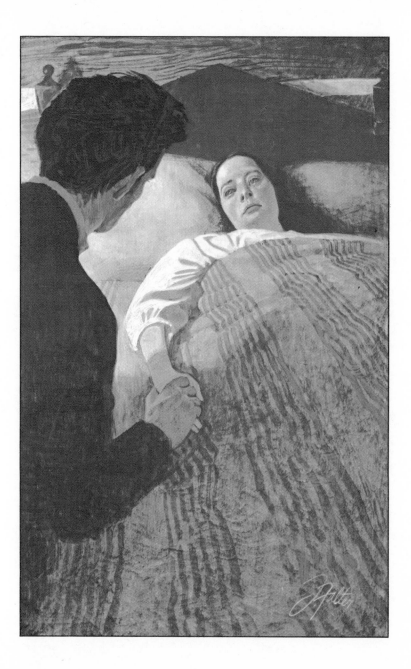

Ann's death went out of his mind, and wandered in the woods mumbling and crazy, all of which was exaggeration and reckless expansion of his taking Ann's death "verry hard." Woven with the recollections of his "insanity" were also the testimonies of what a flaming of lyric love there had been between him and Ann.

John McNamar returned to Illinois three weeks after Ann died, bringing with him his aged mother, and reported that his father had died and he had straightened out the estate. Of what he said of Ann's passing there is no record. In 1838 Mc-Namar married and after the death of his first wife married again. He became county assessor and proved honest and fair. He lived to be seventy-eight unaware that in chronicles to come he would figure as an enigmatic lover.

IN DECEMBER 1835, Lincoln was in Vandalia for six weeks as a lawmaker, and, his term over, he was back in Sangamon County, working away as surveyor, law student, politician. He wrote wills, located roads, settled boundary disputes, and on May 30, 1836, he handed out mail as postmaster for the last time; the New Salem post office was moved to Petersburg.

On June 13, 1836, Lincoln again announced himself as a candidate for election to the legislature. This time writing in the *Sangamo Journal*, he declared that he was for internal improvements, that he would vote for Hugh L. White, the Tennessee Whig, who was running against the Jackson Democrat, Martin Van Buren, for President in November. He also declared that women ought to have the vote. "I go for ... admitting all whites to the right of suffrage, who pay taxes or bear arms (by no means excluding females)."

On the stump he was earning a reputation as a hard man to handle. In Springfield, speaking in the courthouse, he clashed with George Forquer, a lawyer who had switched from Whig to Democrat and then was named by the Jackson Administration at Washington as register of the land office at $3,000 a year. Forquer had just finished building a frame house, the finest in Springfield, and put up a lightning rod on it, the first lightning rod in that part of Illinois. After a speech by Lincoln, Forquer took the platform and said the young man who had just spoken was sailing too high and would have to be "taken down"; and then he made what was termed "a slasher-gaff speech." Lincoln stood by with folded arms and measuring eyes.

When Forquer quit speaking, Lincoln stepped up quietly, apologized, offered his argument and closed as follows: "Mr. Forquer commenced his speech by announcing that the young man would have to be taken down. It is for you, fellow citizens, not for me, to say whether I am up or down. I desire to live, and I desire place and distinction; but I would rather die now than, like the gentleman, live to see the day that I would change my politics for an office worth three thousand dollars a year, and then feel compelled to erect a lightning rod to protect a guilty conscience from an offended God." The speech delighted the audience, and his friends carried him from the courthouse on their shoulders.

In the election on August 1, the Whigs took Sangamon County away from the Democrats, by an average majority of four hundred votes; among seventeen candidates for the legislature, Lincoln was in the lead.

Soon after this sweeping victory Lincoln in stride took his bar examination before two justices of the supreme court, passed, and on September 9, 1836, held in his hands a license to practice law in all the courts of Illinois. On October 5 he was in a Springfield court, appearing in a case for John T. Stuart, the beginning of what would be their partnership as a law firm.

In October and November he made three more known surveys and said good-by to surveying. And in December he went to Vandalia, one of nine tall Whigs who became famous as the "Long Nine." The Long Nine averaged six feet in height, and Lincoln was the longest. Riding the stage to Vandalia, they talked about strategy that would carry through the legislature the one law more important to them than any other, an act to make Springfield the capital of Illinois. Lincoln was to be the Whig floor leader and thus in charge of their strategy.

The Long Nine were also for big projects "commensurate with the wants of the people." They would build some 1350 miles of railroad. They would spend $100,000 to improve the

Rock River; $4,000,000 to complete the Illinois and Michigan Canal; $250,000 for the Western Mail Route.

Altogether, the scheme would cost $10,000,000. Lincoln was among the leaders arguing for it. They would sell bonds to raise the $10,000,000; they would raise the money by promises on paper. And the scheme won out in the legislature, which took the silence of the people of the state for consent. A boom was on, overloaded and sure to collapse. It was the pioneer stock, taking its chances, believing in the future, and believing that future would come sooner if boomed.

That Lincoln, who could not finance himself, should show no ability in financing the state of Illinois in a vast economic project was to have been expected. And yet he had a vision of himself at this time as a constructive statesman, pushing through plans in Illinois for transportation ways, schools, and education.

He was now meeting men of importance from all parts of Illinois; they came from towns and counties wanting appropriations, from banks, railroads, contractors, seeking legislation for special interests. Lincoln, the storyteller, the whimsical, good-natured philosopher, was asked to their game suppers and banquets.

After a day of legislative sessions, committee meetings, conferences, study of bills and measures, and a game supper, Lincoln enjoyed sitting in a hotel room with friendly souls, sitting with his knees up to his chin, drawling out stories, talking about how they were beating the Democrats, emphasizing a good point by drawing his knees again up to his chin and letting both feet down on the floor with a slam.

His colleague, Robert L. Wilson of the Long Nine, later gave this size-up of Lincoln: "He was as much at home in the legislature as at New Salem; he had a quaint and peculiar way, all his own, of treating a subject, and he frequently startled us. He seemed to be a born politician. We followed his lead; but he followed nobody's lead. It may almost be said that he did our thinking for us. He inspired respect, although he was careless and negligent. We recognized him as a master in logic. He was poverty itself, but independent. He seemed to glide along in life without any friction or effort."

On February 24, 1837, the Long Nine found the votes in the legislature to pass the bill moving the capital of the state from Vandalia to Springfield. Other counties besides Sangamon had been hustling for the location; it went to Springfield mainly because of the patient and skilled manipulation of Lincoln. A few members voted for the bill because they liked Lincoln, but most of the votes came through trades, deals, "logrolling." "You scratch my back and I'll scratch yours." And yet as a manipulator Lincoln operated by a code of his own. An all-night session was held by the members favoring Springfield for the state capital; and Lincoln was told of a block of votes he could have if he would give his vote for a certain measure that he considered against his principles; but the members went home at daybreak without having brought him their way. "You will never get me to support a measure which I believe to be wrong," he said, "although by doing so I may accomplish that which I believe to be right."

Just a few days before the legislature adjourned, Lincoln did a thing as independent as the way he wore his hat. He stood almost alone against the whole legislature.

Over the nation the question had come up whether the slavery of the Negro race under the white race was right or wrong, and whether any man or woman, believing it wrong, should be free to say so. The question was being hotly debated.

Forty solemn men and women meeting in a house in Philadelphia four years previous had organized the American Anti-Slavery Society, calling on the free states to remove slavery "by moral and political action, as prescribed in the Constitution of the United States," and announcing, "We shall organize anti-slavery societies, if possible, in every city, town, and village in the land. . . . We shall circulate unsparingly and extensively antislavery tracts and periodicals."

Meanwhile, however, in the southern states it had become unlawful to speak against slavery; any person found guilty of an agitation that might cause an insurrection of slaves was hanged, in accordance with the statutes. The three million Negro workers in the southern states were property, livestock valued by tax assessors at more than a billion dollars; and the

77

cotton belt was spreading westward, adding thousands of acres every month. Legislatures of four southern states were asking that northern states "suppress all associations purporting to be abolition societies"; governors of New York and Massachusetts had asked their legislatures to take such action. Abolitionists, on the other hand, maintained that the United States Constitution in its silent assent to slavery was "a compact with Hell," and from week to week continued to publish their papers. From the government at Washington on down to business partnerships and families, the slavery question was beginning to split the country in two. And aggravations between people south and north were getting worse. Across the northern states the Underground Railway had been organized, a series of routes across the free states and over into Canada. An antislavery man would keep a runaway slave in his house and drive him to the next house or tell him the way. Officers of the law and slave-owners came north with warrants hunting their runaway property; Illinois was seeing them often.

These drifts were known to Abraham Lincoln, as he spent the winter months in Vandalia. The legislature was mostly of southern blood and point of view, and Lincoln could understand his fellow members of the legislature when they passed resolutions declaring: "We highly disapprove of the formation of Abolition Societies . . . the right of property in slaves is sacred to the slaveholding States by the Federal Constitution, and . . . they cannot be deprived of that right without their consent."

But Lincoln voted against these resolutions, though he was joined by only five other members. With one of them, Dan Stone, a former member of the Ohio legislature, he recorded in the *Journal of Proceedings* a protest in language completely courteous but quietly unmistakable in meaning:

> Resolutions upon the subject of domestic slavery having passed both branches of the General Assembly at its present session, the undersigned hereby protest against the passage of the same.
>
> They believe that the institution of slavery is founded on both injustice and bad policy; but that the promulgation of abolition doctrines tends rather to increase than abate its evils.
>
> They believe that the Congress of the United States has no

power under the constitution, to interfere with the institution of slavery in the different States.

They believe that the Congress of the United States has the power, under the constitution, to abolish slavery in the District of Columbia; but that that power ought not to be exercised unless at the request of the people of said district.

The difference between these opinions and those contained in the said resolutions, is their reason for entering this protest.

The end of the legislative session came on March 6, 1837, and the Long Nine started home on their horses, with the exception of Lincoln, whose horse had been stolen. As Lincoln walked, the others pointed to the size of his feet; when he shivered and said, "Boys, I'm cold," another noticed, "No wonder—there's so much of you on the ground."

Arrived at Springfield, the Long Nine sat down to a game supper while spokesmen for Springfield expressed gratitude to those who had arranged to move the state capital from Vandalia to their own city. One toast ran, "Abraham Lincoln: he has fulfilled the expectations of his friends, and disappointed the hopes of his enemies."

He was growing, young Abraham Lincoln. He was a learner, calling himself, and called by others, "a learner always."

Chapter 8

ON A CERTAIN APRIL DAY in 1837, Abraham Lincoln borrowed a horse from Squire Bowling Green, packed his saddlebags, and started the eighteen-mile ride from New Salem to Springfield. He was twenty-eight years old, he had seven dollars in his pocket and he was still more than a thousand dollars in debt. But he was also now a licensed lawyer, a member of the state legislature, and floor leader of the Whig party, and he was about to start practicing law as a member of the new firm of Stuart & Lincoln.

Springfield as he approached it in 1837 was the big town of Sangamon County, having fourteen hundred inhabitants, and selling to the eighteen thousand people of the county a large part of their supplies. Its people, mostly from Kentucky, had come by horse, wagon, and boat across country not yet cleared of wolves and wildcats. But now Springfield was a city, ready to say there was no more wilderness. Farm women coming to town wore shoes where they used to go barefoot; men had changed from moccasins to boots and shoes. Carriages held men riding in ruffled silk shirts, and women in silks and laces. It was civilization which Abraham Lincoln, twenty-eight years old, saw as he rode into town that April day.

Lincoln pulled in his horse at the general store of Joshua Speed. He asked the price of bedclothes for a single bedstead, which Speed figured at $17. "Cheap as it is, I have not the money to pay," he told Speed. "But if you will credit me until Christmas, and my experiment as a lawyer here is a success, I will pay you then. If I fail in that I will probably never pay you at all." Speed said afterward, "The tone of his voice was so melancholy that I felt for him. I looked up at him and thought that I never saw so gloomy and melancholy a face in my life." Speed offered to share his own big double bed upstairs over the store. Lincoln's face lit up. He took his saddlebags upstairs, came down, and said, "Well, Speed, I'm moved." Thus began a friendship that was to last long.

The circuit courtroom was on the lower floor of a two-story building in Hoffman's Row. Upstairs, over the courtroom, was the law office of Stuart & Lincoln: a little room with a few loose boards for bookshelves, an old wood stove, a table, a chair, a bench, and a small bed.

Stuart was running for Congress in the next election, so Lincoln handled all of the law practice in range of his ability. Between law cases he kept up his political fences, writing many letters. Lifting his head from his work, he could look out from the Stuart & Lincoln office window at passersby on Springfield's main street and public square: the doctor going to a birth, the hearse leading a burial party, farmers hauling corn, children going to school. Droves of hogs came past, in muddy weather wallowing over their knees, their curls of tails flipping as they grunted onward to sale and slaughter.

And there were horses, and men riding and driving who loved horses. It was a horse country. They too were passersby—roans, grays, whites, black horses with white stockings, bays with a white star in the forehead.

In a letter to Levi Davis, Esq., of Vandalia, Lincoln wrote on April 19: "We have generally in this country, peace, health, and plenty, and no news."

Then, a few weeks later, he wrote a quaint letter out of an odd, lonely heart.

THE LETTER WAS ADDRESSED to Miss Mary Owens, the daughter of a rich Kentucky farmer whom Lincoln had come to know while she was visiting her married sister in New Salem. Miss Mary Owens, of Green County, Kentucky, four months older than he, was plump-faced, with a head of dark curly hair and large blue eyes. She had first interested Lincoln when she had visited New Salem briefly in 1833. Her sister, Mrs. Bennett Abell, at whose house Lincoln once stayed, had played matchmaker and, during the autumn of 1836, just past, when starting for a visit to Kentucky, had said, perhaps only joking, that she would bring her sister Mary back if Lincoln would marry her. Lincoln had said, perhaps only joking, that he accepted the proposal to become Mrs. Abell's brother-in-law.

It seemed as though Lincoln at this time was looking for a wife. And yet there were things operating against him in the getting of one from among those women who had come his way. He was backward, perhaps bashful, about telling any woman truly how he felt; and without showing that he was bashful he would talk politics or science or the news, or drift into droll humors that would puzzle women. He was odd; he did have a "peculiar manner"; he was homely, ironical, kindly, whimsical, with a fierce physical strength kept under fine control. Yet it was never said of him by those close to him, as was said of his father before him, "He had a way with women."

When Miss Owens had returned to New Salem with her sister in November 1836, Lincoln saw three years had worked changes, Miss Owens having lost bloom, lost teeth, and become stout. She, meanwhile, as one trained in Kentucky schools for refined young ladies, had held off his rather careless overtures. She had noted Lincoln as "deficient in those little links which make up a woman's happiness." He puzzled her; in some things he was so softhearted. He had told her of turning back to get a hog loose when he had seen it mired in mud on the prairie, even though he was in his best clothes. But once when they were in a riding party and came to a treacherous creek crossing, while other men helped their partners, Miss Owens saw Lincoln riding ahead of her without looking back. She had ideas about chivalry and wondered how a man could be so thoughtful about a hog and another time so "neglect" his woman riding partner.

Nevertheless, they had evidently come to some vague understanding that they might marry. From Vandalia that winter Lincoln had written her one or two drawling cryptic letters— letters of hunger for love with hope running low of any answering love. She had not answered these letters. And now, one day early in May, when the stir of new grass was green over the prairie, Lincoln took his pen and wrote another letter to Miss Owens. He wrote of Springfield, and he wrote of marriage. He was telling her he was willing to marry, if she so wished, though his advice would be not to marry. The letter read, in part:

> This thing of living in Springfield is rather a dull business after all, at least it is so to me. I am quite as lonesome here as [I] ever was anywhere in my life. I have been spoken to by but one woman since I've been here, and should not have been by her, if she could have avoided it. . . . I am often thinking of what we said of your coming to live at Springfield. I am afraid you would not be satisfied. There is a great deal of flourishing about in carriages here, which it would be your doom to see without shareing in it. You would have to be poor without the means of hiding your poverty. Do you believe you could bear that patiently? Whatever woman may cast her lot with mine, should any ever do so, it is my intention to do all in my power to make her happy and contented; and there is nothing I can immagine, that would make me more unhappy than to fail in the effort. I know I should be much happier with you than the way I am, provided I saw no signs of discontent in you. . . . You must write me a good long letter after you get this.

That summer Mary Owens and Lincoln saw each other and talked and came to no understanding. When Mary returned again to Kentucky, and Lincoln wrote her, he addressed her as "Friend Mary," and he said: "You must know that I can not see you, or think of you, with entire indifference; and yet it may be, that you, are mistaken in regard to what my real feelings towards you are. . . . I want in all cases to do right, and most particularly so, in all cases with women. I want, at this particular time, more than anything else, to do right with you, and if I *knew* it would be doing right, as I rather suspect it would, to let you alone, I would do it. . . . Do not understand by this, that I wish to cut your acquaintance. I mean no such thing. What I do wish is, that our further acquaintance shall depend upon yourself." And he concluded: "If it suits you best to not answer this—farewell."

So the months passed by and the comedy of man, woman, and destiny worked itself out. The fact that marriages are often accidents later lighted up his brain as his imagination reviewed events. On the first day of April, 1838, when the comedy had ended, he wrote a letter about it. The letter was filled with the chuckles and oddities of a storyteller telling a story with the laugh on himself.

Among his men acquaintances and friends there was not one he could pour out the story to. So he chose a woman, Mrs. Orville H. Browning of Quincy, the wife of a fellow member of the legislature, to hear his confessions. He had found her exceptionally understanding in conversation; she had a sense of humor. On this April Fool's Day he confessed that he had vanity and stupidity, that he had made a fool of himself:

It was, then, in the autumn of 1836, that a married lady of my acquaintance . . . being about to pay a visit to her . . . relatives residing in Kentucky, proposed to me, that on her return she would bring a sister of hers with her, upon condition that I would engage to become her brother-in-law with all convenient dispatch. I, of course, accepted the proposal; for . . . I had seen the said sister some three years before, thought her inteligent and agreeable, and saw no good objection to plodding life through hand in hand with her. Time passed on, the lady took her journey . . . sure enough. . . . We had an interview, and although I had seen her before, she did not look as my immagination had pictured her. I knew she was over-size, but she now appeared a fair match for Falstaff . . . in short, I was not all pleased with her. But what could I do? I had told her sister that I would take her for better or for worse; and I made a point of honor and conscience in all things, to stick to my word.

He went on to describe how, as time went by, he tried to remain "firm" in his resolution to make her his wife, for it did seem as if she and her family approved the "bargain." Nonetheless he found himself "continually repenting" his "rashness"; so in spite of himself he spent his time planning how he might "procrastinate the evil day for a time, which I really dreaded as much—perhaps more, than an irishman does the halter." And then:

After all my suffering upon this deeply interesting subject, here I am, wholly unexpectedly, completely out of the "scrape"; and I now want to know, if you can guess how I got out of it. . . . As the lawyers say, it was done in the manner following, towit. After I had delayed the matter as long as I thought I could in honor do, which by the way had brought me round into the last fall, I concluded I might as well bring it to a consumation without further delay; and so I mustered my resolution, and made the proposal to her direct; but, shocking to relate, she answered, No. At first I supposed she did it through an affectation of modesty . . . [so] I tried it again and again, but with the same success, or rather with the same want of success. I finally was forced to give it up, at which I verry unexpectedly found myself mortified almost beyond endurance. I was mortified, it seemed to me, in a hundred different ways. My vanity was deeply wounded by the reflection, that I had so long been too stupid to discover her intentions, and . . . to cap the whole, I then, for the first time, began to suspect that I was really a little in love with her. But let it all go. I'll try and out live it. Others have been made fools of by the girls; but this can never be with truth said of me. I most emphatically, in this instance, made a fool of myself. I have now come to the conclusion never again to think of marrying; and for this reason; I can never be satisfied with any one who would be block-head enough to have me.

The letter, like those to Miss Owens, was a self-portrait. Mr. and Mrs. Browning took it as the queer prank of a mind of fantasy and humor, having heard Lincoln's storytelling. Had he named the woman he could have had credit as a gossip. But he named no names but his own, and so was able to rollick in the fun of having gotten out of a scrape.

Chapter 9

A SCHOOL FOR YOUNG LADIES in Springfield was announcing that besides ordinary branches of education and training in "intellectual and moral science," it would conduct "a class in Mezzotint painting." A store was offering on sale "cloth, comb, tooth, hair and nail brushes." Civilization and culture were stirring in Illinois. The Alton Literary Society met in the courthouse in that city and debated the question, "Was Brutus justified in killing Caesar?"

Lincoln read newspapers, skirmished through exchanges in the *Sangamo Journal* office. One week in November of 1839, he saw an editorial which he read carefully more than once or twice in the *Illinois State Register*, the Democratic newspaper of Springfield. It was the first time any attempt had been made through the public prints to improve his manners. He had spoken in the courthouse as a candidate for presidential elector on a Tuesday evening, in reply to Stephen A. Douglas, and the *State Register* commented:

> Mr. Lincoln's argument was truly ingenious. He has, however, a sort of *assumed clownishness* in his manner which does not become him . . . he can thus frequently raise a loud laugh among his Whig hearers; but this entire game of buffoonery convinces the *mind* of no man, and is utterly lost on the majority of his audience. We seriously advise Mr. Lincoln to correct this clownish fault before it grows upon him.

In Tuesday's debating, however, Douglas was the loser, the *Register* acknowledged. "Our Democratic 'little giant' . . . had a rough time of it."

85

Also in the same issue of the *Register*, Lincoln could turn a page and read an advertisement of a sort common in all newspapers then. It read:

> $50 Reward. Ran away from the subscriber, living in Lewis County, Mo., four miles from Tully, a slave named Charles, about 20 years of age . . . had . . . a scar on the right wrist, and one between the neck and collar-bone; had also scars on his back.

Reading the newspapers, handling whatever legal work came his way, looking out through the little windowpanes of the law office overlooking the main street and the public square, listening at the street corners in summer and at the circles around wood stoves in the grocery stores in winter, Lincoln came to know the haunts and tabernacles of politics.

On a hot summer day Harvey Ross came to prove ownership of his farm at Macomb, needing the testimony of a witness near Springfield. Court had closed, Lincoln explained, but they would go out to Judge Thomas's farm. With a bundle of papers in one hand and in the other a red handkerchief for wiping sweat, Lincoln with Ross and the witness walked to the farm. The judge had gone to a tenant house on the north part of the farm, to help his men put up a corncrib and hog pen, said Mrs. Thomas. They struck out across the cornfield Indian file, Lincoln still with papers in one hand and red handkerchief in the other. Arriving where the judge and his men were raising logs, Lincoln put the case to the judge, who looked over the papers, swore in the witness, and, with pen and ink from the tenant house, signed the documents. All were in shirt sleeves, and Lincoln remarked it was a kind of shirt-sleeve court they were holding there in the cornfield. Then he offered to roll up some logs and the judge guessed he could stand a little help. They pitched in and when Ross asked the judge his fee the judge said he guessed their help was pay enough.

Once more he carried an election to the legislature, also stumping for his law partner, John T. Stuart, who was elected to Congress in 1838. When Stuart was running against Steve Douglas for Congress the two struck, grappled, and "fought like wildcats" back and forth over the floor of Herndon's

grocery till each was too tired to hit another blow. When Stuart came to, he ordered a barrel of whisky for the crowd.

Lincoln, a while later, sending news to Stuart in Washington, wrote: "Yesterday Douglas, having chosen to consider himself insulted by something in the 'Journal,' undertook to cane Francis [the editor] in the street. Francis caught him by the hair and jammed him back against a market-cart, where the matter ended by Francis being pulled away from him. The whole affair was so ludicrous that Francis and everybody else (Douglas excepted) have been laughing about it ever since."

The Whigs rented the courthouse for a campaign meeting one day, and Edward D. Baker, speaking on the issues of the day, declared that wherever there was a land office there was a Democratic newspaper to defend its corruption. Democrats in the audience yelled, "Pull him down." A riot was starting when Lincoln, who had been listening to the speech through a trapdoor looking from his office down into the courtroom, came dangling down with his long legs through the hole in the ceiling. He helped bring order by saying, "Hold on, gentlemen. This is a land of free speech. Baker has a right to speak, and if you take him off the stand you'll have to take me, too."

At a political meeting in Springfield he replied to an attack on the Long Nine by Jesse B. Thomas; it was a furious and directly personal handling he gave Thomas, with jabs of sarcasm and a mimicking of Thomas; Springfield called it a "terrible skinning," and it was alluded to as "the skinning of Thomas." The crowd had "egged him on" with yells and cheers so that Lincoln gave Thomas a worse skinning than he intended. Afterward he went to Thomas's office and said he was sorry; he told friends he wasn't proud of the performance.

While Stuart was in Washington, Lincoln handled the law practice and kept track of politics. Out of the silences of the little law office he sent letters to Stuart about the many errands he was running from day to day and the items of news, the twists of life he had his eyes and ears bent toward.

"Dear Stuart," he wrote, for example, on December 23, 1839. "Dr. Henry will write you all the political news. I write this about some little matters of business. You recollect you told me you had drawn the Chicago Masack money, and sent it to the claimants. A d—d hawk billed yankee is here, besetting me at every turn I take, saying that Robt Kinzie never received the $80. to which he was entitled. Can you tell me any thing about the matter? Again, old Mr. Wright, who lives up South Fork somewhere, is teasing me continually about some deeds which he says he left with you, but which I can find nothing of. Can you tell me where they are?"

He closed one letter to Stuart with a reference to a local politician's delivering a speech which William May answered. "The way May let the wind out of him was a perfect wonder." To this letter was the postscript: "Japh Bell has come out for Harrison. Ain't that a caution?"

His first published speech in pamphlet form was coming off the printing presses early in 1840 and he wrote Stuart: "Well, I made a big speech, which is in progress of printing in pamphlet form. To enlighten you and the rest of the world, I shall send you a copy when it is finished." The speech was one of a series of discussions of issues of the day, each speaker taking an entire evening, the general public invited to attend, in the hall of the House of Representatives in Springfield.

The thirty-year-old orator ranged across many fierce issues of the hour when he spoke. Not only was he the strong young man who could take an ax handle and go to the polls and alone open a way through a gang blocking passage to the voting place; not only was he the athlete they had seen take two fighting men and throw them apart as though they were two kittens. He was impressionable, with soft spots, with tremulous pools of changing lights. He could stand up loose-jointed and comic with appeals in street-corner slang, yet at moments he was solemn as naked facts of death or hunger.

He declared ten years of Democratic administration had cost more money than the first twenty-seven years of the country's government, including the cost of the War of 1812. "The large sums foolishly, not to say corruptly, thrown away, constitute one of the just causes of complaint against the Administration. The agents of the Government in connection with the Florida [Indian] war needed a certain steamboat; the owner proposed to sell it for $10,000.00; the agents refused to give that sum, but hired the boat at $100.00 per day, and kept it at that hire till it amounted to $92,000.00."

He took up discussion of the subtreasury plan proposed by the Democrats, declaring it "less safe" than the national bank plan of the Whigs; with however much care selections of bank officers might be made, there would be some unfaithful and dishonest. "The experience of the whole world, in all bygone times, proves this true. The Saviour of the world chose twelve disciples, and even one of that small number, selected by super-human wisdom, turned out to be a traitor and a devil. And it may not be improper here to add that Judas carried the bag— was the sub-treasurer of the Saviour and his disciples."

Toward the end of his speech, Abraham Lincoln spoke like a man watching a crazy and cruel horizon. "Many free countries have lost their liberty; and ours may lose hers; but if she shall, be it my proudest plume, not that I was the last to desert, but that I never deserted her. I know that the great volcano in Washington, aroused and directed by the evil spirit that reigns there is belching forth the lava of political corruption in a cur-rent broad and deep, which is sweeping with frightful velocity over the whole length and breadth of the land. . . . Broken by it I, too, may be; bow to it I never will."

The allusions concerned the killing of Elijah P. Lovejoy in Alton, a town seventy miles from Springfield, two years before. Lovejoy, an abolitionist Presbyterian minister, had brought a printing press to Alton from St. Louis, intending through the columns of his weekly newspaper to speak what he believed ought to be spoken; and a mob had thrown his printing press into the Mississippi River. He brought another printing press to Alton; the mob again wrecked it. And a third time he brought a printing press to Alton, and the mob circled by night with torches and guns around the warehouse where he had the print-ing office, and they set the warehouse on fire, and when Lovejoy ran out they shot him and killed him. And over the Illinois prairies and from the frontier to the eastern coast of America there was discussion about whether this young man, Elijah P. Lovejoy, was right or wrong in saying, against repeated warnings, that he must speak what he believed ought to be spoken.

In Springfield, as Abraham Lincoln had read the newspapers, the picture of what had happened at Alton had shocked him. That was his own word for it; he was shocked. Feet on the office table, gazing across the public square, he sat huddled with his thoughts.

When a bill came up in the legislature to throw off to the territory of Wisconsin the fourteen northern counties of the state of Illinois, he fought to defeat it. He wanted Illinois to have Chicago, a port on one of the Great Lakes within its borders, connecting the West with the East. If the measure had won, it would have left Illinois depending on the Ohio and Mississippi rivers for water transportation, with its main economic outlets toward the south, with its future tied closer to the South. The bill was beaten by seventy votes to eleven.

At Page Eaton's carpenter shop one afternoon he stopped and talked. Page Eaton allowed that everybody said Lincoln would never make a good lawyer because he was too honest. And as Eaton told it: "Lincoln said he had a notion to quit studying law and learn carpentering. He thought there was more need of carpenters out here than lawyers."

Watching his fellow citizens, he learned more ways and habits of politics than are told of in the books. The spinning of weaves and webs was going on, schemers winding back and forth trying to piece together their schemes. In order to live and stand up and be one of the men among men in that frontier town and state in the years around 1840, a man had to know schemers, had to know how to spot a scheme when he saw one coming, and how to meet scheme with scheme. It was not only Abe Lincoln's honesty that had put him in the front among leaders of the Whig party, nor only that he had personality and was a vote getter; it was also that he was a schemer: he had a long head and could gun for game far off. He was peering at Stephen A. Douglas, the register of the land office, just as he had peered at unknown lights moving in shallows of the Mississippi River as he drew near in a flatboat.

A young man lit up with wild human enthusiasms had begun

91

clerking in the Speed store, and sleeping upstairs in the big room with Speed and Lincoln. He was William H. Herndon, whose father had taken him out of Illinois College at Jacksonville when the killing of Lovejoy started abolition bonfires among its professors and students. He had been with Lincoln on one or two stumping trips, and he was thinking of studying law.

Between these two men, Lincoln nine years the older, there was a trust and understanding not common among men. They belonged with Speed to a club of young men who met and read their writings to each other; Lincoln once entertained them with rhymes about the mistakes of men and women toward each other, one reading:

> *Whatever spiteful fools may say,*
> *Each jealous ranting yelper,*
> *No woman ever went astray,*
> *Without a man to help her.*

Interest in politics, the science of government, and the destiny of the human race was so keen at this time that the young Democrats and Whigs had a debating tournament that ran eight days straight, Sunday excepted. The future held the thoughts of these young men. What with railroads coming west, the border would move, the Great Plains fill up with settlers.

Peoria ran stages daily to Springfield; seven steamers made trips between Peoria, St. Louis, and Pittsburgh; another ran between St. Louis and the Rock River. History and destiny were in the air; the name of Stone's Landing was changed to Napoleon; the name of Goose Run to Columbus River. The land was now all surveyed; fences were coming. Land speculators held the larger part of the land in Illinois. The wilderness was passing into the hands of landlords and speculators.

In state and national politics, the western public lands became an issue. Martin Van Buren, the New York Tammany Democrat who was picked by Andrew Jackson to follow him in the White House, was beaten in the wild campaign of 1840 partly because of his record of having voted against western internal improvements, against the Cumberland Road, and the reduction of the price of public lands. William Henry Harrison, the first

Whig and the first northern man from west of the Allegheny Mountains, entered the White House. The campaign and the election filled the Illinois Whigs with enthusiasm; some predicted their party had come to stay, that the Democratic party was hitting a slump that would mean its death.

One of Lincoln's early speeches in the campaign was in Alton, where it was announced by large handbills declaring:

ATTENTION! THE PEOPLE!!
A. Lincoln, Esq'r., of Sangamon County,
one of the Electoral Candidates, will Address
the People this Evening!! At Early Candlelighting,
at the   ☞   Old Court Room   ☞   (Riley's
Building). By request of Many Citizens.
Thursday April 9th, 1840.

In this campaign Lincoln did more stumping than in any previous campaign. He was matched against Douglas in many debates. He spoke from a wagon at a big conclave of Whigs in Springfield in June, which was attended by fifteen thousand people, some from as far as Chicago. They came in carriages and wagons, on horseback and on foot. They came with log cabins drawn on wheels by oxen. They came with music and banners, thousands from long distances. Among the Whig orators was Fletcher Webster, a son of Daniel Webster. Delegates from Chicago had been hauled to the gathering by fourteen teams; it took them three weeks to make the trip. One log cabin on wheels had been hauled by thirty yoke of oxen; it had a hickory tree growing by a cabin, with live coons in the tree, and a barrel of hard cider on tap by the cabin door. The Chicago delegates were flying a petticoat, a Democratic symbol of Harrison as a warrior; they had torn it from Democrats on the way. There was singing:

> *Without a why or a wherefore*
> *We'll go for Harrison therefore.*

A large handbill got out by the Whigs, with Lincoln's name printed among other Whig electors, was headed "To the Friends of the National Road." The slogan "Freemen, Strike

Home!" stood in large type. In smaller type were such accusations as, "The scows, pile-drivers, hammers, &c. &c. used in constructing the harbor at Chicago, and which is now unfinished, have been sold by order of the government for $201—having cost more than $6,000."

Illinois voted for Harrison; A. Lincoln as one of the electoral college cast his vote for him. It was a famous campaign proving that sometimes the American democracy goes on a rampage and shows that it has swift and terrific power, even though it is not sure what to do with that power.

Among Illinois Whigs there were regrets. They carried their national ticket, but lost the state to the Democrats. When the newly elected state legislature came into session, it had a Democratic majority. During this session of the legislature there were bitter feelings between the Whigs and Democrats. The voting was often close. Once when the Democrats wanted a quorum and the Whigs didn't, the Democrats locked the door of the house so as to keep the quorum in. Lincoln, Joe Gillespie, and another Whig raised a window and jumped out and hid.

Chapter 10

NINIAN W. EDWARDS, son of a former Illinois governor, lived in Springfield, was one of the Long Nine, was of the same age as Abraham Lincoln, and the two had campaigned and electioneered together over Sangamon County. The Edwards house stood two stories high and was big enough to hold within its walls a dozen prairie-farmer cabins. Its walls and chimneys were of brick, with porches running the lengths of two sides of the house; its tall windows went higher than a tall man's arms would reach. Brocades of wooden scrollwork embellished the eaves; an ornamented railing guarded the second-story portico.

And there had come to the house of Ninian W. Edwards in 1839 a young woman from Lexington, Kentucky. She had been there two years before on a short visit; but now she had come to stay. She was Miss Mary Todd, and was a younger sister of Elizabeth, the wife of Ninian W. Edwards. The sisters were granddaughters of Todds who had fought with Washington through the American Revolution; their father, Robert Smith Todd, had served in both houses of the legislature in Kentucky, and was president of the Bank of Kentucky in Lexington.

Miss Mary Todd was twenty-one years old, plump, swift, beaming, with ready answers slipping from a sharp tongue, in the year that Springfield, and Abraham Lincoln, became acquainted with her. She had her gifts, a smooth soft skin, soft brown hair, and flashing clear blue eyes. With her somewhat short figure sheathed in a gown of white with black stripes, cut low at the neck, her skirt fluffed out in a hoop, shod in modish ballroom slippers, she was a center of likes and dislikes among those who came to the house where her sister was mistress. Though her tongue and its sarcasm that came so quickly and so often brought hates, there was a shine and a bubbling, a foaming over of vitality, that won friends. For Lincoln, as he came to know her, she was lighted with magnets.

She was the first aggressively brilliant feminine creature ever to cross his path. She haunted him and held his attentions by the use of age-old fascinations difficult of analysis. He could keep his head and outguess lights, shoals, and sandbars of the Ohio and Mississippi rivers; with Mary Todd he lost his head. His experience was rich with rivers, starved with women; as one woman remarked, he didn't *go* as much as other young men for "ladies company."

Besides the charm that attached to Mary Todd she was a triumph of cultivation: she had what were known as accomplishments. She had all that the most aristocratic schools of Kentucky could implant. She spoke and read French. Conversation, manners, belles lettres, the piano and approved classical music, had been taught. Punctiliously schooled, she nonetheless had kept a native and bottom fiber of strength and will; she had left her home in Kentucky and had taken up her new home in Illinois because of a dispute with her stepmother. She was impetuous, picked the ridiculous angle, the weak point of anyone she disliked, and spoke it with thrust of phrase. In her first Springfield days Bill Herndon danced a waltz with her, and finding her the most amazingly smooth and easy waltzer he had ever danced with, he told her she seemed to glide through the waltz with the ease of a serpent. She drew back, flashed her eyes, retorted, "Mr. Herndon, comparison to a serpent is rather severe irony, especially to a newcomer," bowed with accomplished dignity, and was gone. She could be hurt, just like that, when no one wanted to hurt her.

Far from ordinary was Miss Mary Todd; she was vivid, perhaps too vivid, ebullient, combative, too quick to fly off the handle. She could shine with radiance at a gift, an arrival, a surprise; a shaft of wanted happiness could strike deep in her. She was informed and versed in apparel and appearance; style was instinctive with her. She hummed gay little ditties putting on a flowered bonnet and tying a double bowknot under her chin. A satisfying rose or ostrich plume in her hair was a psalm.

She embodied a thousand cunning, contradictory proverbs men have spoken about woman as a wildcat and as a sweet angel. While offhand observers spoke of her as having "bounce" and "spunk," it was an understanding among her friends that she had what they chose to call ambition. She was intense with the quality Kentuckians refer to in their horses as high-strung. She chafed at the bit, full of the lust of being vividly and proudly alive, wanting to go, to be a winner known to grandstands, vast amphitheaters of spectators.

Her telling a Kentucky friend, before leaving for Illinois, that she was going to be the wife of some future President of the United States may have been a piece of idle gossip or the evidence of a hope for distinction. In the Edwards circle they believed there were clues to her character in a remark she passed at a party around a fireside one evening. A young woman married to a rich man far along in years was asked, "Why did you marry such a withered-up old buck?" Her answer was, "He had lots of houses and gold." And quick-tongued Mary Todd said in surprise, "Is that true? *I* would rather marry a good man, a man of mind, with a hope and bright prospects ahead for position, fame and power, than to marry all the houses, gold, and bones in the world."

During her first year in Springfield both Abraham Lincoln and Stephen A. Douglas took their turns at being entertained by

Mary Todd in the big parlor of the Edwards house, took their turns at escorting her to parties and balls; she was asked which of the two she intended to have for her husband, and answered, "The one that has the best chance of being President."

ALONG IN THE YEAR 1840 Lincoln and Mary Todd plighted their troth and were engaged to be married. Ninian W. Edwards and his wife had argued she was throwing herself away; it wasn't a match; she and Lincoln came from different classes in society. Her stubborn blood rose; she knew her own mind; Lincoln had a future; he was her man more than any other man she had met.

The months passed. Lincoln, the solitary, the melancholy, was busy, lost, abstracted; he couldn't go to all the parties and concerts Mary Todd was going to; she flared with jealousy and went with other men. She accused him; tears; misunderstandings; they made up, fell out, made up again. The wedding was set for New Year's Day, 1841. In the kitchen of the Edwards house the wedding cakes were put in the oven.

And then something happened. The bride or the groom, or both, broke the engagement. It was a phantom wedding, mentioned in hushes. There was gossip and dispute about whether the wedding had been set for that date at all.

On the day set for the wedding Lincoln took his seat in the legislature and during two months was absent from his seat only seven days. He toiled with the Whigs on an "Appeal to the People of the State of Illinois," on circulars and protests trying to rouse public opinion against the Democrats. He wrote letters, tried law cases.

And yet he was a haunted man. Was he sure he didn't love her? If he did love her it was a terrible wrong to leave her with arms open, waiting for him. So now he walked the streets of Springfield; he brooded, looking out of the windows of the second-story law office; he even consulted a doctor.

On January 20 he wrote to Stuart in Washington: "I have, within the last few days, been making a most discreditable exhibition of myself in the way of hypochondriaism and thereby got an impression that Dr. Henry [Lincoln's physician] is necessary to my existence." The letter closed: "Pardon me for not writing more; I have not sufficient composure to write a long letter." Another time he wrote to Stuart: "I am now the most miserable man living. If what I feel were equally distributed to the whole human family, there would not be one cheerful face on the earth." And he wrote to the *Sangamo Journal* meditations entitled "Suicide."

The legislature adjourned. Josh Speed was selling his store and going back to his folks in Kentucky. Lincoln traveled to Kentucky a little later. As the redbud and the springtime roses of Kentucky came out, the lost Lincoln struggled to come back. Staying with Speed in Louisville, for some three weeks he shared talk and counsel with that rare friend. Speed recalled Lincoln saying that he had done nothing to make any human being remember that he had lived, that what he wished to live for was to connect his name with the events of his day and generation, and to link his name with something that would be to the interest of his fellowmen.

Slowly, he came back. A sweet and serene old woman, Joshua Speed's mother, talked with him, gave him a mother's care, and made him a present of an Oxford Bible.

In mid-September he was in Springfield handling the cases of two clients accused of murder; excitement ran high and hangings were expected; but the man supposed to have been killed turned up alive. And Lincoln ended a long letter to Speed with the remark: "Hart, the little drayman that hauled Molly [Mary Todd] home once, said it was too *damned* bad to have so much trouble, and no hanging after all."

JOSHUA SPEED was a broad, deep-chested man, but he had spots soft as May violets. And he and Abraham Lincoln told each other their secrets about women. Lincoln too had spots soft as violets. "I do not feel my own sorrows more keenly than I do yours," Lincoln wrote Speed in one letter.

Down in Kentucky, the wedding day of Speed and Fanny Henning had been set; and Speed was afraid he didn't love her; it was wearing him down; he wrote Lincoln he was sick.

And Lincoln wrote a letter analyzing Speed. It was a letter as tender as loving hands swathing a feverish forehead, yet direct and logical in its facing of immediate, practical facts. It was a letter showing that the misery of Abraham Lincoln in the unlucky endings of his love affairs with Ann Rutledge and with Mary Todd must have been a deep-rooted, tangled, and baffling misery.

"You are *naturally of a nervous temperament*," he told Speed. "It is out of this, that the painful difference between you and the mass of the world springs." That is, Lincoln believed that he and his friend had exceptional and sensitive personalities. "Though it *does* pertain to you, it *does not* pertain to one in a thousand."

And Lincoln was writing in part a personal confession in telling Speed: "I know what the painful point with you is, at all times when you are unhappy. It is an apprehension that you do not love her as you should. What nonsense!— How came you to court her? Was it because you thought she deserved it; and that you had given her reason to expect it? If it was for that, why did not the same reason make you court . . . at least twenty others of whom you can think, & to whom it would apply with greater force than to *her?* Did you court her for her wealth? Why, you knew she had none. But you say you *reasoned* yourself *into* it. What do you mean by that? Was it not that you found yourself unable to *reason* yourself *out* of it?"

A few days before Speed's wedding, Lincoln wrote again of Speed's fear that he did not love Fanny. "Perhaps this point is no longer a question with you, and my pertenacious dwelling upon it, is a rude intrusion upon your feelings . . . You know the Hell I have suffered on that point, and how tender I am upon it. You know I do not mean wrong."

Speed's wedding day came; the knot was tied. Lincoln wrote from Springfield: "When this shall reach you, you will have been Fanny's husband several days . . . you will always hereafter, be on ground that I have never ocupied, and consequently, if advice were needed, I might advise wrong. I do fondly hope, however, that you will never again need any comfort from abroad. But should I be mistaken in this—should excessive pleasure still be accompanied with a painful counterpart at times, still let me urge you, as I have ever done, to remember in the dep[t]h and even the agony of despondency, that verry shortly you are to feel well again. . . . If I were you, in case my mind were not exactly right, I would avoid being *idle*." So wrote Lincoln.

And when the single man received a letter from his just married friend, he wrote: "Yours of the 16th Inst. announcing that Miss Fanny and you 'are no more twain, but one flesh,' reached me this morning. I have no way of telling how much happiness I wish you both; tho' I believe you both can conceive it. I feel somwhat jealous of both of you now; you will be so exclusively concerned for one another, that I shall be forgotten entirely. . . . I regret to learn that you have resolved to not return to Illinois. I shall be verry lonesome without you. How miserably things seem to be arranged in this world! If we have no friends, we have no pleasure; and if we have them, we are sure to lose them, and be doubly pained by the loss. I did hope she and you would make your home here; but I own I have no right to insist."

A week or so after Joshua Speed's wedding day, he wrote to Lincoln saying that "something indescribably horrible and alarming" haunted him. And Lincoln, in answering Speed's letter, said he was ready to swear it was not the fault of the woman Speed had married.

He went further and ventured the guess that both he and Speed had been dreaming dreams. "I tell you, Speed, our *forebodings*, for which you and I are rather peculiar, are all the worst sort of nonsense." And Lincoln recalled an old saying of his father: " 'If you make a bad bargain, *hug* it the tighter'; and it occurs to me that if the bargain you have just closed can possibly be called a bad one, it is certainly the most pleasant one for applying that maxim to which my fancy can by any effort picture."

A month passed and Speed wrote that he was far happier than he ever expected to be. To which Lincoln replied: "The short space it took me to read your last letter, gave me more pleasure, than the total sum of all I have enjoyed since that fatal first of Jany. '41." Then he referred to Mary Todd for the first time in his letters to Speed. "Since then [the fatal first of January, 1841] it seems to me, I should have been entirely happy, but for the never-absent idea, that there is *one* still unhappy whom I have contributed to make so. That still kills my soul. I can not but reproach myself, for even wishing to be happy while she is otherwise. She accompanied a large party on the Rail Road cars, to Jacksonville last monday; and on her return, spoke, so that I heard of it, of having enjoyed the trip exceedingly. God be praised for that."

Three months later there came to Lincoln thanks from Speed for what he had done to bring and to keep Speed and Fanny together. He wrote to Speed: "I am not sure there was any merit, with me, in the part I took in your difficulty; I was drawn to it as by fate. I could not have done less than I did. I always was superstitious; and as part of my superstition, I believe God made me one of the instruments of bringing your Fanny and you together, which union, I have no doubt He had fore-ordained. Whatever he designs, he will do for *me* yet."

Then he made reference to "our friend here," meaning Mary Todd. Lincoln was now sure he had made a mistake in not going through with his resolve to marry her. "True, that subject is painfull to me; but it is not your silence, or the silence of all the world that can make me forget it. . . . I believe now that, had you understood my case at the time, as well as I understood yours afterwards, by the aid you would have given me, I should have sailed through clear; but that does not now afford me sufficient confidence, to begin that, or the like of that, again."

Such was his pitiless self-revelation. And in one sentence he then sketched himself, "I am so poor, and make so little headway in the world, that I drop back in a month of idleness, as much as I gain in a year's rowing."

Chapter 11

MRS. SIMEON FRANCIS, wife of the editor of the *Sangamo Journal*, often entertained guests in the parlor of the Francis house. She believed with her husband that Abraham Lincoln had a famous career ahead of him. Also she believed her friend Mary Todd to be a rare, accomplished, brilliant woman. She would play her part as a matchmaker. Sometime early in 1842 she invited Lincoln to a party in her parlor, brought the two of them together, and said, "Be friends again."

Whatever of fate or woman-wit was at work, it did happen that they were friends again. But they didn't tell the world so. They had done that before. For a while their quiet meetings in the parlor of the Francis house were known only to Mrs. Francis. Not even Mary Todd's sister, Mrs. Ninian Edwards, knew what was going on till weeks had passed. Mrs. Edwards said later, "I asked Mary why she was so secretive about it. She said evasively that after all that had occurred, it was best to keep the courtship from all eyes and ears."

Out of their meetings came an episode which Lincoln later considered an embarrassment. Julia Jayne, a friend of Mary Todd, joined the little parties in the Francis house, and, to amuse themselves, they concocted a series of four articles to be printed anonymously under the signature "Rebecca" in the *Sangamo Journal*. One of the articles was written by Lincoln; the others were the work of Miss Jayne and Miss Todd. All were Whig attacks on the state auditor of accounts, James Shields, a Democrat. Besides being a political attack on Shields as an official, the articles lampooned his manners and clothes and struts in Springfield society. Written in the lingo of backwoods farmers, they were edged with malice yet often comic.

Shields, a thirty-two-year-old bachelor, was a lawyer and had been a member of the legislature with Lincoln. He was a fighting Irishman born in Dungannon, County of Tyrone, Ireland. He asked the *Sangamo Journal* editor who wrote the articles and was told Lincoln took responsibility for them. Shields challenged Lincoln to a duel.

Lincoln's seconds notified Shields's seconds that Lincoln chose to fight the duel with cavalry broadswords, across a plank ten feet long and nine to twelve inches broad. By horse and buggy, and by an old horse ferry, the two parties traveled on September 22 to a sandbar in the Mississippi River, within three miles of Alton but located in the state of Missouri and beyond the reach of Illinois laws against dueling.

Riding in a rowboat to the sandbar, Lincoln said he was reminded of the time a Kentuckian enlisted for the War of 1812. The sweetheart of the soldier told him she was embroidering a bullet pouch and belt for him to wear in battle and she would stitch in the words "Victory or Death." He asked her, "Ain't that rayther too strong? S'pose you put 'Victory or Be Crippled'!"

Arriving at the sandbar, Lincoln took a seat on a log and practiced swings and swishes in the air with his cavalry broadsword. As one man who made the trip with him recalled, "The absurdity of that long-reaching fellow fighting with cavalry sabers with Shields, who would walk under his arm, came pretty near making me howl with laughter." Meanwhile friends, lawyers, seconds on both sides, held a long confab. Then there were shorter confabs with Lincoln and with Shields. Then a statement was issued declaring that although Mr. Lincoln was the writer of the article signed "Rebecca" in the *Sangamo Journal* of September 2, yet he had no intention of injuring the personal or private character or standing of Mr. Shields as a gentleman or a man, and that Mr. Lincoln did not think, nor does he now think, that said article could produce such an effect; and had Mr. Lincoln anticipated such an effect, he would have forborne to write it; said article was written solely for political effect, and not to gratify any personal pique against Mr. Shields, for he had none and knew of no cause for any.

Afterward, a crowd waiting on the Alton levee for news of the outcome saw the ferryboat come near the shore with what seemed to be a man in blood-soaked clothes in the bottom of the boat. As the boat tied up they saw it was a log covered with a red shirt. The duel had become a joke. Lincoln and Shields came off the boat together, in easy and pleasant chat. But Lincoln never afterward mentioned it and his friends saw it was a sore point that shouldn't be spoken of. A story arose and lived on, that when first told, as the challenged party, he had his choice of weapons, he replied, "How about cow dung at five paces?"

THE YEAR AFTER Lincoln's broken engagement with Mary Todd was a time filled with a good deal of action for Lincoln. The same medicine that he prescribed for the nervous debility of

Joshua Speed he was giving himself in big doses: activity, occupation, work.

In the summer of 1841, Lincoln had acquired a new law partner. With Stuart away months in Congress, and busy with politics when at home, the heavy routine work fell on Lincoln, who had learned about all he could of law from Stuart. They parted cordially and Lincoln went into partnership with Stephen T. Logan, acknowledged leader of the Springfield bar.

That Logan should have picked Lincoln for a junior partner was testimony to Lincoln's unusual ability. Nine years older than Lincoln, Logan was a former circuit judge, Scotch-Irish and Kentucky-born—a short sliver of a man with tight lips and a thin rasping voice. Logan had frowsy hair, wore linsey-woolsey shirts and heavy shoes, and never put on a necktie, yet he was known as one of the most neat, careful, scrupulous, and profoundly learned lawyers in Illinois when it came to preparing cases, writing letters, and filing documents. From him Lincoln was to learn how to be thorough, how to make results come from being thorough.

Since 1839, Lincoln had spent a few months each year traveling the nine, and later fifteen, counties of the Eighth Judicial District or "Eighth Circuit." As he traveled and tried cases, he rode a horse or drove in a buggy, at times riding on rough roads for hours without passing a farmhouse on the open prairie. The journeying could be mean in the mud of spring or in the blowing snow of winter. When rain came, he might stop at a farmhouse, but if court was meeting next day there was nothing to do but plod on in wet clothes. In the taverns where he stayed, the bedrooms had usually only a bed, a spittoon, a washstand with a bowl and pitcher of water, the guest in colder weather breaking the ice to wash his face; though some taverns had big rooms where a dozen or more lawyers slept of a night when "court day" occurred. Among the lawyers were men of rare brains and ability who would be heard from nationally, some of them to be close associates of Lincoln for years. Traveling over the Eighth Circuit area, from Springfield to the Indiana line, Lincoln met pioneer frontier humanity at its best as well as its worst.

He argued before the supreme court in the widely known case of Bailey *vs.* Cromwell. Cromwell had sold Bailey a Negro girl, saying the girl was a slave. Bailey had given a note promising to pay cash for the slave. Lincoln argued, in part, that the girl was a free person until she was proven to be a slave, and, if she was not proven a slave, then she could not be sold nor bought and no cash could be exchanged between two men buying and selling her. The supreme court took practically the same view and Lincoln won his case.

Over in Tazewell County he met a crooked lawyer. An old farmer named Case sold a breaking plow and three yoke of oxen. Two boys named Snow signed notes promising to pay for the plow and oxen. But since signing the notes they had come of age. They admitted on the witness stand they were using the plow and oxen to break prairie, and that they had signed the notes. Their lawyer pleaded they were infants or minors when the notes were signed and therefore they could not be held to pay. Lincoln's speech to the jury stripped the other lawyer of his pretensions.

"Gentlemen," he said, "these boys never would have tried to cheat old farmer Case out of these oxen and that plow, but for the advice of counsel. It was bad advice, bad in morals and bad in law. The law never sanctions cheating, and a lawyer must be very smart to twist it so that it will seem to do so. The judge will tell you what your own sense of justice has already told you, that these Snow boys, if they were mean enough to plead the baby act, when they came to be men should have taken the oxen and plow back. They cannot go back on their contract, and also keep what the note was given for." The jury, without leaving their seats, gave a verdict for old farmer Case.

When Martin Van Buren stopped overnight in the town of Rochester, Illinois, a Springfield party took along Lincoln to help in a night of entertainment for the former President. The two main tavern performers that evening were Lincoln and Van Buren. Lincoln opened his big ragbag of memories and stories of life in Illinois, Indiana, and Kentucky, while Van Buren told about New York ways and New York lawyers as far back as Hamilton and Burr. Lincoln, of course, had a thousand funny, pointed anecdotes such as his father's story of the man who was asked for a warranty bill of a horse he was selling and he guaranteed him "sound of skin and skeleton and free from faults and faculties." When that evening of storytelling was over, Van Buren said his sides were sore from laughing.

One day there came news that hurt Lincoln. Squire Bowling Green was dead, his old friend, teacher, companion from New Salem days. Lincoln rode out to the Green home; he stayed till the day of the funeral, and he was asked to speak at the ceremony. The story goes that he stood at the side of the burial box, looking down for a few moments at the still, white face. He began to tremble, and there were struggles the length of his long, bony frame. He slowly turned and looked around; the room was filled with faces; the faces of old New Salem and Clary's Grove and Sand Ridge friends. A few words came off his lips, broken and choked words. Then tears ran down his face and he couldn't go on.

AT THE MEETINGS of Lincoln and Mary Todd in the Francis home, Miss Todd made it clear to him that if another date should be fixed for a wedding, it should not be set so far in the future as it was the time before. Lincoln agreed with her.

In October he wrote to Speed: "You have now been the husband of a lovely woman nearly eight months. That you are happier now than you were the day you married her . . . is manifested in your letters. But I want to ask a closer question— 'Are you now, in *feeling* as well as *judgement*, glad you are married as you are?' From any body but me, this would be an impudent question not to be tolerated; but I know you will pardon it in me. Please answer it quickly as I am impatient to know."

A few weeks later, on the morning of November 4, 1842, Lincoln came to the room of his friend James Matheny, before Matheny was out of bed, and announced, "I am going to be married today."

On the street that day he met Ninian W. Edwards and told Edwards that he and Mary were going to be married that evening. And Edwards gave notice: "Mary is my ward, and she must be married at my house."

And when Edwards asked Mary Todd if what he had heard was true, and she told him it was true, they all started to make the big Edwards house ready—as best they could on such short notice. Mrs. Edwards sent for her sister Frances, to bake a cake, and the big house was swept and garnished.

Lincoln carefully carried a plain gold ring he had purchased, on the inside band of which the jeweler, a man named Chatterton, had engraved the words, "Love is eternal." And a week or so before he had written his old honest, tried, rugged friend and kinsman, John Hanks of cornfield and flatboat days:

Dear John:
I am to be married on the 4th of next month to Miss Todd. I hope you will come over. Be sure to be on deck by early candlelight.
Yours, A. Lincoln.

At the Edwards house that evening, the Reverend Charles Dresser performed the ring ceremony of the Episcopal Church for the groom, thirty-three years old, and the bride, twenty-three years old. Behind Lincoln stood a supreme court judge, Thomas C. Brown, fat, bluff, blunt, and an able lawyer not accustomed to weddings. As Lincoln placed the ring on the bride's finger and repeated the form, "With this ring I thee endow with all my goods, chattels, lands, and tenements," the supreme court judge blurted out in a suppressed tone that everybody heard, "God Almighty, Lincoln, the statute fixes all that." The minister kept a straight face, and then pronounced Abraham Lincoln and Mary Todd man and wife in the sight of God and man.

Afterward came talk about the wedding, the bride, the groom. Jim Matheny said Lincoln had "looked as if he was going to slaughter." It was told at the Butler house where Lincoln roomed that, as he was dressing, Bill Butler's boy came in and wanted to know, "Where are you going?" Lincoln's answer being, "To hell, I suppose."

However dubious such gossip, Lincoln, seven days after the wedding, sent a letter to his friend and fellow lawyer, Sam Marshall at Shawneetown, in which he discussed two law cases, and ended the letter: "Nothing new here, except my marrying, which to me, is a matter of profound wonder."

In January the new husband wrote Speed: "Mary is very well and continues her old sentiments of friendship for you. How the marriage life goes with us I will tell you when I see you here." And in July: "We shall look with impatience for your visit this fall. Your Fanny cannot be more anxious to see my Molly [Mrs. Lincoln] than the latter is to see her, nor so much as I am— Don't fail to come— We are but two, as yet—"

Chapter 12

MARY TODD, the daughter of a Kentucky bank president, had married Lincoln with all his debts, and they started their married life boarding and rooming at four dollars per week in the plain old Globe Tavern. It was there that their first baby was born, on August 1, 1843. They named the baby Robert Todd.

Though Lincoln was still paying installments on the old debts from New Salem days, the Lincolns, soon after their first son was born, moved into their own home, bought for $1500. It was a story-and-a-half frame house on Eighth and Jackson streets, a few blocks from the Springfield city center. The framework and floors were oak, the doors and doorframes black walnut. The house was painted, wrote one visitor, "a Quaker tint of light brown." In the back lot were a cistern, well, and pump, a barn thirty by thirteen feet, and a carriage house eighteen by twenty. Three blocks east the cornfields began and farms mile after mile.

From this house Lincoln could walk to his law office. Since joining Stephen Logan, he had more cases in the higher·courts in Springfield. In December 1841 he had argued fourteen cases in the supreme court, losing only four. Of twenty-four cases in that court during 1842 and 1843 he lost only seven.

But law practice didn't have the charm for Lincoln that politics did. When Sam Marshall complained that Lincoln was careless about certain cases they were handling together Lincoln explained, "The truth is, when I received your letter, I glanced it over, stuck it away, postponed consideration of the cases mentioned, and forgot them altogether." But he spent days studying the tariff issue, delivered hour-and-a-half speeches as an advocate of the protective tariff, and kept up a running combat of argument against the opposition—taking all comers as he had in wrestling days.

And in February 1843, less than four months after his wedding, he had been actively hunting political support that might make him a congressman. The ways of Lincoln as a mixer in politics were in a letter he wrote at that time to Alden Hall over in Tazewell County: "Your county and ours are almost sure to be placed in the same congressional district—I would like to be its Representative; still circumstances may happen to prevent my even being a candidate— If, however, there are any Whigs in Tazewell who would as soon I should represent them as any other person, I would be glad they would not cast me aside until they see and hear farther what turn things take."

Lincoln did not immediately get the congressional nomination he was seeking. In 1844, with Lincoln's support, Edward D. Baker, another of the party's inner circle in Springfield, was chosen as the Whig nominee. This was part of an understanding, engineered by Lincoln, that the leading Whig candidates would "take a turn a piece" in Congress, and Lincoln's turn would come in 1846. Though "Ned" Baker, a Black Hawk War veteran, a lawyer, a brilliant and dramatic speaker, was one of Lincoln's best friends, Lincoln, campaigning for him, wrote to Speed in Kentucky that he felt "like a fellow who is made groomsman to the man what has cut him out, and is marrying his own dear 'gal.' "

Lincoln also campaigned for the party's national ticket in the 1844 elections, but while Ned Baker was elected to Congress, Henry Clay, the Whig candidate for President, was defeated by Democrat James K. Polk; and Polk also carried Illinois.

IN LATE OCTOBER OF 1844 Lincoln had gone to his old home district in Indiana to campaign for Clay. And Election Day had found him in Gentryville, where he had grown up, where his mother and only sister were buried, where he had not been

ANNE FRANK
The Diary of a
Young Girl

In an attic above a warehouse in wartime Amsterdam, eight hunted people sought to elude the Nazi dragnet. One of them, a thirteen-year-old girl, undertook to write a day-by-day chronicle of this harrowing two-year experience. But Anne Frank was a warm and sensitive child, and her diary fairly bubbles with amusement and love. Eleanor Roosevelt called it "one of the wisest and most moving commentaries on war and its impact on human beings I have ever read."

Anne Frank's story, made into both a film and a Pulitzer Prize-winning stage play, has touched the minds and hearts of audiences that now number in the millions.

PROPHET
IN THE WILDERNESS
The Story of
Albert Schweitzer

by Hermann Hagedorn

The Gospels had for Albert Schweitzer a message of compelling clarity: the true Christian is he who ministers to the neglected, the crippled and the most fearful of God's children. And so this extraordinary man, a brilliantly gifted scholar, musician and theologian, ignored the advice of worldlier colleagues and went into the African jungle to build a hospital. There the beloved doctor of Lambaréné, through his dedication to others, became a unique hero of our time.

Hermann Hagedorn—a teacher, poet and the author of *The Roosevelt Family of Sagamore Hill*—comes from a simple Alsacian background much like that of the great doctor's. Inspired by Schweitzer's utter selflessness, Hagedorn has created a most moving portrait of the man who spent half a lifetime in the service of mankind.

THE GREAT
PIERPONT MORGAN
by Frederick Lewis Allen

Strong men quailed under the glance of J. P. Morgan, the great financier. It was that way in everything he did—from negotiating a corporate merger to purchasing a priceless painting for his collection. Like no other man of his day, Morgan boldly changed the face of industrial America. His life story, by Frederick Lewis Allen, illuminates not only a remarkable personality but an exciting era of our history. Here, then, is a dramatic full-scale portrait of an American titan that perhaps only someone like Allen could have created. Author of such engaging books as *Only Yesterday* and *The Big Change*, Allen has brought to life one of the most fascinating men of our time.

Reader's Digest
Great Biographies

ABRAHAM LINCOLN
The Prairie Years
by Carl Sandburg

The tall stovepipe hat, the deep-set eyes, and the long, lean, careworn face—this is the Abraham Lincoln that Americans know best. But behind this familiar image is one of a younger Abe Lincoln—the adventurous farm boy, the amiable storekeeper, and the maturing lawyer and politician who mixed wisdom, compassion and earthy humor in seeking justice for his fellowman. *The Prairie Years* is the story of that young man and the young nation whose destiny he would so largely shape. A true labor of love by the distinguished poet and historian Carl Sandburg, it has been called "homely but beautiful, learned but simple" and a "noble monument to American Literature."

> "Not often in the story of mankind does a man arrive on earth who is both steel and velvet, who is as hard as rock and soft as drifting fog, who holds in his heart and mind the paradox of terrible storm and peace unspeakable and perfect."
>
> —Carl Sandburg on Lincoln

for fifteen years. The visit brought memories flooding in on him. When he made his speech at Gentryville, his old employer, Josiah Crawford, was in a front seat, proud of the boy that had husked corn in his fields and borrowed books from him. "Where's your books, Abe?" he wanted to know. In Gentryville he also found James Gentry's insane son, Matthew Gentry, who had once been his friend and schoolmate, still alive, drooling, gentle, harmless.

Some time later Lincoln wrote to Andrew Johnston of Quincy, Illinois, that he was sending him "a piece of poetry of my own making." The two men had corresponded about poetry previously. Sending Johnston a series of verses, "My Childhood Home I See Again," he explained that they were inspired by his 1844 campaign visit to Gentryville. Four of the verses read:

> My childhood's home I see again,
>   And sadden with the view;
> And still, as memory crowds my brain,
>   There's pleasure in it too.
>
> Near twenty years have passed away
>   Since here I bid farewell
> To woods and fields, and scenes of play,
>   And playmates loved so well.
>
> Where many were, but few remain
>   Of old familiar things;
> But seeing them, to mind again
>   The lost and absent brings.
>
> The friends I left that parting day,
>   How changed, as time has sped!
> Young childhood grown, strong manhood gray,
>   And half of all are dead.

Andrew Johnston suggested that Lincoln's verses might be published, and some, including one long effort, a piece of doggerel called "The Bear Hunt," did appear in the Quincy *Whig;* but they did not carry Lincoln's name. For he had written

Johnston: "I have not sufficient hope of the verses attracting any favorable notice to tempt me to risk being ridiculed for having written them." And from then on there seemed to be no more exercises of this kind.

LINCOLN AND HIS LAW PARTNER, Stephen T. Logan, both had hopes of going to Congress; they didn't always get along smoothly, and Logan was taking his son into partnership, for he saw Lincoln was about ready to head his own law firm. But Lincoln left the partnership with regrets. For two years they had worked together in the same law office on the same cases. Logan knew how to be a lawyer so that people had fear and respect for lawyers; and Lincoln had his chance to watch Logan every day, close up, to see how Logan did it.

He was sorry to break with Logan, but did not have to look far for a new partner. Young William H. Herndon, who had once clerked in the Speed store and slept upstairs, had been reading law books in the office of Logan & Lincoln on the invitation of Lincoln. In December 1844 young Herndon was admitted to the bar, and shortly afterward Lincoln asked him to be his partner.

Herndon didn't believe his ears; he said, "Mr. Lincoln, don't laugh at me."

"Billy, I can trust you if you can trust me."

They shook hands, opened an office on Hoffman's Row, and hung out the shingle "Lincoln & Herndon." Lincoln was nine years the older; for ten years he had been seeing Herndon, off and on, watching the boy grow up to a young man. Herndon was of medium height, rawboned, with high cheekbones, dark eyes, and a shock of blue-black hair. He was intense, sensitive, and varied as his father and grandfather. His grandfather in Virginia had given slaves their freedom; his father in Illinois had stood fast with those who had fought to make Illinois a slave state. His father had kept a store and had put up the first regular tavern in Springfield. The son had grown up in a tavern, had a tavern eye for judging people, and took pride in the way he could size up men. Bill Herndon knew tavern life, rough country talk and stories, and the slang of men who talk about cards, horse races, chicken fights, women. He liked his liquor, and was close to an element in Sangamon County that Lincoln termed "the shrewd wild boys." Yet he was full of book learning, of torches and bonfires, and had a flamboyance about freedom, justice, humanity. Lincoln had never forgotten how Bill Herndon's father had ordered him home from Illinois College in Jacksonville when the mob at nearby Alton had killed Elijah Lovejoy. The elder Herndon had heard that the college faculty and students were blazing with abolitionist ideas, and declared flatly that he wasn't going to have his boy grow up "a damned abolitionist pup." Now to the upstairs back-room office of Lincoln & Herndon came the abolitionist newspapers week by week, stirring up Herndon with the news of what the American Anti-Slavery Society was doing, of what were the latest actions of the Liberty party. Though slight as a political organization, it had helped sweep Henry Clay out of the political reckoning in 1844, when Polk defeated Clay with a narrow popular majority, and the Liberty party candidate got some 62,000 votes which could have made Clay President.

As young Herndon and his senior law partner looked from their office window to the state capitol, they had a good deal to talk about when there was time. And in their talk from then on, and for years, one was always "Mr. Lincoln" and the other plain "Billy."

ONE DAY down in Coles County, where Tom and Sarah Bush Lincoln were still living, Abraham Lincoln won a slander case for a client who had been called a horse thief. The damages awarded amounted to $200; Lincoln was paid a fee of $35. And old Thomas Lincoln, the father of Abraham Lincoln, living in his log cabin out from Charleston, came in to town and was handed the $35, as requested by Abraham Lincoln, in instructions left with the clerk of the court.

Lincoln's reputation was spreading as a man and lawyer of whom people said, "He'll be fair and square." Two Sangamon County farmers came to see Lincoln one day. They had a dispute concerning a small strip of land, each claiming it. And they agreed in writing to submit their dispute "to the arbitrament of

Abraham Lincoln" instead of a court. In his own mind he did not divide people into good people and bad people. As he walked from his own home near the city limits of Springfield and met people on his way to the courthouse, he saw good mixed in the bad and bad mixed in the good. Perhaps slight yet definite was the influence of Logan in Lincoln's writing later:

> The true rule, in determining to embrace, or reject any thing, is not whether it have *any* evil in it; but whether it have more of evil, than of good. There are few things *wholly* evil, or *wholly* good. Almost every thing . . . is an inseparable compound of the two; so that our best judgment of the preponderance between them is continually demanded.

Fine points in justice came before him, some involving old friends. He pressed the claim of a client against John Calhoun, who had been his chief when he was a surveyor; he questioned Calhoun as to transfers and assignments of property. Then there was the case of a woman who loaned $200 to Mentor Graham, the New Salem schoolmaster who had helped Lincoln learn surveying and who had loaned Lincoln books. She got a note for it, but couldn't collect. She put it in Lincoln's hands. Lincoln sued Graham, won the suit, but didn't force immediate payment. What he asked was that the schoolmaster should do his best to pay the woman.

Once, when another lawyer asked him to go in on a case he didn't believe in, Lincoln said, "You'll have to get some other fellow to win this case for you. I couldn't do it. All the while I'd be talking to that jury I'd be thinking, 'Lincoln, you're a liar,' and I believe I should forget myself and say it out loud."

Chapter 13

THE THIRTY-SEVEN-YEAR-OLD SON of Thomas Lincoln and Nancy Hanks Lincoln had changed with a changing western world. His feet had worn deerskin moccasins as a boy; they were put into rawhide boots when he was full grown; now he had them in dressed calf leather. His head cover had been a coonskin cap when he was a boy; floating down the Mississippi to New Orleans he had worn a black felt hat from an eastern factory and it held the post office mail of New Salem; now he was a prominent politician and lawyer wearing a tall, stiff, silk hat known as a stovepipe, also called a plug hat. In this stovepipe hat he carried letters, newspaper clippings, deeds, mortgages, checks. The hat was nearly a foot high, with a brim only an inch or so in width; it was a high, lean, longish hat and it made Lincoln look higher, leaner, more longish.

Four years after his marriage to Mary Todd, Lincoln was hoping to go to Washington, D.C., as a Whig congressman from Illinois. Ned Baker was not running again. When another baby boy arrived at the Lincoln home in the spring of 1846 he was named Edward Baker.

At his office desk, Lincoln dipped his goose-quill pen into an inkstand and wrote to Whig editors, politicians, voters, sometimes reminding them that "turn about is fair play." He could appeal frankly: "If your feelings towards me are the same as when I saw you (which I have no reason to doubt) I wish you would let nothing appear in your paper which may opperate against me. You understand." The blunt little sentence crept in often, "You understand." Some letters ended, "Confidential, of course."

He had become what was called a public man; and he was taking more care of his looks. He now wore broadcloth, white shirts with white collar and black silk cravat, sideburns down three-fourths the length of his ears. Yet he was still known as carelessly groomed, his trousers mentioned as creeping to the ankles and higher, his hair rumpled, vest wrinkled. Standing he loomed six feet four inches; seated he looked no taller than average, except for his knees rising above the chair's seat level. His loose bones were hard to fit with neat clothes, and once on they were hard to keep neat; trousers go baggy at the knees of a storyteller who has the habit, at the end of a story, of putting his arms around his knees, raising his knees to his chin, and rocking to and fro.

When at home in Springfield, he cut wood, tended to the house stoves, curried his horse, milked the cow. He analyzed the tariff, the national banks, and the annexation of Texas while pailing a cow. He looked like a farmer, it was said. And his very words had a log-cabin smack, the word "idea" more like "idee," and "really" a drawled Kentucky "ra-a-ly." His voice was a tenor that carried song tunes poorly but had clear and appealing modulations when he spoke; in rare moments it rose to a startling, unforgettable high treble. In stoop of shoulders and a forward bend of his head there was a grace and familiarity making it easy for shorter people to look into his face and talk with him.

It was natural that Abraham Lincoln was many things to many people; some believed him a cunning, designing lawyer and politician; some believed him simply a sad, odd, awkward man trying to find a niche in life. On streets, in crowds or gatherings, his tall frame stood out. He was noticed, pointed out, questions asked about him. He couldn't slide into any group of standing people without all eyes finding he was there. His head surmounting a group was gaunt and strange, onlookers remembering the Adam's apple standing out on a scrawny neck, the high cheekbones, deep eye sockets, the coarse black hair bushy and tangled, the nose large and well shaped, the wide full-lipped mouth capable of a thousand shades of meaning, capable of a thousand subtle changes from straight face to wide beaming smile.

He was loose-jointed and comic with appeals in street-corner slang and dialect from the public-square hitching posts; yet at moments he was as strange and far off as the last dark sands of a red sunset.

FOR THE WHIG Congressional nomination, Lincoln's principal rival was a Jacksonville lawyer named John J. Hardin, also an officer in the state militia. Some time before the Whigs' district convention at Petersburg on May 1, 1846, Hardin withdrew from the contest. By acclamation, the convention nominated Lincoln for Congress.

Lincoln's Democratic opponent was Peter Cartwright, an old-fashioned circuit rider, famous as an evangelist and exhorter. Cartwright was twenty-four years older than Lincoln, and years before, while little Abe Lincoln had helped his father at chopping logs for their cabin near Little Pigeon Creek, Cartwright had ridden the Salt River circuit with Bible and rifle. He could count on political support from a big personal acquaintance, including not only church members who believed in his religious faith but also sinners who admired the swift, clean way he could throw drunks and disturbers out of church. Eastern people with their mansions, elegance, and fashions, New York with its dancers from Paris, roused sarcasm from Cartwright; he was proud of Kentucky and Illinois; the Democrats picked him as the one man who had the best chance of taking the Springfield district away from the Whigs.

Cartwright's men spread reports during the campaign that Lincoln's wife was a high-toned Episcopalian, that Lincoln in a temperance speech in Springfield had said that drunkards are as good as Christians and church members, that Lincoln was a "deist" who believed in God but did not accept Christ and the doctrines of atonement and punishment. Lincoln, in spite of warnings, went to a religious meeting where Cartwright was to preach. In due time Cartwright said, "All who desire to lead a new life, to give their hearts to God, and go to heaven, will stand," and a sprinkling of men, women, and children stood up. Then the preacher exhorted, "All who do not wish to go to hell will stand." All stood up—except Lincoln. Then said Cartwright in his gravest voice, "I observe that many responded to the first invitation to give their hearts to God and go to heaven. And I further observe that all of you save one indicated that you did not desire to go to hell. The sole exception is Mr. Lincoln, who did not respond to either invitation. May I inquire of you, Mr. Lincoln, where you are going?"

And Lincoln slowly rose and slowly spoke. "I came here as a respectful listener. I did not know that I was to be singled out by Brother Cartwright. I believe in treating religious matters with due solemnity. I admit that the questions propounded by Brother Cartwright are of *great* importance. I did not feel called upon to answer as the rest did. Brother Cartwright asks me directly where I am going. I desire to reply with equal directness: I am going to Congress." The meeting broke up.

Ink bottles were emptied and filled again as he wrote piles of letters. He took on debaters as carelessly as in the Black Hawk War he took on wrestlers. "If alive and well I am sure to be with you on the 22d. I will meet the trio of mighty adversaries you mention, in the best manner I can."

During his campaign, some Whig friends raised $200 for his personal expenses. After the election he handed them back $199.25, saying he had spent only seventy-five cents in the campaign. "I did not need the money. I made the canvass on my own horse; my entertainment, being at the houses of friends, cost me nothing; and my only outlay was seventy-five cents for a barrel of cider, which some farmhands insisted I should treat to."

The count of ballots had given Lincoln 6340 votes, Cartwright 4829, and Walcott (abolitionist) 249. He had been elected to Congress and was to go to the halls where Clay, Webster, Calhoun had spoken and reached the ears of the nation; after hundreds of speeches and letters, after thousands of handshakes, after scheming and waiting and struggling, he had become a congressman; and he wrote Josh Speed: "Being elected to Congress, though I am very grateful to our friends for having done it, has not pleased me as much as I expected."

NEARLY A YEAR PASSED between the time of Lincoln's election to Congress and his going to Washington. He watched and waited. War began with Mexico.

In declaring a state of war, Congress had authorized an army of 50,000 volunteers and a war fund of $10,000,000. Rifle companies of young men who had drilled regularly, and marched in processions on the Fourth of July, were offering themselves for service; of 8370 volunteers in Illinois 3720 were taken; they went down the Mississippi, across the Gulf to Texas, and on into Mexico. Even Edward D. Baker had returned from Washington to raise an Illinois regiment in June of 1846, had received a commission as colonel, and had gone to Mexico.

Many of the young men who were wild to enlist had heard since 1836 of the Alamo, of San Jacinto, and of how almost incredibly heroic Texans against heavy odds had overwhelmed Mexican armies and won independence for the Republic of Texas. The war now declared was, in part, for the boundary claimed by Texas, the Rio Grande. But a variety of irresistible American forces were acting by fact and dream in "the Texas question" and the Mexican War.

The fact was that Texas, New Mexico, and California were passionately wanted in the domain of the United States because of the immense land and wealth foreseen in them. The dream was of "an ocean-bound republic," an America "from sea to sea." When Congress in March 1845 had passed resolutions to annex Texas, and a Texas convention was unanimous for joining the Union of states, the Mexican government had warned that Texas was still a Mexican province, and voted $4,000,000 for war against Texas. President Polk ordered American troops in "protective occupation" on a strip of land in dispute at the Rio Grande. The inevitable clashes came—and the all-out war was on.

Lincoln saw more shame than glory in the political steps and procedures involved. At this time, however, he adopted the position of most Whigs, including General Zachary Taylor, who commanded the American army in its expedition across the Rio Grande. The Whigs politically had stood against the declaration of war, calling it a fight for a land grab, but with the war started and the nation committed to it, the thing to do, they agreed, was to fight it through, with no stint of sacrifice.

So Lincoln continued to watch events, collect facts and data, and work on the policies he would stand for in Congress, where his term was to start in December 1847. He meanwhile went on riding the Eighth Circuit, driving a rattletrap buggy or on horseback, sometimes perhaps, as he tied his horse to a hitching post, hearing a voice across the street, "That's the new Congressman Lincoln." His yearly income ranged from $1200 to $1500, comparing nicely with the governor's yearly $1200. By now he had probably paid the last of his personal debt. An incomplete fee book of Lincoln & Herndon for 1845–47 showed fees from $3 to $100, most entries $10. Sometimes groceries and farm produce were accepted for fees.

In July 1847 Lincoln was one of hundreds of delegates to the River and Harbor Convention, run by Whigs to promote internal improvements, and held in Chicago, by now a city of sixteen thousand. There Lincoln had his first look at mighty Lake Michigan, a path for ship transport of wheat to New York and Europe. There he met such notable Whigs as Thurlow Weed, the party boss in New York, and editor Horace Greeley, who wrote to his New York *Tribune* that "Hon. Abraham Lincoln, a tall specimen of an Illinoisan . . . was called out, and spoke briefly and happily."

Leasing his Springfield house for a yearly rental of $90, "the North upstairs room" reserved for furniture storage, Lincoln on October 25, 1847, with wife, four-year-old Robert and nineteen-month-old Eddie, took the stage for St. Louis, and after a week of steamboat and rail travel, arrived in Lexington, Kentucky. There relatives and friends could see Mary Todd Lincoln and her congressman husband she took pride in showing.

Lincoln saw the cotton mills of Oldham, Todd & Company, worked by slave labor, driving out with his brother-in-law, Levi Todd, assistant manager. He got the feel of a steadily growing antislavery movement in Kentucky. He saw slaves auctioned, saw them chained in gangs heading to cotton fields, heard ominous news like that of "Cassily," a slave girl, under indictment for "mixing an ounce of pounded glass with gravy" and giving it to her master and his wife.

Lincoln saw in the Todd and other homes the Negro house servants, and in their cleanliness, their handling of food and linen, he saw the chasm between them and Negro field hands who lived in "quarters." He read books in the big library of his father-in-law, Robert Todd, went to parties, and in the capital city of Kentucky met leading figures of state and nation.

He heard that most eminent of Whigs, Henry Clay, speak on November 13 before an immense audience: "Autumn has come, and the season of flowers has passed away . . . I too am in the autumn of life, and feel the frost of age." Clay went on to term the Mexican War one of "unnecessary and offensive aggression," holding, "It is Mexico that is defending her firesides, her castles and her altars, not we." For the United States to take over Mexico and govern it, as some were urging, Clay saw as impossible. And he warned that there would be danger in acquiring a new area into which slavery could move.

The Lincolns stayed three weeks in Kentucky, then left for Washington.

Chapter 14

BY STAGE and by rail the Lincoln family traveled seven days to arrive in Washington on December 2, 1847. Here Abraham Lincoln stood for the first time at the hub of the wheel of government. Here he rested his eyes on the Potomac River, on the slopes where George Washington had lived most of his years, and gazed up the broad pathway of Pennsylvania Avenue, connecting the White House where President James K. Polk lived and the Capitol where the Congress of the United States was to sit in deliberation on laws, and where the name of Abraham Lincoln was to be called in the roll calls.

Here were the stage and footlights where Andrew Jackson, Henry Clay, John Calhoun, Daniel Webster, and John Quincy Adams had spoken their lines so many years. Jackson, the most passionate and forthright of all, had gone; the footlights were out for him; soon another and another was to go; in a few years the stage would be dark for a little row of players who had put their impress on every large issue in the government for thirty years and more. After them were to come other players; they would have lines to speak on a fiercely lighted stage.

The Lincolns stayed first at Brown's Hotel, then moved to Mrs. Sprigg's boardinghouse on ground where later the Library of Congress was built. They were living in a city ten times the size of Springfield, with a population of forty thousand people, among them eight thousand free Negroes and two thousand slaves. It was a planned city with wide streets, squares, parks, and a few noble buildings, yet nearly everywhere a look of the unfinished, particularly the Capitol with its wooden dome, its two wings yet to be built. Here were mansions and slums, cowsheds, hog pens, and privies in backyards; hogs, geese, and chickens roving streets and alleys. Sidewalks were mostly of gravel or ashes. Ragged slaves drove produce wagons; gangs of slaves at times moved in chains along streets. Lincoln saw a jail near the Capitol which he was to term a "sort of Negro livery-stable," where Negroes were kept to be taken south "precisely like a drove of horses."

Yet here too were libraries, fountains, museums, gardens, halls, and offices where historic and momentous decisions were made, where ceremonials, receptions, balls were held. Here were all the dialects of America from Louisiana to Maine, the soft southern drawl, the Yankee nasal twang, the differing western slang.

On the halfway line between the states of the North and of the South they had placed and laid out this city; it was built on something resembling an oath that the states north and south belonged together and should meet at a halfway point.

Here, in this city, Abraham Lincoln was to spend his thirty-ninth-birthday anniversary and round out his fortieth year, as a lawmaker of the American republic.

LINCOLN LIKED Mrs. Sprigg's place, the lodgings and meals. At the table he ate with other congressmen, Patrick Thompson of Mississippi, Elisha Embree of Indiana, Joshua Giddings from Ohio, and others. When the Mississippi and Ohio members between helpings of victuals clashed over the slavery issue, Lincoln sometimes interrupted and steered the discussion into a good-natured channel. At Caspari's bowling alley, near Mrs. Sprigg's place, he tried for ten-strikes with his long right arm and told yarns between plays and games. But Mrs. Lincoln couldn't find company or social events of interest to her, and with her husband one of the busiest men in Congress, missing only seven roll calls in the long session that was opening, after three months of it she traveled with the two boys to her father's home in Lexington.

In the House of Representatives, after the oath of office, Lincoln drew a seat in the back row of the Whig side. He soon was at home in a corner of the House post office where story-tellers met. "By New Year's he was recognized as the champion storyteller of the Capitol," wrote a newspaperman. "His favorite seat was at the left of the open fireplace, tilted back in his chair, with his long legs reaching over to the chimney jamb. He never told a story twice, but appeared to have an endless repertoire always ready."

AT THE TIME Lincoln swore his oath and took his seat as congressman the war with Mexico was nearly over. American armies in Mexico were clinching their hold on that country. The government in Washington had spent $27,000,000 and the lives of 27,000 soldiers. Mexico was beaten. The question of the day was, "What next? What price shall we force Mexico to pay us for what the war has cost us?"

One answer to this question came from a man who stood up on crutches in the Senate; he was six feet high, lean, with wide gray-blue eyes, a thin shrewd nose, bushy eyebrows, proud, independent. He had been shot in the foot at the battle of Buena Vista and stayed in the saddle with his bleeding foot till the battle was won. His name was Jefferson Davis; a graduate of West Point, he had been colonel of the Mississippi Rifles, a crack regiment of young aristocrats from Mississippi; he was a cotton planter with several thousand acres at Biloxi; the governor of Mississippi had appointed him senator to fill a vacancy. Now he was speaking for the Ten Regiments bill, asking Congress to vote money to send ten regiments of soldiers to garrison the cities and provinces of Mexico. He told the Senate, "I hold that in a just war we conquered the larger portion of Mexico and that to it we have a title which has been regarded as valid ever since man existed in a social condition—the title of conquest." The Ten Regiments bill passed the Senate, but when it went to the House it never came to a vote; Whigs controlled the House.

There was confusion. Only five southern states had voted solidly for the Ten Regiments bill. In the other southern states there was opposition to the taking of all Mexico and the annexation of it to the United States. John C. Calhoun, the senator from South Carolina, along with senators from Tennessee and Georgia, voted against the Ten Regiments bill. But while the South was not solid in favor of the dream of the "fire eater" for national expansion southward, still there was in the air the beginnings of a realization of an ocean-bound republic, with the territory from the Atlantic to the Pacific coasts in the hands of the United States. It was a carrying further of the thought of General Jackson years before that Texas must be annexed; more and more western territory must be taken into the Union.

There came into Congress at this time a little piece of writing that called up storms of debate. It was a proviso written to ride with the appropriations bill; introduced by Judge Wilmot of Pennsylvania, it was called the Wilmot Proviso. It provided that any new territory that came into the United States from the Mexican War treaty should be free and not slave territory. Onto one bill after another it was put as an amendment. Voted down, it came back. Lincoln spoke "Aye" for the Wilmot Proviso so many times he couldn't exactly remember how many; he guessed it was "about forty times," at least.

Though other politicians hesitated or were confused, to Lincoln his own way was clear; there were no zigzags in the course of his thinking about the war. His public speeches and his confidential letters to Herndon back home fitted together in all parts, pieces, and dovetails.

Behind the war he saw politics. He believed one motive back of the war was that Polk and the Democratic party wanted to take away public attention from the backdown of the Democratic party on the Oregon boundary; they had said they would take all land up to the "fifty-four forty" or they would fight Great Britain; the slogan had been "Fifty-four forty, or fight!"; they had backed down; and in order to cover up they started a war where they were sure they could win, and the winnings looked good. That was the big reason. Next to that was another reason; the Democrats knew that the war would win more territory into which the southern planters could spread out with cotton, slave labor, and the politics of cotton and slavery.

He saw at a desk in the Senate chamber the spare figure of John C. Calhoun, with a face carved by merciless events, a timeworn forehead with relentless thoughts back of it: "People do not understand liberty or majorities. The will of the majority is the will of a rabble. Progressive democracy is incompatible with liberty." Lincoln did not agree with the thoughts of John C. Calhoun. He could also see, over in the Senate, the Illinois wonder boy, Stephen A. Douglas; Douglas, after two terms in the House, had been reelected but had resigned to start his first term in the upper chamber; as a loyal Democrat, he defended the Administration's war record, quoting Frederick the Great: "Take possession first and negotiate afterward." And Lincoln did not agree with the thoughts of Stephen A. Douglas.

LINCOLN SAT meanwhile as a member of the congressional committee on post offices. One day, in bringing in a report on post office matters, he started to tell the House that all the Whigs in committee voted for the report, and all the Democrats, except one. He was interrupted; didn't he know it was out of order to tell on the floor what happened in the committee room?

"He then observed," said the House minutes, "that if he had been out of order in what he said, he took it all back as far as he could. He had no desire, he could assure gentlemen, ever to be out of order—though he never could keep long in order."

As to making speeches on the floor of the House, Lincoln wrote back to Herndon: "By way of getting the hang of the House, I made a little speech two or three days ago on a post office question of no general interest. I find speaking here and elsewhere about the same thing. I was about as badly scared, and no worse, as I am when I speak in the court."

This was a tryout; a more thorough effort was to come. Getting the floor of the House on January 12, 1848, Lincoln defended the vote of his party given a few days previous, declaring "that the war with Mexico was unnecessarily and unconstitutionally commenced by the President." He spoke of his impression of how he and others believed they ought to behave while their country was engaged in a war they considered unjustly commenced. "When the war began, it was my opinion that all those who, because of knowing too *little*, or because of knowing too *much*, could not conscientiously approve the conduct of the President, in the beginning of it should nevertheless, as good citizens and patriots, remain silent on that point, at least till the war should be ended."

Now he was forced to break silence; the President was telling the country, continually, that votes of the Whigs for supplies to the soldiers in the field were an endorsement of the President's conduct of the war. Then too, the President was holding back documents and information to which the public was entitled.

Lincoln had earlier introduced resolutions and demands that the President should locate the exact "spot" where the war began. He now accused the President of marching an American army out of proven American territory into land not established as American soil, and there shedding the first blood of the war.

Back in Illinois were political enemies murmuring that Lincoln was revealed as a Benedict Arnold in his "spot" resolutions. He now wanted the folks back home to see him pressing the President for the documents of the war, all of them. "Let the President answer the interrogatories I proposed. Let him answer fully, fairly, and candidly. Let him answer with facts and not with arguments." And if the President refused to answer? "Then I shall be fully convinced of what I more than suspect already—that he is deeply conscious of being in the wrong; that he feels the blood of this war, like the blood of Abel crying to Heaven against him."

He dramatized James K. Polk. "Originally having some strong motive to involve the two countries in a war, and trusting to escape scrutiny by fixing the public gaze upon the exceeding brightness of military glory . . . he plunged into it, and has swept on and on till, disappointed in his calculations of the ease with which Mexico might be subdued, he now finds himself he knows not where. . . .

"The President is in no wise satisfied with his own positions. First he takes up one, and in attempting to argue us into it he argues himself out of it. . . . His mind, taxed beyond its power, is running hither and thither, like some tortured creature on a burning surface, finding no position on which it can settle down and be at ease. . . . He knows not where he is. He is a bewildered, confounded, and miserably perplexed man."

If Lincoln could have known what had happened in the White House, he would have known that, behind its closed doors, two men saw President Polk every day and did their best to push him into taking all of Mexico. The two were James Buchanan, Secretary of State, and Robert J. Walker, Secretary of the Treasury. For months the President hesitated; he was precisely what Lincoln had said, a bewildered, confounded, miserably perplexed man. Of Walker the President noted in his diary: "He was for taking all of Mexico"; of Buchanan the notation was similar. Finally, he wrote in his diary, after endless advice to seize the whole Mexico territory: "I replied that I was not prepared to go to that extent."

In rehearsing the start of the Mexican War, Lincoln for the first time told in public his views about revolutions and the rights of peoples to revolutionize. His declarations had a breath of the smoky days of the American Revolution. "Any people anywhere being inclined and having the power have the right to rise up and shake off the existing government. . . . This is a most valuable, a most sacred right—a right which we hope and believe is to liberate the world. Nor is this right confined to cases in which the whole people of an existing government may choose to exercise it. Any portion of such people that can may revolutionize and make their own of so much of the territory as they inhabit. More than this, a majority of any portion of such people may revolutionize, putting down a minority, intermingled with or near about them, who may oppose this movement. Such minority was precisely the case of the Tories of our own revolution. It is a quality of revolutions not to go by old lines or old laws; but to break up both, and make new ones."

All of Mexico, including Texas, he pointed out, had revolutionized against Spain, after which Texas revolutionized against Mexico, raising the question of just how far the boundary line ran that was fixed by the Texas revolution. So far as Lincoln could learn, the "spot" where the first blood of the war was shed was outside the Texas line and over in Mexican territory. It, the spot, was located between two rivers on a strip of land over which the United States government did—or did not—exercise jurisdiction. And Lincoln was trying to get President

Polk to tell just how far the jurisdiction of the United States was exercised over that strip of land—if at all.

He voted for all supplies for soldiers, for every help to the fighting men in the field, yet also for every possible measure that would lay blame on the Administration. He hoped the folks back home would understand from his speeches how he looked at the war. But the folks back home refused to understand.

Even Bill Herndon couldn't see it. He wrote Herndon:

> You fear that you and I disagree about the war. I regret this . . . because if you misunderstand I fear other good friends may also. I will stake my life that if you had been in my place you would have voted just as I did.

What bothered Herndon and the others back home was a resolution maneuvered through Congress by the Whigs, voicing thanks to the officers of the Mexican War—with a stinger for Polk. It added to the thanks the words, "in a war unnecessarily and unconstitutionally begun by the President of the United States." The vote was 82 to 81.

In a second letter to Herndon, Lincoln explained that the President of the United States is the same as a king, in power, if he can do what President Polk had done in commencing the Mexican War. The Constitution gave the war-making powers to Congress. "Kings had always been involving and impoverishing their people in wars," Lincoln wrote, "pretending generally, if not always, that the good of the people was the object. This our convention understood to be the most oppressive of all kingly oppressions, and they resolved to so frame the Constitution that no one man should hold the power of bringing this oppression upon us. But your view destroys the whole matter, and places our President where kings have always stood."

His guess was correct that if Herndon was misunderstanding there would be others misunderstanding. A meeting in Clark County of patriotic Whigs and Democrats adopted this declaration: "Resolved, That Abe Lincoln, the author of the 'spotty' resolutions in Congress, against his own country, may they long be remembered by his constituents, but may they cease to remember him, except to rebuke him."

To the Reverend J. M. Peck, Lincoln wrote a letter. The minister had spoken at a Belleville celebration of the battle of Buena Vista, saying, "In view of all the facts, the conviction to my mind is irresistible that the government of the United States committed no aggression on Mexico." To him Lincoln wrote: "Not in view of all the facts. There are facts which you have kept out of view." And he went on:

It is a fact that the United States army in marching to the Rio Grande marched into a peaceful Mexican settlement, and frightened the inhabitants away from their homes and their growing crops. It is a fact that Fort Brown, opposite Matamoras, was built by that army within a Mexican cotton-field, on which at the time the army reached it a young cotton crop was growing, and which crop was wholly destroyed and the field itself greatly and permanently injured by ditches, embankments, and the like. It is a fact that when the Mexicans captured Captain Thornton and his command, they found and captured them within another Mexican field.

Now I wish to bring these facts to your notice, and to ascertain what is the result of your reflections on them.

Sleuthing for such facts, Lincoln went to the State Department, and he went to the library of the Supreme Court. One evening at the library, after digging in many books and documents, he drew out volumes to read in his room at Mrs. Sprigg's boardinghouse. The library was going to close for the night. And he took his books, pulled a large bandanna out of his pocket, tied it around the books, ran a stick through the knots, slung the stick over his shoulder, and walked out of the library of the Supreme Court in the way natural to him, in the way he carried his belongings from his canoe on the Sangamon River up into New Salem when he was going to clerk in Offutt's store. Over his shoulder was a short circular blue cloak he had bought since he came to Washington.

Thus he walked to his Capitol Hill lodging, where he untied the knots of his bundle, read his books, took a brass key from his vest pocket and wound his watch, put his boot heel into a bootjack and pulled off his boots, blew out the candles, and crept into a warm flannel nightshirt that came down halfway between his knees and ankles. Then he slept the sleep of a man who had been searching Washington dissatisfied with mere claims, looking for the foundations of claims.

He may have dreamed of old Tom Lincoln, who had recently written for money, pleading, "I haven't a thing I could sell."

But there had been sweetness in the fact that Tom had written, "The Old Woman is well."

Chapter 15

LINCOLN by now had got "the hang of the House," as he called it. He had made speeches on internal improvements, public roads, rivers, harbors, canals, saying in one speech that so far as he could see there was the same wrangling in state legislatures and in counties and towns as there was in the national Congress, over improvements. "One man is offended because a road passes over his land, and another is offended because it does not pass over his . . . while not a few struggle hard to have roads located over their lands, and then stoutly refuse to let them be opened until they are first paid the damages."

As a first step toward fair dealing out of the nation's money for needed improvements among the states, Lincoln had suggested statistical information to guide congressmen. He was voicing the wishes of the Chicago River and Harbor Convention. To pay for canals with canal tolls and tonnage duties, before canals were dug, was like the Irishman and his new boots. "I shall niver git 'em on till I wear 'em a day or two, and stretch 'em a little."

Often during the first half of the year 1848, Lincoln was rushed with work, faithfully attending to petitions, appointments, pensions, documents for constituents. He turned out dozens of letters a day, "fixing his political fences." In a typical letter he advised E. B. Washburne on a political campaign matter, "Make Baker help about it. He is a good man to raise a breeze." When back pay was due Joseph Ferguson of Springfield, who had died in Mexican War service, Lincoln made calls at the War Department in Washington until the matter was adjusted.

In April he had written his wife: "Dear Mary: In this trouble-some world, we are never quite satisfied. When you were here, I thought you hindered me some in attending to business; but now, having nothing but business—no variety—it has grown exceedingly tasteless to me. I hate to sit down and direct documents, and I hate to stay in this old room by myself." He wrote of shopping, as she wished, for "the little plaid stockings" to fit "Eddy's dear little feet," and "you are entirely free from headache? That is good—good—considering it is the first spring you have been free from it since we were acquainted. I am afraid you will get so well, and fat, and young, as to be wanting to marry again."

Their children were a common and warm bond. Once he had a dream about bad luck happening to Bobby, which aroused his fears for the boy's safety. "I did not get rid of the impression of that foolish dream about poor Bobby till I got your letter written the same day," he wrote. "What did he and Eddy think of the little letters father sent them? Dont let the blessed fellows forget father." Another long, newsy letter ended, "Kiss and love the dear rascals." He signed his letters to her, "Affectionately A. Lincoln," and hers to him were signed, "Truly yours M. L."

When she wanted to return to Washington she wrote to him asking him about it, as though in such a case it was for her to ask and for him to advise or decide. Her uncle was to travel to Philadelphia to put his eldest daughter in school, and she believed she might travel with her uncle and meet her husband in Washington. "You know I am so fond of sightseeing," she wrote, "& I did not get to New York or Boston, or travel the lake route. . . . How much, I wish instead of writing, we were together this evening, I feel very sad away from you."

In June he wrote to her: "The leading matter in your letter, is your wish to return to this side of the Mountains. Will you be a *good girl* in all things, if I consent? Then come along, and that as *soon* as possible. Having got the idea in my head, I shall be impatient till I see you. . . . Come on just as soon as you can. I want to see you, and our dear—*dear* boys very much."

But campaign duties in that election year of 1848 pressed him and her visit to Washington couldn't be managed.

ONE CONGRESSMAN with whom Lincoln became good friends while he was in Washington was Alexander Stephens of Georgia. Jefferson Davis called Stephens "the little pale star from Georgia." A wizened, dry, wry man who weighed less than a hundred pounds, Stephens drew men to him; in his black eyes, set deep in a large-boned, homely head, there was a smolder. He and Lincoln held similar views on the Mexican War. They had comradeship; scrawls of personal tragedy, pinches of hunger and fate were on their two faces. Each felt it uphill work to act the part of a Great Man. Whereas men looked up toward Lincoln's head and asked, "How's the weather up there?" Stephens said, "Men address me familiarly as 'my son.' "

Both had come up from cabins of poverty. Both were uneasy amid women. And both served in the forefront of Whigs working for the nomination of General Zachary Taylor for President.

In the winter of 1847–48 Stephens, Lincoln, and five other Whigs had organized the Taylor Club, with members nicknamed the "Young Indians." They saw that the Whig war hero would make a candidate the Democrats couldn't keep out of the White House. The name of "Old Zach" carried magic. True enough, Taylor on his Louisiana plantation owned three hundred slaves, and kept quiet on the slavery issue. He was naïve and somewhat ignorant of politics; but he was honest, rugged, plain. And he had spoken of the Mexican War as uncalled for, had moved his troops into action only under direct orders which he obeyed as a loyal soldier, then had gone in and fought as a wildcat from hell. Greatly loved by his troops, he had been nicknamed by them "Old Rough and Ready."

Lincoln went to Philadelphia in June as a delegate to the national convention of the Whig party and as a Taylor man. The first ballot gave Taylor 111, Henry Clay 97, General Winfield Scott 43, Daniel Webster 22. Lincoln voted for Taylor on all ballots, and cheered when he won on the fourth. Lincoln believed the nomination of the hero of the Mexican War for President took the Democrats "on the blind side." He wrote to Illinois: "It turns the war thunder against them. The war is now to them the gallows of Haman, which they built for us, and on which they are doomed to be hanged themselves."

Lincoln knew he was slipping in popularity at home because of his opinions on the Mexican War issue. He was not a candidate for reelection for Congress—though this was due in part to the Illinois Whig party's "turn about is fair play" policy; his old law partner, Stephen T. Logan, was running for Lincoln's seat and in the election would lose to a Democrat who was a Mexican War veteran. But Lincoln was an active campaigner in the 1848 elections, as usual, and he had his personal ways, his own methods of playing politics. A first element to line up, in his plans, was the young men such as those who had been his never-failing guards in Sangamon County, at Clary's Grove. He wrote to Herndon: "As to the young men, you must not wait to be brought forward by the older men. You young men get together and form a Rough & Ready club and have regular meetings and speeches. Take in everybody you can get. As you go along gather up all the shrewd, wild boys about town."

Early in September of 1848, Lincoln stumped New England for the national Whig ticket. There the new Free-Soil party had a threatening strength. They had nominated the former Democratic President Martin Van Buren for President, and their platform called for "Free Soil, Free Speech, Free Labor, and Free Men." Lincoln's trip to Massachusetts lasted three days and carried him into new territory, where he saw the factories, mills, and foundries that made New England so rich and powerful.

As committees of Whigs escorted him, they felt, often, here was a sober, sad man from far west, with a strangeness they could not solve, but as he loosened and lightened, they felt they knew him. In Boston he saw Faneuil Hall and at Cambridge, near the walls of Harvard University, he delivered a speech. He spoke also at Lowell, at Worcester, at Dedham, and in Boston. When he had left Boston he headed west.

At Albany he talked with Thurlow Weed, the Whig boss of New York; they went out and visited Millard Fillmore, the Whig candidate for Vice-President. He rode on the Erie Canal to Buffalo, visited Niagara Falls, which impressed him greatly, and then left Buffalo on the steamer *Globe* for a cruise that had him in Chicago October 5. There he spoke for the Whig ticket to a crowd so large it had to adjourn from the courthouse to the public square. With Mrs. Lincoln and the children he traveled after that to Springfield, stopping over in Peoria for a two-hour speech in which, the *Democratic Press* said, "Mr. Lincoln blew his nose, bobbed his head, threw up his coat tail, and delivered an immense amount of sound and fury."

During the autumn weeks before Election Day he spoke in eight or ten Illinois towns for the Whig ticket, always advising that a vote for the Free-Soil ticket might turn out to be a vote for Lewis Cass, the Democratic nominee for President. His own stand on the Mexican War and the question of the United States reaching out for more territory he sometimes tried to make clear by quoting what the farmer said about land: "I ain't greedy; I only want what jines mine."

Election returns gave Taylor the presidency, though Cass carried Illinois. Ohio elected six Free-Soilers to Congress, other states six more, which forebode that the slavery issue would blaze on.

In late November Lincoln returned to Washington, sat as a congressman who had failed of reelection, introduced resolutions to abolish the slave trade in the District of Columbia, watched the hungry office hunters come swarming in on President Taylor, tried and failed to land a high diplomatic appointment for Ned Baker, looked on the riotous whirl of the President's inauguration ball, had his hat stolen, and walked Washington streets bareheaded at three o'clock in the morning. On March 7 he was admitted to practice before the U. S. Supreme Court; he argued a case appealed from an Illinois court, and lost it. He said good-by here and there—and came home to Springfield, through as a congressman.

Then during four or five months he carried on a furious campaign of letter writing and conferences aimed at getting for himself or for some other Illinois man the appointment of Commissioner of the General Land Office at Washington. Finally the politics of the affair seemed to narrow down to where Lincoln personally would have to go after the office or it would be lost to the Whigs of southern Illinois.

Early in June he was writing friends: "Would you as soon I should have the General Land Office as any other Illinoisan?

If you would, write me to that effect at Washington, where I shall be soon. No time to lose." Later in June he was in Washington wearing a linen duster, carrying a carpetbag, offering President Taylor eleven reasons why he, an original Taylor man, should be named for the land office job. But the appointment went to Justin Butterfield, who had marshaled northern Illinois and Chicago influence, as well as the support of Daniel Webster.

Lincoln's decision then was to stay in Springfield and practice law. And in August 1849, when he was notified that he had been appointed Governor of the Territory of Oregon, he replied to the Secretary of State, "I respectfully decline the office."

Abraham Lincoln was no longer asking for any appointments. He was settling down and straightening out his desk and papers in the Springfield law office with Bill Herndon.

Chapter 16

THE LITTLE FRAME HOUSE which was the Lincoln home on the corner of Eighth and Jackson streets in Springfield was painted white, with green blinds and white chimneys. Under the care of Mary Todd Lincoln, who was spick-and-span about such things, it was a clean, snug-looking place. There the ex-congressman, back from Washington, settled down to law practice, and shoveled snow from the front door to the street, from the back door to the barn and the outhouses.

As he put the currycomb to the horse and slicked axle grease on his buggy wheels, he could think about little Stephen A. Douglas, the short, thick-chested, blue-eyed man who had been a common struggler with the rest of them in Springfield a few years back, now a U. S. senator sitting in conferences with Clay, Calhoun, and Webster at Washington, and fast taking a place as a national leader of the Democratic party. And James Shields, whom Lincoln had met for the duel on the sandbar, was Douglas's colleague from Illinois in the Senate. The mayor of Springfield was John Calhoun, his old friend who had started him as a surveyor. They were all Democrats. Among Illinois Whigs luck was the other way; his old law partners, John T. Stuart and Stephen T. Logan, were practicing law; Edward D. Baker had gone to California.

The slavery question seemed to be settled by what was called the Omnibus bill. Five Negroes were in the Springfield jail down on the public square; they were fugitive slaves and, according to the law, would go back to their owners. And yet, though the slavery question did seem settled, there were more quiet men here and there who were helping to pass on runaway Negroes, up from Jacksonville, Springfield, Bloomington, on up to Galesburg, Princeton, Chicago, and so to Canada, where the British law prohibiting slaveownership made them safe.

The northern part of Illinois had been filling up with settlers. Towns such as Princeton and Galesburg were more Yankee than some towns in New England which, in turn, had filled their factories with newcomers from Europe—men, women, and children who had fled Europe in the dark year of 1848, when there had been revolution all across that continent. The human inflow from Europe was pushing westward, too. Irish and Germans were swarming into Chicago. At Bishop Hill was a settlement as humanly Swedish as Sweden. Near Athens in Sangamon County was a settlement of Norwegians; north of Springfield was a huddle of Portuguese. But the Germans outnumbered all others; and Lincoln carried a German grammar and studied the language in a night class.

Yes, Illinois was changing, just like the country. What was ahead in politics no man could tell. The one sure thing was that the people from Kentucky, Tennessee, and Virginia and the Carolinas, who had controlled Illinois, were to be outnumbered and outvoted at some time in the near future. New men, new issues, were coming. The writing of the history of the country would have to be with new names.

Over the breakfast and supper table at the Lincoln home, the woman of the house told him her hopes that he would move onward and upward. He knew that fame, name, and high place would please her more than anything else. When he made a move in politics he usually knew her view of it; she told him her views, and plainly. She read, she talked with people of influence, she gave him her judgment.

His unwillingness to take the appointment as Governor of the Territory of Oregon had reflected his wife's decision. She was willing to live in Washington as the wife of the General Land Commissioner, but she did not care to live in a pioneer country separated by weeks of wagon travel from the settled regions of the country. So Lincoln stayed in Springfield and studied and worked on law cases. For five years politics was a side issue. He said he was out of politics. He traveled on the Eighth Judicial Circuit as the court moved, staying two days to two weeks in each county seat. From September till Christmas and from February till June, he was away from his home. It was a way of life that kept him in close touch with people, their homes, kitchens, fields, their churches, schools, hotels, saloons, their places for working and worshipping and loafing.

Abraham Lincoln believed in dreams and tried to read his dreams for their connections with his future. Mary Todd Lincoln believed in signs; she told him about signs, portents. Both were superstitious. Both had hopes. And he had his thoughts and his doubts.

IN FEBRUARY 1850 four-year-old Edward Baker Lincoln died. For the first time Abraham Lincoln held in his arms the white still body of a child of his own; he could call the name of Eddie to his boy and the boy had no ears to hear nor breath to answer. The mother took it hard and it was his place to comfort and restore, if he could, a broken woman.

This little still body was his own kith and kin, who had come out of silence and gone back to silence, back where Nancy Hanks had gone the year he helped his father peg together a plank coffin.

He tried to pierce through into the regions of that silence and find replies to questions that surged in him.

On the day Eddie was buried, a funeral sermon was pronounced by the Reverend James Smith of the First Presbyterian Church, and a friendship developed between the Lincoln family and the Reverend Mr. Smith. The minister had been wild in his young days, a scoffer at religion; he could tell a story—he and Lincoln were good company.

The Lincolns rented a pew in the church. Mrs. Lincoln took the sacrament, and joined in membership. The Reverend Mr. Smith presented Lincoln with a copy of his book *The Christian's Defense*, a reply to atheists. Lincoln read the book, attended revival meetings held at the church, and said he was interested. But when asked to join the church he said he "couldn't quite see it."

Close friends of Lincoln, such as his law partner, Bill Herndon, and James Matheny, who stood as best man at his wedding, had a notion Lincoln was a sort of infidel. They said Lincoln told them he could not believe the Bible was the revelation of God, or that Jesus was the Son of God. "An infidel, a theist, a fatalist," was Herndon's notion.

But there were evangelical Christian church members who felt he was a solemn, earnest, religious man. Lincoln read the Bible closely, knew it from cover to cover, was familiar with its stories and its poetry, quoted from it in his speeches and his letters. As a boy he had heard his mother saying over certain Bible verses day by day as she worked. He had learned these verses by heart; the tones of his mother's voice were in them; and sometimes, as he read these verses, he seemed to hear the voice of Nancy Hanks speaking them.

This he once told Mrs. Rankin, a friend over near New Salem. And when Mrs. Rankin had raised the question of what his religion really was, he had said, "Probably it is to be my lot to go on in a twilight, feeling and reasoning my way through life, as questioning, doubting Thomas did." She said that he also told her, "If the church would ask simply for assent to the Saviour's statement of the substance of the law: *Thou shalt love the Lord thy God with all thy heart, and with all thy soul, and with all thy mind,* and *thy neighbor as thyself*—that church would I gladly unite with."

Some friends, like Jesse W. Fell at Bloomington, felt that Lincoln held a good deal the same views as the famous heterodox New England preachers Theodore Parker and William Ellery Channing. When Fell talked with enthusiasm about Channing's sermons, Lincoln showed such a keen interest that Fell gave him a collection of the sermons.

For the Kickapoo Indian, Johnny Kongapod, Lincoln used an epitaph that had the breath of his religion in it:

Here lies poor Johnny Kongapod;
Have mercy on him, gracious God.
As he would do if he was God
And you were Johnny Kongapod.

IN THAT SAME YEAR, 1850, the Lincolns' third son was born; named William Wallace, he was called Willie. Not long after, in January 1851, word came that Lincoln's father down on the Coles County farm was dying.

Lincoln wrote to John D. Johnston, the stepson at the farm:

I feel sure you have not failed to use my name, if necessary, to procure a doctor, or anything else for Father in his sickness. My business is such that I could hardly leave home now, if it were not, as it is, that my own wife is sickabed. . . . I sincerely hope Father may yet recover his health; but at all events, tell him to remember to call upon, and confide in, our great, and good, merciful Maker; who will not turn away from him in any extremity.

The father died January 17, 1851. Later, in 1853, when the Lincolns' fourth baby boy was born, he was named Thomas after his grandfather.

Chapter 17

"THE GREAT CALHOUN is dead," mourned South Carolina and her neighbors in 1850. "The great Henry Clay is dead," cried other mourners in 1852; and in that same year was heard the cry, "The great Daniel Webster is dead."

All three had been congressman, senator, Secretary of State; all three had missed the presidency by narrow margins of whimsical ballots. And they were dying as the country was blundering along with grave problems they had failed to solve.

In their places were rising new young leaders to play with public opinion. Now occupying a chief place in the Democratic party was young Stephen A. Douglas. The names of William Henry Seward of New York; Charles Sumner of Massachusetts; Horace Greeley of the *Tribune* were beginning to count. Among the abolitionists rose young Wendell Phillips, aristocratic, handsome, ironical, scathing, in anguish over slaves chained, flogged, bought and sold. He invented a form of oratory staccato with sneers; he embodied proud yearnings and gifts of contempt.

Far to the south lived Jefferson Davis, the choice of Calhoun for southern leadership. From his cotton plantation at Biloxi, Mississippi, he could look out on the Gulf of Mexico. His home soil was swept by tropic breezes from a gulf whose warm waters touched Mexico, Cuba; the breath of his home outlook in winter was different from that of bleak New England and of the Northwest, where blizzards piled snowdrifts up to the latches of cabin doors. Often Davis could vision the so-called Union of states as two sections or confederacies with two cultures, fated to separate. When it seemed that California was going to be let into the Union as a free state there were mass meetings in all parts of Mississippi; as Davis left for Washington he believed the state of Mississippi would draw out of the Union and be joined by other states.

In Chicago, Abraham Lincoln was trying a law case and was called on to deliver the address at memorial exercises for General Zachary Taylor. For in July of that year President Taylor died, leaving Millard Fillmore to become head of the country. Lincoln spoke mournfully and quoted seven stanzas from the star poem of the album of his memory, "Oh, Why Should the Spirit of Mortal Be Proud?" How Lincoln himself might wish to behave in crises, he intimated in saying of Taylor: "He could not be *flurried*, and he could not be *scared* . . . He was alike averse to *sudden*, and to *startling* quarrels; and he pursued no man with *revenge*."

When Henry Clay, foremost of Whigs, died in 1852, Lincoln was named to deliver a eulogy in the statehouse in Springfield. In the address, Lincoln sketched Clay's long life, how Clay on occasions by his moderation and wisdom had held the Union together when it seemed ready to break. He quoted Clay on the American Colonization Society: "There is a moral fitness in the

141

idea of returning to Africa her children, whose ancestors have been torn from her by the ruthless hand of fraud and violence. Transplanted in a foreign land, they will carry back to their native soil the rich fruits of religion, civilization, law and liberty." How desperate this hope, Lincoln was to learn at cost. Over the South were 3,204,000 slaves valued on tax books at more than $1,500,000,000. How to pay for them as property, if that were conceivable, and then "transplant" them to Africa, was the problem. With Henry Clay, Lincoln at this time was leaning on the hope of buying slave property and colonizing it in Africa. Both laid blame on proud southern hotheads who saw slavery as a sanctioned institution for which they were ready to secede, and laid equal blame on radical abolitionists who were saying they would welcome a breakup of the Union.

Lincoln in 1852 had for twenty years been a loyal Whig party leader who had shaken hands with nearly all local Whig leaders over Illinois. He seemed to be merely a party wheelhorse in his speeches in that year's presidential campaign. He made seven speeches across the state, discussing the candidates and person-alities rather than any great issues. Of General Winfield Scott, the Whig candidate, he said, "Let us stand by our candidate as faithfully as he has always stood by his country."

Election Day came. General Winfield Scott, the hero of Veracruz, was snowed under, carried only four states, and the Democrats sent to the White House the young colonel Franklin Pierce, handsome, well educated, conciliatory. All over the country, in that November of 1852, the question was asked by good Whigs, "Is the party falling to pieces?"

ABRAHAM LINCOLN HAD a family matter to look after down on the Coles County farm where Sally Bush Lincoln, his stepmother, was living.

After his father's death Lincoln, as sole heir, had deeded to his stepbrother, John D. Johnston, the west 80 acres of his father's 120-acre farm, subject to his stepmother's dower rights. This stepbrother bothered him. Once, while Lincoln was in Congress, Johnston had written him asking for $80. Lincoln had refused to lend it. He had husked corn in Indiana with John D. Johnston and knew his ways; he was well aware that Johnston was somewhat of a dude, handy with the girls, at times selling liquor by the jug. At that time he wrote advice: "You are not *lazy*, and still you *are* an *idler*. I doubt whether since I saw you, you have done a good whole day's work, in any one day. . . . This habit of uselessly wasting time, is the whole difficulty; it is vastly important to you, and still more so to your children that you should break the habit." Lincoln had then promised Johnston one other dollar for every dollar Johnston went to work and earned. "In this I do not mean you shall go off to St. Louis, or the lead mines, or the gold mines of California, but I mean for you to go at it for the best wages you can get in Coles County."

On a trip to Coles County, Lincoln found that Johnston was anxious to sell the land he lived on and move to Missouri. He wrote to Johnston, again offering sharp, peremptory advice:

> Such a notion is utterly foolish. What can you do in Missouri, better than here? Is the land any richer? Can you there, any more than here, raise corn, & wheat & oats, without work? Will any body there, any more than here, do your work for you? . . . Squirming & crawling about from place to place can do no good . . . part with the land you have, and my life upon it, you will never after, own a spot big enough to bury you in. . . . Now, I feel it my duty to have no hand in such a piece of foolery. I feel that it is so even on your own account, and particularly on Mother's account.
>
> The Eastern forty acres I intend to keep for Mother while she lives—if you *will not cultivate it;* it will rent for enough to support her—at least it will rent for something. Her Dower in the other two forties, she can let you have, and no thanks to [me]. I do not write in any unkindness. Your thousand pretences for not getting along are all nonsense; they deceive no body but yourself.

Thus a stepson to the son of his stepmother. In all the letters of Lincoln to John D. Johnston there shines far back the feeling of love and care for Sally Bush Lincoln. It was she who tried to tell what there was between her and young Abe in saying, "His mind and mine, what little I had, seemed to run together, more in the same channel."

IN THE LITTLE WHITE HOUSE at Eighth and Jackson streets, Mary Todd Lincoln had in ten years' time borne four children. In the winter of 1850 had come William Wallace; in the spring of 1853 had come Thomas, nicknamed Tad.

At the cradles of these babies, at the grave of one who had died, the mother and father had stood together. For these little ones who came, pink, soft, and helpless, lying on their backs and kicking their heels toward the ceiling, Lincoln was thankful.

To handle them, tickle them, play with them, and watch them grow, had an appeal for his sense both of the solemn and of the ridiculous. Kittens he had always liked; where other men enjoyed hunting and fishing, he found sport in petting kittens. And babies, particularly his own babies, were sacred keepsakes loaned out of a silence.

As the years had passed, the father and mother, these two who had so suddenly and independently married, came to understand that each was strong and each was weak. Habits held him that it was useless for her to try to break. If he chose to lie on the front-room carpet, on the small of his back, reading, or came to the table in his shirt sleeves and ate his meat and potatoes absently, with his eyes and his thoughts far off, she knew that was his way. She tried to stop him from answering the front doorbell; the servant should answer the bell. But he would go to the front door in carpet slippers and shirt sleeves to ask the callers what was wanted. Once two fine ladies wanted Mrs. Lincoln; he looked the house over and came back to ask the callers in, drawling pleasantly, "She'll be down soon as she gets her trotting harness on."

And when his wife wrangled with the iceman claiming an overcharge or when she screamed that she would pay only ten cents a quart for berries, that they were not worth fifteen cents, he spoke quietly to her as "Mary," and did his best to straighten things with the iceman or the berry picker.

He let her manage the house. A workman caring for the Lincoln yard went to Lincoln's office to ask about cutting down a tree. "What did Mrs. Lincoln say?" was Lincoln's question. "She said yes." "Then, in God's name, cut it down to the roots."

There were friends and relatives of Mrs. Lincoln who felt

sorry for her. One said, "Mrs. Lincoln comes of the best stock, and was raised like a lady. Her husband was the opposite, in origin, in education, in breeding, in everything; and it is therefore quite natural that she should complain because he persists in using his own knife in the butter, instead of the silver-handled one intended for that purpose."

Among servant girls in Springfield Mrs. Lincoln had a reputation of being hard to get along with. A girl named Maria came; she would stay a few days, maybe a month, said the other girls. But she stayed two years. Lincoln had arranged to pay her a dollar a week extra, Mrs. Lincoln knowing nothing about the extra dollar. "The madam and I began to understand each other," said Maria. "More than once, when she happened to be out of the room, Mr. Lincoln, with a merry twinkle in his eye, patted me on the shoulder, urging, 'Stay with her, Maria, stay with her.'"

A law student, Gibson W. Harris, in the office of Lincoln & Herndon, often ran errands out to the Lincoln home. Twice, when Lincoln was away on the circuit, he was Mrs. Lincoln's escort at a ball. He remarked, "I found her to be a good dancer; she was bright, witty, and accomplished. The sportive nickname she gave me was Mr. Mister. Mr. Lincoln showed great consideration for his wife. She was unusually timid and nervous during a storm. If the clouds gathered and the thunder rolled, he knew its effect on his wife and would at once hasten home to remain there with her till the skies cleared."

In many important matters Lincoln trusted her judgment. Herndon wrote much against her, yet he noted: "She was an excellent judge of human nature, a better reader of men's motives than her husband and quick to detect those who had designs upon and sought to use him. She was, in a good sense, a stimulant. . . . She kept him from lagging, was constantly prodding him to keep up the struggle. . . . Realizing that Lincoln's rise in the world would elevate and strengthen her, she strove in every way to promote his fortunes."

Living next door to the Lincolns, and watching their ups and downs, was a shoemaker, James Gourley. When the Lincoln cow went dry, Lincoln stepped over to Gourley's for milk.

"I think the Lincolns agreed moderately well," was Gourley's impression. "As a rule Mr. Lincoln yielded to his wife—in fact, almost any other man . . . would have done the same thing. She was gifted with an unusually high temper . . . was very excitable and when wrought up had hallucinations. . . . [At times] her demonstrations were loud enough to be heard by some of her neighbors.

"If she became excited or troublesome, as she sometimes did when Mr. Lincoln was at home, it was interesting to know what he would do. At first, he would apparently pay no attention to her. Frequently he would laugh at her, which is a risky thing to do in the face of an infuriated wife; but generally, if her impatience continued, he would pick up one of the children and deliberately leave home as if to take a walk. After he had gone, the storm usually subsided, but sometimes it would break out again when he returned.

"Notwithstanding her unfortunate temper and her peculiarities generally, I never thought Mrs. Lincoln was as bad as some people here in Springfield represented her. The truth is, she had more than one redeeming trait. She and I rarely differed —in fact, we were good friends. Although I do not believe she could plead justification for many of the things she did, yet, when I hear her criticized by some people, I cannot but recall what she once said to me about her husband, which was that, if he had been at home as much as he ought, she could have been happier and loved him more."

So there was talk about Mrs. Lincoln. She economized in the kitchen in order to have fine clothes; she had a terrible temper and tongue; so the talk ran. That her husband had married her a thousand dollars in debt, that he charged low fees as a lawyer and was careless about money, and that she had managed the household so well that her husband trusted her and let her have her own way in all the household economy, didn't get into the gossip. That she was often sorry, full of regret, after a bad burst of temper, didn't get into the gossip.

She had chosen him at a time when she had a wide range of choices, when an elegant marriage in her own class was planned for her. She had chosen one of the loneliest, strangest men in

the world—had chosen him deliberately, calling him back when he tried to slip away. She had borne him four children. She sewed clothes for herself and her children. She liked fixing herself up, making herself pretty. She read and spoke French, keeping on with her studies. While he was away six months of the year, she kept up connections socially that were of value politically.

As Lincoln sat across from her at the breakfast table, he could see on her hand the plain gold ring engraved, "Love is eternal." He had bought that ring only a little while after he had written his Kentucky chum, Joshua Speed, that his father used to say, "If you make a bad bargain, hug it all the tighter."

Chapter 18

IN THE TEN YEARS now just ahead in the life of Abraham Lincoln, the country grows; its 23,000,000 people become 31,000,000. In the ten years between 1850 and 1860, the United States becomes one of the Powers of the World.

By war and by treaty there had come, on the map of the United States, Texas; and there were the open spaces to be shaped into California, New Mexico, Arizona, Utah, Nevada, Oregon, Washington, Kansas, and parts of Colorado, Wyoming, and Montana. The government owns the land, and in Washington, congressmen and Cabinet officials squabble about what shall be done with it. There are land speculators, powerful business interests, who do not want free land for actual settlers, but homestead bills keep coming up in Congress.

The whistle of the locomotive is heard; the seaboard and the Mississippi Valley are joined by steel rails. Total railroad mileage grows from nine to thirty thousand, a net of lines with cars hauling the pork and grain of the West to the factory towns of the East, to the holds of vessels sailing to the cities of Europe; the cars come back loaded with sewing machines, churns, scissors, saws, steel tools. Some of the tools enable one farmer to do the work of ten. Grain drills, corn planters, and reaping and threshing machines are bought by the farmers. Meanwhile the first undersea telegraph messages are sent; Washington and London exchange words. The breech-loading rifle arrives; man shoots bullets quicker and oftener.

And Lincoln, riding the circuit, living in hotels and court-houses, walking the streets of Springfield, now meets people shaken and stirred by slavery. They have read a book; the book has set their hearts on fire with hate; they hate the South, the people of the South; it is a hate that is making them hate their own country, its laws, its flag; and they have begun to believe their own country guilty of a crime worse than the crimes of any other country in any other time.

HARRIET BEECHER STOWE, a lone little woman, with a house full of children, published her novel, *Uncle Tom's Cabin*, in 1852. Just at that time the antislavery movement was shaping into a sort of religious crusade because of the passage of the Fugitive Slave Law, which required all people in the North to help southern slave hunters capture runaway property. Mrs. Stowe had set out to register in the bosoms of millions of other Christians her own shame of Christian civilization in America. Her hero, Uncle Tom, was a black Christ. He embodied all the implications of the saying, *But the meek shall inherit the earth.* He did what he was told to do; his word was trusted by his master; he could suffer grimly and humbly in his belief that Heaven, a world after this one, would take him in and right all wrongs. He did what he was told to do until he was told to tell which way runaway slaves had run; then, bleeding from whip thongs, his skin and flesh welted and pounded, he died moaning forgiveness to the master who had ordered another obedient Negro to beat him to death. It was the story of Judea located south of the Ohio River, with a whipping post for a cross, slaveowners for Pharisees, ministers and politicians for hypocrites and Pilates, and a cotton plantation for the scene of a passion play. And Mrs. Stowe ended her book with a prophecy: "This is an age of the world when nations are trembling and convulsed. . . . And is America safe? Every nation that carries in its bosom great and unredressed injustice has in it the elements of this last convulsion."

The people Lincoln met in 1852, and the years just after, had read this book; men couldn't pitch hay or fix a wagon, women couldn't wash dishes or knit baby shirts, without thinking of this book and its terrible story.

Abraham Lincoln had begun writing in a notebook some of the points that stood out big for him as he looked north and south at the relations of Man and Master, the upper and lower classes of America. He could see two sorts of inequality, "the British aristocratic sort" and "the domestic slavery sort." Neither was as good as "a society of equals" where every man had a chance.

He had heard southern men declare slaves were better off in the South than hired laborers in the North. Yet he would argue, "There is no permanent class of hired laborers amongst us. Twenty-five years ago I was a hired laborer. The hired laborer of today labors on his own account today, and will hire others to labor for him tomorrow."

He set up the indictment: "Although volume upon volume is written to prove slavery a good thing, we never hear of the man who wishes to take the good of it by being a slave himself." And he writhed as a man under the weight of some heavy conundrum of history in writing: "As labor is the common burden of our race, so the effort of some to shift their share of the burden onto the shoulders of others is the great durable curse of the race."

ACROSS THE STATE of Illinois, in the towns where Lincoln practiced law, men gained different impressions of him. This and that man had his own individual portrait of Lincoln.

Bill Greene, who had clerked in the Offutt store with him in New Salem days, was up in northern Illinois, still telling, with Tennessee skill, stories of "Abe Linkern," the "curi's young feller who used to keep a grocery down whar I live. He kin make a cat laugh. I've seen the whole neighborhood turn out to hear him tell stories. They ain't all jest the kind fer women to listen to, but they's always a pint to 'em. But I've seen him when he was the solumest man in ten states. When he kem back from runnin' a flatboat to New Orleans, ef anybody said anything about niggers he would git so solum, an' tell about a nigger auction he seed in New Orleans—how they sold a fambly, the man to one planter and his wife to another an' passeled the childern out among the highes' bidders, an' he thought it was awful. I've seen him turn pale," Greene went on, "when talkin' about this auction, and seem to take sick to his stomick, and then begin to cuss and take on; and I've heard him say he'd ruther tend sawmill all his life than to sell niggers, and he'd ruther do all the work on a plantation himself than to buy a nigger boy or girl from its mammy. I never once heerd him swar excep' when talkin' o' that nigger auction."

O. H. Browning, a Quincy lawyer who had served in the legislature with Lincoln, told friends that Lincoln was "always a learner," and in that respect was the most notable man he had ever seen. "I have known him for ten years, and every time I meet him I find him much improved. . . . Most young men have finished their education, as they say, at twenty-five; but Lincoln is always a learner."

It was told how Lincoln, asked if he were a temperance man, replied, "I am not a temperance man, but I am temperate to this extent: I don't drink." A Danville man noted, "Lincoln doesn't show at first all that is in him." And there was swift characterization in the remark of Leonard Swett, who often tried cases with and against him. "You can never tell what Lincoln is going to do till he does it."

Other lawyers could not say beforehand just when Lincoln would switch the management of his case and be off on a trail not noticed before. He would speak to a jury and give away one point after another. "Yes, we admit this," and "Yes, we admit that." And it would look as though his case were slipping away, when suddenly he would come down with unexpected power on the weakest point of the opposition and bring up his own strongest point. Once, during a criminal trial, a colleague, Amzi McWilliams, whispered to other attorneys, as Lincoln was speaking, "Lincoln will pitch in heavy now, for he has hid."

In silence and in ways covered from the eyes of other men, he struggled, grew, learned, in the years after he came home from Congress and Washington. The boy who had lain awake nights and wrestled to unravel big words like "in-de-pend-ence" and "pre-des-ti-na-tion" had become a grown man who wrestled to unravel the ways of putting simple words together so that many could understand the ideas he wanted them to understand. He said, "I am never easy when I am handling a thought, till I have bounded it north, bounded it south, bounded it east, and bounded it west." He bought a book on logic and studied the science of explanations, how to analyze the absolutely true and the relatively true, how to untangle fallacies and show mistakes in reasoning.

And he bought the *Elements* of Euclid, a book twenty-three centuries old. It went into his carpetbag as he went out on the circuit. At night, when he was with other lawyers, two in a bed, eight and ten in a hotel room, he read Euclid by the light of a candle after the others had dropped off to sleep. Herndon and Lincoln had the same bed one night, and Herndon noticed his partner's legs pushing their feet out beyond the footboard of the bed, as he held the book close to the candlelight.

John T. Stuart saw Lincoln as a hopeless victim of melancholy. "Look at him now," said Stuart one day in the McLean County courthouse. "I turned a little," wrote Henry C. Whitney, a fellow lawyer, "and there beheld Lincoln sitting alone in the corner . . . wrapped in gloom. I watched him for some time." He seemed to be "pursuing in his mind some specific, sad subject, regularly and systematically through various sinuosities, and his sad face would assume, at times, deeper phases of grief. No relief came till he was roused by the breaking up of court, when he emerged from his cave of gloom, like one awakened from sleep."

He was spending more and more time by himself. Books, newspapers, his own thoughts, kept him alone in his room on evenings when the other lawyers on the circuit had all gone to a party. If he went to a concert, lecture, or Negro minstrel show, he would as soon go alone.

The habit stuck to him of reading out loud to himself what-ever he wanted particularly to remember, and of reading out loud as he wrote. Whitney, who studied him often during a court session, noticed also: "Lincoln had no method, system, or order in his exterior affairs; no library, clerk, no *index rerum*, no diary. When he wanted to preserve a memorandum, he noted it down on a card and stuck it in a drawer or in his vest pocket or his hat. While outside of his mind all was anarchy and confusion, inside all was symmetry and method. His mind was his workshop; he needed no office, no pen, ink and paper; he could perform his chief labor by self-introspection." For his important business matters he had an envelope marked, "When you can't find it anywhere else, look in this."

Herndon found Lincoln had arrived earlier than usual one morning at the office. On his desk were sheets of paper covered with figures and equations. He hardly turned his head as Herndon came in; later he told Herndon he was trying to square the circle. He spent the rest of the day and the next day toiling on the famous problem that has immemorially baffled mathematicians. After a two days' struggle, worn down physically, he gave up trying to square the circle.

"If A can prove, however conclusively, that he may, of right, enslave B, why may not B snatch the same argument, and prove equally that he may enslave A? . . . You say A is white, and B is black. It is *color*, then: the lighter, having the right to enslave the darker? . . . Take care. By this rule, you are to be slave to the first man you meet with a fairer skin than your own. . . ."

The inside changes that began to work in Abraham Lincoln in the four or five years after he came back from Washington had their connection with the changes developing in the heart and mind of the country. He was ready to be the tongue and voice of those changes. As he walked with his long, easy stride, with a head bowed till the chin rested on his collarbone, with a sober face and eyes of deepening mystery, he was already carrying a load, already in the toils, almost ready to cry, "I shall never be glad again." He was to be a mind, a spirit, a tongue and voice.

Out of the silent working of his inner life came forces no one outside of himself could know; they were his secret, his personality and purpose, beside which all other facts of his comings and goings were insignificant. He became a seer and sayer; he took responsibility personally; he solved, resolved, and answered terrible questions; or he said, with out-and-out honesty, that he had no answer; only history and the future could bring the answer. True, he had ambitions; goals beckoned and banners called; but he would wreck and sink the ambition that interfered with his life and personality.

Chapter 19

IN THE FLUSH YEAR and boom times of 1854, the midwest prairie state of Illinois was holding its annual state fair in Springfield, in the harvest month of October.

Shorthorn cattle were feeding in sheds where farmers by hundreds passed through, discussing whether it would pay to try to raise these high-class, high-bred cattle. One shorthorn bull drew particular attention; he had crossed the Atlantic Ocean and the Great Lakes on steamboats. There was keen interest in the exhibits of long yellow or golden-red ears of corn, in the horse races where runners, trotters, and pacers competed, and in the political speakers discussing "purr-ins-a-pulls" and "the Const-ti-too-shun." For the farmers and city people who came it was a high holiday. They went home to talk for a year about what they had seen in Springfield.

The hero of this year's holiday was to be the forty-one-year-old Democratic orator Stephen A. Douglas of Chicago, formerly of Springfield, once land commissioner, then supreme court judge, later a congressman, and then United States senator from Illinois. Blue-eyed, magnetic, with a lionlike head, Douglas was the most daring and forthright personal political force that had held the American stage since Andrew Jackson. In 1852, as spokesman for what he called Young America as against what he called Old Fogyism, Douglas had come close to taking the Democratic nomination for President; the party wheelhorses who pulled the nomination for Franklin Pierce were not yet sure that blind luck had not been the chief reason they had succeeded in defeating Douglas.

To be decisive, to be positive, to win men his way by grand acting, was the sport of Douglas's life. In a typically bold and challenging action earlier that year he had guided, coaxed, and jammed through Congress the Nebraska bill, as it came to be known. And by so doing he had set the slavery issue boiling again in a wild turmoil.

As the representative friend of Chicago business interests allied with New York and Boston interests, he had set out to open the vast stretch of territory west of Iowa to the Pacific Ocean and make it ready for transportation and trade tributary to Chicago. Toward the south in St. Louis other business interests planned a "national central highway" from that city to San Francisco; while the plans of Jefferson Davis, the Secretary of War, favored a railway to the Pacific with Memphis as its eastern terminus. The slavery question, land grants, Indian tribal reservations, railroad routes, territorial government for Nebraska, were snarled in what seemed to be a hopeless tangle.

Douglas cut through the tangle with a bill which would make two territories, Nebraska on the north, Kansas on the south, in each of which the ballots of its voters would decide whether the territory should be free or slave. The Nebraska area then included all or part of the later states of Nebraska, North and South Dakota, Wyoming, and Montana. There, in the future, "they could vote slavery up or down" under the principle of "popular sovereignty," said Douglas. And to get the southern votes required for its passage in Congress, the Illinois senator had accepted a rider to his Nebraska bill expressly repealing the hitherto sacred Missouri Compromise; the line drawn between slave and free soil was wiped out.

"I know it will raise a hell of a storm," Douglas had been quoted as saying at the time of passage; but the opening of this vast western trade tributary to Chicago had come at a higher price than he expected.

As the news went across the country, there had been recoils and explosions of opinion and passion. In New England, 3050 clergymen had signed a widely published memorial to the U.S. Senate: "IN THE NAME OF ALMIGHTY GOD, AND IN HIS PRESENCE," we "solemnly protest against the passage of ... the Nebraska bill." Several longtime Democratic party leaders in Illinois had given it out that they were anti-Nebraska men. Even the Know-

Nothings, a new secret order whose members, on joining, swore never to vote for a foreigner or a Catholic, had joined in the anti-Nebraska outcry. Traveling home to Illinois, Douglas had seen from his train car window the burning of dummies bearing his name. And down in southern Illinois, lawyers on the Eighth Judicial Circuit were remembering the day O. H. Browning had asked Abraham Lincoln how he could keep out of politics. "Nothing going on in politics that I care about," Lincoln had replied. But when Browning and others had discussed the possibility that the Missouri Compromise line between slave and free states might someday be wiped out, Lincoln had said, "Well, if anybody should attempt such an outrage while I live, I think I'd want to take a hand in politics again." Now Lincoln was roused, as he later wrote, as "by the sound of a fire-bell at night."

It was natural that Douglas, at this juncture, should be the central figure of attraction at the state fair. Thousands who hated him and other thousands who loved him were ready to stand in the frosty night air of October to hear him deliver a speech. Douglas knew how to address them; he spoke slowly, measuredly, distinctly: "Neither—to legislate—slavery—into—a territory—nor to exclude it—therefrom—but—to leave—the peo-ple—perfectly free—to form—and regulate—their—domestic institutions—in their own way—subject—only—to the—Constitution—of—the United States: that is—all—there is—of the Nebraska bill. That is 'popular sovereignty'—upon which—I am to speak—tomorrow at the statehouse."

Then he became a little familiar; the words came faster. "I have come home . . . to give an account of my stewardship. I know the Democrats of Illinois. . . . I know, Democrats, that you will stand by me as you have always done. I am not afraid that you will be led off by those renegades from the party . . . who have formed an unholy alliance to turn the glorious old Democratic party over to the black abolitionists. Democrats of Illinois, will you permit it?" And the voices cried: "No! No! Never! Never!"

Between the torches his blue eyes flashed, his lips trembled. "I tell you the time has not yet come when a handful of traitors in our camp can turn the great state of Illinois . . . into a Negro-worshipping, Negro-equality community!"

The next afternoon Douglas spoke for nearly three hours in the statehouse. Was not the real question whether the people should rule, whether the voters in a territory should control their own affairs? If the people of Kansas and Nebraska were able to govern themselves, they were able to govern a few miserable Negroes. The crowd enjoyed it; cries came, "That's so!" "Hit 'em again," and cheers were given for the Little Giant.

Lincoln had a seat up front; he whispered occasionally in the ears of friends, and they chuckled and grinned. When the speech was over, he walked down the main aisle at Douglas's elbow, joking the senator. It was only a few years back they had argued on the stump, in courtrooms, churches, grocery stores. To a pretty young woman abolitionist who told Douglas she didn't like the speech, Lincoln said, "Don't bother, young lady. We'll hang the judge's hide on the fence tomorrow."

There had been a saying around courthouses, "With a good case Lincoln is the best lawyer in the state, but in a bad case Douglas is the best lawyer the state ever produced."

THE NEXT DAY Lincoln stood before the same crowd that Douglas had spoken to. Douglas had arrived at the statehouse in an open carriage, standing bowing to a crowd that cheered him. In the carriage also were the governor of the state, Joel A. Matteson, and Douglas's colleague in the United States Senate, General James T. Shields. Douglas took a seat on the platform.

Lincoln came in, pushing and squirming his way to the platform. After being introduced, he explained he was going to discuss the Missouri Compromise, presenting his own view of it, and in that sense his remarks would not be specifically an answer to Judge Douglas, though the main points of Judge Douglas's address would receive respectful attention.

He began with a short history of the United States and slavery. He dug back into beginnings and traced out the growth of slavery: "Wherever slavery is it has been first introduced without law. The oldest laws we find concerning it are not laws introducing it, but regulating it as an already existing thing."

He gave five burning reasons for hating it as a "monstrous injustice." And he added, "Let me say I think I have no prejudice against the southern people. They are just what we would be in their situation. If slavery did not now exist among them, they would not introduce it. If it did now exist among us, we should not instantly give it up. This I believe of the masses north and south. When southern people tell us they are no more responsible for the origin of slavery than we are, I acknowledge the fact. When it is said that the institution exists, and that it is very difficult to get rid of in any satisfactory way, I can understand and appreciate the saying. I surely will not blame them for not doing what I should not know how to do myself."

Was this oratory? Debating? The man, Abraham Lincoln, was speaking to thousands of people as if he and another man were driving in a buggy across the prairie, exchanging their thoughts.

What to do? There were not ships and money to send the slaves anywhere else; and when shipped anywhere else outside of America they might all die. "What then? Free them all, and keep them among us as underlings? Is it quite certain that this betters their condition? . . . Free them, and make them politically and socially, our equals? My own feelings will not admit of this, and if mine would, we well know that those of the great mass of white people will not. Whether this feeling accords with justice and sound judgment, is not the sole question, if indeed it is any part of it. A universal feeling, whether well or ill-founded, can not be safely disregarded."

And yet, while he could not say what should be done about slavery where it was already established and operating, he was sure it would be wrong to let it spread north. "Inasmuch as you do not object to my taking my hog to Nebraska, therefore I must not object to you taking your slave. Now, I admit that this is perfectly logical, if there is no difference between hogs and Negroes."

The South had joined the North in making the law that classified African slave traders as pirates and provided hanging as the punishment. "If you did not feel that it was wrong, why did you join in providing that men should be hung for it? . . . You never thought of hanging men for catching and selling wild horses, wild buffaloes, or wild bears."

He referred to the man whose business was selling slaves. "You despise him utterly. You do not recognize him as a friend, or even as an honest man. Your children must not play with his; they may rollick freely with the little Negroes, but not with the slave dealer's children. If you are obliged to deal with him, you try to get through the job without so much as touching him, instinctively shrinking from the snaky contact. . . . Now why is this? You do not so treat the man who deals in corn, cotton, or tobacco."

Over the country were 433,643 free black men, at $500 a head worth over $200,000,000. "How comes this vast amount of property to be running about without owners? We do not see free horses or free cattle running at large. How is this? All these free blacks are the descendants of slaves or have been slaves themselves; and they would be slaves now but for something which has operated on their white owners. What is that something? Is there any mistaking it? In all these cases it is your sense of justice and human sympathy continually telling you that the poor Negro has some natural right to himself—that those who deny it and make mere merchandise of him deserve kickings, contempt, and death."

The application of what Douglas called "the sacred right of self-government" depended on whether a Negro was a man. "If he is not a man, in that case he who is a man may as a matter of self-government do just what he pleases with him. But if the Negro is a man, is it not to that extent a total destruction of self-government to say that he too shall not govern himself? When the white man governs himself, that is self-government; but when he governs himself and also governs another man, that is more than self-government—that is despotism."

The Nebraska bill, he noted, said the people were supposed to decide the slavery question for themselves, but no time or place or manner of voting was named in the bill. "Could there be a more apt invention to bring about collision and violence on the slavery question than this . . . ? I do not charge or believe

159

that such was intended by Congress; but if they had literally formed a ring and placed champions within it to fight out the controversy, the fight could be no more likely to come off than it is. And if this fight should begin, is it likely to take a very peaceful, Union-saving turn? Will not the first drop of blood so shed be the real knell of the Union?"

And what should be done first of all? "The Missouri Compromise ought to be restored. For the sake of the Union, it ought to be restored."

The speech was three hours long. Through most of it Lincoln spoke as though he were not debating, trying to beat and crush an opponent, but rather as though he were examining his own mind, his own facts and views.

He stood among neighbors, in his shirt sleeves, on a warm October day. The words came slow, hesitating to begin with, and he spoke often in the tang of his childhood speech. "Just" sounded a little like "jist," and "such" suspiciously like "sich." As his body loosened and swayed to the cadence of his address, and the thoughts unfolded, drops of sweat stood out on his forehead; he was speaking not only with his tongue but with every blood-drop of his body.

A scholarly man said, "His manner was impassioned and he seemed transfigured; his listeners felt that he believed every word he said, and that, like Martin Luther, he would go to the stake rather than abate one jot or tittle of it." A farmer said, "I don't keer fur them great orators. I want to hear jist a plain common feller like the rest on us, thet I kin foller an' know where he's drivin'. Abe Linkern fills the bill."

The speech came to an end. The crowd that heard it scattered out of the statehouse to their homes. But in Peoria twelve days later, Lincoln gave the same speech again to a crowd of thousands and then went home to Springfield and wrote it out for publication, and it became widely known as the Peoria Speech.

Now among many politicians and people in Illinois it was seen there was one man in the state who could grapple and hold his own with Stephen A. Douglas. And among thousands of plain people was an instinct, perhaps a hope, that this voice was their voice.

POLITELY, GENTLY BUT FIRMLY, Lincoln had told Whigs who wanted him to run for the legislature or for Congress again that he wasn't in the running. But now he had other plans. He was studying his chances for election to the U. S. Senate seat of James Shields. Six weeks after the Peoria Speech he was sending out letters in the tone of one written to Joseph Gillespie, who had become a leading lawyer for the Alton Railroad. "I have really got it into my head to try to be United States senator, and, if I could have your support, my chances would be reasonably good. Please write me, and let this be confidential."

Three months later, in February 1855, he sat in the statehouse watching the election for United States senator. He got forty-seven votes. Three more would have elécted him. The balloting went on; his vote slumped to fifteen. The minute came when Lincoln saw that if he held his fifteen loyal votes, Governor Matteson, a Douglas and Nebraska Democrat, would be elected. Lincoln let his votes go to Lyman Trumbull, anti-Nebraska bolter from the Democratic party. Trumbull was elected.

Lincoln wrote to a friend: "I regret my defeat moderately, but I am not nervous about it. . . . Matteson's . . . defeat now gives me more pleasure than my own gives me pain. On the whole, it is perhaps as well for our general cause that Trumbull is elected. The Nebraska men confess that they hate it worse than anything that could have happened. It is a great consolation to see them worse whipped than I am."

JOSHUA SPEED wrote from his Kentucky home in May asking Lincoln, "Where do you stand now in politics?" And Lincoln, busy with law and politics, didn't answer for three months.

Then he wrote: "I think I am a whig; but others say there are no whigs, and that I am an abolitionist . . . I now do no more than oppose the *extension* of slavery. I am not a Know-Nothing. That is certain. How could I be? How can any one who abhors the oppression of negroes, be in favor of degrading classes of white people? Our progress in degeneracy appears to me to be pretty rapid. As a nation, we began by declaring *'all men are created equal.'* We now practically read it 'all men are created equal, *except negroes.*' When the Know-Nothings get control, it will read 'all men are created equal, except negroes, *and foreigners, and catholics.*' When it comes to this I should prefer emigrating to some country where they make no pretence of loving liberty—to Russia, for instance, where despotism can be taken pure, and without the base alloy of hypocracy."

In writing to Speed, Lincoln knew he was searching the mind and heart of an honest man and a southern slaveholder. "You say that sooner than yield your legal right to the slave, especially at the bidding of those who are not themselves interested, you would see the Union dissolved. I am not aware that any one is bidding you yield that right: very certainly I am not. I leave that matter entirely to yourself. I also acknowledge your rights and my obligations under the Constitution in regard to your slaves. I confess I hate to see the poor creatures hunted down and caught and carried back to their stripes and unrequited toil; but I bite my lip and keep quiet."

He reminded Speed of the time on an Ohio River steamboat when they saw a dozen slaves shackled together with irons. "That sight was a continual torment to me, and I see something like it every time I touch the Ohio or any other slave border. It is not fair for you to assume that I have no interest in a thing which has, and continually exercises, the power to make me miserable. You ought rather to appreciate how much the great body of the northern people do crucify their feelings, in order to maintain their loyalty to the Constitution and the Union." He ended: "Yet let me say I am, Your friend forever." And as he mailed the letter he knew he had let his feelings go more freely than he dared to when speaking in public in Illinois.

A peculiar brand of trust and understanding also ran between Lincoln and Owen Lovejoy, the brother of Elijah Lovejoy and a rugged Congregational minister. To him, in August 1855, Lincoln wrote another letter of great candor: "Not even *you* are more anxious to prevent the extension of slavery than I; and yet the political atmosphere is such, just now, that I fear to do any thing, lest I do wrong." Know-Nothing elements would be needed to combat the pro-Nebraska Democrats. "About us here, they [the Know-Nothings] are mostly my old political and personal friends; and I have hoped their organization would die out without the painful necessity of my taking an open stand against them. Of their principles I think little better than I do of those of the slavery extensionists. Indeed I do not perceive how any one professing to be sensitive to the wrongs of the negroes, can join in a league to degrade a class of white men."

Once, between law cases in a courthouse, he had argued with a Chicago lawyer that the slavery question would split the nation. And the two lawyers had beds in the same room at the hotel, and that night sat up in their nightshirts arguing. "At last we went to sleep," said the Chicago lawyer afterward; "and early in the morning I woke up and there was Lincoln half sitting up in bed. 'Dickey,' he said, 'I tell you this nation cannot exist half slave and half free.'" To which the Chicago lawyer answered, "Oh, Lincoln, go to sleep."

Chapter 20

IN THE YEAR 1856, on the Missouri and Kansas border, two hundred men, women, and children were shot, stabbed, or burned to death in the fighting between free- and slave-state settlers and guerrillas. The cost of the fighting, counting crops burned and cattle and horses stolen or killed, ran about two million dollars.

In the month of May the first state convention to organize the Republican party of the state of Illinois met in Bloomington. By then the town of Lawrence, Kansas, had been entered by riding and shooting men who burned the Free State Hotel and wrecked two printing offices. The *Herald of Freedom* had published an editorial, calling: "Come one, come all, slave-ocrats and nullifiers; we have rifles enough, and bullets enough, to send you all to your (and Judas's) own place. If you're coming, why don't you come along?" The governor of Kansas had been arrested in Missouri, his house had been set on fire, and himself chained on a prairie, a jail being lacking.

A Massachusetts senator had said of a South Carolina senator

that every time he opened his mouth "a blunder flew out," and a nephew of the South Carolina senator had walked into the United States Senate chamber and broken a cane over the head of the Massachusetts senator and beaten his victim near to death.

While these issues were in the air, the Republican party was being born; the dissatisfied political elements of Illinois, as of other states, were holding conventions to organize state parties and get up a national organization. Of the delegates who came to Bloomington for the Illinois convention, about one-fourth were regularly elected and the others had appointed themselves. All stripes of political belief outside of the Democratic party were represented: Whigs, bolting anti-Nebraska Democrats, Free-Soilers, Know-Nothings, abolitionists. Some who came were afraid that wild-eyed radicals would control.

Among the delegates was Abraham Lincoln. As he and Henry C. Whitney walked to the depot to see who would come as delegates from Chicago, Lincoln stopped in at a jewelry store and bought his first pair of spectacles; he was forty-seven years old and kind of needed spectacles, he told Whitney.

The convention met in Major's Hall, upstairs over Humphrey's Cheap Store, near the courthouse square; adopted a platform denouncing the Democratic Administration, and declared that Congress had power to stop the extension of slavery and should use that power. Then came speeches to dedicate the new party. After several delegates had loosed their oratory, there were calls for Lincoln. He stood up. There were cries, "Take the platform," which he did.

He looked the convention in the eye. According to a Whitney version written many years later, he observed, "We are in a trying time," which they all knew very well; then suddenly came the thrust: "Unless popular opinion makes itself very strongly felt, and a change is made in our present course, *blood will flow . . . brother's hand will be raised against brother!*" The delegates sat up; it was a sober man speaking. "We must not promise what we ought not, lest we be called on to perform what we cannot. . . . We must not be led by excitement and passion to do that which our sober judgments would not approve in our cooler moments." He noted that the delegates had been collected from many different elements. Yet they were agreed, *"Slavery must be kept out of Kansas."* The Nebraska Act was usurpation; it would result in making slavery national. "We are in a fair way to see this land of boasted freedom converted into a land of slavery in fact."

A terribly alive man stood before them. By this time Joseph Medill, of the Chicago *Tribune*, and the other newspaper writers had felt their pencils slip away; they were going to listen, somebody else would get the report of the speech. Herndon and Whitney had started to take notes, and then forgotten they had pencils. Listeners moved up closer to the speaker. "I read once in a law book, 'A slave is a human being who is legally not a *person* but a *thing*.' And if the safeguards to liberty are broken down, as is now attempted, when they have made *things* of all the free Negroes, how long, think you, before they will begin to make *things* of poor white men?"

Freedom and equality, sacred to the men of the American Revolution, had become words it was fashionable to sneer at. "Suppose Kansas comes in as a slave state, and all the 'border ruffians' have barbecues about it, and free-state men come trailing back to the dishonored North, like whipped dogs with their tails between their legs, is it not evident that this is no more the 'land of the free'? And if we let it go so, we won't dare to say 'home of the brave' out loud."

Monstrous crimes were being committed in the name of slavery by persons collectively which they would not dare commit as individuals. He rehearsed the panorama of current events. "The repeal of the sacred Missouri Compromise has installed the weapons of violence: the bludgeon, the incendiary torch, the death-dealing rifle. . . . We see its fruit in the dying bed of the heroic Sumner; in the ruins of the 'Free State' Hotel; in the smoking embers of the *Herald of Freedom;* in the free-state governor of Kansas chained to a stake on freedom's soil like a horse thief, for the crime of freedom.

"We see it in Christian statesmen, and Christian newspapers, and Christian pulpits applauding the cowardly act of a low bully, who crawled upon his victim behind his back and dealt the deadly blow. We note our political demoralization in the catchwords that are coming into such common use; on the one hand, 'freedom shriekers,' and sometimes 'freedom screechers'; and on the other hand 'border ruffians,' and that fully deserved. And the significance of catchwords cannot pass unheeded, for they constitute a sign of the times."

Should force be met with force? He could not say. "The time may yet come, and if we are true to ourselves may never come. Do not mistake that the ballot is stronger than the bullet."

Applause came regularly. He was saying what the convention wanted said. He was telling why the Republican party was organized. To Bill Herndon and others he seemed taller than ever before in his life. "He's been baptized," said Herndon.

The speech came to its climax with the declaration: "We will say to the southern disunionists, *We* won't go out of the Union, and you *shan't*." The delegates applauded, stamped, cheered, threw hats in the air, and ran riot. He was their tongue and voice.

After it was all over Whitney did the best he could at making notes of the speech, which later became known as Lincoln's Lost Speech. For Whitney didn't write his version from those notes until years had passed. Nor did Lincoln himself write out his speech despite advice from many that he should. What he had said would, he knew, be taken as wild-eyed and radical, and would alienate moderates from the new party. In that particular political hour, his blazing outbursts on human freedom were better kept out of print.

Later that same day, as Whitney and Lincoln were walking to their lodgings at the home of Judge Davis, Whitney told how the Illinois state auditor, Jesse K. Dubois, who was Lincoln's neighbor in Springfield, had burst out to him, "Whitney, that is the greatest speech ever made in Illinois, and it puts Lincoln on the track for the presidency." And Lincoln walked for half a minute with stooped shoulders, not saying a word. Then, said Whitney, "he straightened up and immediately made a remark about some commonplace subject having no relation to the subject we had been considering."

167

Chapter 21

ABRAHAM LINCOLN'S REPUTATION as a lawyer had been rising steadily. And it went up several notches more after a famous decision he had won for the Illinois Central Railroad.

In the McLean County circuit court, Lincoln represented the railroad corporation in a tax case, his retainer $200. His case was beaten in the circuit court; the decision was that the railroad, already paying taxes to the state treasury, must pay a tax in every county through which it passed. The cost would mount into millions and bankrupt the corporation. Lincoln appealed to the supreme court, argued the case twice, and in January 1856 won a decision reversing the lower court.

He presented his bill to the Illinois Central Railroad corporation at their Chicago office. The bill was for $2000. The official handling the bill looked at it and said, "Why, this is as much as a first-class lawyer would have charged!" adding that it was "as much as Daniel Webster himself would have charged." And Lincoln was paid a fee of $200.

Back on the circuit, when he told other lawyers, they didn't know whether to laugh or cry at this treatment of a lawyer by the corporation that had been saved millions of dollars through Lincoln's victory in court. Lincoln started a suit against the Illinois Central for a fee of $5000. The case was called, the lawyer for the railroad didn't show up; Lincoln was awarded his $5000 one morning; in the afternoon the railroad lawyer arrived and begged Lincoln for a retrial. Lincoln said he was willing, the case was called, and Lincoln read a statement signed by six of the highest-priced lawyers in Illinois that the sum of $5000 for the services rendered in the case "is not unreasonable." Before the jury went out he told them he had been paid $200 by the railroad and they should make the verdict for $4800. Which they did.

Thirty-eight days went by and the railroad company failed to pay the $4800 fee. An execution was issued directing the sheriff to seize property of the railroad. Then the fee was paid. And high officers of the railroad stated, "The payment of so large a fee to a western lawyer would embarrass the general counsel with the board of directors in New York."

Lincoln deposited the $4800 in the Springfield Marine Bank, and later, in handing Herndon half of the fee, he said with a smile, "Billy, it seems to me it will be bad taste on your part to keep saying severe things I have heard from you about railroads and other corporations. Instead of criticizing them, you and I ought to thank God for letting this one fall into our hands."

Lincoln was more and more trusted with important affairs of property. The McLean County Bank retained him to bring suit against the city of Bloomington. In Springfield, the gasworks asked him to make certain their title to the two city lots on which they were located, which Lincoln did, later sending the gasworks a bill for $500.

In the famous Rock Island bridge case Lincoln figured as the apostle of the march of civilization. Against threats of lawsuits, the Rock Island Railroad had built a bridge 1582 feet long, across the Mississippi River, from Rock Island on the Illinois side to Davenport on the Iowa side. The bridge was built, even though the chamber of commerce of St. Louis claimed that a bridge across the Mississippi River was "unconstitutional, an obstruction to navigation, dangerous," and threats "to abolish the Rock Island bridge nuisance" were heard in congressional committee rooms in Washington.

Then, on May 6, 1856, came the steamboat *Effie Afton*. She rammed into a pier of the Rock Island bridge, took fire, and burned to a total loss, while part of the bridge burned and tumbled into the river. The owners of the *Effie Afton* sued the bridge company for damages. And Norman B. Judd, general counsel of the Rock Island Railroad, and one of the Bloomington convention organizers of the Republican party, called on Abraham Lincoln to represent the company in the hearing before the District Court of the United States in Chicago.

In his argument Lincoln pointed to the growing travel from east to west being as important as the Mississippi traffic. This east-to-west traffic was building up new country with a rapidity never before seen in the history of the world. In his own memory he had watched Illinois grow from almost empty spaces to a population of a million and a half. One man had as good a right to cross a river as another had to sail up or down it. He asked if the products of the boundless, fertile country lying west of the Mississippi must for all time be forced to stop on its western bank, be unloaded from the cars and loaded on a boat, and after passage across the river be reloaded into cars on the other side. Civilization in the region to the west was at issue.

The jury listened, and then were locked up. When they came out they had agreed to disagree; and their action was generally taken as a victory for railroads, bridges, and Chicago, as against steamboats, rivers, and St. Louis.

Many of his fellow lawyers in Illinois knew that hidden under his brick-dust coloring Lincoln had queer soft spots. He defended an old farmer who had taken a bunch of sheep "on shares," fattened them with his year's crop through the winter, and in the spring, when they all died, couldn't pay the sheep owner for them. The sheep owner sued for the money. The first trial was a mistrial; the second trial was lost, and the costs and damages stripped the old man of nearly all his property. At seventy he was starting west to hunt cheap land and make a new home. As Lincoln shook hands with the old man and spoke good-by, his eyes were wet and he had to hold back tears.

A woman client had Lincoln survey and lay off into lots a piece of land she owned near the Springfield city limits. He found that by some mistake the woman had become owner of three more acres of land than she was entitled to, and Charles Matheny, the former owner, was the loser of the three acres. Lincoln notified her she ought to pay the heirs of Matheny the money owed them at the price per acre first agreed on. The woman couldn't see it; Lincoln wrote her again; the Matheny heirs were poor and needed the money, he told her. And again he wrote explaining what seemed to him plain justice. One day the woman sent him payment in full and he hunted up the heirs and paid them their money.

The home of Lincoln's friend and colleague, Henry C.

Whitney, was in Urbana, and Lincoln came one summer day in 1856 to Urbana to speak at a public meeting in a church. Calling Whitney to one side, he whispered, "There is a boy in your jail I want to see, but I don't want anyone beside yourself to know it. I wish you would speak to the jailer."

The boy, a cripple, had stolen a watch from an old man named Green in Urbana, and was under a charge of stealing a gun in Charleston. Also he was the son of Lincoln's stepbrother, John D. Johnston, and so a grandson of Sally Bush Lincoln. "I'm going to help him out of these two cases," said Lincoln, "but that's the last; after that, if he wants to continue his thieving, I shall do nothing for him."

The jail was a rough log cabin, with a one-foot-square hole through which prisoners talked with callers. And Whitney told later what happened: "The prisoner heard us and set up a hypocritical wailing and thrust out toward us a very dirty Bible. . . . Lincoln cut it [the boy's wailing] short by saying, 'Now, Tom, do what they tell you—behave yourself—don't talk to anyone, and when court closes I will be here and see what I can do for you. Now stop crying and behave yourself.' And with a few more words we left. Lincoln was very sad; I never saw him more so.

"The prosecuting attorney agreed with us that if the Greens would come into court and state that they did not desire to press the case further he would file a *nolle pros.* That same evening . . . Lincoln and I left the [church] meeting and made our way to the house where the Greens lived. They were a venerable old couple, and . . . greatly astonished at our visit. I introduced Lincoln, who explained his position and wishes in the matter in a homely, plain way, and the good old couple assented. The next day they came into court, willing that the boy should be released, which was promptly done."

Lincoln was careless and easygoing sometimes about collecting money owed to him by clients. John W. Bunn, the Springfield banker, was asked by a Chicago firm to have a local attorney help them in an attachment suit involving several thousand dollars; Lincoln won the suit and charged $25; the Chicago firm wrote Bunn: "We asked you to get the best lawyer in Springfield, and it certainly looks as if you had secured one of the cheapest."

A lease on a valuable hotel property in Quincy was handled by Lincoln for George P. Floyd, who mailed a check for $25, to which Lincoln replied: "You are too liberal with your money. Fifteen dollars is enough for the job. I send you a receipt for fifteen dollars, and return to you a ten-dollar bill."

In the town of Danville, Lincoln's law partner there, Ward Hill Lamon, brought the case of a girl named Scott, who was, as they said, "not in her right mind." She had $10,000 in property, mostly cash, and a schemer had struck up an acquaintance with her and asked her to marry him. Her brother wanted a conservator appointed by the court to take care of her and her property, and had agreed with Lamon to pay a fee of $250 when the case was won. On trial it took Lincoln and Lamon only twenty minutes to win their case, and Lamon was paid $250. Lincoln, however, forced Lamon to give back to Miss Scott one half of the $250.

Judge David Davis said, in the wheezing whisper of a man weighing three hundred pounds, "Lincoln, you are impoverishing this bar by your picayune charges of fees, and the lawyers have reason to complain of you." Other lawyers murmured approval. Lincoln stuck to the point: "That money comes out of the pocket of a poor, demented girl, and I would rather starve than swindle her in this manner." In the evening at the hotel, the lawyers held a mock court and fined him; he paid the fine, rehearsed a new line of funny stories, and stuck to his original point that he wouldn't belong to a law firm that could be styled "Catch 'em and Cheat 'em."

THERE CAME A DAY when Lincoln dropped all other law cases, dropped all political affairs, and threw himself with all he had into the defense of young William ("Duff") Armstrong. This young man was the son of Lincoln's good friends Jack and Hannah Armstrong, and had grown up since the days at Clary's Grove when he was a baby and Lincoln rocked him in a cradle.

The Armstrongs had long since moved from Clary's Grove over into Mason County, where Jack Armstrong had recently died, his death coming sooner because his son Duff had been charged with the murder of a man named Metzker in a fight following a drinking bout. A coroner's jury had heard a house painter named Charles Allen from Petersburg swear that he saw the fight between Duff Armstrong and Metzker, that it was between ten and eleven o'clock at night, and, by the light of a moon shining nearly straight over them, he saw Armstrong hit Metzker with a slungshot and throw the slungshot away and he, Allen, picked it up. Duff Armstrong had been arrested. And Jack Armstrong, with whom Abe Lincoln had wrestled on the level green next to Offutt's store twenty-six years before, told Hannah shortly before he died, "Sell everything you have and clear Duff."

Two lawyers were defending Duff when he came to trial at Beardstown, and it was there Lincoln told Hannah Armstrong he remembered all her old-time kindness to him and his services were free to her as long as he should live. The two defending lawyers were glad to have the help of Lincoln. And the trial began.

Lincoln aimed to have young men on the jury; young, hot blood would understand other young, hot blood better, perhaps; the average age of the jurymen, as finally picked, was twenty-three. Then came the witnesses. With each one Lincoln tried to find some ground of old acquaintance. "Your name?" he asked one. "William Killian." "Bill Killian? Tell me, are you a son of old Jake Killian?" "Yes, sir." "Well, you are a smart boy if you take after your dad."

Of the witnesses, the one that seemed to make out that Duff Armstrong was a murderer was Allen, the house painter, who said he had seen Armstrong by the light of a moon nearly overhead, on a clear night, hit Metzker with a slungshot. Against him was a witness, Nelson Watkins, who testified that he had been to camp meeting the day after the fight, that he had with him a slungshot, and that he had thrown it away because it was too heavy and bothersome to carry. He had made the slungshot himself, he testified; he had put an eggshell into the ground, filled it with lead, poured melted zinc over the lead, but the two metals wouldn't stick; then he had cut a cover from a calfskin bootleg, sewed it together with a squirrel-skin string, using a crooked awl to make the holes; and he had then cut a strip from a groundhog skin that he had tanned, and fixed it so it would fasten to his wrist.

Lincoln took out his knife, cut the string with which the slungshot cover was sewed, showed it to be squirrel skin, and then took out the inside metals and showed they were of two different sorts that did not stick together. He had shown that the slungshot which Allen testified he had picked up was identical with one that Watkins testified he had made and thrown away. Meantime, Lincoln had sent out for an almanac, and when the moment came he set the courtroom into a buzz of excitement by showing that, instead of the moon being in the sky at "about where the sun is at ten o'clock in the morning," as Allen had testified, a well-known almanac for 1857 showed that on the night of August 29, 1857, the moon had set and gone down out of sight at three minutes before midnight, or exactly 11:57 p.m. The almanac raised the question whether there was enough light by which a murder could be competently and materially witnessed.

Lincoln told the jury he knew the Armstrongs; the wild boy, Duff Armstrong, he had held in his arms when Duff was a baby; he had rocked the baby in the cradle at the pioneer home at Clary's Grove; he could tell good citizens from bad citizens and if there was anything he was certain of, it was that the Armstrong people were good people; they were plain people; they worked for a living; they made their mistakes; but they were kindly, lovely people and belonged with the salt of the earth. He had told the mother of Duff, "Aunt Hannah, your son will be free before sundown." And so it happened. As the jury had filed out to vote a verdict, one of the jurymen winked an eye at Duff, so he afterward told it.

THERE WAS A PERSONAL TANG or smack in slight things Lincoln did. A man asked him for advice on a point of law and he told the man he'd have to look it up; meeting the man again, he gave him the advice wanted on that particular point of law; but when the man wished to know what the fee would be

Lincoln answered that there would be no fee because it was a point he ought to have known without looking it up.

To a New York firm that wrote asking him about the financial standing of a Springfield man, he replied:

> Yours of the 10th received. First of all, he has a wife and a baby; together they ought to be worth $500,000 to any man. Secondly, he has an office in which there is a table worth $1.50 and three chairs worth, say $1. Last of all, there is in one corner a large rat-hole, which will bear looking into.
>
> Respectfully,
A. Lincoln.

Reading authorities in court once, he suddenly read one against himself, and, drawing up his shoulders and half laughing, finished reading it, first saying, "There, may it please the court, I reckon I've scratched up a snake; but as I'm in for it, guess I'll read it through." Three or four cases were talked about among other lawyers, in which Lincoln had gone in as counsel for the defense, and as the evidence developed, he said to a colleague, "The man is guilty. You defend him; I can't. If I try to speak the jury will see that I think he is guilty, and convict him."

So Lincoln came to know in whispered consultation and public cross-examination the minds and hearts of a quarreling, chaffering, suspicious, murderous, loving, lavish, paradoxical humanity. He once took to the supreme court of the state a case involving a dispute over the payment of three dollars in a hog sale. He became versed in the questions whether a saloon license can be transferred, whether damages can be collected from a farmer who starts a prairie fire that spreads to other farms, whether the divorced wife of a man can compel him to supply her the means for support of their children; these were causes in which he argued before the state supreme court. He also argued before that tribunal in cases involving wills, mortgages, land titles, railroad condemnation proceedings, breaches of contract, validity of patents.

Such were a few of the human causes, disputes, and actions in which Lincoln versed himself thoroughly, carrying his arguments up to the highest court in the state, and winning more than half of his cases there. His memory was indexed and cross-indexed with tangled human causes.

WHEN HE RODE the circuit and likewise when he was at home in Springfield there were little things that interested him, but they were different from the little things that interested a good many other people. He could enjoy watching a duck trying to teach its little one to swim; he played marbles with boys when a grown man, enjoyed holding kittens in his hands. He talked over with Herndon his own theory as to why, when he was kicked by a horse in Indiana and woke to his senses, he finished the sentence he had started to say just as the horse kicked him. The general run of small gossip and community chatter didn't interest him. Herndon noticed: "He didn't care who succeeded to the presidency of this or that association; who made the most money; who was going to Philadelphia, when and for what, and what were the costs of such a trip."

High pretensions didn't wear easy with Lincoln. At hotels he took what was offered him with no complaint. He told Joe Gillespie, his friend who was a lawyer for the Alton Railroad, he never felt easy when a waiter or a flunky was around; he could look a murderer in the eye on the witness stand, and be comfortable, but a hotel clerk made him feel sort of useless. One of his sons pronounced the word "gentleman" with the "g" hard, as in "gas"; and Lincoln told friends about it as if it pleased him to have the dignity of the word "gentleman" mussed up. Several times before posing for an ambrotype he ran his fingers through his hair to rumple it properly.

Often when he was supposed to look and act important, he simply couldn't fill the part or he wouldn't try. He was so easy, so quietly gay and careless, that respectable people found him hard to analyze. The state supreme court, for instance, had appointed Lincoln a member of a committee to examine young law students. When Jonathan Birch came to the hotel in Bloomington to be examined by Lincoln for admission to the bar, Lincoln asked three or four questions about contracts and other law branches. And then, as Birch told it: "He asked

nothing more. Sitting on the edge of the bed he began to entertain me with recollections, many of them vivid and racy, of his start in the profession." Birch couldn't figure out whether it was a real examination or a joke. But Lincoln gave him a note to Judge Logan, another member of the examining committee, and he took the note to Logan, and without any more questions was given a certificate to practice law. The note from Lincoln read:

My Dear Judge:
The bearer of this is a young man who thinks he can be a lawyer. Examine him if you want to. I have done so and am satisfied. He's a good deal smarter than he looks to be.

Yours,
Lincoln.

He read Joe Miller's joke book and repeated some of the jokes on the circuit. But he had a thousand fresher ones of his own; they seemed to sprout by the waysides of his travel. There was the anecdote, for instance, of John Moore, south of Blooming Grove, driving a yoke of red steers to Bloomington one Saturday, starting home with a jug, and emptying the jug into himself. The cart hit a stump and threw the pole out of the ring of the yoke. The steers ran away; Moore slept till morning in the cart, and when he awoke and looked around, he said, "If my name is John Moore, I've lost a pair of steers; if my name ain't John Moore, I've found a cart."

A touch of Aesop, the fable maker, was in him. "If three pigeons sit on a fence and you shoot and kill one of them, how many will be left?" he asked. The answer was, "Two, of course." To which Lincoln responded, "No, there won't, for the other two will fly away."

They had their fun and stories on the circuit. Once in Champaign County Court, Judge Davis absentmindedly sentenced a young fellow to seven years in the *legislature* of the state of Illinois. Prosecutor Ward Hill Lamon whispered to the judge, who then changed legislature to *penitentiary*. Lincoln, one morning in Bloomington, meeting a young lawyer whose case had gone to the jury late the night before, asked what had become of his case; the young lawyer bemoaned, "It's gone to hell," and Lincoln responded, "Oh well, then you'll see it again." When Lamon had a large section of the rear of his trousers torn out in scuffling in front of the courthouse, and was later acting as counsel in a case that same day, a paper was passed around among the lawyers asking contributions for the repair of the trousers. And Lincoln wrote: "I can contribute nothing to the end in view."

Chapter 22

THE DEMOCRATIC NATIONAL CONVENTION, opening in Cincinnati on June 2, 1856, gave unanimous endorsement to the Nebraska Act and voted against a Pacific railway. After the fifteenth ballot it went into a deadlock with 168½ votes for James Buchanan for President, 118½ for Stephen A. Douglas, two-thirds being required to nominate. Douglas, in the interest of party unity, then offered support to Buchanan, who was nominated on the seventeenth ballot. Buchanan had been away as minister to England, had taken no hand in the Kansas-Nebraska mess, and was rated a "safe" candidate. He and the platform faced to the past.

A fresher air and new causes moved the first national Republican convention in Philadelphia in mid-June. The newly born party's platform faced to the future; it called for no extension of slavery, admission of Kansas as a free state, and "a railroad to the Pacific Ocean, by the most central and practicable route." The nomination for President went to John C. Frémont, the explorer and "pathfinder" who had served as U. S. senator from the free state of California. For Vice-President William L. Dayton of New Jersey, an able lawyer and former U. S. senator, was nominated, the first ballot giving him 259 votes and Abraham Lincoln 110.

When the newspapers arrived in Urbana with the information that a person named Lincoln had stood second highest in the vice-presidential balloting, getting the total votes of the Illinois and Indiana delegations, Lincoln, the circuit lawyer at

Urbana, laughed it off to Judge Davis and Henry C. Whitney, saying carelessly to his excited friends, "I reckon that ain't me; there's another great man in Massachusetts named Lincoln and I reckon it's him."

In the campaign that followed, Lincoln delivered more than fifty speeches north and south in the state; and his law practice got little of his time. He sometimes made two speeches a day, traveling by train, stagecoach, buggy, and wagon. When committees met him and escorted him to the hall or courthouse or the grove where the steer was over the fire for a barbecue, he was easy to pick out as the speaker of the day; at the end of his long body and head was a long stovepipe hat that made him look longer; a lengthy linen duster made him look still lengthier; with a little satchel in one hand and a faded brownish green umbrella in the other, he looked as though he came from somewhere and was going somewhere.

On the platform he asked what was the question between the two parties headed by Buchanan and Frémont, answering, "Simply this, Shall slavery be allowed to extend into United States territories now legally free? Buchanan says it shall, and Frémont says it shall not. That is the naked issue and the whole of it."

Lincoln was out to build up the Republican party, elect the state ticket, and put Illinois on the map as a Republican stronghold. But the campaign was complicated by the fact that a February convention of Know-Nothings in Philadelphia, declaring that only "*native*-born citizens" should hold office, and the foreign-born should vote only after "continued residence of twenty-one years," had chosen as their presidential candidate the former Whig Vice-President Millard Fillmore, who had become Whig President on the death of President Taylor. Lincoln knew that in Illinois, as elsewhere, Fillmore had a strong Whig following that would vote for him. In letters and speeches, he hammered it home that a Whig vote for Fillmore was a vote against the Republicans and a vote for Buchanan the Democrat. And he continued to stress the slavery question. He spoke at Princeton with Owen Lovejoy, who was running for Congress. At a Shelbyville rally of Democrats, he debated with a local leader, and the *Register* at Springfield said that his three-hour speech "was prosy and dull . . . all about 'freedom,' 'liberty' and niggers." A crowd of ten thousand heard him in Kalamazoo, Michigan, where an abolitionist wrote he was "far too conservative and Union-loving."

A sober and religious young man, Henry Rankin, who was studying law in the Lincoln & Herndon office, saw a young man come into the office one day and begin to argue with Herndon that Millard Fillmore ought to be elected because he was a "good" man and his "goodness" extraordinary. Lincoln sat at a table writing. As the argument went on he kept on writing. But when he finished writing and was leaving the office Lincoln stopped and said to the young man, "My young friend, I think you are making a mistake in voting for Mr. Fillmore because of his goodness. You can do something so much better. There is One whose goodness and greatness all agree far exceed Mr. Fillmore's and, in fact, all others that could be named. So on the sixth of November I advise you to go to the polls and vote for Almighty God for President. He is unquestionably the best thing that exists. There is practically as much chance of electing God Almighty for President of the United States at this time, as Millard Fillmore." The young man came into the office a few days later and told Lincoln he wasn't going to throw away his vote but would cast his ballot for Frémont.

In Petersburg, only two miles from his old New Salem hilltop, Lincoln met opposition. He had surveyed the town, made the first map of it, walked on its location when it was empty prairie. Now the little Republican committee that escorted him from the stagecoach to the platform in front of the Menard House was lost amid swarming Democrats. When at last Lincoln and the committee managed to squeeze their way up on the platform, the crowd hooted and booed; whistles, tin horns, and cowbells added to the racket. Lincoln moved to the front of the platform and stood there without saying a word. The howling and hooting went on; there were cheers for Buchanan, for Fillmore, curses for abolitionists.

In the crowd was young Henry Rankin, and he photographed Lincoln in his memory that day, and said later, "Nearly half an hour passed. He stood there all that while motionless as a statue. The only change I noticed was that at times he folded both arms across his chest, then releasing them. . . . Then a partial lull came, and he began in his lowest voice to address the assembly. Gradually the tumult near him grew less, then a desire to know what he was saying changed to shouts of 'Louder, louder.' " In less than half an hour the muttering and the chatter had died down; he spoke for two hours.

Rankin explained the situation by pointing out that the clergy of Petersburg and vicinity were nearly all from the South, and strong advocates of the alleged Biblical authority for slavery. Lincoln had met most of them while living in Salem, or at court terms in Petersburg, and in the latter part of his speech he addressed his remarks directly to them.

"We will suppose," said Lincoln, "that the Reverend Dr. Ross has a slave named Sambo, and the question is: 'Is it the will of God that Sambo shall remain a slave, or be set free?' The Almighty gives no audible answer to the question, and His Revelation, the Bible, gives none—or, at most, none but such as admits of a squabble as to its meaning. No one thinks of asking Sambo's opinion on it. So at last it comes to this— that Dr. Ross is to decide the question; and while he considers it, he sits in the shade, with gloves on his hands, and subsists on the bread that Sambo is earning in the burning sun. If he decides that God wills Sambo to be free, he thereby has to walk out of the shade, throw off his gloves, and delve for his bread. Will Dr. Ross be actuated by the most perfect impartiality which has ever been considered most favorable to a correct decision?"

Then from a voice of easy, familiar talk he changed to a high moving wail and cried, "When I see strong hands sowing, reaping, and threshing wheat into bread, I cannot refrain from wishing and believing that those hands, some way, in God's good time, shall own the mouth they feed!"

The gold of October leaves was on the trees; the tawny glow of autumn harvesttime was on the air. He had come and he had spoken; he had known well as he rode along the Sangamon River that morning, as the stagecoach turned at the lovely curve of the stream at Salem and he saw yellow slopes his feet had often wandered over—he had known well he would not change the mind and feeling of Menard County people for that year; what he was counting on was a later time.

Back in his Springfield law office he said to his law partner, "Billy, I never felt so full of just what a crowd ought to hear, and I gave them my best. I soaked that crowd full of political facts they can't get away from."

THAT YEAR OF 1856 saw bonfires for the new Republican party of Illinois; in November they found they had put in their man for governor, and taken away from the Democrats all the state offices. The presidential electors and the legislature were held by the Democrats. The Republicans took over the statehouse; Bill Herndon was appointed bank examiner; Lincoln had a desk in a quiet corner for writing letters when he pleased.

Nationally, the picture was different. When the election returns were all in, Buchanan had 174 electoral votes, Frémont 114, Fillmore 8. But the popular vote was 1,838,169 for Buchanan, 1,341,264 for Frémont, 874,534 for Fillmore; Buchanan had been elected, but by a minority of the popular vote. He carried all the slave states except Maryland, which Fillmore carried.

Lincoln spoke at a Republican banquet in Chicago in December, giving the toast: "*The Union*—the North will maintain it—the South will not depart therefrom." In referring to the fact that the new President had been elected by a minority of voters, he raised the point, that the majority, divided between Frémont and Fillmore, "may not choose to remain permanently rebuked by that minority." He urged that they come together for the future, all stand with the Republicans. The central idea should be not "all citizens as citizens are equal" but the broader and better "all *men* are created equal." He was sure: "The human heart *is* with us—God is with us."

Only four months after the people had, in the combined majority against Buchanan, spoken decisively against slavery extension into new territory, there came from the Supreme Court at Washington the decision in the Dred Scott case that

Congress did not have the power to prohibit slavery in the territories. This decision set the slavery question seething once more. Lincoln, from now on for years, was to stress more than ever what he believed the Declaration of Independence meant by the clause "that all men are created equal." The question would recur, "If those who wrote and adopted the Constitution believed slavery to be a good thing, why did they insert a provision prohibiting the slave trade after the year 1808?" Into Lincoln's speech was to come more often that phrase "the Family of Man," as though mankind has unity and dignity.

A defense of the Dred Scott decision was made by Senator Douglas in a speech in Springfield in June; he said, "Whoever resists the final decision of the highest judicial tribunal aims a deadly blow at our whole republican system of government."

Lincoln two weeks later replied. He pointed to the fact that the Supreme Court had often overruled its own decisions, and said, "We shall do what we can to have it overrule this." There had been days when the Declaration of Independence was held sacred. "But now, to aid in making the bondage of the Negro universal and eternal, it is assailed and sneered at and construed, and hawked at and torn, till, if its framers could rise from their graves, they could not at all recognize it." The speech laid the blame for slavery on the love of money, and closed: "The plainest print cannot be read through a gold eagle; and it will be ever hard to find many men who will send a slave to Liberia, and pay his passage, while they can send him to a new country— Kansas, for instance—and sell him for fifteen hundred dollars." And because Illinois and the Northwest and Lincoln were becoming more important nationally, *The New York Times* printed the speech in full.

Lincoln had become known as one of the active, practical politicians of central and southern Illinois. He was a party man; the other wheelhorses knew him. He kept in close touch with the machinery of the party organization, often holding conferences and exchanging information with other party leaders in the country and state. Caucuses in his own ward, city, county, and congressional district, for the election of delegates to conventions, were watched over by him. He spent hours many a day figuring, tabulating, and estimating as to ballots, candidates, tickets. He gave his ears to the whisperers of political gossip, seeking straws showing the wind; and he wrote endless letters.

Outside of the right and wrong of any issues of justice and humanity in politics, Lincoln enjoyed it as a game. It had some of the skill of billiards, the science of arithmetic, and the hazards of horse racing in it. The foremost national sport was politics and he was at home in the smoke, noise, and hullabaloo of it. The big angles of the game were all the more fascinating to him because he had mastered the little essential details, such, for instance, as electioneering.

Chapter 23

IN THE SPRING OF 1858 Lincoln was writing notes for a speech. At the state gathering of Republicans in June they were going to nominate him for United States senator from Illinois; and he was going to speak; he was to tell the world what Illinois and the Northwest would stand for. As he read the speech to Herndon in their office, it lighted Herndon into saying, "Lincoln, deliver that speech as read, and it will make you President."

Lincoln had spoken the high points of it at Bloomington during the last campaign, and a Chicago judge and a Galena congressman had warned him never to be so radical again. In the state library in Springfield he sat in a chair and read it off to a picked dozen political friends; they said it was too radical; it was "a fool utterance"; it was "ahead of its time"; it would drive away votes in this election year; all were against his delivering the first paragraph of the speech, except Herndon. And Lincoln was polite and decent—and couldn't see where he ought to change the speech.

The convention met in Springfield on June 16, named Lincoln for United States senator to succeed Stephen A. Douglas, and then sent out for Lincoln to come and make a speech. He came, bowed to the applause and cheers, murmured, "Mr. President and Gentlemen of the Convention," and then, for the first time in his life reading a speech from a manuscript, he began:

"If we could first know *where* we are, and *whither* we are tending, we could better judge *what* to do, and *how* to do it. We are now far into the *fifth* year, since a policy was initiated, with the *avowed* object, and *confident* promise, of putting an end to slavery agitation. Under the operation of that policy, that agitation has not only, *not ceased*, but has *constantly augmented*. In *my* opinion, it *will* not cease, until a *crisis* shall have been reached, and passed. 'A house divided against itself cannot stand.' I believe this government cannot endure, permanently half *slave* and half *free*. I do not expect the Union to be *dissolved*— I do not expect the house to *fall*—but I *do* expect it will cease to be divided. It will become *all* one thing, or *all* the other."

This was so plain that any two farmers fixing fences on a rainy morning could talk it over. And to this was added a sentence for all the more thoughtful to follow in all its exact and terrible meanings. The speaker read:

"Either the *opponents* of slavery, will arrest the further spread of it, and place it where the public mind shall rest in the belief that it is in the course of ultimate extinction; or its *advocates* will push it forward, till it shall become alike lawful in *all* the States, *old* as well as *new*, *North* as well as *South*."

In simple Bible language, in short words and in longer words of piercing precision, he had spoken thoughts fresh, beautiful, and terrible, a common-sense telling of what millions of anxious hearts wanted told.

There was more to the speech; he put together this and that circumstance and argued that while on the face of them the people could not be sure that there was a conspiracy on foot to nationalize slavery, yet explanations were required as to why the two Presidents, Franklin Pierce and James Buchanan, a Supreme Court Chief Justice, and the United States senator, Stephen A. Douglas, had all taken parts in moves and acts that seemed to lead straight toward a time when slaves could be owned and worked in all states of the Union. And he mentioned how the Republican party, of strange, discordant, and even hostile elements, "gathered from the four winds," had fought winning battles in the last campaign and with wise counsels should go on.

There was more to the speech—but the part that interested the country, as daily and weekly newspapers published the speech in full, was its opening paragraph. It became known as the "House Divided" speech. The names of agitator and blatherskite were hurled at Lincoln by Democratic newspapers for this speech; and political friends growled that he had been radical, gone too far. He said, "If I had to draw a pen across my record and erase my whole life from sight, and I had one poor gift or choice left as to what I should save from the wreck, I should choose that speech and leave it to the world unerased."

WHEN THE NEWSPAPERS brought to the eye of Stephen A. Douglas, at his Washington home, the speech of A. Lincoln saying that a house divided against itself cannot stand, the senator was more than interested. When he read that the state Republican convention had with cheers resolved "That Hon. Abraham Lincoln is our first and only choice for United States Senator to fill the vacancy about to be created by the expiration of Mr. Douglas's term of office," he was again more than interested. He told a group of Republicans, "You have nominated a very able and a very honest man." To John W. Forney he said, "I shall have my hands full. Lincoln is the strong man of his party, the best stump speaker in the West." And again, "Of all the damned Whig rascals about Springfield, Abe Lincoln is the ablest and the most honest."

Douglas was the leading man at that hour in the great drama of American politics. Against him in his contest for reelection he had not only Lincoln and the young Republican party of Illinois but also President Buchanan and the national Democratic Administration. A split had developed in the Democratic party the year before; Douglas had taken a stand opposing Buchanan in regard to a constitution proposed for Kansas; and Buchanan and the powerful southern planters were interested in breaking Douglas. Already it was believed there would be three candidates for President in 1860; two Democratic parties and the Republican party; and the winner would be the man who could carry the Northwest. Either that, or the election would be so close that it would be thrown into Congress.

Douglas was in a fight for his political life, and, reading the House Divided speech of Abraham Lincoln, he saw that it was important. He studied every thought and phrase in it. He would refer to it and argue it down in nearly every campaign speech he would deliver.

Douglas started west in June. His daily movements were watched by the country; the Chicago *Times* reprinted from the Philadelphia *Press:* "Senator Douglas, accompanied by his beautiful and accomplished wife, arrived at the Girard House, en route for Chicago. He was visited by a large number of our most influential citizens." Sixty miles out from Chicago, a special Illinois Central train with a brass band, flags, streamers, and pennants met Douglas and his party on July 9 and escorted him to Chicago. As he stepped out on the Lake Street balcony of the Tremont House that night, rockets and red fire lit the street; he gazed into what the Chicago *Times* called "an ocean of upturned faces." The crowd in the street started a fight with hack drivers who had tried to plow through the people and deliver distinguished guests at the Tremont House. One man was knocked down with the butt end of a whip; one driver was pulled off his seat three times. As the horses, people, and hack drivers were untangled, Judge Douglas began a speech that lasted an hour and a half.

Lincoln sat nearby and heard Douglas refer to him as "a kind, amiable, and intelligent gentleman, a good citizen, and an honorable opponent." That night he also heard Douglas say to the swarming thousands in the street, "Mr. Lincoln advocates boldly and clearly a war of sections, a war of the North against the South, of the free states against the slave states—a war of extermination—to be continued relentlessly until the one or the other shall be subdued, and all the states shall either become free or become slave."

And the night afterward Lincoln spoke from the Tremont House balcony to a crowd somewhat smaller; rockets blazed; the brass band of the German Republican Club from the Seventh Ward rendered music. And amid much on issues of the day Lincoln said, "I do not claim, gentlemen, to be unselfish; I do not pretend that I would not like to go to the United States

Senate, I make no such hypocritical pretense, but I do say to you that in this mighty issue, it is nothing to you—nothing to the mass of the people of the nation—whether or not Judge Douglas or myself shall ever be he d of after this night."

It was in this same month of July that A. P. Chapman wrote Lincoln that "Grand Mother Lincoln" was doing well, and, "I often take my Republican papers and read Extracts from them that Eulogise you you can hardly form an idea how proud it makes her. She often says Abram was always her best child & that he always treated her like a son. I told her I was a going to write you to day & she says tell you she sent a heap of love to you."

DURING THE HOT SUMMER WEEKS in Illinois, as the corn was growing knee-high and then shoulder-high, Lincoln and Douglas had their coats off, making public speeches, writing private letters, listening to whisperers of gossip, watching various newspapers bawl and bark at each other.

For the first year in nine or ten years Lincoln in 1858 filed no case in the state supreme court of Illinois. His law office was shut up; the reader of lawbooks was out among the people asking them about old laws that needed making over, telling them violence and cunning had taken the place of some of the best laws.

Not since the days of Thomas Jefferson had any American politician reached out with so direct a passion in appealing to the people as though freedom was a word that meant something to be used. He explained the Fourth of July as a day for Americans to be thoughtful and to read the Declaration of Independence.

In Chicago where there were so many different nationalities— German, Irish, French, and Scandinavian—and where they talked about "the old country" and "this new country," he said of the newcomers who had no grandfathers in the American Revolution, "If they look back to trace their connection with those days by blood, they find they have none ... [to] make themselves feel they are part of us; but when they look through that old Declaration of Independence, they find that those old men say that 'We hold these truths to be self-evident, that all men are created equal,' and then they feel that that moral sentiment taught in that day evidences their relation to those men, that it is the father of all moral principle in them, and that they have a right to claim it as though they were blood of the blood, and flesh of the flesh, of the men who wrote that Declaration; and so they are."

In blunt, short words, in a speech in Springfield, he declared, "All I ask for the Negro is that, if you do not like him, let him alone. If God gave him but little, that little let him enjoy." And again as to all men being born equal: "Certainly the Negro is not our equal in color—perhaps not in many other respects; still, in the right to put into his mouth the bread that his own hands have earned, he is the equal of every other man, white or black. In pointing out that more has been given you, you cannot be justified in taking away the little which has been given him."

Lincoln expected trouble, a crisis, perhaps war, between the states. He didn't wish what seemed to be coming. He expected it. That was what he meant in the house-divided-against-itself speech. Whenever Judge Douglas talked for an hour he pulled from inside his Prince Albert coat the opening paragraph of Lincoln's House Divided speech and read, "I believe that this government cannot endure permanently," to show that it meant Lincoln wished for a bloody war between the states. And whenever Lincoln spoke for an hour he too read the paragraph and said it meant just what it said; he expected a crisis; he didn't wish it.

Lincoln meanwhile was reading newspapers from all over the country, trying to fathom what would be happening the next year and the year after. Southern newspapers at times were saying slavery would be a good thing not only for black people but for some classes of white workers. Lincoln got the *Illinois State Journal* to reprint opinions such as one from the Richmond *Enquirer*, reading: "Northern free society is . . . burdened with a servile class of mechanics and laborers, unfit for self-government, and yet clothed with the attributes and powers of citizens. Master and slave is a relation in society as natural and necessary as parent and child; and the Northern States will yet have to introduce it."

Lincoln understood well that these ideas and feelings had sympathizers in the North. He had met it in the faces of that crowd he spoke to in Petersburg when he aimed to "soak them with facts." In that same year the editor of the Mattoon *National Gazette*, a Buchanan organ, advised his readers: "The novelty of free labor is a mere humbug," and predicted the farmers of Illinois would favor slavery for Illinois if a state constitution legalizing slavery should be voted on. The Jackson *Mississippian* joined in this view, declaring: "Establish slavery in Illinois and it would give us the key to the great West."

With irony so sad it was musical, Lincoln told three or four hundred people at Edwardsville one day, "When by all these means you have succeeded in dehumanizing the Negro; when you have put him down and made it impossible for him to be but as the beasts of the field; when you have extinguished his soul, and placed him where the ray of hope is blown out in darkness that broods over the damned, are you quite sure the demon you have roused will not turn and rend you? What constitutes the bulwark of our liberty and independence? It is not ... the guns of our war steamers, or the strength of our gallant army. . . . Our reliance is in the love of liberty which God has planted in our bosoms. Our defence is in the preservation of the spirit which prizes liberty as the heritage of *all men, in all lands everywhere*. Destroy this spirit and you have planted the seeds of despotism around your own doors. Familiarize yourself with the chains of bondage, and you are preparing your own limbs to wear them."

He knew that the challenging, radical tone of what he was saying would interest not only the foreign-born voters but also the young people. The fifteen- and sixteen-year-old boys who had read *Uncle Tom's Cabin* when it was published had grown into twenty-one- and twenty-two-year-old voters. In what he was doing and saying Lincoln kept in mind the young men. He had always had an eye out in politics for the young; his own youth was never forgotten.

Perhaps, after all, only the young people with dreams and

wishes in their eyes would understand his language. When his talk was ended and language had failed to measure off all he wanted to say, it might be the young who would best understand the desperation of his dreams, the unmeasured lengths of the adventure he was for.

Chapter 24

ON AN ILLINOIS Central Railroad train of special coaches, with a brass cannon on a flatcar at the rear, Stephen A. Douglas campaigned downstate. Republican papers said he carried his own brass cannon to make sure he would be saluted when he came to a town. The Democratic papers mentioned him as a friend of civilization in connection with his making the University of Chicago a present of ten acres of land for its buildings to stand on. At Springfield a banner with the name "Douglas" was bestowed on him as a gift from the shopworkers of the Chicago and St. Louis Railroad. He spoke in a picnic grove where five thousand people stood in mud and wet grass, under trees dripping from summer rain.

In several towns Lincoln would stand up when calls came for him, after Douglas's speech, and notify the audience where he would speak. Sometimes handbills were passed out to announce that Lincoln would reply to Douglas later that evening. The Chicago *Times* told its readers: "The cringing, crawling creature is hanging at the outskirts of Douglas meetings, begging the people to come and hear him."

At a Clinton meeting Douglas replied to Lincoln's speeches which had contained facts showing that Douglas was joined in a "conspiracy" to make slavery lawful in the northern states. Douglas said, "My self-respect alone prevents me from calling it a falsehood." A few days later at Beardstown, however, he declared the conspiracy charge "an infamous lie."

Lincoln had run a grocery store and sold whisky, Douglas told a crowd one day. "But the difference between Judge Douglas and myself is just this," Lincoln replied, "that while I was behind the bar he was in front of it."

Suddenly came an event. Lincoln wrote a challenge, Douglas met it. A debate was to be staged. The two men were to stand on platforms together and argue in seven different parts of the state, with all Illinois watching, and the whole country listening.

A new way of taking down speeches—shorthand writing— had been invented; reporters would give the country "full phonographic verbatim reports," newspapers told their readers.

Shade trees were few in the Ottawa public square and most of the twelve thousand listeners were in a broiling summer sun on August 21 when the first of the debates took place. Seventeen cars full of them had come from Chicago. By train, canal boat, wagon, buggy, and afoot they had arrived, waved flags, formed processions, and escorted their heroes. It took a half hour for the speakers and committees to squeeze and wedge their way through the crowd to the platform.

During three hours the acres of people listened, and, the speaking ended, they surged around their heroes and formed escorts. Lincoln was grabbed by a dozen grinning Republicans, lifted onto their shoulders, and, surrounded by a mass of Republicans headed by a brass band, he was carried to the Glover House. "With . . . his long legs dangling nearly to the ground, his long face was an incessant contortion to wear a winning smile that succeeded in being only a ghastly one," said a Democratic newspaper. The reporter for the Philadelphia *Press* noted of Lincoln as a debater: "Poor fellow! he was writhing in the powerful grasp of an intellectual giant. His speech amounted to nothing. . . . Lincoln is the worst used-up man in the United States. He has six appointments to meet Judge Douglas yet. I don't believe he will fill them all." The New York *Evening Post* reporter said: "In repose, I must confess that 'Long Abe's' appearance is *not* comely. But stir him up and the fire of genius plays on every feature. . . . Listening to him on Saturday, calmly and unprejudiced, I was convinced that he has no superior as a stump speaker." President Buchanan's party organ at Washington wished the debaters the worst of luck and called Lincoln and Douglas "a pair of depraved, blustering, mischievous, low-down demagogues."

Lincoln knew there were people whose feeling about the

principles and the politicians involved were like those of Mrs. William Cratty of Seneca, who said, "I felt *so* sorry for Lincoln while Douglas was speaking, and then to my surprise I felt *so* sorry for Douglas when Lincoln replied."

On the afternoon of September 8 at Clinton, Lincoln told the people, "You can fool all the people some of the time, and some of the people all the time, but you cannot fool all the people all the time." And in the office of the lawyer, Clifton H. Moore, he said on the same day, "Douglas will tell a lie to ten thousand people one day, even though he knows he may have to deny it to five thousand the next day."

Then came the debate in Freeport, far in the northwestern corner of Illinois. Douglas was met by a torchlight procession; the Chicago *Times* counted a thousand torches, the Chicago *Press and Tribune* seventy-four. Lincoln rode to the speaking stand in a covered wagon drawn by six white, spanking big horses. Fifteen thousand people sat and stood through three hours of cloudy, chilly weather. A fine drizzle drifted across the air. Some had come on the new sleeping cars from Chicago the night before. The platform in the grove was jammed thick with people.

As Lincoln started to say, "Fellow Citizens, Ladies and Gentlemen," a newspaperman called out, "Hold on, Lincoln. You can't speak yet." The shorthand reporter hadn't come. The debate was put off till a reporter was found. Then the debate could go on. Not only Illinois but the whole country was listening.

From Freeport the two debaters and the shorthand reporters dropped south on the map of Illinois three hundred miles. The Jonesboro crowd numbered about fourteen hundred—most of them rather cool about the great debate. The place was on land wedged between the slave states of Kentucky and Missouri; several carloads of passengers had come from those states to listen. The Chicago *Times* noted: "The enthusiasm in behalf of Douglas is intense." As to Lincoln's remarks, the Louisville *Journal* noted: "Let no one omit to read them. They are searching, scathing, stunning. They belong to what some one has graphically styled the *tomahawking* species."

Three days later, on September 18, the debaters and short-hand reporters were up at Charleston, halfway between the Wabash and Sangamon rivers. Twelve thousand people sat and stood at the county fairgrounds—and listened. They heard Douglas accuse Lincoln of not standing by the soldiers in the field during the Mexican War when Lincoln was in Congress; and they saw Lincoln pause in his reply, step back, and take Orlando B. Ficklin by the collar and drag Ficklin to the front of the platform to testify that when he, Ficklin, was in Congress he knew that Lincoln voted the same as Douglas for the benefit of soldiers. Some said they heard Ficklin's teeth rattle as Lincoln shook him.

On October 7, in the itinerary, came Galesburg, in Knox County. Twenty thousand people and more sat and stood hearing Lincoln and Douglas speak for three hours, while a chilly northwest wind blew at a rate that tore some of the flags and banners to rags.

A procession had met Lincoln in Knoxville. He had been serenaded the night before by a brass band and stepped out on the porch of the Hebard House, and he opened his speech, "My friends, the less you see of me the better you will like me." In the morning he sat in a buggy to ride the five miles to Galesburg in line with a mile of buggies and wagons. Uncle Benny Hebard pointed at a house, saying, "There is where Isaac Gulliher lives." And the mile of buggies and wagons stopped ten minutes while Lincoln stepped in and drank a dipper of water with old Sangamon County friends.

To both of the candidates had come committees of young men and women from Knox and Lombard colleges; they had satin banners to present. The procession that ended at the debating platform on the Knox College campus included floats showing the methods of the Colton Foundry and the George W. Brown Cornplanter Works.

The raw northwest wind blew, ripping banners and bunting; the sky stayed gray; the damp air sent a chill to the bones of those who forgot their overcoats or who didn't have overcoats to forget. For three hours the two debaters spoke to an audience of people who buttoned their coats tighter and listened. They had come from the banks of the Cedar Fork Creek, the Spoon River, the Illinois, the Rock, and the Mississippi rivers, with hands toughened from plow handles, legs with hard bunched muscles from tramping behind a plow team, with ruddy and wind-bitten faces. They were of the earth; they could stand the raw winds of the earth when there was something going on worth hearing and remembering.

Six days later, in Quincy, on the Mississippi River, a crowd of twelve thousand people came from three states, Illinois, Iowa, and Missouri, to hear the debaters. And two days later, farther down the Mississippi, looking from free-soil Illinois across the river to slave-soil Missouri, the two debaters had their final match, in Alton, before six thousand listeners.

One young man, Francis Grierson, kept a sharp impression of Lincoln at Alton, beginning to speak. He "rose from his seat, stretched his long, bony limbs upward as if to get them into working order, and stood like some solitary pine on a lonely summit."

TWO MEN HAD SPOKEN from platforms in Illinois to crowds of people in broiling summer sun and raw winds of fall—to audiences surpassing any in past American history in size and in eagerness to hear. And farther than that they had also spoken to the nation. The main points of the Lincoln-Douglas debates reached millions of newspaper readers. Columns and pages of the debates were published. Some larger newspapers printed the shorthand reports in full. A book of passion, an almanac of American visions, victories, defeats, a catechism of national thought and hope, was in those paragraphs. A powerful fragment of America breathed in Douglas's saying at Quincy, "Let each State mind its own business and let its neighbors alone! . . . If we will stand by that principle, then Mr. Lincoln will find that this republic can exist forever divided into free and slave States. . . . Stand by that great principle and we can go on as we have done, increasing in wealth, in population, in power, and in all the elements of greatness, until we shall be the admiration and terror of the world . . . until we make this continent one ocean-bound republic."

Those who wished quiet about the slavery question, and those who didn't, understood the searching examination for truth in Lincoln's inquiry: "You say it [slavery] is wrong; but don't you constantly . . . argue that this is not the right place to oppose it? You say it must not be opposed in the free States, because slavery is not here; it must not be opposed in the slave States, because it is there; it must not be opposed in politics, because that will make a fuss; it must not be opposed in the pulpit, because it is not religion. Then where is the place to oppose it? There is no suitable place to oppose it."

So many could respond to the Lincoln view: "Judge Douglas will have it that I want a Negro wife. He never can be brought to understand that there is any middle ground on this subject. I have lived until my fiftieth year, and have never had a Negro woman either for a slave or a wife, and I think I can live fifty centuries, for that matter, without having had one for either." Pointing to the Supreme Court decision that slaves as property could not be voted out of new territories, Lincoln said the argument had got down as thin as "soup made by boiling the shadow of a pigeon that had starved to death."

Lincoln was trying to stir up strife and rebellion, according to Douglas, and was "stimulating the passions of men to resort to violence and to mobs, instead of to the law. I take the decisions of the Supreme Court as the law of the land, and I intend to obey them as such." He was the sincere spokesman of powerful men. "Suppose Mr. Lincoln succeeds in destroying public confidence in the Supreme Court, so that people will not respect its decisions, but will feel at liberty to disregard them, and resist the laws of the land, what will he have gained? He will have changed the government from one of laws into that of a mob, in which the strong arm of violence will be substituted for the decisions of the courts."

Lincoln cited a Supreme Court decision as "one of the thousand things constantly done to prepare the public mind to make property, and nothing but property, of the Negro in all the states of this Union." Why was slavery referred to in "covert language" and not mentioned plainly and openly in the United States Constitution? Why were the words "Negro" and "slavery" left out? "It was hoped when it should be read by intelligent and patriotic men, after the institution of slavery had passed from among us, there should be nothing on the face of the great charter of liberty suggesting that such a thing as Negro slavery had ever existed among us."

Was it not always slavery that was the single issue of quarrels? "Does it not enter into the churches and rend them asunder? What divided the great Methodist Church into two parts, North and South? What has raised this constant disturbance in every Presbyterian General Assembly that meets?" This issue somehow operated on the minds of men and divided them in every avenue of society, in politics, religion, literature, morals. "That is the issue that will continue in this country when these poor tongues of Judge Douglas and myself shall be silent. It is the eternal struggle between two principles. . . . The one is the common right of humanity and the other the divine right of kings. It is the same . . . spirit that says, 'You work and toil and earn bread, and I'll eat it.' No matter in what shape it comes, whether from the mouth of a king who seeks to bestride the people of his own nation and live by the fruit of their labor, or from one race of men as an apology for enslaving another race, it is the same tyrannical principle."

The high point of the debates had come when Douglas had framed for Lincoln a series of questions at Ottawa. At Freeport Lincoln took up these questions one by one and replied. Then in his turn he put a series of questions to Douglas, one reading, "Can the people of a United States Territory, in any lawful way, against the wish of any citizen of the United States, exclude slavery from its limits prior to the formation of a State Constitution?" The affirmative answer of Douglas raised a storm of opposition to him in the South, and lost him blocks of northern Democratic friends wishing to maintain connections in the South.

Lincoln showed his questions to advisers beforehand; they told him to drop the main question. He answered, "I am after larger game; the battle of 1860 is worth a hundred of this." His guess was that Douglas's answer would further split the Democratic party and make a three-cornered fight for the presidency two years later.

With only two of the debates over, Douglas had known something had hit him hard and the going would be still harder. From Jonesboro on it was noticed that Douglas's voice did not have the carrying power of Lincoln's. "As a stump speaker, Lincoln used Douglas up," a Galesburg lawyer observed. "In the outskirts of the crowd I could catch every word that Lincoln said, and I had difficulty hearing Douglas." One fairly accurate though slightly partisan reporter wrote from Quincy: "Douglas looked very much the worse for wear. Bad whisky and the wear and tear of conscience have had their effect." As for Lincoln, the open air, the travel and excitement of the speeches threw him back to flatboating days; his voice grew clearer and stronger; in November he was heavier by nearly twenty pounds than he was at the beginning of the campaign.

When Douglas twisted his antislavery position into one of race equality, Lincoln replied it was "a specious and fantastic arrangement of words, by which a man can prove a horse chestnut to be a chestnut horse." He gave the twelve thousand people at Charleston a free lesson in logic, by shaking a finger at a man's face and saying, "I assert that you are here to-day, and you undertake to prove me a liar by showing that you were in Mattoon yesterday. I say that you took your hat off your head, and you prove me a liar by putting it on your head. That is the whole force of Douglas' argument."

He tried to key his openings with good humor or a bit of wisdom touched with nonsense. "Since Judge Douglas has said to you in his conclusion that he had not time in an hour and a half to answer all I had said in an hour, it follows of course that I will not be able to answer in half an hour all that he has said in an hour and a half."

As Lincoln sat in his hotel room in Quincy, there came in a Toledo, Ohio, man named David R. Locke. They found each other good talkers. Would he be elected to the United States Senate? Not quite. He would carry the state in the popular vote, but because of the gerrymandered districts Douglas would be elected by the legislature. He told Locke, "You can't overturn a pyramid, but you can undermine it; that's what I've been trying to do."

They spoke of a puffed-up politician in Illinois who had just died and had a big funeral, Lincoln commenting, "If General Blank had known how big a funeral he would have had, he would have died years ago."

When Locke went away, he told of his visit. "I found Mr. Lincoln surrounded by admirers. . . . I obtained an interview after the crowd had departed. He sat in the room with his boots off, to relieve his very large feet from the pain occasioned by continuous standing; or, to put it in his own words: 'I like to give my feet a chance to breathe.' He had removed his coat and vest, dropped one suspender from his shoulder, taken off his necktie and collar, and he sat tilted back in one chair with his feet upon another in perfect ease."

To Locke it seemed that Douglas played politics, wriggled, dodged, and worked only for Douglas. "Lincoln, on the other hand, kept strictly to the question at issue, and no one could doubt that the cause for which he was speaking was the only thing he had at heart; that his personal interests did not weigh a particle. He was the representative of an idea, and in the vastness of the idea its advocate was completely swallowed up. He admitted frankly all the weak points in the position of his party, and that simple honesty carried conviction with it. His admissions of weakness, where weakness was visible, strengthened his position on points where he was strong. He knew that the people had intelligence enough to strike the average correctly. His great strength was in his trusting the people."

And of Lincoln's face in the hotel room there in Quincy, David R. Locke said, "I never saw a more thoughtful face. I never saw a more dignified face. I never saw so sad a face."

RAIN FELL NEARLY EVERY DAY of the last week of October; wagon wheels sank in the roads; mud stuck to the spokes from hub to rim. Yet on Saturday, October 30, several thousand farmers out around Springfield hitched up their teams and drove in to the public square, where Abe Lincoln was to make his last speech of the campaign. Flags fluttered from wagon seats and from horse collars; cannon and firecrackers boomed and crackled; marchers shouting "Lincoln and Liberty" strode behind banners reading "Abe Lincoln, our next Senator." The crowd swarmed on the east side of the statehouse square, waves of people filling the steps of the courthouse and the Marine Bank, all facing toward the speakers' stand.

Lincoln began his speech at about two o'clock, saying, "I stand here surrounded by friends—some *political, all personal friends,* I trust. May I be indulged, in this closing scene, to say a few words of myself? I have borne a laborious, and, in some respects to myself, a painful part in the contest."

He knew that in the northern counties of Illinois he would have a far heavier vote than in most of the central counties. He was better understood politically in districts where he was personally more of a stranger. Galesburg would vote two to one for him, Jonesboro three to one against him. His final speech faced toward Jonesboro rather than Galesburg.

Facing southward, politically, he said, "The legal right of the Southern people to reclaim their fugitives I have constantly admitted. The legal right of Congress to interfere with their institution in the states, I have constantly denied. In resisting the spread of slavery to new territory, and with that, what appears to me to be a tendency to subvert the first principle of free government itself, my whole effort has consisted. To the best of my judgment I have labored *for,* and not *against* the Union." The issues were so immense, the required decisions so delicate, it was an hour for sinking personal considerations. "As I have not felt, so I have not expressed any harsh sentiment towards our Southern brethren. I have constantly declared, as I really believed, the only difference between them and us, is the difference of circumstances." And with a tone of personal confession, he ended his speech: "Ambition has been ascribed to me. God knows how sincerely I prayed from the first that this field of ambition might not be opened. I claim no insensibility to political honors; but today could the Missouri restriction be restored, and the whole slavery question replaced on the old ground of 'toleration' by *necessity* where it exists, with unyielding hostility to the spread of it, on principle, I would, in consideration, gladly agree, that Judge Douglas should never be *out,* and I never *in,* an office, so long as we both or either, live."

November 2, Election Day, arrived, wet and raw in the northern part of the state. And though Lincoln had a majority of 4085 votes over Douglas, Douglas held a majority of the legislature which would elect a United States senator in January.

Lincoln wrote to loyal friends, "Another explosion will soon come." Douglas managed to be supported as the best instrument both to *break down* and to *uphold* the slave power. "No ingenuity can keep this deception . . . up a great while." He was glad he had made the race. "Though I now sink out of view and shall be forgotten, I believe I have made some marks which will tell for the cause of civil liberty long after I am gone." Also, he joked; he was like the boy who stubbed his toe: "It hurt too bad to laugh, and he was too big to cry."

January 5 came; the legislature would ballot on a United States senator; there had been a lingering hope that Buchanan Democrats or other elements might turn to Lincoln—but Douglas had a majority in the joint ballot, and was elected.

Lincoln sat alone in his law office. Whitney came in, having just talked with a Republican who said he didn't like to follow a leader who was always getting defeated. "I expect everybody to desert me now—except Bill Herndon," Lincoln half groaned. Whitney went out, leaving Lincoln alone. He sat with his thoughts awhile, blew out the light, locked the door, stepped down to the street, and started home. The path had been worn hogbacked, and was slippery. One foot slipped and knocked the other foot from under him. He was falling. He made a quick twist and caught himself, lit square, and said with a ripple, "It's a slip and not a fall!" The streak of superstition in him was touched. He said it again, "A slip and not a fall!"

Chapter 25

ONE EVENING in Bloomington, shortly after the November election in 1858, Jesse Fell was walking on the south side of the public square when he saw Lincoln coming out of the courthouse door. Fell was a landowner and land trader, a railroad promoter, and a railroad contractor. Also he was of Quaker blood, antislavery, Republican, smooth-faced, honest-spoken, and trusted and liked in Bloomington.

Seeing Lincoln come out of the courthouse, he stepped across the street and asked Lincoln to go with him to the law office of his brother, Kersey H. Fell, over the Home Bank. A calm twilight was deepening over the street outside and filtering through the window as Fell said, "Lincoln, I have been east as far as Boston, and up into New Hampshire, traveling in all the New England states, save Maine; in New York, New Jersey, Pennsylvania, Ohio, Michigan, and Indiana; and everywhere I hear you talked about. Very frequently I have been asked, 'Who is this man Lincoln, of your state, now canvassing in opposition to Douglas?' Being, as you know, an ardent Republican, and your friend, I usually told them, we had in Illinois, two giants instead of one; that Douglas was the little one, as they all knew, but that you were the big one, which they didn't all know. But, seriously, Lincoln, Judge Douglas being so widely known, you are getting a national reputation through him . . . your speeches, in whole or in part . . . have been pretty extensively published in the East. . . . I have a decided impression, that if your popular history and efforts on the slavery question can be sufficiently brought before the people, you can be made a formidable, if not a successful, candidate for the presidency."

Lincoln heard Fell, and replied, "Oh, Fell, what's the use of talking of me for the presidency, while we have such men as Seward, Chase, and others, who are . . . so intimately associated with the principles of the Republican party. Everybody knows them. Nobody, scarcely, outside of Illinois, knows me. Besides, is it not, as a matter of justice, due to such men, who have carried this movement forward to its present status?"

Fell analyzed. Yes, Seward and Chase stood out as having rendered larger service to the Republican cause than Lincoln. "The truth is," said Fell, "they have rendered too much service . . . have made long records . . . and said some very radical things, which, however just and true . . . would seriously damage them . . . if nominated. We were defeated on this same issue in 1856, and will be again in 1860, unless we get a great many new votes from what may be called the old conservative parties. These will be repelled by radicals such as Seward and Chase. What the Republican party wants, to insure success in 1860, is a man of popular origin, of acknowledged ability, committed against slavery aggressions, who has no record to defend, and no radicalism of an offensive character. Your discussion with Judge Douglas has demonstrated your ability and your devotion to freedom; you have no embarrassing record . . . depend on it, there is some chance for you."

And Fell went on, "Now, Mr. Lincoln, I come to the business part of this interview. My native State, Pennsylvania, will have a large number of votes to cast for somebody . . . Pennsylvania don't like, overmuch, New York and her politicians. She has a candidate, Cameron, of her own, but he will not be acceptable to a larger number of her own people, much less abroad, and will be dropped. Through an eminent jurist and essayist of my native county in Pennsylvania, favorably known throughout the state, I want to get up a well-considered, well-written newspaper article, telling the people who you are, and what you have done, that it may be circulated not only in that state, but elsewhere, and thus help in manufacturing sentiment in your favor. I know your public life and can furnish items that your modesty would forbid, but I don't know much about your private history: when you were born, and where, the names and origin of your parents, what you did in early life, what were your opportunities for education, etc., and I want you to give me these. Won't you do it?"

Lincoln said, "Fell, I admit the force of much that you say, and admit that I am ambitious, and would like to be President; I am not insensible to the compliment you pay me, and the interest you manifest in the matter, but there is no such good luck in store for me, as the Presidency of these United States; besides, there is nothing in my early history that would interest you or anybody else."

Rising from his chair, Lincoln wrapped a thick gray and brown wool shawl around his bony shoulders, spoke good night, and started down the stairway, with Fell calling out that this was not the last of the affair and Lincoln must listen and do as he asked.

SENATOR SEWARD OF NEW YORK had told the country "an irrepressible conflict" was coming. "The United States must and will, sooner or later, become either a slaveholding nation or entirely a free-labor nation." Douglas had swept south to Memphis and New Orleans to say, "Whenever a territory has a climate, soil, and production making it the interest of the inhabitants to encourage slave property, they will pass a slave code."

Lincoln was the only thinker and leader in the Northwest, of wide and commanding strength, who had won a large confidence among the abolitionist and antislavery forces, without coming out flat-footed for violation of the Fugitive Slave Law.

Not only Jesse Fell, but also newspapers in small towns in midwest states, had begun asking, "Why not Abraham Lincoln for President of the United States?" The Cincinnati *Gazette* printed a letter nominating him, and a mass meeting in Sandusky, Ohio, called for him to head the Republican ticket in 1860. Calls for Lincoln to speak, as the foremost Republican figure of the West, were coming from Kansas, Buffalo, Pittsburgh. Thurlow Weed, the New York boss, wired to Illinois, "Send Abraham Lincoln to Albany immediately."

Long John Wentworth, editor of the Chicago *Democrat*, a Republican paper, saw Lincoln looming, and told him he "needed somebody to run him"; in New York Seward had Weed to run him. Lincoln took a laugh for himself and remarked, "Only events can make a President."

He was at a governor's reception in Springfield, wore a gloomy face as he finished a dance with Mrs. E. M. Haines, and remarked that he was fifty years old. Then he braced himself, brightened, and added, "But, Mrs. Haines, I feel that I am good for another fifty years yet."

LINCOLN BY NOW was a seasoned and hardened player in the great American game of politics, the national sport of watching candidates and betting on who would win. Without the cunning of a fox, without a wilderness sagacity, without natural instincts such as those guiding wild geese on thousand-mile flights, he would have gone under in stalking a presidential nomination.

Outside of himself and Theodore Canisius hardly anyone in Illinois knew that Lincoln was the owner of the German-language newspaper the *Illinois Staats-Anzeiger*. Canisius, the editor, had run into debt, and Lincoln took over the newspaper for $400. So it happened that while the leading German newspaper of Illinois, the Chicago *Staats-Zeitung*, was for Seward for President, Lincoln was the owner of a German newspaper downstate and could walk into its office, ask for favors, and get consideration. Furthermore, he had kept a live political asset from falling into Democratic hands and served his party to that extent in the close fighting for control of the Northwest.

Enemies and events set traps for his feet. Friends and party workers made mistakes. Sometimes he stopped what seemed to him to be a mistake in the making. This was the case in June of 1859 when he wrote to Salmon P. Chase, the Republican governor of Ohio, to watch out or the national Republican party would look like a steamboat with the boilers blown up.

Chase and others were considering a move to have the Republican party take a stand against the federal Fugitive Slave Law. Lincoln wrote to Chase, as one lawyer to another, a lengthy, dry paragraph on the Constitution and the Fugitive Slave Law, and then, as one politician to another, wrote the warning that the proposed move would wreck the party.

In September, Lincoln came into southern Ohio, called to make speeches to help the Republicans in the state campaign. At Columbus, David R. Locke, the newspaperman, asked him why he went out of his way to go on record as favoring the Illinois law forbidding intermarriage of whites and Negroes, and he remarked, "The law means nothing." Public discussion was helping to doom slavery, he told Locke. "What kills the skunk is the publicity it gives itself."

At Dayton, he sat for a daguerreotype, and a young man came in and began painting a portrait of him. "Keep on," he told the artist. "You may make a good one, but never a pretty one."

Then he went back to Springfield to the law office whose walls and bookcases he was seeing so seldom now.

In a cleaning of the office one day it was found that plants had sprouted up from the dirt in one corner. They were government seeds Congressman Lincoln had sent ten years back.

A new student, Littlefield, was digging into Blackstone and Kent. On the big table rested the feet of the new student and of the junior and senior partner—three pairs of feet. And Herndon remarked, "We ought to concentrate enough magnetism, in this way, to run a whole courtroom."

But one day in October the telegraph wires hummed with news that none of them read with his feet on the table.

ABOLITIONISTS had been writing, talking, singing, praying, for thirty years; William Lloyd Garrison had publicly burned a copy of the Constitution, calling it "a covenant with hell" because it sanctioned slavery; Henry Ward Beecher had held mock auctions of slaves in his Brooklyn church; *Uncle Tom's Cabin* had sold hundreds of thousands of copies. In hundreds of runaway-slave cases in the North there had been little or big riots and clashes; in Kansas had been civil war and terrorism.

Out of Kansas came a man who ran slaves to freedom, and for the sake of retaliation and terror burned barns, stole horses, and killed men without trial or hearing. Asked why he had killed young people, he answered, "Nits grow to be lice." He had come to Kansas from Ohio and New York, a child of Pilgrim Fathers; at his house his nineteen children had partaken in prayers and Scripture readings morning and night as they were raised up in his solemn household. As he mixed with abolitionists in the East, he told them action was wanted, bold deeds. "One man and God can overturn the universe," he said often. He was through with talk. And some agreed with him. The thousands of dollars he wanted for rifles, wagons, and stores were secretly given to him by wealthy and respectable citizens.

On Monday, October 17, 1859, telegraph dispatches to all parts of the United States carried terror, strange news. At the junction of the Shenandoah and Potomac rivers, in a rocky little town called Harpers Ferry, a United States government arsenal and rifle factory had been captured, the gates broken, and the watchmen made prisoners; slaveholders had been taken prisoners and their slaves told they were free and should spread the word of freedom to all slaves everywhere.

All of this happened between Sunday night and Monday daybreak. America shivered that Monday as the news spread. What was happening? Was a slave revolt starting? Would the next news tell of rebellious slaves repeating the Nat Turner insurrection on a wider scale, with men, women, and children butchered in their homes? The country breathed easier on Tuesday when Colonel Robert E. Lee, commanding eighty marines, had rushed a little engine-house fort where eighteen men inside had fought till all were dead or wounded except two.

In a corner of the engine house, they found an old man with a flowing long beard who said his name was John Brown. "Who sent you here?" they asked. "No man sent me here. It was my own prompting and that of my Maker, or that of the devil, whichever you please. I acknowledge no man in human form." "What was your object in coming?" "I came to free the slaves." "And you think you were acting righteously?" "Yes, I think, my friends, you are guilty of a great wrong against God and humanity. I think it right to interfere with you to free those you hold in bondage. I hold that the Golden Rule applies to the slaves too. . . ." "You are mad and fanatical." "And I think you people of the South are mad and fanatical. Is it sane to keep five million men in slavery? Is it sane to think such a system can last? Is it sane to suppress all who would speak against this system, and to murder all who would interfere with it? Is it sane to talk of war rather than give it up?"

The state of Virginia gave him a fair trial on charges of murder, treason, and inciting slaves to rebellion; northern friends gave him able lawyers; he was found guilty; a judge pronounced the words, he must hang by the neck till he was dead.

And he looked the judge in the eye and spoke calmly. "Had I taken up arms in behalf of the rich, the powerful, the intelligent . . . or any of their class, every man in this court would have deemed it an act worthy of reward rather than of punishment, but the Court acknowledges the validity of the law of God. I see a book kissed here which is the Bible, and which teaches me that all things that I would have men do unto me, so must I do unto them. I endeavored to act up to that instruction. I fought for the poor; and I say it was right, for they are as good as any of you . . . God is no respecter of persons . . . Now, if it be deemed necessary that I should forfeit my life for the furtherance of the ends of justice . . . I say, let it be done."

Word came from friends who planned to steal him away from the death watch. He sent back word he would be more useful to freedom when dead. Afterward his ghost would come back and walk the earth and tease at men's hearts with questions about freedom and justice and God. He wrote, in jail, a last message before going to the noose: "I, John Brown, am now quite certain that the crimes of this guilty land will never be purged away but with blood. I had, as I now think, vainly flattered myself that without much bloodshed it might be done."

On the day of his doom, the Shenandoah Valley was swept and garnished by sky and weather; beyond the three thousand guardsmen with rifles, he could see blue haze and a shining sun over the Blue Ridge Mountains. "This *is* a beautiful country; I never had the pleasure of really seeing it before." The sheriff asked, "Shall I give you the signal when the trap is to be sprung?" "No, no," came the even voice from the white beard. "Just get it over quickly."

What John Brown had believed came true; his ghost did walk. The governor of Virginia talked about the way he died, without a quaver or a flicker, cool, serene. Emerson, Thoreau, Victor Hugo compared him to Christ, to Socrates. The abolitionists shouted hallelujahs. The antislavery men had regrets; they knew the South was lashed and would retaliate.

Stephen A. Douglas called for a law to punish conspiracies, quoting Lincoln's House Divided speech and Seward's Irrepressible Conflict speech to indicate that Republican politicians and their "revolutionary doctrines" had incited John Brown.

Abraham Lincoln spoke at Troy, Kansas, on December 2, the day Brown was hanged, and made an appeal to southern sympathizers. "Old John Brown thought slavery was wrong, as we do; he attacked slavery contrary to law, and it availed him nothing before the law that he thought himself right. He has just been hanged for treason against the state of Virginia; and we cannot object, though he agreed with us in calling slavery wrong. Now if you undertake to destroy the Union contrary to law, if you commit treason against the United States, our duty will be to deal with you as John Brown has been dealt with. We shall try to do our duty."

"CRAZY" WAS THE WORD for Brown, said many. A plea of insanity had been made for him in the trial; for himself, he had said, "I may be very insane, and I am so, if insane at all. But if that be so, insanity is very like a pleasant dream." Still the plunge of John Brown into the darker valley beyond the Shenandoah kept echoing. Louisa Alcott referred to him as "Saint John the Just," and Longfellow whispered to his diary that the hanging of Brown marked "the day of a new revolution." Brown had been so calmly and religiously glad to be hanged publicly that he could not be dismissed lightly.

All national politics was colored by what he had done. The New York *Herald* published, side by side with the news from Harpers Ferry, the speech, in full, of Senator William H. Seward in which he prophesied the "irrepressible conflict." Seward offered explanations in a Senate speech; he was opposed to conspiracy, invasion, and force as shown by Brown; he favored reason, suffrage, and the Christian spirit. Yet his explanations could not wash off from him the radical stripes. Seward as a candidate for the Republican nomination had been hard hit. Jesse Fell and Judge David Davis worked steadily on their plans to nominate their dark horse in the coming month of May.

Lincoln, on his Kansas trip, meanwhile, spoke in towns on the civil-war border; he battered away at Douglas, politely reciting political history. "Last year, as you know, we Republicans in Illinois were advised by numerous and respectable outsiders to reelect Douglas to the Senate by our votes." He had not questioned the motives of such advisers nor their devotion to the Republican party. But, "Had we followed the advice, there would now be no Republican party in Illinois, and none to speak of anywhere else. The whole thing would now be floundering along after Douglas. . . . It would have been the grandest 'haul' for slavery ever yet made."

Riding in a one-horse open buggy across the prairie, among the rolling gray grasses of Kansas in early winter, Lincoln had

his thoughts of men and history. He knew that he had helped, possibly even he alone had accomplished, the holding of the northwest prairies in the political keeping of people convinced against the spread of chattel slavery. If his life held no more, if he should lose in his dark-horse race for the presidency of the United States, his years had held a large measure.

He had been the Stubborn Man who had erected what in his phrase was "a stumbling-block to tyrants." If there had been any stubborn grandeur at all in his life, it was in his explanations of the Declaration of Independence, and his taking the words, "all men are created equal," not only seriously and solemnly but passionately. That it had paid him politically in support from new American voters from Europe, and in support from anti-slavery and Free-Soil voters, was a factor he reckoned with. He was a gatherer of votes with a keen eye for practical values. But he phrased and thrust forth this very ideal of equality in such a way that it took on new meanings.

He gained and held power, votes, friends, in unknown corners and byways, because he threw some strange accent into the pronunciation of the words, "The People." He was thinker and spokesman for the people. He knew what they wanted more deeply and thoroughly, more tragically and quizzically, than they knew it themselves. He made them believe that he counted the political genius and social control of the masses of people worth more in the long run than the assumptions of those who secretly will not trust the people at all. He had arrived at a sense of history. He looked into the faces of Kansans and said, "Our principle, however baffled or delayed, will finally triumph, I do not permit myself to doubt. Men will pass away—die, die politically and naturally; but the principle will live and live forever."

Chapter 26

LINCOLN WAS BUSY writing in the winter weeks of late 1859 and early 1860. The Young Men's Central Republican Union of New York City had asked him to be its final speaker in a course of lectures on political subjects. He was to lecture on February 27 in New York, and he would have the chance to tell the country what was wrong and what he would do about it.

Just before Christmas that winter Lincoln sent Jesse Fell the story of his life which Fell had requested. His father and mother were born in Virginia, he wrote, of "undistinguished parents," and then, feeling that "undistinguished" might not be understood, he added in his revision that his father and mother came from "second families, perhaps I should say." Indiana, where he grew up, "was a wild region, with many bears and other wild animals still in the woods." He continued, "When I came of age I did not know much. Still somehow, I could read, write, and cipher to the Rule of Three; but that was all. I have not been to school since. The little advance I now have upon this store of education I have picked up from time to time under the pressure of necessity." His own drawl was in the scribbling of, "I was raised to farm work," and when he closed, he said he had a "dark complexion, with coarse black hair, and grey eyes—no other marks or brands recollected."

In the letter sending the sketch to Fell, he noted, "There is not much of it, for the reason, I suppose, that there is not much of me." He had written the facts, for others to use. "Of course, it must not appear to have been written by myself."

Letters kept coming in about the House Divided speech. Just what did it mean? And he would write that it meant just what it said. He would quote its opening paragraph, and write: "It puzzles me to make my meaning plainer."

Lincoln was moving along now with some of his most important decisions and choices in politics dictated by swift-moving, inevitable circumstances. He toiled on, writing and rewriting his speech for New York City, going to the state library nearly every day, tracking down details of history.

As the time came for him to go to New York and tell the country what was wrong with it, the Chicago *Tribune* came out for him for President, and he heard more reports from friends working to get the Illinois and Indiana delegations solid, and Pennsylvania on the second ballot in the coming convention. Then he left Springfield for New York as quietly as though he were going to Bloomington or Jacksonville.

Stopping over in Chicago, he walked into the *Tribune* office and talked with Joseph Medill, the publisher, and Charles H. Ray, editor in chief, about how he was going to speak before a most critical audience in New York and would like to have them look over his speech; the ideas and arguments would have to stand as he had written them but he would like them to make notes as to any changes of words or phrases which they believed would improve it. "Ray and I buckled down to the delicate task," said Medill afterward. "One read slowly while the other listened attentively, and the reading was frequently interrupted to consider suggested improvements of diction, the insertion of synonyms, or points to render the text smoother or stronger. . . . Thus we toiled for some hours, till the revision was completed to our satisfaction. . . . Next morning . . . when he [Lincoln] came in we handed him our numerous notes [and] . . . emendation[s] with a self-satisfied feeling that we had considerably bettered the document. . . . Lincoln thanked us cordially for our trouble, glanced at our notes, told us a funny story or two of which the circumstances reminded him, and took his leave."

ARRIVING IN NEW YORK, Lincoln was told by the lecture committee that he was announced to speak at Cooper Union in Manhattan. In that case, he told the committee, he would have to fix over the manuscript of his speech because he had expected to deliver it at Henry Ward Beecher's church in Brooklyn. At the Astor House he saw visitors, refused invitations to speak in New Jersey, went on working on his speech. He noticed that the New York *Tribune* described him as "a man of the people, a champion of free labor," and also noted his "clearness and candor of statement, a chivalrous courtesy to opponents, and a broad, genuine humor."

A snowstorm interfered with traffic and Cooper Union had that night an audience that didn't fill all the seats. About fifteen hundred people had come, some with complimentary tickets, but most paying their way at twenty-five cents a head; the door receipts were $367. But for all that it was agreed in the *Tribune* office that "since the days of Clay and Webster" there hadn't been a larger assemblage of the "intellect and moral culture" of the city of New York. It included people who had heard Jenny Lind and Adelina Patti warble, who read the newspapers edited by Greeley, James Gordon Bennett of the *Herald*, and Henry J. Raymond of the *Times*. The pick and flower of New York culture was there. Some had heard of the Black Hawk War; but was Black Hawk an Indian chief or a river? Some had heard vaguely that this Lincoln person had once fought a duel out in Illinois; at any rate, he came from a region of corn-fed farmers, steamboat explosions, camp-meeting revivals, political barbecues, and boomtowns. Also, they knew this Lincoln had been the first man to grapple and give stiff handling to the powerful Stephen A. Douglas.

David Dudley Field escorted the speaker to the platform. William Cullen Bryant, editor of the *Evening Post*, author of "Thanatopsis," told the audience that Lincoln had won a majority of the votes for the senatorship in Illinois and that it was the legislative apportionment that gave Douglas the victory. Closing, Bryant said, "I have only, my friends, to pronounce the name of Abraham Lincoln of Illinois [loud cheering], to secure your profoundest attention."

Then came forward on the platform a tall, gaunt frame of bones on which hung a loose and long, new broadcloth suit of clothes, bought just before leaving Springfield, Illinois, and creased in a satchel all the way on the steam cars to New York. Applause began; the orator smiled, put his left hand in the lapel of his broadcloth coat, and stood so as the greeting slowed down. "Mr. *Cheer*man," he began with the Kentucky tang of dialect. He was slow getting started. Some Republicans weren't sure whether they should laugh at him or feel sorry for him.

As he got into his speech there came a change. He was telling them something. It was good to hear. They saw he had thought his way deeply among the issues and angers of the hour. He quoted Douglas: "Our fathers, when they framed the Government under which we live, understood this question [of slavery] just as well, and even better, than we do now."

And who might these "fathers" be? Included must be the thirty-nine framers of the original Constitution and the seventy-six members of the Congress who framed the amendments thereto. And he went into a crisscross of roll calls, quotations, documents in established history connected with the sacred names of bygone times, to prove the "fathers" held the Republican party view of restricting slavery. Did any one of the "fathers" ever say that the federal government should *not* have the power to control slavery in the federal territories? "I defy any man to show that any one of them ever, in his whole life, declared that." He said "neither the word 'slave' nor 'slavery' is to be found in the Constitution, nor the word 'property' even." They called the slave a "person." His master's legal right to him was phrased as "service or labor which may be due." Their purpose was "to exclude from the Constitution the idea that there could be property in man."

If the Republican party was "sectional" it was because of the southern sectional efforts to extend slavery. The Republicans were not radical nor revolutionary but conservative and in line with the "fathers" who framed the Constitution. Yet, "I do not mean to say we are bound to follow implicitly in whatever our fathers did. To do so, would be to discard all the lights of current experience—to reject all progress—all improvement." There were those saying they could "not abide the election of a Republican President," in which event they would destroy the Union. "And then, you say, the great crime of having destroyed it will be upon us! That is cool. A highwayman holds a pistol to my ear, and mutters through his teeth, 'Stand and deliver, or I shall kill you, and then you will be a murderer!' "

Slave insurrections couldn't be blamed on the young Republican party; twenty-eight years before, the slave Nat Turner led a revolt in Virginia where three times as many lives were lost as at Harpers Ferry. "In the present state of things in the United States, I do not think a general, or even a very extensive slave insurrection, is possible. . . . The slaves have no means of rapid communication. . . . The explosive materials are everywhere in parcels; but there neither are, nor can be supplied, the indispensable connecting trains. Much is said by southern people about the affection of slaves for their masters and mistresses; and a part of it, at least, is true." In any uprising plot among twenty individual slaves, "some one of them, to save the life of a favorite

217

master or mistress, would divulge it. . . . John Brown's effort . . . was an attempt by white men to get up a revolt among slaves, in which the slaves refused to participate. In fact, it was so absurd that the slaves, with all their ignorance, saw plainly enough it could not succeed."

His loose-hung, dangling sleeves were by now forgotten, by himself and by his listeners. At moments he seemed to have drifted out of mind that there was an audience before him; he was sort of talking to himself. In the quiet of some moments the only competing sound was the steady sizzle of the gaslights burning.

"And now, if they would listen—as I suppose they will not— I would address a few words to the southern people." Then he dealt in simple words with the terrible ropes of circumstance that snarled and meshed the two sections of the country: "The question recurs, what will satisfy them? Simply this: We must not only let them alone, but we must, somehow, convince them that we do let them alone." What was the nub? "Wrong as we think slavery is, we can yet afford to let it alone where it is, because that much is due to the necessity arising from its actual presence in the nation; but can we, while our votes will prevent it, allow it to spread into the National Territories, and to overrun us here in these Free States? If our sense of duty forbids this, then let us stand by our duty, fearlessly and effectively."

He reasoned: "All they ask, we could readily grant, if we thought slavery right; all we ask, they could as readily grant, if they thought it wrong. Their thinking it right, and our thinking it wrong, is the precise fact upon which depends the whole controversy. Thinking it right, as they do, they are not to blame for desiring its full recognition, as being right; but, thinking it wrong, as we do, can we yield to them? Can we cast our votes with their view, and against our own?"

To search for middle ground between the right and the wrong would be "vain as the search for a man who should be neither a living man nor a dead man." He finished: "Let us have faith that right makes might, and in that faith, let us, to the end, dare to do our duty as we understand it."

There were applause, cheers; hats and handkerchiefs went into the air, the speaker's hand was shaken; Noah Brooks, the *Tribune* man, was blurting out, "He's the greatest man since Saint Paul"; Brooks scurried away to write: "No man ever before made such an impression on his first appeal to a New York audience."

At the Athenaeum Club five or six Republicans gave Lincoln a supper. Then the head of the lecture committee, Charles C. Nott, took Lincoln to show him the way to the Astor House. As they walked along the street, Nott saw Lincoln was limping, and asked, "Are you lame, Mr. Lincoln?" No, he wasn't lame; he had new boots on and they hurt his feet. So they boarded a horse-drawn streetcar and rode to where Nott had to hop off for the nearest way home. He told Lincoln just to keep on riding and the car would take him to the Astor House. And Nott, watching the car go up the street, wasn't sure he had done right to get off; Lincoln looked sad and lonesome like something blown in with the drifts of the snowstorm.

In the morning in the lobby of the Astor, Lincoln saw that four morning papers printed his speech in full, and learned there would be a pamphlet reprint of it. He stayed in New York several days, sizing up "the front door" of the nation. It was a town with sights worth seeing. From his hotel room it was an easy walk to where, not so long before, the Dead Rabbits and the Bowery Boys had been in a gang fight and put up barricades and fought off the police till state troops arrived. Nor was it far to where Laura Keene, the actress manager, had put on her new successful play, *Our American Cousin*. He was taken to the studio of Matthew Brady and photographed; as the picture came out he looked satisfied with himself; it wasn't his usual sad face. But people liked it.

When New York papers carrying the Cooper Union speech arrived in the Chicago *Tribune* office, Medill and Ray were glad to see the compliments paid to Lincoln. "Ray and I plunged eagerly into the report, feeling quite satisfied with the successful effect of the polish we had applied to the address," Medill said afterward. "We both got done reading it about the same time. With a sickly sort of smile, Dr. Ray looked at me and remarked, 'Medill, old Abe must have lost out of the car window

219

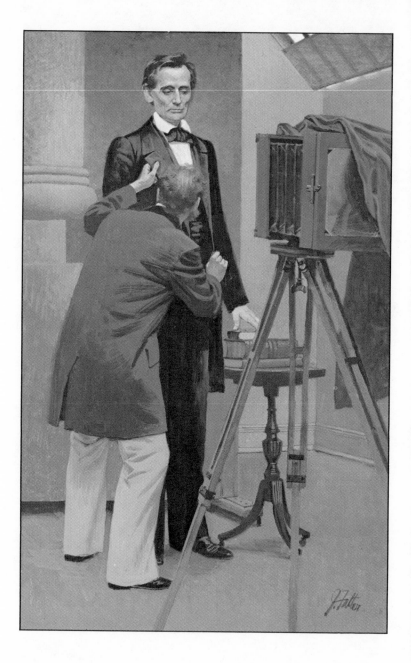

all our precious notes, for I don't find a trace of one of them in his published talk here.'"

Two days after Lincoln's Cooper Union speech, Senator Seward delivered a speech in the Senate, soothing in tone, so different from his Irrepressible Conflict speech that it drew the criticism he was backing down and phrasing his talk "so as to suit Wall Street." For over the country among many of the wealthy and conservative a shifting of view was occurring: slaves were property; slave ownership was property ownership; to disturb the right to own slaves might disturb other rights and interfere with the proper conduct of business in general.

The national muddle was getting more muddled. As it did so, Lincoln made campaign speeches for the Republicans in New England states, and visited his boy, Robert, studying to enter Harvard in a preparatory school at Exeter, New Hampshire. Speaking at Hartford, Connecticut, he discussed property and the property angle of the slavery question. "One-sixth of the population of the United States are slaves, looked upon as property, as nothing but property. The cash value of these slaves, at a moderate estimate, is two billion dollars. This amount of property value has a vast influence on the minds of its owners, very naturally. The same amount of property would have an equal influence upon us if owned in the North."

Lincoln knew that these statements of his, with all their delicate shadings of language, would unlock many secrets of his own conduct. At New Haven the next day he again made allusions to the property phase of slavery. He pointed to its influence on the minds of slaveowners. It carried them into politics "to insist upon all that will favorably affect its value as property, to demand laws and institutions and a public policy that shall increase and secure its value, and make it durable, lasting, and universal. The effect on the minds of the owners is to persuade them that there is no wrong in it." The slaveholder sets about arguing himself into the belief that slavery is right; the property influences his mind.

Shoe-factory workers were on strike in Connecticut and Massachusetts cities; they said they couldn't live on wages of $250 a year. Douglas had said the strike was caused by "this .

unfortunate sectional warfare." Lincoln replied, "Thank God that we have a system of labor where there *can* be a strike."

Thus at Hartford. At New Haven he told the striking shoe workers, "I do not pretend to know all about the matter . . . *I am glad to see that a system of labor prevails in New England under which laborers* CAN *strike* when they want to [cheers], where they are not obliged to work under all circumstances, and are not tied down and obliged to labor whether you pay them or not! [Cheers.] I *like* the system which lets a man quit when he wants to, and wish it might prevail everywhere. [Tremendous applause.] . . . I don't believe in a law to prevent a man from getting rich; it would do more harm than good. So while we do not propose any war upon capital, we do wish to allow the humblest man an equal chance to get rich with everybody else."

He battered away at Douglas. The one personal target he took shots of argument at, in every speech, was Douglas; the one man standing most in the way of the Republican party was Douglas. It was Douglas who had debauched public opinion on the Declaration of Independence more than anyone else. And now "Douglas's new sedition law must be enacted and enforced, suppressing all declarations that slavery is wrong, whether made in politics, in presses, in pulpits, or in private. We must arrest and return their fugitive slaves. So long as we call slavery wrong, whenever a slave runs away they will overlook the obvious fact that he ran because he was oppressed, and declare that he was stolen off. Whenever a master cuts his slaves with the lash, and they cry out under it, he will overlook the obvious fact that the Negroes cry out because they are hurt, and insist that they were put up to it by some rascally abolitionist."

After the strain of facing intellectual and ethical New York at Cooper Union, Lincoln had a good time meeting crowds of Yankee workmen; he let loose his rippling humor in every speech. He spoke in Providence, Concord, Manchester, Dover, New Haven, Meriden, Norwich, and finally in Bridgeport on March 10, usually to "capacity audiences," several times escorted by brass bands and torchlight processions of cheering Republicans. Back in New York, however, he turned down further invitations to speak, being "far worn down." He thanked

James A. Briggs for a $200 check for the Cooper Union speech, and on March 11 went to hear Beecher preach in Brooklyn.

The next day he took the Erie Railroad for Chicago and two days later was home in Springfield, arriving, said the *Journal*, "in excellent health and in his usual spirits."

Chapter 27

LINCOLN WAS fifty-one years old. With each year of his life since he had become a grown man, his name and ways, and stories about him, had been spreading farther and farther among plain people and their children.

So tall, with so peculiar a slouch and so easy a saunter, so bony and sad, so quizzical and comic—he was the Strange Friend and he was the Friendly Stranger. Like something out of a picture book for children—he was. He met the eye as a clumsy, mystical giant that had walked out of a Chinese or Russian fairy story, or a bogey who had stumbled out of an ancient Saxon myth with a handkerchief full of presents he wanted to divide among all the children in the world.

Or again, people said Lincoln looked like a huge skeleton with skin over the bones, and clothes covering the skin.

He didn't wear clothes. Rather, clothes hung upon him as if on a rack to dry. He had clothes to keep the chill or the sun off. His clothes seemed to whisper, "He put us on when he was thinking about something else."

The stovepipe hat sort of whistled softly, "I am not a hat at all; I am the little garret roof where he tucks in little thoughts he writes on pieces of paper." The hat, size seven and one-eighth, had a brim one and three-quarters inches wide. The inside band, in which edges of letters and notes were tucked, measured two and three-quarters inches. The cylinder of the stovepipe was twenty-two inches in circumference. This hat was lined with heavy silk and measured, inside, exactly six inches deep. Written in pencil on the imitation satin paper that formed part of the lining was the signature "A. Lincoln, Springfield, Ill.," so that any forgetful person who might take the hat by mistake would know where to bring it back. Also the hatmaker, "George Hall, Springfield, Ill.," had printed his name in the hat so that Lincoln would know where to get another one just like it.

And people tried to guess what was going on under that hat.

Billy Herndon and Henry C. Whitney had watched at close hand what went on under the hat, the working of Lincoln's mind. Herndon said he might ask Lincoln a question and Lincoln would sit in a moody spell without replying. "Meanwhile, I would forget that I had asked him; but to my surprise a few moments later (once it was over fifteen minutes) he would break the silence and give me a satisfactory answer."

Whitney noted a rare accuracy of memory. "Once we all, court and lawyers, except Lincoln, insisted that a witness had sworn so-and-so, and it turned out that Lincoln was correct, and that he recollected better than the united bench and bar." He had not changed since Josh Speed had said he had a quick mind and he answered, "No, you are mistaken; I am slow to learn and slow to forget. My mind is like a piece of steel—very hard to scratch anything on it, and almost impossible after you get it there to rub it out."

Lincoln liked to test his memory. Driving toward Springfield with his boy, Bob, he recalled he had surveyed the neighborhood they were driving through. He stopped the buggy several times, and each time, with a chuckle, asked Bob to go into the woods and at a certain distance find a blazed tree, which he had more than twenty years ago marked as a survey corner. "And he never made a mistake," said Bob. Yet Lincoln was careless about mental culture for show, just as he was careless about manners and dress for show.

Out of little situations in life he constructed little dramas that he carried with him in the portfolio of his memory. He laughed at himself for helping a pig in a gate or lifting a fledgling bird up into a nest, and philosophized with a relentless sort of reasoning that he wasn't moral; he was selfish; his peace of heart would have been disturbed all day if he had not helped the pig or the bird; he was paid in good feeling.

People looked at Lincoln, searching his face, thinking about his words and ways, ready to believe he was a Great Man. Then he would spill over with a joke or tell of some new horseplay of wit or humor in the next county. The barriers tumbled. He was again a strange friend, a neighbor, a friendly stranger, no far-off Great Man at all.

He could be humble in different ways. When he was in Washington as a congressman and his wife wrote letters addressing the envelopes "Hon.," the abbreviation for Honorable, before his name, he wrote to her: "Suppose you do not prefix the 'Hon.' to the address on your letters to me any more—I like the letters very much but I would rather they should not have that upon them."

As a young man he had played marbles with boys; as an older man he spun tops with his own boys, Tad and Willie. When Tad was late bringing home the milk he hunted the boy and came home with Tad on his shoulders and carrying the milk pail himself. Once he chased Tad and brought the boy home, holding the little one at arm's length; the father chuckled at the son's struggle to kick him in the face. Once as he lugged the howling Willie and Tad, a neighbor asked, "Why, Mr. Lincoln, what's the matter?" The answer: "Just what's the matter with the whole world. I've got three walnuts and each wants two."

He had written angry letters filled with hard names and hot arguments. And such letters he had thrown in the stove. He gave the advice that it was healthy to write a hot letter and then burn it.

Bill Herndon felt sorry for Lincoln, and almost moaned at seeing the "woe-struck face" studying the office floor, the gaze shifting out of the window, desolate with melancholy, the barriers up to all who would speak or interrupt. Yet Herndon knew that his melancholy law partner was a steadying force in his own life, something like a big brother or a shrewd uncle. When Billy got blind drunk, as had happened several times, and tarnished the firm's reputation so that others asked Lincoln if he wouldn't be wise to get rid of a tosspot partner, the answer was "No," and in a tone as though it was nobody's business but his own and Billy's.

Herndon had watched Lincoln grow. The phenomenon of Lincoln's growth was for him close to a miracle. Year by year

Lincoln grew; it was a marvel; Billy was the law partner of a hero; he would someday write the life of this hero; it should tell everything; it should tell, even, how the man walked.

He noticed how Lincoln walked; the walk of Lincoln was a sort of poem to him. "When he walked he moved cautiously but firmly; his long arms and giant hands swung down by his side. He walked with even tread, the inner sides of his feet being parallel. He put the whole foot flat down on the ground at once, not landing on the heel." As to general structure, "The whole man, body and mind, worked slowly, as if it needed oiling." And the face of Lincoln? When lights sprang into the gray eyes and fires of emotion flooded out, then, "sometimes it appeared as if Lincoln's soul was fresh from its creator."

Herndon saw that Lincoln could not trust or use what other minds offered him in certain emergencies. "Hence he tore down to their deepest foundations all arrangements of facts, and constructed new ones to govern himself." Lincoln required not merely proof, but demonstration. He would not believe the circle was unsquarable till he had toiled the limit of his strength and found for himself it was so.

Of Lincoln and whisky Herndon would put it down that Lincoln said, "I am entitled to little credit for not drinking, because I hate the stuff; it is unpleasant and always leaves me flabby and undone." As to eating an apple: "He disdained the use of a knife to cut or pare it. Instead he would grasp it around the equatorial part, holding it thus until his thumb and forefinger almost met, sink his teeth into it, and then, unlike the average person, begin eating at the blossom end. When he was done he had eaten his way over and through rather than around and into it. . . . I never saw an apple thus disposed of by any one else." He would tell about the family Lincoln, the boys, Willie and Tad, in the office with their father on a Sunday morning while the mother was at church; the boys pulled books off shelves, upset ink bottles, threw pencils into the spittoon, and their father worked on as though the office were empty.

Time had been required to grow Lincoln. "He has had a slow build-up, a slow development; he has grown up like the forest oak, tough, solid, knotty, gnarled, standing out with power against the storm, and almost defying the lightning." Thus Herndon's hero. One day, that hero had told Herndon, he would come to some terrible end; he didn't know what; it was a fate that lurked ahead. Like the oak he knew what oaks knew, and murmured out of his shadows.

Everybody knew him and nobody knew him. He seemed to have more secrets that he kept to himself than anyone else in Illinois. "The most secretive, shut-mouthed man I ever knew," said his law partner. "The most reticent man I ever saw," said Judge Davis, in whose court Lincoln practiced twelve years. "I doubt whether he ever asked anybody's advice about anything," said his fellow lawyer Leonard Swett.

One man on the Eighth Circuit became a special sort of chum of Lincoln; they spent many gay hours together. Ward Hill Lamon, the Danville law partner of Lincoln, was a young Virginian of dauntless personal courage, bullnecked, melodious, tall, commanding, aristocratic, and, men said, magnificent in the amount of whisky he could carry. As the years had passed a strange bond of loyalty between the two men grew stronger and was known to other men. "Sing me a little song," was Lincoln's word to Lamon, who brought out a banjo and struck up some nonsensical and rapid staccato such as "Cousin Sally Downard," or "I'll bet my money on de bobtail nag."

The close friendship of Lincoln and Lamon was talked about among the other lawyers. Lamon was considered a second-rate lawyer, and in politics and on the slavery question leaning toward the southern Illinois point of view. He was nineteen years younger than Lincoln. Yet for driving away a spell of melancholy, probably the best friend of Lincoln was this man Lamon, whom he called Hill. Whether it was music or a roistering gaiety he wanted for a dark mood, he treasured and kept the companionship of the reckless and romantic Hill.

The name of the man had come to stand for what he was, plus beliefs and conjectures. Lincoln was spoken of as a "politician" in the sense that politics is a trade of cunning, ambitious, devious men. He himself once had told the Illinois legislature that politicians are a lower breed, more often tricky than honest. He chose a few issues on which to explain his mind fully. Some of his reticences were not evasions but retirements to cloisters of silence. Questions of life and destiny shook him close to prayers and tears in his own hidden corners and byways.

Once when A. J. Grover at Ottawa was in danger of going to jail for helping a runaway slave, he and Lincoln sat and talked over the case. The law was wrong in taking a man's liberty away without trial by jury, Grover told Lincoln, "not only unconstitutional but inhuman." And Lincoln, with his face alive and mournful, brandishing his long right arm, brought it down on his knee, saying, "Oh, it is ungodly! It is ungodly! But it is the law of the land, and we must obey it as we find it."

To which Grover said, "Mr. Lincoln, we propose to elect you President. How would you look taking an oath to support what you declare is an ungodly Constitution, and asking God to help you?"

It was a stinger for Lincoln; his head sloped forward; he ran his fingers through his hair; he dropped into a sad and desperate mood, and came out of it placing his hand on Grover's knee, and saying in a mournfully quizzical manner, "Grover, it's no use to be always looking up these hard spots."

There was a word: democracy. Tongues of politics played with it. Lincoln had a slant at it. "As I would not be a *slave*, so I would not be a *master*. This expresses my idea of democracy. Whatever differs from this, to the extent of the difference, is no democracy."

ONE OF THE LAW STUDENTS in the Lincoln & Herndon office noticed that the junior and senior partners had different ways toward women who came into the office. When a woman was through talking with Herndon about her case, she usually left Herndon at the desk and went to the door alone and stepped out. If she was a good-looking woman, Herndon would step to the door with her and perhaps pat her on the arm or shoulder in bidding her good day, and close the door after her. With women callers who came to see Lincoln the action was different, as this law student observed, for no matter how homely and battered the woman might be, after the conference was ended, Lincoln would step to the door with her, bid good day, and close the door. And no matter what their looks he did not risk a pat on arm or shoulder.

Herndon believed Lincoln cloaked his ways with women by a rare and fine code. "Mr. Lincoln had a strong, if not terrible passion for women," wrote Herndon. "He could hardly keep his hands off a woman, and yet, much to his credit, he lived a pure and virtuous life. . . . I have seen Lincoln tempted and I have seen him reject the approach of woman!"

A woman charged with keeping a house of ill fame had the firm of Lincoln & Herndon for lawyers; they asked for a change of venue; and Lincoln drove across the prairies from one town to another with the madam of the house and her girls. After the trial the madam was asked about Lincoln's talk with her. Yes, he told stories, and they were nearly all funny. Yes, but were the stories proper or improper, so to speak? Well—the madam hesitated—they were funny . . . she and all the girls laughed . . . but coming to think it over she believed the stories could have been told "with safety in the presence of ladies anywhere." Then she added, without being asked, and as though it ought to be part of the story, "But that is more than I can say for Bill Herndon."

About women in general the lawyers of the Eighth Circuit had often joked Lincoln. But in only one case had they ever teased him about being too much in the company of one particular woman. She was a singer, Lois Newhall, of the Newhall Family, a concert troupe who gave programs in churches and town-hall lyceum courses. Though not especially attractive in looks, she was considered a good singer; she had met Lincoln and they took a liking for each other. From the concert platform she would pick him out in the audience and smile to him.

Whitney noticed that if the Newhall Family was to perform in a town where the Eighth Circuit lawyers had arrived, Lincoln would invariably arrange his affairs so that he could be on hand to attend the entertainment. "To most of us," said Whitney, "the thing seemed strange until finally the real reason developed. It was Lincoln's predilection for a woman."

Judge Davis, the lawyer Leonard Swett, and others close to Lincoln saw the affair drifting along to a point where they felt it was somewhat their affair too. With sober faces they reminded him of his duty as a married man. His rejoinder was easy: "Don't trouble yourselves, boys, there's no danger. She's actually the only woman in the world, outside of my wife, who ever dared to pay me a compliment, and if the poor thing is attracted to my handsome face and figure it seems to me you homely fellows are the last people on earth who ought to complain."

One evening at the Macon House in Decatur, the Eighth Circuit lawyers were having a social hour with the Newhall Family, the parents, two sisters, a brother, and a brother-in-law. The singing and fun reached a point where the lawyers tried to get Lincoln to sing for the company. One lawyer said, "Why, over on the Sangamon Abe has a great reputation as a singer. It is quite a common thing over there to invite him to farm auctions and have him start off the sale of stock with a good song." Bashful, Lincoln refused; he never had been a singer in his life, he said. Then, when the others still teased, he showed a threatening face to the lawyers, turned on his heel, and told the company it was late and he was going to bed. Starting upstairs, he had to pass Lois Newhall, sitting at a melodeon; she looked up and said, "Mr. Lincoln, if you have a song that you can sing, I know that I can play the accompaniment.... I can follow you even if I am not familiar with it."

"Why, Miss Newhall"—he laughed, still bashful—"I never sang in my life; and those fellows know it. They are simply trying to make fun of me." He paused; some sort of disappointment crossed her face; and he said, "But ... inasmuch as you and your sister have ... entertained us so generously, I shall try to return the favor.... I can't produce music, but if you will be patient and brave enough to endure it, I will repeat ... several stanzas of a poem of which I am particularly fond."

Then he stepped to the doorway leading from the hotel parlor to the stairway; and leaning against the casing, half closing his eyes, he brought out from the attic of his heart that quaint, faded poem, "Oh, Why Should the Spirit of Mortal Be Proud?" The moods of joking and teasing came to an end.

Lois told her sister afterward that it was all she could do to keep back the tears as that long shadowy riddle of a man wandered through the sorrowful lines. *"A flash of the lightning—a break of the wave— He passeth from life to his rest in the grave."* As he was about to go upstairs, she asked him who wrote the poem. "My dear Miss Newhall, I am ashamed to say that I do not know. But if you really like it, I will write it off for you to-night . . . and leave a copy on the table so that you may have it . . . when you sit down to breakfast."

In the dusk of dawn the next morning, Lois Newhall came down to the hotel dining room and was eating a winter break-fast by candlelight, as she had done many times before. Of this particular breakfast, she said at a later time, "I was eating pan-cakes . . . when I became aware that someone was behind and bending over me. A big hand took hold of my left hand, cover-ing it on the table, and with his right hand . . . he laid down a sheet of paper covered with writing, in front of my plate. I realized it was Mr. Lincoln. He told me that he was due to leave town in a few minutes, and as he moved away, he looked back, waved his hand, exclaiming, 'Good-by, my dear!' and passed through the door. It was the last time I ever saw him."

FRANCES AFFONSA, a black-eyed Portuguese woman who used to do the family washing for the Lincolns, had stayed on and become the regular cook. Frances was a good woman and a good cook. When Frances was once asked how she got along with Mrs. Lincoln, she answered, "If I please Mis' Lincum, she like me, she treat me very well; and she very hard to please, but I please her." And that would about hit off what the husband in the house had learned about getting along with his wife. If he pleased her, she liked him, she treated him very well. And often she was very hard to please, but he pleased her.

Frances Affonsa heard the husband and wife exchange words one day. As she told it, what they said was:

MRS. LINCOLN: You're a very smart man, Mr. Lincoln.
MR. LINCOLN: Well, what have I done now?
MRS. L.: Why, you have put your coat on top of my fresh starched gowns.
MR. L.: Never mind, don't be cross. I'll take my coat away and hang your gowns over it.

As the years had passed Abraham Lincoln and Mary Todd had learned to be more accommodating to each other, though each was so independent and their personalities were so different on important matters that often the marriage ship seemed to be in the troughs. There was gossip in the town. Lincoln had been seen splitting wood at one o'clock in the morning. Hadn't he been turned out of his own house and come home when the rest of the family was in bed, to get his own supper alone in peace?

Herndon told of his partner coming to the office sometimes at seven o'clock in the morning when the usual hour for him to arrive was nine o'clock. Or of Lincoln at noon, having brought to the office a package of grocery crackers and cheese, sitting alone eating. Mrs. Lincoln and Herndon hated each other; they never got along. His first compliment to her, that she danced with the grace of a serpent, had been a slip from the code by which she demanded to be treated. While Herndon was careless as to where he spat, she was not merely scrupulously neat and immaculate; she was among the most ambitious women in Springfield in the matter of style and fashion. It was only natural there should be a clash of these two temperaments.

Mrs. Lincoln knew Herndon as an abolitionist hothead; she knew or had sure intuitions about his wanting to raise cash for rifles to send to Kansas for open combat with proslavery forces. And she felt the radical, unsteady Herndon was a menace to all her dreams of her husband advancing. She knew of such affairs as Herndon getting drunk with two other men and breaking a windowpane that her husband had to hustle the money for so that the sheriff wouldn't lock up his law partner. She didn't like it that her husband had a partner who was too easy about women and whisky, reckless with money, and occasionally touching Lincoln for loans. She carried suspicions and nursed misgivings about this swaggering upstart, radical in politics, transcendentalist in philosophy, antichurch.

At parties, balls, social gatherings, she moved, vital, sparkling, often needlessly insinuating or directly and swiftly insolent. If the music was bad, what was the need of her making unkind remarks about the orchestra? Chills, headaches, creepers of fear came at her; misunderstandings rose in waves so often around her; she was alone, so all alone, so like a child thrust into the Wrong Room.

At such gatherings, she trod the mazy waltzes in crinoline gowns, the curves of the hoopskirts shading down the plump curves of her physical figure as if fashion were cooperating to set off her lines to advantage. With middle age coming on she had spoken less often, in society, of the certainty of her husband going to the White House eventually. But there were those who recollected her replying to the remark that Mr. Lincoln seemed to be a great favorite: "Yes, he is a great favorite everywhere. He is to be President of the United States some day. Look at him! Doesn't he look as if he would make a magnificent President?" Once when talk had turned to a comparison of Lincoln and Douglas, she had said, "Mr. Lincoln may not be as handsome a figure, but people are perhaps not aware that his heart is as large as his arms are long."

Mary Todd and Abe Lincoln had good times together. How often these good times shone for them, when the ship sailed an even moonlit sea, only they two could tell. They were intense and special individuals. Between flare-ups and clashes, between collisions and regrets, the spirit of accommodation rose and offered a way out. Perhaps accommodation was a finer and surer word than Love, less soiled with the lies of hypocrites. He was ten years older than she, with a toiling talent for conciliatory adjustment, a strict genius in the decisions of human accommodation. So he led.

Hours of pleasant reconciliations were in Whitney's mind when he said, "Lincoln loved his wife—I had many reasons to know this." They had good times together, days when she made herself pretty for him, wanting him, and he willing.

She wrote to her sister in the autumn of 1857: "The summer has strangely and rapidly passed away. Some portion of it was spent most pleasantly in traveling East. We visited Niagara, Canada, New York and other points of interest."

She could pronounce on her husband such fine judgments as: "He never joined a church, but still he was a religious man. But it was a kind of poetry in his nature, and he never was a technical Christian."

Much of the gossip about the Lincoln house ran on the theory that in every house there is either a masterman or a henpecked husband, either a domineering woman or a doormat. Some of the gossip rested on solid foundations of fact. Mrs. Lincoln had once discharged, on short notice and with sharp words, a girl in her employ. The uncle of the girl came to ask about it. Mrs. Lincoln met him at the door, blazing, gesticulating, and sent him away with his ears burning. He hunted up Lincoln, finding him in a store, discussing the news of the day with fellow citizens. He stepped into the store, with his ears still burning, and called for Lincoln, who came and listened. When the man had finished telling his grievance, Lincoln said he was sorry, he wanted to be reasonable and fair, but he would ask a question; it amounted to asking, "If I have had to stand this every day for fifteen years, don't you think you can stand it a few minutes one day?" The uncle would have laughed if Lincoln had laughed. But Lincoln's face was mournful, slack, worn. The uncle apologized. The two men parted as friends.

As this scandalous morsel of gossip traveled, the identity of the abused man who came to Lincoln took many forms. It was the iceman who had a spat on the back doorstep of the Lincoln house; or it was a groceryman who was accused of delivering decayed tomatoes. The incident, as it traveled, became a piece of folklore. Men and their wives told it with relish. They liked the Lincolns better for it; it was common and human.

During six months of the year Lincoln was off practicing law on the Eighth Circuit. Other lawyers, starting home at the weekends to spend Sunday with their families, noticed that Lincoln didn't join them; they quietly agreed that the homelife of Lincoln was not all that Lincoln would wish it. Milton Hay, a lawyer with an office on the same floor as Lincoln, used to philosophize that if Lincoln's homelife hadn't sent him out over the state, with free spare hours to think for himself and to build up circles of political friends, Lincoln wouldn't have become the powerful political manipulator that he was in the new controlling party of the Northwest.

Though the tales gathered and spread, Mary Todd Lincoln was proud of her husband and believed he had a genius that would take him farther than any man in Illinois. She joked about his failings and defended his peculiarities. She would say, "He is of no account when he is at home. He never does anything except to warm himself and read. He . . . is the most useless, good-for-nothing man on earth." But if somebody else had said Lincoln was useless, good for nothing, "I would have scratched his eyes out," she flashed. "But really, he is so absorbed with his law, his anecdotes, his reading, and what not, that he is of little use at home." And could one suppose that he never gave his wife any money? "Money!" was Mrs. Lincoln's exclamation. "He never gives me any money—he leaves his pocketbook where I can take what I want."

She was often anxious about her boys, had mistaken fears about their safety or health, exaggerated evils that might befall them. She gave parties for them and wrote with her own pen, in a smooth and even script, gracious invitations.

Young Henry B. Rankin, the sober, scrupulous, religious-minded law student, formed his impressions of the ups and downs in the Lincoln household. As far as he could figure it out nobody was to blame. Mary Todd had married a genius who made demands; when he wanted to work, to isolate himself with every brain cell operating, it was no time for interruptions or errands. For this brooding man she was wife, housekeeper, and counselor insofar as he permitted. She watched his habits of "browsing around" in the pantry, and of skipping meals, and tried to bring him to regular eating habits. She had kept house eighteen years before, too poor for a hired girl; they burned wood then; now they had a coal cookstove with four lids and a reservoir to warm rainwater. She did the shopping and had chosen the beautiful, strong black-walnut cradle, into which she had put four boy babies; one of those babies had died.

Fourteen years after her marriage she was keeping up her readings in the French language. She was not satisfied with a translation of a speech by Victor Hugo on capital punishment published in the *Southern Literary Messenger*. She insisted on getting a copy of the speech in French. In bidding good night to a guest at their home on one occasion, Mrs. Lincoln stepped out on the front porch. The night sky was a dome of clear stars.

She looked up and spoke of what a wonderful display it was; she named several planets and pointed to constellations, and explained that certain stars are suns far larger than our sun, and the center of universes immensely larger than ours. Her interest in the stars matched that of Lincoln himself.

She had moved with him from lean years to the comforts of the well-to-do middle class, and knew of the money cost in 1858 when he had dropped nearly all law cases for months and paid his way at hotels and in 4200 miles of travel, writing in one letter after the campaign closed: "I am absolutely without money now for even household purposes." With their rising income and his taking his place as the outstanding leader of his party, Mary Lincoln enjoyed giving parties occasionally for two or three hundred people, with, as one guest noted, a table "famed for the excellence of many rare Kentucky dishes, and in season, loaded with venison, wild turkeys, prairie chickens, quail," and "every guest perfectly at ease."

Chapter 28

IN MARCH OF 1860, Lincoln was in Chicago on the so-called Sandbar case, defending the title of William Jones and Sylvester Marsh as owners of land at the mouth of the Chicago River. The lawyers on both sides, and the judge, were dinner guests one evening, and finished with a toast, "May Illinois furnish the next President of the United States," to which all Lincoln Republicans and Douglas Democrats present drank heartily.

The mid-May nominating conventions were approaching, and Lincoln-Douglas debate books were selling briskly that spring at fifty cents in paper or one dollar clothbound. The possibility that both Lincoln and Douglas might be presidential candidates had prompted Republican leaders in Ohio, some weeks earlier, to suggest that reprints of the great debates be published "in permanent form." Lincoln had agreed, and had assembled reprints of the debates for this purpose, using his scrapbook of the speech texts clipped from the Chicago newspapers. He urged that they be presented "without any comment whatever." This book held the awesome heave and surge of the slavery issue and its companion, the dark threat of the Union dissolved; that it would go to an immense audience of readers gave Lincoln a quiet pride; it was the first book for which he had furnished a manuscript, and it eventually went into four editions.

Pamphlet reprints of Lincoln's Cooper Union speech, selling at one cent a copy, were also circulating widely. And there was a growing legend spreading of the tall homely man who was log-cabin-born and had been flatboatman and rail splitter, struggling on to where his speech and thought were read nationwide. All this had created an aura about Lincoln that, in the few weeks before the Republican convention, was to be the more effective because it was no forced growth. It had a way of dawning on men, "Why, yes, come to think of it, why not Lincoln? The more you look at him the more he is the man."

He had in 1859 traveled four thousand miles to make twenty-three Republican speeches. He had covered more ground over America than any others of his party mentioned for President; born in Kentucky, he had traversed the Mississippi River in a flatboat to New Orleans, had lived in the national capital, had met audiences over all the Midwest, in New York City, and across New England. He had purposely in public hidden his hopes and strengths as a candidate, following the advice the Chicago editor Long John Wentworth had once given him: "Look out for *prominence*. When it is ascertained that none of the prominent candidates can be nominated then ought to be your time."

The other Republican candidates were indeed prominent. William H. Seward, eight years older than Lincoln, was a New Yorker of Welsh-Irish stock, slim, stooped, white-haired, "a subtle, quick man, rejoicing in power." His friend and manager, Thurlow Weed, publisher of the Albany *Evening Journal*, ran a Seward publicity bureau, was in touch with large special interests, and made free use of money in promoting Seward. When governor of New York, Seward had brought into effect laws requiring jury trial for fugitive slaves, with defense counsel fees paid by the state. His reply to Webster in the U. S. Senate that "there is *a higher law* than the Constitution, which regulates our authority" and his Irrepressible Conflict speech had caused even some of his own advisers to tell him he was too radical. He had retreated into explanations, but a stigma hung on him.

Handsome, portly, overdignified Salmon P. Chase of Ohio, antislavery, radical, had twice been governor and served a term as U. S. senator; he would get delegates from Ohio and elsewhere but didn't seem formidable. Judge Edward Bates of Missouri would have that state's delegates and a scattered following from elsewhere. John McLean, an Ohio Democrat, appointed a Supreme Court Justice by President Jackson, was also in the running, his dissenting opinion in the Dred Scott case in his favor. But he was seventy-five, and his health was failing.

Lincoln himself sized up the situation for an Ohio delegate. Seward, he wrote, "is the very best candidate we could have for the North of Illinois, and the very *worst* for the South of it." With Chase of Ohio it would be likewise in Illinois. Bates of Missouri would be the best candidate for the south of Illinois and the worst for the north. "I am not the fittest person to answer the questions you ask [about candidates]. When not a very great man begins to be mentioned for a very great position, his head is very likely to be a little turned." With Senator Trumbull he could be easier in speech. "As you request, I will be entirely frank. The taste *is* in my mouth a little." He did honestly have some hankerings for the presidency. "And this, no doubt, disqualifies me, to some extent, to form correct opinions."

To an Indiana delegate and others, he wrote they could see his friends Jesse K. Dubois of Springfield and Judge David Davis, who would be in Chicago on May 12 "ready to confer with friends from other States."

He wrote to another Ohio delegate, expressing thanks for confidence, and pointing to his one biggest advantage as a candidate: "If I have any chance, it consists mainly in the fact that the whole opposition would vote for me, if nominated. (I don't mean to include the pro-slavery opposition of the South, of course.) My name is new in the field, and I suppose I am not the first choice of a very great many." And in two sentences there was a shading of color, an indication of the philosophy that often governed Lincoln in tight places. He wrote: "Our policy, then, is to give no offence to others—leave them in a mood to come to us, if they shall be compelled to give up their first love. This, too, is dealing justly with all, and leaving us in a mood to support heartily whoever shall be nominated."

THE ILLINOIS STATE Republican convention was held at Decatur on May 9. Into it came John Hanks carrying two fence rails with flags and streamers tied to them, and the inscription, "Abraham Lincoln, the Rail Candidate for President in 1860: Two rails from a lot of 3,000 made in 1830 by Thos. Hanks and Abe Lincoln—whose father was the first pioneer of Macon County." Shouts followed: "Lincoln! Lincoln! Speech!"

A committee escorted him to the platform. He thanked them with a sober face. Cheers: "Three times three for Honest Abe, our next President." Again came John Hanks and a committee with fence rails, shouting, "Identify your work." "I cannot say that I split these rails," and to the committee, "Where did you get the rails?" "At the farm you improved down on the Sangamon." "Well, that was a long time ago. It is possible I may have split these rails, but I cannot identify them." Shouts from the convention: "Identify your work!"

The sober face of the candidate was loosening into a smile. "What kind of timber are they?" he asked, getting the swing of the fun. "Honey locust and black walnut." "Well, that is lasting timber," and scrutinizing the rails, "It may be that I split these rails," and scrutinizing further, "Well, boys, I can only say that I have split a great many better-looking ones."

Thus the Rail Candidate was brought forth, and the nickname of "Rail Splitter." The idea came from Richard Oglesby, a Decatur lawyer, Kentucky-raised, a plain and witty man, who shared Lincoln's belief in the people. He had hunted out John Hanks and planned the dramatization of Lincoln as "the Rail Splitter."

It was more important that the convention instructed its delegates to the Chicago convention to vote as a unit for Lincoln; seven of the twenty-two delegates personally preferred Seward, and there were peculiar undercurrents against Lincoln. Orville H. Browning, for instance, who had tried cases with

Lincoln and dined often at the Lincoln home, was for Bates for President. Oglesby and other delegates had walked with Lincoln out to a quiet place on a railroad track where they sat down and talked. Oglesby was in favor of cutting off Browning from the list of delegates to the Chicago national convention. Lincoln advised that this would make an enemy of Browning and he might then do more mischief than if he were sent to Chicago as a member of a delegation instructed to vote as a unit for Lincoln's nomination. "Lincoln sat on one of the railroad rails and his legs nearly reached clean across to the other rail," said Oglesby, telling later about the railroad-track conference that guided the Decatur convention.

Only two weeks earlier, the national Democratic convention had met in Charleston, South Carolina, and the Douglas delegates, holding a majority control, but lacking the necessary two-thirds to nominate their man for President, had split the party. Two separate wings of it were planning conventions in June; the powerful political body that had controlled the government practically thirty years was staggering. The answers of Douglas to Lincoln in the Freeport debate had shown him to be a straddler; his break with the Buchanan Administration had also disturbed Southerners; the trust of the South in him, once so loyal, was gone.

William Lowndes Yancey of Alabama, tall, slender, with long black hair, spoke in a soft, musical voice for the minority, the first time in generations of men that the South was in a minority and without the votes to name the Democratic candidate for President. Yancey pronounced a swan song. "We came here with one great purpose, to save our constitutional rights. We are in the minority. . . . In the progress of civilization, the Northwest has grown up from an infant in swaddling-clothes into the free proportions of a giant people."

Yancey was dealing with the fact. The Northwest had grown up; Douglas had captured it politically, and had swung its power as a big stick, calling for a platform pledge to abide by the Dred Scott decision or any future decision of the Supreme Court on the rights of property in the states or territories.

"The proposition you make," said Yancey, "will bankrupt us

of the South. Ours is the property invaded—ours the interests at stake. The honor of our children, the honor of our females, the lives of our men, all rest upon you."

And little Alexander Stephens, "the little pale star from Georgia," who had served with Lincoln in Congress, blazed out, in a talk with a friend: "Men will be cutting one another's throats in a little while. In twelve months we shall be in a war, the bloodiest in history." But why civil war, even if a Republican President were elected? "Because," murmured the little pale star, "there are not virtue and patriotism and sense enough left in the country to avoid it."

In the Senate at Washington, Jefferson Davis and Stephen A. Douglas continued the Democratic clash. "I would sooner have an honest man on any sort of a rickety platform than to have a man I did not trust on the best platform which could be made," said Davis, drawing from Douglas the question, "Why did you not tell us in the beginning that the whole fight was against the man and not upon the platform?"

Senator Seward of New York gazed on what was happening and felt satisfied. He started for his home in Auburn, New York, to write his letter accepting the Republican nomination for President. Would he not have more delegates to start with than any other candidate, and was not there a trend for him even in the supposedly pro-Lincoln Illinois and Indiana delegations?

In Illinois, delegates were outfitting with silk hats and broadcloth suits, to go to the Chicago convention on May 16. Lincoln wrote to Solomon Sturges, the Chicago banker, thanks for the proffered hospitality during the convention. He had decided to stay home. "I am a little too much a candidate to stay home and not quite enough a candidate to go."

THE WEST HAD GROWN powerful, and this fact had operated to give Chicago the national convention of the Republican party. Lincoln's backers had made a special point of getting the convention for Chicago. But their main argument was not that Chicago was a garden city and a center of art and traditions. They challenged the national committee, saying, "Listen to us or run a chance of losing the West."

Chicago was in 1860 a city of 110,000 people, handling hogs, cattle, corn, farming machinery, and the associated finance, transportation, and trade; the depot, crossroads, and point of exchange for thousand-mile prairies. Lifted over the town as memorials and hopes were the tall, overshadowing grain elevators at the railroad yards and the river wharves. And not only bread for man's stomach, but also ideas and opinions for his mind, radiated outward from Chicago. McCormick was shipping out more than fifty thousand reapers a year. Medill was saying, "Chicago is the pet Republican city of the Union, the point from which radiate opinions which more or less influence six states." In and out of Chicago ran fifteen railways with a hundred and fifty railroad trains a day; and on May 16 of 1860 they were to bring forty thousand strangers and five hundred delegates to the Republican national convention.

At the corner of Lake and Market streets the Sauganash Hotel had been torn down, and a lumber shack, to hold ten thousand people, had been put up and named the Wigwam. The big barnlike interior had been made gay with flags, bunting, and streamers; and when it was opened with a mass meeting, it appeared, said the Chicago *Journal*, "large with golden promise of a glorious harvest of truth."

At the Richmond House, Thurlow Weed set up Seward headquarters, called in various state delegations, and addressed them with pleasant arguments. "We think we have in Mr. Seward just the qualities the country will need. He is known by us all as a statesman. . . . We expect to nominate him on the first ballot, and to go before the country full of courage and confidence." Similarly, Judge David Davis set up Lincoln headquarters at Chicago's Tremont House, taking over the entire third floor, paying a rental of $300 to provide rooms for his staff of Lincoln hustlers, pleaders, and schemers.

In the parlor of the Lincoln headquarters were cigars and wine, porter, brandy, whisky, for any delegate or important guest; here were held private talks, and speeches were given to groups. Medill and Ray of the *Tribune* were on hand with ideas and their influence. Others there included Jesse Fell, who could mix with and try to influence the Pennsylvania delegates;

Norman Judd, as a railroad lawyer, who could make promises to the powerful interests who wanted a Pacific railway; Leonard· Swett, Lincoln's lawyer friend who, as a young Maine man, might break, as he did, the Seward unity of Maine's delegates; Richard J. Oglesby, as a Whig Free-Soiler raised in Kentucky, who was doing his best with his hearty jargon among the Kentucky and Missouri delegates. Lincoln's former law partner, Judge Stephen T. Logan, and William Herndon and Ward Hill Lamon were also there; all of them knew Lincoln from close association, could testify where needed in personal talk with doubtful delegates.

Andrew G. Curtin of Pennsylvania and Henry S. Lane of Indiana were each running for governor and were each solemnly positive that their states would be lost if Seward were nominated. A long roll could be called of delegates telling others that Seward couldn't carry the doubtful states of Pennsylvania, New Jersey, Indiana, and Illinois. Still, Seward victory was in the air; champagne fizzed at the Richmond House. Straw votes on all incoming trains had given Seward overwhelming majorities. Six hundred friends, delegates, and henchmen marched and cheered for Seward, their band playing, "Oh, Isn't He a Darling!" Michigan, Wisconsin, and Minnesota were a unit for him; the New York, Massachusetts, and California delegations were pledged to give their totals to him. And Seward sat in his home in Auburn, New York, ready to send a message of acceptance.

The day before the convention opened, May 15, Davis and Dubois wired Lincoln: "We are quiet but moving heaven & Earth. Nothing will beat us but old fogy politicians." The next day Judd's message was: "Dont be frightened. Keep cool. Things is working."

A message from Lincoln was carried to Chicago by Edward L. Baker, editor of the Springfield *Journal;* it was a copy of a newspaper with Seward speeches, with Lincoln's marginal notes, "I agree with Seward's 'Irrepressible Conflict,' but I do not endorse his 'Higher Law' doctrine," and Lincoln underlined words, "Make no contracts that will bind me." Why Lincoln should send such a cryptic message to old companions who were toiling fearfully to make him President was anybody's guess.

Chapter 29

THE CONVENTION was called to order on May 16. The crowd outside the Wigwam was two and three times the size of the one inside; relays of orators made speeches. Processions with brass bands marched, cheering candidates.

On the afternoon of May 17, the platform was adopted in a sweep of yells and cheers. But it left out mention of the Declaration of Independence, and old Joshua R. Giddings, the antislavery war-horse, arose and said it was time to walk out of the Republican party. The convention was shamed; the principle of the equality of men was written in and Giddings stayed on.

The Seward men then wanted to ballot on candidates; a motion to that effect was made but the chair said "the tally-sheets had not been prepared," and on a quick motion to adjourn and a light unrecorded vote the chairman declared the convention adjourned. The moment was fateful; Seward men believed they could have nominated their man that afternoon.

The main Lincoln backers worked all night. They predicted that the Republicans were beaten at the start if Seward headed the ticket; they appealed to antislavery men who believed Seward to be a man of much intellect and little faith, with none of the "mystic simplicity" of Lincoln. At Lincoln headquarters, Davis, Dubois, Swett, Logan, Oglesby, and others struggled to nail down the Pennsylvania and Indiana delegations. Ray of the *Tribune* came to his chief, Medill. "We are going to have Indiana for Old Abe, sure." "How did you get it?" asked Medill. "By the Lord, we promised them everything they asked."

Indiana was nailed down; Caleb B. Smith was to be Secretary of the Interior and William P. Dole, Commissioner of Indian Affairs; Indiana would vote a solid block for Lincoln on the first ballot. The next prospect was Pennsylvania, with its block of fifty-four delegates wearing white hats; they would vote for Simon Cameron, complimenting a favorite son, on the first ballot, and then were willing to go elsewhere.

Judge Davis dickered with them; Dubois telegraphed Lincoln

the Cameron delegates could be had if Cameron was promised the Treasury Department. Lincoln wired back, "I authorize no bargains and will be bound by none." What happened next among Lincoln's convention managers was told by Whitney: "The bluff Dubois said, 'Damn Lincoln!' The polished Swett said, 'I am very sure if Lincoln was aware of the necessities—' The critical Logan expectorated. 'The main difficulty with Lincoln is—' Herndon ventured, 'Now, friend, I'll answer that.' But Davis cut the Gordian knot by brushing all aside with, 'Lincoln ain't here . . . so we will go ahead, as if we hadn't heard from him, and he must ratify it.'"

In that mood they went to the room of the Pennsylvania managers. When they were through they came down to the lobby of the Tremont House, where Joe Medill was waiting. Medill had been thinking about a remark of Lincoln's that Pennsylvania would be important in the convention. As he saw three-hundred-pound Judge Davis come heaving and puffing down the stairs about midnight, he stepped up to the judge and, as he told it later, asked what Pennsylvania was going to do. Judge Davis replied, "Damned if we haven't got them." "How did you get them?" "By paying their price."

And so, with three state delegations solid, and with odd votes from Ohio and other states, the Lincoln men waited for the balloting, seeing to it, however, that the convention seating committee carefully sandwiched the Pennsylvania delegation between Illinois and Indiana.

Ward Hill Lamon had been to the printers of seat tickets to the convention hall. And a staff of young men kept busy nearly a whole night signing names of convention officers to seat tickets so that the next day the Lincoln bucks could jam the hall and leave no room for the Seward shouters. Hour on hour the bulk of the forty thousand strangers in Chicago kept up a shouting and a tumult for Lincoln, for Old Abe, for the Rail Candidate. Judd had fixed it with the railroads so that any shouter who wished to come could set foot in Chicago at a low excursion rate. Men illuminated with moral fire, and also men red-eyed with whisky, yelled and pranced and cut capers and vociferated for Lincoln, swarming around the ramshackle convention hall in an immense mob, the like of which had never before been seen in the assemblages of American politics.

On the first two days of the convention the Seward men had been allowed by the Chicago managers to have free run of the floor. But on May 18, sunrise saw thousands milling about the Wigwam doors. They were the Lincoln shouters, recruited for their lung power and instructed to cut loose every time their leader, seated on the platform, took out his handkerchief, and to keep up till he put it away. They filled all seats and standing room; hundreds of New York hurrah boys couldn't squeeze in.

Nomination speeches were in single sentences. Judd said, "I desire, on behalf of the delegation from Illinois, to put in nomination, as a candidate for President of the United States, Abraham Lincoln, of Illinois." Here the handkerchief came out, and the uproar was enormous. "Five thousand people leaped to their seats," said Swett. "The wild yell made vesper breathings of all that had preceded. A thousand steam whistles, ten acres of hotel gongs, a tribe of Comanches might have mingled in the scene unnoticed."

Seward had $173\frac{1}{2}$ votes, Lincoln 102, and others the remainder on the first ballot. On the second ballot, Lincoln jumped to 181 as against Seward's $184\frac{1}{2}$. On the third, of the 465 votes Lincoln swept $231\frac{1}{2}$ while Seward dropped to 180.

Medill of the *Tribune* whispered to Cartter of Ohio, "If you can throw the Ohio delegation for Lincoln, Chase can have anything he wants." "H-how d'-d'ye know?" stuttered Cartter, Medill answering, "I know, and you know I wouldn't promise if I didn't know."

Cartter called for a change of four votes from his state to the Rail Candidate. Other delegates stood up to announce changes of votes to Lincoln. As the tellers footed up the totals, and the chairman waited for the figures, the chatter of ten thousand people stopped, the fluttering of ladies' fans ended, the scratching of pencils and the clicking of the telegraph dot-dash dot-dot dash-dot-dash could be heard.

The chairman spoke. Of 465 votes, 364 were cast for the candidate highest, and, "Abraham Lincoln, of Illinois, is selected as your candidate for President of the United States."

Chairmen of state delegations arose and made the nomination unanimous. The terrific emotional spree was over. Strong men hugged each other, wept, and laughed. Judge Logan stood on a table brandishing his arms and yelling; he raised his new silk hat and brought it down on somebody's head, smashing it flat.

Inside and outside the Wigwam it was a wild noon hour: hats, handkerchiefs, umbrellas in the air, brass bands blaring; cannon explosions on the roof getting answers from city bells, riverboat and railroad whistles. A Minnesota delegate had tried to voice the feelings of the Seward men, but the stenographic reporters could not catch his words. They wrote, "The audience here became impatient and vociferous in their calls to proceed to business and the speaker could proceed no further."

Hannibal Hamlin, the Maine senator, a former Democrat, was nominated for Vice-President, and thanks were voted to the convention chairman, George Ashmun of Massachusetts. He made a closing speech saying that the Republican party was headed for victory; and he struck the gavel for adjournment. Thurlow Weed pressed the temples of his forehead to hold back tears. Horace Greeley wrote a letter telling a friend it was a fearful week he hoped never to see repeated.

In Albany, New York, a son of Senator Seward was working in the office of Weed's paper, the *Evening Journal*. He read a telegram up a tube to a printing-room foreman, "Abraham Lincoln is nominated for President on the third ballot." The foreman was hesitating; his voice spluttered back, "S-a-y, what damn name was that you said was nominated for President?"

ON THE FRIDAY MORNING of the convention, May 18, Lincoln had walked from home, as usual, to the public square. At Chatterton's jewelry store he turned into a stairway and went up to the office of James C. Conkling, the lawyer, who had just returned by night train from Chicago. With his head on a buggy cushion and his feet over the end of a settee, he listened and quizzed Conkling, and left saying, "Well, Conkling, I believe I will go back to my office and practice law."

Then he met E. L. Baker of the *Journal*, who had also arrived by night train from Chicago, after delivering to Herndon the message from Lincoln; Lincoln and Baker went to Carmody's ball alley for a game; the alley was full. Then, as Baker told it, they went to a saloon to play a game of billiards, but some morning billiard players had already taken the table. "We each drank a glass of beer, and then went to the *Journal* office expecting to hear the result of the convention balloting; we waited awhile; nothing came; and we parted; I went to dinner."

Then shortly after twelve o'clock a messenger boy handed Lincoln a telegram, addressed "Abe," reading: "We did it. Glory to God!" It was from Nathan Knapp. A little flurry of telegrams followed, congratulations from Fell, Swett, Judd, Dubois. Lincoln told the crowd at the *Journal* office he was going home to tell his wife the news. One heard him say, "There is a lady over yonder on Eighth Street who is deeply interested in this news; I will carry it to her."

Boxes, kindling wood, and brushwood went up in bonfire smoke in the Sangamon River country that Friday night. A brass band and a crowd came to Lincoln's house, surged to the front porch, and asked for a speech. He told them the honor of the nomination was not for him personally but as the representative of a cause, and wished that his house were big enough so that he could ask them all to come inside. Shouts and yells of hurrah parties kept up till the gray dawn of the morning after.

Judge David Davis answered a question on what the wild week had cost: "The entire expense of Lincoln's nomination, including headquarters, telegraphing, music, fare of delegations, and other incidentals, was less than seven hundred dollars."

ELEMENTS THAT Lincoln had described as "strange and discordant, gathered from the four winds," had formed a party of youth, pilgrims of faith and candlelight philosophers, besides hopeful politicians. In its platform on a transcontinental railroad, the tariff, land and homestead laws, farm and factory laws to benefit workingmen and business, the Republican party was taking care of issues long neglected or evaded. But the commanding issue before which all others cracked was that of Union and the wage-labor system as against disunion and slave labor.

The man in Springfield picked to carry the banner stood as a shy and furtive figure. He wanted the place—and he didn't. His was precisely the clairvoyance that knew terrible days were ahead. He had his hesitations. And he was in the end the dark horse on whom the saddle was put. He could sit and contemplate an old proverb: "The horse thinks one thing, he that saddles him another."

The notification committee called on Lincoln at his house in Springfield to tell him formally he was nominated; he formally replied. Then he soberly brought them a pitcher of cold water; these were to be the drinks. He loosened the too stiff dignity of the occasion by calling on a tall judge to stand up and measure height with him. Later, after reading the platform, he sent the chairman a letter of acceptance. He would cooperate, "imploring the assistance of Divine Providence."

Chapter 30

IN JUNE the adjourned Democratic national convention met in Baltimore and, after bitter and furious debates, nominated Douglas of Illinois for President and Herschel Johnson, a Georgia unionist, for Vice-President. Delegates from eleven slave states walked out, rejecting with scorn and hate Douglas's "popular sovereignty" and his leadership; bolting their old party, they nominated John C. Breckinridge of Kentucky for President and Joseph Lane of Oregon for Vice-President.

Douglas went out to stump the country. But Lincoln stayed in Springfield. Judge Davis and Leonard Swett probably did more than any others to keep him connected with the main cogs and campaign machinery of the Republican party through the campaign. An immense organization was in the field working for him. Bills for printing, cash vouchers for speakers and their railroad fares and hotel bills, for thousands of torches, oilcloth uniforms, and caps for Wide-Awake clubs had to be met. And Norman Judd's campaign slogan, as Whitney said, was, "Turn on the beer, boys." These details were handled by managers who aimed chiefly at carrying their own states.

Wide-Awake clubs of young men, campaign workers,

marched in torchlight processions. Seward spoke across the northern states. Batteries of orators threatened, promised, appealed to statistics, passions, history. But the chosen spokesman of the Republican party had nothing to say. With the help of his secretary, John G. Nicolay, he wrote a few letters; he shook hands with orators, politicians, and reporters who came by the score out to the two-story cottage on Eighth Street. He made a short speech on August 8 when railroads, buggies, and wagons brought fifty thousand people to Springfield. He greeted them, half joked them. The "fight for this cause" would go on "though I be dead and gone." And he ended with the only important thing he had to say: "You will kindly let me be silent."

To Judge Davis came many letters asking how Lincoln, if elected, would deal with patronage and offices, with party factions, with coming issues and events. Davis had requested Lincoln to guide him in answering such letters, and Lincoln had written for Davis "the body of such a letter as I think you should write . . . in your own handwriting," adding whatever else Davis might "think fit." This letter for Davis's use was wise, comprehensive, yet brief, and indicated what, in that hour of turmoil, was in Lincoln's mind and conscience. It read:

> Since parting with you, I have had full, and frequent conversations with Mr. Lincoln. The substance of what he says is that he neither is nor will be, in advance of the election, committed to any man, clique, or faction; and that, in case the new administration shall devolve upon him, it will be his pleasure, and, in his view, the part of duty, and wisdom, to deal fairly with all. He thinks he will need the assistance of all; and that, even if he had friends to reward, or enemies to punish, as he has not, he could not afford to dispense with the best talents, nor to outrage the popular will in any locality.

Gifts arrived for the candidate, a piece of white-oak wood from Josiah Crawford of Gentryville, Indiana. "It is part of a rail I cut for him in 1825 when I was sixteen years old," said Lincoln; "he sent the wood to have it made into a cane." And pleasant communications came, among them a letter from Nat Grigsby, a brother of the Aaron Grigsby who had married

Lincoln's sister, Sarah. He also received and replied to greetings from Dave Turnham, the constable at Gentryville who had loaned him before he was a voter *The Revised Laws of Indiana*. He would like to visit again the old home and old friends. "I am indeed very glad to learn you are still living and well."

The photographer, Hesler, came one day from Chicago. Politicians there were saying Lincoln seemed to be in "rough everyday rig" in all his pictures. Lincoln had written he would be "dressed up" if Hesler came to Springfield. And Hesler made four negatives of Lincoln in a stiff-bosomed, pleated shirt with pearl buttons. The glister of the shirt was the equal of any in a Douglas photograph, which was what the politicians were demanding.

Leonard W. Volk, the sculptor, arrived one day, was given a rose bouquet by Mrs. Lincoln, and presented her with a bust of her husband. As Lincoln shook him by the two hands, Volk said, "Now that you will doubtless be the next President of the United States, I want to make a statue of you, and shall do my best to do you justice." "I don't doubt it," replied Lincoln, "for I have come to the conclusion that you are an honest man." After sittings, as the likeness emerged from the clay, Lincoln said, "There's the animal himself."

Five biographies of Lincoln were published in June. Medals and coins were struck, advertising soap on one side and the Republican candidate on the other. Requests for autographs came. Newspapers came. A New York *Evening Post* reporter sketched him: "As he gets interested in conversation his face lights up, and his gestures assume dignity. He is fluent, agreeable, and polite, a man of decided and original character. His views are all his own, worked out from a patient and varied scrutiny of life." The reporter added: "I trust I am not trespassing on the sanctities of private life, in saying a word in regard to Mrs. Lincoln. Whatever of awkwardness may be ascribed to her husband, there is none of it in her. She is quite a pattern of ladylike courtesy and polish. . . . Should she ever reach it, [she] will adorn the White House."

Other newspapers came, estimating Lincoln as "a third-rate country lawyer"; he lived "in low Hoosier style"; he "could not speak good grammar"; he was descended from "an African gorilla." Questions came. What was his view on this or that? And his secretary, John G. Nicolay, sent them all the same letter; his positions "were well known when he was nominated; he must not now embarrass the canvass. You perceive it is impossible for him to do so. Yours, etc., John G. Nicolay."

He was beginning to learn more precisely how he was food for the makers of myths. When John G. Scripps of the Chicago *Tribune* had come to him for material for a campaign biography, he told Scripps there would be nothing to it but "the short and simple annals of the poor." He toiled at shaping up a statement of the main facts of his life; it was scrupulous, careful, exact. He personally read the Scripps sketch before it was published, checking for mistakes. When he handed it back to Scripps he said that, before reading it, he hadn't read Plutarch, as the sketch declared, but had since gone and read Plutarch, so the statement could be published as strictly accurate.

"A scrupulous teller of the truth—too exact in his notions to suit the atmosphere of Washington as it now is," Scripps wrote. This thirty-two page pamphlet biography, selling for five cents a copy, was read by millions.

As for Abraham Lincoln himself, grim thoughts sometimes came to him in this summer of 1860 as he sat in his home at Eighth and Jackson streets, watching the making of a legend. He saw a powerful young political party using him, shaping his personal figure into heroic stature, coloring his personality beyond reality. If he should say to himself that he would make the kind of President they said he would make, he could only say it wryly with wry laughter. If he should in the days to come be the historic man of speech and action, of fine wisdom and chilled-steel nerves that they promised, he would be one of God's miracles, he would be one of the storm stars lighting the history of the world.

Yet they were promising, the prophecies were issuing from the mouths of hundreds of stump orators, from the columns of hundreds of newspapers. "Abe," "Old Abe," "the Rail Candidate," "Honest Abe," "the Man of the People"—the Man of the Hour, one who had risen from a dirt-floor cabin of poverty, who knew by firsthand acquaintance the wrongs of the poor, the exploited, the fooled—thus he was proclaimed.

What men there had been who had gone up against the test and met it and gone down before it! What heartbreaking challenge there was in this thing of heading a government where vast sensitive property interests and management problems called for practical executive ability, while millions of people hungry for some mystic bread of life asked for land, roads, freedom! They were the vast groaning, snarling, singing, murmuring, irreckonable instrument through which, and on which, history, destiny, politicians, worked—the people—the public that had to be reached for the making of public opinion.

He could only be solemn about most of it. But he could laugh low over Dick Yates, the Republican candidate for governor of Illinois, saying on the stump, "I know some folks are asking, who is old Abe? I guess they will soon find out. Old Abe is a plain sort of a man, about six feet four inches in his boots, and every inch of him *Man*. I recollect two years ago at a little party a very tall man went up to Lincoln and said, 'Mr. Lincoln, I think I am as tall as you are.' Lincoln began to straighten himself up and up, until his competitor was somewhat staggered. 'Well, I thought I was,' said he, now doubtful. 'But,' says Lincoln, straightening himself up still higher, *'there's a good deal of come-out in me,'* and he came out two inches the higher."

DOUGLAS WAS STUMPING the country; it seemed a losing fight; he went on, tireless; his friends were amazed at the way he wore out, went to bed, and came back to the fight again. Democrats of the southern wing of the party sent Jefferson Davis to dicker with Douglas; if all contenders would shake hands and join on one candidate they would sweep the election; Douglas said it couldn't be done; too many of his friends would go for Lincoln.

At Norfolk, Virginia, in late August he told an audience of seven thousand that he wanted no votes except from men who desired the Union to be preserved. At Raleigh, North Carolina, he said he would "hang every man higher than Haman" who resisted constitutional law. At places in the North he favored "burying southern disunionism and northern abolitionism in

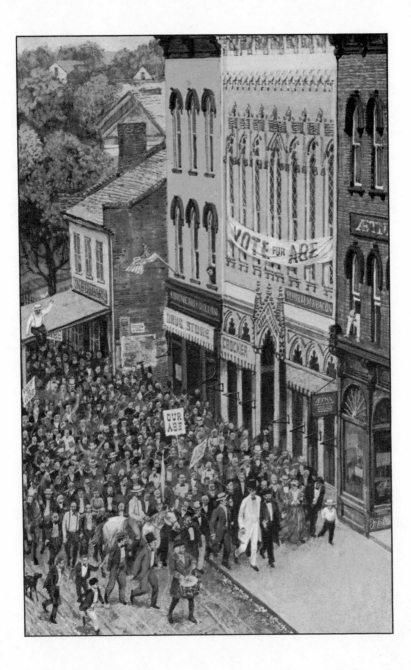

the same grave." The Pacific railway and other dreams would never come true, he told a Boston crowd, "unless you banish forever the slavery question from the halls of Congress and remand it to the people of each state and territory." Going South again, he spoke to large crowds in Tennessee, Georgia, and Alabama, often amid threats and jeers of thugs and rotten fruit and eggs meant to reach his head. In Atlanta, Alexander Stephens, though Douglas was not his first choice for President, introduced him with warm praise. Harassed and in sinking health, Douglas spoke in the Deep South with passion and storm in his voice of the love he held for the Union and his scorn for those who would break up the Union.

"I think there will be the most extraordinary effort ever made to carry New York for Douglas," Lincoln meanwhile wrote to Thurlow Weed. "You and all others who write me from your State think the effort can not succeed, and I hope you are right. Still it will require close watching." Replying to a Southerner, he wrote of receiving many assurances from the South "that in no probable event will there be any very formidable effort to break up the Union." He hoped and believed "the people of the South have too much of good sense and good temper to attempt the ruin of the government rather than see it administered as it was administered by the men who made it." Again and again came letters for Lincoln—just precisely what would he do with slavery if elected? Would he interfere? Would it not be wise to say plainly he wouldn't interfere? One he answered, "Those who will not read, or heed, what I have already publicly said, would not read, or heed, a repetition of it." He wrote to a pro-Douglas Louisville editor: "I have *bad* men also to deal with, both North and South—men who are eager for something new upon which to base misrepresentations—men who would like to frighten me, or, at least fix upon me the character of timidity and cowardice."

A child in a New York town asked whether he had a daughter, and why he didn't wear whiskers. His letter, saluting "My dear little Miss," told her: "I regret the necessity of saying I have no daughter, I have three sons—one seventeen, one nine, and one seven years of age. They, with their mother, constitute my whole family. As to the whiskers, having never worn any, do you not think people would call it a silly piece of affectation if I were to begin it now?"

SHORTLY BEFORE the election Lincoln was in the Illinois statehouse one day, alone with his good friend Newton Bateman, "Little Newt," the state superintendent of public instruction. Lincoln had a Springfield pollbook with notes on how each citizen would probably vote. "I wish particularly to see how the ministers of Springfield are going to vote." They turned the leaves, added up results, and Lincoln said, "Here are twenty-three ministers of different denominations, and all of them are against me but three; and here are a great many prominent members of the churches, a very large majority of whom are against me."

He paused, and after a while rose and walked up and down the room. Bateman saw tears fill his eyes. He stopped in his pacing to say, "I know there is a God, and that He hates injustice and slavery. I see the storm coming, and I know that His hand is in it. If He has a place and work for me I believe I am ready. I am nothing, but truth is everything."

And he went on in a lengthy and dark meditation on God and Christ, slavery, and the teachings of the New Testament. "I may not see the end; but it will come, and I shall be vindicated; and these men will find they have not read their Bibles aright."

Chapter 31

EARLY REPORTS on the evening of Election Day, November 6, told Lincoln he hadn't won his home county of Sangamon. But he had carried his home precinct. From nine o'clock on he sat in the Springfield telegraph office. Lyman Trumbull arrived and summarized reports. "We've got 'em, we've got 'em." Then came a telegram: "Hon. A. Lincoln: Pennsylvania 70,000 for you. New York safe. Glory enough. S. Cameron."

Lincoln and his friends stepped across the street to a room where the Republican ladies' club had fixed a lunch. The ladies rushed him. "How do you do, Mr. President?" Out in the streets, and up around the statehouse, crowds surged, shouting, "New York fifty thousand majority for Lincoln"; lines of men locked arms and sang, "Ain't I glad I joined the Republicans?" The jubilee was still going as Lincoln walked to the Eighth Street cottage and told a happy woman, "Mary, we're elected."

The count showed Lincoln winning with 1,866,452 votes, a majority of nearly a half million over Douglas, the nearest contender. A change of a few votes here and there would have given a different decision. In a total of some 4,700,000 votes the other combined candidates had nearly a million more votes than Lincoln. Fifteen states gave him no electoral votes; in ten states he didn't get a count of one popular vote. And the Congress would have a Democratic majority.

In the whole Northwest, Lincoln's majority was only 6600 over all other candidates. A change of one vote in twenty would have given Douglas the Northwest, and sent the presidential election into the national House of Representatives, where the South would probably have won.

THE ELECTION was a signal. Events came as by clockwork after it. South Carolina legislators voted to raise and equip ten thousand volunteer soldiers; Georgia and Louisiana legislatures voted $1,000,000 and $500,000 for arms and troops. South Carolina through its legislature declared itself a sovereign and independent state and seceded from the Union of States, on December 20, with a flag of its own, with oaths of allegiance; forts, post offices, customhouses of the federal government were taken. Before New Year's Day it was known the whole row of cotton states would follow South Carolina, with a view of forming a Southern Confederacy.

The Atlanta newspaper *Confederacy* spoke for them all: "Let the consequences be what they may—whether the Potomac is crimsoned in human gore, and Pennsylvania Avenue is paved ten fathoms deep with mangled bodies, or whether the last vestige of liberty is swept from the face of the American continent, the South will never submit to such humiliation and degradation as the inauguration of Abraham Lincoln."

A crisscross of facts was operating. Robert Toombs of Georgia was saying, "It is admitted that you seek to outlaw $4,000,000,000 of property of our people in the Territories. Is not that a cause of war?" But was secession the safest way of managing this property? Jefferson Davis had his doubts. He and other high counselors of the South, in their letters and speeches at this time, did not advise secession.

Only later, when secession was accomplished by its radical manipulators, would Southerners till then conservative, and advising against disunion, fall in line as patriots whose first oath of allegiance was to their sovereign state. Alexander Stephens had written: "I consider slavery much more secure in the Union than out of it if our people were but wise." Property suffers in revolutions, he pointed out. "The institution is based on conservatism."

Among the fire-eaters clamoring for secession were those who made a business of buying, breeding, selling slaves. A planter from Georgia had told the national Democratic convention, "I have had to pay from $1,000 to $2,000 a head when I could go to Africa and buy better Negroes for $50 apiece." But in North Carolina, the Raleigh *Banner* was saying: "The big heart of the people is still in the Union. Less than a hundred thousand politicians are endeavoring to destroy the liberties and usurp the rights of more than thirty millions of people. If the people permit it, they deserve the horrors of the civil war which will ensue."

. While southern radicals were calling Lincoln a diabolical abolitionist, Wendell Phillips in Boston sneered at him as "the slave hound of Illinois." Robert Toombs read to the Georgia legislature a defense of secession written and published by Horace Greeley; the advice of Greeley was, "Let the erring sisters depart in peace." Boston heard Phillips declare: "Let the South march off with flags and trumpets, and we will speed the parting guest. . . . Rejoice that she has departed. All hail, disunion! . . . Let the border states go." But the Detroit department-store proprietor, Zachariah Chandler, senator from Michigan, wrote his state governor "a little bloodletting" was wanted. His statement was matched with a Georgian's saying the people must wake up; there was a way to rouse them and get the war going: "Sprinkle blood in their faces."

In the day's mail for Lincoln came letters cursing him for an ape and a baboon who had brought the country evil. Also letters told him he was a satyr, a Negro, a buffoon, a monster, an idiot; he would be flogged, burned, hanged, tortured. Pen sketches of gallows and daggers arrived from "oath-bound brotherhoods." Some letters were specific in statements that a rifle shot would reach him before he reached Washington or the ceremony of inauguration as President.

Across many letters Lincoln wrote for his secretaries the notation, "Need not answer this." The secretaries were two young men. One was a reliable, accurate German editor from Pike County, Illinois, sober as a workhorse, earnest as the multiplication table. This was red-haired, freckled John G. Nicolay, secretive, dependable, carrying messages not to be written but whispered, feeling equally with Lincoln the groaning loads of responsibility.

John Hay, the other secretary, was not strictly engaged as such, but he was going to Washington. Lincoln had said, "We can't take all Illinois with us down to Washington, but let Hay come." A keen and whimsical lad, this Hay. He had been class poet at Brown University, graduated, and had come to Springfield to study law with his uncle Milton Hay, who had an office on the same floor as Lincoln & Herndon. He wrote notes in French to a sweetheart, and had a handsome, negligent elegance all the girls in Springfield liked. He wore a derby hat, buttoned the top button on a long loose sack coat of black, and sauntered with an ease that caught Lincoln's eye. "Let Hay come."

Once more Lincoln and Joshua Speed were exchanging letters. Lincoln hoped he and Speed could meet in Chicago, each with his wife. "Could you not meet me there?" he wrote. "Mary thinks of going with me; and therefore I suggest that Mrs. S. accompany you. Please let this be private, as I prefer a very great crowd should not gather at Chicago."

He went to Chicago, late in November, met Hannibal Hamlin, the Vice-President-elect; they held a reception in the Tremont House, went to St. James's Church together, and in the afternoon, as the *Tribune* reported it, "they visited the North Market Mission where, after the usual services, the President-elect delivered a short address which was received with much pleasure by the destitute children attending the Sabbath school."

Eight little girls stood in a row at the Tremont House; he signed his name in their autograph albums. A four-year-old boy yelled, "Hurray for Uncle Abe!" and was soon in Lincoln's hands getting tossed high toward the ceiling and hugged safe on coming down. He had a good visit with Joshua Speed, asked many questions about Kentucky. Mrs. Lincoln and Mrs. Speed went shopping.

People so crowded in on Lincoln and Hamlin in the Tremont House that they went for their conference to a private home, where they discussed appointments. Lincoln wished to hold a balance between Whigs who had turned Republican and Democrats who had turned Republican. He would trust Hamlin to name the New England member of his Cabinet for Secretary of the Navy, giving Hamlin three names he inclined to favor; Hamlin decided on a former Jackson Democrat, Gideon Welles, a Hartford editor. They both favored Seward for Secretary of State. Lincoln wrote one short letter notifying Seward he would appoint him Secretary of State and a longer letter giving Lincoln's belief "that your position in the public eye, your integrity, ability, learning," made the appointment "preeminently fit." Hamlin was to deliver Lincoln's letters to Seward, who, after pretending to think deeply about it, would accept.

The Lincolns went back to Springfield. On the train Tad and Willie sang a Lincoln campaign song: "Old Abe Lincoln came out of the wilderness."

The trains into Springfield, on a single day, would unload hundreds of passengers arriving to see Lincoln. William Jones dropped in; he was the Jones who kept the store in Gentryville when the boy, Abe, was "the big buck of the lick." An old man from the state of Mississippi came out after his talk with Lincoln and stood at a wall, in tears; men asked the trouble; he wished more people in the South could know Lincoln.

Some carried shining faces; they just wanted to look at him and tell him they hoped to God he'd live and have good luck.

Others, too, carried shining faces, singing, "Ain't we glad we joined the Republicans?" They said they nominated and elected him President, and inquired about post offices, revenue collectorships, clerkships, secretaryships. They wore him. Behind their smiles some had snouts like buzzards, pigs, rats. They were pap seekers, sapsuckers, chairwarmers, hammock heroes, the office-sniffing mob who had killed Zach Taylor, who had killed Tippecanoe Harrison. They wore Lincoln— worse than the signs of war.

The office seekers watched Lincoln's habits, waylaid him, wedged in, and reminded him not to forget them. If personally refused, they sent appeals through friends. One who kept wedging in, by one device and another, was Judge David Davis. Lincoln spoke to Whitney about it, and as Whitney told it: "Lincoln inveighed to me in the bitterest terms against Judge Davis's greed and importunity for office, and summarized his disgust in these words, 'I know it is an awful thing for me to say, but I already wish someone else was here in my place.'"

Hannah Armstrong came, the widow of Jack, the mother of Duff, stronghearted, black-eyed Hannah Armstrong. Lincoln took her two hands. They talked, homely and heartwarming talk. He held the hands that had been good to him, so long ago, when he was young and the sap ran wild in him. They talked. And she was going. "They'll kill ye, Abe." "Hannah, if they do kill me, I shall never die another death."

A joker arose, with a sardonic snort in his jokes. He and Lincoln struck hands of fellowship. In an article in *Vanity Fair*, this joker reported with a horselaugh the tragic swarming to the trough at Springfield. "Hevin no politics, I made bold to visit Old Abe at his humsted in Springfield. I found the old feller in his parler, surrounded by a perfick sworm of orfice seekers. Sum wanted post offices, sum wanted collectorships, sum wanted furrin missions and all wanted sumthin. I thought Old Abe would go crazy."

It was the beginning of a friendship. The writer signed as "Artemus Ward," a twenty-six-year-old wanderer born in Maine, trained on newspapers in Ohio, and doing one sketch a week for *Vanity Fair*. Lincoln adopted him as an unofficial spokesman who could be depended on to say things a Chief Magistrate would like to say if it wouldn't be going too far. Democracy should see and laugh. A republic should have jesters at the overstuffed shirts of dignity and pretense.

Another came whom Lincoln was glad to see. That was Ned Baker, warm, impetuous, song-voiced. Lincoln had named his boy Eddie, the one who died, after Edward D. Baker, who had now become United States senator from Oregon. They talked of the future and of the past. They could recall the story told twenty years before by Lincoln, to tease Baker. The story ran that Baker, who was born on the ocean, from English parents, was found sobbing one morning, and when asked what was the matter had answered that he had just read in a book that only citizens born in the United States could ever become President— and his chance was gone!

Horace Greeley dropped into Springfield, going home from a trip west. He didn't go to Lincoln's house. Lincoln walked to Greeley's hotel. Greeley was cautious, tentative, bewildered, outwardly thinking in straight lines, inwardly running circles. His original advice to "let the erring sisters depart in peace" had changed to counsel against compromise. The two men talked several hours. Lincoln knew what a wide audience of readers Greeley had through the New York *Tribune*, and he was trying to join forces with him. Greeley wanted to be senator from New York. He could use Lincoln's influence. But Lincoln held off from taking a hand in New York state politics. He had written to Weed, Greeley's mortal enemy, politically, the day before, "My name must not be used in the senatorial election in favor of or against any one."

They parted—Greeley and Lincoln—with no fresh understanding of each other, no real arrangement to cooperate. Lincoln, in Greeley's eyes, was just one more common politician. In all of their hours of talk, said Greeley, "I never heard him tell a story or anecdote." The clue was sinister. But Greeley didn't know it. He believed Lincoln wanted to be charioteer of the Greeley chariot, which Lincoln didn't want at all. Lincoln wanted less zigzag driving.

The politicians continued to overrun Springfield. Lincoln

had lost forty pounds' weight in less than a year, so sculptor Leonard Volk said Lincoln told him. "He looks more pale and careworn," said the New York *Herald* writer.

Day by day called for decisions. And Lincoln had no policy, as such, to guide him. He explained to a secretary, "My policy is to have no policy."

Thurlow Weed, the New York boss, came from Albany, where Swett had written to him saying Lincoln wanted to see him about Cabinet matters. They talked politics and issues in general. Lincoln said he had been looking for helpers, for great men. Perhaps he didn't know where the best available timber was. "While the population of the country has immensely increased, really great men are scarcer than they used to be."

Lincoln suggested that Weed was a Cabinetmaker, and while he, Lincoln, had never learned that trade, he had a job of Cabinetmaking on hand and was willing to have the help of friends. Weed came back saying he wasn't exactly a boss Cabinetmaker; he was a journeyman, had helped make state cabinets but not federal. The two men had a good time.

Weed thought it marvelous that Lincoln all the time kept interspersing stories pat to the deal in hand. Weed believed two members of the Cabinet should be from slave states. "Would you rely on such men if their states secede?" "Yes, sir; the men I have in mind can always be relied on." "Well, let us have the names." For one, Weed named Henry Winter Davis of Maryland. Lincoln knew this Davis was a cousin of Judge David Davis, and guessed that the judge was operating through Weed. He laughed. "Davis has been posting you up on this question. He came from Maryland and has got Davis on the brain. Maryland must, I think, be like New Hampshire, a good state to move from." And he told of a witness swearing his age was sixty when the court knew he was much older; the court rebuking the witness got the reply, "Oh, you're thinking about that fifteen years I lived down on the Eastern Shore of Maryland; that was so much lost time and don't count."

Names, personalities, localities, and political shadings were talked over. Would Bates of Missouri do for Attorney General? Yes, Weed was sure; he paid tribute to Bates's personal reliability. He and Lincoln spent two chatty days together. During those two days, Lincoln searched his way through the upstairs and downstairs rooms of Weed's mind and heart; Lincoln had trained himself, for years, to put men at their ease while pumping them with quiet questions, learning by asking. He knew that Weed was in communication with such men of power as A. T. Stewart, the leading New York merchant, and August Belmont, New York representative of the Rothschilds, international bankers, and a leading financier among the northern capitalists to whom the South was in debt two hundred million dollars. Also Lincoln learned how Weed hated and feared the extremists and radicals of the North and South; a man of compromises and adjustments, Weed was for conciliation between North and South; he believed the misunderstandings could be patched up. His visit helped cement loyalty between him and Lincoln, which was Lincoln's main intention.

AMONG THE IMPORTANT MEN who got off the train at Springfield was Salmon P. Chase, then senator from Ohio. He came by invitation, Lincoln having written him: "In these troublous times I would much like a conference with you." Not merely was Chase important; he looked so. Lincoln asked him to become Secretary of the Treasury. Chase wouldn't promise. He'd think it over. And with that he went back to Ohio. "He thinks he's a greater man than you are," said Lincoln's old Springfield friend John Bunn. Lincoln said he would be glad if that were true; he wanted all the great men he could lay hold of for his Cabinet.

Simon Cameron, the Pennsylvania boss, came on. Judge Davis and the Lincoln managers at the Chicago convention had promised Cameron he could be Secretary of the Treasury. Cameron stayed three days. He left with a letter signed by Lincoln to himself, indicating that Lincoln intended to nominate him either as Secretary of the Treasury or as Secretary of War. While Cameron journeyed homeward, his enemies brought evidence to Lincoln intended to show that Cameron was "the very incarnation of corruption." Lincoln wrote Cameron another letter; things had developed which made it impossible to take him, Cameron, into the Cabinet. Would he, Cameron, write a letter publicly declining any Cabinet place? And Cameron's answer was a bundle of recommendations outnumbering the opposition three to one, which Lincoln looked over, and later wrote Cameron that he wouldn't make a Cabinet appointment for Pennsylvania without consulting Cameron. Thus names slipped in and out, though Seward for Secretary of State and Judge Edward Bates of Missouri for Attorney General were well settled from the start.

Often in those days Lincoln took his boy Tad on his knees, and they talked. He could tell Tad many a piece of nonsense with a monkeyshine in it that would have been wasted on a Horace Greeley or a Salmon P. Chase. Tad came into an important conference once and in a loud whisper told his father, "Ma says come to supper." A slow smile spread over the father's face, as he said, "You have all heard, gentlemen, the announcement concerning the interesting state of things in the diningroom. It will never do for me, if elected, to make this young man a member of my Cabinet, for it is plain he cannot be trusted with secrets of state."

Chapter 32

THE WASHINGTON MAN of the Chicago *Tribune* wired on January 3 that President Buchanan had met with his Cabinet the day before, and, "the row recommenced. The President, like a pusillanimous coward, refused to take sides, and, shaken like an aspen leaf, entreated them not to quarrel, and offered them some old whisky—his unfailing remedy. The old man has become little better than a sot." The next day was the one set apart by the President for fasting, prayer, and humiliation. Services were conducted in nearly all churches in the northern states. The Springfield man of the Chicago *Tribune* wired to his paper, "Mr. Lincoln attended church today, in obedience to the presidential proclamation, and it is to be presumed that in his prayers Mr. Buchanan's backbone was not forgotten."

At that hour, as Lincoln was in church, many people believed southern forces would seize Washington, and Lincoln would have to be sworn in at some other place. Twenty-two carloads of troops were starting from Fort Leavenworth across Missouri for Baltimore. Cameron of Pennsylvania was saying, "Lincoln, if living, will take the oath of office on the Capitol steps." Newly organized artillery companies were drilling in Chicago. A thousand Negro slaves were throwing up fortifications in Charleston, South Carolina. "Resistance to Lincoln is Obedience to God" flared a banner at an Alabama mass meeting; an orator swore that if need be their troops would march to the doors of the national Capitol over "fathoms of mangled bodies."

As the cotton states, one by one, left the Union, senators and representatives from the South spoke sad and bitter farewells to Congress; U.S. postmasters, judges, district attorneys, customs collectors, by the hundreds sent their resignations to Washington. Of the 1108 officers of the U.S. regular army, 387 were preparing resignations, many having already joined the Confederate armed forces. Governors of seceded states marched in troops and took over U.S. forts.

THE REVOLUTION was the top headline under which a New York daily paper assembled the news of the country. Nine columns were required on one day to report declarations of southern conventions, and resignations from the army, navy, and training academies. President Buchanan moaned privately that he was the last President of the United States of America.

With the Union broken Stephens of Georgia could see "anarchy" at the North, "and whether we shall be better off at the South will depend on many things I am not satisfied we have any assurance of." Stephens had dug into history. "Revolutions are much easier started than controlled, and the men who begin them, even for the best purposes, seldom end them."

The New York *Herald* advised in an editorial, "A grand opportunity now exists for Lincoln to avert impending ruin, and invest his name with an immortality far more enduring than would attach to it by his elevation to the presidency. His withdrawal at this time from the scene of conflict, and the surrender of his claims to some national man who would be acceptable to both sections, would render him the peer of Washington in patriotism." And the *Herald* added: "If he persists in his present position . . . he will totter into a dishonoured grave, driven there perhaps by the hands of an assassin."

Still, in public, Lincoln had nothing to say. He delivered remarks such as, "Please excuse me from making a speech," and, "Let us at all times remember that all American citizens are brothers of a common country." He indicated he would stand for no further spread of slavery. And his friend Edward D. Baker told the Senate that Lincoln would respect the Fugitive Slave Law. Lincoln also told friends privately that the forts seized by the seceded states would have to be retaken. But as to declaration of policy on this and that, he was waiting.

Some of his Illinois friends were puzzled. They couldn't figure what Lincoln was up to—if anything. It was baffling.

Next to Senator Trumbull, Congressman William Kellogg of Canton, Illinois, was closer to Lincoln than any other Republican in the matter of favors, offices, patronage. And it was Kellogg who stood up in the House of Representatives one day early in February and introduced a bill to amend the Constitution so that slaves could be taken into any territory south of 36° 30' from any state where slavery then lawfully existed.

On January 21, Kellogg had held a long conference with Lincoln in Springfield. Now, when he introduced his compromise bill, he was howled down by the radicals of his party, and read out of the party by the Chicago *Tribune*—as both he and Lincoln had probably expected.

Why had Lincoln and Kellogg done this? One result was that goodwill was created. The Democrats of southern Illinois, Indiana, and Ohio, near the slave-state borders could say to their people that if the southern congressmen had not walked out and left the Union, there might have been a chance for the extension of slavery into the western territories. Then too, the slave state of Missouri had a fresh argument for staying in the Union.

The incident was a piece of Lincoln propaganda. It came in the same week in February in which his closest friend among newspapers, the *Illinois State Journal*, shot the fierce bolt: "Before we talk of concession we want it settled that we have a Government. Let the stolen forts, arsenals, and navy yards be returned to the rightful owners—tear down your Rattlesnake and Pelican flag and run up the ever-glorious Stars and Stripes—disperse your traitorous mobs, and let every man return to his duty. Then come to us with your list of grievances."

The North was crying, "Treason!" the South, "Freedom!" One called the Union sacred; the other spoke of state sovereignty as holy. Propaganda was seething. Southern newspapers were telling of riots and bloodshed in New England factory cities. Northern papers were telling of food shortages in the southern states. That same week, too, on February 4, delegates at Montgomery, Alabama, organized a provisional government named the Confederate States of America, electing Jefferson Davis of Mississippi as President and Alexander Stephens of Georgia as Vice-President.

It was sunset and dawn, moonrise and noon, dying time and birthing hour, dry leaves of the last of autumn and springtime blossom roots.

Chapter 33

A HATTER from Brooklyn, New York, called one day and presented Lincoln with a black silk hat. The President-elect turned to Mrs. Lincoln and remarked, "Well, wife, if nothing else comes out of this scrape, we are going to have some new clothes."

Attentions and incidents of that sort pleased Mrs. Lincoln. She had a sprightly manner of saying, "We are pleased with our advancement." In the hustle of deciding what to take along to the White House, asked about this, that, and the other thing to be done or not done, she would sometimes burst out, "God, no!" One winter morning she was burning papers in the alley when Jared P. Irwin, a neighbor, asked if he could have some of them. She said he was welcome and Irwin scraped from the fire several of the most interesting letters written by Mr. and Mrs. Lincoln to each other.

Pressure came on her to give her husband the names of men who should be appointed to office, with reasons why. Of one woman for whose husband she got a political appointment, Mrs. Lincoln told another woman, "She little knows what a hard battle I had for it, and how near he came to getting nothing." She spoke of fears about her health, would mention "my racked frame" to other women, and would say she hoped the chills she suffered from in earlier years would not return in Washington.

Ugly clouds shaped on the horizons; war would be messy. "If the country was only peaceful, all would be well," wrote Mary Lincoln. And, "I am weary of intrigue," she could remark, while in the same breath saying of a former friend, "She possesses such a miserable disposition and so false a tongue."

She might find Washington a city of tears and shadows. But she would go there with new clothes, fresh ribbons, and see. She made a trip in January to New York City, there meeting Robert, who came down from Harvard. She had as good a time as possible for her, choosing and buying gowns, hats, footwear, and adornments becoming to one to be called "the First Lady of the Land." She wrote such instructions as, "I am in need of two bonnets—I do not wish expensive ones, but I desire them of very fine quality and stylish." She wrote specifications to the milliner. "One bonnet, I wish fine, very fine, pretty shape. This I desire, to be trimmed with black love ribbons—with pearl edge. I cannot have it without the latter."

Henry Villard wrote for the New York *Herald* from Springfield on January 26 of the President-elect "delighted" at the return of Mrs. Lincoln and Bob from the east. "Dutiful husband and father that he is, he had proceeded to the railroad depot for three successive nights in his anxiety to receive them, and that in spite of snow and cold. Mrs. Lincoln returned in good health and excellent spirits; whether she got a good scolding from Abraham for unexpectedly prolonging her absence, I am unable to say; but I know she found it rather difficult to part with the winter gayeties of New York." Villard noted, too, that Robert dressed in an elegance in "striking contrast to the loose, careless, awkward rigging of his Presidential father."

ONE MORNING IN JANUARY, Lincoln started out for Coles County, where he was to say good-by and have his last hour with his stepmother, Sally Bush Lincoln. He rode to Mattoon, missed connections with a passenger train, and took the caboose of a freight train to Charleston. There, with a shawl over his shoulders, and his boots in slush, mud, and ice, he picked his way in the evening dusk alongside the tracks the length of the train to the station, where a buggy was ready. Friends met him and took him to their house, where he stayed overnight, partying with old acquaintances during the evening. The next day he drove to the farm along the road over which he had hauled wood with an ox team. He came to the house he had cut logs for and whose chinks he had helped to smooth; from its little square windows he had seen late winter and early birds.

Sally Bush and he put their arms around each other and listened to each other's heartbeats. They held hands and talked, they talked without holding hands. Each looked into eyes thrust back in deep sockets. She was all of a mother to him. He was her boy more than any born to her. He gave her a photograph of her boy, a hungry picture of him standing and wanting, wanting. He stroked her face a last time, kissed good-by, and went away.

She knew his heart would go roaming back often, that even when he rode in an open carriage in New York or Washington with soldiers, flags, and cheering thousands along the streets, he might just as like be thinking of her in the old log farmhouse out in Coles County, Illinois.

The sunshine of the prairie summer and fall months would come sifting down with healing and strength; between harvest and corn plowing there would be rains beating and blizzards howling; and there would be the silence after snowstorms with white drifts piled against the fences, barns, and trees.

INAUGURATION DAY was only a few weeks off. Letters warned Lincoln he would be killed before he could reach Washington. As they got fiercer, and more came, Lincoln sent Thomas S. Mather, adjutant general of Illinois, to Washington to see General Winfield Scott, military head of the U. S. government, and sound him out on his loyalty. Scott was a Virginian. "Insist on a personal interview. Look him in the face. Note carefully what he says."

Mather came back to Springfield. He had found the seventy-five-year-old Mexican War commander propped up with pillows, in bed, a worn man weighing three hundred pounds, with flesh in rolls over a warty face and neck. What with dropsy, vertigo, and old bullets to carry, he could no longer mount a horse. The general's breathing was heavy, and he wheezed out the words, "You may present my compliments to Mr. Lincoln, and tell him I shall expect him to come on to Washington as soon as he is ready." Also, "I shall consider myself responsible for his safety. If necessary I'll plant cannon at both ends of Pennsylvania Avenue, and if any show their hands or even venture to raise a finger, I'll blow them to hell."

Hearing these assurances that the Washington end of the inaugural was being taken care of, Lincoln went ahead with his plans to be there. When one friend warned him to have a guard, he replied, "What's the use of putting up a gap when the fence is down all around?"

He stepped into the house of Dr. John Todd one evening, holding a gripsack, and talking about the plans for his family to go to Washington. He handed the grip to Mrs. Elizabeth Todd Grimsley, a widow and the only daughter of Dr. Todd, saying it held his "literary bureau." He would leave it in her charge. Speeches, notes, writings of different sorts, filled the grip. He might not come back from Washington, he explained, and in that case she could do what she pleased with the papers.

He cleared out files, burned and threw away letters. He closed up odds and ends. He sold back to Canisius the *Illinois Staats-Anzeiger*. He took walks alone. Whitney ran across him in a section of Springfield where he had no business, unless to be walking alone. His arms were full of papers. Where was he going? "Nowhere in particular," he told Whitney.

The last week of his stay in Springfield arrived. The steps up to the cottage at Eighth and Jackson streets felt the tread of several thousand people who came between seven and twelve o'clock on the night of February 6, some to say good-by, some to see what they would see. It was the Lincolns' good-by house party. The President-elect stood near the front door shaking hands; his son Bob, back from school, and Mrs. Lincoln and four of her sisters assisted. Mrs. Lincoln wore, a St. Louis correspondent noted, a beautiful full trail, white moiré antique silk, with a small French lace collar. Her neck was ornamented with a string of pearls. Her headdress was a simple and delicate vine. She was, the correspondent telegraphed his paper, "a lady of fine figure and accomplished address, well calculated to grace and to do honor at the White House."

Newspapermen were kindly, admiring in their sketches of Mrs. Lincoln, and references to her. She was whirling along in dizzy realizations of her fondest hopes of social importance. She was a woman elevated for gaze.

On one farewell day, as Lincoln was meeting people in Johnson's Block opposite the Chenery House, there came to him an old farmer, in butternut jeans, who had ridden horseback many miles. The old man was bent and worn with age, and nearly blind. He had known the Armstrongs and what Lincoln did for Duff Armstrong. And he came and put his old eyes close to Lincoln's face, peered and studied the lines of the face, burst into tears, and murmured, "It *is* him—it's the *same*." And after mentioning the Duff Armstrong case, he shook the hand of the President-elect and said solemnly two or three times, "God preserve you, Mr. Lincoln."

"LINCOLN IS LETTING his whiskers grow," men had been saying in January. A barber had shaved the upper lip and cheeks, leaving a stubble on the chin. Then along in February, the hairs grew without interference on all the areas of the face and neck, except the upper lip.

Just why Lincoln took to whiskers at this time nobody seemed to know. A girl in New York State had begged him to raise a beard. But something more than her random wish guided him. Herndon, Whitney, Lamon, Nicolay, Hay, heard no explanation from him as to why after fifty-two years with a smooth face he should now change. Would whiskers imply responsibility, gravity, a more sober and serene outlook on the phantasmagoria of life? Perhaps he would seem more like a serious farmer with crops to look after, or perhaps a church sexton in charge of grave affairs. Or he might have the look of a sea captain handling a ship in a storm on a starless sea.

The inaugural address had been written. In a dusty third-story room over his brother-in-law's store, Lincoln had hidden away from all callers at such times as he worked on the writing of the address to be delivered on March 4 in Washington. Two printers, sworn to secrecy, had set up and run off twenty copies of the address. That was in January. Weeks had gone by. Nobody had told or been careless. The inaugural address text was still a well-kept secret.

One special person was going to Washington.

Lamon had been called from Danville and told, "Hill, it looks as if we might have war. I want you with me, I must have you." And Lamon was going along, banjo, bulldog courage, and all.

At sunset on the evening before the day set for starting to Washington, Lincoln and Herndon sat in their office for a long talk. Sixteen years they had been partners, and, said Lincoln, "We've never had a cross word during all that time, have we?" They reviewed old times, exchanged reminiscences; Lincoln was entertaining and cheerful—but suddenly blurted, "Billy, there's one thing I have, for some time, wanted you to tell me, but I reckon I ought to apologize for my nerve and curiosity in asking it even now." "What is it?" "I want you to tell me how many times you have been drunk."

Herndon felt it a blunt question, made his guess as to how many times, perhaps five or six, he had brought disgrace on the law firm. Herndon expected some kind of a warning. But Lincoln changed the subject. What he had done was to give Billy a chance to say he'd keep sober and be fit for any responsible appointment Lincoln would give him.

Herndon said afterward, "I could have had any place for which I was fitted, but I thought too much of Lincoln to disgrace him. And I wanted to be free, drink whisky when I pleased." One request, however, came from Herndon, that Lincoln would speak to Governor Yates and have him reappointed state bank examiner, to which Lincoln agreed. As Lincoln gathered a bundle of papers and stood ready to leave, he told Herndon their law partnership would go on, their shingle would stay up. "If I live I'm coming back and we'll resume practice as if nothing had ever happened." He took a last look around at the old office, and Herndon and he walked downstairs together and parted.

A queer dream or illusion had haunted Lincoln at times through the winter. On election evening he had thrown himself on a haircloth sofa at home, just after the first telegrams had told him he was elected President. Looking into a mirror across the room he saw himself full length, but with two faces.

It bothered him; he got up; the illusion vanished; but when he lay down again there in the glass again were two faces, one paler than the other. He got up again, mixed in the election excitement, forgot about it; but it came back, and haunted him. He told his wife about it; she worried too.

A few days later he tried it once more and the illusion of the two faces again registered to his eyes. But that was the last; the ghost since then wouldn't come back, he told his wife, who said it was a sign he would be elected to a second term, and the death pallor of one face meant he wouldn't live through his second term.

Clothes, furniture, books, the household goods, had been packed in boxes and trunks. The family had taken rooms in the Chenery House; the old cottage home was gone, leased, the horse, buggy, and cow sold off.

At the hotel Lincoln had roped his trunks himself, and had written, "A. Lincoln, The White House, Washington, D.C.," on cards he fastened on the trunks.

A COLD DRIZZLE OF RAIN was falling on the morning of February 11 when Lincoln and his party of fifteen were to leave Springfield on the eight o'clock at the Great Western Railway station. Chilly gray mist hung the circle of the prairie horizon. A short little locomotive with a flat-topped smokestack stood puffing with a baggage car and special passenger car hitched on; a railroad president and superintendent were on board. A thousand people crowded in and around the brick station, inside of which Lincoln was standing, and one by one came hundreds of old friends, shaking hands, wishing him luck and Godspeed, all faces solemn. Even the huge Judge David Davis, wearing a new white silk hat, was a serious figure.

A path was made for Lincoln from the station to his car; hands stretched out for one last handshake. He hadn't intended to make a speech; but on the platform of the car, as he turned and saw his home people, he took off his hat, stood perfectly still, and raised a hand, for silence. They stood, with hats off.

Then he spoke slowly, amid the soft gray drizzle from the sky: "Friends, no one who has never been placed in a like position can understand my feelings at this hour nor the oppressive sadness I feel at this parting. For more than a quarter of a century I have lived among you, and during all that time I have received nothing but kindness at your hands. Here I have lived from my youth till now I am an old man. Here the most sacred trusts of earth were assumed; here all my children were born; and here one of them lies buried. To you, dear friends, I owe all that I have, all that I am. All the strange checkered past seems to crowd now upon my mind. Today I leave you; I go to assume a task more difficult than that which devolved upon General Washington. Unless the great God who assisted him shall be with and aid me, I must fail. But if the same omniscient mind and the same Almighty arm that directed and protected him shall guide and support me, I shall not fail; I shall succeed. Let us all pray that the God of our fathers may not forsake us now. To Him I commend you all. Permit me to ask that with equal sincerity and faith you will all invoke His wisdom and guidance for me. With these few words I must leave you—for how long, I know not. Friends, one and all, I must now bid you an affectionate farewell."

There were voices, "Good-by, Abe."

And bells rang, there was a grinding of wheels, and the train moved, and carried Lincoln away from Springfield.

The tears were not yet dry on some faces when the train had faded into the gray to the east.

ANNE
FRANK

The
Diary
of
a Young
Girl

A CONDENSATION OF

ANNE FRANK

The Diary of a Young Girl

TRANSLATED FROM THE DUTCH BY
B.M.MOOYAART-DOUBLEDAY

▼

ILLUSTRATED BY SCOTT DUNCAN

The sensitive, observant, talented
girl who was Anne Frank lived for two
years in hiding from the Nazi deportation
gangs in Amsterdam. It was a life
inescapably grim, with terror never
far below the surface; yet the record
she left of this experience fairly
bubbles with the joy of living, and her
diary is a beautifully delicate record
of adolescence, depicting with touching
candor the thoughts and feelings of a
young girl.

Now published in many foreign languages
and having sold many millions of copies,
The Diary of a Young Girl is an
acknowledged classic. As both a drama
and a film it has played to vast
audiences all over the world, and in
this country the stage play won a
Pulitzer Prize.

Sunday, 14 June, 1942

ON FRIDAY, June 12th, my birthday, I woke at six o'clock, but of course I was not allowed to get up at that hour, so I had to control my curiosity until a quarter to seven. Then I could bear it no longer, and went to the sitting room to undo my presents. The first to greet me was *you*, possibly the nicest of all. There was a bunch of roses, and I got masses of things from Mummy and Daddy, and was thoroughly spoiled by various friends. I was given a party game, chocolates, a puzzle, a brooch, *Tales and Legends of the Netherlands* by Joseph Cohen, *Daisy's Mountain Holiday* (a terrific book), and some money. Now I can buy *The Myths of Greece and Rome*—grand!

Then Lies called for me and we went to school. During recess I treated everyone to sweet biscuits.

Now I must stop. Bye-bye, we're going to be great pals!

Monday, 15 June, 1942

I had my birthday party on Sunday afternoon. We showed a film *The Lighthouse Keeper* with Rin-Tin-Tin, which my friends thoroughly enjoyed. We had a lovely time. There were lots of girls and boys. For years Lies Goosens and Sanne Houtman were my best friends. Then I got to know Jopie de Waal at the Jewish Lyceum* and she is now my best girl friend. Lies is more friendly with another girl, and Sanne goes to a different school.

Mummy always wants to know whom I'm going to marry. Little does she guess that it's Peter Wessel.

Saturday, 20 June, 1942

I haven't written for a few days, because I wanted to think about my diary. It's odd for someone like me to keep a diary; not only because I have never done so before, but because it seems to me that no one else will be interested in the unbosomings of a thirteen-year-old schoolgirl. Still, does that matter?

There is a saying that "paper is more patient than man"; it came back to me on one of my melancholy days, while I sat chin in hand, feeling bored and limp. I don't intend to show this notebook to anyone unless I find a real friend, boy or girl. And now I come to the root of the matter, the reason for my starting a diary: it is that I have no such friend.

I have darling parents and a sister of sixteen. I have strings of boyfriends who peep at me through mirrors in class. I have a good home. No—I don't seem to lack anything. But with my friends it's just fun and joking, nothing more. We don't seem to be able to get closer.

I want this diary to be my friend for whom I have waited so long. I shall call my friend Kitty. I will begin my letters to Kitty by sketching my life.

My father was thirty-six when he married my mother, who was twenty-five. My sister Margot was born in 1926 in Frankfort on the Main, I followed in 1929, and, as we are Jewish, we emigrated to Holland in 1933, where my father was appointed managing director of Travies N.V., a firm in close relationship with Kolen & Co., of which my father is a partner.

Our family felt the full impact of Hitler's anti-Jewish laws, so life was filled with anxiety. In 1938, after the pogroms, my

---

*A type of secondary school specializing in the classics, common in most continental countries.

two uncles escaped to the U.S.A. After May 1940 good times rapidly fled: first the war, then the capitulation, followed by the arrival of the Germans, which is when the sufferings of us Jews really began. Anti-Jewish decrees followed each other in quick succession. Jews must wear a yellow star,* Jews are banned from trams and are forbidden to drive. Jews are only allowed to do their shopping between three and five o'clock in shops which bear the placard "Jewish Shop." Jews must be indoors by eight o'clock and cannot even sit in their own gardens after that hour. Jews are forbidden to visit places of entertainment. Swimming baths, tennis courts, hockey fields, and other sports grounds are all prohibited to them. Jews may not visit Christians. Jews must go to Jewish schools, and many more restrictions of a similar kind. But life went on.

In 1941, at the end of the school year at the Montessori school, I had to say good-by to Mrs. K. We both wept, it was very sad. Then I went, with my sister Margot, to the Jewish Lyceum, she into the fourth form and I into the first.

Saturday, 20 June, 1942

Dear Kitty,

I've been playing Ping-Pong a lot lately. We ping-pongers are very partial to ice cream, especially in summer, so we usually finish up with a visit to the nearest ice-cream shop, Delphi or Oasis, where Jews are allowed. We've given up scrounging for pocket money. Oasis is usually full and among our large circle we always manage to find some kindhearted boyfriend, who presents us with more ice cream than we could devour in a week.

I expect you will be rather surprised that I talk of boyfriends at my age. One simply can't avoid it at our school. As soon as a boy asks if he may bicycle home with me and we get into conversation, nine out of ten times I can be sure that he will fall head over heels in love immediately. After a while it cools down, as I take little notice of ardent looks and pedal blithely on.

If it gets too far, I swerve slightly on my bicycle, my satchel

---

*To distinguish them from others, all Jews were forced by the Germans to wear, prominently displayed, a yellow six-pointed star.

falls, the young man is bound to get off and hand it to me, by which time I have introduced a new topic of conversation.

These are the most innocent types; you get some who blow kisses or try to hold your arm, but then I get off my bicycle and refuse to go further, or I pretend to be insulted and tell them in no uncertain terms to clear off.

There, the foundation of our friendship is laid, till tomorrow!

Yours, Anne

Sunday, 21 June, 1942

Dear Kitty,

Our whole class is trembling. The teachers' meeting is soon, and there is much speculation as to who will move up and who will stay put. I'm not afraid about my girl friends and myself, though I'm not too certain about my math.

According to me, a quarter of the class should stay where they are; there are some absolute cuckoos, but teachers are the greatest freaks on earth.

I get along quite well with all my teachers. Mr. Keptor, the old math master, was very annoyed with me for a long time because I chatter so much. So I had to write a composition with "A Chatterbox" as the subject. A chatterbox! Whatever could one write?

That evening, when I'd finished my other homework, I pondered. The difficulty was to prove the necessity of talking. I thought and thought and then, suddenly having an idea, filled three sides and felt completely satisfied. My arguments were that talking is a feminine characteristic and I would do my best to keep it under control, but I should never be cured, for my mother talked as much as I, probably more, and what can one do about inherited qualities? Mr. Keptor had to laugh at my arguments.

Yours, Anne

Wednesday, 24 June, 1942

Dear Kitty,

It is boiling hot, we are all positively melting, and I have to walk everywhere. Now I can fully appreciate how nice a tram is; but that is a forbidden luxury for Jews. We are allowed on the ferry and that is all. I had to visit the dentist in the lunch hour yesterday. It is a long way and I nearly fell asleep in school that afternoon. Luckily, the dentist's assistant was very kind and gave me a drink. It is not the Dutch people's fault we are having such a miserable time.

I wish I didn't have to go to school, as my bicycle was stolen in the Easter holidays and Daddy has given Mummy's to a Christian family for safekeeping. But thank goodness, the holidays are nearly here, one more week and the agony is over.

Yours, Anne

Tuesday, 30 June, 1942

Dear Kitty,

I've not had a moment to write to you until today. Jopie slept here on Saturday night, but she went to Lies on Sunday and I was bored stiff. Harry Goldberg, a nice-looking boy I met at my girl friend Eva's, came by in the evening, and we went walking. We passed the bookshop on the corner, and there stood Peter Wessel with two other boys; he said "Hello"—it's the first time he has spoken to me for ages, I was really pleased.

Yours, Anne

Friday, 3 July, 1942

Dear Kitty,

Harry visited us yesterday to meet my parents. I had bought a cream cake, sweets, tea, and fancy biscuits, quite a spread, but neither Harry nor I felt like sitting stiffly side by side indefinitely, so we went for a walk, and it was ten past eight when he brought me home. Daddy was very cross because it is dangerous for Jews to be out after eight o'clock, and I had to promise to be in by ten to eight in future.

Yours, Anne

Sunday morning, 5 July, 1942

Dear Kitty,

Our examination results were announced in the Jewish Theater last Friday. I couldn't have hoped for better. I had a five for

287

algebra, two sixes, and the rest were all sevens or eights. They were certainly pleased at home, although over the question of marks my parents are quite different from most. They don't care a bit whether my reports are good or bad as long as I'm well and happy, and not too cheeky: then the rest will come by itself. I am just the opposite. I don't want to be a bad pupil; I should really have stayed in the seventh form in the Montessori school, but when all the Jewish children had to go to Jewish schools, the headmaster took Lies and me conditionally after a bit of persuasion. He relied on us to do our best and I don't want to let him down. My sister Margot has her report too, brilliant as usual. She is so brainy.

Daddy has been at home a lot lately, as there is nothing for him to do at business; it must be rotten to feel so superfluous. Mr. Koophuis has taken over Travies and Mr. Kraler the firm Kolen & Co. When we walked across our little square together a few days ago, Daddy began to talk of going into hiding. "Anne," he said, "you know that we have been taking food, clothes, furniture to other people for more than a year now. We don't want our belongings to be seized by the Germans, so we shall disappear of our own accord and not wait until they come and fetch us."

"But, Daddy, when would it be?" He spoke so seriously that I grew very anxious.

"Don't you worry about it, we shall arrange everything. Make the most of your carefree young life while you can." That was all. Oh, may the fulfillment of these somber words remain far distant!

Yours, Anne

Wednesday, 8 July, 1942

Dear Kitty,

Years seem to have passed between Sunday and now. So much has happened, it is as if the whole world had turned upside down. But I am still alive, Kitty, and that is the main thing, Daddy says. I will begin by telling you what happened on Sunday afternoon.

At three o'clock (Harry had just gone, but was coming back

later) someone rang the front doorbell. I was lying lazily on the veranda in the sunshine. Margot appeared looking very excited. "The S.S. have sent a call-up notice for Daddy," she whispered. "Mummy has gone to see Mr. Van Daan already." (Van Daan is a friend who works with Daddy.) It was a great shock to me, a call-up; everyone knows what that means. I picture concentration camps and lonely cells. "Of course he won't go," declared Margot. "We should move into our hiding place tomorrow. The Van Daans are going with us, so we shall be seven in all." Silence. We couldn't talk any more, waiting for Mummy, thinking about Daddy, who, little knowing what was going on, was visiting some old people in the Joodse Invalide.

Suddenly the bell rang again. "That is Harry," I said.

"Don't open the door." Margot held me back, but it was not necessary as we heard Mummy and Mr. Van Daan downstairs, talking to Harry, then they came in and closed the door behind them. Margot and I were sent out of the room. Van Daan wanted to talk to Mummy alone. When we were in our bedroom, Margot told me that the call-up was not for Daddy, but for her. I was frightened and began to cry. Margot is sixteen; would they really take girls of that age away? But thank goodness she won't go, Mummy said so herself; that must be what Daddy meant when he talked about us going into hiding.

Where would we go, in the country, in a house or a cottage, when, how . . . ? These were questions I was not allowed to ask, but I couldn't get them out of my mind. Margot and I began to pack some of our most vital belongings into a school satchel. The first thing I put in was this diary, then hair curlers, handkerchiefs, school books, a comb, old letters; the craziest things, but memories mean more to me than dresses.

At five o'clock Daddy finally arrived. Van Daan went and fetched Miep. Miep has been in the business with Daddy since 1933 and has become a close friend, like her brand-new husband, Henk. Miep came and took shoes, dresses, coats, underwear, and stockings away in her bag, promising to return. Then silence fell; not one of us felt like eating anything, it was hot and everything was very strange. We let our large upstairs room to a Mr. Goudsmit, a divorced man in his thirties, who appeared to have nothing to do this evening; we simply could not get rid of him without being rude; he hung about until ten o'clock. At eleven o'clock Miep and Henk Van Santen arrived. Once again, shoes, stockings, books, and underclothes disappeared into Miep's bag and Henk's deep pockets, and at eleven thirty they too disappeared.

I was dog-tired and on my last night in my own bed I fell asleep immediately and didn't wake up until Mummy called me at five thirty the next morning. It was raining and, luckily, not so hot as Sunday. We put on heaps of clothes as if we were going to the North Pole. No Jew in our situation would have dreamed of going out with a suitcase. I had on two vests, three pairs of pants, a dress, a skirt, jacket, summer coat, two pairs of stockings, lace-up shoes, woolly cap, scarf, and still more; I was nearly stifled before we started, but no one inquired about that.

Margot filled her satchel with school books, fetched her bicycle, and rode off behind Miep. I still didn't know where our secret hiding place was to be. At seven thirty the door closed behind us. Moortje, my little cat, was the only creature to whom I said farewell. She would have a good home with the neighbors. This was all written in a letter addressed to Mr. Goudsmit.

There was one pound of meat in the kitchen for the cat, breakfast things lying on the table, stripped beds, all giving the impression that we had left helter-skelter. But we didn't care about impressions, we only wanted to escape safely, nothing else. Continued tomorrow.

Yours, Anne

Thursday, 9 July, 1942

Dear Kitty,

So we walked in the pouring rain, Daddy, Mummy, and I, each with a school satchel and shopping bag filled to the brim with all kinds of things thrown together. We got sympathetic looks from people on their way to work. You could see by their faces how sorry they were they couldn't offer us a lift; the gaudy yellow star spoke for itself.

Only when we were on the road did Mummy and Daddy begin to tell me bits and pieces about the plan. For months as many of our goods as possible had been sent away. They were ready for us to have gone into hiding on July 16. The plan had had to be speeded up ten days because of the call-up, so our quarters would not be so well organized, but we had to make the best of it.

The hiding place itself would be in the building where Daddy has his office. Daddy didn't have many people working for him: Mr. Kraler, Koophuis, Miep, and Elli Vossen, a twenty-three-year-old typist; all knew of our arrival. Elli's father and two boys worked in the warehouse; they had not been told.

Exterior view of the "Secret Annexe"

I will describe the building: there is a large warehouse on the ground floor which is used as a store. The front door to the house is next to the warehouse door, and inside the front door is a second doorway which leads to a staircase. There is another door at the top of the stairs, with a frosted-glass window in it, which has "Office" written in black letters across it. That is the large main office, very big, very light, and very full. Elli, Miep, and Mr. Koophuis work there in the daytime. A small dark room containing the safe, a wardrobe, and a large cupboard leads to a small dark second office. Mr. Kraler and Mr. Van Daan used to sit here, now it is only Mr. Kraler. One can reach Kraler's office from the passage, but only via a glass door which can be opened from the inside, but not easily from the outside.

From Kraler's office a long passage goes past the coal store, up four steps, and leads to the private office. Dark, dignified furniture, linoleum and carpets on the floor, radio, smart lamp, everything first-class. Next door there is a roomy kitchen with a hot-water faucet and a gas stove. Next door the W.C. That is the first floor.

A wooden staircase leads from the downstairs passage to the next floor. There is a small landing at the top. There is a door at each end of the landing, one leading to a storeroom at the front of the house and to the attics. One of those really steep Dutch staircases runs from the side to the other door opening on to the street.

The other door leads to our "Secret Annexe." No one would

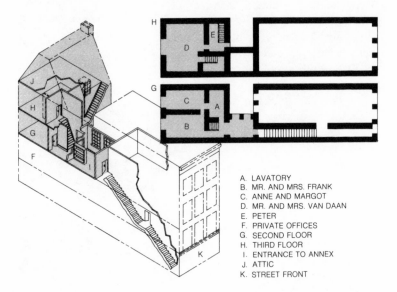

A. LAVATORY
B. MR. AND MRS. FRANK
C. ANNE AND MARGOT
D. MR. AND MRS. VAN DAAN
E. PETER
F. PRIVATE OFFICES
G. SECOND FLOOR
H. THIRD FLOOR
I. ENTRANCE TO ANNEX
J. ATTIC
K. STREET FRONT

ever guess that there would be so many rooms hidden behind that plain gray door. There's a little step in front of the door and then you are inside.

There is a steep staircase immediately opposite the entrance. On the left a tiny passage brings you into a room which was to become the Frank family's bed-sitting-room, next door a smaller room, study and bedroom for the two young ladies of the family. On the right a little room without windows containing the washbasin and a small W.C. compartment, with another door leading to Margot's and my room. If you go up the next flight of stairs and open the door, you are simply amazed that there could be such a big light room in such an old house by the canal. There is a gas stove in this room (thanks to the fact that it was used as a laboratory) and a sink. This is now the kitchen for the Van Daans, besides being general living room, dining room, and scullery.

A tiny little corridor room will become Peter Van Daan's apartment. Then, just as on the lower landing, there is a large attic. So there you are, I've introduced you to the whole of our beautiful Secret Annexe.

Yours, Anne

Friday, 10 July, 1942

Dear Kitty,

When we arrived, Miep took us quickly upstairs and into the Secret Annexe. She closed the door behind us and we were alone. Margot was already waiting for us, having come much faster on her bicycle. Our living room and all the other rooms were chock-full of rubbish, indescribably so. All the cardboard boxes which had been sent to the office in the previous months lay piled on the floor and the beds. The little room was filled to the ceiling with bedclothes. We had to start clearing up immediately, if we wished to sleep in decent beds that night. Mummy and Margot were not in a fit state to take part; they were tired and miserable, and lay down on their beds. But the two "clearers-up" of the family—Daddy and myself—wanted to start at once.

The whole day long we unpacked boxes, filled cupboards, hammered and tidied, until we were dead beat. We sank into clean beds that night. We hadn't had a bit of anything warm the whole day, but we didn't care; Mummy and Margot were too tired and keyed up to eat, and Daddy and I were too busy.

On Tuesday morning we went on where we left off the day before. Elli and Miep collected our rations for us, Daddy improved the poor blackout, we scrubbed the kitchen floor, and were on the go the whole day long again. I hardly had time to think about the great change in my life until Wednesday. Then I had a chance, for the first time since our arrival, to realize what had actually happened to me and what was still going to happen.

Yours, Anne

Saturday, 11 July, 1942

Dear Kitty,

Daddy, Mummy, and Margot can't get used to the sound of the Westertoren clock which tells us the time every quarter of an hour. I loved it from the start, and especially in the night it's like a faithful friend.

I expect you will be interested to hear what it feels like to "disappear"; well, all I can say is that I don't know myself yet. I don't think I shall ever feel really at home in this house, but that does not mean that I loathe it here, it is more like being on vacation in a very peculiar boardinghouse. The Secret Annexe is an ideal hiding place. You'd never find a better or more comfortable one anywhere in Amsterdam, perhaps even in the whole of Holland. Our little room looked very bare at first with nothing on the walls; but my film-star collection and picture postcards have transformed the walls into one gigantic picture. It looks much more cheerful.

Margot and Mummy are a bit better now. Mummy felt well enough to cook some soup yesterday. The four of us went to the private office yesterday evening and turned on the radio. I was so terribly frightened that someone might hear it that I begged Daddy to come upstairs with me. Mummy understood how I felt and came too. We are very nervous that the neighbors might hear us or see something. We made curtains straightaway on the first day. Really one can hardly call them curtains, they are just light, loose strips of material, all different shapes, quality, and pattern, which Daddy and I sewed together in a most unprofessional way. These works of art are fixed in position with thumbtacks, not to come down until we emerge from here.

There are some large business premises on the right of us, and on the left a furniture workshop; there is no one there after working hours but we have to whisper and tread lightly during the day as sounds could travel through the walls. We have forbidden Margot to cough, although she has a bad cold, and make her swallow large doses of codeine.

I am looking for Tuesday when the Van Daans arrive; it will be much more fun and not so quiet. It is the silence that frightens me so in the evenings and at night. I can't tell you how oppressive it is *never* to be able to go outdoors, also I'm very afraid that we shall be discovered and shot. That is not a pleasant prospect.

Yours, Anne

Friday, 14 August, 1942

Dear Kitty,

I have deserted you for a whole month, but there is so little news here that I can't find amusing things to tell you every day. The Van Daans arrived on July 13. We thought they were coming on the fourteenth, but between the thirteenth and sixteenth of July the Germans called up people right and left so they played for safety, better a day too early than a day too late. At nine thirty in the morning (we were still having breakfast) Peter arrived, the Van Daans' son, not sixteen yet, a rather shy, gawky youth; can't expect much from his company. He brought his cat (Mouschi) with him. Mr. and Mrs. Van Daan arrived half an hour later, and to our great amusement she had a large pottie in her hatbox. "I don't feel at home without my chamber," she declared; its permanent resting place is under her divan.

From the day they arrived we all had meals cozily together and after three days it was just as if we were one large family. Naturally the Van Daans were able to tell us a lot about the extra week they had spent in the inhabited world. Among other things we heard what had happened to our house and to Mr. Goudsmit. Mr. Van Daan told us:

"Mr. Goudsmit phoned at nine o'clock on Monday morning and asked if I could come around. I went immediately and found G. in a state of great agitation. He let me read a letter that the Franks had left behind and wanted to take the cat to the neighbors as indicated in the letter, which pleased me. Mr. G. was afraid that the house would be searched so we went through all the rooms, tidied up a bit, and cleared away the breakfast things. Suddenly I discovered a writing pad on Mrs. Frank's desk with an address in Maastricht written on it. Although I knew that this was done on purpose, I pretended to be very shocked and urged Mr. G. to tear up this unfortunate piece of paper.

"I went on pretending that I knew nothing of your disappearance all the time, but after seeing the paper, I got a brain wave.

'Mr. Goudsmit'—I said—'it suddenly dawns on me what this address may refer to. Now it all comes back to me, a high-ranking officer was in the office about six months ago, he appeared to be very friendly with Mr. Frank and offered to help him. He was stationed in Maastricht. I think he must have kept his word and somehow or other managed to get them into Belgium and then on to Switzerland. I should tell this to any friends who may inquire. Don't, of course, mention Maastricht.'

"With these words I left the house. Most of your friends know already, because I've been told myself several times by different people."

We were highly amused at the story and, when Mr. Van Daan gave us further details, laughed still more at the way people can let their imagination run away with them. One family had seen us pass on bicycles very early in the morning and another lady knew quite definitely that we were fetched by a military car in the middle of the night.

Yours, Anne

Friday, 21 August, 1942

Dear Kitty,

The entrance to our hiding place has now been properly concealed. Mr. Kraler thought it would be better to put a cupboard in front of our door, but of course it had to be a movable cupboard that can open like a door.

Mr. Vossen, Elli's father, made the whole thing. We let him into the secret and he can't do enough to help. If we want to go downstairs, we have to first bend down and then jump, because the step has gone.

I'm not working much at present; I'm giving myself holidays until September. Then Daddy is going to give me lessons; it's shocking how much I've forgotten already. There is little change in our life. Mummy sometimes treats me like a baby, which I can't bear. I still don't like Peter Van Daan, he is so boring; he flops lazily on his bed half the time.

It is lovely weather. We make the most of it by lying on a bed in the attic, where the sun shines through an open window.

Yours, Anne

Dear Kitty,

Mr. and Mrs. Van Daan have had a terrific quarrel, I've never seen anything like it before. Mummy and Daddy would never dream of shouting at each other. The cause was so trivial that the whole thing was a waste of breath. Naturally it is very unpleasant for Peter, who has to stand by. No one takes him seriously, he is so frightfully touchy and lazy.

It is not all honey between Mummy and Mrs. Van Daan either; Mrs. Van Daan has taken all three of her sheets out of the common linen cupboard. She takes it for granted that Mummy's sheets will do for all of us. It will be a nasty surprise for her when she finds that Mummy has followed her good example.

Also, she is thoroughly piqued that her dinner service and not ours is in use. I always have bad luck; I smashed one of Mrs. Van Daan's soup plates into a thousand pieces yesterday. "Oh!" she cried angrily. "Couldn't you be careful—that's the last one I've got."

Last week we had a little interruption in our monotonous life; it was over a book about women—and Peter. Margot and Peter are allowed to read all the books that Mr. Koophuis lends us, but the grown-ups held back this particular book. Peter's curiosity was aroused at once. He got hold of the book on the sly and disappeared to the attic. All went well for a few days. His mother knew what he was doing, but didn't tell tales, until Mr. Van Daan found out. He was very angry, took the book away, and thought that that would finish the whole business. However, he had not allowed for his son's curiosity.

Mrs. Van Daan, meanwhile, asked Mummy what she thought about it all. Mummy thought this particular book was not suitable for Margot, but she saw no harm in letting her read most books. "There is a great difference, Mrs. Van Daan," said Mummy, "between Margot and Peter. In the first place Margot is a girl and girls are always more grown-up than boys; secondly, Margot has read a lot of serious books, and does not go in search of things that are forbidden her; and thirdly, Margot is far more intelligent."

In the meantime Peter found a time when no one bothered

about this enthralling book he was determined to finish: seven thirty in the evening—then everyone was in the private office listening to the radio. He took his treasure to the attic again. He should have been downstairs again by eight thirty, but because the book was so thrilling he forgot the time and was just coming downstairs as his father came into the room. You can imagine the consequences! With a slap and a snatch, the book lay on the table and Peter was in the attic. That's how matters stood as we sat down to table, chattering gaily, when suddenly we heard a piercing whistle; we all stopped eating and looked from one to another. Then we heard Peter's voice, calling down the chimney, "I say, I'm not coming down anyway." Mr. Van Daan sprang to his feet, his napkin fell to the floor, and scarlet in the face he shouted, "I've had enough of this." Daddy took his arm, afraid of what might happen, and the two men went together to the attic. After a good deal of resistance, Peter landed in his room with the door closed. We went on eating. Mrs. Van Daan wanted to save one slice of bread for the dear boy, but his father stood firm. "If he doesn't apologize soon, he will sleep in the attic." Loud protests from the rest of us, as we thought missing supper was quite enough punishment. Besides, Peter might catch cold and we couldn't call a doctor.

Peter did not apologize, but I noticed the next morning that his bed had been slept in. Peter was back in the attic at seven o'clock, but Daddy managed with a few friendly words to persuade him to come down again. Sour faces and obstinate silences for three days and then everything went smoothly once more.

Yours, Anne

Monday, 21 September, 1942

Dear Kitty,

Mrs. Van Daan is unbearable. This is the latest: she doesn't want to wash the pans if there is a fragment of food left; instead of putting it into a glass dish, as we've always done, she leaves it in the pan to go bad. After the next meal Margot sometimes has about seven pans to wash up.

I'm busy with Daddy working out his family tree: as we go along he tells me little bits about everyone—it's terribly interesting. Mr. Koophuis brings a few special books for me every other week.

Term time has begun again, I'm working hard at my French and manage to pump in five irregular verbs per day. Peter sighs and groans over his English. A few school books have just arrived; we have a good stock of exercise books, pencils, erasers, and labels, as I brought these with me. I sometimes listen to the Dutch news from London; Prince Bernhard recently said that Princess Juliana is expecting a baby next January. I think it is lovely.

I have just waked up to the disturbing fact that I have one long-sleeved dress and three cardigans for the winter. I've received permission from Daddy to knit a jumper of white sheep's wool; it's not very nice wool, but as long as it's warm that's all that matters. We have some clothes deposited with friends, but unfortunately we shall not see them until after the war, if they are still there then.

Mrs. Van Daan just came in. Slap! I closed the book. It gave me a frightful shock, because there was an unflattering description of her on this particular page.

Yours, Anne

Friday, 25 September, 1942

Dear Kitty,

Yesterday evening I went upstairs and "visited" the Van Daans. Sometimes it can be fun. We have moth biscuits (the biscuit tin is kept in the wardrobe which is full of mothballs) and drink lemonade. We talked about Peter. I told them how Peter often strokes my cheek and that I wished he wouldn't as I don't like being pawed by boys.

In the typical way parents have, they asked if I couldn't get fond of Peter, because he certainly liked me very much. Imagine it! I thought, "Oh dear!" and said that I thought Peter rather awkward, but that it was probably shyness, as many boys who haven't had much to do with girls are like that.

The Refuge Committee of the Secret Annexe is very ingenious. To get news of us to Mr. Van Dijk, Travies' chief representative who has hidden some of our things, they typed a letter to a chemist in South Zeeland, who does business with our firm, in such a way that he has to send an enclosed reply back in an envelope addressed to the office. When this envelope arrives from Zeeland, the enclosed letter is taken out and replaced by a message in Daddy's handwriting. Van Dijk will think we are in Zeeland when he reads the note. They specially chose Zeeland because it is so close to Belgium and the letter could have easily been smuggled over the border; in addition no one is allowed into Zeeland without a special permit, so if he thought we were there, he couldn't look us up.

Yours, Anne

Sunday, 27 September, 1942

Dear Kitty,

Just had a big bust-up with Mummy for the umpteenth time; we simply don't get on together these days. Our ideas are completely opposite. And Margot and I don't hit it off any too well either. Margot's and Mummy's natures are completely strange to me. I can understand my friends better than my own mother.

The Van Daans are the kind of people who adore bringing up other people's children. Margot doesn't need it, she is such a goody-goody, but I seem to have enough mischief in me for the two of us put together. You should hear the reprimands and cheeky answers flying to and fro at mealtimes. Mummy and Daddy always defend me stoutly. I'd have to give up if it weren't for them. Although they do tell me that I mustn't talk so much.

If I take a small helping of some vegetable I detest and make up with potatoes, the Van Daans can't get over it.

"Come along, Anne, have a few more vegetables," she says straightaway.

"No, thank you, Mrs. Van Daan," I answer, "I have plenty of potatoes."

"Vegetables are good for you. Have a few more." When Daddy comes to my rescue, she says: "Anne's frightfully spoiled. I wouldn't put up with it if Anne were my daughter." These are always her last words, "if Anne were my daughter." Thank heavens I'm not!

Yours, Anne

Dear Kitty,

Extraordinary things happen to people hiding. Just imagine, as there is no bath, we use a washtub. All seven of us take this great luxury in turns.

Each member of the family has found his own place for carrying out the performance. Peter uses the kitchen in spite of its glass door. When he is going to have a bath he tells us that we must not walk past the kitchen for half an hour. Mr. Van Daan goes right upstairs; to him it is worth the bother of carrying hot water all that way, so as to have the seclusion of his own room. Mrs. Van Daan simply doesn't bathe at all; she is waiting to see which is the best place. Daddy has his bath in the private office, Mummy behind a fireguard in the kitchen; Margot and I have chosen the front office for our scrub. The curtains there are drawn on Saturday afternoons.

However, I don't like this place any longer, and since last week I've been on the lookout for more comfortable quarters. Peter gave me an idea and that was to try the large office W.C. There I can sit down, have the light on, lock the door, pour my own bath water away, and I'm safe from prying eyes.

I tried my beautiful bathroom on Sunday for the first time and although it sounds mad, I think it is the best place of all. Last week the plumber was at work downstairs to move the drains and water pipes from the office W.C. to the passage, a precaution against frozen pipes. The plumber's visit was far from pleasant for us. Not only were we unable to draw water the whole day, but we could not go to the W.C. either. Now it is rather indecent to tell you how we overcame this difficulty; however, I'm not such a prude that I can't talk about these things.

The day we arrived here, Daddy and I improvised a pottie for ourselves; not having a better receptacle, we sacrificed a glass preserving jar for this purpose. During the plumber's visit, nature's offerings were deposited in these jars in the sitting room during the day.

This was bad, but there was an even greater trial for "Miss Quack-Quack." I have to whisper on ordinary days; but not being able to speak or move the whole day was ten times worse.

Who, three months ago, would ever have guessed that quick-silver Anne would have to sit still for hours—and, what's more, could?

Yours, Anne

Thursday, 1 October, 1942

Dear Kitty,

Suddenly at eight o'clock yesterday the bell rang loudly. Of course, I thought that someone had come: you'll guess who I mean. But I calmed down when everyone said it must be some urchins or perhaps the postman.

The twenty-ninth was Mrs. Van Daan's birthday. We managed a little party in her honor, with a specially nice meal, and she received some small presents, and red carnations from her husband. To pause for a moment on the subject of Mrs. Van Daan, I must tell you that her attempts to flirt with Pim (Daddy's nickname) and attract his attention are a source of continual irritation for me. Pim doesn't find her attractive or funny. Mummy doesn't behave like that with Mr. Van Daan; I've said that to Mrs. Van Daan's face.

Now and then Peter comes out of his shell and can be quite funny. We have one thing in common: we both love dressing up. He appeared in one of Mrs. Van Daan's very narrow dresses and I put on his suit. He wore a hat and I a cap. The grown-ups were doubled up with laughter. Elli has bought new skirts for Margot and me. The material is just like sacking. What a difference compared with before the war!

Another nice thing: Elli has ordered a correspondence course in shorthand for Margot, Peter, and me. You wait and see what perfect experts we shall be by next year. It's extremely important to be able to write in a code.

Yours, Anne

Saturday, 3 October, 1942

Dear Kitty,

Mummy kicked up a frightful row yesterday and told Daddy just what she thought of me. Then she had an awful fit of tears so, of course, off I went too; and I'd got such an awful headache anyway. Finally I told Daddy that I'm much more fond of him than Mummy, to which he replied that I'd get over that. But I don't believe it. I have to simply force myself to stay calm with her. Daddy wishes that I would volunteer to help Mummy, when she doesn't feel well or has a headache; but I shan't.

Why do grown-ups quarrel so much over the most idiotic things? Of course, there is sometimes a reason for a quarrel, but this is just plain bickering. I suppose I should get used to it. But I can't as long as I am the subject of nearly every discussion (they use the word "discussion" instead of quarrel). I'm expected (by order) to swallow the harsh words in silence and I am not used to this. Am I really so bad-mannered, conceited, headstrong, stupid, lazy, etc., etc., as they say? Oh, of course not. I have faults just like everyone else, I know, but they exaggerate everything. Kitty, if only you knew how I sometimes boil under so many gibes and jeers. And I don't

Anne Frank

know how long I shall be able to stifle my rage. I shall just blow up one day.

Anyhow, I've learned one thing. You only really get to know people when you've had a jolly good row with them.

Yours, Anne

Friday, 9 October, 1942

Dear Kitty,

I've got dismal, depressing news today. Our Jewish friends are being taken away by the dozen. These people are treated by the Gestapo without a shred of decency, loaded into cattle trucks and sent to Westerbork, the big Jewish camp in Drenthe. Westerbork sounds terrible: only one washing cubicle for a hundred people and not nearly enough lavatories. There is no separate accommodation. Men, women, and children all sleep together. One hears of frightful immorality because of this; a lot of the women, and even girls, are expecting babies. It is impossible to escape; most of the people in the camp are branded by their shaven heads and Jewish appearance. If it is as bad as this in Holland whatever will it be like in the distant and barbarous regions they are sent to? We assume that most of them are murdered. The English radio speaks of their being gassed. Perhaps that is the quickest way to die.

I feel terribly upset. I couldn't tear myself away while Miep told these dreadful stories. Just recently, for instance, a poor old crippled Jewess was sitting on her doorstep; she had been told to wait there by the Gestapo, who had gone to fetch a car to take her away. The poor old thing was terrified by the guns that were shooting at English planes overhead, and by the glaring beams of the searchlights. But Miep did not dare take her in; no one would undergo such a risk. The Germans strike without the slightest mercy. Elli is very quiet: her boyfriend has got to go to Germany. Dirk is not the only one: trainloads of boys leave daily.

This, however, is not the end of my bad news. Have you ever heard of hostages? That's the latest thing in penalties for sabotage. Can you imagine anything so dreadful? Prominent citizens —innocent people—are thrown into prison. If the saboteur can't be traced, the Gestapo simply put five hostages against the wall. Announcements of their deaths appear in the papers frequently. These outrages are described as "fatal accidents." Nice people, the Germans! To think that I was once one of them! No, Hitler took away our nationality long ago. In fact, Germans and Jews are the greatest enemies in the world.

Yours, Anne

Friday, 16 October, 1942

Dear Kitty,

I'm terribly busy. I've just done a perfectly foul math problem and three pages of French grammar. I flatly refuse to do math problems every day. Daddy agrees that they're vile. Neither of us are much good and we often have to fetch Margot.

Mummy, Margot, and I are as thick as thieves again. Last evening Margot and I got on to the subject of the future. I asked her what she wanted to be. But she wouldn't say and

made a great secret of it. I gathered something about teaching.
I shouldn't be so curious!

I asked Margot if she thought I was very ugly. She said that
I was quite attractive and that I had nice eyes. Rather vague,
don't you think?

Yours, Anne

Tuesday, 20 October, 1942

Dear Kitty,

My hand still shakes, although it's two hours since we had
the shock. I should explain that there are five fire extinguishers
in the house. We knew that someone was coming to fill them,
but no one had warned us when.

We weren't making any attempt to keep quiet, until I heard
hammering outside on the landing opposite our cupboard door.
I thought of the workman at once and warned Elli, who was
having a meal with us, that she shouldn't go downstairs. Daddy
and I posted ourselves at the door to hear when the man left.
After he'd been working for a quarter of an hour, he laid his
tools down on top of our cupboard and knocked and pulled at
our door. We turned absolutely white. Perhaps he had heard
something and wanted to investigate our secret den. The knocking, pulling, and wrenching went on. Then, just as I thought
my last hour was at hand, I heard Mr. Koophuis say, "Open the
door, it's only me." We opened it immediately. The hook that
holds the cupboard, which can be undone if you know the
secret, had got jammed. That was why no one had been able to
warn us about the workman. The man had now gone downstairs and Koophuis wanted to fetch Elli, but couldn't open the
cupboard again. It was a great relief, I can tell you.

Yours, Anne

Thursday, 29 October, 1942

Dear Kitty,

I am awfully worried, Daddy is ill. He has a high temperature
and a red rash, it looks like measles. Think of it, we can't even
call a doctor! Mummy is letting him have a good sweat. Perhaps
that will send his temperature down.

This morning Miep told us that all the furniture has been removed from the Van Daans' home. We haven't told Mrs. Van Daan yet. She's such a bundle of nerves already, and we don't feel like listening to another moan over all the lovely china and beautiful chairs that she left at home. *We* had to leave all our nice things behind; what's the good of grumbling about it?

I'm allowed to read more grown-up books lately. I'm now reading *Eva's Youth* by Nico van Suchtelen. I can't see much difference between this and schoolgirl love stories. It is true there are bits about women selling themselves to unknown men in back streets. They ask a packet of money for it. I'd die of shame if anything like that happened to me. Also it says that Eva has a monthly period. Oh, I'm so longing to have it too; it seems so important.

Yours, Anne

Saturday, 7 November, 1942

Dear Kitty,

Is it just chance that Daddy and Mummy never rebuke Margot and always drop on me for everything? Yesterday evening, for instance: Margot was reading a book with lovely drawings in it; she put the book down and went upstairs. I started looking at the pictures. Margot came back, saw "her" book in my hands, and asked for it. Just because I wanted to look a little further on, Margot got angry. Then Mummy joined in: "Give the book to Margot; she was reading it." Daddy came into the room. He didn't even know what it was all about, but saw the injured look on Margot's face and promptly dropped on me: "I'd like to see what you'd say if Margot ever started looking at one of your books!" I gave way at once, laid the book down, and left the room—offended, as they thought. It so happened I was neither offended nor cross, just miserable.

Margot is the sweetest, most beautiful girl in the world. I have always been the dunce of the family, but all the same I feel I have some right to be taken seriously too. I've always had to pay double for my deeds, first with the scolding and again because my feelings are hurt. I'm not satisfied with this apparent favoritism. I want something from Daddy that he is not able to give me. I'm not jealous of Margot, never have been. I don't envy her beauty. It is only that I long for Daddy's real love: not only as his child, but for me—Anne, myself.

I cling to Daddy because it is only through him that I am able to retain a remnant of family feeling. Daddy doesn't understand that I need to give vent to my feelings over Mummy sometimes. He doesn't want to talk about it; he simply avoids anything which might lead to remarks about Mummy's failings. Just the same, I find Mummy and her failings are harder to bear than anything else. I don't know how to keep it all to myself. I can't always be drawing attention to her untidiness and her sarcasm, neither can I believe that I'm always in the wrong.

We are exact opposites in everything; so naturally we are bound to run up against each other. I don't pronounce judgment on Mummy's character, for that is something I can't judge. I only look at her as a mother, and she just doesn't succeed in being that. I have an image of what a perfect mother should be; and in her whom I must call "Mother" I find no trace of that image.

Mr. Frank

I am always making resolutions not to notice Mummy's bad example. I want to see only the good side of her and to seek in myself what I cannot find in her. But it doesn't work; and the worst of it is that neither Daddy nor Mummy understands this gap in my life, and I blame them for it. I wonder if anyone can ever succeed in making their children absolutely content.

Sometimes I believe that God wants to try me. I must become good through my own efforts, without examples and advice. Then later on I shall be all the stronger. From whom but myself shall I get comfort? As I need comforting often, I frequently feel weak, and dissatisfied with myself; my shortcomings are too great. I know this, and every day I try to improve myself.

My treatment varies so much. One day Anne is so sensible and is allowed to know everything; and the next day I hear that

Anne is just a silly little goat who doesn't know anything and imagines that she's learned a wonderful lot from books. I'm not a baby to be laughed at. I have my own views and ideas, though I can't put them into words yet. That's why in the end I always come back to my diary, because Kitty is always patient.

I shall persevere, in spite of everything, and find my own way. I only wish I could occasionally receive encouragement from someone who loves me.

Yours, Anne

Monday, 9 November, 1942

Dear Kitty,

Yesterday Peter was sixteen. He had some nice presents: a game of Monopoly, a razor, and a lighter.

The biggest surprise was the announcement that the British had landed in Tunis, Algiers, Casablanca, and Oran. "This is the beginning of the end," everyone was saying, but Churchill, the British prime minister, said: "It is not even the beginning of the end. But it is, perhaps, the end of the beginning."

But to return to our secret den. I must tell you about our food supply. As you know, we have some greedy pigs on the top floor. We get our bread from a nice baker, a friend of Koophuis. We don't get so much as we used to at home, but it's sufficient. Four ration cards have been bought illegally. Their price is going up all the time; it has now gone up from twenty-seven florins to thirty-three, for a little slip of printed paper! In order to have something in the house that will keep, apart from our 150 tins of vegetables, we have bought 270 pounds of dried peas and beans. They are not all for us, some are for the office people.

We decided it would be better to put our winter store in the attic and Peter was given the job of dragging it all up there. He had managed to get five of the six sacks upstairs intact, and was busy pulling up number six, when the bottom seam of the sack split and a positive hailstorm of brown beans rattled down the stairs. The noise was enough to waken the dead. Downstairs they thought the house was coming down. (Thank God there were no strangers in the house.) It gave Peter a fright. But he was soon roaring with laughter, especially when he saw me standing at the bottom of the stairs, up to my ankles in beans. Quickly we started to pick them up. But small, slippery beans rolled into all the corners and holes. Now, every time anyone goes downstairs they are able to present Mrs. Van Daan with a handful of beans.

I'd almost forgotten to mention that Daddy is better again.

Yours, Anne

Tuesday, 10 November, 1942

Dear Kitty,

Great news—we want to take in an eighth person. Yes, really! We've always thought that there was quite enough room and food for one more. We were only afraid of giving Koophuis and Kraler more trouble. But now that the appalling stories we hear about Jews are getting even worse, they thought it was an excellent plan. "It is just as dangerous for seven as for eight," they said. This settled, we ran through our circle of friends, trying to think of a single person who would fit in well with our "family." We chose a dentist called Albert Dussel, whose wife was fortunate enough to be out of the country when war broke out. He is quiet, and from a superficial acquaintance, both families think he is a congenial person. Miep will make arrangements for him to join us. If he comes, he will have to sleep in my room instead of Margot, who will use the camp bed.

Yours, Anne

Tuesday, 17 November, 1942

Dear Kitty,

Dussel has arrived. Miep had told him that he must be in front of the post office at eleven o'clock, where a man would meet him. Dussel was standing at the rendezvous dead on time. Mr. Koophuis, who knows Dussel, went up to him and told him that the gentleman could not come, but asked whether he would go to the office. Koophuis got into a tram and went back to the office, while Dussel walked. At twenty past eleven Dussel tapped at the office door. Miep helped him off with his coat, so that the yellow star would not be seen, and took him to the private office, where Koophuis engaged him in conversation until the charwoman had gone. Then Miep went upstairs with Dussel under the pretext that the office was needed for something, opened the swinging cupboard, and stepped inside before the eyes of the dumbfounded Dussel.

We sat around the table upstairs, waiting with coffee and cognac to greet the newcomer. Miep showed him in. He sank into a chair, and looked at us, speechless. After a while he stuttered, "But . . . you are not in Belgium then? The escape is *sie nicht* successful?"

We explained everything to him, that we had spread the escape-to-Belgium story on purpose to put the Germans on the wrong track should they try to find us. Dussel was struck dumb by such ingenuity and, when he had explored further our superpractical little Secret Annexe, he could do nothing but gaze about him in astonishment.

We all had lunch together. Then he had a little nap and joined us for tea, tidied up his things a bit (Miep had brought them beforehand), and began to feel more at home. Especially when he received the following typed "Secret Annexe Rules" (Van Daan product).

Guide to the Secret Annexe
Special temporary residence for Jews and suchlike

Open all year round. Beautiful, quiet, in the heart of Amsterdam.

Board and lodging: Free. Special fat-free diet.

Running water in the bathroom (alas, no bath) and down various inside and outside walls.

Own radio center, direct communication with London, New York, Tel Aviv, and other stations. For residents' use only after six p.m. No stations are forbidden, but German stations are only listened to in special cases, such as classical music.

Rest hours: 10 o'clock in the evening until 7:30 in the morning. 10:15 on Sundays. For reasons of public security rest hours must be strictly observed!

Holidays (outside the home): Postponed indefinitely.

Use of language: Speak softly at all times! All civilized languages are permitted, therefore no German!

Mealtimes: Breakfast, every day except Sundays and bank holidays, 9 a.m. Sundays and bank holidays, 11:30 a.m.

Lunch (not very big): 1:15 p.m. to 1:45 p.m.

Dinner (cold and/or hot): No fixed time (depending on the news broadcast).
Duties: Residents must always be ready to help with office work.
Baths: The washtub is available for all residents from 9 a.m. on Sundays.

Yours, Anne

Thursday, 19 November, 1942

Dear Kitty,

Dussel is a very nice man. Of course he thought it was all right to share my little room. Quite honestly I'm not so keen that a stranger should use my things, but one must be prepared to make some sacrifices. "If we can save someone, then everything else is of secondary importance," says Daddy, and he's absolutely right.

The first day that Dussel was here, he asked me all sorts of questions: When does the charwoman come? When can one use the bathroom? When is one allowed to use the lavatory? You may laugh, but these things are not so simple in a hiding place. I explained all this carefully to Dussel. But he is very slow on the uptake. Perhaps it's only that he's upset by the sudden change.

Dussel has told us a lot about the outside world. He had very sad news. Countless friends and acquaintances have gone to a terrible fate. Evening after evening the Germans ring at every front door to inquire if any Jews live in the house. If there are, the whole family has to go at once in gray army lorries. If they don't find any, they go on to the next house. No one has a chance of evading them unless one goes into hiding. Often they go around with lists; sometimes they let them off for cash —so much per head. It seems like the slave hunts of olden times. In the evenings when it's dark, I often see rows of good, innocent people with crying children, walking on and on, in charge of a couple of these chaps, bullied and knocked about. No one is spared—old people, babies, expectant mothers, the sick.

How fortunate we are here, so well cared for and undisturbed. But I feel wicked sleeping in a warm bed, while my dearest friends have been delivered into the hands of the cruelest brutes that walk the earth. And all because they are Jews!

Yours, Anne

Dear Kitty,

We have used more than our ration of electricity. Result: no light for a fortnight, a pleasant thought. It's too dark to read in the afternoons after four or half past. We pass the time in all sorts of crazy ways: asking riddles, physical training in the dark, talking English and French, criticizing books. But it all begins to pall in the end. Yesterday evening I discovered something new: to peer through a powerful pair of field glasses into the lighted rooms of the houses at the back. In the daytime we can't allow even as much as a chink to appear between our curtains, but it can't do any harm after dark. I never knew that neighbors could be such interesting people. I found one couple having a meal, one family was taking a home movie; and the dentist opposite was just attending to an old lady, who was awfully scared.

It was always said about Mr. Dussel that he could get on wonderfully with children. Now he shows himself in his true colors; a stodgy, old-fashioned disciplinarian, and preacher of long, drawn-out sermons on manners. As I'm considered to be the most badly behaved of the three young people, I have to put up with old, much-repeated warnings.

You needn't think it's easy to be the "badly brought-up" member of a hypercritical family in hiding. When I lie in bed at night and think over the many sins and shortcomings attributed to me, I get so confused by it all that I either laugh or cry; it depends what sort of mood I am in.

Yours, Anne

Monday, 7 December, 1942

Dear Kitty,

Hanukkah and St. Nicholas' Day came almost together this year. We didn't make much fuss about Hanukkah: we just gave each other a few little presents and then we had the candles. Because of the shortage of candles we only had them alight for ten minutes, but it is all right as long as you have the song.

Saturday, the evening of St. Nicholas' Day, was much more fun. Miep and Elli were whispering with Daddy, so we guessed that something was on. And so it was. At eight o'clock we all filed down the wooden staircase through the passage in pitch-darkness (it made me shudder and wish that I was safely upstairs again) into the little dark room. There, as there are no windows, we were able to turn on a light. Daddy opened the big cupboard. "Oh! how lovely," we all cried. A large basket decorated with St. Nicholas paper stood in the corner.

We took the basket upstairs with us. There was a present for everyone, with a poem attached. I got a doll whose skirt is a bag for odds and ends; Daddy got bookends. As none of us had ever celebrated St. Nicholas, it was a good way of starting.

Yours, Anne

Thursday, 10 December, 1942

Dear Kitty,

Mr. Van Daan used to be in the meat, sausage, and spice business. It was because of this that he was taken on in Daddy's business. Now he is showing the sausagey side of himself, which is by no means disagreeable.

We had ordered a lot of meat (under the counter, of course) for preserving in case we should come upon hard times. It was fun to watch as the pieces of meat went through the mincer two or three times, then all the accompanying ingredients were mixed with the meat, and then the intestine was filled to make the sausages. We fried the sausage meat and ate it with sauerkraut for supper that evening, but the Gelderland sausages had to be thoroughly dried first, so we hung them over a stick tied to the ceiling with string. They looked terribly funny!

The room was in a glorious mess. Mr. Van Daan was wearing one of his wife's soiled aprons round his substantial person and was busy with the meat, hands smothered in blood, his face red. Mrs. Van Daan was trying to do everything at once, learning Dutch from a book, stirring the soup, watching the meat, complaining about her injured rib. That's what happens to elderly ladies (!) who do idiotic exercises to reduce their large behinds!

Dussel had inflammation in one eye and was bathing it with camomile tea by the fire. Pim was sitting in a beam of sunlight that shone through the window. I think his rheumatism was bothering him; he sat rather hunched up with a miserable look on his face, watching Mr. Van Daan at work. He looked like some shriveled-up man from an old people's home. Peter was doing acrobatics with his cat. Mummy, Margot, and I were peeling potatoes; and, of course, all of us were doing everything wrong because we were so busy watching Mr. Van Daan.

Yours, Anne

Sunday, 13 December, 1942

Dear Kitty,

I'm sitting cozily in the main office, looking outside through a slit in the curtain. It is dusk but just light enough to write.

It is very queer as I watch the people walking by; it looks as if they are all in a terrible hurry. The people in this neighborhood don't look very attractive. The children are so dirty; real slum kids with running noses.

Yesterday afternoon Margot and I were having a bath and I said, "Supposing we were to take the children who are walking past, one by one, hoist them up with a fishing rod, give them each a bath, wash and mend their clothes, and then let them go again, then . . ." Margot interrupted me, "By tomorrow they would look just as filthy and ragged as before."

I'm gradually getting to know all the women at a glance, blown out with potatoes, wearing a red or a green coat, trodden-down heels and with a bag under their arms. Their faces either look grim or kind—depending on their husbands' dispositions.

Yours, Anne

Tuesday, 22 December, 1942

Dear Kitty,

Joyful news: each person will receive an extra quarter pound of butter for Christmas. It says half a pound in the newspapers, but that's only for the lucky mortals who get their ration books from the government, not for Jews who have gone into hiding, who can only afford to buy four illegal ration books, instead of eight. We are all going to bake something with our butter. I made some biscuits and two cakes this morning.

Mrs. Van Daan is in bed with her bruised rib, complains the whole day long, and isn't satisfied with anything. I shall be glad when she's on her feet again, because I must say this for her, she's exceptionally industrious and tidy. She is cheerful too.

As if I didn't hear enough during the day about my making too much noise, my bedroom companion now calls "ssh-ssh" to me at night too. I am not even allowed to turn over! I refuse to take the slightest notice of him, and shall go "ssh-ssh" back

Mrs. Van Daan

at him the next time. He makes me furious, on Sundays especially, when he turns the light on early to do his exercises. It seems to take simply hours. Then His Lordship begins his toilet. His pants are hanging up, so he must go to collect them. But he forgets his tie, which is lying on the table. Once more he pushes past the chairs to get it, while I, poor tormented creature, feel the chairs, which are placed at the head of my bed to lengthen it, slide backwards and forwards continually under my sleepy head.

But I won't bore you any longer on the subject of old men. It won't make things any better and all my plans of revenge (such as disconnecting the lamp, hiding his clothes) must be abandoned to keep peace. Oh, I'm becoming so sensible! One must apply one's reason here, learn to hold your tongue, to help, to give in.

Yours, Anne

Wednesday, 13 January, 1943

Dear Kitty,

Everything has upset me again this morning. It is terrible outside. Day and night more of these poor miserable people are being dragged off. Families are torn apart, women and children separated. Children coming home from school find that their parents have disappeared. Women return from shopping to find their homes shut up and their families gone. The Dutch people are anxious too, their sons are being sent to Germany. Everyone is afraid.

And every night hundreds of planes fly over Holland to German towns, where the earth is plowed up by their bombs, and every hour hundreds and thousands of people are killed in Russia and Africa. The whole globe is waging war and, although it is going better for the Allies, the end is not yet in sight.

We are luckier than millions of people. It is quiet and safe here. We are even so selfish as to talk about "after the war," and brighten up at the thought of having new clothes, whereas we really ought to save every penny to help other people.

The children run about in just a thin blouse and clogs; no coat, no hat, no stockings, no one helps them. Their tummies are empty, they go from cold homes into the cold street and when they get to school find themselves in an even colder classroom. It has got so bad that children stop passersby and beg for a piece of bread. I could go on for hours about the suffering the war has brought. The whole earth waits; and there are many who wait for death.

Yours, Anne

Saturday, 30 January, 1943

Dear Kitty,

I'm boiling with rage, and yet I mustn't show it. I'd like to stamp my feet, scream, give Mummy a good shaking, because of the horrible words, mocking looks, and accusations which are leveled at me repeatedly every day. I would like to shout to Margot, Van Daan, Dussel—and Daddy too—"Leave me in peace!" But I can't let them see the wounds they cause.

If I talk, everyone thinks I'm showing off; when I'm silent they think I'm ridiculous; rude if I answer, sly if I get a good idea, lazy if I'm tired, selfish if I eat a mouthful more than I should, stupid, cowardly, crafty, etc., etc. The whole day long I hear nothing else but that I am an insufferable baby, and although I laugh about it and pretend not to take any notice, I *do* mind. I would like to ask God to give me a different nature, so that I didn't put everyone's back up. But that can't be done. I've got the nature that has been given to me. I do my very best to please everybody, far more than they'd ever guess.

Yours, Anne

Saturday, 27 February, 1943

Dear Kitty,

Pim is expecting the invasion any day. Churchill has had pneumonia, but is improving slowly. Gandhi is holding his umpteenth fast.

Henk brought us a copy of the bishop's fine and inspiring letter to churchgoers. "Do not rest, people of the Netherlands, everyone is fighting to free the country, the people, and their religion." It won't help the people of our religion.

You'd never guess what has happened now. The owner of these premises has sold the house without informing Kraler and Koophuis. One morning the new owner arrived with an architect to have a look at the house. Luckily, Mr. Koophuis was present and showed the gentlemen everything except the Secret Annexe. He professed to have forgotten the key of the communicating door. The new owner didn't question any further. It will be all right as long as he doesn't come back.

Daddy has emptied a card-index box for Margot and me, and put cards in it. It is to be a book card system; then we both write down which books we have read, who they are by, etc.

Lately Mummy and I have been getting on better together, but we still *never* confide in each other. Margot is more catty than ever and Daddy remains the same darling.

New butter and margarine rationing. Each person has their little bit of fat put on their plate. In my opinion the Van Daans don't divide it at all fairly. However, my parents are much too afraid of a row to say anything.

Yours, Anne

Wednesday, 10 March, 1943

Dear Kitty,

Last evening the guns kept banging away all the time. I haven't got over my fear of shooting and planes, and I creep into Daddy's bed nearly every night for comfort. I know it's childish but you don't know what it is like. The guns roar so loudly that you can't hear yourself speak. Mrs. Van Daan, who claims to be a fatalist, was nearly crying, and said in a timid little voice, "Oh, it is so unpleasant!" by which she really means, "I'm so frightened." I was shivering and begged Daddy to light the candle. He was relentless, the light remained off. Suddenly there was a burst of machine-gun fire ten times worse than guns. Mummy jumped out of bed and, to Pim's annoyance, lit the candle. It didn't seem nearly so bad by candlelight as in the dark. When he complained her answer was firm: "After all, Anne's not exactly a veteran soldier."

You must know about Mrs. Van Daan's other fears. One night she thought she heard burglars in the attic and was so frightened that she woke her husband. But the only sounds that Mr. Van Daan could hear were the heartbeats of the frightened fatalist herself. A few nights after that the whole Van Daan family was wakened by ghostly sounds. Peter went up to the attic with a torch—and scamper—scamper! What do you think it was? A swarm of enormous rats! When we knew who the thieves were, we let Mouschi sleep in the attic and the guests didn't come back.

Yours, Anne

Friday, 12 March, 1943

Dear Kitty,

A bottle of preserved sole has gone bad: gala dinner for Mouschi and Boche. You haven't met Boche yet. She is the warehouse cat and keeps down the rats in the storerooms. Her political name requires an explanation. For some time the firm had two cats; one for the warehouse and one for the attic. Occasionally the two met and the result was always a terrific fight. The aggressor was always the warehouse cat; yet the attic cat always managed to win—just like among nations. So the storehouse cat was named the German or "Boche" and the attic cat the English or "Tommy." Tommy was got rid of later. We are all entertained by Boche when we go downstairs.

We have eaten so many kidney beans that the mere sight of them makes me feel quite sick. Bread is no longer served in the evenings now.

Horrible air raids on Germany. Mr. Van Daan is in a bad mood; the cause—cigarette shortage.

I can't get into a single pair of shoes anymore, except ski boots, which are not much use about the house. A pair of rush sandals costing 6.50 florins lasted me just one week. Perhaps Miep will scrounge something under the counter. I must cut Daddy's hair. Pim maintains that he will never have another barber after the war, as I do the job so well. If only I didn't snip his ear so often!

Yours, Anne

Friday, 19 March, 1943

Dear Kitty,

Five-hundred- and one-thousand-guilder notes have been declared no longer valid. It is a trap for black marketeers and people in hiding. If you wish to hand in a one-thousand-guilder note you must be able to prove exactly how you got it.

The *Führer* has been talking to wounded soldiers. Listening in to it was pitiful:

"My name is Heinrich Scheppel."

"Wounded where?"

"Near Stalingrad."

"What kind of wound?"

"Two feet frozen off and a broken joint in the left arm."

In this frightful puppet show on the radio the wounded seemed to be proud of their wounds—the more the better. One of them felt so moved at being able to shake hands with the Führer (that is, if he still had a hand!) that he could hardly get the words out of his mouth.

Yours, Anne

Thursday, 25 March, 1943

Dear Kitty,

Yesterday Mummy, Daddy, Margot, and I were sitting pleasantly together when Peter came in and whispered in Daddy's ear. I heard something about "a barrel fallen over" and "fumbling at the door." Daddy and Peter went off immediately and the three of us waited in suspense. A minute later Mrs. Van Daan joined us. She'd been listening to the wireless in the private office, and Pim had asked her to turn it off and go softly upstairs.

Five minutes later Pim and Peter appeared, white to the roots of their hair. They had hidden under the stairs and waited. Suddenly they heard two loud bumps, as if two doors were banged in the house. Pim was upstairs in one leap. Peter warned Dussel and we all went up in stockinged feet to the Van Daans where Mr. Van Daan had already gone to bed. We waited and waited, but we heard no more and finally came to the conclusion that thieves had been in the warehouse and taken to their heels when they heard footsteps in the house.

The wireless downstairs, the chairs neatly arranged round it, was still turned to England. If the air-raid wardens had had to force the door for any reason and had noticed, the results might have been very unpleasant. So Mr. Van Daan got up and put on his coat and followed Daddy cautiously downstairs, Peter took up the rear, armed with a large hammer in case of emergencies. They reappeared five minutes later and told us that all was quiet. Nevertheless, we arranged that we would not draw any water or pull the plug in the lavatory.

Mr. Vossen having left earlier than usual the previous evening, we didn't know whether Elli had been able to get the key, and had perhaps forgotten to shut the door. We did feel reassured by the fact that from about eight o'clock, when the burglar had alarmed the house, until half past ten we had not heard a sound. It also seemed very unlikely that a thief would have forced open a door so early in the evening, while there were still people about in the street. It was possible that the "thief" was the caretaker of the warehouse next door who was still at work. With the thin walls, one can easily make a mistake, and one's imagination can play a big part at critical moments.

So we all went to bed; but none of us could sleep. This morning the men went downstairs to see whether the outside door was still shut, and everything turned out to be quite safe. We gave everyone a detailed description of the nerve-wracking event. They all made fun of it, but it is easy to laugh at such things afterwards. Elli was the only one who took us seriously.

Yours, Anne

Saturday, 27 March, 1943

Dear Kitty,

We have finished our shorthand course—our time-killing subject. I call it that because we have got nothing else to do but make the days go by as quickly as possible. I'm mad on mythology, especially the gods of Greece and Rome. They think here that it is just a passing craze, they've never heard of an adolescent being interested in mythology. Well, then, I shall be the first!

Rauter, one of the German big shots, has made a speech. "All Jews must be out of the German-occupied countries before July 1. Between April 1 and May 1 the province of Utrecht must be cleaned out (as if the Jews were cockroaches). Between May 1 and June 1 the provinces of North and South Holland." Wretched people are sent to filthy slaughterhouses like a herd of sick cattle. But I won't talk about it, I only get nightmares from such thoughts.

One good piece of news: the German department of the Labor Exchange has been set on fire by saboteurs. A few days after, the registrar's office went the same way. Men in German police uniforms gagged the guards and managed to destroy important papers.

Yours, Anne

Thursday, 1 April, 1943

Dear Kitty,

Misfortunes never come singly. To begin with, Mr. Koophuis, the one who always cheers us up, has had hemorrhage of the stomach and has to stay in bed for three weeks. Secondly, Elli has flu. Thirdly, Mr. Vossen has got an abdominal ulcer. And fourthly, some important business conferences, the main points of which Daddy had discussed in detail with Mr. Koophuis, were due to be held, but now there isn't time to explain everything thoroughly to Mr. Kraler.

Yours, Anne

Friday, 2 April, 1943

Dear Kitty,

Oh dear: I've got another terrible black mark against my name. I was lying in bed yesterday evening waiting for Daddy to come and say my prayers with me when Mummy came into my room, sat on my bed, and asked very nicely, "Anne, Daddy can't come yet, shall I say your prayers with you tonight?" "No, Mummy," I answered.

Mummy got up and walked slowly towards the door. Suddenly she turned around, and with a distorted look on her face said, "I don't want to be cross, love cannot be forced." There were tears in her eyes as she left the room.

I lay still, feeling that I had been horrible to push her away so rudely. But I knew too that I couldn't have answered differently. I felt very sorry for Mummy because I had seen for the first time in my life that she minds my coldness. I saw the look of sorrow on her face.

Mrs. Frank

It is hard to speak the truth: she herself has pushed me away, her tactless remarks and her crude jokes have now made me insensitive to any love from her. Just as I shrink at her hard words, so did her heart when she realized that the love between us was gone. She cried half the night, and now Daddy doesn't look at me, or if he does I read in his eyes: "How can you be so unkind to your mother?"

They expect me to apologize, but I can't. I spoke the truth and for the first time they are both aware of something which I have always felt. I can only feel sorry for Mummy.

Yours, Anne

Tuesday, 27 April, 1943

Dear Kitty,

The Carlton Hotel is smashed to bits. Two British planes loaded with incendiary bombs fell right on top of the *Offiziersheim* [German Officers' Club]. The whole corner of the square is burned down. The air raids on German towns are growing in strength every day. We don't have a single quiet night. I've got dark rings under my eyes from lack of sleep. Our food is miserable. Dry bread and coffee substitute for breakfast. Dinner: spinach or lettuce. Potatoes twenty centimeters long and tasting sweet and rotten. Whoever wants to follow a slimming course should stay in the Secret Annexe!

All the men who fought in 1940 or were mobilized have been called up to work for the Führer as prisoners of war. Suppose they're doing that as a precaution against invasion.

Yours, Anne

Saturday, 1 May, 1943

Dear Kitty,

Our life here must be paradise compared with that of other Jews not in hiding. Even so, it is amazing to think that we, who were so spick-and-span at home, should have allowed our manners to decline to such a low level. For instance, ever since we have been here, we have had one oilcloth on our table which by now is not one of the cleanest, although I often try to clean it with a dirty, ragged dishcloth. The table doesn't do us much credit either, in spite of hard scrubbing. The Van Daans have been sleeping on the same sheet the whole winter; one can't wash it here because the soap powder we get on the ration isn't sufficient, and besides it's not good enough. Daddy goes about in frayed trousers and his tie is beginning to show signs of wear too. Mummy's corsets have split today and are too old to be repaired, while Margot goes about in a brassiere two sizes too small for her. Mummy and Margot have managed the whole winter with three undershirts between them, and mine are so small that they don't even reach my tummy.

These are small things. Still, I sometimes realize with a shock: "How are we ever going to get back to our prewar standards?"

They were banging away so much last night that four times I gathered all my belongings together. Today I have packed a suitcase with the most necessary things for an escape. But Mummy quite rightly says: "Where will you escape to?"

Yours, Anne

Tuesday, 18 May, 1943

Dear Kitty,

I witnessed a terrific air battle between German and British planes. Unfortunately a couple of Allies had to jump from burning machines. Our milkman saw four Canadians sitting by the roadside, one of them spoke fluent Dutch. He asked the milkman to give him a light for his cigarette, and told him that the crew had consisted of six men. The pilot was burned to death, and their fifth man had hidden himself somewhere. The German police came and fetched the four men.

Although it is fairly warm, we have to light our fires every other day, to burn vegetable peelings and refuse. We can't put anything in the garbage pails, because of the warehouse boy. How easily one could be betrayed by being a little careless!

All students who wish to get their degrees this year, or continue their studies, are compelled to sign that they are in sympathy with the Germans and approve of the New Order. Eighty percent have refused to go against their consciences. Naturally they had to bear the consequences. All the students who do not sign have to go to a labor camp in Germany. What will be left of the youth of the country if they have all got to do hard labor in Germany? Mummy shut the window last night because of all the banging; I was in Pim's bed. Suddenly Mrs. Van Daan jumped out of bed above us, just as if Mouschi had bitten her. A loud clap followed immediately. It sounded just as if an incendiary bomb had fallen beside my bed. I shrieked out, "Light, light!" Pim turned on the lamp and we all hurried upstairs. Mr. and Mrs. Van Daan had seen a red glow through the open window. He thought that there was a fire in the neighborhood and she thought that our house had caught fire. When the clap came Mrs. Van Daan was already on her feet with her knees knocking. Nothing more happened and we all crept back into our beds.

Yours, Anne

Sunday, 13 June, 1943

Dear Kitty,

My birthday poem from Daddy is too good to keep from you. Judge for yourself whether he didn't do it brilliantly:

> *Though youngest here, you are no longer small,*
> *But life is very hard, since one and all*

Aspire to be your teacher, thus and thus:
"We have experience, take a tip from us."
"We know because we did it long ago."
"Elders are always better, you must know."
At least that's been the rule since life began!
Our personal faults are much too small to scan;
This makes it easier to criticize
The faults of others, which seem double size.
Please bear with us, your parents, for we try
To judge you fairly and with sympathy.
Correction sometimes take against your will,
Though it's like swallowing a bitter pill,
Which must be done if we're to keep the peace,
While time goes by till all this suffering cease.
You read and study nearly all the day,
Who might have lived in such a different way.
You're never bored and bring us all fresh air.
Your only moan is this: "What can I wear?
I have no knickers, all my clothes are small,
My shirt might be a loincloth, that is all!
To put on shoes would mean to cut off toes,
Oh dear, I'm worried by so many woes!"

Don't you think my birthday poem is good? I have been thoroughly spoiled and received lovely things. Among other things a book on my pet subject—the mythology of Greece and Rome. I can't complain of a shortage of sweets either—everyone has broken into their last reserves. I am really more honored than I deserve.

Yours, Anne

Tuesday, 15 June, 1943

Dear Kitty,

Lots of things have happened. When Mr. Vossen was on the operating table for his duodenal ulcer, the doctors saw that he had cancer, which was far too advanced to operate. So they stitched him up again, kept him in bed for three weeks and gave him good food, and finally sent him home. I do pity him terribly and think it is rotten that we can't go out, otherwise I should visit him to cheer him up. It is a disaster for us that good old

Vossen won't be able to keep us in touch with all that goes on in the warehouse. He was our best security adviser; we miss him very much indeed.

It will be our turn to hand in our radio next month. Koophuis has a clandestine baby set at home that he will let us have to take the place of our big Phillips. It certainly is a shame to have to hand in our lovely set, but in a house where people are hiding, one daren't, under any circumstances, take wanton risks and so draw the attention of the authorities. Everyone is trying to get hold of an old set to hand in instead of their "source of courage." As the news from outside gets worse, the miraculous voice helps to keep up our morale and to say again, "Chins up, better times will come!"

Yours, Anne

Sunday, 11 July, 1943

Dear Kitty,

To return to the "upbringing" theme for the umpteenth time, I really am trying to be helpful and friendly. And I do really see that I get on better by shamming a bit, instead of my old habit of telling everyone exactly what I think.

I have decided to let my shorthand go, firstly to give me more time for my other subjects and secondly because I've become very shortsighted and ought to have had glasses for a long time already (phew, what an owl I shall look!). Yesterday Mummy suggested sending me to the oculist with Mrs. Koophuis. I shook in my shoes at this announcement, for it is no small thing to go out of doors, imagine it, in the street. I was petrified at first, then glad. But it doesn't go as easily as that, because all the people who would have to approve such a step could not reach an agreement quickly. In the meantime I got out my gray coat, but it was so small that it looked as if it belonged to my younger sister. I don't think the plan will come off because the British have landed in Sicily now and Daddy is again hoping for a "quick finish."

Elli gives Margot and me a lot of office work—filing correspondence, etc. It makes us feel important and is a great help to her. Miep is just like a pack mule, she fetches and carries so much. Almost every day she manages to get hold of some vegetables for us and brings everything in shopping bags on her bicycle. We always long for Saturdays when our books come. Just like little children receiving a present.

Yours, Anne

Tuesday, 13 July, 1943

Dear Kitty,

Yesterday afternoon, with Daddy's permission, I asked Dussel whether he would please be so good as to allow me to use the little table in our room twice a week in the afternoons, from four o'clock till half past five. I sit there every day from half past two till four, while Dussel sleeps, but otherwise the room plus table are out of bounds. In our common room there is too much going on; it is impossible to work there.

So it was quite a reasonable request, and the question was put very politely. Now honestly what do you think Dussel replied: "No." Just plain "No!" I was indignant and refused to be put off. I asked him the reason. This barrage followed:

"I have to work too, and if I can't work in the afternoons, then there is no time left. Anyway, you don't work seriously at anything. Your mythology, your knitting and reading, now what kind of work is that? I am at the table and shall stay there."

My reply was: "Mr. Dussel, I do work seriously and there is nowhere else for me to work in the afternoons. I beg of you to kindly reconsider my request! When you first came here we arranged that this room should be for both of us; if we were to divide it fairly, you would have the morning and I all the afternoon! But I don't even ask that much, and I think that my two afternoons are really perfectly reasonable."

At this Dussel jumped up as if someone had stuck a needle into him. "And where am I to go, then? I simply can't work anywhere. With you one always gets trouble. If your sister Margot, who after all has more reason to ask such a thing, would have come to me with the same questions, I should not think of refusing. But you, one simply can't talk to you. You are outrageously selfish. I've never seen such a child. But after all, I suppose I shall be obliged to give you your own way, because otherwise I shall be told later on that Anne Frank failed her exam because Mr. Dussel would not give up the table for her."

After giving final vent to his fury, Master Dussel left the room in mixed wrath and triumph. I dashed to Daddy and told him. Pim decided to talk to Dussel the same evening. They talked for over half an hour. Dussel thought that I should not speak as if he was an intruder who tried to monopolize everything, but Daddy stuck up for me firmly, defending my "trifling" work. Finally, Dussel gave in; I could work undisturbed two afternoons a week. But he looked down his nose and didn't speak to me for two days—frightfully childish. A person of fifty-four who is so small-minded will never improve.

Yours, Anne

Friday, 16 July, 1943

Dear Kitty,

Burglars again, but real this time! This morning Peter went to the warehouse at seven o'clock as usual, and noticed that both the warehouse door and the door opening onto the street were ajar. He told Pim, who tuned the radio to Germany and locked the door. Then they went upstairs together.

The standing orders for such times were observed: no taps turned on, no washing, silence, everything finished by eight o'clock and no lavatory. We were all very glad that we had slept well and not heard anything. Not until half past eleven did we learn from Mr. Koophuis that the burglars had pushed in the outer door with a crowbar and had forced the warehouse door. However, they did not find much to steal, so they tried their luck upstairs. They stole two cashboxes containing forty florins, postal orders and checkbooks and then, worst of all, all the coupons for 150 kilos of sugar. The typewriters and money, which are brought upstairs every evening, were safe.

Yours, Anne

Monday, 19 July, 1943

Dear Kitty,

North Amsterdam was very heavily bombed on Sunday. The destruction seems to be terrible. Whole streets lie in ruins, and it will take a long time before all the people are dug out. Up till now there are two hundred dead and countless wounded; the hospitals are crammed. You hear of children lost in the smoldering ruins, looking for their parents. I shudder when I recall the dull droning in the distance, which marked the approaching destruction.

Yours, Anne

Friday, 23 July, 1943

Dear Kitty,

Just for fun I'm going to tell you each person's first wish, when we are allowed to go outside again. Margot and Mr. Van Daan long for a hot bath filled to overflowing and want to stay in it for half an hour. Mrs. Van Daan wants to eat cream cakes immediately. Dussel thinks of nothing but seeing Lotje, his wife; Mummy of her cup of coffee; Daddy is going to visit Mr. Vossen first; Peter a cinema, while I should find it so blissful, I shouldn't know where to start! But most of all, I long for a home of our own, and school.

Yours, Anne

Monday, 26 July, 1943

Dear Kitty,

Nothing but uproar yesterday. We had the first warning siren while we were at breakfast, but that only means that planes are crossing the coast. Then at half past two the sirens began to wail, and five minutes later they began shooting so hard that we went and stood in the passage. The house rumbled and shook, and down came the bombs.

I clasped my "escape bag" close to me, more because I wanted to have something to hold than with an idea of escaping. If ever we come to the extremity of fleeing from here, the street would be just as dangerous as an air raid. This one subsided after half an hour. I went upstairs to see columns of smoke rising above the harbor. You could smell burning, and outside a thick mist hung everywhere. That evening at dinner: another air-raid alarm! My hunger vanished at the sound of it. Nothing happened and three-quarters of an hour later it was all clear.

The dishes were stacked ready to be done: air-raid warning, ack-ack fire, an awful lot of planes. According to the British, the bombs once again rained down on Schiphol [Amsterdam airport]. The planes dived and climbed. Each moment I thought, "One's falling now. Here it comes."

When I went to bed at nine o'clock I couldn't hold my legs still. I woke up at the stroke of twelve: planes. At the first shot, I leaped out of bed, wide awake. Two hours with Daddy and still they kept coming. Then they ceased firing and I was able to go to bed. I fell asleep at half past two.

Seven o'clock. I sat up in bed with a start. Mr. Van Daan was with Daddy. Burglars was my first thought. I heard Mr. Van Daan say "everything." I thought everything had been stolen. But no, this time it was wonderful news, such as we have not heard in all the war years. "Mussolini has resigned, the King of Italy has taken over the government." We jumped for joy. After the terrible day yesterday, at last something good again—hope. Hope for it to end, for peace.

Yours, Anne

Tuesday, 3 August, 1943

Dear Kitty,

We've just had another air raid; I clenched my teeth together to make myself feel courageous. Mrs. Van Daan, who has always said, "A terrible end is better than no end at all," is the greatest coward of us all. This morning she even burst into tears. When her husband, with whom she has just made up after a week's squabbling, comforted her, the expression on her face almost made me feel sentimental.

Mouschi has proved that keeping cats has disadvantages. The whole house is full of fleas, and the plague gets worse every day. Mr. Koophuis has scattered yellow powder in every nook and corner, but the fleas don't seem to mind a bit. It's making us all quite nervous; one keeps imagining an itch on various parts of one's body, which is why a lot of us are doing gymnastics to look at the back of our legs. We're too stiff to even turn our heads properly. We gave up real gymnastics long ago.

Yours, Anne

Wednesday, 4 August, 1943

Dear Kitty,

Now that we have been in the Secret Annexe for over a year, you know something of our lives, but some of it is quite indescribable. Everything is so different from ordinary people's lives. To give you a closer look, I intend to give you a description of an ordinary day. Today I'm beginning with the evening and night.

Margot Frank

Nine o'clock in the evening. The bustle of going to bed in the Secret Annexe begins. It is quite a business. Chairs are shoved about, beds are pulled down, blankets unfolded, nothing remains where it is during the day. I sleep on the little divan, which is so short that chairs have to be used to lengthen it. A quilt, sheets, pillows, blankets, are all fetched from Dussel's bed where they remain during the day.

Terrible creaking in the next room: Margot's concertina bed being pulled out. Everything is done to make the wooden slats a bit more comfortable. It sounds like thunder above, but it is only Mrs. Van Daan's bed being shifted to the window to give Her Majesty in the pink bed jacket fresh air.

After Peter's finished, I step into the washing cubicle, for teeth cleaning, hair curling, manicure, and a thorough wash. Occasionally there is a flea floating in the water.

Half past nine. Quickly into dressing gown, soap in one hand, pottie, hairpins, pants, and curlers in the other, I hurry out of the bathroom; but usually I'm called back for the hairs which decorate the washbasin in graceful curves, which are not approved of by the next person.

Ten o'clock. Put up the blackout. Good night! For at least a quarter of an hour there is creaking of beds and broken springs, then all is quiet, at least that is if our neighbors upstairs don't quarrel in bed.

Half past eleven. The bathroom door creaks. A narrow strip of light falls into the room. A squeak of shoes, a coat even larger than the man inside it—Dussel returns from his night work in Kraler's office. Shuffling on the floor for ten minutes, and a bed is made. Then the form disappears again and one hears noises from the lavatory.

Three o'clock. I have to get up for a little job in the metal pot under my bed, which is on a rubber mat for safety's sake in case of leakage. When this has to take place, I always hold my breath, as it clatters into the tin like a brook from a mountain. Then the pot is returned to its place and the figure in the white nightgown, which evokes the same cry from Margot every evening: "Oh, that indecent nightdress!" steps back into bed.

Then a certain person lies awake for about a quarter of an hour, listening to the sounds of the night, and to hear whether there might not be a burglar downstairs.

It can happen that we get a bit of shooting between one o'clock and four. Sometimes I'm so busy dreaming about French irregular verbs or a quarrel upstairs that it is some time before I realize that guns are firing and that I am standing at my bedside. I quickly grab a pillow, put on my dressing gown and slippers, and scamper to Daddy, like Margot wrote in this birthday poem:

> *The first shot sounds at dead of night.*
> *Hush, look! A door creaks open wide,*
> *A little girl glides into sight,*
> *Clasping a pillow to her side.*

Once in the big bed, the worst is over, except if the firings get very bad.

Quarter to seven. Trrrr—the alarm clock that raises its voice at any hour of the day (if one asks for it and sometimes when one doesn't). *Crack—ping*—Mrs. Van Daan has turned it off. *Creak*—Mr. Van Daan gets up. Puts on water and then full speed to the bathroom.

Quarter past seven. The door creaks again. Dussel can go to the bathroom. I take down the blackout—and a new day in the Secret Annexe has begun.

Yours, Anne

Thursday, 5 August, 1943

Dear Kitty,

Today I am going to take lunchtime.

It is half past twelve. The whole crowd breathes again: the warehouse boys have gone home. Above, one can hear Mrs. Van Daan's vacuum cleaner on her only carpet. Pim, with his Dickens, tries to find peace in a corner. Mummy hurries upstairs to help the industrious housewife, and I go to the bathroom to tidy it and myself at the same time.

Quarter to one. The place is filling up with "the soup eaters," the people from the office who often come in for a cup of soup. First Mr. Van Santen, then Koophuis or Kraler, Elli and sometimes Miep as well.

One o'clock. We're all listening to the B.B.C., seated around the baby wireless; these are the only times when the members of the Secret Annexe do not interrupt each other.

Quarter past one. The great share-out. Everyone from below gets a cup of soup and if there is a pudding, some of that as well. Koophuis tells us the latest news from town.

Quarter to two. Everyone rises from the table and goes about his business. Margot and Mummy to the dishes. Mr. and Mrs. Van Daan to their divan. Peter to the attic. Daddy to the divan downstairs. Dussel to his bed and Anne to her work. Then follows the most peaceful hour. Time goes fast and at five o'clock the pedantic Dr. Dussel is standing, clock in hand, because I'm one minute late in clearing the table for him.

Yours, Anne

Monday, 9 August, 1943

Dear Kitty,

To continue the Secret Annexe daily timetable. I shall now describe the evening meal:

Mr. Van Daan is first to be served, takes a lot of what he likes. Usually talks at the same time. He has the best opinion, he knows the most about everything. All right then, he has got brains, but "self-satisfaction" has reached a high grade with this gentleman.

Madame. At table, Mrs. Van Daan doesn't go short, although she thinks so at times. The tiniest potatoes, the sweetest mouthful, the best of everything; picking is her system. Then talking. Whether anyone is interested, whether they are listening or not. Coquettish smiles, giving everyone advice and encouragement, that's *sure* to make a good impression. She is industrious, gay— and, occasionally, pretty. This is Petronella Van Daan.

The third table companion. One doesn't hear much from him. Young Mr. Van Daan doesn't draw much attention to himself. As for appetite: a vessel which is never full and after the heartiest meal declares quite calmly that he could have eaten double.

Number four—Margot. Eats like a little mouse—only vegetables and fruit—and doesn't talk at all. "Spoiled" is the Van Daans' judgment; "not enough fresh air and games" our opinion.

Beside her—Mummy. Good appetite, very talkative. No one has the impression, as Mrs. Van Daan: this is the housewife. What is the difference? Well, Mrs. Van Daan does the cooking, and Mummy washes up and polishes.

Numbers six and seven. I won't say much about Daddy and me. The former is the most unassuming of all at table. He looks first to see if everyone else has something. He needs nothing himself, for the best things are for the children. He is the perfect example, and sitting beside him, the Secret Annexe's "bundle of nerves."

Dr. Dussel. Never looks up, and doesn't talk. And if one must talk, then for heaven's sake let it be about food. Enormous helpings go down and the word "No" is never heard. He is always working, alternated only by his afternoon nap, food, and—his favorite spot—the lavatory.

Number nine isn't a member of the Secret Annexe family, but a companion. Elli has a healthy appetite. Leaves nothing on her plate and is not picky. She is easy to please and that is just what gives us pleasure. Cheerful and good-tempered, willing and good-natured, these are her characteristics.

Yours, Anne

Tuesday, 10 August, 1943

Dear Kitty,

If I have to eat something that I simply can't stand, I put my plate in front of me, pretend that it is something delicious, look at it as little as possible, and before I know it, it is gone. When

I get up in the morning, also a very unpleasant process, I jump out of bed thinking to myself: "You'll be back in a second," go to the window, take down the blackout, sniff at the crack of the window, until I feel a bit of fresh air, and I'm awake. The bed is turned down as quickly as possible and then the temptation is removed. Do you know what Mummy calls this? "The Art of Living"—an odd expression.

For the last week we've all been in a muddle, because our beloved Westertoren clock bell has apparently been taken away for war purposes, so that we never know the exact time.*

My feet are the admiration of all, glittering in a pair of (for these days) exceptionally fine shoes. Miep got them secondhand for 27.50 florins, wine-colored suede leather with fairly high wedge heels. I feel as if I'm on stilts and look much taller.

Dussel has indirectly endangered our lives. He actually let Miep bring him a forbidden book which abuses Mussolini and Hitler. On the way she happened to be run into by an S.S. car. She lost her temper, shouted, "Miserable wretches," and rode on. It is better not to think of what might have happened if she had had to go to their headquarters.

Yours, Anne

Friday, 20 August, 1943

Dear Kitty,

Half past five. The men in the warehouse go home and we are free. Elli comes upstairs, where she usually has a bite from our second course. Before Elli is seated, Mrs. Van Daan begins thinking of things she wants. "Oh, Elli, I have only one little wish. . . ." Elli winks at me; Mrs. Van Daan never misses a single opportunity of letting them know what she wants.

Quarter to six. Elli departs. I go two floors down to have a look around. First to the kitchen, then to the private office, after that the coalhole, to open the trapdoor for Mouschi. After a long tour of inspection I land up in Kraler's room. Van Daan is looking in all the drawers and portfolios to find the day's post.

---

*The clock bell was taken away for repairs. When it was later reinstalled, it stroked continually.

Peter is fetching the warehouse key and Boche; Pim is hauling the typewriters upstairs; Margot is looking for a quiet spot to do her office work; Mrs. Van Daan puts a kettle on the gas ring; Mummy is coming downstairs with a pan of potatoes; each one knows his own job.

Yours, Anne

Monday, 23 August, 1943

Dear Kitty,

Continuation of the Secret Annexe daily timetable. As the clock strikes half past eight in the morning, Margot and Mummy are jittery: "Daddy, quiet, Otto, ssh. It is half past eight, come back here, you can't run any more water; walk quietly!" As the clock strikes half past eight, he has to be in the living room. Not a drop of water, no lavatory, no walking about, everything quiet. Everything can be heard in the warehouse. At twenty minutes past eight in my room, everything goes at terrific speed: do my hair, put away my noisy pottie, bed in place. Upstairs Mrs. Van Daan has changed her shoes and is shuffling about in bedroom slippers. Hush, the clock strikes! All is quiet.

Now we have a little real family life. I read or work, Margot as well. Daddy is sitting (with Dickens and the dictionary, naturally) on the edge of the sagging, squeaky bed. Mummy sits on the *opklapbed*,* sewing or knitting. She suddenly thinks of something: "Anne, do you know . . ."

Margot closes her book with a clap. Daddy raises his eyebrows, Mummy begins to chatter with Margot, I become curious and listen. Pim is drawn into the discussion . . . nine o'clock! Breakfast!

Yours, Anne

Friday, 10 September, 1943

Dear Kitty,

Last Wednesday evening, listening to the seven-o'clock news, the first thing we heard was: "Here follows the best news of the war. Italy has capitulated!" Italy's unconditional surrender!

---

*Dutch type of bed which folds against the wall to look like a bookcase with curtains hanging before it.

"God Save the King," the American national anthem, and the "Internationale" were played.

Still we have troubles. As you know, we are all very fond of Mr. Koophuis, he is always cheerful and brave, although he has a lot of pain, and is not allowed to eat or walk much. Now he has to go into the hospital for a very unpleasant abdominal operation and will have to stay for at least four weeks. You ought to see how he said good-by to us, just as usual—he might have simply been going out to do a bit of shopping.

Yours, Anne

Thursday, 16 September, 1943

Dear Kitty,

Relations between us are getting worse all the time. At meal-times, no one dares open their mouths because you either annoy someone or it is misunderstood. We've almost forgotten how to laugh. I feel afraid sometimes that from having to be so serious I'll grow a long face and my mouth will droop at the corners. The others don't get any better either, everyone looks with fear and misgivings towards that great terror, winter. Another thing: the warehouseman, V.M., is becoming suspicious about the Secret Annexe.

We really wouldn't mind what V.M. thought if he wasn't so exceptionally inquisitive and, moreover, not to be trusted. One day Kraler wanted to be extra careful, put on his coat at ten minutes to one, and went to the chemist round the corner. He was back in less than five minutes, and sneaked like a thief up the steep stairs that lead straight to us. At a quarter past one Elli came to warn him that V.M. was in the office. He sat with us until half past one. Then he took off his shoes and went in stockinged feet to the front attic stairs. Elli had been freed of V.M. in the meantime, and came up to fetch Kraler, but he was still on the staircase with his shoes off. After balancing there for a quarter of an hour to avoid creaking, he landed safely in the office, having entered from the outside. Whatever would the people in the street have thought if they had seen the manager outside in his socks!

Yours, Anne

339

Wednesday, 29 September, 1943

Dear Kitty,

Elli had a fit of nerves this week; she had been sent out so often; time and time again she had been asked to go and fetch something quickly, which meant yet another errand or made her feel that she had done something wrong. She has to finish her office work downstairs, Koophuis is ill, Miep at home with a cold, and she herself has a sprained ankle, love worries, and a grumbling father; it's no wonder she's at her wit's end. We comforted her and said that if she puts her foot down once or twice and says she has no time, then the shopping lists will automatically get shorter.

Yours, Anne

Sunday, 17 October, 1943

Dear Kitty,

Koophuis is back again, thank goodness! He still looks rather pale, but in spite of this sets out cheerfully to sell clothes for Van Daan. It is an unpleasant fact that the Van Daans have run out of money. Mrs. Van Daan won't part with a thing from her pile of coats, dresses, and shoes. Mr. Van Daan's suit isn't easily disposed of, because he wants too much for it. They've had a terrific row upstairs about it, and now the reconciliation period of "oh, darling Putti" and "precious Kerli" (their nicknames) has set in.

I am dazed by all the abusive exchanges that have taken place during the past month. Daddy goes about with his lips tightly pursed; when anyone speaks to him, he looks up startled, as if he is afraid he will have to patch up some tricky relationship again.

Mummy has red patches on her cheeks from excitement. Margot complains of headaches. Dussel can't sleep. Mrs. Van Daan grouses the whole day and I'm going completely crazy! I sometimes forget who we are quarreling with and with whom we've made it up.

The only way to take one's mind off it all is to study, and I do a lot of that.

Yours, Anne

Dear Kitty,

There have been resounding rows again between Mr. and Mrs. Van Daan. One day Koophuis spoke about a furrier with whom he was on good terms; this gave Van Daan the idea of selling his wife's fur coat. It's rabbit, and she has worn it seventeen years. He got 325 florins for it—an enormous sum. However, Mrs. Van Daan wanted to keep the money to buy new clothes after the war, and it took some doing before Mr. Van Daan made it clear to her that the money was urgently needed for the household—you can't possibly imagine the yells and screams, stamping and abuse! It was frightening.

Mr. Koophuis is away again; his stomach gives him no peace. For the first time, he was very down when he told us that he didn't feel well and was going home.

I have no appetite. I keep being told: "You don't look at all well." I must say that they are doing their very best to keep me up to the mark. Grape sugar, cod-liver oil, yeast tablets, and calcium have all been lined up. My nerves often get the better of me, especially on Sundays. The atmosphere is so oppressive, you don't hear a single bird singing, and a deadly close silence hangs everywhere, catching hold of me as if it will drag me down into an underworld. I wander from one room to another, downstairs and up again, feeling like a songbird hurling himself against the bars of his cage. "Laugh, and take a breath of fresh air," a voice cries within me, but I don't even feel a response anymore; I go and lie on the divan and sleep to make the time pass more quickly, and the stillness and the terrible fear, because there is no way of killing them.

Yours, Anne

Monday evening, 8 November, 1943

Dear Kitty,

If you were to read my pile of letters one after another, you would certainly be struck by the many different moods in which they are written. It annoys me that I am so dependent on the atmosphere here. At the moment I'm going through a spell of being depressed. I believe it's just because I'm a coward.

This evening, while Elli was here, there was a long, loud ring at the door. I turned white at once, got a tummy-ache and heart palpitations, all from fear. At night, when I'm in bed, I see myself alone in a dungeon, without Mummy and Daddy. Sometimes our Secret Annexe is on fire, or they come and take us away. I see everything as if it is actually taking place, and this gives me the feeling that it may all happen to me soon! Miep often says she envies us for possessing such tranquillity here. That may be true, but she is not thinking about our fear. I simply can't imagine that the world will ever be normal for us again. I talk about "after the war," but it is only a castle in the air, something that will never really happen. If I think back to our old house, my girl friends, the fun at school, it is just as if another person lived it all, not me.

I see the eight of us in our Secret Annexe as if we were a little piece of blue heaven, surrounded by heavy black rain clouds. The round, clearly defined spot where we stand is still safe, but the clouds gather more closely about us and the circle which separates us from the approaching danger closes more and more tightly. Now we are so surrounded by danger and darkness that we bump against each other, as we search desperately for a means of escape. We all look down below, where people are fighting each other, we look above, where it is quiet and beautiful, and meanwhile we are cut off by the great dark mass, which will not let us go upwards, but which stands before us as an impenetrable wall; it tries to crush us, but cannot do so yet.

Yours, Anne

Thursday, 11 November, 1943

Dear Kitty,

My fountain pen has always been one of my most priceless possessions; I value it especially for its thick nib, for I can only write neatly with a thick nib. My fountain pen has had a long and interesting pen-life:

When I was nine, my pen arrived in a packet from Aachen, where my grandmother, the kind donor, used to live. The glorious fountain pen had a red leather case and was at once shown around to all my friends. I, Anne Frank, the proud owner of a fountain pen! When I was ten I was allowed to take the pen to school. When I was twelve and went to the Jewish Lyceum, my fountain pen received a new zippered case in honor of the great occasion. At thirteen the fountain pen came with us to the Secret Annexe, where it has raced through countless diaries and compositions.

Now I am fourteen, we have spent our last year together.

It was on a Friday afternoon after five o'clock. I had come out of my room and wanted to sit at the table to write, but I was roughly pushed aside to make room for Margot and Daddy, who wanted to practice their Latin. The fountain pen remained on the table unused while, with a sigh, its owner contented herself with a tiny little corner of the table and started rubbing beans. "Bean rubbing" is making moldy beans decent again. I swept the floor at a quarter to six and threw the dirt, together with the bad beans, into a newspaper and into the stove. A terrific flame leaped out and I thought it was grand that the fire should burn up so well when it was practically out. The "Latinites" had finished, and I went to clear up my writing things, but my fountain pen was nowhere to be seen. I looked again, Margot looked.

"Perhaps it fell into the stove together with the beans," she suggested.

"Oh, no, of course not!" I answered. When my fountain pen didn't turn up that evening, however, we all took it that it had been burned, as celluloid is terribly flammable.

And so it was, our fears were confirmed; when Daddy did the stove the next morning the clip used for fastening was found among the ashes. Not a trace of the gold nib was found. "Must have melted," Daddy thought. I have one consolation, although a slender one; my fountain pen has been cremated, just what I want later!

Yours, Anne

Wednesday, 17 November, 1943

Dear Kitty,

Shattering things: diphtheria reigns in Elli's home, so she is not allowed to come into contact with us for six weeks. It makes shopping very awkward and we miss her companionship. Koophuis is still in bed and has had nothing but porridge and milk for three weeks. Kraler is frantically busy.

Yesterday, the sixteenth, Dussel had been exactly one year in the Secret Annexe. Mummy received a plant in honor of the occasion.

Yours, Anne

Monday, 6 December, 1943

Dear Kitty,

When St. Nicholas' Day approached, none of us could help thinking of the prettily decorated basket we had last year and thought it would be very dull to do nothing at all this year. I consulted Pim, and a week ago we started composing a little poem for each person.

On Sunday evening at a quarter to eight we appeared upstairs with the large laundry basket, decorated with little figures, and bows of pink and blue carbon paper, and covered with a piece of brown paper, on which a letter was pinned. Everyone was rather astonished at the size of the surprise package.

I took the letter and read:

> *"Santa Claus has come once more,*
> *Though not quite as he came before;*
> *We can't celebrate his day*
> *In last year's fine and pleasant way.*
> *For then our hopes were high and bright,*
> *All the optimists seemed right,*
> *None supposing that this year*
> *We would welcome Santa here.*
> *Still, we'll make his spirit live,*
> *And since we've nothing left to give,*
> *We've thought of something else to do:*
> *Each please look inside his shoe."*

As each owner took his shoe from the basket there was a resounding peal of laughter. A little paper package lay in each shoe with the address of the shoe's owner on it.

Yours, Anne

Wednesday, 22 December, 1943

Dear Kitty,

A bad attack of flu has prevented me from writing to you until today. It's wretched to be ill here. When I wanted to cough I crawled under the blankets and tried to stifle the noise. Milk and honey, sugar or lozenges had to be brought. It makes me dizzy to think of all the cures we tried. Sweating, compresses, wet cloths on my chest, dry cloths on my chest, hot drinks, gargling, throat painting, lying still, hot-water bottles, lemon squashes, and—the thermometer every two hours!

Miep

Can anyone really get better like this? The worst moment of all was certainly when Mr. Dussel thought he'd play doctor, and came and laid his greasy head on my naked chest in order to listen to the sounds within. Not only did his hair tickle unbearably, but I was embarrassed, in spite of the fact that he studied medicine and has the title of Doctor.

But that is enough about illness. I'm as fit as a fiddle again, one centimeter taller, two pounds heavier, pale, and with a real appetite for learning.

We are all getting on well together for a change! There's no quarreling—we haven't had such peace for half a year. We received extra oil for Christmas, sweets and syrup; Mr. Dussel gave Mummy and Mrs. Van Daan a lovely cake which he had asked Miep to bake. With all her work, she has to do that as well! I have also something for Miep and Elli. For at least two months I have saved the sugar from my porridge, you see, and with Mr. Koophuis's help, I'll have it made into fondants.

Yours, Anne

Friday, 24 December, 1943

Dear Kitty,

I have previously written about how much we are affected by atmospheres here, and I think that in my own case this is getting much worse lately, as happened today, for example. Mrs. Koop-huis comes and tells us about her daughter Corry's hockey club, canoe trips, theatrical performances, and friends. I couldn't help feeling a great longing to have lots of fun, and to laugh until my tummy ached. Especially at this holiday time. Still, I really ought not to write this, because it seems ungrateful. But whatever you think of me, I can't keep everything to myself, so I'll remind you of my opening words—"Paper is more patient."

When someone comes in from outside, with the wind in their clothes and the cold on their faces, then I could bury my head in the blankets to stop myself thinking: "When will we be granted the privilege of smelling fresh air?" I know I must not bury my head in the blankets; I must keep my head high and be brave. But if you have been shut up for a year and a half, it can get too much for you some days. Cycling, dancing, whistling, looking out into the world, feeling young, to know that I'm free—that's what I long for; still, I mustn't show it, because I sometimes think if all eight of us began to pity ourselves, or went about with discontented faces, where would it lead us? I am simply a young girl badly in need of some rollicking fun, but I couldn't talk about it to anyone, because then I know I should cry.

Yours, Anne

Monday, 27 December, 1943

Dear Kitty,

For the first time in my life I received something for Christmas. Koophuis, Kraler and the girls had prepared a lovely surprise. Miep made a Christmas cake, on which was written "Peace 1944." Elli provided a pound of sweet biscuits of prewar quality. For Peter, Margot, and me a bottle of yogurt, and a bottle of beer for each of the grown-ups. Everything was so nicely done up, and there were pictures stuck on the different packages.

Yours, Anne

Sunday, 2 January, 1944

Dear Kitty,

This morning I turned over some of the pages of my diary and several times I came across letters dealing with Mummy in

such a hotheaded way that I was quite shocked, and asked myself: "Oh, Anne, how could you?" I remained sitting with the
open book in my hand, and thought about how it came about
that I should have been so filled with hate. I have been trying to
understand the Anne of a year ago and to excuse her, because my
conscience isn't clear.

I suffered then from moods which only allowed me to see the
things subjectively. I hid within myself; I only considered myself and quietly wrote down all my joys, sorrows, and contempt
in my diary. Those violent outbursts on paper were only giving
vent to anger which in a normal life could have been worked
off by stamping my feet a couple of times in a locked room, or
calling Mummy names behind her back.

This diary is of great value to me, because it has become a
book of memoirs in many places, but on a good many pages I
could certainly put "past and done with." I used to be furious
with Mummy, and still am sometimes. It's true that she doesn't
understand me, but I don't understand her either. She did love
me very much and she was tender, but as she landed in so many
unpleasant situations through me, and was nervous and irritable
because of other worries and difficulties, it is certainly understandable that she snapped at me. I took it much too seriously,
and was rude to Mummy, which, in turn, made her unhappy. So
it was really a matter of unpleasantness and misery rebounding
all the time. It wasn't nice for either of us, but it is passing.

I have grown wiser and Mummy's nerves are not so much
on edge. And I soothe my conscience now with the thought that
it is better for hard words to be on paper than in her heart.

Yours, Anne

Wednesday, 5 January, 1944

Dear Kitty,

I have two things to confess to you today. The first is about
Mummy. It is suddenly clear to me what she lacks. Mummy
has told us that she looked upon us more as her friends than
her daughters. Now that is very fine, but a friend can't take a
mother's place. I need my mother as an example which I can
follow, I want to be able to respect her. I have the feeling that

Margot thinks differently about these things and would never be able to understand this. And Daddy avoids all arguments about Mummy.

The second is very difficult to tell you, and I don't blush easily. Yesterday I read an article by Sis Heyster that might have been addressed to me personally. This article said that a girl in the years of puberty begins to think about the wonders that are happening to her body. I experience that, too. I think all that is taking place inside me is wonderful. Each time I have a period —and that has only been three times—I have the feeling that in spite of all the pain and unpleasantness, I have a sweet secret, although it is nothing but a nuisance to me in a way.

Sis Heyster also writes that girls of my age don't feel certain of themselves, and discover that they are individuals with ideas, thoughts, and habits. After I came here, when I was just fourteen, I began to think about myself as a "person." Sometimes, in bed at night, I have a terrible desire to feel my breasts and to listen to the quiet rhythmic beat of my heart.

I had these feelings before I came here; I remember once when I slept with a girl friend I had a strong desire to kiss her, and I did. I could not help being terribly inquisitive over her body, for she had always kept it hidden from me. I go into ecstasies every time I see the naked figure of a woman, such as Venus, for example. It strikes me as so exquisite that I have difficulty in stopping the tears rolling down my cheeks.

If only I had a girl friend!

Yours, Anne

Thursday, 6 January, 1944

Dear Kitty,

My longing to talk to someone became so intense that I took it into my head to choose Peter.

I've been in Peter's room during the day, but I never dared stay long, because I was afraid he might think me a bore. I tried to think of an excuse to stay in his room and get him talking, and my chance came yesterday. Peter has a mania for crossword puzzles at the moment and hardly does anything else. I helped him with them and we soon sat opposite each other at his little table, he on the chair and me on the divan. He sat there with that mysterious laugh playing round his lips. I could see that he was uncertain as to how to behave, and, at the same time, feeling a sense of manhood. His shy manner made me feel very gentle; I couldn't refrain from meeting those dark eyes again and again, and with my whole heart I beseeched him: "Oh, tell me, what is going on inside you, can't you look beyond this ridiculous chatter?" But the evening passed and nothing happened. Still, I have made up my mind to go and sit with Peter more often and to get him talking. Don't think I'm in love with Peter—not a bit! If the Van Daans had had a daughter instead of a son, I should have tried to make friends with her too.

I woke this morning and remembered at once what I had dreamed. I sat on a chair and opposite me sat Peter . . . Wessel. We were looking at a book of drawings. Suddenly Peter's eyes met mine and I looked into those fine, brown eyes for a long time. Then Peter said very softly, "If I had only known, I would have come to you long before!" I turned around brusquely because the emotion was too much for me. And after that I felt a soft, and oh, such a cool cheek against mine and it felt so good. I awoke at this point, while I could still feel his cheek against mine. Tears sprang into my eyes, and I was very sad that I had lost him, but glad because it made me feel quite certain that Peter Wessel was still the chosen one.

It is strange that I should often see such vivid images in my dreams.

Yours, Anne

Friday, 7 January, 1944

Dear Kitty,

What a silly ass I am! I am quite forgetting that I have never told you the history of myself and all my boyfriends.

When I was quite small—I was still at kindergarten—I became attached to Karel Samson. He had lost his father, and he and his mother lived with an aunt. One of Karel's cousins, Robby, was a slender, good-looking boy, who aroused more admiration than the little, humorous Karel. But looks did not count with me and I was very fond of Karel for years.

Then Peter Wessel crossed my path, and in my childish way I really fell in love. We were inseparable for one whole summer. I can still remember us walking hand in hand together, he in a white cotton suit and me in a short summer dress. At the end of the summer holidays he went into the first form of the high school and I into the sixth form of the lower school. He used to meet me after school. Peter was a very good-looking boy, tall, handsome, and slim, with an earnest, intelligent face. He had dark hair, and wonderful brown eyes, ruddy cheeks, and a pointed nose. Above all, I was mad about his mischievous laugh!

I went to the country for the holidays; when I returned, Peter had moved, and had started going around with girls of his own age. He didn't even think of saying "Hello" to me anymore; but I couldn't forget him.

Lots of boys in our class at the Jewish Lyceum were keen on me—I thought it was fun, felt honored, but I never fell in love again. I imagined that I had forgotten Peter and that I didn't like him a bit anymore. However, I admitted to myself sometimes I was jealous of the other girls, and that was why I didn't like him anymore.

This morning I knew that nothing has changed; on the contrary, as I grew more mature my love grew with me. I can understand now that Peter thought me childish, and yet it still hurt that he had so completely forgotten me.

I am upset by the dream. When Daddy kissed me this morning, I could have cried out: "Oh, if only you were Peter!" I think of him all the time. I must live on and pray to God that Peter will cross my path when I come out of here, and that when he reads the love in my eyes he will say, "Oh, Anne, if I had only known, I would have come to you long before!"

I saw my face in the mirror and it looks quite different. My eyes look so clear and deep, my cheeks are pink—which they haven't been for weeks—my mouth is much softer; I look as if I am happy, and yet I'm not because I know that Peter's thoughts are not with me.

Once, when we spoke about sex, Daddy told me that I couldn't possibly understand the longing yet; now I understand it fully.

Yours, Anne

Wednesday, 12 January, 1944

Dear Kitty,

Elli has been back a fortnight. Miep and Henk were away from their work for two days—both had tummy upsets.

I have a craze for ballet at the moment, and practice dance steps every evening diligently. I have made a supermodern dance frock from a light blue petticoat edged with lace. I tried in vain to convert my gym shoes into real ballet shoes. My stiff limbs are well on the way to becoming supple again.

Margot has grown so sweet; she isn't nearly so catty these days and is becoming a real friend.

Yours, Anne

Saturday, 15 January, 1944

Dear Kitty,

There is no point in telling you of our rows and arguments. Let it suffice that we have divided up a great many things, such as butter and meat, and that we fry our own potatoes.

For Mummy's birthday she got some extra sugar from Kraler, which made the Van Daans jealous. But what's the use of annoying each other with unkind words and angry outbursts. I keep asking myself whether one would not have trouble whoever one shared a house with. Are most people so selfish and stingy? Or did we strike it extra unlucky? I think it's all to the good to have learned a bit about human beings, but now I think I've learned enough. The war goes on whether we quarrel or not.

I believe that if I stay here I shall grow into a dried-up old beanstalk. And I did so want to grow into a real young woman!

Yours, Anne

Saturday, 22 January, 1944

Dear Kitty,

I wonder why people always try so hard to hide their real feelings? Why do we trust one another so little? I've grown up a lot since my dream the other night. I'm much more of an "independent being." Even my attitude towards the Van Daans has changed. I suddenly see all the arguments in a different light, and am not as prejudiced as I was. You see, it suddenly struck me that if Mummy had been different, the relationship might have been different. It's true that Mrs. Van Daan is by no means a nice person, but still, half the quarrels could be avoided if it weren't for the fact that Mummy is a bit difficult too.

Mrs. Van Daan has one good side: you can talk to her. Despite all her selfishness and underhandedness, you can make her give in easily as long as you don't irritate her.

I know exactly what you'll say, Kitty: "But, Anne, do these words really come from *your* lips? From you, who have had to listen to so many harsh words from the people upstairs, from you, the girl who has suffered so many injustices?" And yet they come from me.

I want to examine the whole matter carefully myself and find out what is true and what is exaggerated. I shall seize every opportunity to discuss things openly with Mrs. Van Daan and not be afraid of declaring myself neutral. It is not that I shall be going against my own family, but from today there will be no more unkind gossip on my part.

Yours, Anne

Monday, 24 January, 1944

Dear Kitty,

Whenever anyone used to speak of sexual problems at home, it was either mysterious or revolting. Words on the subject were whispered, and often if someone didn't understand he was laughed at. It struck me as very odd and I thought, "Why are people so secretive and tiresome when they talk about these things?" But I kept my mouth shut and sometimes asked girl friends for information. When I had spoken about it with my parents, Mummy said, "Anne, let me give you some good advice; never speak about this subject to boys and don't reply if they begin about it." I said, "No, of course not! The very idea!"

When we first came here, Daddy often told me about things that I would really have preferred to hear from Mummy, and I found out the rest from books. Peter Van Daan was never as tiresome over this as the boys at school—he never tried to get me talking. Mrs. Van Daan told us that she never talked about these things to Peter, and for all she knew neither had her husband. Apparently she didn't even know how much he knew.

Yesterday, when Margot, Peter, and I were peeling potatoes, the conversation turned to Boche. "We still don't know what sex Boche is, do we?" I asked.

"Yes, certainly," Peter answered. "He's a tom. You can go look at him. Once when I was playing with him, I noticed that he's a tom."

I couldn't control my curiosity, and went with him to the warehouse. Boche stood on the packing table. Peter picked up the animal and turned him over on his back. "These are the male organs, these are just a few stray hairs, and that is his bottom." The cat did another half-turn and was standing on his white socks once more.

If any other boy had shown me "the male organs," I would never have looked at him again. But Peter went on talking quite normally on an otherwise painful subject, and finally put me at my ease. We played with Boche, chattered together, and then sauntered through the large warehouse towards the door.

"Usually, when I want to know something, I find it in some book or other, don't you?" I asked.

"Why on earth? I just ask my father."

Really I shouldn't have discussed these things in such a normal way with a girl. I know that Mummy didn't mean it that way when she warned me not to discuss the subject with boys. There really are people of the opposite sex who can discuss these things naturally without making fun of them.

Yours, Anne

Thursday, 27 January, 1944

Dear Kitty,

Lately I have developed a great love for family trees and genealogical tables of the royal families, and have come to the conclusion that, once you begin, you want to delve still deeper into the past, and can keep on making fresh and interesting discoveries. I am extraordinarily industrious over my lessons, and can already follow the English Home Service quite well on the wireless. I still devote many Sundays to sorting my collection of film stars, which is quite a respectable size by now.

I am awfully pleased whenever Mr. Kraler brings the *Cinema and Theater* with him. Although this little gift is called a waste of money by the less worldly members of the household, they are amazed at how accurately I can state who is in a film, even after a year. Not so long ago, Mum said that I wouldn't need to go to a cinema because I knew the plots, the stars, and the opinions of the reviews all by heart.

Yours, Anne

Friday, 28 January, 1944

Dear Kitty,

I asked myself this morning whether you don't sometimes feel rather like a cow who has had to chew over all the old pieces of news again and again, and who finally yawns loudly and wishes that Anne would occasionally dig up something new.

Alas, I know it's dull for you, but try to put yourself in my place. If the conversation at mealtimes isn't over politics, then Mummy or Mrs. Van Daan trot out the stories of their youth, which we've heard so many times before; or Dussel twaddles on about his wife's extensive wardrobe, beautiful racehorses, leaking rowboats, boys who can swim at the age of four, muscular pains and nervous patients. What it all boils down to is that if one of the eight of us opens his mouth, the other seven can finish the story for him! The various milkmen, grocers, and butchers of the two ex-housewives have grown beards in our minds, so often have they been praised to the skies or pulled to pieces; it is impossible for anything in the conversation here to be fresh.

Still, all this would be bearable if the grown-ups didn't tell the stories ten times over, adding their own little frills and furbelows, so that I often have to pinch my arm under the table to prevent myself from putting them right. Little children such as Anne must never know better than grown-ups, no matter how they allow their imaginations to run away with them.

One favorite subject of Koophuis's and Henk's is people in hiding and in the underground movement. Anything to do with other people in hiding interests us tremendously. We sympathize with the sufferings of people who get taken away, and rejoice with the liberated prisoner.

There are a number of organizations which forge identity cards, supply money to people "underground," and find hiding places for people; it is amazing how much noble, unselfish work these people are doing, risking their own lives to save others. Our helpers are a very good example. They have pulled us through so far and we hope they will bring us safely to dry land. Otherwise, they will have to share the same fate as the many others who are being searched for. Never have we heard *one* word of the burden which we certainly must be to them, never has one of them complained of all the trouble we give.

They all come upstairs every day, talk to the men about business and politics, to the women about food and wartime difficulties, and about newspapers and books with the children. They put on the brightest possible faces, bring flowers and presents for birthdays, are always ready to help. That is something we must never forget; although others may show heroism in the war or against the Germans, our helpers display heroism in their cheerfulness and affection.

New ration books are being handed out. In order that the people in hiding may also draw rations, the officials have given instructions to them to come at a certain time, so that they can collect their documents from a separate table. They'll have to be careful that such impudent tricks do not reach the ears of the Germans.

Yours, Anne

Thursday, 3 February, 1944

Dear Kitty,

Invasion fever in the country is mounting daily. All the newspapers are driving people mad by saying that "In the event of the English landing in Holland, the Germans will do all they can to defend the country; if necessary they will resort to flooding." Maps have been published, on which the parts of Holland that will be under water are marked. As this applies to large parts of Amsterdam, the first question was, what shall we do if the water floods the streets? The answers vary considerably.

"We shall have to wade through stagnant water."

"We shall all put on our bathing suits and swim underwater, then no one will see that we are Jews."

"I'd like to see the ladies swimming if the rats started biting their legs!" (That was naturally a man: just see who screams the loudest!)

"We shan't be able to get out of the house anyway; the warehouse will collapse, it is so wobbly already."

"We shall get a boat."

"I shall walk on stilts: I used to be an expert at it in my youth."

This chatter is all amusing, but the truth may be otherwise. A second question about the invasion was bound to arise: what do we do if the Germans evacuate Amsterdam?

"Leave the city and disguise ourselves as best we can."

"The only thing to do is to remain here! The Germans are quite capable of driving the whole population right into Germany."

"This is the safest place. We'll fetch Koophuis and his family here to live with us."

"We'll order some extra corn and more peas and beans; we have about sixty pounds of beans and ten pounds of peas in the house at present, as well as fifty tins of vegetables."

"Mummy, count up how much food we've got, will you?"

"Ten tins of fish, forty tins of milk, ten kilos of milk powder, three bottles of salad oil, four preserving jars of butter, four ditto of meat, two wicker-covered bottles of strawberries, two bottles of raspberries, twenty bottles of tomatoes, ten pounds of rolled oats, eight pounds of rice; and that's all."

"We have sufficient coal and firewood in the house."

"Let's all make lists of the most important things to take, should we have to run for it, and pack rucksacks now."

I hear nothing the whole day long but invasion, hunger, dying, bombs, fire extinguishers, sleeping bags, Jewish vouchers, poisonous gases, etc., etc. I will spare you further examples. I keep very quiet and don't take any notice of all the excitement. I don't care much whether I live or die now. The world will keep on turning without me; what is going to happen, will happen, and it's no good trying to resist.

Yours, Anne

Saturday, 12 February, 1944

Dear Kitty,

The sun is shining, the sky is a deep blue, there is a lovely breeze and I'm longing for freedom, for friends, to be alone. And I do so long to cry! I feel as if I'm going to burst, and I know that it would get better with crying; but I can't, I'm restless, I go from one room to the other, breathe through the crack of a closed window, feel my heart beating.

I believe it's spring awakening within me, in my whole body and soul. It is an effort to behave normally, I feel utterly confused, don't know what to do, I only know that I am longing . . . !

Yours, Anne

Sunday, 13 February, 1944

Dear Kitty,

Since Saturday a lot has changed for me. I longed—and am still longing—but something happened which made it a little, just a little, less.

To my great joy I noticed that Peter Van Daan kept looking at me all morning. Not in the ordinary way, I don't know how, I just can't explain. I used to think that Peter was in love with Margot, but yesterday I suddenly had the feeling that it is not so. I made a special effort not to look at him too much, because whenever I did, he kept on looking too and it gave me a lovely feeling inside, which I mustn't feel too often.

I desperately want to be alone. Daddy has noticed that I'm not my usual self, but I can't tell him everything. "Leave me in peace, leave me alone," I'd like to cry out. Who knows, the day may come when I'm left alone more than I would wish!

Yours, Anne

Wednesday, 16 February, 1944

Dear Kitty,

It's Margot's birthday. Peter came to look at the presents and stayed much longer than was necessary—a thing he'd have never done otherwise. I went to get some potatoes, because I wanted to spoil Margot one day in the year. I went through Peter's room and asked whether I should close the trapdoor to the attic. "Yes," he replied, "knock when you come back, then I'll open it for you."

I thanked him, went upstairs, and searched in the barrel for the smallest potatoes. Then my back began to ache and I got cold. Naturally I opened the trapdoor myself, but still he came to meet me, and took the pan. He gave me a warm look which made a tender glow within me. I could see that he wanted to please me, and I was very grateful.

When I reached the door, I asked, "What are you doing?" "French," he replied. I asked if I might glance through the exercises, and went and sat on the divan opposite him.

We soon began talking. He told me that he wanted to go to the Dutch East Indies and live on a plantation. He talked about his early life, and he said he felt useless. I told him that he had a strong inferiority complex. He said it would have been much easier if he'd been a Christian and if he could be one after the war. Who was to know that he was really a Jew after the war? he said. This gave me a pang; there's always a tinge of dishonesty about him. Then we chatted pleasantly about all kinds of things. It was half past four when I left.

In the evening he said something I thought was nice. We were talking about some pictures of film stars that I'd given him, which have been hanging in his room for a year and a half. He liked them very much and I offered to give him more. "No," he replied, "I'd rather leave it like this. I look at these every day and they have grown to be my friends." Now I understand why he always hugs Mouschi. He needs affection, of course.

Yours, Anne

Friday, 18 February, 1944

Dear Kitty,

Whenever I go upstairs now I keep on hoping that I shall see "him." My life now has an object, I have something to look forward to, and everything has become more pleasant.

At least I needn't be afraid of rivals, except Margot. Don't think I'm in love, because I'm not, but I feel that something fine can grow between us, something based on confidence and friendship. If I get half a chance, I go up to him now. It's not like it used to be when he didn't know how to begin. Now he's still talking when I'm half out of the room.

Mummy doesn't like it much, and says I'll be a nuisance. Honestly, doesn't she realize that I've got some intuition? She looks at me so queerly every time I go into Peter's room. If I come downstairs from there, she asks me where I've been. I think it's horrible.

Yours, Anne

Saturday, 19 February, 1944

Dear Kitty,

It is Saturday again, and the morning was quiet. I helped a bit upstairs, but I didn't have more than a few words with "him." At half past two, when everyone had gone to their rooms to sleep or read, I went to the private office, with my blanket, to write. It was not long before tears were streaming down my cheeks; I felt desperately unhappy. Oh, if only he had come to comfort me. At four o'clock I went upstairs again with hope of a meeting, but while I was still smartening up my hair, he went down to see Boche in the warehouse. Suddenly I felt tears coming back and I hurried to the lavatory. There I sat while the tears made dark spots on my apron.

Oh, I'll never reach Peter. Who knows, perhaps he doesn't need anyone to confide in. Perhaps I shall have to go on alone once more, without friendship or anything to look forward to again. Oh, Peter, if that were the truth it would be more than I could bear.

Yours, Anne

Wednesday, 23 February, 1944

Dear Kitty,

Lovely weather and I've quite perked up since the other day. I went to the attic, where Peter works, to blow the stuffy air out of my lungs. From my favorite spot on the floor I looked up at the blue sky and the bare chestnut tree, on whose branches little silver raindrops shine, and at the sea gulls as they glide on the wind. We breathed the fresh air, and felt that the spell should not be broken by words. We remained like this for a long time, and when he had to go up to the loft to chop wood, I followed; he chopped for a quarter of an hour, doing his best to show off his strength. But I looked out the window over all the roofs of Amsterdam to the horizon, which was such a pale blue that it was hard to see the dividing line. As long as I may live to see this sunshine, these cloudless skies, I cannot be unhappy.

I firmly believe that nature brings solace in all troubles. The best remedy for those who are lonely or unhappy is to go where they can be alone with nature and God. Only then does one feel that all is as it should be and that God wishes to see people happy.

Yours, Anne

Sunday, 27 February, 1944

Dearest Kitty,

From early morning till late at night, I hardly think of anything else but Peter. I even dream about him. Peter and I are really not so different as we would appear, and I will tell you why. We both lack a mother. His is too superficial, and doesn't trouble about him or what he thinks. Mine does bother about me, but lacks sensitiveness, real motherliness. Peter and I both wrestle with our inner feelings. If we are roughly treated, however, my reaction is to hide my feelings, throw my weight about, and be noisy and boisterous. He, on the contrary, shuts himself up, hardly talks at all, and daydreams.

But how will we finally reach each other? I don't know how long my common sense will keep this longing under control.

Yours, Anne

Monday, 28 February, 1944

Dearest Kitty,

It is becoming a bad dream—in daytime as well as at night. I see him all the time and can't get at him, I mustn't show anything, must remain gay while I'm really in despair. Peter Wessel and Peter Van Daan have grown into one Peter, who is beloved and good, and for whom I long desperately.

Peter didn't come to me in the attic. He went up to the loft and did some carpentry. At every creak some of my courage seemed to seep away and I grew more unhappy. In the distance a bell was playing "Pure in body, pure in soul."* I'm sentimental, desperate and silly—I know that. Oh, help me!

Yours, Anne

Wednesday, 1 March, 1944

Dear Kitty,

My own affairs have been pushed into the background by a burglary. I'm becoming boring with all my burglars, but what can I do, they seem to take such a delight in honoring Kolen & Co. with their visits. This burglary is much more complicated than the one in July 1943.

When Mr. Van Daan went to Kraler's office at half past seven, as usual, he saw that the glass doors to the office were open. Surprised, he walked through and was even more amazed to see the doors of the little dark room open too, and a terrible mess in the main office. "A burglar," he thought at once, and he went straight downstairs to look at the front door, tried the Yale lock, and found everything closed. "Both Peter and Elli must have been very slack this evening," he decided. He switched off the lamp, and went upstairs, without worrying about the open doors or the untidy office.

Early this morning Peter knocked at our door with the not so pleasant news that the front door was wide open. The projector and Kraler's new portfolio had both disappeared from the cupboard. Peter was told to close the door. Van Daan told us of his discoveries the previous evening and we were all awfully worried. The thief must have had a skeleton key, because the lock was undamaged. He must have crept into the house quite early, hidden when disturbed by Mr. Van Daan, and fled with his spoils, leaving the door open in his haste. Who can have our key? Why didn't the thief go to the warehouse? Might it be one of our own warehousemen, and would he betray us, since he certainly heard Van Daan and perhaps even saw him? It is all very creepy, because we don't know whether this burglar may not visit us again.

Yours, Anne

---

*The bells in old clock towers play tunes.

Dear Kitty,

During dishwashing Elli began telling Mummy and Mrs. Van Daan that she felt very discouraged at times. And what do you think Mummy's advice was? She should try to think of all the other people who are in trouble! What is the good of thinking of misery when one is already miserable? I said. I would have so liked to say something to poor Elli, something that I know from experience would have helped her. But Daddy came between us and told me, "You keep out of this conversation." Aren't grown-ups stupid! Even if people are still very young, they shouldn't be prevented from saying what they think.

Only great love and devotion can help Elli, Margot, Peter, and me, and none of us gets it. And no one, especially the mothers here, can understand us. We are much more sensitive and advanced in our thoughts than anyone here would ever imagine.

I managed to get hold of Peter this afternoon and we talked for an hour. He told me how often his parents quarrel over politics, cigarettes, and all kinds of things. He was amazed that we don't always like his parents. "Peter," I said, "you know I'm always honest, so why shouldn't I tell you that we can see their faults too." And among other things I said, "I would so like to help you, Peter; can't I? You are in such an awkward position and, although you don't say anything, it doesn't mean that you don't care."

"Oh, I would always welcome your help."

"Perhaps you would do better to go to Daddy, you can tell him anything."

"Yes, he is a real pal, a first-rate chap."

Peter is a first-rate chap, too, just like Daddy!

Yours, Anne

Friday, 3 March, 1944

Dear Kitty,

When I looked into the candle this evening* I felt calm and happy. Oma seems to be in the candle and it is Oma who pro-

---

*In Jewish homes candles are lit on the Sabbath eve.

tects me and makes me feel happy again. But there is someone else who governs all my moods . . . Peter. When I went up to get potatoes today he asked, "What have you been doing since lunch?" I sat on the steps and we started talking. An hour later the potatoes finally reached their destination.

I believe I'm pretty nearly in love with him. He talked about that this evening. I went into his room, after peeling the potatoes, and said that I felt hot.

"You can tell what the temperature is by Margot and me; if it's cold we are white, and if it is hot we are red in the face," I said.

"In love?" he asked.

"Why should I be in love?" My answer was rather silly.

"Why not?" he said.

Would he have meant anything by that question?

Kitty, I'm just like someone in love, who can only talk about her darling. And Peter really is a darling. When shall I be able to tell him so? Naturally, only if he thinks I'm a darling too. I have no idea how much he likes me. In any case, we are getting to know each other a bit. I wish we dared to tell each other much more already.

Yours, Anne

Saturday, 4 March, 1944

Dear Kitty,

This is the first Saturday for months and months that hasn't been boring, dreary, and dull. And Peter is the cause. First we talked French; then we did some English. Daddy read out loud to us from Dickens and I was in the seventh heaven, because I sat very close to Peter. We talked until a quarter to one. If he gets a chance after a meal, and if no one can hear, he says: "Good-by, Anne, see you soon."

Oh, I am so pleased! And no one knows what lovely talks I have with him! Mrs. Van Daan quite approves, but she asked today teasingly, "Can I really trust you two up there together?"

"Of course," I protested, "really you quite insult me!"

From morn till night I look forward to seeing Peter.

Yours, Anne

Dear Kitty,

My life in 1942 all seems so unreal now. It was quite a different Anne who enjoyed that heavenly existence from the Anne who has grown wise within these walls. Yes, it was a heavenly life. Boyfriends at every turn, many friends my own age, the darling of nearly all the teachers, spoiled from top to toe by Mummy and Daddy, lots of sweets, enough pocket money, what more could one want?

You will certainly wonder how I got around all these people. Peter's word "attractiveness" is not altogether true. All the teachers were entertained by my cute remarks, my smiling face, and my questioning looks. That is all I was—a terrible flirt, coquettish and amusing. I had one or two advantages which kept me in favor. I was industrious, honest, and frank. I would never have dreamed of cribbing from anyone else. I shared my sweets generously, and I wasn't conceited.

At school I was the one who thought of new jokes and pranks, always "king of the castle," never in a bad mood. No wonder everyone liked to cycle with me, and I got their attentions. Peter said quite rightly about me: "You were always the center of everything!"

It was a good thing that, at the height of all this gaiety, I suddenly had to face reality; it took me a year to get used to the fact that there was no more admiration forthcoming. I look back at that Anne as an amusing but superficial girl, who has nothing to do with the Anne of today. What is left of that girl? Oh, don't worry, I haven't forgotten how to laugh or to answer back readily, and I can still flirt if I wish. I'd like that sort of carefree, gay life again for a few days, or even a week; but at the end of that week, I should be only too thankful to listen to anyone who began to talk about something sensible. I don't want followers, but friends who fall not for a flattering smile but for one's character. I know quite well that the circle around me would be much smaller. But what does that matter, as long as one keeps a few sincere friends?

Yet in spite of everything I wasn't entirely happy in 1942. I often felt deserted, but because I was on the go the whole day

long, I didn't think about it and enjoyed myself as much as I could. I tried to drive away the emptiness with jokes and pranks. Now I think seriously about life.

The carefree school days are gone forever. I don't even long for them anymore; I have outgrown them.

I look upon my life up till the New Year, as it were, through a powerful magnifying glass. The sunny life at home, then coming here in 1942, the sudden change, the quarrels, the bickerings. I couldn't understand it, I was taken by surprise, and the only way I could keep up some bearing was by being impertinent.

The first half of 1943: my fits of crying, the loneliness, how I slowly began to see all my faults and shortcomings. I tried to draw Pim to me, but couldn't. Alone I had to face the difficult task of changing myself, to stop the everlasting reproaches which reduced me to such terrible despondency.

Things improved slightly in the second half of the year, I became a young woman and was treated more like a grown-up. I started to write stories. And it struck me that even Daddy would never become my confidant over everything.

At the beginning of the New Year: the second great change; I discovered my longing for a boyfriend. I also discovered inward happiness.

In the evening I end my prayers with the words, "I thank you, God, for all that is good and dear and beautiful." Then I think with joy about going into hiding, my health, and the dearness of Peter, of that which is still embryonic and impressionable and which we dare not name; of love, the future, nature, and all that is exquisite and fine in the world.

Whoever is happy will make others happy too. He who has courage and faith will never perish in misery!

Yours, Anne

Tuesday, 14 March, 1944

Dear Kitty,

Perhaps it would be entertaining for you—though not in the least for me—to hear what we are going to eat today. I'm sitting on the Van Daans' table at the moment. I have a handkerchief soaked in scent (bought before we came here) over my mouth

367

and nose. You won't gather much from this, so let's "begin at the beginning."

The people from whom we obtained food coupons have been caught, so we just have our five ration cards, no extra coupons, and no fats. As both Miep and Koophuis are ill, Elli hasn't time to do any shopping, so the atmosphere is dreary and dejected, and so is the food. From tomorrow we shall not have a scrap of fat, butter, or margarine left. We can't have fried potatoes (to save bread) for breakfast any longer, so we have porridge instead, and as Mrs. Van Daan thinks we're starving, we have bought some full cream milk "under the counter." Our supper today consists of hash made from kale which has been preserved in a barrel. Hence the precautionary measure with the handkerchief! It's incredible how kale can stink when it's a year old! The mere thought of eating that muck makes me feel sick.

Added to this, our potatoes are suffering from such peculiar diseases that out of two buckets only one ends up on the stove. We amuse ourselves by searching for different kinds of diseases, and have come to the conclusion that they range from cancer to measles! It's no joke to be in hiding during the fourth year of the war.

I wouldn't care so much about the food, if it were more pleasant here. This tedious existence is beginning to make us all touchy. The following are the present views of the five grown-ups:

Mrs. Van Daan: "The job as queen of the kitchen lost its attraction long ago. It's impossible to cook without fats, and these nasty smells make me feel sick. Nothing but ingratitude and rude remarks do I get in return for my services. I'm afraid we're going to starve."

Mr. Van Daan: "I must smoke and smoke and smoke, and then the food, the political situation, and Kerli's moods don't seem so bad. Kerli is a darling wife."

But if he hasn't anything to smoke, then nothing is right, and this is what one hears: "I'm getting ill, we don't live well enough. I must have meat. Frightfully stupid person, my Kerli!" After this a terrific quarrel is sure to follow.

Mrs. Frank: "Food is not very important, but I would love

a slice of rye bread now, I feel so terribly hungry. If I were Mrs. Van Daan I would have put a stop to Mr. Van Daan's everlasting smoking a long time ago. But now I must definitely have a cigarette, because my nerves are getting the better of me. I must be thankful I'm not in Poland."

Mr. Frank: "Everything's all right, I don't require anything. Give me my potatoes and then put some of my rations on one side for Elli. The political situation is very promising, I'm extremely optimistic!"

Mr. Dussel: "I must get my task for today, everything must be finished on time. Political situation 'outschtänding' and it is 'eempossible' that we'll be caught."

I, I, I . . . !

Yours, Anne

Wednesday, 15 March, 1944

Dear Kitty,

The warehouse people are getting a free day tomorrow; Elli can stay at home, then the cupboard door will remain locked and we shall have to be as quiet as mice, so that the neighbors don't hear us. Henk is coming to visit the deserted ones at one o'clock—playing the role of zoo-keeper, as it were. For the first time in ages he told us something about the great wide world this afternoon. He talked about food, of course, and Miep's doctor. Miep hasn't recovered from her flu yet. You should have seen the eight of us sitting around him; it looked exactly like a picture of grandmother telling a story.

Yours, Anne

Thursday, 16 March, 1944

Dear Kitty,

Now I know why I'm so much more restless than Peter. He has his own room where he can work, dream, and think. I am shoved about from one corner to another. I hardly spend any time in my "double" room and yet it's something I long for so much. That is the reason why I so frequently escape to the attic. There I can be myself for a while. I don't want to moan about myself, on the contrary, I want to be brave. Thank goodness the others can't tell what my inward feelings are. No one must know that war between desire and common sense reigns incessantly within. The latter has won up till now; yet will the former prove to be the stronger of the two? Sometimes I fear that it will and sometimes I long for it to be!

Oh, it is so terribly difficult never to say anything to Peter, but I know that the first to begin must be he; I've lived it all in my dreams, it is so hard to find that yet another day has gone by, and none of it comes true! Yes, Kitty, Anne is a crazy child, but I live in crazy times and under still crazier circumstances.

Yours, Anne

Friday, 17 March, 1944

Dear Kitty,

Margot and I are getting a bit tired of our parents. When you are as old as we are, you do want to decide just a few things for yourself.

If I go upstairs, then I'm asked what I'm going to do, I'm not allowed salt with my food, every evening regularly at a quarter past eight Mummy asks whether I ought not to start undressing, every book I read must be inspected. I must admit that they are not at all strict, and I'm allowed to read nearly everything, and yet we are both sick of all the remarks and questioning that go on the whole day long.

Something else that doesn't please them: I don't feel like giving lots of kisses anymore and I think fancy nicknames are terribly affected. In short, I'd really like to be rid of them for a while. Margot said last evening, "I think it's awfully annoying, the way they ask if you've got a headache, or whether you don't feel well, if you happen to give a sigh and put your hand to your head!" It is a great blow to us both, suddenly to realize how little remains of the confidence and harmony that we used to have.

Although I'm only fourteen, I know quite well what is right and wrong, I have my opinions, my own ideas and principles, and although it may sound mad from an adolescent, I feel more a person than a child, and quite independent of anyone.

Yours, Anne

Dear Kitty,

Yesterday was a great day for me. I had decided to talk things out with Peter. As we were going to supper I whispered to him, "I'd like to talk to you later!" He agreed. After the dishes were done, I stood by the window in his parents' room for the look of things, but it wasn't long before I went to Peter's room. He was standing on the left side of the open window, I went and stood on the right side, and we talked. It was much easier to talk in semidarkness than in bright light, and I believe Peter felt the same.

We told each other so very very much, it was lovely; the most wonderful evening I have ever had in the Secret Annexe. First we talked about the quarrels and the estrangement between us and our parents. How his parents would have loved to have his confidence, but that he didn't wish it. How I cry my heart out in bed, and he goes up into the loft and swears. How Margot and I really don't tell each other everything, because we are always together. Over every imaginable thing—oh, he was just as I thought!

Then we talked about 1942, how different we were then. How we simply couldn't bear each other in the beginning. He thought I was much too talkative and unruly, and I couldn't understand why he didn't flirt with me, but now I'm glad. He mentioned how he had isolated himself, but I said there was not much difference between my noise and his reserve. I said that I love peace and quiet too, and have nothing for myself, except my diary. How glad he is that my parents have children here, and how glad I am he is here, and how I would love to be able to help him.

"You do help me," he said. "How?" I asked, very surprised. "By your cheerfulness."

I am so grateful and happy. I feel now that Peter and I share a secret. If he looks at me with those eyes that laugh and wink, then it's just as if a little light goes on inside me. I hope it will remain like this and that we may have many, many more glorious times together!

Your grateful, happy Anne

Monday, 20 March, 1944

Dear Kitty,

This morning Peter asked me if I would come again. I said that I couldn't come every evening, because they wouldn't like it downstairs, but he thought that I needn't let that bother me. Then I said that I would love to come one Saturday evening and especially asked him to warn me when there was a moon. "Then we'll go downstairs," he answered, "and look at the moon."

I had a little ticking off yesterday evening from Mummy, which I certainly deserved. I mustn't overdo my indifference towards her. In spite of everything, I must try to be friendly and keep my observations to myself. Even Pim is different lately. He is trying not to treat me as such a child, and it makes him much too cool. See what comes of it!

In the meantime a little shadow has fallen on my happiness. I've thought for a long time that Margot liked Peter quite a lot too. How much I don't know, but I must cause her terrible pain each time I'm with Peter, and the funny part of it is that she hardly shows it. I'd be desperately jealous, but Margot only says that I needn't pity her.

"I think it's so rotten that you should be the odd one out," I added. "I'm used to that," she answered, somewhat bitterly.

Evidence of Margot's goodness: I received this today,

March 20th, 1944

Anne, when I said yesterday that I was not jealous of you I was only fifty-percent honest. I only feel a bit sorry that I haven't found anyone yet, and am not likely to for the time being, with whom I can discuss my thoughts and feelings. But I should not grudge it to you for that reason. One misses enough here anyway.

I know for certain that I would never have got far with Peter, anyway, because if I wished to discuss a lot with anyone, I should want to be on rather intimate terms with him. I would want to have the feeling that he understood me through and through. But it would have to be someone who was my superior intellectually, and that is not the case with Peter.

You are not doing me out of anything which is my due; do not reproach yourself in the least on my account. You and Peter can only gain by the friendship.

My reply:

Dear Margot,

I thought your letter was exceptionally sweet, but I still don't feel quite happy about it.

At present there is no question of such confidence as you have in mind between Peter and myself, but in the twilight beside an open window you can say more to each other than in brilliant sunshine. Also it's easier to whisper your feelings than to trumpet them forth out loud. I believe that you are beginning to feel a kind of sisterly affection for Peter, and that you would love to help him as much as I. Perhaps you will be able to sometime.

Let's not talk about it anymore; but if you still want anything please write to me about it, because I can say what I mean much better on paper.

You don't know how much I admire you, and I only hope that I may yet acquire some of the goodness that you and Daddy have.

Yours, Anne

Wednesday, 22 March, 1944

Dear Kitty,

I received this from Margot last evening:

Dear Anne,

After your letter yesterday I have the unpleasant feeling that you will have prickings of conscience when you visit Peter; but really there is no reason for this.

I do feel just as you say, that Peter is a bit like a younger brother; the affection of a brother and sister might grow, perhaps later—perhaps never; however, it has certainly not reached that stage yet.

Therefore you really needn't pity me. Now that you've found companionship, enjoy it as much as you can.

In the meantime it is getting more and more wonderful. I believe, Kitty, that we may have a real great love in the Secret Annexe. Don't worry, I'm not thinking of marrying him. I don't know what he will be like when he grows up, nor do I know whether we should ever love each other enough to marry. I know that Peter loves me, but whether he only wants a great friend, or whether I attract him as a girl, I can't yet discover.

I asked him yesterday what he would do if there were a dozen Annes here who always kept coming to him. His reply was, "If they were all like you, it certainly wouldn't be bad!" He's tremendously hospitable towards me and I really believe he likes to see me. Oh, when I think about Saturday evening and recall it all, word for word, I don't feel discontented about myself.

He is so handsome when he laughs; he is such a darling and so good. I believe what surprised him most about me was that I'm not the superficial worldly Anne that I appear, but just as dreamy, with just as many difficulties as he himself.

Yours, Anne

Reply:

Dear Margot,

I think the best thing we can do is wait and see what happens. Which way it will go I don't know. But I shall certainly do one thing, if Peter and I decide to be friends, I shall tell him that you are very fond of him and would always be prepared to help him.

You are always welcome to join us in the attic, or wherever we are; you honestly won't disturb us. We have a silent agreement to talk only in the evenings when it's dark.

Keep your courage up! Your time may come sooner than you think.

Yours, Anne

Thursday, 23 March, 1944

Dear Kitty,

Things are running more or less normally again now. Our coupon men are out of prison again, thank goodness!

I often go upstairs after supper nowadays and take a breath of the fresh evening air. I like it up there, sitting on a chair beside him and looking outside. Sometimes he comes and gets me from downstairs, but he turns simply scarlet, and can hardly get the words out of his mouth.

Van Daan and Dussel make feeble remarks when I disappear into his room; "Anne's second home," or, "Is it suitable for young gentlemen to receive young girls in semidarkness?" Peter shows amazing wit in his replies to these so-called humorous sallies. Mummy is curious and would love to ask what we talk about, if she wasn't secretly afraid of being snubbed. Peter says it's nothing but envy on the part of the grown-ups, because we are young. We don't take much notice of this chatter. Have the two sets of parents forgotten their own youth? It seems like it.

Yesterday I received a genuine compliment from Peter, and just for fun I will tell you how the conversation went:

Peter often used to say, "Do laugh, Anne!" This struck me as odd, and I asked, "Why?"

"Because I like it; you get such dimples in your cheeks when you laugh; how do they come, actually?"

"I was born with them. That's my only beauty!"

"Of course not, that's not true."

"Yes, it is, I know quite well that I'm not a beauty."

"I don't agree. I think you're pretty. And if I say so, then you can take it from me it is true!"

Yours, Anne

Monday, 27 March, 1944

Dear Kitty,

One chapter of our history in hiding should be about politics, but as this subject doesn't interest me very much, I've rather let it go. So today I will devote my whole letter to politics.

There are many different opinions on this topic, and it's logical that it should be a favorite subject for discussion in such critical times, but—it's just stupid that there should be so many quarrels over it.

During these countless arguments in the Secret Annexe over invasion, air raids, speeches, etc., etc., one hears cries of "Impossible!" or "However long is it going to last?" "It's going splendidly!" Optimists and pessimists, and don't let's forget the realists; they give their opinions with untiring energy, each one thinking he is right. They never seem to tire of it.

As if the German and English news bulletins were not enough, they have now introduced "Special Air-Raid Announcements." The British are making nonstop air attacks with the same zest as the Germans are lying. The radio is listened to at all hours of the day, from early morning until ten, and often eleven o'clock in the evening. This is certainly a sign that the grown-ups have infinite patience, but it also means the power of absorption of their brains is pretty limited, with exceptions, of course—I don't want to hurt anyone's feelings. One or two news bulletins per day would be ample! It gets so boring!

I must mention one shining exception—a speech by our beloved Winston Churchill. Nine o'clock on Sunday evening. The teapot stands with the cozy over it, on the table. The gentlemen puff at their pipes, Peter's eyes are popping out of his head with the strain of listening, Mummy wearing a long dark negligee, and Mrs. Van Daan trembling because of the planes, which take no notice of the speech but fly blithely on towards Essen, Daddy sipping tea, Margot and I united in a sisterly fashion by the sleeping Mouschi, who is monopolizing both our knees. Margot's hair is in curlers, and I am wearing a nightdress which is much too narrow and too short.

It all looks so intimate, snug, peaceful; yet I await the consequences with horror. They can hardly wait till the end of the speech, so impatient are they to discuss it.

Yours, Anne

Tuesday, 28 March, 1944

Dearest Kitty,

I have heaps of things to tell you today. First, Mummy has forbidden me to go upstairs so often, because, according to her, Mrs. Van Daan is jealous. Secondly, Peter has invited Margot to join us upstairs; I don't know whether it's just out of politeness or whether he really means it. Thirdly, I asked Daddy if he thought I need pay any regard to Mrs. Van Daan's jealousy, and he didn't think so. Mummy is cross, perhaps jealous too. Daddy doesn't grudge us these times together, and thinks it's nice that we get on so well. Margot is fond of Peter too, but feels that two's company and three's a crowd.

Mummy thinks that Peter is in love with me; quite frankly, I wish he were, then we'd really be able to get to know each other. She also says that he keeps on looking at me. I suppose that's true, but I can't help it if he looks at my dimples, can I?

I'm in a very difficult position. Mummy is against me and I'm against her, Daddy closes his eyes and tries not to see the silent battle between us. Mummy is sad, because she does really love me, while I'm not in the least bit sad, because I don't think she understands. And Peter—I don't want to give Peter up, he's such a darling.

When he lies with his head on his arm with his eyes closed, then he is still a child; when he plays with Boche, he is loving; when he carries anything heavy, he is strong; when he watches the shooting, or looks for burglars in the darkness, he is brave; and when he is so awkward and clumsy, then he is just a pet.

I like it much better if he explains something to me than when I have to teach him; I would really adore him to be my superior in almost everything.

What do we care about the two mothers? Oh, but if only he would speak!

Yours, Anne

Wednesday, 29 March, 1944

Dear Kitty,

Bolkestein, an M.P. speaking on the Dutch News from London, said that they ought to make a collection of diaries and letters after the war. Of course, they all made a rush at my diary immediately. Just imagine how interesting it would be if I were to publish a romance of the Secret Annexe. The title* alone would be enough to make people think it was a detective story.

But it would seem funny ten years after the war if we Jews were to tell how we lived and what we ate and talked about here. I tell you a lot; even so, you know very little of our lives. For instance, on Sunday, when 350 British planes dropped half a million kilos of bombs, the houses trembled like grass in the wind; and who knows how many epidemics now rage. You don't know anything about these things, and I would need to write the whole day if I were to tell. People have to line up for vegetables and other things; doctors are unable to visit the sick, because if they turn their backs for a moment, their cars are stolen; burglaries abound. Little children break windows of

---

*The original title of this diary was *Het Achterhuis*. There is no exact translation into English, the nearest being the "Secret Annexe."

people's homes and steal whatever they can lay their hands on. No one dares to leave his house unoccupied for five minutes. Every day there are announcements in the newspapers offering rewards for the return of lost property, typewriters, Persian rugs, electric clocks, cloth, etc., etc. Electric clocks in the streets are dismantled, public telephones are pulled to pieces—down to the last thread. Morale among the population can't be good, weekly rations are not enough to last for two days except the coffee substitute. The invasion is a long time coming, and the men have to go to Germany. The children are ill or undernourished, everyone is wearing old clothes and old shoes. Hardly any shoemakers will accept shoe repairs or, if they do, you have to wait months, during which time the shoes often disappear.

One good thing: as the food gets worse and the measures against the people more severe, sabotage against the authorities increases. The people in the food offices, the police, officials, they all either work with their fellow citizens and help them or they tell tales on them and have them sent to prison. Fortunately, only a small percentage of Dutch people are on the wrong side.

Yours, Anne

Friday, 31 March, 1944

Dear Kitty,

It's still pretty cold, but most people have been without coal for about a month. Public feeling over the Russian front is optimistic again; they have reached Rumania, close to Odessa. They fire off so many salvos in Moscow to celebrate their victories that the city must rumble and shake every day.

The chatter about Peter and me has calmed down a bit. We are very good friends, are together a lot and discuss every imaginable subject. It is awfully nice never to have to keep a check on myself as I would have to with other boys, whenever we get onto precarious ground. We were talking, for instance, about blood and via that we began talking about menstruation. He thinks women are pretty tough. Why on earth? My life here has greatly improved. God has not left me alone and will not leave me alone.

Yours, Anne

Dear Kitty,

And yet everything is still so difficult; I am so longing for a kiss, the kiss that is so long in coming. I wonder if all the time he still regards me as a friend? Am I nothing more?

I simply can't forget that dream of Peter's cheek, when it was all so good! Wouldn't he long for it too? Is it that he is just too shy to acknowledge his love? Why does he want me with him so often? Oh, why doesn't he speak?

I'd better stop, I must be quiet, I shall remain strong and with a bit of patience the other will come too, but—and that is the worst of it—it looks as if I'm running after him; *I* am always the one who goes upstairs, *he* doesn't come to me.

But that is just because of the rooms, and he is sure to understand the difficulty.

Yours, Anne

Monday, 3 April, 1944

Dear Kitty,

Contrary to my usual custom, I will for once write more fully about food because it has become a very difficult and important matter, not only here in the Secret Annexe but in the whole of Holland, all Europe, and even beyond.

In the twenty-one months that we've spent here we have been through a good many "food cycles"—periods in which one has nothing to eat but one kind of vegetable. We had nothing but endive for a long time, day in, day out, endive with sand, endive without sand, stew with endive, boiled or *en casserole;* then it was spinach, and after that kohlrabi, salsify, cucumbers, tomatoes, sauerkraut. It's really disagreeable to eat a lot of sauerkraut for lunch and supper every day, but you do it if you're hungry.

Now we don't get any fresh vegetables at all. Our weekly menu for supper consists of kidney beans, pea soup, potatoes with dumplings, potato-chalet, and occasionally turnip tops or rotten carrots. We eat potatoes at every meal because of the bread shortage. We make our soup from kidney beans, potatoes, julienne soup in packets, French beans in packets, kidney beans in packets. Everything contains beans.

In the evening we always have potatoes with gravy substitute and—thank goodness we've still got it—beetroot salad. The dumplings, which we make out of government flour, water, and yeast, are so sticky and tough, they lie like stones in one's stomach—ah, well!

The great attraction each week is a slice of liver sausage, and jam on dry bread. But we're still alive, and quite often we even enjoy our poor meals.

Yours, Anne

Tuesday, 4 April, 1944

Dear Kitty,

For a long time I haven't had any idea of what I was working for anymore; the end of the war is so terribly far away, so unreal, like a fairy tale. Peter filled my days—nothing but Peter, until Saturday, when I felt so utterly miserable it was terrible. I was holding back my tears all the while I was with Peter. I knew that the moment I was alone I would cry my heart out. So, that night, clad in my nightdress, I let myself go and slipped down onto the floor. I said my long prayer very earnestly, then I cried with my head on my arms, knees bent, completely folded up, on the bare floor. One large sob brought me back to earth again, and I quelled my tears because I didn't want them to hear anything in the next room. Then I began trying to talk some courage into myself. I could only say: "I must, I must, I must . . ." Completely stiff from the unnatural position, I climbed into bed just before half past ten.

And now it's all over. I must work to become a journalist, because that's what I want! I can write, a couple of my stories are good, my descriptions of the Secret Annexe are humorous, there's a lot in my diary that speaks, but—whether I have real talent remains to be seen.

"Eva's Dream" is my best fairy tale, and the queer thing about it is that I don't know where it comes from. I am the best and sharpest critic of my own work. I know myself what is not well written. Anyone who doesn't write doesn't know how wonderful it is; I used to bemoan the fact that I couldn't draw, but now I am more than happy that I can at least write. I want to send in to some paper or other to see if they will take one of my stories, under a pseudonym, of course. And if I haven't any talent for writing books or newspaper articles, then I can always write for myself.

I can't imagine leading the same life as Mummy and Mrs. Van Daan and all the women who do their work and are then forgotten. I must have something besides a husband and children, something that I can devote myself to! I want to go on living even after my death! And therefore I am grateful to God for giving me this gift, this possibility of developing myself and of expressing all that is in me.

Yours, Anne

Thursday, 6 April, 1944

Dear Kitty,

You asked me what my hobbies and interests were. I warn you, there are heaps of them!

First of all: writing, but that hardly counts as a hobby.

Two: family trees. I've been searching for family trees of the French, German, Spanish, English, Austrian, Russian, Norwegian, and Dutch royal families in all the newspapers, books, and pamphlets I can find. I've been taking down notes from the biographies and history books that I read.

My third hobby is history. Daddy has already bought me a lot of books. I can hardly wait for the day that I shall be able to comb through the books in a public library.

Number four is Greek and Roman mythology.

Other hobbies are film stars and family photos. Have a great liking for history of art, poets, and painters. I have a great loathing for algebra, geometry, and figures.

Yours, Anne

Tuesday, 11 April, 1944

Dear Kitty,

My head throbs, I honestly don't know where to begin.

On Sunday evening (Easter Sunday) at half past nine Peter knocked softly on the door and asked Daddy if he would just help him over a difficult English sentence. "That's a blind," I said to Margot, "anyone could see through that one!" I was right. Someone was in the act of breaking into the warehouse. Daddy, Van Daan, Dussel, and Peter were downstairs in a flash. Margot, Mummy, Mrs. Van Daan, and I stayed upstairs and waited.

Four frightened women just have to talk; we did, until we heard a bang downstairs. After that all was quiet. The clock struck a quarter to ten. The color had vanished from our faces, we were quiet, we were afraid. What was that bang? Where could the men be? Fighting the burglars? Ten o'clock, footsteps on the stairs: Daddy, white and nervous, entered, followed by Van Daan. "Lights out, creep upstairs, we expect the police in the house!"

There was no time to be frightened; the lights went out, I quickly grabbed a jacket, and we were upstairs. The men had disappeared downstairs again. Only at ten past ten did they reappear; two kept watch at Peter's open window, the door to the landing was closed, the swinging cupboard shut.

Then they told us what had happened: Peter heard two loud bangs on the landing, ran downstairs, and saw there was a large plank out of the left half of the front door. He dashed upstairs, warned the "Home Guard," and the four of them proceeded downstairs. When they entered the warehouse, the burglars were in the act of enlarging the hole. Without further thought Van Daan shouted: "Police!"

The burglars fled. In order to avoid the hole being noticed by the police, a plank was put against it, but a good hard kick from outside sent it flying to the ground. The men were perplexed at such impudence. A married couple outside shone a torch through the opening, lighting up the whole warehouse. "Hell!" muttered one of the men, and now they switched over from their role of police to that of burglars. The four of them sneaked upstairs, Peter quickly opened the doors and windows of the kitchen and private office, flung the telephone onto the floor, and finally the four of them landed behind the swinging cupboard.

The married couple with the torch would probably have warned the police: it was Easter Sunday evening, no one would be at the office on Easter Monday, so none of us could budge until Tuesday morning. Think of it, waiting in such fear for two nights and a day! No one had anything to suggest, so we simply sat there in pitch-darkness, talked in whispers, and at every creak one heard "Sh! Sh!"

It turned eleven, but not a sound. Then at a quarter past eleven, a bustle and noise downstairs. Everyone's breath was audible, no one moved. Footsteps in the house, in the private office, then . . . on our staircase. No one breathed now, then a rattling of the swinging cupboard. "Now we are lost!" I said, and could see us all being taken away by the Gestapo that very night. Twice they rattled at the cupboard, then nothing, the footsteps withdrew. A shiver seemed to pass from one to another, no one said a word.

There was not another sound in the house, but we found a light burning on our landing, right in front of the cupboard. Would someone come back to put it out? Was someone on guard outside?

Next we did three things: we went over again what we supposed had happened, we trembled with fear, and we had to go to the lavatory. All we had was Peter's tin wastepaper basket. Van Daan went first, then Daddy, but Mummy was too shy. Daddy brought the wastepaper basket into the room, where Margot, Mrs. Van Daan, and I gladly made use of it. Finally Mummy decided to do so too. People kept asking for paper—fortunately I had some in my pocket!

The tin smelled ghastly, we were tired, it was twelve o'clock. Margot and I were each given a pillow and one blanket; Margot lying just near the store cupboard and I between the table legs. The smell wasn't quite so bad when one was on the floor, but still Mrs. Van Daan quietly brought some chlorine and also put a tea towel over the pot.

Whispers, fear, stink, and trying to go to sleep! However, by half past two I was so tired that I knew no more until half past three. I awoke then, and lay shivering. I prepared myself for the return of the police; they would either be good Dutch people, then we'd be saved, or N.S.B.-ers [the Dutch National Socialist Movement], then we'd have to bribe them!

"In that case, destroy the radio," sighed Mrs. Van Daan.

"Yes, in the stove!" replied her husband.

"They will find Anne's diary," added Daddy.

"Burn it then," suggested the most terrified member of the party. This, and when the police rattled the cupboard door, were my worst moments. "Not my diary; if my diary goes, I go with it!" But luckily Daddy didn't answer.

Mr. Van Daan

I comforted Mrs. Van Daan, who was very scared. We talked about being questioned by the Gestapo, and being brave.

"We must behave like soldiers, Mrs. Van Daan. If all is up now, then let's go for Queen and Country, for freedom, truth, and right, as they always say on the Dutch News from England. The only really rotten thing is that we get a lot of other people into trouble too."

After an hour Daddy came and sat beside me. The men smoked nonstop; now and then there was a deep sigh. Four o'clock, five o'clock, half past five. I went and sat with Peter by his window and listened, so close together that we could feel each other's bodies quivering; we spoke a word or two now and then.

In the other room they decided to call up Koophuis at seven o'clock. The risk that the police on guard at the door might hear the telephone was very great, but the danger of the police returning was even greater. If Koophuis would send Henk around, perhaps on the pretext of feeding the cat, he could see what had happened downstairs, and inform us.

They wrote down everything they wanted to tell Koophuis, and after phoning him we sat around the table again and waited for Henk.

Peter had fallen asleep and Van Daan and I were lying on the floor, when we heard loud footsteps downstairs. I got up quietly. "That's Henk."

"No, no, it's the police," some of the others said.

Someone knocked at the door, then Miep whistled. This was

too much for Mrs. Van Daan, she turned as white as a sheet and sank limply into a chair.

Henk and Miep were greeted with shouts and tears when they entered. Henk mended the hole in the door and went off to inform the police of the burglary. Miep found a letter under the warehouse door from the night watchman Slagter, who had noticed the hole and warned the police.

We had half an hour to tidy ourselves. I've never seen such a change take place in half an hour. Margot and I took the bedclothes downstairs, went to the W.C., washed, and did our teeth and hair. After that I tidied the room and went upstairs again. We made coffee and tea, boiled the milk, and laid the table for lunch. Daddy and Peter emptied the potties and cleaned them with warm water and chlorine.

Slowly things began to be more normal. At eleven o'clock we sat round the table with Henk, who was back by that time, and heard his story, which went as follows:

Mr. Slagter said he had found the hole in our door when he was doing his tour round the canals, and had called a policeman, who had gone through the building with him. At the police station they told Henk they knew nothing of the burglary yet, but the policeman had made a note of it at once and would come and look round on Tuesday.

On the way back Henk happened to meet our greengrocer at the corner, and told him that the house had been broken into. "I know that," he said quite coolly. "I was passing last evening with my wife and saw the hole in the door. My wife wanted to walk on, but I just had a look with my torch; then the thieves cleared at once. To be on the safe side, I didn't ring up the police, as I didn't think it was the thing to do. I don't know anything, but I guess a lot."

The man obviously guesses that we're here, because he always brings the potatoes during the lunch hour. Such a nice man!

It was one o'clock by the time Henk had gone and we'd finished the dishes. We all took a nap.

This affair has brought quite a number of changes. Mr. Dussel no longer sits in Kraler's office in the evenings, but in the bathroom. Peter goes round the house for a checkup at half past eight and half past nine. Peter isn't allowed to have his window open at night anymore. No one is allowed to pull the plug after half past nine. This evening there's a carpenter coming to make the warehouse doors even stronger.

Now there are debates going on all the time in the Secret Annexe. Kraler reproached us for our carelessness. Henk, too, said that in a case like that we must never go downstairs. We have been pointedly reminded that we are in hiding, that we are Jews, chained to one spot, without any rights, but with a thousand duties. We Jews mustn't show our feelings, must be brave and strong, must accept all inconveniences and not grumble, and trust in God. Surely when this terrible war is over we will be people again, and not just Jews.

Who has inflicted this upon us? Who has made us Jews different from all other people? Who has allowed us to suffer so terribly up till now? It is God that has made us as we are, but it will be God, too, who will raise us up again. If we bear all this suffering, then Jews, instead of being doomed, will be held up as an example.

Be brave! A solution will come. God has never deserted our people. Through all the ages Jews have had to suffer, but it has made them strong; the weak fall, but the strong will never go under!

My first wish after the war is that I may become Dutch! I love this country, I love the language and want to work here. And if God lets me live, I shall not remain insignificant, I shall work for mankind! And now I know that first and foremost I shall require courage and cheerfulness!

Yours, Anne

Friday, 14 April, 1944

Dear Kitty,

When Peter and I are sitting together on a hard, wooden crate in masses of rubbish and dust, our arms around each other, and very close; when the birds sing outside and you see the trees changing to green, the sun invites one to be out in the open air, when the sky is blue, then—oh, I wish for so much!

One sees nothing but dissatisfied, grumpy faces here, nothing but sighs and suppressed complaints; it really would seem as if suddenly we were very badly off. Every day you hear, "If only it was all over."

My work, my hope, my love, all these things keep my head above water and keep me from complaining.

I really believe, Kitty, that I'm slightly bats today. Everything here is so mixed up, nothing's connected anymore, and sometimes I very much doubt whether in the future anyone will be interested in all my tosh. "The unbosomings of an ugly duckling," will be the title of all this nonsense.

Yours, Anne

Saturday, 15 April, 1944

Dear Kitty,

Shock upon shock. Will there ever be an end? Guess what's the latest. Peter forgot to unbolt the front door (which is bolted on the inside at night) and the lock of the other door doesn't work. The result was that Kraler could not get into the house, so he went to the neighbors, forced open the kitchen window, and entered the building from the back. He is livid at us for being so stupid.

I can tell you, it's upset Peter frightfully. At one meal, when Mummy said she felt more sorry for Peter than anyone else, he almost started to cry. We're all just as much to blame as he is, because nearly every day the men ask whether the door's been unbolted and, just today, no one did.

Perhaps I shall be able to console him a bit later on; I would so love to help him.

Yours, Anne

Sunday morning, just before eleven o'clock,
16 April, 1944

Darlingest Kitty,

Remember yesterday's date, for it is a very important day in my life. Surely it is a great day for every girl when she receives her first kiss?

How did I suddenly come by this kiss? Well, yesterday evening at eight o'clock I was sitting with Peter on his divan, it wasn't long before his arm went round me. "Let's move up a bit," I said, "then I won't bump my head against the cupboard." He moved up, almost into the corner, I laid my arm under his and across his back, and he just about buried me, because his arm was hanging on my shoulder. Now we've sat like this on other occasions, but never so close together. He held me firmly against him, my left shoulder against his chest; already my heart began to beat faster. My head was on his shoulder and his against it. When I sat upright again after about five minutes, he took my head in his hands and laid it against him once more. Oh, it was so lovely, I couldn't talk much, the joy was too great. He stroked my cheek and arm a bit awkwardly, played with my curls and our heads lay touching most of the time. I was too happy for words, and I believe he was as well.

At half past eight Peter got up to put on his gym shoes, so that when he toured the house he wouldn't make a noise, and I stood beside him. How it came about so suddenly, I don't know, but before we went downstairs he kissed me, through my hair, half on my left cheek, half on my ear; I tore downstairs without looking round, and am simply longing for today!

Yours, Anne

Monday, 17 April, 1944

Dear Kitty,

Do you think that Daddy and Mummy would approve of my kissing a boy? I don't really think they would, but I must rely on myself over this. It is so peaceful to lie in his arms and dream, it is so thrilling to feel his cheek against mine, so lovely to know that there is someone waiting for me. But there is indeed a big "but," because will Peter be content to leave it at this? I haven't forgotten his promise, but he *is* a boy!

I know that I'm starting very soon, not even fifteen, and so independent already! I know Margot would never kiss a boy unless there had been some talk of marriage, but neither Peter nor I have anything like that in mind. I'm sure too that Mummy never touched a man before Daddy. What would my girl friends say if they knew that I lay in Peter's arms, my head on his shoulder and his head against mine!

Oh, Anne, how scandalous! But honestly, I don't think it is; we are shut up here, away from the world, in fear and anxiety, especially lately. Why, then, should we who love each other wait until we've reached a suitable age? He would never cause me sorrow or pain. Why shouldn't I follow the way my heart leads me? All the same, Kitty, you can sense that I'm in doubt. I think it must be my honesty which rebels against doing anything on the sly! Do you think it's my duty to tell Daddy? Should we share our secret with a third person? A lot of the beauty would be lost, but would my conscience feel happier? I will discuss it with "him."

Peter Van Daan

Oh, yes, there's still so much I want to talk to him about, for I don't see the use of just cuddling each other. To exchange our thoughts, that shows confidence and faith in each other, we would both be sure to profit by it!

Yours, Anne

Tuesday, 18 April, 1944

Dear Kitty,

Everything goes well here. Daddy's just said that he definitely expects large-scale operations to take place in May, both in Russia and Italy; I find it more and more difficult to imagine our liberation from here.

Yesterday Peter and I finally got to talk; I explained everything about girls to him and didn't hesitate to discuss the most intimate things. The evening ended by each giving the other a kiss, just beside my mouth, it's really a lovely feeling.

We are having a superb spring after our long, lingering winter; April is really glorious, not too hot and not too cold, with little showers now and then. Our chestnut tree is already quite greenish and you can even see little blooms here and there.

I must do some algebra, Kitty—good-by.

Yours, Anne

Wednesday, 19 April, 1944

My darling,

Is there anything more beautiful in the world than to sit before an open window and enjoy nature, to listen to the birds singing, feel the sun on your cheeks and have a darling boy in your arms? It is so soothing and peaceful to feel his arms around me, to know that he is close by and yet to remain silent, this tranquillity can't be bad.

Yours, Anne

Friday, 21 April, 1944

Dear Kitty,

It's the eighteenth birthday of Her Royal Highness Princess Elizabeth of York. The B.B.C. has said that she will not be declared of age yet, though it's usually the case with royal children. We have been asking ourselves what prince this beauty is going to marry, but cannot think of anyone suitable. Perhaps her sister, Princess Margaret Rose, can have Prince Baudouin of Belgium one day.

Yours, Anne

Tuesday, 25 April, 1944

Dear Kitty,

Dussel has not been on speaking terms with Van Daan for ten days. Ever since the burglary, a whole lot of fresh security measures have been made that don't suit him, and he maintains that Van Daan has been shouting at him.

"Everything here happens upside down," he told me. "I am going to speak to your father about it." He is not supposed to sit in the office on Saturday afternoons and Sundays anymore, but he goes on doing it just the same. Van Daan was furious and Father went downstairs to talk to him. Naturally, he kept on inventing excuses, but this time he could not get around even Father. Father now talks to him as little as possible, as Dussel has insulted him.

I have written a lovely story called "Blurr, the Explorer," which pleased the three to whom I read it very much.

Yours, Anne

Thursday, 27 April, 1944

Dear Kitty,

What doesn't a schoolgirl get to know in a single day! Take me, for example. First, I translated a piece from Dutch into English, about Nelson's last battle. After that I landed up in Brazil, read about tobacco, the abundance of coffee and the inhabitants of Rio de Janeiro, not forgetting the river Amazon; about more than fifty percent of the population being illiterate, and the malaria. As there was still some time left, I quickly ran through a family tree.

Twelve o'clock: In the attic, I continued my program with the history of the Church—phew! Till one o'clock.

Just after two, the poor child sat working again, this time studying narrow- and broad-nosed monkeys. Kitty, tell me quickly how many toes a hippopotamus has!! Then followed the Bible, Noah and the Ark, Shem, Ham, and Japheth. Then with Peter: *The Colonel*, in English, by Thackeray. Heard my French verbs and then compared the Mississippi with the Missouri.

I have a cold and have given it to Margot as well as to Mummy and Daddy. As long as Peter doesn't get it! He called me his "Eldorado" and wanted a kiss. Of course, I couldn't! Funny boy! But still, he's a darling.

Yours, Anne

Friday, 28 April, 1944

Dear Kitty,

I have never forgotten my dream about Peter Wessel (see beginning of January). I can still feel his cheek against mine, and recall that lovely feeling that made everything good. Sometimes I have had the same feeling with Peter, but never to such an extent, until yesterday, when we were, as usual, sitting on the divan, our arms around each other's waists. Then suddenly the ordinary Anne slipped away and a second Anne took her place, a second Anne who is not reckless and jocular, but one who just wants to love and be gentle.

I sat pressed closely against him and felt a wave of emotion come over me, tears sprang into my eyes, the left one trickled onto his dungarees, the right one ran down my nose and also fell onto his dungarees. Did he notice? He made no move or sign. He hardly said a word.

At half past eight I stood up and went to the window, where we always say good-by. He came towards me, I flung my arms around his neck, kissed his left cheek, and was about to kiss the other cheek, when my lips met his and we pressed them together. In a whirl we were clasped in each other's arms, again and again, never to leave off.

Oh, Peter does so need tenderness. For the first time in his life he has shown his real self.

Once more there is a question which gives me no peace. "Is it right? Is it right that I am as ardent and eager as Peter himself? May I, a girl, let myself go to this extent?" There is but *one* answer: "I have longed so much and for so long—I am so lonely—and now I have found consolation."

In the mornings we just behave in an ordinary way, in the afternoons more or less so; but in the evenings the suppressed longings of the whole day, the happiness and the blissful memories of all the previous occasions come to the surface and we only think of each other. Every evening, after the last kiss, I would like to dash away, not to look into his eyes anymore—away, away, alone in the darkness.

And what do I have to face, when I reach the bottom of the staircase? Bright lights, questions, and laughter; I have to swallow it all and not show a thing. My heart still feels too much. The Anne who is gentle shows herself too little anyway and, therefore, will not allow herself to be suddenly driven into the background. Oh Peter, what have you done to me? What do you want of me? Where will this lead us? If I were older and he should ask me to marry him, what should I answer? Anne, be honest! You would not be able to marry him, but yet, it would be hard to let him go. Peter hasn't enough character yet, not enough courage and strength. He is still a child in his heart of hearts; he is only searching for tranquillity and happiness.

Am I only fourteen? Am I really still a silly little schoolgirl, so inexperienced about everything? I have more experience than most; I have been through things that hardly anyone of my age has undergone. I am afraid of myself, I am afraid that in my longing I am giving myself too quickly. How, later on, can it ever go right with other boys? Oh, it is so difficult, always battling with one's heart and reason.

Yours, Anne

Tuesday, 2 May, 1944

Dear Kitty,

On Saturday evening I asked Peter whether he thought that I ought to tell Daddy a bit about us; when we'd discussed it a little, he came to the conclusion that I should. I was glad, for it shows that he's honest. Downstairs, I spoke with Daddy alone. "I expect you've gathered that when we're together Peter and I don't sit miles apart. Do you think it's wrong?" Daddy didn't reply immediately, then said, "No, I don't think it's wrong, but you must be careful, Anne; you're in such a confined space here."

On Sunday morning he called me to him and said, "Anne, I have thought more about what you said." I felt scared already. "It's not really very right—here in this house. Under normal circumstances, it is quite different. You are free, you see other boys and girls, you can get away sometimes, play games and do all kinds of other things; but here, you see each other every hour of the day—in fact, all the time. Be careful, Anne, and don't take it too seriously!"

"I don't, Daddy, but Peter is a decent boy, really a nice boy!"

"Yes, but he is not a strong character; he can be easily influenced, for good, but also for bad; I hope for his sake that his good side will remain uppermost, because, by nature, that is how he is." We talked on for a bit and agreed that Daddy should talk to him too.

On Sunday morning in the attic Peter asked, "Have you talked to your father, Anne?"

"Yes," I replied. "Daddy doesn't think it's bad, but he thought we were just pals; do you think that we still can be?"

"I can—what about you?"

"Me too, I told Daddy that I trusted you. I do trust you, Peter, and I believe you to be worthy of it. You are, aren't you?"

"I hope so." (He was very shy and rather red in the face.)

"I believe in you, Peter," I said.

After that, we talked about other things.

In the meantime the Dussel drama has righted itself again. At supper on Saturday evening he apologized in beautiful Dutch. Van Daan was nice about it straightaway; it must have taken Dussel a whole day to learn his speech by heart.

Yours, Anne

Wednesday, 3 May, 1944

Dear Kitty,

Have I told you that Boche has disappeared? We haven't seen a sign of her since Thursday of last week. I expect she's already in the cats' heaven, while some animal lover is enjoying a succulent meal from her. Perhaps some little girl will be given a fur cap out of her skin. Peter is very sad about it.

Since Saturday we've changed over, and have lunch at half past eleven in the mornings, so we have to last out with one cupful of porridge; this saves us a meal. Vegetables are still very difficult to obtain: ordinary lettuce, spinach and boiled rotten lettuce, there's nothing else. With these we eat rotten potatoes, a delicious combination!

We often ask ourselves despairingly: "What, oh, what is the use of the war? Why can't people live peacefully together? Why all this destruction?" No one has found a satisfactory answer so far. Yet, why do they make still more gigantic planes, still heavier bombs and, at the same time, prefabricated houses for reconstruction? Why should millions be spent daily on the war and yet there's not a penny available for medical services, artists, or for poor people? Oh, why are people so crazy?

I don't believe that the big men, the politicians and the capitalists, are guilty of the war. Oh no, the little man is just as guilty, otherwise the peoples of the world would have risen in revolt long ago! There's in people simply an urge to destroy, to murder, and until all mankind undergoes a great change, wars will be waged, everything that has been built up, cultivated, and grown will be destroyed and disfigured, after which mankind will have to begin all over again.

I have often been downcast, but never in despair; I regard our hiding as a dangerous adventure, romantic and interesting. In my diary I treat all the privations as amusing. I have made up my mind now to lead a different life from other girls and, later on, different from ordinary housewives. My start has been so very full of interest, and that is why I have to laugh at the humorous side of the most dangerous moments.

I possess many buried qualities; I am young and strong and have been given a happy nature. I am in the midst of living a great adventure and can't grumble the whole day long. Every day I feel that I am developing inwardly, that the liberation is drawing nearer and how beautiful nature is, how good the people are about me. Why, then, should I be in despair?

Yours, Anne

Friday, 5 May, 1944

Dear Kitty,

Daddy is not pleased with me; he thought that after our talk on Sunday I automatically wouldn't go upstairs to see Peter every evening. He doesn't want any "necking," a word I can't bear. It was bad enough talking about it, why must he make it so unpleasant now?

I shall talk to him today. Margot has given me some good advice, so listen; this is roughly what I want to say:

"I believe, Daddy, that you expect a declaration from me, so I will give it you. You are disappointed in me. You had expected more reserve from me, and you want me to be just as a fourteen-year-old should be. But that's where you're mistaken!

"Since we've been here, from July 1942 until a few weeks ago, I haven't had an easy time. If you only knew how unhappy I was, how lonely I felt, then you would understand that I want to go upstairs!

"I have now, after a bitter, hard struggle, reached the stage that I know that I'm a separate individual. I tell you this so you will know why I don't feel in the least bit responsible to any of you. When I was in difficulties you all closed your eyes and stopped up your ears. I received nothing but warnings not to be so boisterous. I was only boisterous so as not to be miserable all the time. I was reckless so as not to hear that persistent voice within me continually. Now the battle is over. I have won! I am independent both in mind and body, for all this conflict has made me strong.

"I want to be able to go on in my own way, the way I think is right. You mustn't regard me as fourteen, for all these troubles have made me older. You can't coax me into not going upstairs; *either* you forbid it, *or* you trust me through thick and thin."

Yours, Anne

Saturday, 6 May, 1944

Dear Kitty,

I put a letter, in which I wrote what I explained to you yesterday, in Daddy's pocket. After reading it, he was, according to Margot, very upset for the rest of the evening. (I was upstairs doing the dishes.) Poor Pim! He hasn't said any more about it to me. Is that yet in store, I wonder?

Here everything is going on more or less normally again. What they tell us about the prices and the people outside is almost unbelievable: half a pound of tea costs 350 florins [a florin is equal to approximately twenty-eight cents], a pound of coffee 80 florins, butter 35 florins per pound, an egg 1.45 florin. People pay 14 florins for an ounce of Bulgarian tobacco! Everyone deals in the black market, every errand boy has something to offer. Our baker's boy got hold of some sewing silk, 0.9 florin for a thin little skein, the milkman manages to get clandestine ration cards, the undertaker delivers the cheese. The police and night watchmen join in burglaries just as strenuously as the professionals, everyone wants something in their empty stomachs and people simply have to swindle. Every day the police are tracing girls of fifteen, sixteen, and older, who are reported missing.

Yours, Anne

Sunday morning, 7 May, 1944

Dear Kitty,

Daddy and I had a long talk yesterday afternoon, I cried terribly and he joined in. Do you know what he said to me, Kitty? "I have received many letters in my life, but this is certainly the most unpleasant! You, Anne, who have received such love from your parents, can you talk of feeling no responsibility towards us? Anne, you have done us a great injustice! We haven't deserved such a reproach as this!"

This is certainly the worst thing I've ever done. And it's right that for once I've been taken down from my inaccessible pedestal, that my pride has been shaken a bit, for I was becoming much too taken up with myself again. What Miss Anne does is by no means always right! Anyone who can cause such unhappiness to someone else, someone he professes to love, and on purpose, too, is low, very low!

Even yesterday, I was only trying to show off with my crying and my tears, just trying to appear big, so that Daddy would respect me. And the way he has forgiven me makes me feel more than ever ashamed of myself. He is going to throw the letter in the fire and is so sweet to me now, just as if he had done something wrong.

No, Anne, you still have a tremendous lot to learn. I have had a lot of sorrow, but who hasn't? I have felt lonely, but hardly in despair! I am deeply ashamed of myself.

What is done cannot be undone, but one can prevent it happening again. I want to start from the beginning again and it can't be difficult, now that I have Peter. With him to support me, I can and will! I'm not alone anymore; he loves me. I love him, I have my books, and my diary, I'm not so frightfully ugly, not utterly stupid. I have a cheerful temperament and want to have a good character!

Yes, Anne, you've felt deeply that your letter was too hard and that it was untrue. To think that you were even proud of it! I will take Daddy as my example, and I *will* improve.

Yours, Anne

Monday, 8 May, 1944

Dear Kitty,

Have I ever really told you anything about our family?

I don't think I have, so I will begin now. My father's parents were very rich. His father had worked himself right up and his mother came from a prominent family, who were also rich. So, even though their money was lost during the World War and the inflation that followed, Daddy was extremely well brought up: parties every week, balls, beautiful girls, dinners, a large home, etc., etc. He laughed yesterday when, for the first time in his fifty-five years, he scraped out the frying pan at table.

Mummy's parents were rich too and we often listen open-mouthed to stories of engagement parties of two hundred and fifty people. One certainly could not call us rich now, but all my hopes are pinned on after the war. I'm not keen on a narrow, cramped existence like Mummy and Margot. I long to see something of the world and meet interesting people. I'd adore to go to Paris and London for a year to study languages and the history of art. Margot wants to be a midwife in Palestine!

Miep told us this morning about a party she went to, to celebrate an engagement. Both the future bride and bridegroom came from rich families and everything was very grand. Miep told us about the food they had: vegetable soup with minced meat balls, cheese, rolls, hors d'oeuvre with eggs and roast beef, fancy cakes, wine and cigarettes, as much as you wanted of everything (black market). Miep had ten drinks—can that be the woman who calls herself a teetotaler? Naturally, everyone at the party was a bit tipsy. There were two policemen from the fighting squad there as guests. It seems we are never far from Miep's thoughts, because she took down the addresses of these men at once, in case anything should happen, and good Dutchmen might come in useful.

She made our mouths water. We, who get nothing but porridge and half-cooked spinach (to preserve the vitamins) and rotten potatoes day after day. If Miep had taken us to the party we shouldn't have left any rolls for the other guests. We positively drew the words from Miep's lips, as if we'd never heard about delicious food in our lives before! And these are the granddaughters of a millionaire. The world is a queer place!

Yours, Anne

Tuesday, 9 May, 1944

Dear Kitty,

Mr. Kraler came upstairs this afternoon with the news that Mrs. B., who used to act as demonstrator for the business, wants to eat her box lunch in the office here at two o'clock every afternoon. Think of it! No one can come upstairs anymore, the potatoes cannot be delivered, Elli can't have any lunch, we can't go to the W.C., we mustn't move. We thought up the wildest suggestions to wheedle her away. Van Daan thought that a good laxative in her coffee would be sufficient.

Oh, Kit, it's such wonderful weather, if only I could go outdoors!

Yours, Anne

Wednesday, 10 May, 1944

Dear Kitty,

Our beloved Queen spoke to us this evening. She used words like "speedy liberation, heroism, and heavy burdens." A clergyman concluded with a prayer to take care of the Jews, the people in concentration camps, and in Germany.

Yours, Anne

Thursday, 11 May, 1944

Dear Kitty,

I'm frightfully busy at the moment, and although it sounds mad, I haven't time to get through my pile of work. Let me explain. By tomorrow I must finish reading the first part of *Galileo Galilei*, as it has to be returned to the library. I only started it yesterday, but I shall manage. Next week I have got to read *Palestine at the Crossroads* and the second part of *Galilei*. Next I finished reading the first part of the biography *Emperor Charles V* yesterday, and it's essential that I work out all the diagrams and family trees that I have collected from it. After that I have three pages of foreign words gathered from various books, which have all got to be recited, written down, and learned. Number four is that my film stars are all mixed up together and are simply gasping to be tidied up; however, as such a clearance would take several days, and since Professor Anne, as she's already said, is choked with work, the chaos will have to remain.

Next Theseus, Oedipus, Peleus, Orpheus, Jason, and Hercules are all awaiting their turn to be arranged, as their deeds lie crisscross in my mind like fancy threads in a dress. It's the same with the seven and nine years' war; I'm mixing everything together at this rate. What can one do with such a memory! Think how forgetful I shall be when I'm eighty!

Oh, something else, the Bible; how long is it still going to take before I meet the bathing Suzanna? And what do they mean by the guilt of Sodom and Gomorrah? Oh, there is still such a terrible lot to find out and to learn.

Kitty, can you see that I'm just about bursting?

You've known that my greatest wish is to become a journalist someday and later on a famous writer. I want to publish a book entitled *Het Achterhuis* after the war. Whether I shall succeed or not, I cannot say, but my diary will be a great help. I have other ideas as well, but I will write about them when they have taken a clearer form in my mind.

Yours, Anne

Saturday, 13 May, 1944

Dearest Kitty,

It was Daddy's birthday yesterday. Mummy and Daddy have been married nineteen years. The charwoman wasn't below and the sun shone as it has never shone before in 1944. Our horse chestnut is in full bloom, thickly covered with leaves and much more beautiful than last year.

Daddy received a gigantic box from Van Daan, beautifully decorated, containing three eggs, a bottle of beer, a bottle of yogurt, and a green tie. It made our pot of syrup seem rather small. He was certainly spoiled. Fifty fancy pastries have arrived, heavenly! Daddy treated us to spiced gingerbread, beer for the gentlemen, and yogurt for the ladies.

Enjoyment all around!

Yours, Anne

Friday, 19 May, 1944

Dear Kitty,

I felt really rotten yesterday (unusual for Anne!). I'm much better today, but I'd better not touch the kidney beans we're having.

All goes well with Peter and me. The poor boy blushes every evening when he gets his good-night kiss and simply begs for another. I don't mind, he is so happy now that he knows that someone loves him.

I've got the situation more in hand now, but my love hasn't cooled off.

Yours, Anne

Monday, 22 May, 1944

Dear Kitty,

On May 20th Daddy lost five bottles of yogurt on a bet with Mrs. Van Daan. The invasion still hasn't come yet; the whole of Europe, right down to Spain, talks about the invasion day and night, makes bets on it and . . . hopes.

The suspense is rising to a climax. People want to see deeds, great, heroic deeds. But no country is going to sacrifice its men for nothing, certainly not in the interests of another. The invasion, with liberation and freedom, will come sometime, but England and America will appoint the day, not the occupied countries.

To our great horror and regret we hear that the attitude of a great many people towards us Jews has changed. There is anti-Semitism now in circles that never thought of it before. This news has affected us very deeply. The cause of this hatred of Jews is understandable, but not good. The Christians blame the Jews for giving secrets away to the Germans, for betraying their helpers and for causing a great many Christians to suffer terrible punishments.

This is all true, but would Christians behave differently in our place? The Germans have means of making people talk. Can a person, Jew or Christian, entirely at their mercy, always remain silent? Everyone knows that is practically impossible. Why, then, should people demand the impossible of the Jews?

When one hears this one wonders why we are carrying on this long and difficult war. We're fighting together for freedom, truth, and right! Is discord going to show itself while we are still fighting, is the Jew once again worth less than another? Oh, it is sad, very sad, that for the umpteenth time the old truth is confirmed: "What *one* Christian does is his own responsibility, what *one* Jew does is thrown back at all Jews."

I can't understand that the Dutch, good, honest, upright people, should judge us like this, we, the most oppressed, the unhappiest, perhaps the most pitiful of all peoples of the whole world. I hope that this hatred will be a passing thing, that the Dutch will never lose their sense of right.

It's being murmured in underground circles that the German Jews who emigrated to Holland and who are now in Poland may not be allowed to return here; they once had the right of asylum in Holland, but when Hitler has gone they will have to go back to Germany again.

If this terrible threat should come true, then the pitiful little collection of Jews that remain will have to leave this beautiful country, which offered us such a warm welcome and which now turns its back on us.

I love Holland. I, having no native country, had hoped that it might become my fatherland, and I still hope it will!

Yours, Anne

Thursday, 25 May, 1944

Dear Kitty,

There's something every day. This morning our vegetable man was picked up for having two Jews in his house. It's a great blow to us, not only that those poor Jews are balancing on the edge of an abyss, but it's terrible for the man himself.

The world has turned topsy-turvy, respectable people are being sent off to concentration camps and lonely cells, and the dregs that remain govern young and old, rich and poor. One person walks into the trap through the black market, a second through helping the Jews or other people who've had to go underground; anyone who isn't a member of the N.S.B. doesn't know what may happen to him from one day to another.

The girls aren't allowed to haul our share of potatoes, so the only thing to do is to eat less. It's certainly not going to make things any pleasanter. We shall cut out breakfast, have porridge and bread for lunch, and for supper fried potatoes and possibly vegetables once or twice per week, nothing more. We're going to be hungry, but anything is better than being discovered.

Yours, Anne

Friday, 26 May, 1944

Dear Kitty,

I feel so miserable, I haven't felt like this for months; even after the burglary I didn't feel so utterly broken. On the one hand, the vegetable man, the Jewish question, which is being discussed over the whole house, the invasion delay, the bad food, the strain, the miserable atmosphere; and on the other hand, Elli's engagement, Whitsun, flowers, Kraler's birthday, fancy cakes, and stories about cabarets, films, and concerts. That huge difference, it's always there; one day we laugh and see the funny side of the situation, but the next we are afraid, despair staring from our faces.

Miep and Kraler carry the heaviest burden through the enormous responsibility, which is sometimes so much for Kraler that he can hardly talk from pent-up nerves. Koophuis and Elli look after us well too, but they can forget us, even if it's only for a few hours. They have their own worries, Koophuis over his health, Elli over her engagement, but they also have the life of ordinary people. For them the suspense is sometimes lifted, but for us it never lifts for a moment. We've been here two years now; how long have we still to put up with this ever increasing pressure?

The affair of the vegetable man has made us more nervous, and we're being quieter over everything. The police forced the door there, so they could do it to us too! If one day we too should . . . no, I mustn't write it, but I can't put the question out of my mind. On the contrary, all the fear I've already been through seems to face me again in all its frightfulness.

Again and again I ask myself, would it not have been better for us if we had not gone into hiding, if we were dead now and not going through this misery, especially as we shouldn't be running our protectors into danger. But we all recoil from these thoughts, for we still love life; we haven't yet forgotten hope, we still hope about everything. I hope something will happen soon, shooting if need be—nothing can crush us *more* than this suspense. Let the end come, even if it is hard; then at least we shall know whether we are finally going to win or go under.

Yours, Anne

Dear Kitty,

It was so frightfully hot on Saturday, Sunday, Monday, and Tuesday that I simply couldn't hold a fountain pen in my hand. It was impossible to write to you. The drains went phut again on Friday, were mended on Saturday; Mr. Koophuis came to see us in the afternoon and told us masses about Corry and her hockey club.

There's seldom been such a beautiful, warm Whitsun. The heat here in the Secret Annexe is terrible; I will give you a sample of the sort of complaints that arise:

Saturday: "Lovely, what perfect weather," we all said in the morning. "If only it wasn't quite so warm," in the afternoon when the windows had to be closed.

Sunday: "It's positively unbearable, this heat. The butter's melting, there's not a cool spot anywhere in the house, the bread's getting dry, the milk's going sour, windows can't be opened, and we, wretched outcasts, sit here suffocating while other people enjoy their Whitsun holiday."

Monday: "My feet hurt me, I haven't got any thin clothes. I can't wash the dishes in this heat," all this from Mrs. Van Daan. It was extremely unpleasant.

I can't put up with heat and am glad there's a stiff breeze today, and yet the sun still shines.

Yours, Anne

Monday, 5 June, 1944

Dear Kitty,

Fresh Secret Annexe troubles, a quarrel between Dussel and the Franks over something very trivial: the sharing of the butter. Dussel's capitulation. Mrs. Van Daan and the latter very thick, flirtations, kisses and friendly little laughs. Dussel is beginning to get longings for women. The Fifth Army has taken Rome. The city has been spared devastation by both armies and air forces, and is undamaged. Very few vegetables and potatoes. Bad weather. Heavy bombardments against the French coast continue.

Yours, Anne

Tuesday, 6 June, 1944

Dear Kitty,

"This is D day," came the announcement over the English news at eight o'clock this morning, "this is *the* day."* The invasion has begun!

As a safety measure for occupied territories, all people who live within a radius of thirty-five kilometers from the coast are warned to be prepared for bombardments. If possible, the English will drop pamphlets one hour beforehand.

According to German news, English parachute troops have landed on the French coast, English landing craft are in battle with the German Navy, says the B.B.C. We discussed it over breakfast: Is this just a trial landing like Dieppe two years ago?

English broadcast in German, Dutch, French, and other languages at ten o'clock. "The invasion has begun!"—that means the "real" invasion.

English broadcast in German at eleven o'clock: speech by the Supreme Commander, General Dwight Eisenhower.

The English news at twelve o'clock in English: "This is D day." General Eisenhower said to the French people: "Stiff fighting will come now, but after this the victory. The year 1944 is the year of complete victory; good luck."*

English news at one o'clock (translated): 11,000 planes are flying to and fro nonstop, landing troops and attacking behind the lines; 4000 landing boats, plus small craft, are landing troops and matériel between Cherbourg and Le Havre. English and American troops are already engaged in hard fighting. Speeches by Gerbrandy, by the Prime Minister of Belgium, King Haakon of Norway, De Gaulle of France, the King of England, and last, but not least, Churchill.

Great commotion in the Secret Annexe! The long-awaited liberation still seems *too* wonderful, *too* much like a fairy tale. Could we be granted victory this year, 1944? We don't know yet, but hope is revived within us. The great thing now is to remain calm and steadfast. Now more than ever we must clench our teeth and not cry out.

---

*Original English.

Oh, Kitty, the best part of the invasion is the feeling that friends are approaching. We have been oppressed by Germans for so long, that the thought of friends and delivery fills us with confidence!

Now it doesn't concern the Jews anymore; no, it concerns Holland and all Occupied Europe. Perhaps, Margot says, I may yet be able to go back to school in September or October.

Yours, Anne

Friday, 9 June, 1944

Dear Kitty,

Super news of the invasion. The Allies have taken Bayeux, a small village on the French coast, and are now fighting for Caen. It's obvious they intend to cut off the peninsula where Cherbourg lies. Every evening war correspondents give news from the battlefront. The air force are up all the time in spite of the miserable weather. We heard that Churchill wanted to land with the troops on D day; however, Eisenhower and the other generals managed to get him out of the idea. What pluck he has for such an old man.

We're hoping that the war will be over at the end of this year.

Yours, Anne

Tuesday, 13 June, 1944

Dear Kitty,

Another birthday has gone by; now I'm fifteen. I received quite a lot of presents.

All five parts of Sprenger's *History of Art*, a set of underwear, a handkerchief, two bottles of yogurt, a pot of jam, a spiced gingerbread cake, and a book on botany from Mummy and Daddy, a double bracelet from Margot, a book from the Van Daans, sweet peas from Dussel, sweets and exercise books from Miep and Elli and, the high spot of all, the book *Maria Theresa* and three slices of full-cream cheese from Kraler. And a lovely bunch of peonies from Peter.

There's still excellent news of the invasion, in spite of gales, heavy rains, and high seas. Yesterday Churchill and Eisenhower visited French villages which have been liberated. The torpedo boat that Churchill was in shelled the coast. He appears, like so many men, not to know what fear is—makes me envious!

Yours, Anne

Wednesday, 14 June, 1944

Dear Kitty,

I'm really not as conceited as people seem to think, I know my faults and shortcomings better than anyone. And the trying part about me is that I criticize and scold myself far more than anyone else does. So if Mummy adds her bit of advice the pile of sermons becomes so insurmountable that I become rude and start contradicting and then, of course: "No one understands me!" I know it sounds silly, yet there is truth in it. I often accuse myself to such an extent that I long for a word of comfort, for someone who could give me sound advice and also draw out some of my real self; but, alas, I haven't found anyone yet.

I know that you'll immediately think of Peter, won't you, Kit? Peter loves me as a friend and grows more affectionate every day. But what is the mysterious something that holds us both back? I don't understand it. Sometimes I think that my terrible longing for him was exaggerated, yet that's not it, because if I don't go up to see him for two days, I long for him more desperately than ever. Peter is a darling, but still there's a lot about him that disappoints me. Yet I feel quite convinced that we shall never quarrel. Pete is a peace-loving person; he's tolerant and he lets me say a lot of things to him that he would never accept from his mother. Yet why should he keep his innermost self to himself? By nature he is more closed-up than I am, I agree, but I know—and from my own experience—that at some time or other even the most uncommunicative people long to find someone in whom they can confide.

Yours, Anne

Thursday, 15 June, 1944

Dear Kitty,

I wonder if it's because I haven't been able to poke my nose outdoors for so long that I've grown so crazy about everything to do with nature? There was a time when a deep blue sky, the

song of the birds, moonlight and flowers could never have kept me spellbound. That's changed since I've been here.

At Whitsun, when it was so warm, I stayed awake on purpose until half past eleven one evening in order to have a good look at the moon by myself. The sacrifice was all in vain, as the moon gave far too much light and I didn't dare open a window. Some months ago, I happened to be upstairs one evening when the window was open. The dark, rainy evening, the gale, the scudding clouds held me entirely in their power; it was the first time in a year and a half that I'd seen the night face-to-face. After that I went downstairs all by myself and looked out the windows in the kitchen. Alas, I had to look through dirty net curtains hanging before very dusty windows. And it's no pleasure looking through these, because nature is one thing that must be unadulterated.

Yours, Anne

Friday, 16 June, 1944

Dear Kitty,

New problems: Mrs. Van Daan is desperate, talks about a bullet through her head, prison, hanging, and suicide. She's jealous that Peter confides in me and not her. She's offended that Dussel doesn't enter into her flirtations with him, as she'd hoped, afraid that her husband is smoking all the fur-coat money away, she quarrels, uses abusive language, cries, pities herself, and then starts a fresh quarrel. What can one do with such a foolish, blubbering specimen? No one takes her seriously, she hasn't any character. The worst of it is that it makes Peter rude, Mr. Van Daan irritable, and Mummy cynical. It's a frightful situation! There's *one* golden rule to keep before you: laugh about everything and don't bother yourself about the others! It sounds selfish, but it's honestly the only cure for anyone who has to seek consolation in himself.

Yours, Anne

Friday, 23 June, 1944

Dear Kitty,

Nothing special going on here. The English have begun their

big attack on Cherbourg; according to Pim and Van Daan, we're sure to be free by October 10. It's exactly three years to a day since the Germans attacked. We've hardly got any potatoes; from now on we're going to count them out for each person, then everyone knows what he's getting.

Yours, Anne

Tuesday, 27 June, 1944

Dearest Kitty,

The mood has changed, everything's going wonderfully. Cherbourg fell today. A tremendous achievement! In the three weeks since D day not a day has gone by without rain and gales, both here and in France, but a bit of bad luck didn't prevent the English and Americans from showing their enormous strength, and how! Certainly the "wonder weapon" is in full swing, but when they really realize in "Bocheland" that the Bolshevists are on the way, they'll get even more jittery.

How far do you think we'll be on July 27?

Yours, Anne

Thursday, July 6, 1944

Dear Kitty,

It strikes fear to my heart when Peter talks of later being a criminal, or of gambling; although it's meant as a joke, of course, it gives me the feeling that he's afraid of his own weakness. Again and again I hear from Peter: "If I was as strong and plucky as you, if I always stuck to what I wanted, if I had such persistent energy, yes then . . . !"

I wonder if it's really a good quality not to let myself be influenced. Is it really good to follow almost entirely my own conscience?

Quite honestly, I can't imagine how anyone can say: "I'm weak," and then remain so. After all, if you know it, why not fight against it, why not try to train your character? The answer was: "Because it's so much easier not to!" This reply rather discouraged me. Does that mean that a lazy, deceitful life is an easy life? Oh, that can't be true.

Peter's beginning to lean on me a bit and that mustn't happen.

How can I make it clear to him that what appears easy and attractive will drag him down into the depths, from which it is almost impossible to raise oneself? Laziness may *appear* attractive, but *work* gives satisfaction.

I can't understand people who don't like work, yet that isn't the case with Peter; he just hasn't got a fixed goal, and he thinks he's too stupid and too inferior to achieve anything. Poor boy, he's never known what it feels like to make other people happy, and I can't teach him that. He scoffs at religion and swears, using the name of God; it hurts me every time I see how deserted, how scornful, and how poor he really is.

People who have a religion should be glad, for not everyone has the gift of believing in heavenly things. You don't necessarily have to be afraid of punishment after death; a lot of people can't accept purgatory or hell. But still a religion, it doesn't matter which, keeps a person on the right path. It isn't the fear of God but the upholding of one's honor.

Whoever doesn't know it must learn and find by experience that: "A quiet conscience makes one strong!"

Yours, Anne

Saturday, 8 July, 1944

Dear Kitty,

The chief representative of the business, Mr. B., has managed to get strawberries at the auction sale.* Large quantities arrived here dusty, covered with sand. That very evening we bottled six jars and made eight pots of jam.

Next morning Miep wanted to make jam for the office people. At half past twelve, no strangers in the house, front door bolted, trays fetched, Peter, Daddy, Van Daan clattering on the stairs: Anne, get hot water; Margot, bring a bucket; all hands on deck! I went into the kitchen, which was chock-full, with a queer feeling in my tummy, Miep, Elli, Koophuis, Henk, Daddy, Peter: the families in hiding and their supply column, all mingling together, in the middle of the day!

People can't see in from outside because of the net curtains,

---

*It is compulsory in Holland for all growers to sell their produce at public auction.

but, even so, the loud voices and banging doors positively gave me the jitters. Are we really in hiding? It gives one a very queer feeling to appear in the world again. The family was seated round our kitchen table stalk-picking—though more went into mouths than into buckets. The remainder are being sterilized and bottled. If the jars come unsealed, as two did that evening, Daddy quickly makes them into jam.

For two whole days we eat strawberries and nothing but strawberries; strawberries with our porridge, skimmed milk with strawberries, bread and butter with strawberries, strawberries for dessert, strawberries with sugar, strawberries with sand. Then the supply was finished or in bottles and under lock and key.

"I say, Anne," Margot calls out, "the greengrocer on the corner has let us have nineteen pounds of green peas." "That's nice of him," I replied. But oh, the work . . . ugh!

So this morning at half past nine we began the boring job of shelling peas. Perhaps it's all right for pedantic dentists or precise office workers, but for an impatient teen-ager like me, it's frightful. Bend the top, pull the skin, remove the string, throw out the pod; they dance before my eyes, green, green, green maggots, strings, rotten pods, green, green, green. Just for the sake of doing something, I chatter the whole morning, any nonsense that comes into my head, make everyone laugh, and bore them stiff. But every string that I pull makes me feel certain that I never, never want to be just a housewife only!

Yours, Anne

Saturday, 15 July, 1944

Dear Kitty,

I have one outstanding trait in my character, which must strike anyone who knows me, and that is my knowledge of myself. I can watch myself and my actions, just like an outsider. The Anne of every day I can face entirely without prejudice, without making excuses for her, and watch what's good and what's bad about her. This "self-consciousness" haunts me, and every time I open my mouth I know as soon as I've spoken whether "that ought to have been different" or "that was right as it was." There are so many things about myself that I condemn. I understand more and more how true Daddy's words were when he said: "All children must look after their own upbringing." Parents can only give good advice or put them on the right paths, but the final forming of a person's character lies in their own hands.

In addition, I have lots of courage, I feel strong, as if I can bear a great deal, I feel so free and so young! I was glad when I first realized it, because I don't think I shall easily bow down before the blows that inevitably come to everyone.

But I've talked about these things so often before. Now I want to come to the chapter of "Daddy and Mummy don't understand me." Daddy and Mummy have always thoroughly spoiled me, were sweet to me, defended me, and have done all that parents could do. And yet I've felt so terribly lonely for a long time, so left out, neglected, and misunderstood. Daddy tried all he could to check my rebellious spirit, but it was no use. He always talked to me as a child who was going through difficult phases. It sounds crazy, because Daddy's the only one who has always taken me into his confidence, and no one but Daddy has given me the feeling that I'm sensible. But you see, he hasn't realized that I didn't want to hear about "symptoms of your age," or "other girls," or "it wears off by itself"; I didn't want to be treated as a girl-like-all-others, but as Anne-on-her-own-merits.

Pim always takes up the older, fatherly attitude, tells me that he too has had similar passing tendencies. These things have made me never mention my views on life nor my well-considered theories to anyone but my diary and, occasionally, to Margot. I concealed from Daddy everything that perturbed me; I never shared my ideals with him. I was aware of the fact that I was pushing him away from me. I couldn't do anything else. I have acted that way because I knew I should completely lose my repose and self-confidence if, at this stage, I were to accept criticisms of my half-completed task.

This is a point that I think a lot about: why is it that Pim annoys me? So much so that I can hardly bear him teaching me, that his affectionate ways strike me as being put on, that I want to be left in peace and would really prefer it if he dropped me a bit, until I felt more certain in my attitude towards him? Because I still have a gnawing feeling of guilt over that horrible letter that I dared to write him when I was so wound up. Oh, how hard it is to be really strong and brave in every way!

Yet this was not my greatest disappointment; no, I ponder far more over Peter than Daddy. I know very well that I conquered him instead of he conquering me. I created an image of him in my mind, pictured him as a quiet, sensitive, lovable boy, who needed affection and friendship. I needed a living person to whom I could pour out my heart; I wanted a friend who'd help to put me on the right road. I achieved what I wanted, and, slowly but surely, I drew him towards me.

We talked about the most private things, and yet up till now we have never touched on those things that fill my heart and soul. I still don't know quite what to make of Peter, is he superficial, or does he still feel shy of me? But I committed one error in my desire to make a real friendship: I tried to get at him by developing it into a more intimate relation, whereas I should have explored all other possibilities. He longs to be loved and I can see that he's beginning to be more and more in love with me. And yet I don't seem able to touch on the subjects that I'm so longing to bring out. Now he clings to me, and for the time being, I don't see any way of putting him on his own feet.

"For in its innermost depths youth is lonelier than old age." I read this saying in some book and I've always remembered it. Is it true then that grown-ups have a more difficult time here than we do? No. I know it isn't. Older people have formed their opinions about everything, and don't waver before they act. It's twice as hard for us young ones to hold our ground, and maintain our ideals when people are showing their worst side.

It's really a wonder that I haven't dropped all my ideals, dreams, and cherished hopes, because they seem so absurd and impossible to carry out. Yet, in spite of everything I still believe that people are good at heart. I simply can't build my hopes on a foundation of confusion, misery, and death. I see the world gradually being turned into a wilderness, I hear the ever approaching thunder which will destroy us, I can feel the sufferings of millions and yet, if I look up into the heavens, I think that it will all come right, that this cruelty will end, and that peace and tranquillity will return again.

I must uphold my ideals, for perhaps the time will come when I shall be able to carry them out.

Yours, Anne

Friday, 21 July, 1944

Dear Kitty,

Now I am getting really hopeful. Super news! An attempt has been made on Hitler's life and not by Jewish communists or English capitalists this time, but by a proud German general, and what's more, he's a count. The Führer's life was saved by Divine Providence and, unfortunately, he managed to get off with just a few burns. The chief culprit was shot.

It certainly shows that there are lots of officers who are sick of the war and would like to see Hitler descend into a bottomless pit. Hitler has announced that from now on everyone in the armed forces must obey the Gestapo, and that any soldier who knows that one of his superiors was involved in this low, cowardly attempt upon his life may shoot same on the spot, without court-martial.

What a perfect shambles it's going to be. Little Johnnie's feet begin hurting him during a long march, he's snapped at by his officer, Johnnie grabs his rifle and cries out: "You wanted to murder the Führer, so there's your reward." One bang and the proud chief who dared to tick off little Johnnie has passed into eternal life (or is it eternal death?). In the end, whenever an officer finds himself up against a soldier, he'll be wetting his pants from anxiety.

Do you gather a bit what I mean, or have I been skipping too much from one subject to another? I can't help it; the prospect that I may be sitting on school benches next October makes me feel far too cheerful to be logical! Oh, dearie me, hadn't I just told you that I didn't want to be too hopeful? Forgive me, they haven't given me the name "little bundle of contradictions" for nothing!

Yours, Anne

Dear Kitty,

"Little bundle of contradictions." That's how I ended my last letter and that's how I'm going to begin this one.

I've told you before that I have a dual personality. One half embodies my high-spiritedness, cheerfulness, and the way I take everything lightly: a flirtation, a kiss, an embrace, a dirty joke. This side is usually lying in wait and pushes away the other, which is much better and deeper. No one knows Anne's better side and that's why most people find me so insufferable. I loathe having to tell you this, but my superficial side will always be too quick for the deeper side of me. That's why it will always win. I've tried to push this Anne away, because after all, she's only half of Anne; but it doesn't work and I know why.

I'm awfully scared that everyone who knows me as I always am will discover that I have another, finer and better side. I'm afraid they'll laugh at me, think I'm ridiculous and sentimental. I'm used to not being taken seriously but only the "lighthearted" Anne can bear it; the "deeper" Anne is too frail for it. Sometimes, if I compel the good Anne to take the stage for a quarter of an hour, she shrivels up as soon as she has to speak, and lets Anne number one take over.

Therefore, the nice Anne is never present in company, but almost always predominates when we're alone. I know exactly how I'd like to be, but I'm only like that for myself. I am guided by the pure Anne within, but outside I'm nothing but a frolicsome little goat who's broken loose. That's how I've acquired the name of chaser-after-boys, flirt, know-all, reader of love stories. The cheerful Anne laughs about it, gives cheeky answers, shrugs her shoulders, but, oh, the quiet Anne's reactions are just the opposite. If I'm to be quite honest, then I must admit that it does hurt me, that I try terribly hard to change myself, but that I'm always fighting against a more powerful enemy.

A voice sobs within me: "There, that's what's become of you: you're uncharitable, you look supercilious, people dislike you and all because you won't listen to the advice given you by your own better half." Oh, I would like to listen, but if I'm quiet and serious, everyone thinks it's a new comedy and then I have to turn it into a joke; my family thinks I'm ill, makes me swallow pills for headaches and nerves, feels my head to see whether I'm running a temperature, asks if I'm constipated and criticizes me for being in a bad mood. I can't keep that up: if I'm watched to that extent, I start getting snappy, then unhappy, and finally I twist my heart round again, so that the bad is on the outside and the good is on the inside, and I keep on trying to find a way of becoming what I would so like to be, and what I could be, if there weren't any other people living in the world.

Yours, Anne

EPILOGUE

Anne's diary ends here. On August 4, 1944, the *Grüne Polizei* made a raid on the Secret Annexe. All the occupants, together with Kraler and Koophuis, were arrested and sent to German and Dutch concentration camps.

The Secret Annexe was plundered by the Gestapo. Among a pile of old books, magazines, and newspapers left lying on the floor, Miep and Elli found Anne's diary. Apart from a very few passages which are of little interest to the reader, the original text has been printed.

Of all the occupants of the Secret Annexe, Anne's father alone returned. Kraler and Koophuis, who withstood the hardships of the Dutch camp, were able to go home to their families.

In March 1945, two months before the liberation of Holland, Anne died in the concentration camp at Bergen-Belsen.

PROPHET
IN THE
WILDERNESS

A CONDENSATION OF

PROPHET
IN THE
WILDERNESS

The Story of
Albert
Schweitzer

by
HERMANN
HAGEDORN

Albert Schweitzer was one of the outstanding men of our time, a protean genius whose life was dedicated to his fellowman. The world remembers him chiefly as the selfless doctor of Lambaréné, where in his jungle hospital he labored for half a century in the service of suffering African humanity.

But this was only a fraction of his accomplishment. He was also one of the leading interpreters of the music of Johann Sebastian Bach, a scholar of theology who shook the seminaries with a revolutionary interpretation of Jesus, a world-famous virtuoso of the organ, and a respected philosopher of history. He was honored with the Nobel Peace Prize, but a more enduring monument is his principle of "reverence for life," which guided his own endeavors and which for us becomes more meaningful each year.

From the simple Alsatian boyhood, the poet Hermann Hagedorn has traced the inspiring life of an extraordinary man.

Chapter 1

Albert Schweitzer speaking:
"River and forest . . . ! Who can describe the first impression
they make? . . . Pictures of antediluvian scenery which elsewhere
had seemed to be merely the creation of fancy, are now seen
in real life. It is impossible to say where the river ends and the
land begins. . . . Clumps of palms and palm trees, ordinary trees
spreading out widely with green boughs and huge leaves, . . .
wide fields of papyrus clumps as tall as a man, with big fan-like
leaves, and amid all this luxuriant greenery the rotting stems of
dead giants shooting up to heaven. . . . In every gap in the
forest a water mirror meets the eye; at every bend in the river
a new tributary shows itself. A heron flies heavily up and then
settles on a dead tree-trunk; . . . and high in the air a pair of
ospreys circle. Then—yes, there can be no mistake about it!—
from the branch of a palm there hang and swing—two monkey
tails. . . . We are really in Africa!"

"The operation is finished, and in the hardly-lighted dormitory I watch for the sick man's awaking. Scarcely has he recovered consciousness when he stares about him and ejaculates

again and again: 'I've no more pain! I've no more pain!' His hand feels for mine and will not let it go.

"Then I begin to tell him and the others who are in the room that it is the Lord Jesus who has told the doctor and his wife to come to the Ogowe, and that white people in Europe give them the money to live here and cure the sick. . . . Black and white, [we] sit side by side and feel that we know by experience the meaning of the words: *And all ye are brethren.*"

"At first, however, I had not the heart to practice [the organ]. I had accustomed myself to think that this activity in Africa meant the end of my life as an artist. . . . One evening, however, as, in melancholy mood, I was playing one of Bach's organ fugues, the idea came suddenly upon me that I might after all use my free hours in Africa for the very purpose of perfecting and deepening my technique.

"I immediately formed a plan to take, one after another, compositions by Bach, Mendelssohn, Widor, César Franck, and Max Reger, study them carefully down to the smallest detail, and learn them by heart, even if I had to spend weeks or months on any particular piece."

"We get, as a rule, about fifteen workers, which in view of the overwhelming amount that has to be done is far too few. . . . One of us must go with them as supervisor; left to themselves they would hardly do anything. Why should they, who happen to be here just now, exert themselves so that others, who will be in the hospital a few months hence, may have maize to eat, and even be housed in good wards!

"A day with these people moves on like a symphony.

"*Lento:* They take very grumpily the axes and bush-knives that I distribute to them on landing. In snail-tempo the procession goes to the spot where bush and tree are to be cut down. . . . With great caution the first blows are struck.

"*Moderato:* Axes and bush-knives move in extremely moderate time, which the conductor tries in vain to quicken. The mid-day break puts an end to the tedious movement.

"*Adagio:* With much trouble I have brought the people back

to the work-place in the stifling forest. Not a breath of wind is stirring. One hears from time to time the stroke of an axe.

"*Scherzo:* A few jokes . . . are successful. The mental atmosphere gets livelier, merry words fly here and there, and a few begin to sing. It is now getting a little cooler, too. . . .

"*Finale:* All are jolly now. The wicked forest, on account of which they have to stand here instead of sitting comfortably in the hospital, shall have a bad time of it. . . . Howling and yelling they attack it, axes and bush-knives vie with each other in battering it. But—no bird must fly up, no squirrel show itself. . . . With the very slightest distraction the spell would be broken. Then the axes and knives would come to rest, . . . and there would be no getting them into train for work. . . . If this finale lasts even a good half-hour the day has not been wasted."

"If the day has not been too exhausting I can give a couple of hours after supper to my studies in ethics and civilisation. . . . Strange, indeed, are the surroundings amid which I study. . . . From the forest come harsh and terrifying cries of all sorts. Caramba, my faithful dog, growls gently on the verandah, to let me know that he is there, and at my feet, under the table, lies a small dwarf antelope. In this solitude I try to set in order thoughts which have been stirring in me since 1900. . . . Solitude of the primeval forest, how can I ever thank you enough for what you have been to me?"

"On December 4th the canoes are surprised on their return journey by a terrible thunderstorm. . . . We wait for an hour and a half in dreadful anxiety, but at last the storm abates. One after the other the canoes arrive in pitch darkness and under a deluge of rain. They had had just time to reach the bank somewhere or other, and no one was drowned. I mount to the doctor's house almost dizzy with joy."

WHO IS THIS SURGEON who practices Bach and César Franck, and makes a symphony of the ordeal of bossing a crew of native laborers; this musician who writes far into the night concerning civilization; this philosopher who is "dizzy with joy" because a boatload of black men ride through a tropical storm and reach home without the loss of a single life?

Scientists recognize him as a notable experimental physician in the field of tropical medicine, musicians acclaim him as one of the world's leading organists. He is the author of the most comprehensive and profound biography of Johann Sebastian Bach, and one of Bach's greatest interpreters. He is a theologian whose conclusions concerning the relations of Jesus to the popular thought of His own time have shaken every theological seminary in the world; a prophet who foresaw, in the degeneration of the nineteenth-century ethics, the doom that has overcome the Western world in the twentieth; a revolutionary, whose insistence on "reverence for life" sets him in dramatic antithesis to the assailants as well as the defenders of Western civilization. He is, finally, a humanitarian, whose example may do for millions more than his skillful fingers have done for the thousands he has rescued from physical agony—men who are among the most backward inhabitants of the globe.

He burns like Francis of Assisi, and he looks like Joseph Stalin before Stalin reduced his luxuriant mustache. His great muscular frame, the masterful nose, the broad forehead, the unruly hair, the large, humorous mouth, keep the mustache in proportion; the eyes are black wells of concentrated sorrow and compassion, faintly lighted by hope. He knows that above the dark canopy there are stars; and there are flowers where he goes which he will greet with simple gaiety. He is a great laugher.

Outwardly he is Teutonic, but he is in fact the product of two cultures. He is neither German nor French, he insists, but an Alsatian. "I have my roots in the Vosges country, but I am preoccupied first of all and always with what I want to be doing as a man, serving humankind." Nor can he be confined within any religious orthodoxy. Devoted to the teachings of Jesus, devoted to the Christian church, he is not only tolerant of other faiths but eloquent in his enthusiasm for the ethical wisdom of the great Asiatic thinkers.

He has been called a modern saint, but there is about him nothing of the detached ascetic. He knows the world and he confronts it with toleration, kindliness and mercy. His con-

426

"... you will find light
and help and
human kindness."

versation glows rather than sparkles, and humanity and power stream out of him. As a rule he reproaches, when he has to, with a joke or a play on words.

Yet Schweitzer rules himself as firmly as he rules his hospital, demanding more from himself than from any of his subordinates. When World War II ended he sent one after another of his doctors and nurses home, but he himself remained in Africa, though he was seventy and had been in the tropics for six years without a break. The hospital needed him, that was enough. The burning sympathy for the sufferings of the black people which impelled him to give up a great European career has not been dulled with the passing years. He identifies with each patient, suffering in his suffering, tormented with his anxieties.

He is often so tired that, at mealtimes, he will not say a word. But he is never too tired to take the table scraps to his pets or to visit the children's ward.

As a thinker and as a human being, he is a plain man. Asked by the chairman of a meeting he is about to address how he wants to be introduced, he suggests: "See that fellow over there who looks like a Scotch collie? That's Albert Schweitzer." Whether in Africa or in Europe, he lives with the simplicity of a hermit, traveling third-class, carrying his own luggage, and eating in simple restaurants. In Alsace the shoes that he wears, the big black hat, the cape floating in the wind, are such as a countryman might don on a trip to the city.

In Africa he is not only the physician; he is the carpenter and builder, the boss of the pick-and-shovel gang, the one who does the marketing and starts the gasoline engine in the morning. This "genius in compassion," as he has been called, builds a hospital largely with his own hands, swings the axe, hauls huge beams, when the black men he is feeding loll under the trees in maddening indifference. A white-clad native he calls on for help looks down his nose at him. "I am an intellectual. I don't drag timbers around." Schweitzer replies, "You're lucky. I too wanted to become an intellectual. But I didn't make it."

In his large heart the natives, irresponsible though they seem, find shelter. He does not ask if they are worthy of the love and the patience he gives them. Who is he to balance his qualities of mind and spirit against theirs? "It is an uncomfortable doctrine. ... You are happy; ... therefore you are called upon to give much. Whatever more than others you have received in health, natural gifts, working capacity, success, a beautiful childhood, ... you must not accept as being a matter of course. You must pay a price for them."

Chapter II

ALBERT SCHWEITZER was a puny thing when he was born on January 14, 1875, in an old, gray, tile-roofed house in Kaysersberg, Alsace. For weeks he was not expected to live. Even six months later, at the time of his father's installation as pastor of the church in nearby Günsbach, the parish ladies who inspected him were so pessimistic about his survival that his mother drenched his face with her tears. But the clear, pine-scented air blowing down the slopes of the Vosges Mountains, and the milk of neighbor Leopold's cow together worked a miracle.

He defeated Death, but he had more difficulty with the Devil. Periodically, at Sunday-morning service, Satan peered at the child around the edge of the organ, hiding when the pastor spoke, but reappearing when he fell silent. Albert was rather proud of his father's power over the Evil One, but was not sorry when he found that the Devil was only the bearded organist coming into range of the organ mirror when he wanted to follow the pastor's movements.

His father's parsonage was damp and gloomy, but there was nothing gloomy about the pastor or his energetic, self-contained wife. Albert's father came of a line of pastors, schoolmasters, organists and tillers of the soil. His mother was a parson's daughter from up the valley. Music and piety twined like strong vines through his ancestry, music that was a form of piety, piety that sought expression in music. His mother's father, Pastor Schillinger, a noted character in the Münster Valley, had been a devotee of the organ, improvising on it in a way that his neighbors talked about for decades after his death. Albert's father, too, was no mean hand at improvisation.

The pastor was a kindly man in whose theology the sunshine of the Christian faith was more conspicuous than the thunder. By a law of Louis XIV, which the Germans left unchanged when they retook Alsace, his Lutheran flock shared with the predominating Catholic population the only church in the village.

Young Albert was thrilled with the splendor of the gilded altar with its huge bunches of artificial flowers, its tall majestic candles and, on the wall above, the gilt statues of Joseph and the Virgin. No strain of inherited puritanism made this magnificence unholy in his eyes. He was precocious in his deep response to religion and music. Church services filled him with a kind of rapture. But he did not communicate his joy. He had a way of driving his elders frantic at what looked like indifference when he was fairly burning up inside.

He loved his father's sermons because, in his father, the homily and the life were so obviously of a piece. The sermons were the reflections of day-by-day experience, and knowing his father, he recognized, in later years, the effort it cost him to lay his heart bare to his congregation. Once a month, in the less formal afternoon services, his father would tell stories of missionaries in the far corners of the earth, and on successive Sundays one year read the reminiscences of an Alsatian named Casalis who had labored among the Negroes of South Africa.

Sermons and stories alike so impressed themselves on the boy's mind that he could recall them a half century later. But what meant more to him was the sense of consecration in the little church and the reverence he felt glowing in his own heart.

Akin to this reverence was the emotion that the beauty of the natural world excited in him. At seventy he remembered how, even as a child, he was "like a person in an ecstasy in the presence of nature, without anyone suspecting it."

If he was precocious in his relation to the Deity and to natural beauty, he was even more so in his perception of moral values. Outwardly, as he grew, he was quite like the other Günsbach boys. He insisted on clattering about on wooden sabots weekdays and going without an overcoat in the winter, because the other boys wore sabots and had no overcoats. When a boy whom he had subdued in a wrestling bout cried that he, too, might be strong if he had broth twice a week like the pastor's son, how the broth gagged in Albert's throat after that! He did not want what the other village boys did not have.

Inwardly, too, he wanted to be like them, but this was not so easy. He might taunt a Jewish peddler because the other boys were doing it, but he fell back crushed before the victim's embarrassed, good-natured smile and went home thinking about persecution and what it meant to be silent under it. A sense of the sorrow that was in the world awoke in him early.

He was especially sensitive to the suffering of animals. The sight of an old limping horse, tugged forward by one man while another beat it from behind, haunted him for weeks. Driving the neighbor's ancient chestnut horse one day, he could not resist whipping him into a trot, though he knew the old nag was tired. It was only when he unharnessed the poor animal and saw how his flanks were pumping that Albert recognized what he had done. What use now, he asked himself in misery, to look into the tired eyes and silently implore forgiveness?

The sufferings of animals were so real to him that he could not understand why, in his bedtime prayers, he was told to pray for human beings only. When his mother had spoken his prayer with him, put out the light and left the room, he returned to his devotions with a whispered prayer of his own: "O heavenly Father, protect and bless all things that have breath. Guard them from all evil, and let them sleep in peace."

The village boys had no patience with what to them was unmanly squeamishness, and he learned to keep his convictions to himself. When a friend called him to come with his beanshooter to take a shot at a robin or a thrush, he felt his heart sink but dared not refuse. On a leafless tree a flock of birds sang, wholly unafraid of the boys advancing toward them. The friend fell on one knee and took aim. When he ordered Albert to do as he had done, Albert meekly obeyed. Suddenly the church bells began to ring, mingling their jubilation with the birdsong. To young Albert, aged seven, they were a voice from on high, crying *Thou shalt not kill*. He waved his arms, so the birds took flight, and leaving his enraged companion, he fled.

The experience shook him and remained in his memory.

For it not only deepened his conviction that killing was not for him; it gave him courage to emancipate himself from the attitudes of the majority.

EVEN BEFORE he went to the dame school in the village, his father gave him lessons on Grandfather Schillinger's square piano. He found shortly that without effort he could do things on the keys that made melodious patterns. He asked his first schoolteacher why she played the hymn tunes with one finger when you could play them so much more enjoyably with two hands, and promptly gave an illustration with full chords. He noted that the teacher gave him a strange look, and he felt ashamed at having shown off.

He was about eight when he began to play the organ, though his legs were scarcely long enough to reach the pedals. A year later he took the place of the organist for the first time at a service in his father's church.

At school he was slow in learning to read and write, but he questioned everything he read. The story of the Magi, for instance, entranced him. But what did Joseph and Mary do with the gold and other valuables the kings brought them? How could they have been poor after that? And why did the Wise Men never bother again to look up the Christ Child?

Albert was sent to school in an ancient little town with an elevation called Monk's Hill behind it, in memory of the Benedictine abbey which had dominated the valley for centuries. He so loved the beauty of the countryside that he evaded the company of other Günsbach boys at the school in order to be alone with his thoughts. Through those colorful, checkered fields, down the long aisles of the smooth-barked beeches, surely God Himself walked to protect His children—the hares, the chipmunks, the stag Albert himself saw now and again at dusk. The birds that sang in the early sunlight—surely God would see to it that they should not suffer when the icy winds came and the snow fell?

Walking through the woods or sitting on the rocky promontory that jutted out from the vineyards above the village, he was thinking a good deal about the suffering that seemed to leave no man or beast untouched. There was suffering in his own home, for his father dragged himself about for years with muscular rheumatism and stomach disorders. There was always too much work for his mother, with five children to feed and clothe, and only a country parson's salary.

What did it mean, all this suffering, and what could anyone do about it? How diligently careful you must be not to add to the sum of it! He began to see that man had no right to inflict pain and death on another living creature unless the necessity for it was unavoidable. How horrible to cause suffering and death by mere thoughtlessness! His playmates thought him a sentimental fool. All right, if that were folly, he would be a fool.

In spite of his consciousness of suffering around him, the boy recognized early that he had a goodly heritage. His mother might lose the famous Schillinger temper and briefly rock the timbers, but the family all loved one another, and were united in the love of God and man. Parental discipline was firm, but so transfused with love and lit with laughter that it was the love rather than the restraint which remained in the children's memory. Five boys and girls made for tumult. But Pastor Schweitzer and his busy wife knew that even tumult must somehow be fitted into the pattern of a Christian home.

WHEN ALBERT WAS TEN he was sent to the classical high school, the Gymnasium, at Mulhouse. The town was famous for its long tradition of independence. It had been a free city under the Holy Roman Empire, and subsequently a republic with a code of civil liberties beyond anything a modern democracy would demand. If a man were accused even of murder, no bailiff might enter his house, and the judge conducted the trial from the sidewalk!

But Albert heard less of liberty than of discipline from the paternal great-uncle and great-aunt with whom he was lodged. Uncle Louis was superintendent of the elementary schools of Mulhouse, and therefore had a professional interest in seeing that his godchild took the education which was offered him. Aunt Sophie, like many other women who have no children of their own, had firm convictions about the upbringing of the young. Albert's days were regulated to the last minute. School in the morning, piano practice after the midday meal, more school, homework and more piano. Sunday afternoons a formal promenade, perhaps. So much, and no more, for recreation.

Life in the cheerless flat was inclined to be bleak for the ten-year-old from the happy, uninhibited country manse. He was desperately homesick for his kindly father and his devoted, energetic mother, homesick for the fields and flowers, the clean-swept forest. He took refuge in dreams when he was supposed to be studying fractions and Latin conjugations.

The principal sent for his father. If Albert did not do better he would lose the scholarship which was his as a pastor's son. Perhaps it might be well to withdraw Albert from the Gymnasium. Some boys were fitted for higher education, others . . . His father didn't scold him. The boy sensed that the disappointment went too deep for anger, and still felt no impulse to pull himself together.

Yet three months later he was in the upper group of his class. The miracle was performed quite unconsciously by a new teacher who did his own work with such precision that the boy could not bear to face what such a paragon must think of him. His grades rose sharply. More important, he began to have a glimmer of what teaching meant. To present an example of conscience in action—that was teaching.

He began to read prodigiously. To begin a book meant finishing it at one sitting. Aunt Sophie protested against such "devouring" of good literature. Having been a schoolteacher, she read for style, lingered over the paragraphs. Albert consumed even the daily press in a way that roused Aunt Sophie's indignation. A boy of eleven had no business reading accounts of murders, she declared, even when they were played down to the bare fact in the discreet manner of the Teutonic press.

"But it's not the murders I'm interested in," Albert protested. "It's the politics. Politics is history—contemporary history."

"We'll find out right now whether the youngster is really reading politics," Uncle Louis said. "Tell me the names of the sovereigns of the Balkan states."

The boy gave him the difficult names. He managed next to tell his uncle the composition of the three most recent French cabinets, and the gist of a speech by a prominent member of the Reichstag. That settled the question of newspaper reading.

But he still had to practice scales. Something in Aunt Sophie, or in him, kept him from finding a connection between scales and the harmonies his father evoked from Grandfather Schillinger's square piano. Not even Eugene Münch, the organist of St. Stephen's Church, to whom he was sent for formal instruction, seemed able to help him to it. Instead of studying the pieces his teacher prescribed, he played what he wanted to play or lost himself in dreamy improvisations. Yet there was something else behind his hit-or-miss execution of the masters. Did this man think that he, Albert, was going to let him see what this wonderful piece of music meant to him? Never!

Once too often the boy murdered Mozart. Herr Münch raged, then flung open a book at one of Mendelssohn's briefer "Songs without Words." "I suppose you will pollute this song as you have polluted the rest. When a boy hasn't any feeling I can't give it to him."

Albert knew the piece well, having frequently read it at sight for his own pleasure when he should have been doing finger exercises. Through the week that followed, he threw himself into the study of it. In the next lesson, he took a deep breath, resigned himself to baring his soul, and played the Mendelssohn piece with everything he had.

Herr Münch said little, but he pressed the boy's shoulder and gave Albert a Beethoven piece to bite into. A few weeks later he offered his pupil the privilege of trying his hand at the master of masters, Johann Sebastian Bach. Not long after, the boy was at Eugene Münch's own organ at St. Stephen's, learning to deal with three keyboards and twenty-six registers. He fairly glowed with delight.

In the Germany of the 1880's confirmation was an inescapable part of the ritual of adolescence. You went to the Gymnasium (if your father could afford it and you had the brains), you lengthened your trousers, you agonized in first love and you were confirmed. This solemn act was preceded by a year of weekly class instruction in the elements of the Lutheran faith.

At fourteen Albert's mind and his spirit alike were incandescent. Move mountains? Why not? An idealist? Of course. How could you be a Christian and be anything else? Yet when he asked that question of his elders, it seemed to him that everyone he respected gave an unhappy sigh and fell silent. Those who visited his father's parsonage or sat at Aunt Sophie's table frequently talked of idealism, but their talk always ended in a sigh. Yes, it was fine to have ideals, and how wonderful it had been to believe in them! Once you had flamed with enthusiasm, but, of course, when you became a man, you put aside such things. Albert gathered that disillusionment was regarded as an essential step in achieving that maturity which was expected of a man.

The boy listened to their talk and made no comment. But inwardly he rebelled. Was disillusionment really a part of this business of growing up? Would he someday look back upon his own youth with the same melancholy recognition of noble futility? Not if he could help it!

What could he do about it? Pastor Wennager's confirmation class loomed as a God-sent opportunity to find out. But he discerned shortly that asking questions was the prerogative solely of the teacher. The Gospel was a matter not of reason but of faith. Albert had his own ideas about that. Reason is given us, he said to himself, in order that we may comprehend the highest conceptions of religion. The thought, becoming conviction, filled him with a serene joy. Approaching the solemn hour of his union with the church, he was so moved by the sacredness of the impending rite that he came near to being ill. When, on the great day, Eugene Münch at the organ evoked the rolling splendors of Handel's "Lift up your hearts," his own seemed ready to burst.

TO A BOY as mentally alert and as independent as Albert Schweitzer, school was inevitably bound to be exciting. The passion for reading Aunt Sophie had tried so hard to bring within the bounds of respectable temperance served him well. But books and instructors alike seemed to Albert too reluctant to admit how little really was known of what went on in the natural world. Once more he began to dream. A raindrop could make him forget time, food, even duty. But not only in the natural world did he confront the mystery of the Unknowable. He came gradually to realize that no man could ever truly understand the past. All he could do was describe such fragments of it as he could fitfully discern.

His hunger to know (combined, no doubt, with a clever boy's realization of his cleverness) made him a nuisance and a pest. Forgotten was the reserve he had inherited from his mother, forgotten the Teutonic tradition of modesty of youth. He thrust his opinions into every talk, argued every point, seeking with others that which they could accept as true. If man were to progress, intelligence and knowledge must supplant ignorance, and he himself must get started upon his major business of human existence. Like the Ancient Mariner, he buttonholed everyone who crossed his path into earnest discourse. Conversation? To converse meant to enlighten!

Too often, both in Günsbach and Mulhouse, the result was merely sharp exchanges and ruined tempers. He was, in fact, as unbearable as a well-brought-up youth could be.

Albert's immature pursuit of truth was responsible for the only friction that father and son ever suffered in their relationship. When the pastor went visiting anywhere with his son he exacted a promise in advance that the boy would not spoil his day with his "stupid behavior" in conversation.

Being humble at heart, devoted to his fellowman only a little less than he was devoted to truth, Albert did what he could. It became one of the chief disciplines of his life to endure conversations which are that and nothing more. Gradually he became a civilized member of society, outwardly at least.

HARMONY RETURNED to the parsonage in Günsbach. Indeed, after many frowns, fortune was fairly beaming on the Schweitzer family. A remote cousin had left Albert's mother a modest fortune, and the Protestant community had acquired a new manse, open to the sun, with a garden. The pastor's health was improving day by day. Albert was at home through every vacation, reveling in its unrestrained joyousness.

Between him and his father there was none of the friction which so often mars the relations between generations. They were friends and seemed contemporaries. He could talk to his father about the thoughts that were agitating his mind—the sense of the suffering in the world that had been with him since his early childhood and was growing more acute and more persistent as he grew toward manhood; and the realization that had come to him of late that he had no right to take for granted the exceptional happiness he had known. He wanted to believe that his gifts were just good luck. But a voice in him was saying that he who has been blessed with joy and beauty has incurred a debt which he cannot evade.

He did not want to hear the voice, and there were times when he did not hear it. But it always returned and spoke ever more insistently. There is too much suffering in the world. A man must pay God for high fortune.

Strange thoughts, no doubt, on the lips of a boy of sixteen, strange perhaps on any lips at the opening of the last decade of a complacent century, but not strange to the parson of Günsbach, preaching the gospel of Christ to hardworking peasants who knew from time immemorial the weight of the burden of sorrow.

Chapter III

FOUR MONTHS AFTER GRADUATING from the Gymnasium Albert Schweitzer, now eighteen, went to Paris. The tall, sturdy youth with the eyes of the artist, set deep under the broad forehead and the unruly dark hair, had never seen a city larger than the Alsatian capital, Strasbourg. Yet he was a thinker of exceptionally independent mind and a musician of such distinction that Herr Münch had told him he was ready to study under Charles Marie Widor, the organist of St. Sulpice, in Paris.

Early in October 1893 Schweitzer found himself in the presence of Monsieur Widor, who was also a professor of the organ at the Conservatoire and a virtuoso whose works had been performed before the most discriminating audiences of Europe.

The young man asked whether he might play Widor something on the organ.

"Play what?" asked Widor.

"Bach," was the answer. "Bach, of course."

The Frenchman could not guess the emotions sweeping through this youth as he took his place at the majestic instrument. Why, the boy was wondering, had he ever imagined that the great Widor would bother to teach an unknown young man from Alsace? If Widor wondered about that himself he did not wonder long. Here, he recognized, was a musician with a mind, an imagination and unfathomable depths of feeling.

Breathlessly the young man awaited the verdict. Yes, said the master, he would take Monsieur Schweitzer as a pupil. The young man was to have a number of lessons before he returned home for the opening of the university, and return to Paris now and again as he could.

Late that month Schweitzer matriculated at Strasbourg as a student of theology and philosophy. German universities made much of independent investigation. Lectures on the first three Gospels started Schweitzer reading commentaries. The passion for truth was still intolerant of compromise. The inquiring mind which, in his early boyhood, had wondered how the Holy Family could have been poor when the Magi had showered the Child with precious stones, started wondering about more vital theological problems. There were passages in the Gospels, he thought, that did not make sense on the basis of accepted dogmas. There were, on the other hand, episodes which had the ring of historical fact.

How about that episode in the Gospel of Matthew in which Jesus sends forth His disciples to tell people that the end of the natural world is at hand and the supernatural Kingdom is imminent? It will be no easy mission, He says. Being followers of His, they will be persecuted. But they will not have gone the rounds of the towns and villages of Israel before the Kingdom will have come. The disciples had presumably made the rounds and come back. But so far as the record goes, nothing had happened. The world was quite as it had been.

Apparently Jesus had been mistaken. But how could He be

in error if He were divine? Schweitzer's teacher explained that the passage was obviously a later addition to the Christ story.

But Schweitzer was not persuaded. Could anyone believe that a later generation would have put into Jesus' mouth words which were belied by the subsequent course of events? What, then, were the historical facts?

While the youthful theologian was pondering the problem, the kaiser stretched out his arm and drew him into the German army for his year of compulsory service. He was strong as an ox, and drilling for hours under a hot sun had no terrors for him. But he took a New Testament with him, and a copy of biblical commentaries.

Was there ever a conscript before, one wonders, who, after a day in the field pursuing an imaginary foe, kept awake at night asking himself searching theological questions? How could Jesus have led His disciples to expect events which never happened? Was it possible that Jesus had shared the popular delusion of the time that the Kingdom of God was coming in an apocalyptic convulsion of nature and man? Up and down the warm, green hills of Lower Alsace these queries pursued the conscript.

AT THE UNIVERSITY once more, Schweitzer had a wonderful time. Such exciting thoughts, shaking the foundations of belief, testing whether a man's faith had the stamina to maintain itself! Old Testament, New Testament, the church, dogma, ethics, practical theology.

With what radiance the great speculative philosophers, Kant, Fichte, Hegel, had filled a century! Eagerly Albert turned to their contemporary, Goethe, to see how they had affected Europe's great poet of the period. To his bewilderment he found that Goethe had not been affected at all. How was it possible that this titanic intellect should have remained within the aura of the ancient Stoics and let such original thought pass him by? Schweitzer went to the Stoics and found the answer. The Stoics had chosen to wrestle with the immediate issues troubling men's hearts—the meaning of life, the nature of the good. They had done it, moreover, in a way that was understandable to the ordinary mind. How straight to the mark the Stoic went in his thinking! How firmly he faced reality, even though it appalled him! The budding theologian could not escape the conviction that this simple kind of philosophizing was right. The important thing for the human creature was how to come to grips with the ordinary issues of life—sorrow and pain; marriage, children and death; the sense of individual littleness under the stars; the hunger for security; the humble minds seeking nothing vaster than merely to find out how to endure life or enlarge it and to discern whatever design there might be in its frustrations and raptures.

During his university years Albert also became one of a group of gifted students drawn to each other by a common love of nature and a proud faith that they were the forerunners of a new time. They covered a dozen fields, from social science to fine arts; each a specialist, yet able to talk intelligently in the others' domains. They went bicycling together, made music and wrestled with social and aesthetic problems.

The bicycle was the veritable magic carpet to the middle nineties. To wheel out of the city at dusk and look for wild iris along the Rhine was adventure, and to hide Easter eggs in some ruined castle rising out of the forest was enchantment. To Schweitzer the call of the green world was never-ceasing. "People call me a man of action," he wrote in his seventh decade, "but actually, at bottom, I am a dreamer."

And always, weaving like a golden thread throughout these days, his music. He studied theory under Ernest Münch, the brother of his music teacher in Mulhouse and organist at St. William's Church a few blocks from the university. Münch persuaded Strasbourg's civic orchestra to join him in performances of Bach's cantatas, calling on his prime pupil to play the organ at the rehearsals and occasionally even at the performances. Already Albert knew more about Bach than most of the organists in Strasbourg. One pompous gentleman played him a great Bach fugue. When he finished he turned patronizingly to the young student. "Now, boy, play that if you can!" Schweitzer took his place at the bench, shut the music book and played the fugue from end to end, by heart.

He supplemented his instruction at St. William's by trips to

Paris and stimulating hours with Widor and the organ in St. Sulpice. In Paris, too, he studied piano. He had two teachers, in fact. The two had no high opinion of each other, so Schweitzer, determined to get the best each had to give, shuttled between them, keeping each unaware that he was the pupil of the other.

Schweitzer also went to Stuttgart to hear the new organ in the Liederhalle, which he had heard acclaimed by musicians. Did it really represent a great step forward in organ building? He had noted with dismay that, here and there, fine old church organs were being "brought up-to-date" and ruined, or ripped out of churches and replaced by new instruments inferior in every respect except technical facility. Was something undermining men's standards?

The chaos of sound issuing harshly from the Stuttgart organ confirmed the misgivings which had haunted him. Organ building, like other fields of contemporary activity, was going backward. Why? He made up his mind to find the answer.

Similar fundamental questions were roused in him regarding the state of the world in which he had that year reached his twenty-first birthday. Everybody he met and all the books he read, summarizing the progress of the nineteenth century, took Western civilization for granted and assumed that it would go on indefinitely from triumph to triumph, but the young student was not convinced. No one seemed shocked anymore when governments and nations did things which a generation earlier would have seemed intolerable. Expediency was the new word on everybody's lips. Justice—the passion of the Enlightenment of the eighteenth century—seemed to have few friends, and these only lukewarm.

He was conscious of a peculiar intellectual and spiritual fatigue among the men who were directing the affairs of the world. "Our hopes for mankind were pitched too high," they seemed to be saying. "Practical men must concentrate on what they can reasonably expect to attain." He remembered that when he was a boy his elders had recognized the validity of youthful ideals, but he also remembered their unhappy conviction that man must make the best of life as he found it. Was the fatigue of this generation the result of that compromise? Or

442

"...actually
...I am a dreamer."

was the compromise itself the result of a fatigue which had set in even earlier?

Was this fatigue of the mind and spirit, in fact, a sign that Western civilization had run its course? Was this inspiring century of scientific achievement merely the last glow of the dying day? Schweitzer could accept no such fatalism. There was decadence, indeed; but decadence was not destiny.

SCHWEITZER'S STUDENT YEARS passed as happily as a summer vacation. Happiness! Once he had told himself you had to pay for it. You had to give something to those who had never had it. He thrust the idea from his mind. Why shouldn't he enjoy this? What loftier passion was there than the pursuit of beauty and truth?

"You must pay," said the voice in his heart.

"Pay? How?"

"In service to those who are starving, in body or soul, to those who are writhing in pain."

"Is not scholarship service? Is not art service?"

"The fortunate, the greatly blessed, are called to more immediate service, the service of the heart and of the hand. The simple, unheroic act, the day-in, day-out giving of yourself to people who cannot possibly compensate you."

"All this?"

"Is it too much?" the voice asked.

"No. It is not too much for what I have had."

In the parsonage at Günsbach one bright Whitsunday morning, Albert Schweitzer lay in bed listening to the birds singing in the first warmth of the new year. The lilacs shouting with scent, the young green almost covering the windows of the church. Who would not, at twenty-one, feel the heart throb with delicious joy? The rapture of living lifted him clear out of himself so that the voice he had fled from and sought to silence spoke as it had never spoken before. Into his consciousness leaped words that were familiar yet obscure: *He that loseth his life . . . shall find it.* "You must pay."

But how *did* one pay for such benefactions, so freely given? How . . . had . . . Jesus . . . paid?

A carpenter's shop till he was thirty. His skill with tools; the hills of Judea, sunrises, sunsets and the young moon; his friends. All these to enjoy until he was thirty; then service to God, and man, for as long a time as might be granted him.

Thirty. That meant nine years. And what then? What would be expected of him then? He would know when the time came. The main thing was never to let the resolution fail, the irrational fire be quenched. The rest was in God's hands.

NINE YEARS!

Examinations, theses and more examinations. A dissertation and a doctorate in theology. A doctorate in philosophy. And always organs: in remote country churches, in huge new concert halls. A traveling fellowship took the brilliant young scholar to Paris. He found the teaching methods of the Sorbonne antiquated. But Paris was Paris, though it was not to gaiety in Montmartre that Schweitzer gave his nights. The philosopher Kant had those. He got his relaxation at the organ under Widor's direction. The great organist now freely admitted that his pupil knew more about Bach than he did.

One day Widor confessed that the choral preludes baffled him. "Naturally many things in the chorales must seem obscure to you," Schweitzer answered, "since they can be explained only by the choral texts." As Schweitzer explained them, one after the other, the great organist began to recognize that he was meeting the real Bach for the first time.

"My friend," Widor told him earnestly, "for the sake of my colleagues of the organ in France, you must write down what you have said to me about Bach's choral preludes."

FROM PARIS SCHWEITZER went to Berlin to continue the study of philosophy at the university. The Alsatian liked the overgrown provincial town that Berlin was in the late nineties, liked its assurance, its music, its theaters, its intellectual life. But here, too, Schweitzer noted a sense of moral and spiritual fatigue. In Berlin the great new word was *Realpolitik*. It meant that you did what benefitted your country, without regard to principles or decency. In plain words, might made right.

What was the answer?

Schweitzer found it in the eighteenth century, the century of Bach, Kant, Goethe, Rousseau and Voltaire. How radiant with wisdom it had been! It had kept clear its perception of the large issue of human rights and the worth of the individual!

In Berlin Schweitzer also met many of the leading minds of the new Germany, the scholars and scientists, the artists and men of letters. One evening, through the din of general conversation, Schweitzer caught an exclamation of sharp disgust: *"Ach was! Wir sind ja doch alle nur Epigonen!"* "Pshaw! We are all of us nothing but inheritors of the past!" As Schweitzer walked home to his quarters that night the words kept ringing through his mind. Evidently this age in which he was living was not an advance but retrogression! A great civilization was relinquishing, in its pride of secondary achievements, the ethical principles on which its existence depended.

HE WOULD LIVE his own life, he had said, until he was thirty.

Three of the nine years had passed in study and thought and the joyous exercise of his gift for music. He established himself at the university and made a place for himself as curate at the Church of St. Nicholas and assistant to the two pious old gentlemen who were its regular pastors. The Sunday-afternoon services in the old church with the long slanting roof were his particular delight. He had a gift "of taking one's own immature thoughts," as one of his audience put it, "and carrying them farther than they knew how to go by themselves." The number of his listeners grew from Sunday to Sunday. But a complaint was registered against him: his sermons were too short!

Schweitzer deprecated his fault. "You see, I am a very young man and I have to stop when my ideas give out."

Three times a week he taught the boys' confirmation class. Characteristically, he played down dogma. The traditional beliefs were important, of course, but the word of Saint Paul still held: *Where the Spirit of the Lord is, there is liberty*. It was well to remember, moreover, that there were limits to what men could know in the field of religion, as in history; and to some questions—they might as well face it—there were no answers this side of infinity. That was where faith came in. His boys should not beware of reality corrupting their ideals, but rather should grow into their ideals, so that life could not take those ideals from them.

In addition to his work as a curate, his teaching, his research and his writing, he had administrative duties as warden of the theological college, which included, in his mind, personal relations with the young "theologs." If in spite of him they neglected their studies, he was a kindly spur. He worked with students coming up for examination to all hours of the night, not asking, "How much do you know?" but demonstrating to them how much they actually did know, so that a shy youth could gain assurance. He also wanted to help neglected or destitute children to an education and offered a portion of his official quarters for that purpose. But he found the German official mind incapable of grasping so novel a conception as voluntary cooperation. A government bureau was charged with such matters; that was all that was needed.

Since Schweitzer could not help waifs, he determined to do what he could for vagrants. Bicycling from one end of the city to the other to seek out some applicant for charity, he told himself it was sentimental nonsense for him to spend time in this fashion. But then he remembered that Goethe on one occasion put aside important work to seek out a friend in a distant town who was in spiritual need. Yes, you had to do more in life than study and preach. This had been made abundantly clear to him that Whitsunday morning eight years ago. But was it to vagrants that he was to render the "immediate service" to which he had been called? No, not vagrants. To whom then? The answer would come when the time was ripe. . . .

Meanwhile Johann Sebastian Bach went with him night and morning. The essay he had promised Widor was taking on unexpected proportions. If he were to say what must be said, he wrote Widor, he would have to do a full-length book. So much the better, Widor replied, enthusiastically. Schweitzer, up to his neck in historical studies, preaching, teaching and lecturing, took a deep breath and set to work.

In his room at the College of St. Thomas in Strasbourg,

Schweitzer was also pursuing the researches into the life of Jesus which had excited him during the first year at the university, questions reaching to the very heart of the Christian faith. His initial purpose was to destroy the compelling but, in his judgment, untrue conception of the story of Jesus with which the nineteenth-century theologians tried to make Jesus comprehensible to their time.

Schweitzer sought the Jesus of history as other men have sought an elusive mathematical formula or a new star. He studied all previous attempts to reconstruct the supreme story. What was legend, what was fact? Had Jesus actually been the gentle liberal the theological writers and sentimental painters of the age had depicted? Had he not, rather, been a fiery warrior, heralding the supernatural Kingdom of God? If the young scholar shrank from the affirmative answer, he gave no indication of it.

As he gathered the books he needed for each chapter, he piled them in various corners of his study, to the dismay of the housekeeper. Month after month, year after year, visitors to his quarters picked their way among the leaning, occasionally sprawling towers.

The man who, on a bright May morning, had resolved that at thirty he would give himself to the service of mankind was now twenty-eight. His exultation in preaching and teaching grew year by year. His historical studies and the idea of interpreting Bach excited him. To exchange ideas with his associates, to stride through the lovely rolling countryside and think his way into the book about civilization he intended someday to write—all this was unadulterated happiness. Asked forty years later whether the temptations to give up his high purpose had not been all but irresistible, he replied that there had been no temptations at all. He had been too busy to think about himself, and too happy.

But his joy had a somber undercurrent. He recognized that the world was full of suffering. Sympathy for the neglected peoples of the world was fed by everything he read of the white man's exploitation of the black in the Congo and by accounts of conditions in Africa given him by missionaries home on leave.

It was a dark record of white barbarism matching black. How could the European mind be so callous, calling it no concern of theirs? Only a few hundred doctors in all the vast colonial possessions of the great powers. Perhaps someday someone would rouse the Europeans from their apathy, someone who cared enough to offer his life to the cause.

Chapter IV

PHILOSOPHY, THEOLOGY, fellowship, talk. But excellent talker though he was, Schweitzer listened more than he talked, glad to sit humbly before great minds and personalities. In Paris he met Romain Rolland, the great novelist, playwright, poet, historian and biographer. A shy, seemingly detached figure, he was an internationalist, passionately seeking the integration of Europe by transcending national fears and prejudices. A pioneer, he stood alone. Those few aware of him scoffed at him.

The two men met as musicians, and found shortly that, beneath the artist in each, was a man of transcendent idealism. When in Rolland's drama King Louis IX says on his deathbed, "It is glorious to fight for the unattainable when the unattainable is God," he was speaking out of Schweitzer's own heart, as Schweitzer was to speak out of Rolland's when he wrote in his autobiography, "There are no heroes of action: only heroes of renunciation and suffering."

In Rolland's little attic, high above the rumbling trucks of the Boulevard Montparnasse, talking for hours, or, now one, now the other, letting his fingers roam over the piano, these dreamers of a fellowship wider than any national borders became friends. Self-reliant as Schweitzer was, it was heartening to him to find, in a generation intoxicated with materialistic success, a man possessed by a great ethical idea.

But if Rolland widened Schweitzer's international horizon, his friends in Strasbourg stimulated his social consciousness. A young man named Schwander had recently been appointed burgomaster—an official who combines the impressive character of a mayor with the political detachment of a city manager. Dr. Schwander was a new and brilliant type of German public servant. He called upon the high-minded elements in the city to take a hand in the work of its welfare agencies and persuaded Protestants and Catholics, workingmen and university professors to work together.

Among the group with whom Schweitzer bicycled, argued and made music, was Helene Bresslau, the daughter of a distinguished history professor. Talking with Schweitzer one day about his sermons, she expressed astonishment at having heard him use French sentence forms which were habitual in Alsatian daily speech but uncommon in formal addresses. Albert thereupon proposed that she go over his manuscripts with a critical eye. Discussions of form led to discussions of content, and deepening interest in each other's ideas. Both had set a terminal date beyond which they must take on responsibility for other lives than their own. Schweitzer had set his at age thirty; Helene had set hers at age twenty-five. She had already taken a teacher's degree and a nursing course, and was doing social work. Both young people recognized that they were obligated to God and their fellowmen to pass on to others the good that life had bestowed on them. They had a further bond in their search to find the particular field in which their gifts might be most usefully employed.

New horizons, new impulses, new visions. And always the old warm fellowship. The group bicycled through quaint Alsatian villages to secluded glades in the Black Forest where there was always a tavern serving coffee and butter cake. Occasionally they trooped to church to hear Schweitzer preach or to hear him play Bach.

It was against this background of human fellowship that Schweitzer carried on his theological research. He still challenged not only his scholarship and his imagination, but the deepest resources of his spirit as well. His researches were leading him to revolutionary conclusions. He knew that the only way that the popular myth of Jesus could be dispelled would be to present the historical figure of Him in such sharp outline that no myth could exist beside it. But what would his discoveries do to the Christian world? What if he brought confusion into the hearts of the devout? The question troubled but did not deter him. The pain of adjustment would be sharp for many; but let Christians face the fact that the world into which Jesus had been born was not the world of the twentieth century. Religious truth varies from age to age, but the religion of love is forever the same. What matter in what garments succeeding generations clothe it?

Besides his studies of the life of Jesus, the essay Schweitzer had contemplated on Johann Sebastian Bach had grown to a book of four hundred and fifty pages. Its publication stirred Bach enthusiasts throughout Europe, giving Bach's music, in the words of one critic, "the aspect of a new revelation."

NINE YEARS. By the fall of 1904 the ninth was almost spent. Though Albert's resolve was as sharp and clear as ever, he had no idea what form his "direct service to mankind" should take.

Then one day, when he was three months under thirty, he picked up a magazine of the Paris Missionary Society. He had a soft spot in his heart for the society. Had it not sent out the devoted missionary Casalis? His eye was caught by an article pointing out how starved for workers the French Congo was. The picture of savages tortured by superstition and pain came to life for Schweitzer in a blaze of revelation. When he closed the magazine, he knew at last what his direct service should be.

The man in the parable, *intending to build a tower, . . . counteth the cost, whether he have sufficient to finish it*. What were the essentials, Schweitzer asked himself, for carrying out his own resolution? Health he had abundantly, with sound nerves, energy, practical sense, toughness, prudence. As for personal wants, he had none that the jungle could not satisfy. And he had the temperament to bear possible failure. But one thing more. Had he any thought of heroism? If he had, the undertaking was wrong. Only a man with a sense of obligation, undertaken with sober enthusiasm, was capable of becoming the kind of "spiritual adventurer" the world needed.

To talk about the religion of love was not enough. The immediate need in the Congo was obviously not for another teacher or preacher but for a doctor. He must go there as a medical missionary. How long would it take to become a physician, a surgeon? Six years, perhaps seven? Well, he could face it.

Schweitzer did not immediately tell anyone of his decision. "I am by nature very uncommunicative as to everything which concerns my personal life," he explained in a private letter forty years later. He hated the implication of self-righteousness in so drastic a determination. So he said nothing, only quietly cleared the road for the beginning of his medical studies.

It was months before Schweitzer wrote his family and closest friends of his decision to go to Africa as a medical missionary. The news was a bombshell.

In Paris Rolland was noncommittal, while Widor scolded him: "You are like a general going into the firing line with a rifle." His father and mother did not pretend to understand, but they recognized that there must be a very deep reason behind their son's revolutionary decision, and they supported him with their faith.

His colleagues at the university and his other friends were less trusting. Had he, Albert Schweitzer, gone crazy? they asked. *Umsatteln*—to shift from one career to another—was then to most Germans the sign of instability of judgment. And to do it when he was more than halfway up the ladder! So to wreck what promised to be a great career!

"The waste of it!"

"Why bury yourself alive in the most neglected corner of the earth? Did not the Gospels have something to say about buried talents?"

Yes, Schweitzer said, but they had something to say also about losing your life in order to gain it.

"But is not scholarship service? Is not preaching service? Other men can work among the Africans, men without your gifts."

True. But not enough were doing it.

His friends called him a sentimentalist. "The nations who live in the bosom of nature are never so ill as we are, and do not feel pain so much."

He wondered.

"You are casting pearls before swine. Christianity is something too high for primitive man."

Most painful to Schweitzer were his encounters with men and

women who professed to be—and in most areas of their lives were—Christians. They were familiar with New Testament stories of lives turned radically from their courses in answer to the call of Christian love. Surely they must understand. It was torture to him to open his heart to the point of declaring the depths that had moved him to his decision; and all he received in return was incredulity, the charge of conceit and suspicion. Was he disappointed in the public recognition that had come to him? Had he been crossed in love? For weeks well-meaning colleagues battered him with arguments and probed his heart for hidden motives.

But twenty years later a French writer suggested possibly the chief reason for the opposition Schweitzer encountered: to accept the conceptions motivating Schweitzer obligated a man either to go and do likewise or to face the fact that he himself did not possess the love and courage required.

THUS LATE in October 1905 Schweitzer became a student again, to the disgust of the dean of the medical faculty, who was inclined to turn him over to the psychiatric department.

As a scholar and artist, the ordeal of finding his way into an understanding of the sciences taxed all of Albert's intellectual and physical stamina. Partly to support himself but also, one suspects, for deeper reasons, he continued to carry on all his former activities. He could not bear to give up his teaching at the university; his preaching, his research, his music. He would give them up only when he had to. One thinks of Augustine, pledged to godliness, yet clinging still to his Carthaginian mistress. "God, make me pure. But not yet!"

Night after night he studied the life of Jesus, and as he did, the true significance and power of Jesus began to dawn on him. If this world is to be worth living in, the individual must be transformed "by the personal rejection of the world," preached in the sayings of Jesus, and by his own determination not to let the hate, the lust and the greed of the world possess and direct his life.

As he worked, it seemed to Schweitzer that his own relation to the Jesus of history unfolded without any conscious reasoning of his own. Month by month the young man came to know Jesus not only as the protagonist of the world's supreme story of love and sacrifice, not even as history's greatest teacher and prophet, but as a Person having authority over him. The one thing Jesus had asked of His followers was that they prove themselves men who had been compelled by Him to leave behind the ego-centered and take up the God-centered life.

The long labor drew at last to a close. The final paragraph was under his hand:

> ". . . Follow thou Me!" . . . He commands. And to those who obey, be they wise or simple, He will reveal Himself through all they are privileged to experience in His fellowship of peace and activity, of struggle and suffering, till they come to know, as an inexpressible secret, who He is. . . .

The publication of what, in its English edition, would be called *The Quest of the Historical Jesus* stirred scarcely a ripple on the smooth current of German academic life. Schweitzer's personality was so disarming in its modesty and charm that none of his colleagues could bring themselves to recognize how revolutionary he really was. But in England scholars accepted his conclusions as authoritative and their enthusiastic comments began to be heard in Europe. Something cataclysmic was stirring in Christian theology! Pastors were shocked to learn that the historical Jesus must be regarded as capable of error. The confusion and pain among Christian believers was manifested in eloquent abuse of Schweitzer himself.

Schweitzer had no time to worry about this. The six years that he pursued his scientific and medical studies were a time of increasing and finally desperate fatigue, for he could not, even yet, bear to give up his parish work or his lectures, and he must give concerts to meet his living expenses. In his passion for music, his joy in teaching, his delight in the work of the mind, he seemed driven to crowd every atom of possible achievement into the time that was yet to be given him.

He published a pamphlet on organ building and organ playing. It made him Europe's chief authority on the organ and a storm center in a new field.

Nor could he give up his ten-year campaign to keep short-sighted men from scrapping magnificent old organs. He wrote letters by the hundreds to bishops, mayors, organ builders, organists. He pleaded before consistories and church committees: "Don't be seduced by the harsh new organs with their noisy confusion of sound! Get back to the clear-cut, tender tones of the old instruments of the eighteenth century."

He was laughed at and cold-shouldered, but the effort was worth the cost, since the struggle for the good organ was essentially a part of the everlasting struggle for truth.

As the years passed on the long journey to his medical degree, his fatigue became an octopus wrapping writhing arms about him. But the beauty of music and nature helped save him from collapse. On his infrequent holidays he would slip off to Günsbach and sit for hours in the woods listening to the birds and the wind, and return to his work with renewed energy. More often, he would wander into the Church of St. Nicholas, and climbing to the organ loft, let body and mind float blissfully on billows of sound.

There was a yet deeper source from which at intervals he drew fresh life. His path and Helene Bresslau's were drawing closer. Ever since he had reached his decision to study medicine and go to Africa they had had a tacit understanding that they would be going together. But they never talked about it, not even to each other.

Late in 1911 he passed his final medical examination. As he strode out of the examination room into the darkness of the winter evening, he was in a kind of daze, unable to grasp that the long ordeal was over. He still had a year's internship to serve and a thesis to write, but that seemed child's play.

Six months later Helene Bresslau and he were married. Since she would be working in a foreign land where recognized credentials were essential, Helene had taken a further nursing course, leading to the government certificate.

By the end of 1912 they were ready to start for Africa, but Schweitzer's superhuman exertions had taken their toll and he needed another six months to restore his energy. When, at last, he resigned from the theological faculty of the university, and from his post at St. Nicholas, it was as though he were tearing the heart out of his body.

Next, Schweitzer went to Paris to take a course in tropical medicine and get his credentials as a medical missionary. He did not ask the Paris Missionary Society for funds. He would not be trammeled by an organization. All he asked was a place to plant his hospital within the compound of the mission at Lambaréné in the colony of Gabon in French Equatorial Africa. The director of the society begged his committee not to miss this priceless opportunity to secure the doctor they had desperately prayed for. But the orthodox saw only that *M. le docteur* might be tempted to confuse the natives by his preaching. Let him appear before the committee and subject his beliefs to its scrutiny.

Schweitzer balked. Even a Mohammedan might be eligible for service, he said, so long as he relieved the suffering of the natives. The committee raised its hands in shocked dissent. Thereupon Schweitzer rang doorbells, calling on the individual members. He pledged his word that he would be a doctor and nothing but a doctor, remaining "mute as a fish" in matters of theology. The committee was mollified and, over the resignation of one irreconcilable member, finally agreed to give this radical a few acres of its hallowed precinct.

Back in Germany, Schweitzer faced the ordeal of raising funds for his hospital with characteristic self-forgetfulness, fortified by humor. But the presumption of asking support for a project which was still solely in the domain of hope weighed upon him: his friends gave, not because they believed in what he was doing but because they believed in him. Contributions came from St. Nicholas and from other parishes. Concerts here and there yielded heavily. Schweitzer took particular delight in the contributions to his fund provided by the royalties on the Bach book, now in English, French and German. In all, he gathered enough to operate the hospital for a year.

On Easter Sunday 1913, with his wife at his side, seventy cases of supplies in the hold, and all the bells of France pealing the gospel of the Resurrection, Albert Schweitzer set sail for Africa.

Chapter V

WHERE THE Ogowe River flows into the Gulf of Guinea, some seven hundred miles north of the Congo, Africa received them. A stern-wheeler bore them slowly up the wide stream flowing sluggishly between dark jungle walls. Water and wilderness, all that day and half the next. Sullen yellow water and dark green foliage, thickets aflame with bloom. Bright-feathered birds—parrots, butterfly finches, flycatchers and weaverbirds. A river? A river system, with branches intertwined like the creepers on the matted banks, and among them, lakes, dazzling in the sunlight.

The boat stopped at a village where the captain purchased logs for engine fuel—with alcohol as currency. They passed other villages—deserted. Why? A French trader at Schweitzer's side shrugged his shoulders. *L'alcohol.* . . .

Night. . . . Pain and fear filled the dark with their presence. The vessel grazed the jungle wall and the heat that came from it was almost unendurable. In a quiet bay the steamer anchored, waiting for daylight.

Dawn. . . . The paddle wheels churned the water once more. The river narrowed, the water moved more swiftly, the forest walls seemed to increase in height. The steamer stopped at another landing: N'Gomo, the nearest mission station to Lambaréné. Five hours later there rose ahead the green slopes the Doctor had traveled so far to reach. As the boat lay moored at the village, a long canoe, rowed by black boys with radiant faces, darted around its bow. Schweitzer and his wife slid into the hollow tree trunk, not too confidently. The paddlers stood, singing as they drove the canoe forward. After a half hour they turned up a side stream, beside green slopes rising on the right to a hill bathed in the warm glow of the late afternoon. The Doctor noted the small white buildings, each on its own elevation. The canoe slid safely into smooth waters. At a primitive landing white hands and black reached out.

Albert Schweitzer was at his post.

The Lambaréné Mission had been established almost forty

years earlier by an American medical missionary, and taken over by the Paris Missionary Society when Gabon became a French possession. Twenty yards back of the hilltops, crowned with the square white mission buildings, crouched the forest, huge and black, encroaching day and night upon the little area the missionaries had conquered for their flimsy, fern-thatched structures, their citrus trees and cocoa trees, mangoes and coffee bushes. At the foot of the hills was the ruthless river. The narrow area between the forest and the water was no place for the undisciplined spirit or the feeble will; nor, indeed, was any part of Gabon. Its flat lowlands and swamps, sluggish water and impenetrable forest were stiflingly hot. It had once been densely populated, but three hundred years of alcohol and the slave trade had disposed of most of the aborigines. The cannibal tribes which swarmed into the region from the interior had been prevented from eliminating the rest only by the guns of the white men who came for mahogany and other timber.

The situation of the mission was highly strategic for a hospital, since patients could be brought by water from hundreds of miles away. Schweitzer had been promised a building of corrugated iron for his use, but the timber trade absorbed all available labor along the Ogowe, and the framework had not been set up. Against all edicts issued by the mission, moreover, restricting applications for medical aid to the most serious cases, patients began to arrive in disconcerting numbers. They came not singly but in families.

Treating and bandaging the sick in the open before the little white bungalow which had been set aside for his wife and himself, Schweitzer learned something of the savage force of equatorial sunshine and equatorial rain. Since any shelter would be better than none, he transformed a henhouse into a hospital. His wife assisted with the operations. One of his patients, a tall, lean native who had been a cook and had acquired some knowledge of French and English, developed gifts both as an interpreter and an orderly. Having learned in the kitchen such anatomy as he knew, Joseph Azvawami provided comic relief in desperate moments by his references to a patient's "right leg of mutton" or "upper left cutlet."

"*Oganga*," the natives called the new doctor, meaning fetish-man, working magic with mysterious, shining tools. Anesthesia baffled them. "Since the Doctor came here," wrote a native girl in the mission school, "we have seen the most wonderful things happen. First of all, he kills the sick people; then he cures them, and after that he wakes them up again."

Such a man was good to have as your friend, but dangerous as your enemy. The man who could heal could, obviously, also cause disease. For was not all pain and disease caused by evil spirits? The Doctor began to see that pain was not the worst enemy he had to meet and somehow subdue. Fear lay over the jungle and was its very spirit; fear of a hundred subtle poisons in the hands of any man who might become possessed by the will to slay; fear of the evil fetish against which no counter-fetish is proof. Schweitzer must heal their disease but heal too their fear.

If the Doctor had had any qualms about "wasting" his energies in the African jungle, they would have evaporated during his first fortnight at Lambaréné. If he had had any illusions that, as some of his friends in Strasbourg had insisted, the natives did not feel pain as sensitized Europeans felt it, he would have buried them in shame. He was treating thirty or forty people a day—people suffering from malaria, heart disease, dysentery, elephantiasis, suppurating bone injuries and skin diseases of every description. He was left in no doubt regarding their pain.

"Here among us, everybody is sick," a young native said.

"Our country devours its own children," said an old chief.

Schweitzer decided that the site selected for his hospital was impractical, and journeyed by canoe to Samkita, a mission station thirty-five miles up the river, to attend a mission conference and to secure permission to use a more convenient location. The conference brought Schweitzer his first opportunity to note the quality of other French missionaries in the Ogowe area, so far from their native France, yet so content, so self-forgetful, so united. He stayed with them for a week and returned not only with permission to build his hospital where he wanted but with four thousand francs in cash.

Immediately he set to work. He hired the crew of a local

timber merchant who recognized that a hospital might have its uses, even for timber merchants. Schweitzer himself wielded a spade but failed to shame into activity the crew's foreman who lay in the shade contributing occasional encouraging words. When neither he nor the foreman was present no work was done at all. On one occasion Schweitzer blew up.

The natives remained unperturbed. "Don't shout," one protested. "It's your own fault. Stay here and we'll work, but when you are in the hospital with the sick, we are alone."

The Doctor's temperature might rise because time was precious, but he could not join the white merchants in their indignation at the laziness of the Negro. The Negro was a free man who refused to sell his birthright for a few pieces of silver he did not need, for he derived his shelter and his food from the bounty of nature. The eight-hour day and other conceptions of modern industry were as remote from his thinking as thermodynamics.

The laborers took their pay after two days and made for the nearest village. They returned blind-drunk, and Schweitzer—a theologian-musician-philosopher-surgeon—and his gifted ex-cook were left alone to convert a pile of lumber and corrugated iron into a hospital. Happily, the mission could spare two workers with experience as mechanics.

The rainy season was in full course before the building was completed in early November. It contained a consultation room and an operating theater, a sterilization room and a dispensary. The windows were wide and high, the floor cement, the roof of palm leaves held down with slender tree stems. Along a path leading from the hospital to the river, Schweitzer built— largely with his own hands—a waiting room and a dormitory made like native huts, of unhewn logs and raffia leaves, persuading the natives who brought and tended the patients to build the beds. Dried grass served for mattresses.

From the base of the hill on which the Doctor's bungalow stood, the primitive medical center looked over a body of dazzling water that was like a lake with green wooded banks. Behind the dormitory at the water's edge a magnificent mango tree provided welcome shade. Near it Joseph built a hut of his own.

"Our country devours
its own children."

Joseph was wholly justifying the title he had assumed of "first assistant to the doctor of Lambaréné." He spoke eight African dialects, in addition to French and English, and though he could not read or write, could identify any medicine by the look of the words on its label. He spent half the money he earned on clothes, neckties and shoes, and the Doctor smiled, noting how much better Joseph dressed than he did.

Teaching at the mission was a shy young African named Oyembo, to whom Schweitzer was instantly drawn. As a rule even a little education made the native swagger and pose as an intellectual, but "the song," for his name meant that, was kindly and unassuming, with a refinement that was reflected in his orderly home, his capable wife and their disciplined children. "I look upon him," Schweitzer wrote in a report to his European supporters, "as one of the finest men that I know anywhere."

He cherished not only the exceptional natives. Most of the common villagers were savagely primitive in their way of life, and the converts were frequently arrogant; but almost all thought about life, some with a depth that would have shamed the average white man. Schweitzer found that they were as curious about the habits and customs of the world from which he had come as he was about their own.

"What is different in the white man's country from what it is here?" they would ask.

They never tired of his answer: For one thing, there were forest fires where he came from. They could not imagine that. Even in the dry season the jungle was so damp that they could scarcely burn the logs they felled to establish new banana plantations. Another point of difference, the Doctor would go on, was that in Europe people rowed for pleasure.

His listeners fairly rocked with laughter at that. "Who orders them to row?"

"Nobody."

"But somebody must give them a present for doing it?"

"No, they do it of their own free will. Often they even row until they are quite exhausted."

They took the Doctor's word for it. But when he came to the third point of difference, they protested loudly that he was spoofing them. "In Europe a man can marry without having to pay for his wife." That was too much. Scarcely an adult male in the whole region was not paying installments on his wife and endlessly bickering with her relatives. Was it possible that anywhere in the world man was not exploited by his in-laws?

Day in, day out, the patients came with wives and families and friends. All he could do for some was to ease the final agony. He sent others home with boxes of medicine and instructions which he knew half would disregard. But many he raised from beds of suffering to active life and work.

Even with the help his valiant wife gave him the work was sometimes almost beyond enduring. The daily pressure now and again awakened the temper he had inherited from his mother. He never seemed to have enough time. Again and again his determination to make a diagnosis certain kept his eye glued to the microscope while twenty patients were waiting. He was, moreover, his own apothecary and his own commissary. Providing food for his patients and the friends who brought them taxed his ingenuity. He might issue an edict that he would give treatment to no one who did not bring so many bananas or cassava sticks. But if patients came without bringing contributions to the larder or had none to bring, he would take pity on their condition and devise some way to gather the provisions needed.

With all this he must always be ready for emergency operations. He was the only doctor within a radius of hundreds of miles. What was weariness when he could lay his hand on the forehead of a man tortured with pain, and say with assurance, "Don't be afraid, you shall be put to sleep and when you wake up you won't feel any more pain."

Music helped him maintain his spiritual balance. One day a metal-lined case was borne on the shoulders of a dozen natives up the hill to the Doctor's little house. It contained a piano built for the tropics—an upright with organ-pedal attachments—the gift of the Paris Bach Society. For months Schweitzer did not dare do more than let his fingers roam casually over the keys. Music was one of the delights he had renounced. But one twilight as, tired and homesick, he was playing a Bach organ fugue, he thought, What, after all, was wrong in using such free hours as he could find to perfect his technique, to deepen his understanding of great organ music? The thought made his heart beat faster. "I have a passion for music," he once told an English friend, "like other men's passion for tobacco or wine."

In the quiet hours he was able to spend with his favorite masters, he learned much that had escaped him in the rush of life at Strasbourg. There might be pressure in the hospital, but there was no concert to prepare for, no train to catch for Dresden or Paris. He might salvage only a half hour out of the day, but that half hour he could spend on a single passage if he wanted, a single bar. There were compensations in the jungle.

And the greatest was the opportunity to give the Christian message to men and women for whom it still held the excitement of fresh discovery. He had promised in Paris he would be "mute as a fish" in Africa, but his mission associates released him from his promise. They did not share the fears of the orthodox concerning the inner peace of the African native. Dogma did not matter in the jungle. What mattered was the life and basic teachings of Jesus. The missionaries were too busy trying to learn from each other how to develop in their districts some approximation of Christian living.

So Schweitzer was encouraged to give the natives the message of Jesus one day a week with his lips as he was already giving it seven days a week with his life.

CARPENTER, BUILDER, physician, preacher and judge.

In the hospital compound Schweitzer himself administered justice on the pattern of Solomon. Hearing an altercation on the riverbank, he discovered that one of the natives had borrowed another's canoe the night before without a by-your-leave and had gone fishing. The owner of the canoe claimed his haul.

The Doctor heard the complaint and the defense and established the fact that both men were in the right and both in the wrong. "You are in the right," he said to the owner of the canoe, "because the other man ought to have asked for permission to use your boat. But you are in the wrong because you were careless, merely twisting the chain of the canoe around a palm tree instead of fastening it with a padlock as we all do here. Your carelessness led this other man into temptation. You are guilty of laziness besides, being asleep in your hut instead of taking advantage of the moonlight night for fishing."

He turned to the other. "You were in the wrong when you took the boat without permission. You were in the right because you were not so lazy as he was."

Thereupon Schweitzer pronounced sentence: The man who went fishing was to give one third of the catch to the owner of the canoe and keep one third. The remaining third the Doctor claimed for the hospital, because the affair had taken place on its land and he had had to waste his time adjusting it.

THE TRADITIONAL CALENDAR lost its meaning along the Ogowe when January was hotter than July and your feet were like weights at any time of year. The Doctor himself needed a doctor and took the little stern-wheeler downriver to Cape Lopez to have a military surgeon deal with an abscess. For four days, with his wife beside him, he luxuriated on a veranda overlooking the Atlantic, drinking in the cool, salt breezes. He used the enforced idleness to write an account of the lumbermen and raftsmen of the forest. He wanted his friends and supporters to know all about this land whose people they were salvaging.

At intervals in his work the Doctor and his wife talked hopefully of a visit home. There were families and friends to see, and it was a law of the tropics that white men and women return north for a few months every second year, if they wanted to keep their health. Moreover, he could raise money now with an assurance which had been impossible while the hospital was still no more than a plan. He had pictures to show, stories to tell.

Two days after the Doctor and his wife returned to the mission on August 2, 1914, Schweitzer received a note from the white trader at the village of Lambaréné. "In Europe they are mobilizing and probably already at war."

Schweitzer had had no word from Europe for a month; he knew nothing of the tragic tangle of ultimatums and counter-ultimatums which had filled the last week of July. But the long lash of war struck him that very day. He was a German subject, living in a French colony. He and his wife were told that they must regard themselves as prisoners of war. They might remain in their own house, but must not communicate with either the natives or the Europeans at the mission, and must obey unquestioningly the orders of the black soldiers set to watch over them.

The hospital? *C'est la guerre.* A colonial bureaucracy shrugged its shoulders. Schweitzer found himself at his desk in the morning for the first time since he had begun his medical studies. If the world were intent on going crazy, there was no reason why he should not complete his book on the Apostle Paul. But he found he could not concentrate. His mind was in Günsbach with his father and mother; in Strasbourg with his friends and former teachers; in his enchanted Vosges where young men would soon be charging through the quiet fields to die. His mind was in Paris with Widor and Rolland and a dozen other beloved friends. How many of them were now confronting one another as enemies!

Then one day a native presented a note from the local French administrator. Since the bearer was sick the Doctor might prescribe for him. Other men came bearing other notes. The administrator was recognizing that common sense had its claims. In Paris, meanwhile, Widor was doing what he could to inject reason into a war-harried Colonial Office. The district commandant received orders from the Colonial Office that Monsieur Schweitzer was no longer regarded as a menace and informed the Doctor that he might as well return to his hospital.

Nineteen fourteen ended. Life went on in the hospital, but it seemed to Schweitzer that wherever he went he heard the wounded and the dying in the valleys of France and the forests of Russia.

When the news went around that ten of the whites who had gone home in answer to the mobilization call had been killed, an old native exclaimed, "Ten men killed already in this war! Why don't the tribes meet for a palaver? How can they pay for all these dead men?" It seemed that in the native fighting all who fell in a war, whether vanquished or victors, had to be paid for by the other side.

The natives also asked a simple, penetrating question: How was it possible that the white men who had brought them the gospel of Love should be at each other's throats?

Schweitzer had no answer. Mankind was face to face with something "terrible and incomprehensible," he would say. He thanked God every morning, as he strode down the hill to the hospital, that it was given to him to save life rather than destroy it.

Shortly, the French colonial armies needed porters, and war came close along the jungle trails. Schweitzer saw a company of impressed carriers being taken away by boat, and ached, hearing the wailing of their women at the dock. On the riverbank an old woman whose son had been taken sat weeping silently. The Doctor tried to comfort her, but she seemed not to hear; and then he too was weeping, with the setting sun in his eyes.

In Europe the armies thrust forward, drew back and thrust again. At Lambaréné the rains undermined the hospital so that the Doctor was forced to construct retaining walls and gutters; the termites got into the supplies; the traveler ants, on the march, presented a drama of ruthless militarism second only to what Europe was demonstrating. Food became scarce and the Schweitzers had to learn to like monkey flesh. "People may think what they like about Darwinism and the descent of man," Schweitzer wrote in a letter home, "but the prejudice against monkey flesh is not so easily got rid of."

Death and destruction. . . . What did it matter what he ate? A great civilization was crumbling before men's eyes. A civilization that Socrates, Jesus, Paul, Augustine, Saint Thomas Aquinas had helped to build. A generation which had pinned its faith on the power of progress, which had been so sure that ethical ideals were out of date, was hearing from history. Schweitzer would write a book pointing out what would happen if men persisted in building houses on sand. *Would* happen? The house built on the sand had already collapsed. All he could do now was to analyze the folly of the builders and the nature of the sand.

But what was he doing, rehearsing the reasons for downfall and decay? Hindsight was easy. Was there not something bigger that he should be doing? Why not move from the study of the decay of civilization to the promise of its revitalization?

Night by night, when the last patient had been bandaged and he had had his supper in the little house on the hill, the jungle doctor groped through the tangled wilderness of thought. What was the approach to life on which Western man's hunger for a more satisfying world and his belief in ethical principles alike were founded? Was it not this—that he accepts life as worth living, and accepts the world as worth the effort to live in it? What had blighted this high ardor? Schweitzer asked. How had it happened that a philosophy of life which had led men from triumph to triumph had lost its ethical content and was tragically adrift? Could one find one's way to an idea which should embrace both ethics and that faith in life which impelled men to action and progress? The aspiration became a determination, the determination an obsession. Schweitzer could think of nothing else. It was in his mind as he examined his patients, as he bent over his microscope, bandaged sores, operated.

He carried his impassioned queries downriver to Cape Lopez, for he and his wife were beginning to feel the effects of the climate. A white timber trader had offered them his house; they lived on herrings which the Doctor fished from the estuary, and felt the lassitude of the jungle give way before the soft air blowing across the long Atlantic combers. Even in this paradise of wide blue waters and darkly wooded shores, Schweitzer was still pursued by the query: What is it that ethics and the affirmation of life and the world have in common?

While he was pondering this the Doctor received a call to N'Gomo, about a hundred and sixty miles upriver, to attend the wife of one of the missionaries. The captain of a small steamer gave him space on the already overladen barge he was towing. As the steamer crept slowly upstream, Schweitzer sat on the barge's deck lost in thought. To keep his mind concentrated, he scrawled on paper from time to time isolated words, phrases, disconnected sentences. All one day he sat thus, and all the next. At sunset on the third day, as the boats were making

"...an indescribable
sympathy"

their way upstream, the phrase "reverence for life" flashed at him from the paper in his hand.

He had found the conception common to ethics and to that affirmation of life and the world which was the dynamic of progress. Civilization, then, did not rest upon a beautiful sentiment, a tradition, which was at the mercy of any skeptic. It rested upon an idea.

Reverence for life!

Chapter VI

DECEMBER 1915. The second Christmas of the war arrived. Belatedly, European newspapers came and seemed irrelevant in the jungle, where the Doctor labored to save life; life which seemed to have no significance except that it *was* life and therefore precious in whatever body it throbbed. One day the war hit the Doctor himself with ruthless savagery. News came that his mother had been trampled to death by cavalry in the village of Günsbach.

Nineteen sixteen, nineteen seventeen. At Lambaréné the Doctor worked on. In Europe his friends, taxed into penury, failed to renew their subscriptions to his work. Yet the patients came in ever-increasing numbers. He was forced to borrow from the missionary society in Paris to keep his hospital in supplies, and wondered darkly through anxious nights how, if ever, he would be able to pay this obligation. Yet was not a life, was not an hour of agony relieved, worth any risk?

The Schweitzers had been in Lambaréné four and a half years when orders came that they were forthwith to be taken to France to be interned as prisoners of war. Schweitzer made no complaint, then or later. With the help of the missionaries and a few natives, he and his wife stowed away their personal belongings, the piano-organ, the surgical instruments and the drugs, and after three days of frantic preparations, embarked. For the first time since Schweitzer's boyhood, the direction of his life was out of his hands.

In the barracks at Bordeaux, in France, the Doctor, who had

never been sick in his life, developed dysentery. He was still in a weakened state when he and his wife were packed off in the night to an internment camp at Garaison in the Pyrenees.

Through a long cold winter they lived in an abandoned monastery, with an aggregation of the homeless—bank managers, cooks, waiters, architects, musicians, tailors, artists, engineers, shoemakers and priests. Schweitzer was elected an honorary member of a gypsy orchestra, and generous and outgoing, he was shortly camp doctor. With practically no books at his disposal, he satisfied his thirst for knowledge by systematically pumping his fellow prisoners in fields new to him. Every day, on a plank marked as an organ keyboard, and on imaginary pedals on the floor, he memorized Bach or Widor. He sketched the outline of the final volume of his work on the decay and restoration of civilization.

The clear crisp air of the Pyrenees restored to Helene much of the strength Equatorial Africa had drained, but the Doctor himself failed to respond. His attack of dysentery had left a languor which deepened as the months passed. The transfer of the prisoners to another abandoned monastery, not far from Arles, was a blow to the Schweitzers. In a room immortalized by the painter Van Gogh, who had been confined there shortly before his death, they suffered from the bleak winds and the stone floors. Schweitzer's weakened body burned with fever.

In midsummer they were exchanged, and went home via Switzerland. Nothing had prepared them for the thrill of finding a half-dozen friends waiting for them at the railroad station at Zurich, nor for the pang of seeing at Constance, after they crossed the German border, the pale, emaciated faces of men, women and children, undernourished through four years of war. Strasbourg was under a blackout. Schweitzer could scarcely find his way in the night through the dear, familiar streets he had returned to so often in imagination these past five years.

Günsbach was in the front lines, under fire much of the time and, feeble as he was, Schweitzer had to cover the final ten miles there on foot. He found his father vigorous, and defiant of gunfire. His mother was in every room, a living, heartbreaking presence. The hills and valleys he had loved as long as he could remember were devastated, the enchanted beechwoods of his boyhood were wildernesses of broken, blackened trunks. Old friends were dead, one or two by their own hands.

Even years after, Schweitzer would not talk of his war experiences. "They were part of the madness of the world," he told a Quaker friend. "We must forget that time of hate and fear."

Nineteen eighteen. The armistice was signed; the war was over. But in the manse at Günsbach Schweitzer tossed in his bed with mounting fever and pain. He recognized the symptoms. An immediate operation was necessary.

The prospect that lay before him through the long weeks of convalescence in the hospital in Strasbourg was not such as to hasten his recovery. His health was broken; his hospital ruined. He had no income; only huge debts owed to the missionary society and to personal friends. He did not know how he would earn enough to support his wife and the little girl who had been born on his own birthday two months after the armistice. He might, of course, teach again; but no one knew what would become of the university now that Strasbourg was once more to be French.

His friend the burgomaster, the same Dr. Schwander who had done so much to awaken social consciousness in Strasbourg, asked him to serve on the staff of the municipal hospital, and the Church of St. Nicholas invited him to resume his post of curate and live in the parsonage. He accepted both offers. They met his immediate needs, but they did not relieve the sense of impotence which possessed him. He had staked everything he had on a great dream and had lost. It was scant solace to know that the loss was no fault of his. He had hoped not only to relieve some of the misery of the stepchildren of the world but to stir the imagination and rouse the conscience of mankind. He had failed. The jungle would have his hospital, the natives would sink back into the old patterns of suffering and fear.

Schweitzer's activities in the hospital and at St. Nicholas reminded him at every turn of the exuberant, fruitful years preceding his departure for Africa. What joy in work, what aspiration, what hope! All that was over. Even among the learned he felt he was no more than a ghost from the past.

The necessity for a second operation, and the operation itself a year after his return home, deepened his sense of fellowship with all who suffered. What a bond pain was! An idea took possession of him—*the fellowship of those who bear the mark of pain*. A great, unorganized world company; every man, woman or child who has known pain, committed, while life endures, to relieve pain. He became a familiar figure to German customs officials, carrying rucksacks full of food to friends weak with hunger in Germany.

The fellowship of those who bear the mark of pain!

Then, late in 1919, the Orféo Català of Barcelona invited him to play the organ at a concert. The world of art seemed still to have a place for him.

Even among the learned he was not as forgotten as he supposed. In Sweden a distinguished philosopher and ecclesiastic, Archbishop Nathan Söderblom, remembered a young scholar's pursuit of the historical Jesus and his studies on Saint Paul, and made inquiries as to what had happened to Albert Schweitzer. No one seemed to know. However, the archbishop was a man of action. He communicated with the archbishop of Canterbury in England.

Schweitzer did not dream of the stir he had caused in the highest ecclesiastical circles. One evening, just before Christmas, he returned to find an impressive-looking envelope awaiting him. It contained a letter from Archbishop Söderblom inviting him to deliver a course of lectures in the field of ethics at the University of Uppsala. Tears blurred the Doctor's eyes as he read. So he was not completely forgotten! And to have Söderblom want him to speak, Söderblom, whose influence on his own thinking he had long acknowledged!

Schweitzer was a tired, sick man when, in April 1920, he and his wife arrived in Uppsala. The Söderbloms—ten of them besides the archbishop and his wife—enveloped them in their warm family life. The big, handsome primate spoke French and German fluently, and proved to have a sense of humor and a mind that worked like a well-oiled engine.

Schweitzer's Uppsala lectures dealt with the affirmation of life and the world, in relation to ethics, and his audiences gave him a response which warmed his heart. When, in the final lecture, he presented the fundamental ideas of "reverence for life," the reaction of his hearers was so electric that Schweitzer was barely able to overcome his emotion and complete his address.

He had spoken from the depths of his being, and there were people who cared! He had presented thoughts he had been led to believe were hopelessly out of key with the spirit of the age, and thus doomed to be scoffed at. But these leaders of the intellectual and religious life of Sweden had acclaimed them.

Schweitzer began to get well.

The archbishop had a personal part in that process. A singularly engaging personality, he was not likely to remain unaware that his guest still had something on his mind. On a walk in the rain, touching shoulders under a single umbrella, the archbishop asked discreet questions and discovered that the Doctor was sicker in his heart than he ever had been in his body. His debts, the appeals that were coming to him from Lambaréné, the recognition that he might never be in a position to reestablish his African work, all this was weighing on him like a mountain.

"Look here," said the archbishop, "we may be able to do something there. Sweden has made a lot of money during the war. Why not give organ recitals and lectures on your African work? If we manage things right you ought to get enough to pay a large part of your debts."

The archbishop was not one to hatch an idea and trust it to the ravens. Night after night he sat down with Schweitzer, working on his itinerary and writing letters of introduction to bishops, deacons, organists and friends. He also tipped off a publisher that this jungle doctor had a great story in him.

The middle of May Schweitzer began his tour. It took him through all the major cities of Sweden as well as the remote parishes. He spoke of the needs of the African natives, the guilt of the white race, the opportunity to make restitution; he spoke of "the fellowship of those who bear the mark of pain."

The public flocked to hear. Missions were nothing new to the Swedes, but never had such a mind, such a spirit, presented so glowingly the duty that lay on Western civilization to do something about the children of the African night.

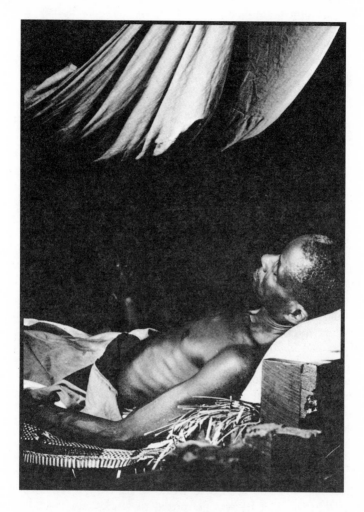

"...the fellowship
of those who bear the
mark of pain."

Playing Bach and Mendelssohn and César Franck, Schweitzer roused one congregation after another to the beauty of the organs they had been ready to scrap. By the time he ended his six weeks' journey, two movements were taking form—one for an association of the friends of Lambaréné, the other for the safeguarding of the public taste in organs.

Schweitzer returned to Strasbourg a new man. Sweden had given him back his assurance, welcomed his ideas and poured into his hands enough to pay his most pressing debts. Sweden had also given him the courage to think of reopening his hospital at Lambaréné. There were people in the world who cared! That was all he needed to know. He could begin again, rebuilding what was destroyed.

As a first step toward Lambaréné, he wrote the book of African reminiscences which the Uppsala firm had asked for. *On the Edge of the Primeval Forest* appeared in Swedish and German the following year and in English shortly after, creating a widening company of friends and supporters. And it brought its author royalties.

But the tropical climate had borne heavily on his wife. He could not ask her to return to Africa, or to bring their child. In the interludes of quiet permitted them on their tour, the Doctor and his gallant partner faced the issues and came to a decision. Schweitzer must return to Lambaréné, but he must go alone. The decision was costly for both, costliest, the Doctor recognized, for the woman who would be waiting year after year in Europe, bringing up their child without a husband at her side. "I have never ceased to be grateful," he wrote years later, "for the fact that she sacrificed herself... [for] Lambaréné."

Schweitzer resigned his posts in Strasbourg and moved with his wife and child to the Günsbach parsonage, where he could have the quiet he needed to work on his trilogy, *Philosophy of Civilization*. But he was permitted to work only sporadically. He gave recitals in many of the great churches of England and the Continent. He was called to lecture in Switzerland, Copenhagen, Prague, and a second time in Sweden. And everywhere Schweitzer found occasion to talk in behalf of his hospital; and wherever he talked he made friends, roused men's consciences.

Like some prophet out of the wilderness, aflame with vision, he preached of Africa. "Who can describe the injustice and the cruelties that in the course of centuries they have suffered at the hands of the Europeans? . . . We are not free to confer benefits on these men, or not, as we please; it is our duty. Anything we give them is not benevolence but atonement."

He had been back in Europe almost four years before he realized what had happened in his life.

When eighteen years before he had made up his mind to work in Africa, he had consciously accepted the renunciations which such work seemed inevitably to entail. Now what he had renounced was being given back to him in greater measure. Had he surrendered the joy of the organ? He was playing in many more countries now! Had he renounced university teaching? He had taught at a single university; now he was teaching at a dozen! Had he renounced his financial independence? He had it back to a degree he could barely have imagined a decade before!

He that loseth his life . . . shall find it.

IN THE INTERVALS of his tours across Europe, Schweitzer established a new base for himself and his family in the Black Forest. Here at Königsfeld, as his lecture and concert tours permitted, he pushed forward his history of civilization, writing it for the ordinary man who thought, or might be persuaded to think.

Men talked lightly of the death of civilization as though there were another ready to take its place. But Europe was sick, the whole world was sick.

"It is clear now to everyone," Schweitzer wrote, "that the suicide of civilization is in progress. What yet remains of it is no longer safe. . . . The problems involved in salvaging civilization . . . are in the last resort to be solved only by an inner change of character. . . . The only conceivable way of bringing about a reconstruction of our world on new lines is first of all to become new men ourselves. . . ."

Page by page Schweitzer hammered out his relentless truths. He corrected the proofs of the second volume of his trilogy, *Civilization and Ethics*, as he was packing supplies for a new beginning at Lambaréné.

Chapter VII

ONCE MORE the long voyage south, accompanied, alas, not by his wife, but by a young Oxford student of chemistry, Noel Gillespie. Once more the mile-wide estuary of the Ogowe, the stern-wheeler, shabbier than ever, the slow journey inland; once more the green slopes of Lambaréné, the outstretched hands, white and black.

To be back again after seven years—and such years!—that was much. But to come back—to this! He went over the familiar scene as though in a nightmare. He had underrated the efficiency of the armies of decay and the rapacity of the jungle. The little medical center lay buried in brushwood and overarching trees. The path up to the slope to what had been his home was so overgrown that he could scarcely trace its windings.

The Doctor faced the desolation and, characteristically, felt the impulse to wring a blessing from it. He would build a bigger hospital on a larger area, where there would be room to expand. He knew the exact site, less than two miles up the river. A village had once stood there. The ground had been cultivated, and the forest was therefore young and not too difficult to clear.

But the labor problem was as bad as ever. The timber trade was booming again and every man who could work was felling the great trees or helping to pilot the lumber rafts to the sea. What folly to think of building a new hospital when he scarcely knew whether he could repair the old!

The missionaries at the station had done what they could to keep the palm-leaf roofs intact but had finally given up a year before. No tiles of woven foliage were to be had. Three hours after his arrival he was in a canoe with his youthful companion, being paddled to a distant village to find tiles. He greeted old friends, begged, cajoled, flattered. He even threatened: not another sick man would he receive from that village unless tiles were forthcoming.

The natives smiled, not taking "our Doctor's" threats too seriously. But, when the white men turned homeward through the late afternoon deluge, they had forty-six tiles in the canoe.

The sick began arriving next morning and with them, happily, a half-dozen laborers, supplied by a native merchant. Two weeks of watchful supervision on young Noel's part, and the apothecary and the room for the examination of patients were usable. But the roof of the hospital itself was still open to the storms. Many of the patients were drenched nightly, and caught cold. In an agony of despair the Doctor saw two of them die.

Afternoon after afternoon Schweitzer went from village to village begging leaf tiles. He was called to restore life to a newborn baby, and exacted a promise of five hundred tiles if he succeeded, feeling like a dog as he did it. Leaf tiles had become an obsession. On them might depend the whole future of the hospital. Up and down the river they were clamoring for the Doctor's healing touch—lepers, sufferers from sleeping sickness, children covered with sores. He offered his medicines and injections for a price—leaf tiles, or bananas to keep the patients fed. No leaf tile or banana, no cure. But in the presence of a pitiful mother he weakened, bearing even chieftains no ill will if they failed to produce the five hundred tiles they had promised in return for healing.

Somehow, the hospital roof was patched. The Doctor was eagerly starting work on a new building when his laborers quit. Their contract with the lumberman was up, they wanted to go home; and no amount of money would persuade them to stay. The Doctor was forced to utilize such volunteers as he could raise from among those who had come to the hospital accompanying sick relatives or friends. He never knew from day to day how many there would be, and for days no work would be done. He himself had to serve as foreman, with the job of summoning his reluctant laborers in the mornings by flattery and the promise of food and presents, and keeping them at work when their energy flagged.

He did it generally with a laugh, accompanied occasionally by a little discreet pressure. There was the time, for instance, when his men were patching a roof and decided at noon that they had had enough of it for the day. The Doctor beamed up at them. "You're not coming down from that roof until you have finished the job, even if you have to spend the night." There-upon he went off with the ladder. The men took it in good humor and fell to, and were rewarded with an extra portion of rice, bananas and dried fish when night fell on a sound roof.

The Doctor had to send a canoe twenty miles for the fiber to fasten the tiles to the roof. He had no sizable canoe himself and had to beg or borrow one from a neighbor; but too often when he had secured the canoe, he had no men to send for the bamboo, and when he had the men, he had no canoe. And only for three weeks in the spring when the water was high was the bamboo accessible.

He developed sores on his feet so that he could not wear shoes, and had to hobble painfully about in such wooden sabots as the villagers in Günsbach had worn in his boyhood. He needed bricks for foundations and walls and, lacking any native willing to make them, set to work himself. Here, too, time was a factor, since only two months in the dry season were free of rain for the drying of the bricks. The Doctor's call for helpers impelled every available native to go fishing. Along the river ran the word: "Keep away from the Lambaréné doctor. He is oppressing the people in order to get bricks."

Schweitzer was not one to give up anything he had decided to do. But he found that he had to fight against the white man's most insidious temptation in dealing with the natives: the temptation to get hard. To rule with the whip, figuratively or literally, created more problems than it solved. Yet to assume an equality which did not exist had no better results. There was only one basis of real authority, Schweitzer found. To keep yourself humane: that was the perpetual challenge.

With all its complications and delays, the rebuilding program was moving forward.

But as the months passed and the work of reconstruction went on, fatigue, such as he had known only in the later years of his medical course, seized the Doctor. It was also one of the great disappointments of his return to Lambaréné to find that his mission friend, Oyembo, had apparently gone the way of self-seeking, had given up teaching and was deep in the lumber trade. The Doctor had had high hopes for the shy, sensitive little man and felt so badly about his black friend that he could not bring himself to ask the missionaries about him. He learned the truth only after years. Oyembo had merely ceased teaching children; but he was educating his whole village, establishing new plantations, building a school and setting up a thriving cooperative lumber business.

Yet now there was so much to do and no time to do it. The advent of a trained nurse from Strasbourg was a help, but he needed a doctor even more. He suffered, recognizing how superficial his examinations of patients had become. The microscope, too often neglected, seemed to eye him reproachfully. "Why didn't you ask me? I could have told you." His gorge rose at the consciousness of doing slipshod work. Not another day could he bear the double load of physician and builder. . . .

He heard the whistle of the river steamer and leaped into a canoe. On the deck a tall young man called to him, and a minute later a strong hand clasped his own. "You are going to get a rest now," the son of a friend of his medical school days in Strasbourg was saying. "I'm going to do everything."

"Good!" Schweitzer cried exultantly. "You can begin by getting your baggage into the canoes."

He had an assistant at last, and was so filled with the realization that, on the slow trip up the river, he could scarcely speak. The blessed luxury of being able to admit to yourself how deadly tired you really are!

Everything became different with Dr. Nessmann at his side. The young man seemed made for Africa, with his practical sense, his humor, his gift for organization, his skill with the natives. Help in other forms came also—a second nurse from Alsace, another doctor, this time from Switzerland; and, of all God's gifts the most welcome, a carpenter who had read of the Doctor's troubles and decided to volunteer his services. He sent no word; he came. Schweitzer set him to work on a ten-room house he had been dreaming of.

He was seeing light at last. The hospital would soon be restored. He could at last get back to his volume on Saint Paul that he had been working on sporadically for over twenty years.

But nature and human nature together interposed. Patients

came flooding into Lambaréné as never before. Many were homeless migrants from the interior, sucked into the lower Ogowe region by the decline of the local population and the needs of the timber industry. Schweitzer saw them come with a heavy heart, for their coming meant famine in the interior, where their labor was needed to cultivate plantations, and famine in the Ogowe country, where they raised nothing and only helped consume the dangerously low stocks of food.

They came to him suffering from malaria and dysentery and foot ulcers such as no mind unacquainted with the tropics could imagine. Schweitzer felt "an indescribable sympathy" for them in their misery, mingled with despair. Time and rules meant nothing to them. The simplest regulations could not, in fact, even be communicated, for where, in the early days, only two languages were spoken in the hospital, there were now ten. But Schweitzer had not been in Africa so many years without learning to communicate without words. He never forgot that the native fetishman also professed to heal and that in the mind of the patient he must out-magic the magician. Dr. Nessmann noted how the Doctor occasionally took on the manner of a sorcerer, looking slyly at the black nurse who acted as interpreter, as he devised elaborate ruses to persuade the black man that the worm, Pain, was being exorcised.

But nothing could make the Doctor forget that these people were his brothers and sisters. He would sit all night at a bedside or have himself waked every two or three hours to look after a sick man. Something went out of him every time a black body was wrapped in linen and palm leaves and lowered to its final resting place in the forest graveyard.

The famine of the interior spread into the Ogowe region and became desperate when a ship, laden with rice, was shipwrecked.

Schweitzer collected what rice was available and spent sleepless nights wondering how, in case he were forced to close the hospital, he would ever get his patients home to their villages. Meanwhile, an epidemic of dysentery developed. His helpers were forced to carry out a never-ending battle to keep dysentery patients from spreading pollution. The natives would not observe the hospital rules, slipping surreptitiously out of bed in the dark to drink the polluted river water rather than walk a hundred feet to the unpolluted spring.

If only he had a contagious ward, groaned the Doctor, where he could isolate the dysentery patients! He tried to lead them with such laughter as remained in him, but one day his overstrained patience finally cracked. He threw himself into a chair. "What a blockhead I was," he exclaimed, "to come out here to savages like these!"

"Yes, Doctor," remarked his faithful black assistant, Joseph, "here on earth you are a great blockhead, but not in heaven!"

The famine and the dysentery deepened the conviction that had come to Schweitzer that he must move the hospital to a site that would give him space to expand and land to raise crops. He must have an isolated unit for contagious cases, cells for the insane; above all, general wards that were better than stifling black holes. It was characteristic of him that he shared his conviction with no one, but went time after time alone to the place he had picked a year and a half ago on his return to Lambaréné.

If he could wave a wand and move the hospital! But the labor would be prodigious and he would have to supervise every detail. Besides, he had told his wife he would be back in Europe in two years! If he moved the hospital it would be three, at least. . . .

With a heavy heart, he made his decision and applied to the district commissioner for the right to utilize some hundred and seventy acres. Then he gathered his little staff and told them what was to be. There was a minute of dumb stupefaction ending in shouts of delight.

THE NATIVES WORKED, of course, only under surveillance. But Schweitzer expected nothing else. It was with dismay, however, that he found that they would bow to no authority but that of "the old Doctor." For months he stood over his refractory workers, striving to wrest from the forest the land on which his house of healing should stand, the land that must provide food for patients, doctors and nurses. Now and then his temper wore thin and he saw sharply the incongruity of a philosopher, a musician, a surgeon, spending months out of his life acting as an overseer.

The hospital buildings that rose slowly through the next year were of corrugated iron, whereas the old hospital structures were of bamboo and leaf tile. Schweitzer had sent to Europe for the iron, on a gamble, trusting that friends of the hospital would support the cost. He himself, in baggy trousers and suspenders over his white shirt, assisted by some convalescents, sank the piles on which the buildings were to be set to keep them clear of floods.

Upstream, the welcome green shoots of cabbage appeared and beans elbowed their way out of the soil. The hospital had a vegetable patch at last. He called it his Garden of Eden and lined it with fruit trees. He had long dreamed of the day when his patients might steal fruit to their heart's content and there would still be enough.

Meanwhile, two miles away, the work of healing the sick went on in the old hospital, and the doctors and nurses alternated operations and house painting. The Doctor had long resigned himself to relinquishing all thought of working on Saint Paul. But he managed to keep up his daily organ practice. His fingers must remain supple for the concerts in Europe that must support Lambaréné.

A year and three months after he had announced his decision to move the hospital, the patients were transferred to the new buildings. As Schweitzer strode through the wards the first evening, the blacks greeted him with the cry, "It's a good hut, Doctor, a good hut!" In an exaltation of joy he sent his thoughts in gratitude to God and to the friends in Europe who were His instruments.

In this spirit of almost overwhelming thankfulness, six months after the removal of the patients to the new hospital, Schweitzer started on the journey home to his wife and child. As he watched the green African shore recede, he knew that, for the first time since he had established the hospital fourteen years before, he had the right to feel the thrill of success.

As the dark continent's last thin line slipped under the horizon, two of the nurses, homeward bound, stood at Schweitzer's side.

All three were thinking of Africa: the terror of it and the beauty; the natives, so maddening and so dear; the work, so exhausting and so satisfying. They solemnly shook hands and went below to their cabins.

Chapter VIII

AT KÖNIGSFELD in the Black Forest, the little girl who had been five when her father went to Africa for the second time was eight. The altitude and the pine woods had restored her mother's health, and a happy household made the comfortable little house vibrate with accounts of three years of separation.

The Doctor could not stay with them long. There were appeals for lectures and concerts, and the hospital went with him day and night: by every mail he wrote personal letters to the doctors and nurses.

In the late summer he went to Scandinavia, then to England, for, being so near, he would not miss the opportunity of seeing again the friends who had for years been supporting his hospital. It was at the urging of these English friends that Schweitzer set down his convictions on the basic political and social issues in Africa for publication in the *Contemporary Review*.

Did the white races have a right to colonize Africa? he asked in this article. *No*, if they regarded the black races merely as raw material for their industries. *Yes*, if they felt a responsibility for their moral health and their growth toward a better order. Schweitzer drew up a list of the fundamental rights of man which the Negro might expect to enjoy: the right to habitation, the right to circulate freely, the right to the soil and to its development and use, the right to work, to justice, to national organization, the right to education. Out of the depths of personal experience, he dealt with these rights with such understanding and moderation that the revolutionary character of the article did not immediately reveal itself. What he actually did in the innocent-appearing essay was to draw up a bill of rights for subject races, and the program of a new social order for Africa.

In the spring of the following year Schweitzer was in Holland, proceeding, in May, through fields carpeted in flowers, into Amsterdam and Haarlem.

He worked on a sixteen-hour schedule on such tours, with an occasional excursion to examine some fine old church organ—his only recreation. "The very sight of the organ," he would say, "must make music in the spectator."

Another tour through England followed, with the high point a new acquaintance. Maude Royden, pastor of a congregation known as the Guildhall for Fellowship, recognized in Schweitzer "one of the greatest living personalities" whose life was "Christianity in practice." Her community adopted Lambaréné as its own, even as she herself became one of Schweitzer's most penetrating interpreters to the English-speaking world.

At the end of August Schweitzer was in Germany. The municipality of Frankfort on the Main had established a Goethe Prize of ten thousand marks, almost twenty-five hundred dollars, to be awarded annually to a writer who expressed in his life and work the qualities associated with the noblest of German poets. The prize for 1928 had been awarded to Albert Schweitzer.

Worldly honors meant little to Schweitzer but this award shook him. From his student days the spirit of Goethe had gone with him, speaking the guiding word, helping him to endure, stimulating him to grow.

On the anniversary of Goethe's birth he was welcomed by the lord mayor in the presence of the leaders in the scientific, literary and artistic life of Frankfort. The burgomaster was eloquent in his citation: Schweitzer had "commanded the admiration of lovers of humanity throughout the world."

Schweitzer responded with felicity, telling of the great poet, who, "amid the deep and widely varied experience of his age, cared for his age and labored for it," sought to understand it and "grew to be part of it."

"A spirit like Goethe's," he pointed out, "lays three obligations upon us. We have to wrestle with conditions, so as to make sure that men who are imprisoned in work, and being worn out by it, may nevertheless preserve the possibility of a spiritual existence. We have to wrestle with men, so that, in spite of our being continuously drawn aside to the external things . . . they may find the road to inwardness and keep it. We have to wrestle with ourselves . . . so that in a time of confused ideals, ignoring every claim of humanity, we may remain faithful to the great humane ideals of the eighteenth century, translating them into the thought of our own age and attempting to realize them today." It was a part of the same philosophy he had expressed to the children of England years before. When a British writer, gathering a collection of hero stories, asked for a personal word for his chapter on "Oganga, the Jungle Doctor," Schweitzer sent this message:

> Tell the boys and girls of England that the truths they feel deep down in their hearts are the real truths. God's love speaks to us in our hearts and tries to work through us in the world. We must listen to this voice . . . as to a pure and distant melody that comes across the noise of the world's doings . . . that we may become the children of God. Happy are those who listen.

THE GOETHE PRIZE built the Doctor a new house. He enjoyed the quiet charm of Königsfeld, but he had to face the fact that he no longer belonged wholly to himself or his family. He had to keep his contact with the Alsatian churches which were largely supporting his hospital. Friends, moreover, could not always take the tortuous journey into the Black Forest. He needed a substantial house, finally, to hold his library and to serve as headquarters for the Lambaréné staff when they were on leave.

Günsbach was still home to him, though his father was dead and a new pastor was in the old family manse. He determined to use the Goethe prize money to build a house of his own there. With the hospital firmly established at last, he would be able, as old age came upon him, to spend longer vacations in Europe. How satisfying to be surrounded by the mountains, woods and valleys he had loved in his youth, and to complete the books he had been working on for thirty years.

The house, designed from Schweitzer's own sketches, was completed the following year. But the thought that he was taking money out of Germany, barely recovering from her orgy of inflation, tormented him. He made arrangements to give lectures and concerts in Germany in behalf of charitable causes, and did not rest until the sums received equaled the amount of the Goethe award.

In 1929 Schweitzer also completed his monumental work on the mysticism of Saint Paul. The book was, in a sense, a sequel to *The Quest of the Historical Jesus*, revealing Paul as sharing the illusion of an imminent, cataclysmic coming of the Kingdom which, Schweitzer believed, had governed the acts of Jesus and determined His message. He completed the final chapter in December on the ship that was taking him from Bordeaux to Cape Lopez. The preface was written the day after Christmas on the deck of the dirty little riverboat steaming up the Ogowe to Lambaréné. Once more his wife accompanied him, while their daughter remained in a Moravian school in Königsfeld.

Schweitzer's two years in Europe had brought him refreshment of mind and body, new friends and the opportunity to bind old supporters to his cause. He was grateful for the applause and honors, but with all its satisfactions, his visit also brought him profound misgivings.

For he saw the postwar world as he could not see it from Lambaréné. He saw all the tendencies toward decay which he had noted and deplored thirty years before. Men seemed no longer to have any spiritual self-confidence, the simple, elemental thinking which could help them endure and somehow master the strain of labor and sorrow, the mystery of life and death. In "reverence for life," men must again find the desire and the ability to think.

Schweitzer was conscious as never before of a mission, of which his work in Africa, his books, his lectures and his music, all, were the multiple expression. The mission was definite—and clear: to wake men's sleeping souls.

AFRICA ONCE MORE . . . for both the Schweitzers. "The sky above the palms in front of my window is bright blue. A scarcely perceptible breeze comes up from the river. Some of the hospital goats graze on the mown meadow, each accompanied by a white heron. . . ." The new hospital crowded with patients . . . a real unit for the insane at last, the gift of Maude Royden's Guild-

"I have a passion
for music ..."

house for Fellowship . . . The Garden of Eden expanding into ever more rows of vegetables, bananas and oil palms . . .

On the wharf a lamp burned nightly, carrying into the tropic darkness the Doctor's message: "Here, at whatever hour you come, you will find light and help and human kindness." On a wooden campanile now hung a bell from an Alsatian foundry, which called only to prayers, in contrast to a gong which called the men to work. "The gong is the Doctor's voice," said the natives; "the bell is God's."

The middle of January Schweitzer turned fifty-five, but his activity showed no sign of waning energy. With two and sometimes three doctors besides himself on the staff, he fulfilled a dream of many years and began sending out a traveling unit to serve those who were unable to make the journey to Lambaréné. He himself worked as hard as ever, not only as physician but as carpenter, mason, painter and electrician, until he was able to write his supporters that he had "at last reached finality in building operations. How it lightens our work to have at last a sufficiency of rooms to do it in!"

At the insistence of two of his medical colleagues, he devoted most of his mornings now to writing an account of his life. The story unfolded under his hands into a singularly attractive record of a great life, becoming finally an exultation on the theme of "reverence for life."

If man affirms life, Schweitzer wrote, he accepts it as having meaning and validity for him, he deepens and exalts his own will to live and feels a compulsion to give to every other living thing the same reverence for life that he gives to his own. Then he experiences that other life in his own. Surely, a man was truly ethical only when life, as such, was sacred to him, that of plants and animals as that of his fellowmen, and he helped all life that needed what he could give. "The ethic of Reverence for Life is the ethic of Love widened into universality. It is the ethic of Jesus, now recognized as a logical sequence of thought."

He ended his drama on a note of hope. He was convinced that the spirit generated by truth was even stronger than the force of circumstances. "I do not believe that [mankind] will have to tread the road to ruin right to the end. . . . Because I have confidence in the power of truth and of the spirit, I believe in the future of mankind."

Not long after he had completed the autobiography Schweitzer received a message from the municipality of Frankfort, inviting him to give the address that March on the centenary of Goethe's death. He heard the call with dismay, but having accepted the Goethe Prize, he was in no position to refuse this second distinction.

Happily, he had Goethe's collected works in his Lambaréné library, so he immersed himself in the poet-philosopher's writings. He wrote the address himself on the eighteen-day voyage, completing it as the ship steamed into Bordeaux.

On March 22, 1932, the Frankfort sky was clear; wreaths lay against the base of Goethe's monument; cars began to roll to the opera house bearing civic notables. At a quarter past eleven Schweitzer began to speak to a house conscious of such national tragedy as the poet in his darkest moments had never divined. The German people were hanging on the edge of an abyss. The depression, lying like an incubus on all the world, was suffocating a people humiliated by defeat, devastated by inflation. Six million and more were unemployed, hundreds of thousands quietly starving to death. Every day brought reports of street fighting, bloodshed and death. Across the confusion rang the strident voice of the psychopathic pied piper, Adolf Hitler.

It was against this background that Albert Schweitzer said one thing insistently and unforgettably: that the supreme need of man is to be himself and to grow in ethical perception and action.

Did this message seem alien to a generation seeking salvation in mass movements and political formulas? Schweitzer spoke of "the most awful hour of destiny which has ever struck for mankind," this "fateful hour," in which Goethe was called to speak.

What is it that Goethe says to this time?

Don't give up the ideal of man as a person! Remain human beings whose souls are their own! "Once surrender it," said Schweitzer, "and man as a thinking, an aspiring being, is destroyed, and that is the end of civilization, yes, even of humanity."

From beginning to end his address was a challenge to Hitler

and his hordes who, even as he spoke, were hypnotizing the German people and who, within a year, would be showing the world what *they* thought of the ideals of man.

LATER THAT SUMMER visitors entering the house in Günsbach which the Goethe Prize had built found Schweitzer at work on the third volume of his history of civilization. They noted that the tall vigorous frame was a little stooped, but the black hair and mustache were only slightly streaked with gray and his blue eyes still twinkled at the slightest provocation. Busy as he was, he seemed always to have time for those who came. He entertained them at his own table, plying them with questions; and took them through the village in which he had lived as a boy, to the dame school he had attended, to the woods to which he had carried his first boyish agonizings at the pain that was in the world.

Frequently he would bring a guest into the organ loft of the church that had been his father's and let his fingers roam over the keys. Whatever Schweitzer played, it seemed to come out without conscious effort, a kind of harmonious emanation of his inner life. For the organ had always been his solace, the organ he had so persistently defended against attacks of a generation of declining standards, the organ to which since his boyhood he had given so richly of his mind and spirit.

An old friend, Stefan Zweig, the biographer, novelist and poet, recorded a picture of Schweitzer's face bent over the keys. "Never," he wrote, "have I felt Johann Sebastian Bach's metaphysical power as I felt it in that Protestant church, awakened by a truly religious man and given substance there in utmost self-abnegation."

As Schweitzer talked of Lambaréné or of his philosophical work, his visitor noted with satisfaction that the Doctor's eyes were clear and warm as ever and the sharply chiseled features showed no blurring of the heroic power. "In him," Zweig wrote, "one is aware of a power which, invisible to us, expresses itself in another continent in acts of mercy and ethical creativeness, and at the same time awakens or augments similar power in thousands of others."

The Doctor also opened his hospitable door that summer to a stranger from his own Münster Valley, a crusty peasant, dressed up for a call and not at all happy about it. "I'm going round trying to raise money," explained his visitor. "My God, what a job!" He mopped his brow. "One and all, they make excuses and some even bang the door in my face. I suppose you won't give me anything either."

"What are you raising money for?" Schweitzer asked.

"The new church."

"Well, well. Come in. We'll talk about it." The upshot was a contribution and the peasant's acceptance of the Doctor's invitation to share his evening meal. "I know how you feel," his host remarked as they sat at supper. "I'm a hardened beggar myself. Let me give you a piece of advice. Never say die. If one door shuts, another opens. Keep hoping."

"What is it that you are raising money for?"

"Oh, an old hospital in Africa," Schweitzer replied.

Abruptly, the peasant pushed his chair back. "*Herr Jesu!* Are *you* the famous Dr. Schweitzer? I can't take anything from *you!*"

NINETEEN THIRTY-THREE, nineteen thirty-four. Europe and Africa, Europe and Africa. A year in Europe, six months in Africa; eighteen months in Europe, two years in Africa. Günsbach . . . and oh, how quieting to the mind, how comforting to the body to be among the scenes of his boyhood, to hear the deep call of the church bell, to play on the organ and to preach in his father's pulpit. He spent a winter at Lausanne with his wife and their daughter, now sixteen, but when he was in Europe he was seldom allowed to remain long in one place. The calls for him were incessant and he could not afford, for his hospital's sake, to refuse any of them. But his Teutonic sense of duty would not let him accept the one that meant most to him: the opportunity to thank his American friends for the support they had given him over the years. He hungered to join the assembly of the world's great scholars receiving honorary degrees at the Harvard Tercentenary, and it was "with a heavy heart," he wrote a friend, that he sent his regrets. "I must finish the philosophy," he explained. "Then I can die in peace."

It was the *Philosophy of Civilization* that he had been working on for many years, the thinking of a lifetime that should be his contribution to his time.

To a friend who asked him whether he were happy, Schweitzer answered, "Yes, when I am working, and getting somewhere. As an individual I have really ceased to exist, and I don't know personal happiness any more."

An echo of the elegiac yet challenging words rang through a talk he gave to boys in an English school: "I don't know what your destiny will be. But one thing I know: the only ones among you who will be really happy are those who will have sought and found how to serve."

Chapter IX

FOR ALL HIS traveling through those middle thirties there was one country in Europe to which he did not go. He issued no denunciation of Germany from Lambaréné or from the security of his Alsatian home, which was once more a part of the French republic. That sort of fighting, he seemed to say, was not for him. To Schweitzer, Hitler was no supernatural phenomenon, spawned in hell and let loose in the hearts of a people. Hitler was a product of forces which had been at work in the world for a hundred years and more. In Schweitzer's childhood, in the spiritual fatigue of so many of his elders, he had become vaguely conscious of those forces. In his early manhood he had begun clearly to note their effect on the political thought of his generation. The First World War had made him aware that without ethical standards men were beasts, and it should not be surprising to anyone if they acted like beasts.

So in the face of the crumbling structure of Western civilization, Schweitzer—in Africa and in Europe, in his hospital, at his desk, on the lecture platform, at the organ—preached "reverence for life," and lived it through eighteen waking hours of each crowded day.

Lambaréné was "reverence for life" in action. Year by year, along the Ogowe, through the spoken word and the unspoken sermon of the Doctor's daily living, "reverence for life" took on reality in dark and haunted minds. Men began to understand why they must not kill wantonly, or torture, or steal, or seek revenge; women began to nurse babies whose mothers had died in childbirth rather than let them die for fear of the curse assumed to have killed the mother.

To the Doctor, "reverence for life" meant reverence for all life. Almost twenty years before he had written, "A man is truly ethical only when he obeys the compulsion to help all life which he is able to assist, and shrinks from injuring anything that lives."

Early in the hospital's history Schweitzer had issued the decree that, within the area over which he had jurisdiction, no animal was to be wantonly killed, and that anyone bringing wounded or orphaned animals to the hospital would be greeted as a benefactor and given a present. The compound was a veritable zoo of wild creatures, made pets by the Doctor; in the early years a miniature antelope that would venture to the Doctor's desk for his caress; subsequently, monkeys without number, a stork, some white goats which had a bad habit of eating the bark off the young fruit trees; and a gorilla, a porcupine, a fluffy white owl.

But Schweitzer recognized that reverence for all life, and not for human life only, presented problems which man could not evade. So that no leopard might invade the hospital grounds and no elephant tear up the plantations on which the life of the hospital depended, Schweitzer had to kill. Anywhere in the world man must kill to live. What then became of "reverence for life"? Was not this the answer?—that man must indeed destroy life, but destroy it only to preserve or advance life in its higher forms. Man must live daily from judgment to judgment, deciding each case as it arises, as wisely and mercifully as he may, with no hope of an easy conscience.

Thus it was torment to him in the dry season to see the heavy smoke clouds over the forest where the natives were burning felled timbers to make new plantations. It had to be, if human beings were not to starve, but he was seized by compassion for the animals that perished by thousands in the conflagrations.

The essential thing was that man never let his sensibilities become blunted and dull, and that he never be too sure that his highest judgments are really high enough. Look out, when your conscience tells you that all is well. "The good conscience is an invention of the Devil."

SCHWEITZER STILL WORKED with his old energy, from six in the morning until midnight, himself astonished at the amount he could still do. "At the moment," he wrote to a friend, "I am working on the drains that carry off the water. That's a big problem here because the hospital stands at the foot of a little hill. . . . For a year and a half, I haven't had a day free, or been as much as five kilometers from the hospital. Can you imagine such sticking in one place? But there is something rather nice and healing about it."

The news coming from Europe fell like intimations of winter on his fertile fields. The diplomatic maneuverings between France and Germany in the autumn of 1938 convinced him that war was imminent. A stock of provisions and medicines had to be provided in case war came.

In January 1939 he went to Europe. He wanted to see his wife and daughter. Besides, he had to admit how tired he was and how much he felt the need of shifting to other shoulders for a time the manifold duties he carried at Lambaréné. Had he not told himself that, as age crept on him, he would spend longer and longer vacations among the mountains and memories of Günsbach?

Before he reached France he knew how illusory his expectations were. At every port at which the vessel touched he saw warships gathering; in every broadcast that he heard he recognized the note of doom. Before he landed at Bordeaux on February first he had made up his mind to return to Africa on the same boat a fortnight later. When war came he would be needed there.

He spent his two weeks in Alsace and in Switzerland with his wife and daughter, setting his personal affairs in order and making purchases for his hospital. His friends did not share his apprehensions, least of all, ironically, those in Strasbourg, living

"... the only ones among you
who will be really happy are those
who will have sought
and found how to serve."

as it were between the leveled guns. They gently ribbed him as an alarmist who, remote from the scene, had lost his perspective. He did not argue. He prayed.

He was back at Lambaréné the first week in March. He set to work at once to lay up stores of medicines, surgical materials and food.

He expected war in July. It came in September, and like another Joseph, he prepared for the seven lean years—never guessing they would actually be that—purchasing all available supplies of rice. Reluctantly, he sent home the sick who were not in immediate need of treatment or operating, for surgical supplies as well as food must be conserved. "What sad days we spent," wrote the Doctor, "sending these people home!"

He sent home also a considerable group of native attendants, laborers and field workers. A Swiss doctor on the staff, called for service in his own country, went home by steamer; one of the nurses, due for a furlough, caught the last plane carrying civilian passengers for Europe. Since the service of the hospital was greatly reduced, other nurses accepted posts in the crowded colonial hospitals. Daring the submarine-infested seas, a woman doctor came from Latvia; and from France, to share his exile once more, came the Doctor's wife.

Closer and closer the war came. In the middle of its first year, the old steamer, which had so often carried the Doctor to Europe and back was torpedoed and carried down with her the last consignment of drugs and surgical materials he had counted on. Seven months later the war was literally at the gate. For weeks the forces of the Free French fought the Vichy government troops for Lambaréné, but happily both commanders ordered their bombers to spare the hospital, two or three miles from the town. Through the furious bombardment the Doctor protected patients and nurses against stray shots by reinforcing the walls with thick sheets of corrugated iron.

With ocean traffic at the mercy of the submarines, the forest lumberyards were shut down and the trade in coffee, cocoa and palm oil, too, came to a standstill. But rubber was in sharp demand and the industry, which the competition of the East Indies had choked a quarter century before, revived.

The war brought changes in the Ogowe area that were not all evil. Strategic roads were thrust into the forest, bridges were built over the lesser streams and ferries established to carry traffic over the rivers. To Lambaréné came the road builders, carrying the Cape Town to Algiers highway. The roads were rough and travel by them was no luxury, but they brought motor transportation into the area. The Doctor was now able to travel in a day to stations he had in the past been able to reach only by a twelve-day journey on foot.

The collapse of the lumber trade made labor cheap, and the Doctor saw an opportunity to keep some of the natives from starvation and at the same time to undertake certain works he had long deferred. He prepared a number of acres for the young fruit trees in his nursery, cleared other acres from the bushes and creepers choking the oil palms, and constructed retaining walls to keep his Garden of Eden from sliding into the river.

Gradually the hospital began to function again at something like the old pace. But when the war was in its second year, his supplies began to run out. The purchases of provisions he had made, moreover, and the wages he had to pay his native workers, were draining his financial resources. But how could he send back patients who had made their way to him down two hundred and fifty miles of jungle trails?

Happily the Free French won the colony, and in spite of their own losses and deprivations, friends in England began to resume their contributions and to forward donations from loyal supporters in Sweden. Continental Europe, enclosed in an iron ring, could do nothing, but American friends jumped into the breach. They sent word that they were organizing what was in effect a rescue party, and volunteered to send medical supplies.

As the months passed the gaps on his shelves widened and the promised shipment did not arrive. In the spring of 1942 it came at last. Money came, too, and the Doctor was able to give the sick better nourishment and send his co-workers on furlough to the mountains of the interior to restore the energies the perpetual heat drained out of them.

But the Doctor refused the pleas that he himself go on furlough. The work, in fact, was increasing. The white Europeans in the area, exhausted by their enforced stay in the jungle country, were crowding into the hospital, suffering from anemia, stomach ulcers or malaria. The natives were coming, as before the war, in a steady stream.

"You want to make me take a vacation," Schweitzer wrote an American friend. "It can't be done. If the hospital is to function normally, I must be in my place every day for many reasons. . . . If I came back from a holiday, I would find so many building repairs would be awaiting me, so many things would not have been done!

"For there are too few of us. I have to do other jobs alongside that of a doctor. I'm the one who starts up the motors every morning, who has been for some time doing the marketing at half-past eight in the morning, when you buy bananas, manioc, and corn for the food for the sick, it is I who go to the plantation every day to look over what the workers have done (or haven't done). I'm the one who has to see that the fruits are gathered and put on straw to keep them. . . . No one could take my place.

"Believe, dear friend, that I am doing the right thing staying at my post, doing my work day by day and dreaming that a day will come when, after the war, I shall take a real vacation, when I shall sleep as long as I like, when I shall go for walks, when I shall work all day long and half the night at philosophy without having to break up the concentration, when I shall play the organ. . . . Don't worry about me."

But by the end of the fifth year of war, the incessant work and strain induced in the Doctor and his indomitable wife a fatigue which put to the test their last resources of body and spirit. "Sometimes our feet drag as if they were made of lead," Madame Schweitzer admitted in a letter to a friend, "but we keep going."

Each day they seemed to draw on their final reserves to meet the demands of the hospital, and each night found a little still left to carry them into another day. Not to fall ill, to keep fit for work, became an obsession. No one must collapse. There would be no replacements. Somehow, by the grace of God, everyone must carry on.

"So," wrote Schweitzer in his first postwar report, "we carried on."

He marveled, himself, at the strength and the endurance which were still his and thanked God for them out of a full heart. Had he not dreamed of delegating the hospital work to his assistants when he came to be sixty-five, to spend months of every year in Europe, to study and write, to give concerts for the hospital and even—not impossibly—take a few weeks off for a vacation? That had certainly been a dream!

He reached seventy on January 14, 1945, and the world took note of it in editorials, sermons, radio broadcasts and Lambaréné benefits. Schweitzer spent the day—and it was a Sunday—in more than the usual round of work, operating, looking after cases that had worried him; in the hospital from dawn to nightfall. Seventy! he said to himself. For the sake of the work he had to do and the years that the hospital would still have need of him, he ought to be thirty, not seventy!

Four months later Schweitzer was sitting at his desk after the midday meal when one of his white patients appeared at his window breathless.

"There's a German report on the radio that an armistice has been concluded in Europe!"

The Doctor finished the letter he was writing. In midafternoon, after a succession of appointments in the hospital, he asked that the gong be rung, and gave the hospital family the news: the war in Europe was over.

He was aching with fatigue, aching for quiet and the chance to send his mind out to meet what might come. But there was work to be done. Not until evening fell did he have a chance to sit down at last and let the thoughts that had been darkly milling about in his brain come to some sort of focus. What did the end of hostilities mean? What were the millions thinking who this night at last should have no fear of bombs? After slaughter, what follows?

He drew down the little book of sayings of Lao-tzu, the Chinese sage who had known wars and victories two centuries before Socrates, six centuries before Christ.

"Weapons are disastrous implements," Schweitzer read aloud

to his wife, "and are no tools for a noble being. Only when he can do no otherwise, does he make use of them. For him, quiet and peace are the highest."

"Reverence for life!" And, after twenty-five hundred years, scarcely a handful really believing in it! All the more reason to "stand and work in the world as one who aims at deepening men's inner life and making them sounder of heart by making them think."

Albert Schweitzer speaking:

"But to everyone, in whatever state of life he finds himself, the ethics of reverence for life do this: they force him without cessation to be concerned at heart with all the human destinies and all the other life-destinies which are going through their life-course around him, and to give himself as man, to the man who needs a fellow-man. They will not allow the scholar to live only for his learning, even if his learning makes him very useful, nor the artist to live only for his art, even if by means of it he gives something to many. They do not allow the very busy man to think that with his professional activities he has fulfilled every demand upon him. They demand from all that they devote a portion of their life to their fellows."

EPILOGUE

Albert Schweitzer died on September 5, 1965, at the hospital he built in Lambaréné, Gabon. He was ninety years of age and active almost up until the moment of his death. His grave on the banks of the Ogowe River is marked by a simple cross he made himself.

THE
GREAT
PIERPONT
MORGAN

A CONDENSATION OF

THE
GREAT
PIERPONT
MORGAN

by
FREDERICK
LEWIS
ALLEN

J. P. Morgan was the mightiest financier in American history. He created United States Steel, he welded America's railroads into a system that ran from coast to coast, and on one occasion the United States Treasury itself appealed to him to save it from bankruptcy.

All this took incredible energy, boldness, and imagination; but John Pierpont Morgan had other remarkable qualities that distinguished him from many of the get-rich-quick robber barons of his time—among them an interest in the beautiful and rare that built the greatest private American art collection. With his high silk hat, his yachts, his wide travels, and fabulous collection of paintings and rare books, he appeared the very image of the ruthless international financier. Yet his credo was simple: "The first thing is character"—and he lived up to it.

This is the superbly told story of one of the most powerful, fascinating, and enigmatic personalities ever to appear on the American scene.

Chapter 1

Judgment Day

A FEW DAYS before Christmas in the year 1912, John Pierpont Morgan, the most influential banker in the world and the mightiest personal force in American business life, was called to testify before an investigating committee in Washington. This group—a subdivision of the House Committee on Banking and Currency—was popularly known as the Pujo Committee, because its chairman was Arsène Pujo of Louisiana. Its aim was to demonstrate that there existed in America a "money trust," that a small group of New York bankers, headed by Pierpont Morgan, held such a grip on the money and credit resources of the country, and so dominated the big industrial and railroad corporations, that in effect the whole American economy lay under its control. Day after day the Pujo Committee had spread its evidence on the record, and now the inquiry was coming to its climax. Pierpont Morgan himself was going to take the stand.

After traveling from his hotel to the Capitol in a big square-topped limousine, he walked beside his daughter Louisa and his son, Jack, through the staring crowds to the committee room— an old-fashioned figure in a heavy velvet-collared overcoat and high silk hat, walking slowly, with a stick. The committee room was packed, and the crowd outside was kept in order by policemen.

Morgan was old now, well along in his seventy-sixth year. His hair was white and thin. His big straggling mustache, which had remained black until old age approached, was graying. Now, as always, the first thing that caught the attention of anyone who saw him for the first time was his nose. It was bulbous and flaming red as the result of a baffling skin disease. Only when one was accustomed to the sight of this dismaying feature did one note the burning intensity of his eyes. But those eyes were tired now. The vital force in him was waning; though no one in the committee room could know it, he was within four months of his death.

Morgan was a direct and cooperative witness. He took no refuge in the evasions or lapses of memory which often afflict business executives when they confront congressional committees. He answered clearly and stoutly; when he could not remember a fact or figure he said he would be glad to have it looked up. And he spoke with completely satisfied assurance.

Samuel Untermyer, counsel for the committee, a shrewd and well-prepared lawyer, conducted the examination. Having established that some seventy-eight interstate corporations carried bank accounts totaling over eighty-one million dollars with J. P. Morgan & Co., Untermyer asked Morgan if he thought it was a wise thing to permit publicly owned corporations to make deposits with a private banker.

Morgan answered firmly, "I do, sir."

Untermyer further brought out that a great many railroad corporations had made J. P. Morgan & Co. their fiscal agent, so that the Morgan firm had become the designated channel through which these railroads must sell all their securities to the public.

"Don't you think it would be better," Untermyer asked, "for these great interstate railroad corporations if they were entirely free to sell their securities in open competition, than that they should be tied to any banking house, however just might be its methods in the issue of such securities?"

Morgan answered, "I should not think so."

Untermyer asked if the fact that the same few men served on the boards of directors of many banks did not tend to prevent those banks from competing for deposits.

"I should doubt it," said Morgan. "I have been in business for a great many years in New York and I do not compete for any deposits. I do not care whether they ever come. They come."

With all the ingenuity of a trained trial lawyer, Untermyer tried to get Morgan to admit that he exercised great power. Morgan said he exercised no power at all.

The audience in the committee room was ready for this sort of denial; of course this organizer of huge corporations, this consolidator of banks, this master of the authority of money would be expected under such circumstances to minimize his own status; but Morgan was denying too much. He was not only denying that he controlled the reorganized railroads for which he had named the voting trustees; he was actually denying that if he himself were voting trustee for all the railroad systems of the United States, this would concentrate control of them in him. He was denying that there was any way in which one man could get a monopoly of money, or control of it. Presently Untermyer would find a weak spot.

Yet as the questioning persisted, it became apparent that the old man's denials were not merely tactics in his battle of wits with Untermyer; they came from something deeper in his nature that commanded the audience's respect.

"Is not commercial credit based primarily upon money or property?" asked Untermyer.

"No, sir," said Morgan. "The first thing is character."

"Before money or property?"

"Before money or anything else. Money cannot buy it. . . . Because a man I do not trust could not get money from me on all the bonds in Christendom."

How could anybody hear those words—so dubiously applicable to the business world in general, yet clearly so valid to the old gentleman in the witness chair—without wondering what manner of man this was, and by what circumstances he had come to a place where people could honestly believe that he was the ruler of America?

Chapter 2

The Materials of a Career

AMONG THE MEN of authority in American business at the beginning of the twentieth century, Morgan was unusual in his origins. John D. Rockefeller had begun his working life at sixteen as a $4-a-week clerk in Cleveland. Andrew Carnegie had gone to work at thirteen as a $1.20-a-week bobbin boy in a Pittsburgh cotton mill. And the great railroad organizer, E. H. Harriman, though he had prosperous relatives, had started as a broker's office boy at $5 a week. The prevailing pattern was of the sort prescribed by Horatio Alger: begin work as a boy, without benefit of higher education; work furiously, with a single eye to business; and thus rise to the top. By contrast, Morgan had been born to rising wealth and social position, and before he was twenty had enjoyed opportunities for travel, university education, and international acquaintance.

Morgan's grandfather Joseph Morgan came from a Massachusetts farm to Hartford, Connecticut, in 1817; ran a tavern, and then sold it to become the proprietor of the City Hotel in Hartford. He prospered as a hotelkeeper, and invested in Hartford real estate; he helped to organize a canal company and steamboat lines and the new railroad which connected Hartford with Springfield; and finally became one of the founders of the Aetna Fire Insurance Company. He was a solid citizen, hearty, hardworking, shrewd in a bargain, and God-fearing withal.

His son, Junius Spencer Morgan, who was born before his father arrived in Hartford, was put into business without benefit of a college education. After a taste of commercial life in New York, he spent a number of years in a dry-goods firm in Hartford. But by his late thirties he had moved to Boston to become a partner in the booming firm of James M. Beebe & Co., which conducted and financed foreign trade transactions, particularly in cotton. As a result of his father's expanding wealth, he was able to bring considerable capital with him.

After only a few years he was invited to go to London to become a partner of George Peabody, a Yankee who had built up an international banking house there. And when, during our Civil War, George Peabody retired, the Peabody firm—an important link in the system of financial communications between London and industrializing America—took the name of J. S. Morgan & Co.

Junius Morgan's son, John Pierpont Morgan, was born on April 17, 1837, in his grandfather's substantial house in Hartford. Young Pierpont—Pip, as they called him in his boyhood—went first to a small private school in Hartford, then to a public grammar school, then to a boarding school at Cheshire, Connecticut; after that to the English High School in Boston, a public school of exceptionally high standards; next to a private school in Vevey, Switzerland; and finally for more than a year to the University of Göttingen in Germany.

As a boy he absorbed certain traditions and tastes characteristic of the Yankee business community. First, there was the tradition of businesslike thrift. There was nothing finer than to be a good businessman, and the very mechanics of a business operation were alluring. When Pierpont was just reaching his twelfth birthday, he and his cousin Jim Goodwin got up a show for which they sold tickets to their families and indulgent friends—a *Grand Diorama of the Landing of Columbus*. Not only did Pierpont keep strict account of every penny received and disbursed, but he prepared an accurate balance sheet of the whole operation, headed "Morgan & Goodwin, Grand Diorama Balance Sheet, April 20, 1849."

He kept a diary as well as a series of precise personal account books. When he was married and traveling abroad with his wife and children, he still committed to a blue leather account book the exact record of the francs he had spent on such items as: *3 bouquets, 18; postage 1.40; cab, 1.80; oranges, 1.70; mineral water, 18; postage, 1.50.*

Along with the thrift went godliness: church attendance twice on Sundays and family hymn singing Sunday evenings. Morgan's friend, Dr. William S. Rainsford, the rector of St. George's Church in New York, wrote that Morgan's faith was like a "precious heirloom—a talent to be wrapped in its own napkin and venerated in the secret place of his soul . . . in safe disuse." To Morgan religion was something as solid and unquestionable as the stones of St. George's, even though most of the time it was out of sight and out of mind. In the Hartford and Boston of the mid-nineteenth century, devotion to business and devotion to God and the church and the creed had been two mutually comfortable parts of a whole life.

In his youth Morgan collected the autographs of Episcopal bishops. He went on to become a tireless vestryman and church warden, a giver of parish houses and cathedral chapels, an energetic attender of Episcopal conventions. When in 1913 he died and his will was made public, those who had known him only by his reputation as monarch of Wall Street, worldly yachtsman, and lordly spender of millions, gasped at the way in which the document began:

> I commit my soul into the hands of my Saviour, in full confidence that having redeemed it and washed it in His most precious blood He will present it faultless before my Heavenly Father; and I entreat my children to maintain and defend, at all hazard and at any cost of personal sacrifice, the blessed doctrine of the complete atonement for sin through the blood of Jesus Christ, once offered, and through that alone.

There was no mystery: this was the faith in which Pierpont Morgan had been raised.

Yankee thrift was often mitigated by the conviction that travel was a sound investment; and as Junius Morgan moved along from Hartford to Boston and then to London, his son had increasing chances to see the wide world. When Pierpont was a pupil at the English High School in Boston he was crippled by a bad attack of inflammatory rheumatism. His family packed him off in a sailing ship to the Azores, in company with their friend Mr. Dabney, the American consul at Horta on the island of Fayal.

His letters home from Horta give us a revealing glimpse of him at fifteen. They showed a zeal for precision, as when, in his account of the voyage from the States on the sailing ship *Io*, he noted, "We had five ladies on board and three gentlemen besides myself. Of course, three ladies and one gentleman were seasick, and as it very singularly happened those who escaped with the exception of Mr. Dabney were those who had never been to sea before." He set down for his parents careful accounts of the whitewashed stuccoed-over houses, of the gardens and what grew in them, of the currency and prices of Horta, and of the ships and shipping; the latter he studied with especially close attention, liking to go aboard the ships in port and hear about their trade. He was methodical, too: he noted in his diary the temperature on rising, at noon, and at bedtime.

Some signs of aesthetic appreciation appear: "Pico is a very beautiful mountain and it seems to me as if I should never tire of looking at it. It varies so both as to clearness and color. I often sit before a window facing it and watch the various changes which take place so often." But mainly he was a tireless observer with an eye for the business aspect of events. When the *Io*, on a subsequent visit to Horta, was badly damaged in a heavy storm while in port, Pierpont reported: "Had the *Io* gone ashore the Underwriters would have had a nice bill to pay, for she is insured for $25,000 and her cargo for $10,000 more, and none of the cargo had been landed at all."

When Pierpont arrived at Horta he had been very weak from his illness. He spent much of his time playing chess and reading and writing letters. But his condition improved so rapidly that before long he was taking long walks and going to parties with the Dabney girls. His gain in size was prodigious. On his arrival in November 1852 his weight was one hundred and twenty-six pounds; a month later he was complaining that his pantaloons were too tight; by March he weighed one hundred and fifty pounds.

This prolonged boyhood expedition, along with his later schooling at Vevey, Switzerland, and at the University of Göttingen, and his holiday visits to his family in London, gave Pierpont Morgan while he was still in his teens a familiarity with foreign life and ideas which in those days of slow ocean travel was exceptional for a young American. The farthest west he ever went in the United States as a boy was to Buffalo and

Niagara Falls. Not a very extended American trip for a young-ster who was about to live for years abroad; but in those days the merchants and the bankers of New England faced east.

THE LEVEL-EYED, METHODICAL BOY was growing up to be a big bulky man, a six-footer. You would hardly have called him handsome, but he was responsible-looking, with round strong features, a rather large and expressive mouth, and a fine direct gaze. He was not athletic, though he liked to walk and climb mountains and had a normal enjoyment of sports.

Like many youths, he was cursed with a bad complexion; at least once, when he was nineteen, he stayed away from a dance at Göttingen because he was ashamed of the eruption on his forehead. In school he was by no means a conspicuous student, though in his later years at English High he stood near the top of his class. But he developed a very sharp head for mathematics, and when he left Göttingen, the professor of mathematics there urged him to stay on, perhaps become the professor's assistant, and even possibly succeed to the professor's own chair.

He was a sociable fellow, with a relish both for playing chess and for organizing dances at Vevey, where—as he wrote to his cousin Jim Goodwin—his participation would cost him "about $5.75 a night, but that is dog cheap when you can laugh, talk, and dance with such a beautiful girl as Miss H. as much as you choose."

In the year 1857, when Pierpont was twenty, there was a fare-well party at Göttingen and his university days were over. After a short visit to England, he left his family and crossed to America to begin his business career as a junior accountant with Duncan, Sherman & Co., private bankers in Pine Street, Manhattan.

Here he soon demonstrated his enterprise and confidence in a way that brought acute if momentary alarm to his business seniors. He had gone to New Orleans to make a firsthand study of the cotton and shipping business. Ranging from dock to dock, one day he boarded a ship, and learned that the man to whom the ship's cargo of coffee had been consigned could not be found. The captain had been instructed to dispose of the coffee as best he could. Pierpont saw an opportunity. He went off with samples of the coffee in his pockets, made the rounds of the local merchants, collected orders, returned to the ship, and bought *the entire cargo* with a sight draft on Duncan, Sherman & Co. The next day, while his superiors in New York were spluttering with rage, he telegraphed them that he had sold every bag of coffee at a neat profit, and was forwarding the checks to Duncan, Sherman & Co. It had been a bold transaction for a neophyte of twenty-one, and characteristic in that he had not bargained for a quarter or a half of the cargo but for the whole thing.

After four years with Duncan, Sherman & Co., Morgan at twenty-four went into business on his own. It was very much of a one-man show that he ran at first as George Peabody & Co.'s American representative. At first he did not even have a clerk to help him; he sold bills all morning, posted his books in the afternoon, and spent half his evenings writing letters to the London branch or to his father, who was a partner in the firm. His letters to his father were detailed reports of his business operations and the general state of affairs in America. He continued writing them until his father's death in 1890.

Meanwhile he had settled into the agreeable life of a young gentleman-about-town. He roomed with Joe Peabody, a nephew of George Peabody of London, in what was then the fashionable uptown district of Manhattan, West Seventeenth Street. In those pre-Civil War days the solid blocks of brownstone houses reached up Fifth Avenue only to about Thirty-seventh Street. The chief center of polite society was still the neighborhood of Washington Square.

The city skyline was broken not by skyscrapers but by church spires. Pierpont's account books throw light upon his life as well as upon the prices of 1857–58: they contain such items as: *Lunch .30, Paper .02; Horse and Buggy to Middletown 3.; Cap 2., Gloves 1., Barber .12; Tickets to Philharmonic Concert 3., Church collections 1.25, Opera tickets 8., Adele 1., Sleighride 13.62.*

Gradually, young Morgan made a considerable acquaintance among the substantial families of the city. He threw himself with gusto into Sunday-evening hymn singing at the Babcocks', country walks at the Osborns' in the highlands of the Hudson, and evening gatherings of young people at the Sturgeses', who owned what was said to have been the first grand piano in New York. He had a sizable income from his family, good prospects, high spirits, and the sort of enthusiasm that made every party of young people revolve about him.

A FEW YEARS BEFORE, when he was at Göttingen, Morgan had written to Jim Goodwin: "Your career in life, like mine, depends on our own individual exertions, our courses though widely apart will both be in the mercantile sphere, and from this cause it becomes our duty to select for our wives those who, when we go home from our occupations, will ever be ready to make us happy and contented with our homes." Pierpont might have seemed to be following his own sage advice when he fell in love with Amelia Sturges, a girl of impeccable Manhattan antecedents. Yet what happened next took him out of the calculated pattern which he seemed to have been setting for himself.

In the spring of 1861, just as the Civil War was beginning, Amelia Sturges—or Mimi, as she was generally called—came down with tuberculosis. By autumn she was gravely ill. Pierpont decided that he would marry her and take her to a warmer climate. His business? That could go hang; and anyhow loyal Jim Goodwin could be persuaded to come down from Hartford and look after the office for an indefinite time.

On October 7, 1861, he and Mimi were married. By that time she was so weak that she could not stand alone. A few close friends gathered in the Sturges house as Pierpont carried Mimi downstairs in his arms and held her upright during the brief ceremony. Then he carried her to a carriage, drove with her to the pier, and took her abroad—first, by way of England, to Algiers and then, in desperation when her strength continued to fail, across the Mediterranean to Nice. It was all to no avail. Mimi died only a little over four months after the wedding.

A widower at the age of twenty-four, Pierpont Morgan returned to New York. Slowly he began to pick up the pieces of his life. On the first of September of that year 1862 there appeared in *The New York Times* a modest advertisement to the effect that he was now ready to engage in business under the name of J. Pierpont Morgan & Co.

Chapter 3

Groping for Direction

THE NEW YORK to which Morgan returned after his brief and tragic marriage was seething with Civil War business. Because of his health Morgan did not enlist. For some time he had been subject to dizzy spells, which seemed to have some obscure relation to the state of his complexion, for when his skin was clear the dizzy spells were more severe. When the draft was instituted in 1863, he took advantage of the curious regulation which permitted one to hire a substitute to take one's place in the army. This was a fully accepted practice.

Meanwhile, the shifting fortunes of battle, the expansion of manufacturing under the impact of war orders, and the westward push of trade toward the Pacific kept the speculative markets in turmoil. During these wild years young Morgan got mixed up in two dubious enterprises. One was the Hall Carbine Affair.

In the summer of 1861—just before he married Mimi—Morgan lent $20,000 to one Simon Stevens, who was engaged in selling outmoded carbines to General Frémont for $22 apiece. They had been bought by one Arthur M. Eastman *from the War Department itself* for $3.50 apiece. The deal was a scandalous one, reflecting gross incompetence on the part of the War Department and profiteering greed on the part of Stevens. Although the Hall Carbine scandal was promptly investigated by two congressional committees and by a special War Department commission, Morgan himself was never called before any of them; apparently they were convinced that his connection with the business was not only brief but incidental. Nevertheless it was an ugly thing to have been involved in, however inadvertently; Morgan, at the age of twenty-four, had at least been headstrong, injudicious, and a bad judge of character.

In the other dubious episode, which took place during 1863, Morgan and a young man named Edward Ketchum, having bought gold quietly and in small amounts, conspicuously

THE SUSQUEHANNA WAR.

The Case Before the Supreme Court—Motion to Vacate Appointment of Receiver and to Dissolve Injunction—Decision Reserved Until the Next Special Term.

ALBANY, Aug. 31.—Judge HOGEBOOM held a special term of the Supreme Court to-day to hear motions relative to the Receivership of the Susquehanna Railroad.

Mr. HALE, of counsel for the Ramsey interest, asked for a postponement till to-morrow, owing to the illness of Judge ALLEN, who was to argue the motions on the part of the Railroad Company.

Mr. FIELD objected, saying that they were unable to find the books of the Company, though he understood they had been kept at the residence of one of the opposing counsel. It was of the greatest consequence to them that these books should be produced so that they might be examined to ascertain who were legal stockholders of the road.

Mr. SMITH replied, admitting that the books were temporarily at his residence, but said th___ ___ the custody of the officers of t___ ___ to hold them.

___ ___ to vacate the order of Ju___ ___ pointing Mr. PRUYN Re___ ___ dissolve the injunction is___ ___CKHAM ___ FINK and ___cting___ ___he inju___ ___by ___ Judg ___spec___ an___ ___arked ___ covere

The Drexel Building

Pierpont Morgan, age twenty-four

Amelia Sturges, the first Mrs. Morgan

Frances (Fanny) Tracy, his second wife

shipped abroad half of what they had acquired in order to lift the price and sell the remainder at a handsome profit. The scheme worked, and according to some reports they divided a profit of $160,000.

Although a legitimate speculative coup, this gold deal was a shabby operation, since it was in effect an attempt to depreciate, at least temporarily, the national currency in a time of acute emergency. When at about this time Charles H. Dabney joined Pierpont as senior partner (the firm became Dabney, Morgan & Co.), it is quite possible that Morgan's father breathed more easily in the knowledge that his son would have an older and wiser head in the office with him. For once again the young man had been a bad judge of character: his crony in the gold deal, Edward Ketchum, later got into other speculations which turned out disastrously, forged a large number of gold checks, and went to prison.

QUITE ASIDE from these adventures, Morgan had his hands full putting through sales of American securities on behalf of his firm's English clients, who doubted if the Union would survive and wanted to unload their American holdings. What with a variety of other sorts of transactions, he prospered strikingly; his personal income for the year 1864 was no less than $53,286.

Just as the Civil War came to an end Morgan married again. His bride was Frances Louisa—Fanny—Tracy, whose father was one of the leading lawyers of the city. The Tracys had several charming daughters, and their house on Seventeenth Street had long been a favorite haunt of Pierpont's. He and Fanny were married at St. George's Church on May 31, 1865.

He now settled down, first at 227 Madison Avenue and then at 243, in what were then the northernmost residential reaches of the city proper. Within the next decade Pierpont's wife bore him four children: Louisa (who later became Mrs. Herbert L. Satterlee); John Pierpont (who succeeded him in 1913 as head of the family firm); Juliet Pierpont (who became Mrs. William P. Hamilton); and Annie Tracy (who, as Anne Morgan, was to become well known for her work in French war relief and other charities).

519

A hulking, solid-shouldered young man with a strong, large-featured face and an emphatic mustache and striking hazel eyes, Morgan settled into the role of active young businessman, citizen, and churchman. Apparently he had now learned greater circumspection. He was elected to the highly respectable Union Club. He became a member of the board of managers of St. Luke's Hospital, was busy in the affairs of the Y.M.C.A., helped to organize both the Metropolitan Museum of Art and the Museum of Natural History, and became a vestryman of St. George's Church in Stuyvesant Square. In those days if you had a good cause to promote and wanted on your committee a young fellow with good connections, a wide acquaintance, unlimited energy, and a sort of force which made people tend to go his way, people would suggest that you consider young Morgan. But it was not until the late summer of 1869, when he was thirty-two, that his career gave signs of the direction in which his character and peculiar talents would lead him.

The Northern victory in the Civil War had opened up the expanding country to the railroads and the exciting prospect of the industrial exploitation of a continent. In the rush to take advantage of the new opportunities, ethical scruples were being heedlessly tossed aside.

In that summer of 1869, when Jay Gould, a stock-market gambler who was the undisputed master of the Erie Railroad, cast covetous eyes on the newly completed Albany & Susquehanna line, between Albany and Binghamton, New York, he sent agents to buy up shares subscribed to by towns along its right-of-way, and tried to displace the existing management and directors of the road by getting complaisant judges to issue a flock of injunctions against them. Gould was vigorously countered by President Ramsey of the Albany & Susquehanna, who induced other judges to issue counterinjunctions against Gould. The conflict between the two factions became a minor civil war, with arrests being made in accordance with the dictates of Manhattan judges who took orders from Gould and the decrees of upstate judges who sided with Ramsey. At one point, hired thugs battling for control of a tunnel along the way manned two locomotives and collided. Day after day the

New York papers carried news stories about "The Susquehanna War." As the date of the annual stockholders' meeting at Albany approached, it was clear that the Gould forces would try to unseat the directors favorable to President Ramsey.

On the day of the meeting Gould's right-hand man, the dandified Jim Fisk, was on hand accompanied by a gang of forty or more ruffians whom he had brought up by train from New York. Each carrying a proxy—for they were now to play the part of Albany & Susquehanna stockholders—these ragged and muscular characters were lined up by Fisk in a meeting room already crowded with railroad officials, lawyers, and stockholders.

Just before the meeting, President Ramsey was arrested on a charge engineered by Gould. Apparently the Gould-Fisk tactics were to disorganize the Ramsey forces and then to hold an election which their gang of "stockholders" would control. But Ramsey managed to get bail in the nick of time. What then happened was that *two* stockholders' meetings took place. Surveying the tangled results of these rival elections, and of assorted injunctions, arrests, and lawsuits, the governor of New York called upon the Supreme Court to settle the whole issue. Weeks later it delivered judgment—in favor of the Ramsey board and all its works.

As one of Ramsey's chief aides, Pierpont Morgan took part in this incredible episode, but just how much part is not clear. It is certainly true, however, that Morgan was called upon to help Ramsey, and that his name headed the list of directors chosen by the Ramsey faction and subsequently confirmed by the upstate court. Undoubtedly the victory of his side added to the solidity of Morgan's reputation in downtown New York. But the battle for control of the Albany & Susquehanna may have had a deeper effect.

Earlier that summer Pierpont Morgan, accompanied by his wife and two friends, had taken his first far-western trip over the newly completed transcontinental railroad line. On the way out they had spent twelve days in Chicago; as they crossed the plains, they could see a Pawnee war party, squads of United States Cavalry, herds of antelopes, and immigrant wagon trains winding slowly westward. They had visited Salt Lake City and San Francisco and the Yosemite. It is not unreasonable to guess that this expedition gave Morgan a fresh and lively sense of what new frontiers there were for the railroad industry to conquer, and that it must have been a shock to him to see a part of that industry demoralized by a lawless battle for control.

In 1869, monopoly, as an alternative to competition, had no such connotations as it carries today. It is hardly an accident that most of the Americans who at the beginning of the twentieth century were charged with being monopolists had got a good look in their youth at competition at its savage and unbridled worst. At the age of thirty-two Pierpont Morgan saw at close range what the Battle of the Susquehanna did to a small fragment of the railroad industry. It brought corruption, confusion, waste, and loss; and his systematic soul detested it. Surely, he may well have thought, it would be better if people could be brought together to combine forces for the orderly and profitable development of railroad properties.

DURING THE NEXT YEAR or two Morgan became deeply depressed about his health. He felt perpetually tired, slept badly, had severe headaches, and recurrences of his old fainting-spell trouble. He began to think that, having already made a good deal of money, he might as well retire. The partnership of Dabney, Morgan & Co. was coming to an end; the elderly Mr. Dabney wanted to retire. Why not get out of business and take as much time as might be necessary to recover his own physical well-being? So he reasoned in a letter to his father in London.

It happened that at about this time his father was engaged in one of the boldest operations ever known in international finance. The French had just been soundly defeated in the Franco-Prussian War of 1870; Paris was surrounded by German forces. Junius Morgan, head of the London firm of J. S. Morgan & Co., agreed with the French ministers in Tours to float a loan to the French government of two hundred and fifty million francs—fifty million dollars—in the form of six percent bonds which he would take at the price of 80. It was a stiff price, but it was also a dangerous gamble. At first the sale of bonds went badly, and Morgan had to buy back a considerable number of them at a discount. But French credit rallied; the value of the bonds quickly rose to par, and Morgan's judgment was justified. His firm not only made a resounding profit on the French bonds—probably five million dollars or more—but won for itself in the world of international finance a place second only to that of the Rothschilds.

Junius Morgan now appreciated more than ever the value of having his son in a strongly entrenched position to sell European securities in the United States and to negotiate for American securities which J. S. Morgan & Co. might distribute in Europe. And here was that son flirting with the idea of retirement at the age of thirty-three!

Somewhere about this time Junius Morgan wrote to his son, "I have had a visit from Mr. A. J. Drexel, of Drexel & Co., Philadelphia. It is possible he may want to see you about a certain matter, and if he does I hope you will go to see him."

Drexel & Co.—established by old Joseph Drexel, an immigrant portrait painter turned financier—had become an important private banking house in Philadelphia. It had set up a London branch and it also had a Paris house. But its New York connections were unsatisfactory. What could be more promising than an alliance with young Pierpont Morgan, who not only was building up a sturdy reputation of his own but also was the son and American representative of the great J. S. Morgan of London? One day in May 1871, Anthony J. Drexel, old Joseph's son, wired young Morgan asking him to come on to Philadelphia for dinner.

Morgan took a train to Philadelphia and dined with the Drexel family. After dinner Drexel and he adjourned to the library.

When Drexel proposed that they join forces to set up in New York the firm of Drexel, Morgan & Co., Morgan protested that he was in wretched health and that he had been thinking of leaving business altogether. He could not enter such an alliance unless he took a year off at the outset. Drexel saw no objection, and that evening they reached an agreement, written down by hand on a small sheet of paper. On the first of July, 1871, the new firm of Drexel, Morgan & Co. began business—whereupon Pierpont Morgan promptly sailed with his wife and young children to spend over a year abroad.

THE NEW ASSOCIATION proved highly profitable. By 1873 Drexel, Morgan & Co. began to break into the field of distributing United States government bond issues, a field which for some time had been monopolized by Jay Cooke's banking house in Philadelphia. When, a few months later, Cooke plunged into bankruptcy in the panic of 1873, Morgan found himself without an equal rival. For in those days there were far more wealthy investors in England and on the Continent than in the United States, and there was nothing more important to a distributor of government bonds than to have the means of selling them abroad. With the Drexel capital and his connections abroad, Morgan suddenly found himself one of the key figures of American finance.

He had his offices, now, in a sumptuous and strategically located building just erected by the Drexels at the corner of Broad and Wall streets—a six-story white marble building with a corner entrance and, high above it on the roof, a hexagonal cupola. These splendid new quarters were to serve him throughout the rest of his business life, for it was not until within two or three years of his death that the Drexel Building was removed to make way for the present building at 23 Wall Street.

Uptown, he and Fanny and the children occupied a brownstone house at 6 East Fortieth Street, just a few steps from Fifth Avenue, across which rose the embankment of the Croton Reservoir (on the site of the present Public Library). It was a very proper house by the standards of the Rutherford B. Hayes period. In its high-ceilinged, heavily curtained drawing room there were upholstered chairs, a fringed sofa, and sundry small tables of maximum inutility and instability; there were fine rugs superimposed upon a flowered carpet; every mantel, table, and shelf carried ornaments and knickknacks; and there was hardly a foot of wall space not covered with pictures elaborately framed in gold, hanging one above the other.

The Morgans also had a country place at Highland Falls, just south of West Point. Cragston was one of the most comfortable estates in what was then a fashionable summer district. Standing on a knoll just above the west bank of the Hudson, the house was a very ample, broad-eaved, gabled structure three stories high, built of white clapboard; its front windows looked southward across a fine lawn toward the hills opposite Bear Mountain. This commodious country house, surrounded by rolling acres of field and grove with the river glittering below it, well suited a man who enjoyed exercising a substantial hospitality and appreciated the English county tradition. Here the growing Morgan family now spent a good part of the year.

Still Pierpont's health troubled him. He had frequent colds and headaches, and to his humiliation the recurring inflammation of the skin of his face began to settle in his nose; this was the beginning of the unending affliction of *acne rosacea*, which was destined to disfigure him increasingly as time went on. But there were compensations. He was a rich man now, and life was beginning to expand.

He was beginning to think of breeding collies as well as cattle at Cragston, and wondering whether he might not acquire, in addition to the pair of smart horses which drew Fanny's carriage, a pair of fast trotters. And might not the launch *Louisa* soon be superseded by a real steam yacht?

The depression which followed the financial follies of the post-Civil War years was slow to depart, and it was a hungry time for a great number of Americans; but Morgan was a coming man with an ample income, and it was fun to use it amply.

He took his family on frequent trips abroad. In England they stayed either in Junius Morgan's fine city house at Prince's Gate, facing Hyde Park, or at his country estate, Dover House, at Roehampton, in the western outskirts of London. In 1877 the Morgans chartered a steamer to go up the Nile and had their pictures taken in front of the ruins of Karnak in a group of eighteen—family, friends, doctor, maid, dragoman, waiter, and consular agent—Pierpont standing very straight and solid-looking, with pith helmet, knickerbocker suit, wing collar, and a long walking stick.

IN A DAY WHEN AMERICAN RAILROADS and American industry depended largely upon Europeans to provide them with capital, Morgan was a sort of colonial administrator: a representative in America of the financial might of Britain. Now this very fact was about to bring a new turn in his career.

In 1879 William H. Vanderbilt—son and heir of the old "Commodore"—came to Pierpont for aid. The Vanderbilts had brought together a number of small railroads to form the New York Central System, which reached from New York all the way to Chicago. The younger Vanderbilt, who owned no less than eighty-seven percent of its shares, had begun to realize that this virtual one-man ownership had its embarrassing aspect. He was unpopular with the general public, and he knew it.

Now Vanderbilt wanted to unload the onus of sole ownership and went to consult Morgan because of Morgan's English connections. Though he wanted to sell a considerable part of his interest in the road, he did not want the word to go around that either he or the Central must be in trouble. Could Morgan manage a private and unpublicized sale to English investors?

Morgan leaped at the chance, and working quietly, disposed of 150,000 shares of New York Central stock directly to overseas purchasers at $120 per share, with an option to dispose of another 100,000 shares within the following year at the same price. When the news broke, the financial community was amazed. In the words of the *Commercial & Financial Chronicle* for November 29, 1879, "There has been one topic in Wall Street this week—the great New York Central & Hudson stock sale."

As holder of proxies for the English purchasers, Morgan sat on the New York Central's board as a wielder of great potential influence. For years, on his visits to London, Englishmen had asked him why so many things went wrong with their investments in American securities. Why was America having such hard times? Why was the United States currency so unsound? Why were so many American railroads scandalously mismanaged? Why were men like Gould permitted to plunder right and left the properties in which honest Englishmen had invested? Now he had become the representative of these skeptical Englishmen on the New York Central board. They had been persuaded by his assurances. To himself he must admit that lawless feuds continued to sully the record of American railroading. Now he could be something more than a banker and international dealer in securities; he was in a position to do something about this economic anarchy. At the age of forty-two he moved out from his father's shadow and took his place as a regularizing and disciplining force in American industry.

Chapter 4

Morgan the Peacemaker

ON A WARM MORNING in July 1885, two gentlemen from Philadelphia boarded a sleek black steam yacht at a dock in Jersey City. The two Philadelphians were George B. Roberts and Frank Thomson, president and vice-president of the Pennsylvania Railroad. They had come at the invitation of Pierpont Morgan to talk with him and Chauncey Depew, the president of the New York Central Railroad.

The yacht was Morgan's *Corsair*, a 185-foot vessel which he had bought three years earlier to supersede the *Louisa*. And the purpose of the excursion—ostensibly to offer the two Philadelphians a few hours of respite from the summer heat—was really to try to negotiate a peace treaty to end the most menacing railroad war of the day.

The six years since Morgan had taken a seat on the New York Central's board of directors in 1879 had been years of furious and undisciplined railroad building. All over the country new railroads were being projected, big lines were buying up little ones to form connected systems. Railroad corporations were the most powerful units of big business. They were attracting inventive and ambitious men who could foresee how a well-run railroad would transform a wilderness into a chain of thriving communities. But they also attracted adventurers and knaves, and their financing, construction, and operation offered extraordinary spectacles of ruthlessness and buccaneering.

To begin with, railroad rates were wildly anarchic. At one time it cost only half as much to ship steel from Chicago to the Atlantic seaboard as to ship it the much shorter distance from Pittsburgh to the seaboard, simply because there were several lines competing for the Chicago traffic and there was only one line available for the Pittsburgh traffic. Passenger fares, too, fluctuated wildly as the roads sought to grab one another's business: at one time the New York Central charged only seven dollars for the long ride from New York to Chicago, and the "immigrant" rate between these two cities fell all the way to one dollar. Even worse was the practice of charging reduced rates to big companies whose business was especially valuable while the small and friendless paid through the nose. The anarchy in rates made business hazardous not only for those who shipped their goods over the roads but for the railroad corporations themselves.

There was also widespread buccaneering in railroad ownership—getting control of a company only to play its stock up and down in the market for one's personal profit; or getting control of two railroads and using one of them to enrich the other; or organizing a construction company to build a road at such padded "cost" that the construction company made millions and the railroad company (whose stock one could always sell) became saddled with overwhelming fixed debts.

Finally, there was an epidemic of building needlessly competitive roads. If, for example, there was already a prosperous line running between two cities, there was nothing to prevent the building of another, parallel line, in the hope that the management of the existing road would buy it out at a blackmail price.

This last was more or less what had brought about the conference on the *Corsair* in 1885. Some years previously a group of men including Jay Gould, George M. Pullman, and General Horace Porter, had conceived the idea of building a railroad on the west shore of the Hudson that would run roughly parallel to William H. Vanderbilt's New York Central all the way from New York to Buffalo.

This West Shore Road was a losing venture from the first. But Vanderbilt did *not* buy it out, and before 1885 it was bankrupt. Lately, however, a group of men interested in the Pennsylvania Railroad had been quietly buying up the West Shore's depreciated bonds. Suppose they got control of the ailing company and then put the mighty resources of the Pennsylvania into an effort to steal from the New York Central much of the valuable New York–Great Lakes traffic?

Earlier the Central had begun a foray into Pennsylvania territory. Knowing that Pittsburgh industrialists like Andrew Carnegie were angry at the high rates exacted by the Pennsylvania for carrying their products to the Atlantic seaboard, William H. Vanderbilt had proposed to them in 1883 that a parallel line be built across the Allegheny Mountains from the Philadelphia region to Pittsburgh.

"What do you think of it, Carnegie?" asked Vanderbilt.

"I think so well of it," said the little Scotsman, "that I and my friends will raise five million dollars as our subscription."

Whereupon Vanderbilt himself agreed to put in five million, and presently construction of the South Pennsylvania Railroad began.

Morgan had watched the building of the West Shore with acute distaste—a distaste accentuated by the fact that its new tracks ran along the Hudson River shore just below his beloved Cragston; during two or three summers its construction gangs had made an infernal noise blasting at the ledges along the route and shaking the windows of his house. More importantly, Morgan felt responsible for the Central's future prosperity; were not English investors counting on him to see that dividends were steady? And because the Drexel firm had done financing for the Pennsylvania in the past, he had every reason to want to remain in the Pennsylvania's good graces too. Surely this war was folly. Here, perhaps, was a chance to do something for the cause of order.

Coming back from Europe, Morgan took pains to return on the same liner with Vanderbilt and talk him into permitting peace negotiations. After several futile conferences, he also finally succeeded in inducing Roberts and Thomson of the Pennsylvania to come for a little run on the *Corsair*.

When his guests were settled on the yacht's deck he proposed that the Pennsylvania drop all interest in the West Shore line, permitting the Central to buy it out of bankruptcy and take a long lease on it. In return the Central would turn over the control of the South Pennsylvania project to the Pennsylvania, to do with as it pleased.

The four men—Roberts, Thomson, Depew, and Morgan—sat under an awning aft of the *Corsair*'s single funnel while the sharp-prowed vessel steamed slowly up and down the Hudson and out of New York Harbor as far as Sandy Hook. Depew talked, argued, reasoned. Roberts argued back. Morgan sat mostly silent, smoking a big black cigar. Thomson appeared to have been won over, but Roberts, who had begun his career as a rodman and had been a railroad builder throughout, didn't like to succumb to the will of an investment banker.

The afternoon drew to a close and the *Corsair* steamed back to the Jersey City docks; still there seemed to be no meeting of minds. Not until Roberts was leaving the boat did he capitulate. As he shook hands with Morgan and stepped upon the gangplank he said, "I will agree to your plan and do my part." The war was over.

Presently weeds began to grow over the unfinished South Pennsylvania embankments and moss over the tunnel walls. Not for over half a century was work resumed for the completion not of a railroad but of a great automobile highway. The Pennsylvania Turnpike uses the embankments and tunnels built during the railroad war of the early eighties; and modern motorists would not be following that particular route through the Pennsylvania hills if Pierpont Morgan had not in the summer of 1885 taken two Philadelphians for a little spin on the *Corsair*.

With this bold success to his credit, Morgan's prestige became immense. One by one the managements of financially sick railroads came to him for help. Within the next few years he was deep in the reorganization plans of the Reading, the Baltimore & Ohio, the Chesapeake & Ohio, and other lines. What matter that he was ignorant of the technical knowledge of railroading which it took railroad executives long years to master? In matters of life and death for the corporations which stood behind these executives, it was his word which counted most.

530

WITHIN ONLY A FEW WEEKS of Morgan's successful peacemaking between the Pennsylvania and the Central the principle of co-operation was being eagerly embraced by the other trunk lines. There was a new feeling in the air that the owners and heads of the companies meant business, and freight rates and passenger fares began to rise from the low points to which harsh competition had driven them.

By the following spring the *Commercial & Financial Chronicle* reported that passenger fares between New York and Chicago, which had gone all the way down to seven dollars, had advanced to twenty dollars for first class and seventeen dollars for second class. And in the same journal there was another announcement, which read:

> *Anthracite Coal Combination*—Representatives of the various coal companies met at the house of Mr. J. Pierpont Morgan this week, and informally decided to limit coal production and maintain prices. The new coal combination agrees to mine 33,500,000 tons of coal this year. Last year's output was 31,600,000 tons. An advance of 25 cents a ton was made by the companies on the following day. . . .

Morgan, having succeeded with one peace conference, had decided to try another. The anthracite coal business was then almost wholly in the control of several railroad companies which served eastern Pennsylvania—the Reading, the Pennsylvania, the Lehigh Valley, the Delaware & Hudson, and others. He was now reorganizing the Reading; what better way of showing his interest in its future than by a conference on prices and production between the heads of these railroads?

There was then no Sherman Anti-Trust Act so the agreement was perfectly legal. But it was, of course, monopolistic and throttled competition, and there was a loud public outcry. As *The New York Times* said indignantly: "In plain language, this means . . . a tax upon an important commodity at the will of the combination. . . ."

It is doubtful if Morgan saw much difference between ending railroad wars and ending competition in the coal industry. This, too, in his eyes, was cooperation in order that all might prosper.

IN THE RAILROAD INDUSTRY there remained a semblance of co-operation among the trunk lines largely as a result of Morgan's influence; but over the country as a whole the granting of rebates and the sale of blocks of tickets by railroad passenger agents to scalpers went right on, as did the building of rival and blackmail lines, especially in the West. In short, the industry was still in an anarchic condition.

Public fury at the behavior of the railroads led Congress to adopt the Interstate Commerce Act early in 1887. It sternly forbade rebates and any sort of discrimination in rates, and it set up an Interstate Commerce Commission to see that freight and passenger rates were reasonable and just, and to require public disclosure of all rates charged.

But Congress had given the law enforcers so little authority that there were dozens of ways of circumventing them. Abuses and cutthroat competition continued. By the end of 1888 so few American railroads were earning enough money to pay dividends on their swollen capital that the English investors to whom Morgan felt responsible were protesting vehemently, and he decided that it was time to turn on the heat.

So now he called a much larger and more ambitious conference; and this time he allied with him several other investment banking houses. It was as much as to say, We represent the owners of your companies. These owners are sick and tired of the way you are behaving. They want earnings. And to that end they want you people to cooperate.

One can measure the height to which Morgan's prestige and influence had risen by the fact that the great company of railroad presidents from all over the country who gathered at Morgan's brownstone house in December 1888 represented nearly every major railroad west of Chicago and St. Louis. Even Jay Gould, who at the time was head of the Missouri Pacific, had accepted Morgan's invitation. The presidents of the trunk lines were there too, and representatives of several leading investment banking houses on both sides of the water.

Morgan wanted the railroad presidents to make among themselves a definite agreement not to cut rates and not to build unnecessary competing lines. He wanted them to put teeth into this agreement, so that any man who broke it would suffer penalties.

It was too much of a gathering of lions to be an altogether calm occasion. At one point Roberts of the Pennsylvania pointed out sharply that there wouldn't be much trouble about the building of ruinously competing lines if investment bankers didn't provide the money to finance them. Morgan replied with a firm pledge that the investment bankers were ready to play ball and would no longer provide such funds.

The meeting appeared to end successfully. The men who sat in Morgan's library agreed to set up an association of presidents, pledged to live up to the Interstate Commerce Act and also to maintain rates, with a board of managers to arbitrate disagreements. But after the presidents had filed out of the library, a group of the Westerners adjourned to hold a rump session of their own at the Hotel Windsor, and one of them was quoted as saying, "We did not swallow whole the arrangement evidently prepared for us."

Rate wars and competitive gouging did not come to an end. The following year Morgan held another conference, and that one, too, failed to end the chaos in the industry. He began to realize that wherever he really *must* have order, he would have to impose it himself.

Chapter 5

No. 219

IN 1880 IT HAD BECOME CLEAR to Morgan that the house on East Fortieth Street was no longer adequate for the needs of his family, so he bought a more massive brownstone house at the corner of Thirty-sixth Street and Madison Avenue.

He employed Christian Herter, head of Herter Brothers, interior decorators for the post-Civil War millionaires, to remodel it. He moved the entrance to Thirty-sixth Street, utilizing the whole Madison Avenue front for a bay-windowed drawing room, and added a conservatory on the eastern side, where it would catch the morning sunlight. In the autumn of 1882 the Morgans moved in; and this house, 219 Madison Avenue, remained their town residence throughout the rest of Pierpont's life.

In those days New York's native brownstone was beginning to seem a little old-fashioned; the apt material for a millionaire's house was limestone, or even marble; and American architects trained at the École des Beaux-Arts vied with one another in adapting the designs of famous European châteaus, castles, and palaces to residential uses. It became fashionable also to import bodily various architectural details and accessories, much as if Western Europe were one great builders' supply store.

With such nonsense Pierpont Morgan would have no truck. He shared the rising veneration for the art of the Old World and became a collector and importer of it on a tremendous scale, but he didn't want to subdue his domestic life to it. His brownstone house was large, dignified, and comfortable. In due course he consented to have his drawing room done over from more or less Pompeian into more or less French; and still later, when his collection of books had long since overflowed all the book-shelves of the house, he built a marble Renaissance library on Thirty-sixth Street next door to his house, and incorporated into its interior design many of the architectural trophies of his chase for art. But he never changed the original library at No. 219. It was just about right for him, and that was that.

This large, high-ceilinged room was the center of his life at home, and it was here that he held his important conferences. Paneled with Santo Domingo mahogany, the general effect was so imposingly dark that in later years the household staff referred to it as the "black library." In an arched alcove there was a tiled fireplace flanked by settees, and near the middle of the carpeted floor there was a big, ornate walnut kneehole desk. The room reflected the late-Victorian unwillingness to leave any foot of wall space unoccupied; there were even paintings hung between the wainscoting and the ceiling. But above all it conveyed a sense of somber and dignified comfort.

Here at No. 219 the Morgan family spent the winter months. During the rest of the year—from April to October or thereabouts—they made their headquarters at Cragston; and just as they stood fast on Thirty-sixth Street despite the northward drift of wealth and fashion, so they remained loyal to the highlands of the Hudson when its popularity waned in favor of Newport or the north shore of Long Island. To such decrees of fashion the Morgans were indifferent. In the complex of social groups in Manhattan, they belonged neither to the aristocracy of the old Dutch families nor to that Society with a capital S aspired to by upcoming millionaires and their wives. Pierpont Morgan, for one, didn't care for balls, cotillions, gilt chairs, chatter, lackeys in livery, or social emulation. He preferred solid comfort, solid dinners, solid people; butlers in discreet black coats; and if there was occasion for splendor, his own sort, on his own terms.

He belonged to what in Europe would be called the *haute bourgeoisie*—a vaguely defined group of men who had plenty of money, were engaged in large corporate business or finance, voted the Republican ticket, subscribed to conservative newspapers, held a low view of most politicians and an even lower view of "labor agitators"; who belonged to the right sort of church (preferably Episcopal); served on the boards of well-established charities, hospitals, and museums; joined clubs where they would be unlikely to be troubled by hearing any queer ideas; had a proper taste for good cigars and good wines; had decent manners, at least toward one another; and expected their wives to be charming and angelic but ignorant of business affairs or, for that matter, any affairs of moment.

Morgan's life at No. 219 followed a strict routine. Church at St. George's on Sunday morning, with perhaps a walk home afterward. Friends or relatives in to supper Sunday evening. Hymn singing after Sunday supper. Dr. Rainsford of St. George's Church to breakfast Monday morning. For some years, the Mendelssohn Club, a choral society, on Wednesday evening—presumably to please Fanny, for Pierpont was unable to hold a tune, despite his undaunted appetite for what his son-in-law Herbert R. Satterlee called "strenuous, tuneful hymns."

He dressed for a business day in a frock coat, a hard winged collar, and an ascot tie; this was the costume of his kind in Wall Street, and only on the hottest days was it considered proper to remove the coat for certain chores, such as the signing of papers. He ate a solid breakfast, and delighted in having his children—in later years, his grandchildren—on hand then.

In the pre-telephone days there was a private wire between his house and his office, on which reports and quotations were printed on a tape, news-ticker fashion; he would send a child into the next room to bring him the tape, so that he could scan it at the breakfast table and write messages or orders for the child to type off on the machine; he liked to get the quotations on foreign exchange and perhaps to do a little arbitraging—simultaneously buying and selling dollars, pounds, and other currencies to net a profit on the fluctuations of the moment. A lightning mathematical mind enabled him to see at a glance what the winning operation would be. Then he would proceed to his office—preferably, as the years went by, not by the elevated railroad but by horse-drawn cab.

At the end of the day's work he might stop off at the Whist Club or the Union Club for some cards, or call briefly on a friend; but as often as not he would go straight home, lie down on the sofa in his study, pull an afghan over him, and sleep until it was time to dress for dinner: he prided himself on being able to hurry upstairs just as the first guests arrived, and come down again only six minutes later in tails and white tie. The Morgans gave a good many dinner parties and dined out often. The last item of his daily routine was a few games of solitaire, his constant solace.

During the warm months he always spent Thursday at Cragston as a midweek holiday—a custom which dated back to his earliest business days, when he had had to spend most of Saturday at his desk. Now the *Corsair* took him to Cragston for the Thursday respite and again—usually with a house party of guests—for a short weekend. There he could show his guests his new cow barn and his prize cattle, as well as the Cragston Kennels and his blue-ribbon collies. Yet for all the amplitude of the place, with its stables of driving horses, saddle horses, and ponies, its farm buildings, its grass tennis courts, its subordinate buildings to house the servants, and its numerous guests, it remained essentially a place of unostentatious domestic comfort.

UPON THIS DOMESTIC ROUTINE, however, was superimposed another pattern more individual and more splendid. First of all, there was the magnificent *Corsair*. When the family were at Cragston, he spent most of his leisure time aboard the great yacht anchored in the North River. He would pile guests into a little launch to go out and dine aboard her; usually he slept there. She frequently took him off on cruises, sometimes with his family, sometimes with a party of friends. She was a big yacht, but not big enough to suit him as his fortunes waxed, and so in 1890 he ordered the building of *Corsair II*, to measure 204 feet on the waterline and 241 feet overall. On such a superb pleasure boat one could live and entertain like a prince.

Each year he had been accustomed to go to London, usually in the spring, to maintain touch with his father's old office at 22 Old Broad Street and to take a short holiday on the Continent; now these annual expeditions became longer and more elaborate. As time went on, Fanny no longer accompanied him. Usually he took along one of his daughters. A busy stay at Prince's Gate or Dover House and he would be off for Paris, where the Hotel Bristol (run by his father's ex-butler) always let him have the same corner suite; he might go on to the Riviera, or visit Rome, or take the cure at one of the great watering places. Several months might elapse before he spied the *Corsair*, decked with pennants, coming down New York Harbor to welcome him home.

These were months when he moved out from under the strict conventions of his domestic routine and enjoyed the more varied company of men and women of the world. Like many an American man of that era of sheltered womankind, Pierpont Morgan believed that the wives and daughters of all right-thinking men should be kept unsullied from contact with anything so gross as outspoken talk, or politics and business affairs. He also enjoyed with unashamed gusto not only the freer talk and freer conduct of gentlemen apart from their ladies, but also the company of those women whose wit and beauty had escaped the confines of a dulling respectability. Despite his swollen nose and his often brusque manner, Pierpont Morgan was immensely attractive to women of all ages. He liked to shower gifts upon them; at least one or two he presented with houses or set up financially for life. In an age when an unmarried woman was considered lost to decency if she dined alone with a man, gossip portrayed in flaming colors many companionships that today would attract no attention whatever. Like many men in that era, part of the time Morgan lived by the rules of nineteenth-century gentility, and part of the time he was free to make his own rules. He had his own standard of personal conduct—to try to behave like a gentleman—and there is no reason to believe that it did not govern him throughout.

THERE WAS A STRONG conservative strain in Pierpont Morgan's temperament. He cherished old family rites. There must always be a gathering of the Morgan clan for Thanksgiving dinner, with an invariable menu. He loved the traditional Christmas ceremonies: the dressing of the tree on Christmas Eve, a carriage trip with one of the children to distribute presents; church on Christmas morning, and then a family dinner. (For several years, when his children were young, he used to dress up as Santa Claus.) In his religion he especially warmed to what was venerably traditional. When he liked anything—the furnishings of his library or of his yacht, a certain suite at a hotel, a house or scene hallowed by association—he wanted to keep it unchanged.

In politics and economics, too, he was deeply conservative. He voted the Republican ticket except in 1884, when he disapproved of Blaine and cast his ballot for Cleveland, who was certainly no apostle of quick change or government intervention in business. His son-in-law's biography describes the prosperity of 1881 and reflects the conservative nineteenth-century attitude:

"There were not many problems in the national life of the day. Immigration was practically unrestricted. Work was plentiful. Food and clothing were cheap. Everybody was busy. Labor was not yet unionized. The organized attempts to stir up discontent and raise class feeling had not been begun. Pierpont was making money, as was almost everybody else who was engaged in sound business. . . ."

That passage would probably have struck Morgan himself as reasonable. If you had reminded him that the Reading Railroad's anthracite workers in the valleys of Pennsylvania, for example, had little share in the national prosperity, being overworked and underpaid, he would have given you a glare signifying that this was irrelevant: that new inventions and new industrial processes, sensibly applied by well-financed companies, were one of the answers to general poverty; that churches and charities were another.

As for politicians being of any value in combating poverty, Morgan had seen enough of them in the Albany & Susquehanna business and in subsequent litigations to be convinced that they were low fellows who were always ready to sell their services for a handout from the rich. People like himself, who helped business secure capital and tried to keep it on an orderly and solvent basis, were doing more for the general well-being than all these yawpers put together.

Most of us would call such sentiments extremely conservative. Yet the label is misleading to the extent that it suggested that Morgan wanted to see things stand still. In a real sense it was he and the other fabricators of giant industries who were the radicals of the day, changing the face of America; it was those who objected to the results who were conservatives seeking to preserve the individual opportunities and the folkways of an earlier time.

Nor did his love for tradition prevent him from hastening technological change. He put money into the Edison Electric Light Co. as early as 1878, when the coming of electric lighting was only a hope. When, in September 1882, Edison's first power station for lower Manhattan was completed, the Drexel Building was one of the first ones to be equipped (with 106 bulbs).

At that time Morgan was completing the alterations to 219 Madison Avenue, and he seized the opportunity to install the new lights there, making his house the first residence in the world to be thus lit throughout. Then began a chapter of troubles. Since there was no central power station in that part of the city, an engine had to be installed in a cellar under his stable, and an engineer had to visit this plant daily to get up steam so that the generator would operate. The electric wiring of the gas lamps which had been installed in the house caused

SHERMAN ANTI-TRUST A

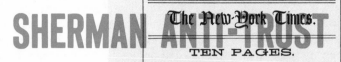

CORSAIR I and CORSAIR II

Lawn tennis at Dover Hou[se]
about 1876

---

r denotes the time when the
n expires.

y up-town office of THE TIMES
1,269 Broadway, between Thirty-
first and Thirty-second Streets.

The New-York Times.

TEN PAGES.

NEW-YORK, WEDNESDAY, DEC. 10, 1890.

The Signal Service Bureau report indi-
cates for to-day, in this city, fair, warmer
weather.

A GROWING INDUSTRY.

We hope it has not escaped the attention of Mr. JOHN SHERMAN that the en-
actment of his so-called Anti-Trust law
stimulated the Trust-making
possibly this has not been
y the high-tariff journals
uring the campaign to this
hat their party had "kept
nd made ample provision
row of every "combine" in
they do not s
e of them
atches in
T

the next atte
next general
successful. I
Mr. PARNELL
sure that nece
pathies of th
class, which f
the Liberal a
Parties, from
the champion
might have na
the Irish lead
have put the
during his ow
cidally selfish
Irish Parliame
tions, and ha
paralyzed the
It is evident
the Irish Parl
absolutely un
thing for ho
united ever s
the leadership
it was due th
to Ireland ha
just before t
personal clai
destruction of
the present c
be most absu
rward any
use of C
xior

frequent short circuits or failures of power; once the lights died out at eleven p.m. while the house was full of guests. Neighbors complained of the noise of the motor; one even alleged that it gave off smoke which tarnished her silver. And when the lamp on the big desk in the middle of Pierpont Morgan's library was wired there was a short circuit and then a fire which ruined the rug and the desk.

The next morning (according to Satterlee) Edison's assistant, Everitt H. Johnson, arrived when Morgan was at breakfast. He went into the library and surveyed the wreckage, apprehensive lest the banker lose interest in financing Edison's enterprise. "Suddenly he heard footsteps and Pierpont appeared in the doorway . . . and looked at him over the tops of his eyeglasses. 'Well?' he said. Johnson had been formulating an explanation ever since he had heard of the fire and was preparing to make excuses. Just as he opened his mouth to speak, he saw Mrs. Morgan. Catching Johnson's eye she put her finger on her lips. Johnson took the hint. . . . After a long minute's silence, Pierpont said, 'Well, what are you going to do about it?'

"Johnson answered, 'Mr. Morgan, the trouble is not inherent in the thing itself. It is my own fault, and I will put it in good working order so that it will be perfectly safe.'

"Pierpont asked, 'How long will it take to fix it?'

"Johnson answered, 'I will do it right away.'

" 'All right,' said Pierpont, 'see that you do.' And he turned and went out.

"The . . . new installation was so satisfactory that Pierpont gave a reception, and about four hundred guests came to the house and marveled at the convenience and simplicity of the lighting system."

The morning after the reception, when the financier Darius Ogden Mills visited the Drexel Building to buy a thousand shares of Edison stock, Morgan waylaid him and told him that he would permit his partners to make such a sale on one condition, "that for every share of Edison stock that they buy for you, they buy one for me." And later, when a million dollars was needed to build an uptown power station, he subscribed half of the amount himself.

Chapter 6

Railroad Reorganizer—and Emperor?

LIKE A GENERAL whose supreme tactical opportunity comes when the battle is going badly, Morgan had to wait for a time of financial disaster to become a really decisive power in the railroad industry. During the eighteen eighties he had ended one railroad war, had reorganized several bankrupt or hard-pressed railroad companies, and had tried, with indifferent success, to persuade the railroad chiefs of the country to end the corporate knifing and gouging that seemed to be imperiling the investment standing of the nation's most important industry. Now, during the financial hurricanes of the mid-nineties, he was to step into a position of unprecedented authority in that industry.

For more than four years—from 1893 into 1897—the United States was tormented by a major depression. Factories shut down, bankruptcies multiplied, wages were cut, workers by the millions lost their jobs, and there was industrial strife, bitterness, and unrest. The Homestead Strike of 1892, the Pullman Strike of 1894, the pathetic march upon Washington by "Coxey's Army," reveal the anger and bewilderment of the time.

One of the most dismaying things about that depression was the epidemic of financial bankruptcy among the railroads. As passenger and freight traffic declined, the moment came when the managers of a line could no longer pay their debts and joined the melancholy procession to the courts. Within two years nearly one-fourth of the total railway capitalization of the country passed through these courts, and by the middle of 1895 no less than 169 railroads with 37,855 miles of track—amounting to more than one-fifth of the total mileage of the country—were being operated by receivers. Nor were little lines the only ones to suffer; many of the largest failed—including the Baltimore & Ohio, the Erie, the Northern Pacific, the Union Pacific, the Santa Fe, the Reading, and the Norfolk & Western.

In every such case the railroad corporation had to be reorganized; for even the sorriest backwoods line was too vital to the life of the community to be permitted to go out of business. This meant that somebody had to invent a plan by which the debts could be whittled down to a point where the company could safely meet all its interest payments out of current revenue. If the plan was to succeed, it must look fair and workable not only to the courts but also to the various groups of creditors; and it must also assure new investors that the reorganized company would be a safe and profitable thing to put their money into. The job called for a mastery of money and the paper instruments which provide money. It was a job for an investment banker, with an expert in corporation accounting at one elbow and a corporation lawyer at the other. Here was Morgan's opportunity.

Nobody in the country could match Morgan's experience as a negotiator among railroad executives and financiers, or his reputation for financial impregnability, reliability, and personal authority. His plans had a way of working. Thus it came about that during the middle nineties Morgan's firm acquired the lion's share of the business of reorganizing the larger railroads. Within the space of four years he reorganized the Richmond Terminal, the Erie, the Reading, and the Norfolk & Western; in alliance with James J. Hill, the great railroader of the Northwest, he reorganized the Northern Pacific; and he played a part also in the reorganization of the Baltimore & Ohio.

The Morgan method, as it developed during those years, might be summed up as follows:

First, his experts estimated the minimum earning capacity of the road. Then the fixed debt of the company was ruthlessly pared down until, even with minimum earnings, it could readily meet its interest payments on that debt—holders of bonds being forced to accept bonds of lower yield, or stock, or both.

Second, the present holders of stock were assessed to provide the reorganized road with working funds.

Third, new stock was issued as lavishly as was necessary to keep everybody happy. In many cases so much stock was issued that thereafter, if the company should need new capital, it could not raise it by selling more stock but would have to sell bonds instead—thus increasing once more its burden of fixed debt. In this respect the Morgan pattern of financing was shortsighted. But for the time being it worked.

Fourth, the reorganizers charged heavily for their services. Of the Erie Railroad reorganization plan, for example, the London *Economist* said wryly, "Messrs. Morgan state, with a candor which, as far as we know, has no precedent in such cases, that they are to get $500,000 cash for their trouble; and as, in addition, the syndicate which guarantees the success of the scheme is likely to get a good commission on the $15,000,000 bonds it purchases, the doctor's bill is sure to reach a million, and perhaps even two million dollars."

In fact, only a small fraction of the syndicate's commission would go to Morgan's own firm. *The Economist* found the Morgan plan fair and reasonable otherwise.

If you had remarked on the size of the bill to Morgan or one of his partners, you would have been reminded that every one of these operations involved great risk. For if the new securities could not for any reason be sold at a good price, his firm would at the least have tied up a lot of capital and at the worst would incur a whopping loss.

Fifth, the future control of the railroad was tied up so tightly that prudent management could be enforced. For Morgan had learned a lesson from what had happened to the Baltimore & Ohio and to the Reading after he had reorganized them, and was resolved that it should not happen again.

In the case of the Baltimore & Ohio, after Morgan had reorganized it in 1887 everything seemed to go well for a while. Samuel Spencer, who had been vice-president of the company, was installed as president. But presently the Garrett family and their friends, under whose leadership the road had run into difficulties, decided to take over again; and since they still owned a majority of the company's stock they were able to do it. They resumed their improvident course, and by 1896 the Baltimore & Ohio was once more in trouble. Investigators looking over the company books found that it had been scandalously overstating its income and understating its liabilities.

The second reorganization of the Baltimore & Ohio was indicative of Morgan's resolution that no one again should have a chance to run away with the property and ruin it. For the voting control of the reorganized road was placed for five years in the hands of a voting trust of five men, including Charles H. Coster (a Morgan partner), Louis Fitzgerald (a firm ally), and three other men whom he and Hill regarded as trustworthy.

The Philadelphia & Reading, too, had been reorganized by Morgan during the eighteen eighties. For a brief time it had been in the grip of a voting trust. But after it was freed, a head-strong president, A. Archibald McLeod, embarked upon a course of management more ambitious than prudent. He leased or bought other railroad lines with the notion of getting a monopoly of the anthracite coal business and launched a scheme for getting a lion's share of the business of carrying coal to New England.

Morgan was furious. In the first place, the Reading Railroad's treasury could ill afford such large expenditures and commitments. In the second place, what McLeod was doing offended Morgan's conviction that each railroad should develop its own territory and not invade other roads' spheres of influence. The Reading had no business going into New England.

When Morgan remonstrated with him, McLeod had been openly defiant. Had he not been heard to say that he would rather run a peanut stand than be dictated to by J. P. Morgan?

Morgan was no peacemaker when he felt that he or his interests had been attacked. Now he made it known that he was through with McLeod's management of the Reading, and that he would have no use in the future for anyone who came to McLeod's aid. Then, on February 17, 1893, there was a sudden onslaught on the stock of the Reading Railroad on the Stock Exchange: a cascade of selling orders which was, probably with good reason, attributed to Morgan's hostility to McLeod.

Only a few days later the officials of the Reading Railroad had to go into court and ask for the appointment of a receiver. Thereupon the job of reorganizing the road went to Morgan. McLeod departed and—lest anybody try such nonsense again—the reorganization provided for a Morgan-appointed voting trust to run the road for at least five years.

Morgan also meant to make it impossible for any speculator to upset his orderly plans. During this same period the officers of the Richmond Terminal—the nucleus of a group of loosely connected southern railroads—came to him and suggested that he reorganize the property. Its stock had long been a football of speculation. Morgan found that most of the common stock was held by a few men, and decided that he would not touch the reorganization unless these men would deliver their shares into his keeping. He didn't want to risk any speculative games while he was at work. When one of the principal owners refused, Morgan was content to have somebody else try to reorganize the Richmond Terminal. The Central Trust Company undertook the job and failed. Morgan was reapproached, and only when the owners agreed to deposit their shares with him did he proceed. And this time, in order that the future of what became the Southern Railway might not be jeopardized by speculators, he tied up its control under the direction of a voting trust composed of himself and two trusted collaborators.

IN EACH OF THESE CASES the company in question came—as many other concerns were in the future to come—under Morgan's control. This involved immense power, but the nature and limitations of that power have often been misunderstood.

Any large business concern is a loose aggregation of departments which run to a large extent on their own; and if this is true of a single company, it is all the more true of a collection of companies and of the men who supposedly "control" them. Usually the representatives of the House of Morgan on the board of directors of a company were content to listen to what went on, merely assuring themselves that the company's funds were not being wasted, that its executives were not going berserk in their competitive battles with other concerns, and that stock-market plungers were not playing hob with it. Even when—as in the three cases of the Baltimore & Ohio, the Reading, and the Richmond Terminal—voting trusts were set up to prevent such abuses, the grasp of Morgan and his friends upon the company's affairs, while strong as iron, was sometimes so loose as to be almost impalpable.

Yet that is not quite all. For beyond this reached the Morgan influence, a thing impossible to measure because it was based upon imponderables. These included the desire of the men of the business community to remain on good terms with a man whose backing had a solid dollars-and-cents value; the knowledge that business deals in which he took part had a way of becoming profitable; the feeling that his judgment was weighty among bankers they might need in the future, and the final fact that there emanated from Morgan himself a personal force which men felt it was rash to challenge.

There is one more thing to be noted. Pierpont Morgan felt that the corporations for whose securities he had assumed responsibility must be in "safe hands." By safe hands he meant those of honest and capable men who lived by a code of conduct which permitted one to rely upon oral agreements. There were a good many businesses in which, if one were dealing with the head executives, one knew one would have to watch one's step. Some of these men one couldn't avoid dealing with, for they had indispensable knowledge and authority. But he preferred to deal with men of his own sort, who followed the code of the gentleman. This often meant men who belonged to the same club, as it were, whose intellectual and social background was similar. With them one knew just where one stood and the understanding could be complete. And it was better yet to deal with tried and trusted friends; their hands were the safest of all.

Now as it happened, Morgan was a man of increasingly formidable will, whose friends tended to agree with him or to be swayed by him. These friends were likely to deal with things very much as he would. They even consulted him and did as he advised. And so, in the end, it often turned out that the "safe hands" were hardly distinguishable from his own.

From the evidence available, it was not Morgan's intent to build a "railroad empire." He believed in order, in reducing competition, in protecting the solvency of properties which he had backed. And so great was his confidence in his own rightness that the logical way of producing this state of affairs seemed to be to provide the railroads with supervisors who would see things as he did. (It was not always clear whether the offense of a man like McLeod was that he had been reckless or that he had got in Morgan's way.) And so the pattern of domination and influence that had emerged by 1897 looked to observers very much indeed like a railroad empire, with Pierpont Morgan as the emperor.

Chapter 7

Gold for the Government

PRESIDENT GROVER CLEVELAND had been established in the White House only a few weeks when the panic of 1893 had convulsed the business world. Other troubles followed—widespread unemployment, the Pullman Strike, destruction of the corn crop by drought, and a fall in the price of wheat. Worst of all, in the eyes of this conservative President, the Treasury's reserve of gold—the buttress of its stability—had been dwindling.

This reserve, alarmingly depleted when Cleveland had taken office, had been shored up by emergency measures only to crumble away again. As the month of January 1895 drew to a close, it seemed likely to vanish altogether. The President faced the grim prospect of a new panic.

The trouble was multifold. In the first place, legislation not only permitted men who held the kind of paper dollars called legal tender (or greenbacks) to turn them in, in exchange for gold, but also provided that the notes must be reissued, and could thus be used again and again as a means of drawing out gold. But this was not the only reason for the gold shortage. The government's revenues were not keeping pace with its expenditures; it was running at a loss, and at times actually had to dip into its gold reserves to pay its day-to-day expenses. Meanwhile a succession of bankruptcies in the United States had so disturbed European investors that they were unloading their American securities, thus hastening the flow of gold away from America.

Several times Cleveland's Secretary of the Treasury, John G. Carlisle, had gone to the New York bankers and persuaded them to exchange some of the gold in their vaults for government notes, or else had issued bonds and with the proceeds of their sale had bought gold for the Treasury; thus disaster had been deferred. But now, on the morning of Monday, January 28, 1895, the gold remaining in the reserve had fallen far below the amount considered the minimum for safety, which was one hundred million dollars. It had been reduced to only a little over fifty-six millions, and the amount was shrinking daily.

On that Monday, January 28, three and three-quarter millions were withdrawn. On Tuesday, three millions were taken out. On Wednesday, nearly three and three-quarter millions. At that rate, the reserve would last scarcely three weeks—and who could tell when the trickle of gold might not become a torrent?

On Monday the twenty-eighth Cleveland turned to Congress for help. But the chances of relief from Congress were small indeed. For during the early nineties the long-gathering resentment of farmers, small businessmen, and workers against business abuses of the time had boiled over, and led them to form the Populist Party. This party's 1892 platform contained many drastic proposals which went to the roots of the abuses of the day. The Populists carried four states and swept into office five senators and ten representatives. But as time went on Populist indignation was concentrated more and more upon the cause of "free silver." The perennial susceptibility of desperate men to panaceas led millions of people to believe that it was gold which was at the root of their troubles; that the wider circulation of silver would enable Kansas farmers to make a profit on their wheat, and would restore the reduced wages of Pennsylvania steelworkers; and that any plan to protect the government's gold supply was an attempt by the money interests to enslave the plain people of America.

Now, at the beginning of 1895, the Senate was dominated by men to whom President Cleveland's insistence upon the protection of the government's gold was the surest sign of his alliance with Wall Street. And when in his emergency message of January 28 he spoke of "the preservation of our national honor and credit," they turned deaf ears.

What, then, could Cleveland do to avert panic? Could the government borrow money through private bankers, who could raise it more rapidly than the government itself through a publicly advertised bond issue? Could private bankers with European connections possibly help to bring back some of the gold which was currently being shipped abroad? On Wednesday, January 30, Secretary of the Treasury Carlisle sent Assistant Secretary Curtis to New York to consult with August Belmont, a banker whose firm was allied with the Rothschilds in England, France, and Germany. Curtis talked with Belmont at his home that evening, and Belmont said there was one man without whose aid no plan could succeed: Pierpont Morgan.

MORGAN WAS NOW emphatically master in his own house. Junius Spencer Morgan, his father, had died in 1890 as the result of a carriage accident. Pierpont had succeeded him as senior partner of the London house of J. S. Morgan & Co. Then, three years later, Anthony J. Drexel died. After a long delay caused by the troubled financial conditions of the time, Morgan in late 1894 had proposed that the Philadelphia and New York firms should become one, the name to become J. P. Morgan & Co. in New York, and Drexel & Co. in Philadelphia. This arrangement went into effect at the end of 1894, so that by the end of January 1895, when Curtis went to New York to consult August Belmont about the gold crisis, Pierpont Morgan's firm in New York had for almost a month been known by his name alone.

Foremost among his partners in New York was the brilliant Charles H. Coster, described by John Moody as "a white-faced, nervous figure, hurrying from directors' meeting to directors' meeting; at evening carrying home his portfolio of corporation problems for the night." Other partners were George S. Bowdoin, an old and dear friend; J. P. Morgan, Jr., who had graduated from Harvard in 1889, and the young Bostonian Robert Bacon. If Coster's endless labor and his untimely death in 1900 did much to give currency to the Wall Street saying, that Morgan partners were likely to die young of overwork, Bacon's spectacular good looks bore out another generalization about the firm: that Pierpont Morgan liked handsome men.

Perhaps there was in this preference an element of compensation for a man who, suffering from *acne rosacea*, knew that his own physical appearance sometimes struck beholders with dismay.

All these men stood in awe of Pierpont Morgan. Everything hung on his word.

On Thursday, January 31—the morning after Curtis' conference with Belmont—Pierpont Morgan received a cable from J. S. Morgan & Co. in London saying that the Rothschild firm there was being requested to handle a new issue of U. S. government securities and was asking the Morgan firm to act with them in marketing the issue. According to the cable, the Rothschild firm doubted that European investors would be willing to take the bonds at an interest rate the U. S. government was willing to offer unless the bonds were backed by gold.

Since there seemed to be little hope that Congress would authorize a bond issue specifically payable in gold, it looked unlikely to Morgan that the government could borrow money quickly on terms satisfactory to European investors.

Presently August Belmont appeared and the two of them walked across the street to confer with Assistant Secretary Curtis at the U. S. Subtreasury. Curtis was consulting the heads of most of the chief international banking houses that day, but it was Morgan and Belmont with whom his negotiations took definite form. Morgan was able to cable London that very day:

. . . The situation, however, is critical and we are disposed to do everything our power avert calamity and assist government under the power it actually possesses . . .

We have requested Secretary Curtis to obtain from government answer to following questions: Would the government make a private contract with a syndicate for the sale of 50,000,000 with option of 50,000,000 additional, such a contract to be considered a state paper and confidential and not to be divulged until syndicate issue completed?

After further financial details, Morgan's cable added:

If can obtain such exclusive contract should feel inclined form syndicate on $3\frac{5}{8}$ to $3\frac{3}{4}\%$ [interest] basis provided at least 25 million could be sold or underwritten in Europe. It is essential restoration confidence and stoppage gold withdrawals that it be known such negotiations made, and £5,000,000 in banks of England, Germany, France available shipment here if necessary.

When Curtis went back to Washington, rumors began to circulate that a syndicate of bankers headed by Pierpont Morgan was coming to the rescue of the gold reserve by an immediate loan of money to the government. There was suddenly a new feeling of hope in the air; the stock market closed strong; and although on that day nearly two and a half million dollars in gold had been withdrawn from the Treasury reserve—all for export by Saturday's steamer—by evening it was said that some of it might not be exported at all.

The tension in Washington was terrific. Night after night the Cabinet was meeting at the White House, and some of the men most directly concerned with the problem of the gold reserve— the President, Secretary of the Treasury Carlisle, Attorney General Olney, and the President's onetime private secretary and present Secretary of War, Daniel Lamont—would on occasion stay in session till dawn. They considered the proposal brought by Curtis, and the next day, Friday, February 1, Morgan cabled London, "Curtis telephones from Washington indications favorable. He will reach here eleven tonight." That Friday morning *The New York Times* ran a front-page news report headed BOND ISSUE COMING SOON. Again the stock market leaped. Better yet, only $1,257,000 was withdrawn from the gold reserve—and $1,800,000 was returned to it! As Morgan cabled to London, "Improvement public feeling today, with nothing known and nothing done, indicative what will follow successful conclusion business."

There seemed to be only one likely hitch in the negotiations. The press and public had acquired the idea that the four percent bonds would be issued to the syndicate at a price to yield $3\frac{1}{2}$ percent. The Treasury insisted on $3\frac{1}{2}$ percent. Morgan was asking for $3\frac{3}{4}$ percent, expecting privately to be able to compromise on $3\frac{5}{8}$ percent. But surely that gap could be closed. Curtis took the detailed proposal back to Washington, promising to telephone the answer at three o'clock Sunday afternoon.

The West Room of the Morgan Library, where the financier held important conferences as well as relaxed, played solitaire, and answered his mail.

On Sunday a telephone message came that the matter was still under consideration and that a messenger would soon start for New York bearing a letter from Secretary Carlisle. The letter, which arrived in New York the next morning, was a bombshell. The negotiations were off.

The Administration's change of heart had been induced by three things: the fact that the price was high, the fact that the drain of gold from the Treasury reserve had for the moment ceased, and the political hazard of the undertaking. Already Democratic newspapers were dismayed at the notion of a private deal between the government and a Republican Wall Street capitalist. Joseph Pulitzer's New York *World* was warning Cleveland and Carlisle that they were delivering themselves to the money interests, and was advising the President to hold out for a three percent loan, saying, "If the banks won't take it, the people will." And so the decision had been made to make a public call for the purchase of government bonds.

Morgan was appalled. He did not believe that a public sale of bonds could possibly succeed. He consulted with Belmont. To abandon the negotiations for a private sale would be disastrous for the government, they agreed. While Belmont started for Washington on Monday morning, Morgan reached Assistant Secretary Curtis by telephone and told him that it would be fatal to announce a public issue of bonds. Curtis presently reported that Secretary Carlisle would delay the announcement for a day.

That afternoon Morgan took the *Congressional Limited* for Washington. Only one thing, he thought, could prevent the failure of his plan—and a panic of incalculable severity: he himself must talk to Grover Cleveland.

IT WAS COLD AND WINDY when he arrived in Washington that Monday evening. He was met at the station by Daniel Lamont, who told him that President Cleveland would not see him. According to Herbert Satterlee, Morgan said shortly to Lamont, "I have come down to Washington to see the President, and I am going to stay here until I see him."

The Hotel Arlington was Morgan's usual Washington headquarters, but, knowing that there he would be under close observation by reporters, he went to the house of his old friend Mrs. J. Kearney Warren on K Street.

He told Mrs. Warren that he could not explain his sudden visit to her, but he was in hiding, awaiting a telephone call; nobody must be admitted to the house while he was there; she must tell her servant that she was not at home to callers. Then—to quote Satterlee—he "sat and smoked before the fire, apparently listening to Mrs. Warren's talk." At the end of an hour or so the telephone rang. It was his partner Bob Bacon, who had persuaded Attorney General Richard Olney to talk to Morgan. Morgan then took a cab to Olney's house, explained to him the importance of a conference with Cleveland, and went on to the Arlington Hotel, where he settled down to play "Miss Milliken," his favorite game of solitaire, for hours while he thought the situation out.

SOMETIME THAT NIGHT or early in the morning a message came from the White House: the President would see Mr. Morgan. With Belmont, Bacon, and his counsel, Francis Lynde Stetson, he walked to the White House through the bitter cold of that February morning.

At the White House they were shown upstairs and ushered into the presence of the President and Secretary Carlisle. Cleveland said that a public issue of bonds had been decided upon. There was a delay while the two officials went over early reports from New York which indicated further withdrawals of gold that day—possibly disastrous withdrawals. There were more interruptions—telephone calls, messages. At last Cleveland turned to Morgan and asked him what he had to say.

Morgan made his argument. Withdrawals of gold had begun again. There was no time for a public issue. He introduced a new idea: that in a certain law dating from Civil War days, Section 3700 of the Revised Statutes, the government was authorized *to buy coin and pay for it in bonds*. Why should the government not buy gold coin from the syndicate—coin gathered partly in the United States, partly in Europe—and pay for it with this new private bond issue?

According to Satterlee, Morgan had recalled the provision as he played solitaire during the night. According to Allan Nevins' life of Cleveland, it was Assistant Secretary Curtis' idea. In any case, the law books were sent for, and Section 3700 was found to be the perfect answer to the situation.

At first, as Cleveland said many years later, "I had a feeling, not of suspicion, but of watchfulness. . . . I had not gone far, however, before my doubts disappeared. I found I was in negotiation with a man of large business comprehension and of remarkable knowledge and prescience . . . of clear-sighted, far-seeing patriotism."

"Mr. Morgan," said the President, "what guarantee have we that if we adopt this plan, gold will not continue to be shipped abroad and while we are getting it in, it will go out, so that we will not reach our goal? Will you guarantee that this will not happen?"

"Yes, sir," answered Mr. Morgan instantly. "I will guarantee it during the life of the syndicate, and that means until the contract has been concluded and the goal has been reached."

Morgan was pledging himself to control what for years had been uncontrollable—the course of international exchange and international gold shipments. And he was a man who did not make pledges lightly.

Cleveland was persuaded. As Pierpont Morgan got up to leave, someone noticed what looked like brown dust on his knees and on the carpet by his feet. Without realizing it, he had been crushing the cigar which, long hours before, he had brought into the room unlighted.

Later that day he cabled London, "Received your cable of yesterday. Impossible convey any just idea of what have been through today, but we have carried our point and are more than satisfied."

The message went on to outline the basis of the forthcoming deal. The syndicate would deliver to the government gold equivalent to sixty million dollars, payment for it to be made in bonds at a rate "equivalent to a purchase of the bonds on a $3\frac{3}{4}$ percent basis, one half gold to come from Europe. . . ." And the syndicate, as far as lay in its power, would "make all legitimate efforts to protect the Treasury of the United States against the withdrawal of gold pending the complete performance of this contract."

An uproar of protest arose at the news of the bankers' intervention. The price of their aid looked high. In the final contract they had secured the bonds on the basis of a $3\frac{3}{4}$ percent yield, not the $3\frac{5}{8}$ percent that they had been ready to compromise on, nor the $3\frac{1}{2}$ percent that the public had expected.

On February 14, young William Jennings Bryan of Nebraska, not yet renowned as a presidential candidate, said in a speech in Congress, "I only ask that the Treasury shall be administered on behalf of the American people and not on behalf of the Rothschilds and other foreign bankers."

The New York *World*, speaking scornfully of "bank-parlor negotiations," called the agreement "an excellent arrangement for the bankers. It puts at least $16,000,000 into their pockets. . . . For the nation it means a scandalous surrender of credit and a shameful waste of substance."

Nor was this all, for it was widely—and baselessly—whispered that Cleveland had profited personally by the deal.

But the syndicate operation proved a thumping success. On February 20 the new United States government bonds were put on sale simultaneously in New York and London, and presently the cables were ticking off messages of triumph. From London, J. S. Morgan & Co. sent word, "Subscription enormous. Subscription books closed noon; open only two hours." And from New York came the return message from J. P. Morgan & Co., "We have closed our books. Subscriptions something enormous. We offer you all our sincere congratulations."

Within a few weeks the New York banks associated with the syndicate had turned in to the Treasury large amounts of gold collected in the United States; and a steady stream of gold also was crossing the Atlantic westward. To protect the Treasury against simultaneous withdrawals of gold which would have nullified these gains was a more difficult undertaking; but so well did the members of the syndicate keep their pledged word that before the end of June the Treasury's reserve of gold had crossed the safety line of one hundred million dollars.

The Morgan-Belmont bond issue did not bring permanent relief to the Treasury. But it had brought instant temporary relief. To say that it had prevented a panic is to indulge in guess-work. Certain it is, however, that a later cable of Morgan's to London, which spoke of "dangers so great scarcely anyone dared whisper them," was written not to impress the public—it was a private message—but out of well-informed conviction.

IN VIEW OF THE PUBLIC OUTCRY and the whispers of graft, there was a congressional investigation of the Treasury's dealings; and on June 19, 1896, Pierpont Morgan took the stand at a hearing in the Hoffman House in New York. His forthright answers to questions reflected his complete satisfaction in the course he had taken. Let us listen to him for a moment, as Senator Platt of Connecticut and Senator Vest of Missouri interrogate him.

SENATOR PLATT: And so your real purpose, as I understand you, in this transaction was not the idea that you could take this bond issue and make money out of it, but that you could prevent a panic and distress in the country?

MORGAN: . . . I will say that I had no object except . . . to save the disaster that would result in case that foreign gold had not been obtained.

SENATOR VEST: If that was your sole object, why did you specify in your telegraphic communication to Mr. Carlisle that your house, or you and Mr. Belmont, were to have exclusive control of the matter?

MORGAN: Because it was absolutely impossible for more than one party to negotiate—to make the same negotiation for the same lot of gold. It would only have made competition.

VEST: If the gold was abroad, I take for granted that anybody could get hold of it who had the means to do so. If you were actuated by the desire to prevent a panic, why were you not willing that other people should do it, if they wanted to?

MORGAN: *They could not do it.*

VEST: How did you know?

MORGAN: That was my opinion. . . .

VEST: Do you believe that the government could have made any better terms with anybody else than it made with yourself and Mr. Belmont at that juncture?

MORGAN: I do not, sir.

VEST: Do you believe that gold could have been obtained from abroad on any better terms?

MORGAN: I do not. It was difficult enough to obtain it, as it was.

VEST: Was your house engaged in shipping gold abroad up to this time, or at about this time?

MORGAN: We never have shipped one dollar of gold abroad for the last three years.

When Senator Vest asked, "What profit did your house make upon this transaction?" Morgan replied: "That I decline to answer. . . . I am perfectly ready to state to the committee every detail of the negotiation up to the time that the bonds became my property and were paid for. What I did with my own property subsequent to that purchase I decline to state, except this, that no member of the government in any department was interested directly or indirectly. . . ."

J. P. Morgan, Jr., used to say that his father told him that he himself was quite willing to disclose his profit, but that August Belmont asked him not to. Nobody seriously questioned the banker's right to keep silence if he chose—a fact which seems somewhat remarkable to us today, since the transactions of the syndicate were emphatically vested with a public interest.

As we have noted, the New York *World* charged in 1895 that "the bankers" made at least sixteen million dollars. In his book *The House of Morgan*, published in 1930, Lewis Corey said that "the syndicate profits ranged from seven to twelve million dollars." Even the conservative historian Alexander Dana Noyes wrote that "the terms were extremely harsh . . . they measured with little mercy the emergency of the Treasury." But according to Francis Lynde Stetson the American syndicate realized "only five percent and interest"; and Satterlee declared that "from my talks with Mr. Morgan I can confidently state that there was no profit for him at all."

Among these divergent statements Stetson's was the most accurate. Here are the actual figures from the original Syndicate

Book of the American syndicate. (It must be recalled that there were two syndicates, one American, one European, with the business divided about evenly between them.) The American syndicate took bonds totaling $31,157,000, and allotted them among no less than sixty-one syndicate members—banks and private banking and investment houses. The House of Morgan took less than a tenth of the total. The largest holdings of bonds were $2,753,875 by August Belmont & Co. and $2,678,825 by J. P. Morgan & Co. When the transaction was over and the books were closed, the total profit of the American syndicate was $1,534,516.72, which was a shade less than the five percent figure given by Mr. Stetson.

Of the American syndicate's profit, J. P. Morgan & Co.'s share was $131,932.13. In addition the Morgan firm received half of the American Syndicate Managers' commission of three-quarters of one percent; that brought in $116,841.37 more. These two sums total $248,773.50—a little less than a quarter of a million dollars. And this, by the way, was gross profit, against which could reasonably be charged some of the general costs of doing business.

To people outside the banking world, a profit of a quarter of a million dollars on a single transaction looks large. But considering that it amounted to less than one percent of the value of the bonds it was not large at all—especially when one took into account the duration and complexity of the operation and the risks it involved. And to Morgan himself, who was accustomed to thinking in large sums, it undoubtedly seemed a modest recompense for saving the credit of the United States.

Chapter 8

As Others Saw Him

LINCOLN STEFFENS, writing in his *Autobiography* about the days when he was a young financial reporter for the New York *Evening Post*, depicts Morgan at about the time of the gold crisis. In those days of the eighteen nineties, "I had to do with the private bankers who are the constructive engineering financiers.

"Of these last, J. P. Morgan, Senior, was the greatest. I did not see much of him, of course; nobody did. He was in sight all the time. He sat alone in a back room with glass sides in his banking-house with his door open, and it looked as if any one could walk in upon him and ask any question. One heard stories of the payment of large sums for an introduction to him. I could not see why all the tippers with business did not come right in off the street and talk to him. They did not. My business was with his partners or associates . . . but I noticed that these, his partners, did not go near him unless he sent for them; and then they looked alarmed and darted in like officeboys. 'Nobody can answer that question except Mr. Morgan,' they would tell me. Well, Mr. Morgan was there; why not go in and ask him? The answer I got was a smile or a shocked look of surprise. And once when I pressed the president of one of the Morgan banks to put to him a question we agreed deserved an answer, the banker said, 'Not on your life,' and when I said, 'But why not?' he said, 'You try it yourself and see.' And I did.

"I went over to J. P. Morgan and Company, walked into his office, and stood before him at his flat, clean, clear desk. I stood while he examined a sheet of figures; I stood for two or three long minutes, while the whole bank seemed to stop work to watch me, and he did not look up; he was absorbed, he was sunk, in those figures. He was so alone with himself and his mind that when he did glance up he did not see me; his eyes were looking inward. . . . I thought . . . that he was doing a sum in mental arithmetic, and when he solved it he dropped his eyes back upon his sheet of figures and I slunk out. . . ."

But one afternoon Steffens' paper received a statement from J. P. Morgan & Co. about some bonds, a statement that did not make sense as written. So, says Steffens, "ready for the explosion, I walked into Morgan's office and right up to his desk. He saw me this time; he threw himself back in his chair so hard that I thought he would tip over.

" 'Mr. Morgan,' I said as brave as I was afraid, 'what does this statement mean?' and I threw the paper down before him.

" 'Mean!' he exclaimed. His eyes glared, his great red nose seemed to me to flash and darken, flash and darken. Then he roared. 'Mean! It means what it says. I wrote it myself, and it says what I mean.'

" 'It doesn't say anything—straight,' I blazed.

"He sat back there, flashing and rumbling; then he clutched the arms of his chair, and I thought he was going to leap at me. I was so scared that I defied him.

" 'Oh, come now, Mr. Morgan,' I said, 'you may know a lot about figures and finance, but I'm a reporter, and I know as much as you do about English. And that statement isn't English.'

"That was the way to treat him, I was told afterward. And it was in that case. He glared at me a moment more, the fire went out of his face, and he leaned forward over the bit of paper and said very meekly, 'What's the matter with it?'

"I said I thought it would be clearer in two sentences instead of one and I read it aloud so, with a few other verbal changes.

" 'Yes,' he agreed, 'that is better. You fix it.'

"I fixed it under his eyes, he nodded and I, whisking it away, hurried back to the office. They told me in the bank afterward that 'J.P.' sat watching me go out of the office, then . . . asked what my name was, where I came from, and said, 'Knows what he wants, and—and—gets it.' ' "

FROM THE TIME that the Reverend William Stephen Rainsford had accepted the pulpit of St. George's in 1882 at a vestry meeting in Morgan's house, Morgan had been Rainsford's devoted friend and backer. Morgan had become senior warden of the church on his father-in-law's death; had passed the plate every Sunday when he was in New York; and had Rainsford to breakfast every Monday morning at No. 219 to discuss the affairs of the church. When in 1889 Rainsford suffered a nervous breakdown from overwork, Morgan saw to it that he was well cared for, and during Rainsford's absence made a point of reaching St. George's each Sunday morning a half hour before the service began and standing at the church door, "welcoming those he knew and did not know," helping them to feel "that St. George's was a going concern."

After Rainsford returned to the pulpit he found that he had lost vitality and was often tired. "Mr. Morgan saw most things he wanted to see," writes Rainsford, "and he noticed the change in me. Soon after my return, in his quiet way, he drew me aside one day and, slipping a paper into my hand, said, 'Don't work too hard; you ought not to have to worry about money. Don't thank me, and don't speak of it to anyone but your wife.' He had created a modest trust fund for me and mine. So he lifted from my shoulders a burden that has crushed the life out of many a good soldier. . . ."

The close association between these two men was a strange one. For Rainsford was by nature a radical reformer, a passionate democrat. He believed in the "social gospel"—the preeminent importance, in Christ's teaching, of the duty of active neighborliness to all men. Morgan was a conservative and traditionalist. As Rainsford interpreted him, "His mental qualities drew him strongly to the ecclesiastical side of the Episcopal Church's life. Its very archaic element, its atmosphere of withdrawal from the common everyday affairs of men, answered to some need of his soul." Morgan regularly attended the triennial national Episcopal conventions, and according to Rainsford, "The floor of the convention, the association with men who were, by virtue of their office, guardians and exponents of a religious tradition, beautiful and venerable, had for him an attraction stronger than any other gathering afforded. He would cast all other duties aside and sit for hours, attentively following the details of the driest of debates, on subjects that could interest only an ecclesiastic."

It is likely that the chief reason for Morgan's loyalty to Rainsford was that when he believed in a man he believed in backing him with full faith and with few questions; and Rainsford, a big, handsome, straightforward fellow who knew how to meet loyalty with loyalty, attracted his belief. But the story of Morgan and Rainsford would not be complete if it omitted a rift between them which opened up in the middle eighteen nineties.

This episode is from Rainsford's autobiography, *The Story of a Varied Life.*

One night, at a meeting of the vestry of St. George's Church, out of a clear sky Pierpont Morgan rose and read a motion that the vestry be reduced from two wardens and eight members to two wardens and six members, adding, "I think the vestry will agree with me that when I get a seconder it had better be passed without debate."

Rainsford, who presided at these meetings, was stunned. Morgan had given him no warning whatever of any intention to propose such a change.

"Since I stood in your study that night when you called me to the church," he told Morgan, "I think you will bear witness that I have never advocated any important matter in this, our church's council, without first discussing it with you. Here now you spring this revolutionary proposition on me, and on the vestry, without any warning whatever; and you ask that we should proceed to pass it without any discussion. This I cannot agree to, and I must ask you, before you get a seconder, to explain to me and to this vestry your reasons for proposing so important a change. We have done good work together, constituted as we are. If a small vestry is for St. George's a better vestry, there must be some reasons for it. What are your reasons for it?"

Thereupon Morgan explained that the vestry's role in the church was fiduciary and its obligations were financial. "I am its senior warden and responsible officer," said Morgan. "I am aging. I want at times to have these vestry meetings held in my study. This vestry should be composed, in my judgment, of men whom I can invite to my study, and who can help me to carry the heavy financial burden of the church. . . . The rector wants to democratize the church, and we agree with him and will help him as far as we can. But I do not want the vestry democratized. I want it to remain a body of gentlemen whom I can ask to meet me in my study."

Rainsford realized that if Morgan had his way, the vestry would cease to represent the congregation in any true sense; they—and the church—would inevitably fall under Morgan's control. (Perhaps what Morgan really wanted was a group of men so well-heeled that he could pass the hat among them without being embarrassed by the presence of men who could not contribute their share; if so, either he failed to make this point clear or Rainsford thought that anyhow it involved a distortion of the vestry's function.) He reminded Morgan that he, Rainsford, had long believed that the vestry ought to be not reduced but enlarged to include at least one representative of the increasing number of wage earners in the congregation.

A long, embarrassing, and vehement debate followed. Rainsford asked Morgan to withdraw his motion. Seth Low, subsequently mayor of New York, who was among the vestrymen, joined Rainsford in asking that the motion be withdrawn. Morgan remained immovable.

Then another vestryman, "one of his oldest friends, one to whom in these financially troublesome times . . . Mr. Morgan had been of immense service (I did not know this till later), slowly rose. He was white to the lips, and turning to Mr. Morgan he said, 'Mr. Morgan, I am compelled to agree with our rector in this matter, and I move that this vestry be increased to eleven.'"

Mr. Low seconded this motion. Morgan could get no seconder for his. Thereupon the motion to enlarge the vestry was put and carried, seven votes to one.

For a moment the group of men sat silent. Then Morgan got up and said, "Rector, I will never sit in this vestry again," and walked out of the room and out of the building.

From this point on I shall quote Rainsford verbatim:

"Next day I had Mr. Morgan's written resignation, with a request to submit it to the vestry without delay. I acknowledged his letter, and nothing more, going to breakfast next week at 219 Madison Avenue as usual. As I expected he was very grumpy, and at the breakfast table conversation was limited to the weather. Next week I went again to breakfast. He had nothing to say to me at the table.

"As I asked for a cigar, in his study afterward, he said, 'Have you submitted my resignation?'

" 'I have not, and I will not.'

" 'Why not?'

" 'When I first came to you I came because you gave me

your hand and your promise to stand by me in the hard work that lay ahead. I told you I was a radical. I told you I would do all I could to democratize the church. I am only keeping my word. I certainly shall not now, nor at any time, do anything to help you break yours.'

"Dead silence. So I lit my cigar and walked away.

"I think after that I went to breakfast three times before Mr. Morgan sailed for Europe. He never made another allusion to his resignation, nor did he enter into any private conversation with me. The day he sailed, I did what I had not done before, I went to the dock to bid him good-bye. On this occasion, in the days I am writing of, the late nineties, a rather miscellaneous crowd was wont to gather to bid him good-bye. It had become quite a function, and I did not usually care to take part in it. As I went up the gangplank, I saw Mr. Morgan standing at some distance surrounded by his friends. At the same instant he saw me and, coming out of the group, signed to me to follow him. He made for his cabin, entered quickly, without saying a word, and shut and bolted the door behind us. We never had another falling out."

What was said in that cabin Rainsford would not divulge. But Morgan remained senior warden the rest of his life.

IN THE EIGHTEENTH and nineteenth centuries collecting had become one of the standard preoccupations of men of means both in England and on the Continent. Even in the United States, those who had been able to visit Europe or Asia and had been entranced by the exquisite workmanship achieved under older civilizations, were bringing fine things back with them to their homeland, and many of these collectors had been men of real taste.

As the century drew to a close there began a new period in which a swarm of American millionaires ransacked Europe for masterpieces, near masterpieces, and pseudo masterpieces of painting, sculpture, architectural accessories, and fine workmanship in all sorts of materials. This new surge of the collectors gathered momentum during the eighteen nineties, rushed at full tilt from 1900 to 1914, and continued, though at a less sensational pace, after the First World War. At the head of this company of American purchasers was Morgan, the pacesetter for them all.

Morgan had always enjoyed bringing home with him fine things that caught his fancy, whether in New York or on his annual trips to Europe. As a youngster he had picked up fragments of old stained glass which he had found on the ground beneath cathedral windows, and he had occasionally bought paintings.

When he moved into 219 Madison Avenue, at the age of forty-five, he was sufficiently vain of his books to engage one J. F. Sabin to prepare a pamphlet, *Catalogue of the Library of Mr. J. Pierpont Morgan.* This was the sort of thing that a gentleman of taste and means did. But an examination of the catalogue shows that the books themselves were, with very few exceptions, nothing special. It was not until 1888, when he was fifty-one, that he bought his first manuscript; not until 1891, when he was fifty-four, that he began to concentrate on the purchase in quantity of manuscripts, first editions, and fine volumes generally; and it was only gradually, in the years that followed, that he shifted part of his attention from books to other lovely relics of the past: paintings, bronzes, terra-cottas, jades, ivories, enamels, crystals, glass, tapestries, bas-reliefs, miniatures, snuffboxes, watches, Bibles, Church of England rituals, and autographs. The twentieth century had arrived before he began making serious plans to construct the library building next to his house, and in 1904, when he was sixty-seven, he became the president, wholesale benefactor, and supreme ruler of the Metropolitan Museum.

According to his admiring son-in-law, Herbert L. Satterlee:

> It was really Pierpont's nephew, Junius S. Morgan, who interested him in collecting manuscripts and rare editions. Junius knew that a young friend of his, F. Wheeler, had acquired a Thackeray manuscript, but he himself could not afford to buy it; so he introduced Wheeler to his uncle at the latter's office. As far as we know, this is the first manuscript that Pierpont himself bought; and the interview (as Wheeler wrote it down) is characteristic.

When young Wheeler was shown in, Pierpont asked, "What have you got to show me?"

"A Thackeray manuscript which came to me from Thackeray's daughter, Mrs. Ritchie."

Pierpont took it and turned over the leaves. In a moment he asked, "Are you sure that this is in Thackeray's own handwriting?"

"Quite certain."

"You are too young to be quite certain."

"I think not, sir, because I have been dealing in manuscripts since I was seventeen."

"Very well. What's the price?"

"One hundred pounds."

"Is that 'cash'?"

"No, sir. Ninety pounds cash."

"Very well. My secretary will give you a check. Let me know if you get any more really good authors' manuscripts."

That was the end of the interview.

Pierpont carried this manuscript uptown to his house and showed it to his family and friends. Eventually he put it into the little room in the basement which gradually became the storage place of many of the manuscripts and books that he bought during the next eighteen years. Before the Morgan Library was built the room became so crowded that it was difficult to get into it to find anything; books, pictures, and manuscripts were piled on the floor, after every table and chair had been filled.

There we have many of the elements of the Morgan collecting pattern: a chance beginning through a family introduction; a brief interview; no haggling, and a satisfaction in acquisition. But it throws little light upon either Morgan's motive or his method. Satterlee's account of Morgan's purchase in 1907 of a Spanish painting, *Portrait of a Child*, which was submitted to him, in London, as a Velásquez, tells us more:

At the time this picture was shown him he told the dealer to leave it until he could study it and consider the matter. This was quite according to his custom. The dealer left it on a chair at Prince's Gate [the Morgan town house in London]. There was no documentary evidence that went with it, but it was a charming little picture, painted undoubtedly in Velasquez's time. . . . Of course, when a picture like that was left for Mr. Morgan to consider, it was not hidden. The other dealers who came saw it in turn. One of them might say, "Oh, I know where that came from. I was offered that a year ago at such-and-such a price. It is not an original." Another would remark: "That picture was sold at Christie's ten years ago, but its authenticity is in question. I hope, Mr. Morgan, that you have not bought it as an original, nor paid much for it as a picture." And so on. Mr. Morgan always listened to it all without comment. Before he made up his mind whether he wanted the picture or not he would get someone from the Berlin Museum who happened to be in London, or an expert connected with one of the great London public galleries, to stop in and look at the picture. If it was not documented and the preponderance of the best opinion was against it, he rejected it.

In the case of this picture of the Spanish child, when the dealer came back and said, "Well, Mr. Morgan, what do you think?" he answered, "You cannot prove the picture is Velasquez's, and I feel quite sure it is not."

"All right," said the dealer. "I will take it away." And he started to pick it up.

"No," said Mr. Morgan. "Leave it right where it is. No matter who painted it, I have become very fond of it and I am going to keep it."

This anecdote not only illuminates Morgan's method of collecting but suggests that he may have been moved by a love for exquisite things, whether or not attributable to recognized masters. Satterlee, however, adds the unconsciously devastating comment, "It might be a Velasquez after all!"—thereby demolishing Morgan the amateur and substituting for him Morgan the speculator in attributions.

A consciously adverse view of Morgan the collector is supplied by Roger Fry, who served as curator of paintings and then as European adviser on paintings for the Metropolitan Museum from 1906 to 1910. According to Virginia Woolf's life of Fry, his connection with the Metropolitan was terminated because he tried to buy for the museum a picture which Morgan—who was then its president—wanted for his own personal collection.

Certain it is that during the summer of 1909 something happened which deeply offended Morgan. The few directors of the museum who knew of this episode considered it discreditable to Fry. At any rate Fry had long tried the patience of the officers of the museum; his connection with it had been a chapter of misunderstandings, mistakes, differences of judgment, inefficiencies, and cross-purposes.

From the outset Fry had resented Morgan's influence at the Metropolitan. He had described him as "the most repulsively ugly" man, "with a great strawberry nose," and had said that he "behaved like a crowned head." Fry had written home from New York, "I don't think he wants anything but flattery. He is quite indifferent as to the real value of things. All he wants experts for is to give him a sense of his own wonderful sagacity. I shall never be able to dance to that tune. . . . The man is so swollen with pride and a sense of his own power that it never occurs to him that other people have any rights." And years later Fry, writing an account of a trip which he took with Morgan in Italy in the summer of 1907, described the financier with venom.

He recounted in detail how Morgan—who at the age of seventy was accompanied on his travels by his close friend, the "stately and enameled" Mrs. Douglas, by his sister, Mrs. Burns, and by a courier, "a lank, hungry Italian cadger"—was beset by dealers and cringing aristocrats who took lavish pains to please Morgan in the hope that some of his money might be enticed in their direction.

> There jumped out from a dark corner of the room a little Levantine or Maltese gibbering in broken English and broken Italian. He had in his hands a large seventeenth-century crucifix which he handed me with feverish gestures. It was not a remarkable work of art and [I] was beginning the usual process of getting out when he whipped out a stiletto from the shaft of the cross. This was the *clou* of the piece and I knew my Morgan well enough to guess how likely he was to be taken by it. "Shows what the fellows did in those days! Stick a man while he was praying! Yes, very interesting." For a crude historical imagination was the only flaw in his otherwise perfect insensibility.

Fry's harshness in judging Morgan may be attributed in part to the probability that Fry, a sensitive man not immune to self-pity, hated to be under the domination of someone who knew less about Renaissance art than he did; and to the fact that anyhow the two men were utterly dissimilar in temperament. Fry was complex, articulate, humorous, fastidious, and a student of minutiae; Morgan by contrast was simple, a man of a few short words, lacking in humor, and impatient of fine discriminations. Fry's judgment upon Morgan may therefore be likened to the judgment of a cavalryman upon a thirty-ton tank.

Perhaps the truth about Morgan the collector includes both Satterlee's and Fry's view and also that of Edward P. Mitchell, editor of the New York *Sun*, who found in the banker "a genuine affection and hunger for the rarest and finest and most beautiful achievements in the arts." Unquestionably Morgan had such an affection and hunger. But he took no noticeable interest in encouraging contemporary artists. He thought of art in the past tense, not the future.

What turned Morgan to collecting was a romantic reverence for the archaic, the traditional, the remote, for things whose beauty took him far away from prosaic, industrial America—the same feeling, in essence, which made him delight in the ceremonies of the church.

Once Morgan became enamored of collecting, he went at it in the same way in which he went at a business reorganization. As *The Burlington Magazine* said of him after his death, "Having become the greatest financier of his age, he determined to be the greatest collector." So completely did this ambition occupy him that, as *The Burlington* said, he "had little leisure left for contemplation"—or even, one might add, for studious examination of works of art. He relied rather upon the quick verdicts of experts, upon his own instinct for quality, and upon a strategy of concentrated attack—buying a whole collection rather than picking and choosing among its component parts, and coming instantly to his decision, cost what it might, without wearisome bargaining.

It may be that the editorial in *The Burlington Magazine* was the soundest witness as to Morgan the collector:

571

In the world of art quite as much as in the world of finance, Mr. Morgan was above everything a man of action. His successful raids upon the private collections of Europe were organized and carried out with the rapid decisive energy of a great general. He believed in military methods; he regarded rapidity and irrevocability of decision as more important than accuracy of judgment; he considered discipline more effective than a nice discrimination. And in spite of many instances of failure it would be rash to say that for the end he had in view his choice of means was a wrong one.

Morgan never made money on the gigantic scale of John D. Rockefeller, who during his lifetime was able to give away something like five hundred million dollars without dissipating the family fortune; or Andrew Carnegie, whose benefactions totaled some three hundred and fifty millions. When Morgan died in 1913 the public—which had thought of his wealth as limitless—was surprised at the comparatively modest size of the estate he left. If one excluded his art collections, which were variously estimated to be worth from twenty to fifty millions, the amount was only a little over sixty-eight millions. Morgan not only made less money than many other multimillionaires; he spent most of what he earned. He lived on an increasingly magnificent scale; his collecting during the last fifteen years or so of his life must have cost him millions a year; and he was also a lavish giver.

Most of his gifts were connected with his personal loyalties and affections. He felt a close link with Hartford, where he had been born and brought up, and gave over a million dollars to its museum, the Wadsworth Athenaeum. He was long a vestryman and then senior warden of St. George's Church, and Rainsford was his loved and trusted friend; hence his gifts to it of a Memorial House, a building for its Trade School, a Deaconess House, a new organ. Another close friend was Dr. James Markoe, who aroused his interest in the work of the Lying-In Hospital, to which Morgan presented a million and a quarter dollars for the construction of a modern building. He was an energetic Episcopal layman, hence many large gifts toward the construction of the Cathedral of St. John the Divine and its

Synod House. He was the president of the Metropolitan Museum; hence his many gifts of works of art, his contributions toward its excavations in Egypt and other enterprises, and his plan (largely carried out after his death) to turn over to it the bulk of his collections.

There were quantities of other gifts—to the American Museum of Natural History, of which he was for fifteen years the treasurer; to the Metropolitan Opera, of which he was a director; to the American Academy in Rome; to St. Paul's Cathedral in London, the city where he had inherited his father's house and business; to a hospital in Aix-les-Bains, a resort which he enjoyed visiting. Not all, but most, of these involved some tribute to loyalty.

Perhaps the most striking thing about Morgan's giving was its speed. Unlike other men of wealth, he did not ask committees of experts to study appeals made to him. When he saw something worth giving to, he liked to do it without delay or ceremony.

There is a story of what happened when Harvard University wanted to build a new group of buildings for its medical school and approached Morgan for a gift. Morgan liked the idea. Harvard was a good place; his son, Jack, had gone there and the results had seemed satisfactory. President Eliot was an excellent man. Medicine was a good thing, and the Harvard Medical School was well spoken of. So he said he would be glad to see the plans for the new buildings.

When he had been approached by Harvard, John D. Rockefeller had taken six months to have the school's needs investigated. But Morgan, when representatives of the school were taken to an inside room at 23 Wall Street, walked in watch in hand.

"Gentlemen," said he, "I am pressed for time and can give you but a moment. Have you any plans to show me?"

The plans were unrolled.

Said Morgan, moving his finger quickly from point to point, "I will build *that*—and *that*—and *that*. Good morning, gentlemen." And he departed, having committed himself to the construction of three buildings at a cost of over a million dollars.

Chapter 9

Billion-Dollar Adventure

DURING THE SUMMER and autumn of 1897 there came a change in the economic weather. For more than four years America had been beset with depression, unemployment, unrest, and uncertainty. Now all at once men began to look ahead with hope. In the words of the financial chronicler Alexander Dana Noyes, "the crippled industrial and financial state of 1894, with the country's principal industries declining, its great corporations drifting into bankruptcy, and its government forced to borrow on usurious terms from Europe to maintain the public credit" had been transformed within half a dozen years into "a community whose prosperity had become the wonder of the outside world."

The conservative William McKinley, having demolished William Jennings Bryan in the campaign of the preceding autumn, now sat in the White House, with Mark Hanna, the friend of the corporations, at his elbow. The silver heresy was no longer a menace; the government's gold reserve was once again adequate; a bumper wheat crop on the plains was bringing good prices because of a wheat famine in Europe, and as the revenues of all manner of businesses began slowly to swell, confidence at last returned. A new era of growth and activity for American business was beginning.

The prosperity of this new era was singularly restricted. While Andrew Carnegie was enjoying a personal income of something like fifteen million dollars a year (with no income taxes to pay), the mass of unskilled workers in the North were receiving less than four hundred and sixty dollars a year in wages, and in the South less than three hundred dollars. And this in a period when one millionaire's domestic staff was said to be ready at an hour's notice to serve a hundred guests; when another was basking in a Scotch castle with forty guest suites, eight footmen whose sole function was to serve wine, and a personal bagpiper whose assignment was to march around the

The Times does not undertake to return rejected manuscripts. In all cases where a return of manuscript is desired postage must be inclosed.

SHALL WE REPUDIATE?

There is a considerable number of men, especially in the Senate, from the West and the South who, we are sure, if they could be made to see whither the downward path leads on which our national finances are tending would draw back with horror from the consequences of the policy they are now advocating. These men are the obstinate opponents of a gold loan to maintain gold payments. They say that gold is no more legal tender than silver, which is true, and that what is good enough for our own citizens is good enough for our foreign creditors. And they say further that even if we do not maintain gold payments it is only the capitalists of the East, it is only "Wall Street," it is only the "gold bugs" that will suffer. And this is not true. It is the exact opposite of the truth. It would be impossible for all the capitalists north of the Potomac and east of the Mississippi, if they could conspire together, to inflict upon the West and South, upon the classes that gain their living by labor or by trade on borrowed capital, so terrible an injury as would come from the failure of the Government to maintain gold payments.

For gold payments are, in the first place, a matter of national honor, and, in the second place, a matter of equal and universal justice between all classes of the people of the United States. What are the greenbacks? They are promises to pay issued to carry on the war for the Union, and to meet its burdens. They were promises to pay gold, and nothing else. They were so issued by the Congressmen who voted for them. They were so taken by the creditors of the Government to whom they were given. They could not have got one vote in Congress on any other understanding. They would never have been accepted on any other. Congress declared that again and again. The customs dues were made payable in gold in order that the notes might be paid in gold, and remained so until specie payments had been resumed. If a contract is to be read in the light of what both parties to it believed that the contract was at the time that it was

the main line, upon which it holds a second lien, but the terminals and branches, upon which it has no mortgage, and it would also have to take poss⸺ of the Central Pacific if it was to m⸺ tem effective. To become⸺ the first mortgage ⸺ the ⸺ cil Bluffs to Ogden, a⸺ of ⸺ and terminals, would⸺ of $180,000,000, which⸺ have to be met by a l⸺ out of account an u⸺ the Central Pa⸺ sides, there ⸺ ment of G⸺

To mo⸺ ⸺row the who⸺ ⸺ng scheme⸺ ⸺t over a⸺ est th⸺ back, ⸺ By a⸺ it is a⸺ it assu⸺ ⸺ties of⸺ ⸺ll worse. ⸺nly one to w⸺ ⸺seri- ous attent⸺ ⸺ plan of refunding ⸺ fall due or sooner.

THE PRESIDENT WILL DO HIS DUTY.

In closing the message sent to Congress on Monday President Cleveland said:

"In conclusion, I desire to frankly confess my reluctance to issuing more bonds in present circumstances and with no better results than have lately followed that course. I cannot refrain, however, from adding to an assurance of my anxiety to co-operate with the present Congress in any reasonable measure of relief an expression of my determination to leave nothing undone which furnishes a hope for improving the situation or checking a suspicion of our disinclination or disability to meet with the strictest honor every national obligation."

Curiously enough, this language, plain and direct as it is, has been either misunderstood or ignored in some quarters. There were those yesterday in "the Street" who believed, or chose to assert, that the message to Congress was an abandonment by the President of all independent action, leaving the responsibility for the consequences with the National Legislature. And there are others —silver men these, in Washington—who pretend to think that if they do not adopt the President's recommendations he will be helpless and will let things take their course, which these gentlemen think

ments. To have the p by a large very much prove suffi ance of the carrying ⸺ndation ⸺hattan ⸺t th⸺ ⸺, th⸺ ⸺e r⸺

E EXⁱ It is stra changes in istration o so little he of Brookly in 1888, th conclusive tions made seems to b charter of ures a goo well, and the same p ner of app evil conse⸺

In Broo ments are Commissic serving w Board of forty-five The Comm is the sole ment the ⸺ ing with b Whatever Brooklyn to the fac headed, n that fact politics o⸺

In Broo Elections, Departme it was imp duties an its duties, in the lea the ballot consists o san. The Mayor for gin in th been no c not effect elections

castle in the morning playing to wake the guests; and when the vast new residence of a third was to contain a swimming pool, a gymnasium, a billiard room with ten tables, a private chapel with a marble altar weighing ten tons, a fifty-thousand-dollar organ, and a refrigerator that could hold twenty tons of beef!

In the polite journals of the eighteen nineties there was only one group of people who appeared to matter much: ladies and gentlemen and those of the new rich who aspired to be ladies and gentlemen. Scant notice was taken of the vast middle group of the population—the proprietors of little businesses, the more successful farmers, and those hosts of small-salaried business employees and professional people among whom *The Saturday Evening Post* and the *Ladies' Home Journal* were presently to recruit armies of readers. To the polite journalists of the eighteen nineties, such men and women were untutored and negligible. As for "the poor," the polite journalists referred to them almost as if they were residents of a foreign land.

Nor was there then any widespread realization of the existence of what we today call the national economy. The statistics of business were elaborately recorded in the financial journals of that time, but one looks in vain for any adequate measurement of the prosperity of the country as a whole. Not for many years to come would Willford I. King produce the idea that there was such a thing as the national income. But as business accumulated momentum during the McKinley days, an idea precedent to the idea of the national income seized the minds of businessmen: the idea of national—and even international—markets.

The concept was of course not new. Before the eighteen nineties many manufacturers—like the Singer Sewing Machine people, let us say—had sold their goods in so many areas of the country as to conceive of the United States as a single market for their wares. And Pierpont Morgan, calling together the chief railroad presidents of the country, surely had at least a vague concept of all these separate lines making together something of a national pattern. But the vast majority of businesses were local, and during the depression of the mid-nineties almost all grand schemes for new business combinations had been held in abeyance or slowed down.

But now, in 1897, the nation was linked by railroads from Maine to California; the frontier was closed; the South was at last recovering from the Civil War; manufacturers were learning the techniques of mass production, and, all at once, among shrewd and well-heeled business proprietors, the idea spread that a national market awaited them if only they could expand or combine to exploit it. The easy victory of the United States in the Spanish-American War in 1898 encouraged an extension of this idea: why not an international market for that matter?

But how could a business or group of businesses grow so big as to capture the whole American market?

The answer to this question had been found, even before the Sherman Anti-Trust Act was passed in 1890. The machinery for combining businesses had already been invented by a cheerful, rosy-faced New Jersey lawyer named James B. Dill. In 1889 Dill suggested to the governor of New Jersey that a state law be passed permitting one corporation to hold the stock of another corporation—a thing previously considered improper, and only rarely sanctioned by special legislation.

The law was accordingly passed, and New Jersey's revenues swelled as businessmen discovered that now the door was open to legal combination. If you wanted to combine ten companies into one, all you had to do was to go to New Jersey, incorporate a holding company under the New Jersey laws, make a series of agreements by which this company would buy the stock of the ten companies, giving its own shares in return—and the thing was done. The ten companies had now become subsidiaries of one big concern—which now might be big enough to capture the whole national market.

By the time the business tide turned in 1897, the wonderful possibilities of Dill's law had become very well known. But how could anyone persuade the owners of, say, ten businesses to sell out to a holding company? Supposing each of these businesses represented an investment of one million dollars, the promoter of the new holding company would offer the owners *two* million dollars' worth of shares in the new company. Would these shares actually *be worth* two million dollars? Possibly not—but to the eye of optimism the advantages of monopoly, plus the gain in efficiency that should come from integrating all these concerns, plus the appeal of a big and forward-looking scheme, would be very persuasive.

As soon as the shares of the new holding company were launched on the Stock Exchange, the public swarmed to buy them; and the man who had sold his control of the Podunk Street Railway Company to a new Consolidated Traction Company, accepting stock in the latter as payment, found he could sell his new stock at a fat price—and would suddenly be a rich man. Not only that, but if the promoter, merging ten companies into one, was increasing their total capitalization from ten million to twenty million, why not increase it still more, say to twenty-two million, and award the additional stock to himself for his services in organizing the syndicate? The idea began to get around that there was nothing so remunerative as promoting New Jersey holding companies.

IT WAS IN THE LATE SUMMER of 1897 that Pierpont Morgan got his first real glimpse of the possibilities of combination.

Returning from Europe in June, he had divided his summer attention between financial affairs and his plans for the annual regatta of the New York Yacht Club, of which he had recently been elected commodore.

They were big plans, for the new commodore liked to do things in a spacious way. The yachts were to assemble at Glen Cove, Long Island, proceed to New London, Newport, Vineyard Haven, and then race around Cape Cod all the way to Mount Desert, Maine. Morgan offered gold and silver cups for the winners. And at the beginning of August he filled his 241-foot black *Corsair* with guests and set out upon the festivities of regatta week.

The yacht club had never had such a gala cruise. When on the afternoon of August 4 the schooners and sloops and steam yachts slipped into Newport Harbor past the gleaming white warships of the Atlantic squadron, there was "a constant coming and going of launches and gigs filled with gay people, sunburnt yachtsmen and pretty women, carriages and traps bringing down favored ones for dinners on the yachts, and other favored ones driven off for dinners on shore"; after dusk fell, the harbor glittered with moving lights and on the shore there was a grand show of fireworks.

It was not long after this regatta that Morgan was visited in New York by Judge Elbert H. Gary, a Middle Westerner whom Morgan had met before. Gary had come to New York on behalf of John Warne Gates, a rising manufacturer of barbed wire who had already, with Gary's help, combined a number of steel and wire companies into one, and now wanted to combine a great many more—to form an eighty-million-dollar American Steel & Wire Company.

Charles Coster had already examined the data which Gary had brought with him, and had reported that the project was worth his chief's attention. Morgan talked with Gary, was favorably impressed, and gave his provisional okay to the ambitious project; and Gary and Gates thereupon went to work trying to line up the numerous manufacturers of wire for the great merger.

Morgan was dealing with two quite different men. Gary, born and bred in an Illinois farm town, had become a leading Chicago lawyer, had been mayor of Wheaton, Illinois, had served two terms as a county judge, and had been president of the Chicago Bar Association. As legal adviser for Gates, he became an expert matchmaker among corporations. A shrewd, diplomatic man, Gary was described as resembling, in appearance and manner, "a Methodist bishop—benign, suave, cordial, and earnest."

But there was nothing about his friend Gates that remotely resembled a bishop. Gates was a gambler, a large, genial all-night poker player, once described by his secretary as a "great boy with an extraordinary money sense annexed." He had made his start in business as a barbed-wire salesman; had gone to San Antonio, rented a tract of land there, built a corral of his barbed wire, and challenged the ranchers to find a steer that could get out of it. He had accumulated so many orders for wire that he abandoned his employer, went to St. Louis, raised some capital, and went into the wire business himself. Now he had become a big shot in the wire industry. They called him

"Bet-a-Million" Gates; he was said to have spent a rainy afternoon on a train betting with a companion on which of the raindrops coursing down the windowpane would reach the bottom first—at a thousand dollars a race.

All that fall and early winter the negotiations over the proposed wire combine went on. By February, Morgan would go no further, saying that he was disturbed by the financial showing of one of the companies that was to be included in it, though the main reason may have been distaste for Gates and his "Waldorf crowd" of speculative plungers. Gates and Gary went ahead without him, forming first a small combination and then, a few months later, a larger one called the American Steel & Wire Company, put together without aid from 23 Wall Street.

Morgan had had his initiation into the steel industry, and he found Gary both able and reliable. So the following summer he willingly embarked with Gary upon a scheme, tying together the Illinois Steel Company, an ore company, and several other concerns, to form the Federal Steel Company. When, by September 1898, the job was done, he called Gary to his office and said with his customary brevity:

"Judge Gary, you have put this thing together in very good shape. We are all very well pleased. Now you must be president."

Gary was amazed. He had had no inkling of any such plan. He said he couldn't think of it.

"Why not?" said Morgan.

"Why, Mr. Morgan, I have a law practice worth seventy-five thousand dollars a year and I cannot leave it."

"We'll take care of that," said Morgan. "We must make it worth your while."

"But I must think it over," said Gary desperately.

"No, we want to know right now."

"But who are the directors to be?"

"You can select the directors, name the executive committee, choose your officers, and fix your salary."

Gary begged for a week to think the matter over. Morgan gave him twenty-four hours. Gary accepted.

And so, the following month, the Chicago lawyer Gary came

east to head what had become the second biggest steel concern in the country. He knew little about steel manufacturing; he was there because Morgan trusted him.

DURING THE NEXT TWO YEARS it was as if a giant magnet moved over the surface of the steel industry, pulling together the separate particles into compact groups: the National Tube Company and the American Bridge Company, which Morgan himself helped to bring together; the National Steel Company, the American Tin Plate Company, the American Sheet Steel Company, and the American Steel Hoop Company. Each of these constituted a merger of a number of hitherto competing businesses; and each, as it acquired a partial monopoly in its special field of steel manufacture, lifted its prices. The profits accordingly rolled in.

Inevitably, now, a new notion popped into many minds. *Why not combine the combinations?* Why not make a mammoth supercorporation? Since its victory in the Spanish-American War, America had become conscious of being a world power; could not a colossus of American steel capture the market not only of its own continent but of other continents?

There was one thing which stood squarely in the way of such a dream. The huge, efficient, and fabulously successful Carnegie Steel Company, tightly controlled by that twinkling little genius, white-bearded Andrew Carnegie. And while the new combinations concentrated on making finished articles—wire, pipe, rails, girders, steel plate—Carnegie dominated the making of the crude steel from which they fashioned their wares. Obviously any supercombination must include Carnegie's company, or its life would be precarious indeed. Carnegie, who was in his middle sixties, was known to be looking forward to retirement. Perhaps he would sell. The trouble was that his company had become so incredibly prosperous that hundreds of millions of dollars would be required to buy out the principal stockholder.

Two of Carnegie's colleagues, Henry Clay Frick and Henry Phipps, toyed with various plans for buying Carnegie out. In 1899 they induced Carnegie to give them an option on the purchase of his company on behalf of some unidentified clients. Their clients were the Moore brothers, who were notoriously successful speculator-promoters, but the scheme failed because too many possible investors, Morgan among them, would have no part of any deal with the Moores. Later, in the spring of 1900, Carnegie's chief aide, the young and brilliant Charles M. Schwab, went to Gary to propose that Federal Steel should buy Carnegie out. Gary consulted Morgan. "I would not think of it," said Morgan. "I don't believe I could raise the money." He was aware that so many New Jersey holding companies had been launched during the past two or three years with lavish issues of stock, that the stock market was suffering from what he called "undigested securities."

Thus the matter rested in the summer of 1900, when there began a ferocious struggle within the steel industry. The various new combinations which made finished steel products, in the hope of making themselves independent of Andrew Carnegie, made ready to go into the manufacture of crude steel. On behalf of American Steel & Wire, John W. Gates sent word to the Carnegie Company that he was canceling his contract for crude steel; in the future he would make his own. The Moore brothers sent identical notices on behalf of Steel Hoop and Sheet Steel. And word came that National Tube and American Bridge expected likewise to stop ordering from Carnegie.

Carnegie was idling that summer at Skibo Castle in Scotland, but when the full scope of the impending crisis became clear he decided on a full declaration of war.

"Urge prompt action essential," he cabled; "crisis has arrived, only one policy open: start at once hoop, rod, wire, nail mills; no halfway about last two. Extend coal and coke roads, announce these; also tubes . . . have no fear as to the result; victory certain. . . ."

Schwab, Carnegie's right-hand man, took plans to Scotland for a great new steelworks to be constructed on Lake Erie. "How much cheaper, Charlie, can you make tubes than the National Company?" asked Carnegie. Schwab said he could save at least ten dollars a ton. "Go on and build the plant," ordered Carnegie, the fire of battle in his eyes.

The prospect that this decision opened up was staggering. All the steel combinations that had been effected during the past three years were in deadly peril. For Carnegie could produce steel more cheaply than anyone else on earth. He had immense resources. And he didn't mind stopping dividends entirely in order to pour earnings into new construction. If there were a price war, he could cut and cut his prices until his heavily capitalized rivals were doomed.

Morgan was uneasy; and not on the score of Carnegie's steel operations alone. The Pennsylvania Railroad had raised Carnegie's freight rates, and now Carnegie was negotiating for the building of a new railroad link to connect Pittsburgh with the eastern seaboard. "Carnegie," Morgan was heard to say, "is going to demoralize railroads just as he has demoralized steel." Morgan tried to get Schwab to come and see him for a talk. Schwab did not come. Carnegie drove ahead with his plans.

Then on the evening of December 12, 1900, Morgan was invited to attend a dinner for Schwab at the University Club in New York. After dinner, Schwab, who had a fine voice and was something of an orator, made a speech on the future of the American steel industry. He told how the demand for steel was growing, and how America could dominate the steel trade of the entire world if only the industry could be fully integrated for complete efficiency and every cost-cutting measure could be taken. Only a single corporation which could carry the manufacture of steel through every stage from the mining of the ore to the completion of the finished product could accomplish this, said Schwab. And so great would be the economies of such a company that it could cut prices and still make millions.

Morgan was impressed. "After the cheers had subsided"— I quote from Burton J. Hendrick's life of Carnegie—"he took Schwab by the arm and led him to a corner. For half an hour the two men engaged in intimate conversation. The banker had a hundred questions to ask, to which Schwab replied with terseness and rapidity." In the days that followed it was clear that Morgan was wondering how Schwab's idea could be turned into a reality. He would have to negotiate with Andrew Carnegie. How could this best be done?

He sent for Bet-a-Million Gates, who even if unreliable knew his way around, and asked whether Gates thought Carnegie would sell. Gates thought he might and suggested that since Carnegie and Frick were then on bad terms, Schwab was the man to work through.

Schwab didn't like to talk with Morgan without telling Carnegie in advance; but Gates persuaded him that there would be no disloyalty to Carnegie if he, Schwab, were to be in Philadelphia on a certain day when Morgan happened to be there—say at the Hotel Bellevue. The date was accordingly set, and Schwab went to Philadelphia—only to find a message that Morgan was laid up with a cold, and wouldn't Schwab be so good as to go on to New York and talk with him?

Schwab took the train to New York, and that night a momentous conference began in the library at No. 219 that lasted until daylight. Four men took part in it: Morgan, Robert Bacon, Gates, and Schwab. They discussed what companies should be included in a possible merger. Gates, who knew the whole of the industry, explained why such concerns as Bethlehem and Cambria and Jones & Laughlin should remain independent. Gradually the picture of a new giant steel company began to take shape. When at last the session came to an end, Morgan asked Schwab to convey a firm proposal of purchase to Carnegie.

It has occurred to a great many people that Carnegie had all this time been playing an elaborate game with a view to inducing the Morgan offer. Had his announced invasion of the territory of the other steel companies, his threat to do battle with the Pennsylvania Railroad, and the carefully contrived oratory at the dinner for Schwab been conceived to this very end? Perhaps; but there is no evidence of anything quite so Machiavellian.

Like many men who one moment dream of retiring and then the next are filled with the lust of activity, Carnegie wanted to be bought out and yet didn't. And so when Schwab broke the news, Carnegie at first was dismayed. But presently he realized that this was the inevitable and desirable end of his years as a steelmaster. On a slip of paper he jotted down in pencil a few figures. He gave the slip to Schwab and asked him to present it to Morgan.

What Carnegie proposed was that for every $1,000 in bonds of the Carnegie Company there should be exchanged $1,000 in securities of the new corporation; that for every $1,000 in stock of the Carnegie Company there should be given $1,500 in securities of the new corporation. He would take his own personal payment wholly in bonds. For Carnegie, who owned some fifty-eight percent of Carnegie Company stock, this would mean a payment in bonds of no less than $225,639,000 (par value). For all the bonds and stocks of the Carnegie Company, it would mean a payment of bonds and stocks to the amount of $400,000,000—later increased by throwing in some extra common stock for Carnegie's partners, so that the total reached $492,556,766 (par value).

Schwab took the slip of paper to Morgan. Morgan glanced at it and said, "I accept."

It was not until weeks later that Morgan suddenly woke up to the fact that he had nothing from Carnegie at all but those penciled figures on a slip of paper. Suppose Carnegie should drop dead? Or change his mind? Hurriedly Morgan had a suitable letter prepared which Carnegie obligingly signed.

A year or two later the two men met on shipboard. Carnegie said, "I made one mistake, Pierpont, when I sold out to you."

"What was that?" asked Morgan.

"I should have asked you a hundred million more than I did."

"Well," said Morgan, "you would have got it if you had."

AFTER CARNEGIE AGREED to sell, the terms were worked out for acquisition of one big company after another.

There were, of course, difficulties. John W. Gates proved to be one of them. Representing American Steel & Wire, he demanded what seemed an altogether impossible sum, holding out through hour after hour of bargaining in a room at 23 Wall Street. Finally Morgan, who had not been present at the session, entered the conference room and said sternly, "Gentlemen, I am going to leave this building in ten minutes. If by that time you have not accepted our offer, the matter will be closed. We will build our own plant." And he left the room.

"I don't know whether the old man means that or not," said Gates to a colleague.

Gary assured him that Morgan meant it. "Then I guess we will have to give up," Gates concluded.

The Rockefellers were difficult too. It had been decided that the new supercorporation should acquire the Lake Superior Consolidated Iron Mines, which controlled the largest deposits of ore in the great Mesabi Range. Carnegie had leased these properties from John D. Rockefeller—but with Carnegie out of the picture, would not ownership of them be safer?

"How are we going to get them?" Morgan asked.

"You are to talk to Mr. Rockefeller," said Gary.

"I would not think of it," said Morgan.

"Why?"

"I don't like him."

But the next morning, according to Gary's account, Morgan threw up his arms in exultation as he cried to Gary, "I have done it!"

"Done what?"

"I have seen Rockefeller."

"How did he treat you?"

"All right."

Rockefeller, when Morgan had asked to see him, had replied that he was out of business but would be glad to have a personal chat at his home. When Morgan arrived and began to talk business, Rockefeller told him that the man to see was his son.

Not long afterward the son—young John D. Rockefeller, Jr., then only twenty-seven years old—showed up at 23 Wall Street accompanied by Henry H. Rogers, one of the head men of Standard Oil. As they came in, Morgan was deep in talk with his partner Charles Steele and seemed entirely oblivious of their arrival. When the conversation was completed and Steele left the room, Rogers introduced Rockefeller.

Morgan asked in a stern voice, "Well—what's your price?"

Rockefeller mustered courage to say firmly, "Mr. Morgan, I think there must be some mistake. I did not come here to sell. I understood you wished to buy."

For a moment Morgan glared. Then, as usual when his brusqueness was boldly met, he thawed, and the negotiations began in a more friendly vein.

In the newspapers of March 3, 1901—less than three months after the dinner at the University Club—a large advertisement announced that under the laws of New Jersey there had been organized the United States Steel Corporation, which would acquire not only the outstanding stocks and bonds of the Carnegie Company but also the preferred and common stocks of Federal Steel, National Steel, National Tube, American Steel & Wire, American Tin Plate, American Steel Hoop, and American Sheet Steel. A little later, the Lake Superior Consolidated Iron Mines and the American Bridge Company were added. This new concern would embrace roughly three-fifths of the steel business of the entire country; and its total capitalization would reach—at par value—the unprecedented figure of $1,402,846,817.

The news provoked a great outcry of dismay. The Philadelphia *Evening Telegraph* said that if a "grasping and unrelenting monopoly" should be the outcome of the current trend, it might provoke "one of the greatest social and political upheavals that has been witnessed in recent history." President Hadley of Yale said in a speech that unless trusts were regulated by effective public sentiment, there would be "an emperor in Washington within twenty-five years." William Jennings Bryan's *Commoner* struck a note of unexpected humor as it commented: "'America is good enough for me,' remarked J. Pierpont Morgan a few days ago. Whenever he doesn't like it, he can give it back to us." And as usual Finley Peter Dunne's "Mr. Dooley" put into the mouth of an Irish saloonkeeper sentiments which suggested what millions of people were vaguely feeling:

Pierpont Morgan calls in wan iv his office boys, th' prisidint iv a national bank, an' says he, "James," he says, "take some change out iv th' damper an' r-run out an' buy Europe f'r me," he says. "I intind to re-organize it an' put it on a paying basis," he says. "Call up the Czar an' th' Pope an' th' Sultan an' th'

Impror Willum, an' tell thim we won't need their savices afther nex' week," he says. "Give thim a year's salary in advance. An', James," he says, "ye betther put that r-red headed bookkeeper near th' dure in charge iv th' continent. He doesn't seem to be doin' much," he says.

The new corporation represented a very large gesture of faith. For not only did it issue its own stock on a lavish basis to the owners of the constituent companies, but almost all of these companies had already issued their own stock equally lavishly to the owners of still smaller concerns. According to the Bureau of Corporations, the value of all the Steel Corporation's property, tangible and intangible, was $793 millions; and yet its total capitalization amounted to $1,402 millions. How on earth could it expect to pay dividends upon such a mass of securities? Large numbers of the stockholders of the constituent companies, finding themselves the startled possessors of Steel Corporation stock in amounts beyond their wildest dreams, would hasten to cash in on at least part of the bonanza. Could the market absorb their sales?

To make a market in Steel Corporation stock James R. Keene was engaged by the Morgan syndicate; and so actively did the skilled operator keep the market churning that the preferred stock, starting on the Stock Exchange at a price of $82\frac{3}{4}$, soon went to $101\frac{7}{8}$, while the common stock, starting at 38, rose to 55.

Many of the chief beneficiaries of the high prices paid for the stock of the constituent companies were Pittsburgh steelmen, and now Pittsburgh witnessed a carnival of spending such as it had never known before. According to Herbert N. Casson, one of the sudden millionaires "ordered a special brand of half-dollar cigars made in Cuba, each with his name and coat of arms on the wrapper"; another "had his wife's portrait painted by every obtainable foreign and American artist"; the city became "a Klondike for artists, book agents, curio dealers, and merchants who had expensive gewgaws for sale. A young [Carnegie] partner would say, 'See that painting? Cost me twenty-two thousand dollars; but I could get twenty-eight thousand dollars

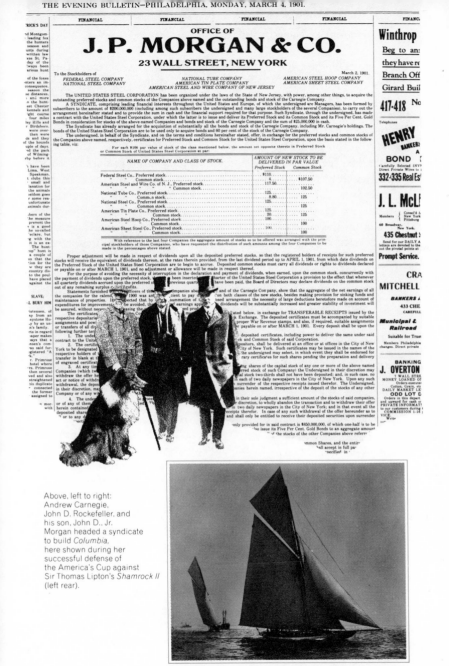

Above, left to right:
Andrew Carnegie,
John D. Rockefeller, and
his son, John D., Jr.
Morgan headed a syndicate
to build *Columbia*,
here shown during her
successful defense of
the America's Cup against
Sir Thomas Lipton's *Shamrock II*
(left rear).

for it. Have a cigar. Fine brand. Seventy-five cents apiece wholesale.'"

The Morgan syndicate did very well too. It had been paid for its services in launching the new combination with a block of stock amounting to nearly 1,300,000 shares. When this had been sold on the Exchange, the syndicate's profit, including the managers' fee, came to $57,515,000, plus some preferred stock and the right to participate in a subsequent U. S. Steel Retirement Syndicate, which increased the total to $60,000,000 or more. The House of Morgan's share in these profits—its fee for managing the syndicate—came to $11,503,000, again plus stock and participation in the new syndicate; this enabled the firm, at the close of the year 1902, to transfer to profit and loss the sum of exactly $12,000,000.

Morgan himself remained in New York for a month after the great announcement. By that time he felt assured that all was well. The reliable Gary was going to be chairman of the board of the Steel Corporation; Schwab was going to be president; Bacon, head of the finance committee. Gates he vetoed even for membership in the board of directors. Whatever the future might hold for the new corporation, it was off to a favorable start. On April 4, well satisfied, he sailed for Europe on the *Teutonic*, accompanied by his sister, Mrs. Burns.

Wherever he went now, crowds gaped at him. He slipped aboard the *Teutonic* by the second cabin gangway to outwit the reporters and photographers; when he reached Euston Station in London there was another small army of them and another great crowd. He could not learn to stomach the staring and crowding and reportorial inquisitiveness that must be the lot of one of the mightiest personages in the world. It was said that certain English brokers were taking out three-month insurance policies on his life to protect their American investments if he should die while overseas.

And why not? Was there not much truth in what John Brisben Walker had written in the *Cosmopolitan:* that "the world, on the 3rd day of March, 1901, ceased to be ruled by ... so-called statesmen," and that now "the world's real rulers" were "those who control the concentrated portion of the money supply"? Perhaps; but Pierpont Morgan wanted to settle down in his great house at Prince's Gate and enjoy the beautiful things that the dealers would bring him.

And so he did. Within a very few days he had bought Gainsborough's famous portrait of the Duchess of Devonshire.

Chapter 10

Pomp and Circumstance

IT IS DOUBTFUL if any citizen of the United States ever led—or ever will lead—a life more regal than that of Pierpont Morgan during the early years of the twentieth century. Not that he led all comers in wealth or in lavishness. What set him apart from all others was a combination of large wealth, large spending, social assurance, international social experience, love of grandeur, and restrained taste.

His home base during these years continued to be 219 Madison Avenue. There his family enjoyed the ministrations of some twelve servants (including a butler, two or three other menservants, a lady's maid, a cook, two kitchen maids, two chambermaids, a laundress, and a gardener). The Murray Hill region where Morgan remained, and the house itself, represented not fashion but rather the strict brownstone tradition of conservative Manhattan respectability. He kept accumulating property in the neighborhood for his children and enough land just to the east of No. 219, on Thirty-sixth Street, for a separate lawn-surrounded building in which he could house the books and manuscripts that had long since overflowed the storage room in his basement.

Upon this library building—completed in 1906—he lavished loving pains. He chose as his architect Charles F. McKim, who produced a one-story white marble building in early sixteenth-century Italian Renaissance style. From the day it was completed Morgan spent more and more of his time in its large west room. Its grandeur, its masculine comfort, the Florentine paintings that hung on its red walls, the statuette of Eros that stood on a pedestal by the fireplace, the other bits of choice craftsmanship that decorated it, all satisfied him completely.

There was also the Morgan country house, Cragston, and for winter holidays a thousand-acre place in the Adirondacks. For less spartan intervals in the cold months, he had a furnished apartment at the Jekyll Island Club, on a piny Georgia coast island, and, for stopovers when his yacht was in Narragansett Bay, a small "fishing box" at Newport, with an expert cook in readiness to satisfy the palates of his guests.

In London his headquarters was the big double house at Prince's Gate which had formerly been his father's town residence. This, too, was unpretentious in aspect, but contained paintings by Rubens, Rembrandt, Hobbema, Velásquez, Gainsborough, Reynolds, Constable, Turner, and other artists of wide renown, as well as a special room designed to display a series of Fragonard panels. And outside London there was Dover House, a comfortable country seat with gardens, orchards, and a dairy farm. When Morgan ended his English visit in 1902 his special railway carriage, attached to the boat train for Southampton, was piled high at one end—according to Herbert Satterlee's account—with "the boxes from Dover House that contained melons, hothouse grapes, peaches, nectarines, and bottles of cream sufficient for the voyage."

But the finest of his residences was the *Corsair III*. (The *Corsair II* had been sold to the government for use in the Spanish-American War, where it saw service as the *Gloucester*.) *Corsair III*, which was completed at the end of 1898, was 304 feet long, as against 241 for *Corsair II* and 185 for *Corsair I*. There have not been many larger private pleasure craft, and few of such regal dimensions are produced today.

The graceful black steamer served many uses. She could ferry him up the Hudson to Cragston. When he was working in Wall Street during the summer, he could dine and sleep aboard her between weekends. A launch would meet him and his friends at the West Thirty-fifth Street dock and take them to where the *Corsair* lay at anchor off the Jersey shore; in the morning they would return, after Morgan had worked his way through a monumental breakfast of fruit, porridge, eggs, hash, fish, and tomatoes. Or the party would board the *Corsair* at the East Twenty-third Street landing of the New York Yacht Club, and she would take them through Hell Gate to an anchorage off Great Neck in Long Island Sound. In warm weather this was cooler than the Hudson, and in the evening the *Corsair* might steam slowly up and down the Sound, while the company sat in wicker chairs on the deck and conversed, Morgan perhaps dozing off, his cigar between his fingers.

Morgan also used the *Corsair* as a floating residence in the quiet waters of the Mediterranean. Although he himself never crossed the Atlantic in her, that mattered hardly more than the fact that she could not ascend the Nile. In the last years of his life he engaged Thomas Cook and Sons to build for him a private all-steel Nile steamer, the *Khargeh*, with paddle wheels. As for his voyages across the Atlantic, he nearly always traveled by the ships of the White Star Line—a part of the great ship combination, the International Mercantile Marine, which he himself organized in 1902—and was therefore treated almost exactly as if he were the owner of the line.

A frequently quoted remark of Morgan's deserves repetition here. Some successful man who was thinking of buying a steam yacht asked him about the cost of maintaining it. Said Morgan shortly, "Anybody who even has to think about the cost had better not get one."

When traveling within the United States, Morgan customarily used a private railroad car. He did not own one; he would simply use one owned by a railroad in which he was influential. And on occasion he used a special train, as when he took the bishops to the San Francisco Episcopal Convention in 1901, putting them up at the large Crocker residence, to which he had sent in advance Louis Sherry and a catering staff; and afterward conveying them home by a roundabout route which included a stop at Seattle, where he took his guests to a fur store and invited them to pick out fur rugs or fur collars or gloves as keepsakes from him. The wife of a Morgan partner said that her most vivid recollection of a trip she made on a Morgan private car was of the entranced expression on the porter's face when the banker tipped him with a hundred-dollar bill.

He once remarked that he could do a year's work in nine months, but not in a year; and after he reached the age of sixty he was usually absent from the office routine for some three or four months of each twelve. Usually he would leave New York for England around March, and from then until June or July would divide his time between London and the Continent. Wherever he was, whether at Prince's Gate or Dover House, or at the Bristol in Paris, or at Aix-les-Bains, or at the Grand Hotel in Rome, or journeying about to inspect works of art, or taking a look at the excavations conducted in Egypt by the Metropolitan Museum, he was in touch with his office by coded cable. But on these holidays he liked to throw off responsibility, leaving the conduct of affairs wholly to his associates. After his return to New York there might be other interruptions of the working routine—a voyage up the coast in the *Corsair*, a yacht club cruise, a church convention trip, or a few days in the Adirondacks or at Jekyll Island during the winter.

So accustomed was he to vacationing on this generous scale that it was not easy for him to understand that such a life was not possible for many people. When a young partner-to-be, preparing to enter the firm, said he would like to be able to manage three months off each year, Morgan was all affability. "Why certainly. Of course. Let's see: you're coming in January first—why don't you pick up your family on February first and take them up the Nile? Have you ever been up the Nile?" The young man demurred. He and his wife had young children. He doubted if this would be possible. But Morgan made light of his doubts. "Nonsense. Take a couple of nurses. Take a doctor if you want to." It was all very simple to him and he was cordial and enthusiastic, planning a trip which—as the young partner later said—"of course never came off."

MORGAN WAS VERY LOYAL to family ties and family rituals—the Sunday-evening hymn singing (at which he loved to hear, and sometimes to sing in a voice of uncertain pitch, old favorites such as "Blest Be the Tie That Binds," "The Church's One Foundation," "Rock of Ages," or "Jesus, Lover of My Soul"); the family Thanksgiving dinner (with four kinds of pie); the

Christmas festivities (a tree for the grandchildren, an expedition in a cab to leave presents at friends' houses, and a big Christmas dinner with the choir of St. George's Church to sing for the company with the famous Negro baritone Harry Burleigh as soloist).

When he was at breakfast at No. 219, he liked to have one of his daughters with him because Mrs. Morgan had her coffee upstairs; and nothing pleased him more than to have one or two small grandchildren playing about in the dining room. With Mrs. Morgan he was always affectionate and deferential. But she was seldom with him on the *Corsair* or on the European trips of his later years. Being shy, domestic by taste, and in uncertain health, she became settled in the habit of remaining behind at No. 219 and at Cragston while he with his overpowering energy and hunger for human society roamed widely.

Usually on his voyages abroad it was a daughter who accompanied him—most likely Louisa Satterlee; and he was surrounded wherever he went by considerable parties of friends. The frequent presence of attractive women on his trips abroad or on the *Corsair* caused gossip, especially as he liked nothing better than to escort one of them to the jewelers' shops in the rue de la Paix and ask her to choose what she liked.

Naturally, Morgan's lamentable nose was attributed by some people to high living. As a matter of fact, he drank very moderately: ordinarily nothing more than some wine at dinner and perhaps a cordial afterward. There was usually a cigar between his lips or between his fingers from breakfast until bedtime, though it was often unlighted. He breakfasted hugely, but lunched lightly—perhaps a chicken sandwich and a slice of pie set in the back room in the office where he ate alone. No coffee, no milk; just a glass of water.

But if his lunch was usually light, he enjoyed dining largely and well. He belonged to a small dining group who called themselves the Zodiac Club and whose members vied with one another in offering sumptuous meals. Here is the menu of one Zodiac dinner, given at the University Club. Satterlee, from whose book I quote it, swears that it was devised to be eaten right through from start to finish:

Amontillado Sherry
Cotuit oysters
Bisque of crabs à la Norfolk
Consommé de volaille Sévigné
Hors-d'oeuvres variés
Rhine Wine, 1893
Soft clams à l'ancienne
Château-Latour, 1878
Saddle and rack of spring lamb
Mint sauce
Peas à la Française
Bermuda potatoes rissolées
Moët & Chandon, 1893
Terrapin, Maryland Club
Grapefruit au Kirsch
Clos-Vougeot, 1893
Canvasback ducks
Fried hominy
Celery à l'université
Parfait noisettes
Cheese
Fruit
Coffee
Cognac, 1805

WHATEVER MORGAN DID, he did in a big way. There is a story that two men who owned a steel mill decided, on the way to Morgan's office, that they would take five million dollars for it but might as well begin by asking for ten; whereupon Morgan said to them abruptly as they entered, "Now, I don't want to hear any talk from you men; I know all about your plant and what it's worth; I haven't time for any haggling; I'm going to give you twenty million dollars—now take it or leave it."

Douglas and Elizabeth Rigby, in their book on collectors, produce two equally characteristic anecdotes. In one, the dealer George S. Hellman brought Morgan a Vermeer to look at, and finding that "the great Dutchman's name was strange to the Morgan ear," delivered a brief lecture on Vermeer, his place in the history of art, and the value set upon his work.

"Morgan gazed at the picture; abruptly asked the price.

" 'One hundred thousand dollars,' said the dealer.

" 'I'll take it,' snapped Morgan, and the deal was concluded."

The Rigbys' other story is that after Morgan had bought the famous Garland collection of Chinese porcelain, he remarked to James H. Duveen, the dealer who had acted for him, "I understand that Mr. Garland did not complete the collection. I shall be glad if you will complete it for me"—an instruction which, in view of the expense of Chinese porcelains, was enough to take a dealer's breath away.

He showered the Metropolitan Museum with gifts in great variety; in 1906, when he bought the great Hoentschel collection of eighteenth-century French decorative art and of Gothic decorative art, he gave the eighteenth-century part of it to the museum outright, and announced that he would deposit the entire Gothic part of it on loan. He loaned treasures in quantity to this museum and that, yet still the works of art piled up in storage and he could not stop. He was engaged in assembling a big thing—as big in its way as the Steel Corporation—the very biggest aggregation of lovely things that there was or ever could be.

AFTER BREAKFAST at No. 219, and perhaps a business conference or a call from an art dealer, Pierpont Morgan would proceed downtown in a horse-drawn box cab or, in his very latest years, in a large automobile. Arriving at the Drexel Building he would establish himself at a corner desk on the Broad Street side of the ground-floor banking rooms. At intervals he would retire to a back room which was in the adjoining Mills Building; he had another desk in this room, and his partner Charles Steele had one, and there was a pleasant open fire; here he could work out of sight of people who came to ask for him. There was a stream of these, some of whom had no idea of being granted an audience but came merely in order to be seen going in and out of the building. On one occasion a broker carefully dropped on the steps of 23 Wall Street an unsigned buying order for securities, in the hope that a passerby might pick it up and the report might go about that the great House of Morgan was interested in the stock.

At some time between twelve and three o'clock, "the Senior," as they called him in the office, would make a tour to look at the books. It was a nervous moment for the clerks, for he seemed to be able to take in a whole page of figures in an instant; if a clerk had put down a 4 percent bond as $4\frac{1}{2}$ he would pick up the error without fail. His manner was ordinarily quiet and kindly, but if he found anything he disapproved of, he would shout something like "Who gave that order, Kinnicut?" in a deep voice—and if he caught a mistake that he attributed to carelessness he would thunder. He often took his lunch in the back room as late as two or even three o'clock; by four the box cab would be waiting outside the door—often to remain there for an hour or two before he was ready to proceed to his beloved library or to drop off at a friend's house for a call.

When people first met him the one thing they saw was his nose; trying not to look at it, they met his blazing eyes and were speechless. One woman said that for the first few weeks of her acquaintance with him she was terrified; only gradually did she come to realize that behind his alarming front were courtesy and kindness. Edward Steichen, who photographed him, says that meeting his gaze was a little like confronting the headlights of an express train bearing down on one. If one could step off the track, they were merely awe-inspiring; if one could not, they were terrifying.

His gestures were abrupt. In the office he would snatch up a piece of paper, glance at it, and either lay it down or crumple it up so suddenly that he seemed angry. While almost everybody who has written about him has applied to him the word "brusque," people who worked with him worshipped him and emphasized the graciousness of his manners.

He was given to sudden acts of goodwill. Once when a reception was being held at the Metropolitan Museum, a young woman in plain attire with a baby in her arms was in line with ladies and gentlemen in evening dress to meet the president of the museum. Some of those about Morgan wondered whether she should not be asked to step out of line. Not so Morgan; he greeted her affably and then, as she went on, whispered to the museum official who stood beside him, "Quick—get that baby's name so that I can make it a life fellow of the museum."

"That will cost you a thousand dollars," said the official.

"So much the better," said Morgan. Nor did he forget. The woman proved to be the wife of a new museum attendant; at the next meeting of the museum board, her baby was formally elected a life fellow, and Morgan footed the bill.

There are many stories of friendly acts: of his lending a million dollars to a friend who had great losses during the grim days of 1893, and refusing collateral, saying, "You may need your collateral with the banks—I am lending you the money on your business record and on what I know your character to be"; of his getting word of the business failure of a man who had been a companion of his earliest years in New York, and at once writing to him, "Why didn't you let me know?"; of his taking pains to concoct a job for an elderly lady which would give her a sense that she was earning her way.

In his life of Henry P. Davison, Thomas W. Lamont tells of an incident that happened on his very first day as a partner—January 2, 1911. The Carnegie Trust Company in New York was in trouble, and by a process of contagion runs had started on two other small banks in poor neighborhoods in uptown Manhattan. Representatives of the two banks came to Lamont and another Morgan partner, William H. Porter, to see if the House of Morgan could be persuaded to stand behind the banks. An examination of the banks' last balance sheets indicated that this would be risky, and the young partners were inclined to say no; but Porter called up Morgan to get his advice.

According to Lamont, Morgan, learning that the two banks had some thirty thousand depositors, mostly poor East-Siders, said, "Well, some way *must* be found to help those poor people. We mustn't let them lose all they have in the world. Suppose that, at worst, we were to guarantee the payment of these deposits in full. You say the total is only six million dollars? That means that the firm can't lose more than six million dollars, doesn't it?" The firm backed the two banks, and escaped with a limited loss of about $190,000.

It is hard to believe that in the banking world anybody would think or talk in those terms, yet the incident did happen. And it was characteristic. No competition was involved. Nobody could be trying to get the better of Morgan. And under such circumstances he could astonish people with his openhandedness.

He had a way of saying to partners entering his firm that he wanted its business done "up here" (raising his hand high in the air) "not down there" (dropping his hand near the floor). It was as if an old king were instructing his young princes in the moral responsibilities attending the royal function. For kingly Morgan was—in the range of his possessions, in the splendor of his journeyings, in the bigness of his plans, and in his limitations too. His royal manner of living and of traveling insulated him from the mass of men and women; and though he might by an impulsive act of kindness make connection with them, most of the time they were to him creatures apart.

Morgan thought of industry not in terms of the thousands of workers whose sweat made its production possible, nor in terms of the engineering advances which contributed to its efficiency, but in terms of the investors whose money supported it, and of the officers and directors whose duty it was to protect and enrich the investors. These officers and directors had better be honest, and it was preferable that they be gentlemen. Morgan would have liked to see the United States run by gentlemen. That these gentlemen, too, might have swollen ideas of their proper share of the fruits of industry did not apparently occur to him. In short, though he was unswervingly loyal to the United States and believed in its government, his ideas were kingly, like his conduct of life; the idea of democracy evaded him.

Chapter 11

The Limits of Triumph

IN MAY 1901, two months after his successful launching of the Steel Corporation, Morgan was vacationing at Aix-les-Bains in the hills of southeastern France when his holiday was disturbed by the arrival of a disquieting telegram from New York. It informed Morgan that he had almost lost control of the "safe" Northern Pacific Railroad in a surprise raid by Edward H. Harriman. A shrewd little man with sharp bespectacled eyes and a drooping mustache, Harriman had crossed swords with Morgan back in 1887 when he had taken control of the Dubuque & Sioux City Railroad by a trick that Morgan regarded as crafty. Some years later, when Jacob Schiff, of the New York banking firm of Kuhn, Loeb & Company, was trying to reorganize the Union Pacific Railroad, suspecting that Morgan was trying to upset his plan, he called to investigate. Morgan replied that he was not interested in the Union Pacific. "It's that little fellow Harriman," he said. "You want to look out for him."

Schiff thereupon conferred with Harriman, and made a treaty of peace by which Harriman would have a part in the new Union Pacific management. Presently Harriman was not only running the whole Union Pacific Railroad, with Schiff as his firm backer and ally, but was transforming this run-down property into an efficient, up-to-date, and highly profitable one. The little man was a genius; he was also a man of Napoleonic ambition, ready to challenge Morgan's influence. His moment for attack came that spring of 1901.

The reason behind Harriman's attack lay in the fact that both the Union Pacific and the rival Northern Pacific, controlled by Morgan and James J. Hill, were seeking access to Chicago and St. Louis by gaining control of the most important railroad in the Iowa region: the Chicago, Burlington & Quincy, known sometimes as the Burlington. In March 1901 the Morgan-Hill group purchased a large majority of the Burlington stock and thus achieved what looked like a secure grasp. Apparently Harriman had lost his chance to bring the Union Pacific farther east.

But he would not accept defeat. With credit from Schiff and other bankers, he tried to buy not merely the Burlington but the *Northern Pacific itself*.

The fact that Morgan and Hill and their friends owned considerably less than half of the stock of the Northern Pacific, sufficient under ordinary circumstances to guarantee control, gave Harriman his opportunity. Acting through Schiff, he began to buy Northern Pacific stock on the open market. The recent launching of the Steel Corporation had set off a furious stock-market boom, and Harriman rightly reasoned that if his heavy purchases caused the price of Northern Pacific to rise, people would assume that speculators were responsible. He bought and bought, and the price climbed and climbed.

Yet it wasn't many days before old James J. Hill, who was in Seattle, decided that the rise must be investigated and set out for New York by special train. Arriving on Friday, May 3, he went to see Schiff, and learned that Harriman and Schiff had almost succeeded in buying control of the road. He at once reported the situation to Morgan's partners.

In Morgan's absence, Robert Bacon was in charge at 23 Wall Street. Bacon and his colleagues thought that the Harriman group was buying to gain representation on the Northern Pacific board of directors, but they had no idea of the scale of the operation.

The shocked Morgan partners conferred—and Bacon sent off a cable to Pierpont Morgan in Europe asking for authority to buy 150,000 shares of Northern Pacific common. As Morgan later testified, "We had reorganized the Northern Pacific. . . . I feel bound in all honor when I reorganize a property, and am morally responsible for its management, to protect it, and I generally do protect it; so I made up my mind that it would be desirable to buy 150,000 shares of stock, which we proceeded to do, and with that I knew we had a majority of the common stock, and I knew that actually gave us control, and they couldn't take the minority and have it sacrificed to Union Pacific interests."

But it was only by an accident that the Morgan purchases—which did not begin until Monday—prevented a Harriman victory. For on Saturday morning Harriman decided to buy 40,000 additional shares of Northern Pacific common to make his own position unassailable. He called up Schiff's office and put in the order, but it couldn't be executed because Schiff, a devout Jew, was at the synagogue.

Was it simply devoutness that took Schiff there, or had he decided that further purchases might cause trouble? If so, he was quite right. For when, on Monday, May 6, the Morgan buying orders poured into the market, they caused a panic.

What Harriman and Morgan, between them, had succeeded in doing was to buy more Northern Pacific common shares than there were in the market. (There were only 800,000 in existence, of which Harriman held over 370,000; Morgan's order would bring the number that he and Hill held to some 410,000. That would make the total of shares going into the strongboxes of the two groups at least 780,000, leaving very few of the 800,000 for anybody else.) Morgan brokers were buying, in part, stock that didn't exist. Traders were selling the stock short—selling stock that they didn't own, in the hope of buying it later at a lower price to make delivery. And having sold this nonexistent stock, they were finding to their dismay that there was little stock to borrow and almost none to buy.

On Monday, as the Morgan brokers in New York bought no less than 127,500 shares of Northern Pacific, the price climbed from 114 to 127½. On Tuesday they continued buying, and it touched 149¾. On Wednesday they had stopped buying, but it reached 180. And on Thursday, May 9, it leaped wildly all the way to 1000—while the price of all other stocks cascaded furiously downhill. Brokers, realizing that their inability to deliver the Northern Pacific shares they had sold might make them liable for terrific sums of money, sold everything they could lay their hands on to escape bankruptcy.

The panic was brief. For that very Thursday the Morgan and Harriman forces made an agreement which saved the short sellers from destruction. By their agreement Morgan, who now held a clear majority of Northern Pacific common, would give Harriman places on the new board of directors. Harriman and Morgan would consider setting up a New Jersey holding company to hold the shares of both the Northern Pacific and Hill's Great Northern; and in this new concern, which would be called the Northern Securities Company, Harriman as well as Morgan would have representation. Thus at last "community of interest" would be achieved.

The Northern Pacific battle was over, but Morgan's prestige had suffered a heavy blow. Not only had his organization been caught napping, but his headlong financial barrage in reaction

Cragston, Morgan's country estate

Playing his favorite version of solitaire

CALL LOAN RATES ADVANCED TO 70 PER CENT THIS MORNING.

Large Decline in Stocks as a Result of the Latest Banking Developments—Heavy Deposit Withdrawals Closed a Big Trust Company.

WASHINGTON, Oct. 22.—The Comptroller of the Currency, Ridgley, said this morning:

"My advices are reassuring and the situation in New York should now improve. The storm has broken and the damage known without any failures of the national banks, which have lately been criticised. The clearing house confirms my reports that these banks are all solvent and is standing by them. Their debt balances at the clearing house this morning are less than expected, and I understand one bank paid its balance without help.

not for alarm."

however, that the Secretary was ready to meet

for call money and the worst break that the stock market has had since last March were the results this morning of the announcement made last night of the resignation of President Barney of the Knickerbocker Trust company and the tempo-

to Harriman's attack had outraged public opinion. Is this, people asked, the way in which the monarchs of American finance preserve order and peace in the business community?

"ON THE AFTERNOON of September 14 [1901]," writes Herbert Satterlee, "Mr. Morgan had just finished his day's work and . . . we were both just starting to the front door of the office when half a dozen newspapermen rushed in. The first one cried out, 'Mr. Morgan, President McKinley is dead.' He turned and went back to his closed desk, took off his hat, and sat down heavily as if he were very tired.

"The newspapermen gathered around, and nothing was said for a full minute. Finally the spokesman of the group said, 'Mr. Morgan, what have you got to say about the news I gave you?'

"Again there was a long pause. Then Mr. Morgan got up and, looking at the reporters, said, 'It is the saddest news I ever heard. I can't talk about it.'"

The loss was more than personal. For the assassination of McKinley and the arrival in the White House of Vice-President Theodore Roosevelt might mean the end of an era.

Behind McKinley stood Mark Hanna of Ohio, chief of the bosses of the Republican Party, who believed that whatever was good for the big corporations was good for the country; with the unpredictable Roosevelt in power, who could tell what might happen? Hanna himself, when he received the news, exclaimed, "And now look—that damned cowboy is President of the United States!"

Morgan had felt he could rely on Hanna. He had met him in 1896, before McKinley's election; had him out on the *Corsair* for dinner, and, as the two men sat smoking on the afterdeck, Morgan had argued that the Republican Party must back the gold standard. It had done so, and had won; and from that time forward Morgan felt that the government in Washington was sound. But this young Roosevelt was an upsetter of apple carts.

During his vice-presidency Roosevelt had given a dinner for Morgan, and had even written to Secretary of War Root that this dinner represented "an effort on my part to become a conservative man in touch with the influential classes." But

Roosevelt was headstrong and sometimes said wild things. Could one be sure that he would not become the instrument of rising popular discontent?

That discontent was partly a delayed reaction from the suffering caused by the depression of the mid-nineties. Partly it was due to reports by a group of journalists—"muckrakers," as Roosevelt was later to call them—who described in lurid detail facts about business excesses and political corruption. Partly it was a natural consequence of the spectacle of unbridled wealth—of men making millions at a stroke when the average wage earner's family was struggling along on less than a thousand dollars a year. Partly it was due to the fact that many of the so-called trusts brought about monopoly—followed by rising prices. These discontents had been sharpened by the formation of the Steel Corporation and by the Northern Pacific panic.

Up to now the rebellion had lacked an effective leader. During Theodore Roosevelt's seven and a half years in the White House he was destined to be only intermittently and uncertainly its leader, for after every sally against big business he would go back to touch base with the conservative leadership of the Republican Party. But he became the most enthusiastic mouthpiece of the reform movement. As Finley Peter Dunne described business combinations through the person of "Mr. Dooley," " 'Th' trusts,' says he, 'are heejous monsthers built up by th' inlightened intherprise iv th' men that have done so much to advance progress in our beloved counthry,' he says. 'On wan hand I wud stamp thim undher fut; on th' other hand not so fast.' " But only a few weeks later the blow fell.

One evening in February 1902, Morgan was told by a friend that the Attorney General of the United States was about to announce the prosecution of the Northern Securities Company for breach of the Sherman Anti-Trust Act of 1890. The company was the holding concern which Morgan had set up in order to settle the Northern Pacific dispute with Harriman.

When the news of the government's action came out the next day, there was frightened selling on the Stock Exchange. So seldom had any corporation been prosecuted under the Sherman Act that it had come to be regarded almost as a dead letter; and anyhow the best lawyers—following the decisions of the United States Supreme Court—had long since made up their minds that a combination brought about through a holding company was immune.

Morgan went to Washington and had an interview with Roosevelt, in the presence of Attorney General Knox, who had brought the government's suit. He protested that Roosevelt might have shown him the courtesy of advance warning.

"That is just what we did not want to do," said the President.

"If we have done anything wrong," persisted Morgan, "send your man to my man and they can fix it up." (He meant the Attorney General and one of his own lawyers.)

"That can't be done," said Roosevelt.

Then Knox added, "We don't want to fix it up, we want to stop it."

Morgan wanted to know whether the President were going to attack any of his other interests. "Certainly not," answered Roosevelt, "unless we find out that in any case they have done something that we regard as wrong."

The lawyers who felt the government's case against the Northern Securities Company was doomed to defeat were wrong. The change that was taking place in the climate of opinion had reached even the judiciary. But it was not until March 14, 1904—two years later—that the Supreme Court said the final word on Northern Securities; then, reversing its former position on holding companies, it voted, five to four, that the company was illegal. In the words of Justice John M. Harlan, "No scheme or device . . . could more effectively and certainly suppress free competition."

Before that decision had been handed down Morgan had been thrust into another dispute—the anthracite coal strike of 1902. This was a rebellion of the miners, under their idolized leader John Mitchell, against the virtually feudal conditions of work imposed by the mine operators headed by George F. Baer. As president of the Reading Railroad, Baer was subject—in certain financial matters at least—to Morgan's authority.

That spring, in London, Pierpont Morgan had completed arrangements for combining the White Star, American, Red

Star, Leyland, Atlantic Transport, and Dominion lines into a shipping combine to be called the International Mercantile Marine. This was a project that was to mitigate the mutually damaging competition between transatlantic steamship lines. It was big, very big; the combined fleet numbered over one hundred and twenty steamships. And if the investing public would buy shares of International Mercantile Marine at solid prices, the profit to his firm would run into millions.

Many Englishmen were disturbed at the news that so large a British-American combination would be under the aegis of an American; was Britain to be no longer mistress of the seas? Peddlers on the London streets were selling for a penny a "license to stay on the Earth," signed by "J. Pierpont Morgan."

But Morgan didn't mind. He was having a gay time in England, giving large dinner parties at Prince's Gate and Dover House and making lavish purchases of art. Soon he was off on a real holiday round—a voyage on the *Corsair* from the Riviera to Venice and back to Brindisi; another voyage to Kiel, where Kaiser Wilhelm of Germany came aboard for luncheon; an expedition to Berlin in the private railway car used by members of the imperial family; and finally, attendance at the coronation of King Edward VII. Late in August he returned to the United States, to find the coal strike awaiting him.

The anthracite miners had been out on strike since May. They would not return to work unless the coal operators would negotiate with their union, the United Mine Workers. But the operators were adamant; they would talk with their own men but not with the union. The strike went on and on. Though the acute shortage of coal troubled Morgan and he contributed twenty thousand dollars toward the maintenance of a coal depot on New York's Lower East Side, he felt that labor relations lay outside the range of his authority and that he could not lay down the law to Baer and the other operators.

By the first of October matters had reached such a pass that President Roosevelt intervened by calling John Mitchell and the chief operators to the temporary White House on Lafayette Square (the Executive Mansion was being repaired). Mitchell promptly agreed to accept the findings of an arbitration commission to be appointed by the President; Baer and the other operators not only refused but insolently told the President that "the duty of the hour is not to waste time negotiating with the fomenters of this anarchy."

It was at this juncture that Elihu Root, the Secretary of War, thought of a formula for bridging the gap. He thought he knew who would make the operators see reason. With Roosevelt's approval he got in touch with Morgan, went to New York by train, and was taken by launch to the *Corsair*, lying at anchor in the North River. There he talked for hours with Morgan.

Under Morgan's eye Root wrote out a brief memorandum to be adopted by the mine owners for settlement. Then he and Morgan went ashore and drove by cab to the Union Club, where some of the operators had gathered at Morgan's request.

At this session, and in a meeting the next day with Baer, Morgan secured the operators' acceptance of the memorandum. The proposal they had agreed to was for arbitration of the strike by a commission appointed by the President, the commission to consist of an engineer officer of the Army or Navy, an expert mining engineer, one of the federal judges in eastern Pennsylvania, "a man who by active participation in mining and selling coal is familiar with the physical and commercial features of the business," and finally "a man of prominence eminent as a sociologist."

Roosevelt was delighted. Morgan had brought the operators a long way from their previous position. When he submitted the proposal to the miners, they naturally suggested that the commission should include a representative of organized labor, and also, since most of the miners were Catholics, a Catholic bishop. Roosevelt thought these revisions should be allowed, but the operators would not accept a representative of organized labor. Then Roosevelt suddenly discovered that they were quite willing to accept the Grand Chief of the Order of Railway Conductors as a member of the board, *provided he was labeled "a man of prominence eminent as a sociologist."* With that ludicrous face-saving arrangement, the operators said yes—and the strike was settled.

To all of this a footnote should be added. When Morgan was

accused in the press of having intervened because he had a personal financial interest in stopping the coal strike, John Mitchell came to his defense: "To my personal knowledge Mr. Morgan had been trying to settle the coal strike ever since he came back from Europe two months ago. If others had been as fair and reasonable as Mr. Morgan was, this strike would have been settled a long time ago. . . ."

From this time on there was an armed truce between President Roosevelt and Morgan. In 1904, when Roosevelt was up for election, Morgan and his partners contributed $100,000 to the Republican campaign fund; but although, as the campaign approached, Roosevelt had prudently become more discreet in his references to business, it may be guessed that Morgan made these contributions less out of enthusiasm for the President than out of a sense that a Republican Administration was best for business even if led by a man of unfortunate tendencies.

During 1905 and 1906 Roosevelt, after a landslide victory at the polls, resumed his forays against business excesses. He fought energetically and successfully for the passage of the Hepburn Bill, which would widen the powers of the Interstate Commerce Commission over the railroads and give it authority to fix maximum rates; and in the course of the battle he said a great many severe things about big business men.

Although Roosevelt was held in leash by the necessity of keeping together the conservative Republican Party with its super-conservative financial backers, the truth was that when he spoke—or more rarely acted—to keep the power of big business within bounds, he represented a very large body of increasingly influential American opinion. And the further truth was that Morgan was building up a sphere of influence so very much more formidable than that of any other individual or group in the business world, that no one could speak of keeping the power of big business within bounds without thinking of him. The two men had become symbols—Roosevelt, of the authority of government; Morgan, of the authority of private business. There was never an open break between the two men. Nevertheless the relations between them were not easy.

Another set of difficulties confronted Morgan in these years of his mature power—economic difficulties brought on by the methods he had chosen to reorganize the railroads and amalgamate industrial corporations.

When Morgan reorganized a railroad, he had to make his plan palatable to the creditors and stockholders of the road while reducing its fixed debt. This meant issuing stock lavishly. When he pulled together a group of corporations to make a supercorporation, this too meant issuing stock lavishly. The result was that both the reorganized railroads and the newly organized supercorporations were overcapitalized; only if these concerns achieved high success could they pay adequate dividends. And sometimes they could not achieve it.

In the case of the Steel Corporation, the results were good—but only after periods of anxiety. During the "rich men's panic" of 1903—when there were so many "undigested securities" on the market that all values fell on the exchanges—dividends on the common stock had to be interrupted and its price fell all the way to $8\frac{3}{4}$.

Slowly the Steel Corporation pulled out of the doldrums; for not only had the amalgamation permitted some economies in production, but also the steel industry was still capable of great growth. When the International Harvester Company of New Jersey was incorporated under the Morgan aegis in 1902—pulling together the McCormick Harvesting Machine Co., the Deering Co., and three other rival concerns, and thus assembling into one enterprise some eighty percent of the harvester trade—it was also a success, acquiring as it did a partial monopoly of a young and lusty industry.

But the International Mercantile Marine proved a grievous disappointment. There was such a small public demand for its securities that in 1906 the Morgan firm had to report to the syndicate participants that "the prices at which the company's securities ruled in the market have been so low that we have not felt justified in attempting to dispose of those held for the account of the Syndicate"; the participants had to pay up their subscriptions in full and receive in return I.M.M. bonds and stock of limited value. And the company itself, beset by tribulations such as the *Titanic* tragedy, did not prosper.

However, the most dismaying of Morgan's ventures was his attempt to expand the New York, New Haven & Hartford Railroad into a great integrated New England system. Morgan had a sentiment for the New Haven road, as an old Hartford boy whose grandfather had invested in one of the little lines out of which it was pieced together. When in 1892 he became a member of its board of directors, he began to try to build it into a real system; and when President McLeod of the Reading invaded its territory in 1893 he fought back. A decade later, President Charles S. Mellen of the Northern Pacific was induced to take over the management of the New Haven. With Morgan's continuing encouragement Mellen embarked upon an ambitious plan of expansion.

Some steamship lines which plied Long Island Sound, carrying passengers and freight from New York to Fall River and other points, appeared to menace the New Haven Shore Line by offering low rates which undercut those of the railroad. Very well, those steamship lines must be bought by the New Haven or put out of business. Another menace was the interurban trolley lines, which were then the very latest thing in transportation; people could travel imposing distances by transferring from one to another of these careening electric car lines. Very well, the New Haven must buy up all the competing trolley lines. There were other railroads in New England which, if acquired by the New Haven, might extend it into an all-New England system. Very well, the New Haven must buy control of the Boston & Maine and bring other lines into alliance. Some New York men had acquired franchises for two little lines to carry commuters from the New York suburbs as far as the Bronx terminal of the New York subway. Very well, these projects must be bought up and the New Haven must build such a suburban line of its own.

As Morgan confidently moved issue after issue of stocks and bonds to pay for the expansion, the total capitalization of the railroad climbed from 93 millions in the middle of 1903 all the way to 417 millions in the middle of 1913. Such aggressive purchasing in New England by the New Haven management provoked legal and political opposition, led by the Boston lawyer Louis D. Brandeis, and this both delayed the fruition of the plans and weakened public confidence in the New Haven. In 1913, shortly after Morgan's death, affairs had come to such a pass that Mellen was forced out of the presidency of the road by Morgan's own firm. Presently the New Haven passed its dividend; it never recovered its former standing. Moreover, in two investigations the Interstate Commerce Commission disclosed gross scandals in the management of the line.

And in the hue and cry that took place after Morgan's death, Mellen claimed that in this whole campaign of expansion he had been following Morgan's lead. When asked in the investigation whether he had been "Morgan's man," he answered, "I have been called by the newspapers his office boy." When asked how important the rest of the directors were as compared with Morgan, he said that there were other strong men on the New Haven board, but that he "could not recall anything where Mr. Morgan was determined, emphatic, insistent . . . where he did not have his way." In another part of his examination Mellen, who prided himself on his picturesque language, declared that the record of the New Haven, without Morgan, would have been "as tame and uneventful, as devoid of interest and incident, as would the record of a herd of cows deprived of the association of a bull."

Mellen also testified, apparently correctly, that the New York, Westchester & Boston project—which up to 1914 had cost over thirty-six million dollars and had resulted in a suburban line only 18.03 miles long which was losing money at the rate of over a million dollars a year—had been pushed through the board of directors by Morgan. He, Mellen, had never been given an adequate account of the way in which millions of dollars were spent. Mellen complained on the witness stand that if anything went wrong with the New York, Westchester & Boston scheme he had known that he himself would be "the goat." "I was a president," he testified, "and I knew, if trouble came, that lots of people would go to Carlsbad or some other place where they would be inaccessible, and I would have to stay and fight it out."

Despite these insinuations, we may dismiss any notion that

Morgan had any direct part in the financial irregularities of the New Haven. He was absent from his desk for months at a time and preoccupied with large decisions. His way was to pick a man, trust him, and leave everything to him. If Mellen said there was nothing to Brandeis' charges that the New Haven was overextended, that was enough. Morgan's judgment of men was not always reliable. He once confessed to Rainsford, "I am not a good judge of men. My first shot is sometimes right. My second never is." He had left too much to Mellen and Mellen's henchmen.

In his later years, his judgment of enterprises was likewise not always reliable. The idea of rounding out the New Haven system came as naturally as the idea of rounding out the Garland art collection; and if it cost a few extra millions, what did that matter? It was not his way to look into details—except on the books of his own firm. It was totals he dealt with. The details were up to the men he trusted.

Chapter 12

Rock of Defense

PIERPONT MORGAN was seventy years and six months old when, in the autumn of 1907, his influence was put to its most inexorable test.

He had been taking business much less strenuously that year, as befitted his age. During the winter and early spring he had often been absent from 23 Wall Street, preferring to remain uptown in the big red-walled West Room of his recently completed library, where he could interview business callers or art dealers at leisure. In March he was off to Europe—shuttling back and forth between London and Paris, visiting Rome, Florence, and Aix, and, as always, collecting indefatigably. Not until August 19 was he back in New York.

He arrived to find the business situation threatening. There had been minor panics abroad; the New York stock market had been subject to sinking spells since early in the year; new issues of securities had languished; commodity prices were sagging; and there was an ominous feeling that an economic storm was brewing. But still Morgan was intent upon leaving as much work and responsibility as possible to his younger partners. The triennial Episcopal convention was to be held at Richmond, Virginia, the first three weeks of October, and, since it had become his custom to attend these assemblages, he set out as usual. Two special cars took him and his guests—including three American bishops and the gaitered bishop of London—to Richmond. There they took up residence in the Rutherford house on Grace Street, which Morgan had engaged for the occasion, with Louis Sherry once more serving as majordomo.

During the last few days of the convention Morgan began to receive telegrams from New York with increasing frequency. As Bishop Lawrence of Massachusetts later wrote, "One day a member of the party said, 'Mr. Morgan, you seem to have some bad news.' He shot his eyes across the table at the speaker and said nothing. No question of that sort was asked again. The fact was that we were so busy in our convention work, we were not aware of the clouds gathering in New York and the country which was to break in the great financial panic of October 1907."

In New York a group of speculators headed by F. Augustus Heinze made a disastrous attempt to corner the stock of the United Copper Company, and went to the wall. Heinze was head of the Mercantile National Bank, and naturally rumors flew about that it might have been involved in his speculations. When a run on the bank began, it appealed to the Clearing House for aid. (There was at that time no Federal Reserve System, and therefore the Clearing House—an association of banks set up for the clearing of checks—was the logical agency to turn to if one's bank was in trouble.) Two of Heinze's associates in his stock-market ventures, Charles W. Morse and Edward R. Thomas, also headed banks; and presently these banks, too, were beset by suspicion. Whereupon the conservative bankers who headed the New York Clearing House demanded the resignation of all three speculators from their banking connections. Although the Clearing House announced simultaneously that these men's banks were in sound condition, rumors of trouble were redoubled.

People began to question the reliability of a certain type of bank. For several years before 1907 there had been an epidemic of setting up trust companies, which were permitted by law to engage in banking operations without being subject to the strict regulations that surrounded national banks. A good many plungers had got into the managements of some of these trust companies and invested in more adventurous enterprises than ordinary banks were permitted to.

Investors, speculators, and bank depositors began selling stock, calling loans, drawing their funds out of suspect banks. The whispers multiplied. "You say your company's funds are deposited in the Knickerbocker Trust Company? Better watch out; didn't you know that the president was mixed up in deals with Morse?" "What, you're holding three hundred shares of Union Pacific on margin? Sell. Get out of the market. In a few days more, the way things are going, some of the biggest brokerage houses will go under." "Did you realize that these trust companies don't belong to the Clearing House, and have to rely on a national bank to clear their checks for them? Well, suppose the bank decides it won't do this anymore? That will be nice for the trust company's depositors, won't it?" Thus the talk ran. It was the beginning of panic.

Some of Morgan's friends wanted him to come back from Richmond, but he and his partners thought he had better remain, lest his return be taken as a sign of alarm, until the convention broke up on Saturday, October 19. That night he traveled back to New York on the special cars with his Episcopal guests. And the next morning, like a general arriving at the headquarters of a beleaguered army, he climbed the steps of the library on East Thirty-sixth Street and entered its massive doors.

He spent the rest of that Sunday, until after midnight, studying the problem—talking with partners and friends, with bank presidents, with trust company heads; hearing about the demoralized condition of the Stock Exchange, the widespread calling of loans, the runs on bank after bank; looking at financial statements; listening to the appeals of men who wanted him to lend cash to this institution or that. His own banking house was secure unless everything went. What concerned him was the general mood of panic. Everybody seemed to look to him for leadership. Reporters took up their watch in Thirty-sixth Street outside the library gate, and noted who arrived and who left, but there was no news.

Monday morning Morgan asked his son-in-law, Herbert Satterlee, to get in touch with some able young bankers who could assemble figures and facts for him. Then he went downtown. Among the banks which appeared to be headed for trouble was a big trust company, the Knickerbocker. Some of its funds were said to have been dubiously invested and depositors were beginning to draw out their cash. A committee of the Knickerbocker's directors came to see Morgan and reported that because the popular president of the Knickerbocker, Charles T. Barney, had been closely linked in the public mind with Heinze and Morse, they had called for Barney's resignation. That afternoon the National Bank of Commerce, which customarily cleared checks for the Knickerbocker, had sent word that it would do so no longer. The committee appealed to Morgan for help.

Morgan himself was a stockholder in the Knickerbocker, some of his own firm's money was on deposit there, and it had been founded by an old school friend of his; but he doubted it could be saved. There would be no sense in throwing valuable funds into a sinking institution. He advised the committee to assemble a meeting of all the Knickerbocker directors to see whether they could devise a plan to prevent its downfall.

The meeting was held that evening—at Sherry's restaurant, in a room so unprivate that strangers wandered in and out, picking up fragments of the talk, telephoning their friends, spreading the news that the Knickerbocker was in jeopardy. That evening Morgan went to bed after midnight, with a cold coming on—a tired and uncertain man.

On Tuesday, the twenty-second, as expected, depositors swarmed to Fifth Avenue and Thirty-fourth Street to draw out their funds from the Knickerbocker. One of Morgan's team of examiners had been making a quick examination of the bank's condition, and his report was unfavorable: there was nothing to be done. The run continued—and by two o'clock in the afternoon the Knickerbocker had failed.

The news of its failure came like a thunderclap in the midst of a gathering storm. Every banker, and especially every trust company president, knew that he faced the same possibility. The Secretary of the Treasury, George B. Cortelyou, sped to New York to see what use could be made of government funds. Again Morgan conferred with anxious financiers half the night. "It was at this time," says Satterlee, that he "organized the group or committee of bankers who voluntarily submitted their statements to him and permitted him to allocate each one the sum of money which he felt was appropriate and necessary to make up the total amount needed to carry the weaker institutions through the panic." He tried to get the heads of the trust companies to organize for mutual aid, but failed. Not until after three o'clock did he turn in, still miserable with a heavy cold.

Among the bankers who discussed possible plans of action that night with Secretary Cortelyou was George W. Perkins, one of Morgan's partners. When the session was over the reporters clustered around, and Perkins attempted to brief them on the situation to date. As a result there appeared the next morning in *The New York Times* and the *Sun* a statement that "the sore point" was now the Trust Company of America; the company had applied for help, provision had been made to supply it with all the cash it might need the next morning, and it was sound and would pull through. That statement was so injudicious that the Associated Press refused to send it out. Under the circumstances it was not surprising that the next day the Trust Company of America was besieged.

On that Wednesday morning "Morgan could not be waked up." (I am quoting Satterlee, at whose house on Thirty-sixth Street he was staying, for Mrs. Morgan was at Cragston and the house at No. 219 was closed.) "If he could not be aroused, the consequences were too serious to contemplate. He seemed to be in a stupor. I finally got him to open his eyes and answer my questions. His cold had made fast progress owing to his fatigue. He could hardly speak above a whisper. Dr. Markoe was summoned by telephone and came down provided with

MARKET FALLS AND PANIC SOON REIGNS.

Northern Pacific Corner Causes a Tremendous Break.

GRAVEST RESULTS PREDICTED

Financiers Appeal to Mr. Morgan—Cornered. "Shorts' " Loss Uncounted Millions—Far-Reaching Combinations Menaced.

The long-predicted panic in the stock market came upon Wall Street yesterday, and, like all other panics, it found market operators so completely unprepared for, and so utterly astounded, and dumbfounded, by it and this notwithstanding the many warnings put out—that prices fairly melted away in the wild scramble of holders of stock to "stand from under."

sprays, gargles, etc. After half an hour's heroic work Mr. Morgan dressed and went down to breakfast."

A cup of coffee revived him, and after a few conferences in the library he went downtown by cab. His voice was hoarse and his eyes teared so that it was hard for him to read. He found Wall Street full of crowds, and outside the door of the Trust Company of America there was a long line of depositors. President Oakleigh Thorne had opened seven paying tellers' windows that morning instead of the customary one, hoping to reduce the crowd of panicky depositors. Two members of Morgan's team of examiners had been inside, appraising the securities in its vaults, since four o'clock that morning. Morgan could not yet know whether the bank was worth saving.

Meanwhile he invited the presidents of all the other trust companies to meet in his office, and urged them to get together funds to help such of their own group as might be in trouble. And he also asked the two most important national bankers in the city, George F. Baker of the First National and James Stillman of the National City, to meet with him. They joined him in one of the back rooms of the Morgan office—while frantic messages came from Thorne that the cash in the tills of the Trust Company of America was dwindling fast.

At about half past twelve Morgan sent for the men who had been examining Thorne's bank. One of them, Willard King, went into the meeting of the trust company heads to make a report. The other, Benjamin Strong, joined Morgan and Baker and Stillman in the back room. Morgan listened while Strong consulted Baker and Stillman. Minutes dragged by—half an hour, three-quarters of an hour. Morgan was well aware that meanwhile Thorne's cash was getting lower and lower. Finally Morgan asked Strong whether he believed the Trust Company to be solvent. "Yes," said Strong.

"This, then, is the place to stop this trouble," said Morgan.

At once, with the aid of Baker and Stillman, he made cash available to Thorne's bank. It arrived in the nick of time, and the Trust Company of America did not close.

It was a very tired man of seventy who heaved himself into a cab on Fifth Avenue late that evening and rode to the Satterlee house. He had spent the entire evening with the committee of trust company presidents which he had succeeded in getting organized. He had told them that they must subscribe a fund of ten million dollars which could be used for the support of their weaker brethren. Secretary Cortelyou was going to put federal funds at the disposal of certain national banks, which would pass them on to the trust companies; but there was no time now to wait for that. They must act at once. When that evening they subscribed up to eight and a quarter millions, he told them that his firm and the leading national banks would be responsible for the remaining million and three-quarters.

It had been a terrible day. The Westinghouse Company had failed. The Pittsburgh Stock Exchange had suspended. Western banks with money on deposit in New York were drawing it away, for the panic was now national. No one could tell what turn it would take next. But it looked as if the forces of defense were at last getting organized. So far, so good. Morgan played a last game of solitaire and went slowly up to bed.

At about ten o'clock Thursday morning, Morgan drove downtown with Satterlee "in the Union Club brougham drawn by the white horse and driven by the faithful Williams." Satterlee has given an account of that ride:

> All the way downtown people who got a glimpse of him in the cab called the attention of passers-by. Policemen and cabbies who knew him well by sight shouted, "There goes the Old Man!" or "There goes the Big Chief!" ... Near Trinity Church a way through the crowd was opened as soon as it was realized who was in the cab. The crowd moved with us. ... All this time he looked straight ahead and gave no sign of noticing the excitement, but it was evident that he was pleased. Wall Street and Broad Street were filled ... with an excited throng. ... As Mr. Morgan got out of the cab and hurried up the steps into his office the hubbub ceased, and there was a moment's pause; and then the struggling mob fought their way on, all looking up at the windows of J. P. Morgan & Co.

There was new aid available now. John D. Rockefeller put up ten millions to aid the trust companies. Cortelyou stood ready to follow the leading bankers' advice as to where the United

States government's money should be applied. But the bank runs continued, especially at the Trust Company of America; the ten-million-dollar fund subscribed the preceding evening was "swallowed up . . . so quick you couldn't tell where it went to," as George W. Perkins later testified. Now the storm center shifted to the Stock Exchange. Prices were tumbling; that morning Union Pacific fell from $108\frac{1}{2}$ to 100, Reading from $78\frac{5}{8}$ to $70\frac{1}{2}$, Northern Pacific from 110 to $100\frac{1}{2}$. Toward the end of the morning, sales almost stopped—there was no money with which to buy stocks. President Thomas of the Stock Exchange thereupon crossed the street to 23 Wall.

The accounts of what happened next vary somewhat, for it was a confused time and memories of it were jumbled. According to Satterlee's version, Thomas walked into the back room where Morgan was talking with some men, and said:

"Mr. Morgan, we will have to close the Stock Exchange."

"What?" said Morgan, turning sharply.

Thomas said he didn't see how the Exchange could be kept open till the regular closing time of three o'clock.

" 'It must not close one minute before that hour today!' " said Morgan—"emphasizing each word by keeping time with his right hand, the middle finger of it pointing straight at Mr. Thomas." At once he sent for the presidents of all the national banks in the neighborhood. Some of Cortelyou's federal funds were available. From these and other sources he raised within a few minutes the twenty-five millions to be lent on the Exchange to keep it open.

But how long could such rescue operations continue? Once more, on Friday, there was a total shortage of cash on the Stock Exchange; once more Morgan had to call upon the bank presidents to take up a subscription. This time the meeting produced not the fifteen millions that Morgan had considered necessary but thirteen—which might or might not be enough to save the day. As Perkins later testified, "If twenty millions had been needed that day, the Stock Exchange and a hundred or more firms would have gone up, it was just that close. It was touch and go." But the Exchange stayed open. As things turned out, thirteen millions *were* enough. Just.

"Anyone who saw Mr. Morgan going from the Clearing House back to his office that day will never forget the picture," writes Satterlee. "With his coat unbuttoned and flying open, a piece of white paper clutched tightly in his right hand, he walked fast down Nassau Street. His flat-topped black derby hat was set firmly down on his head. Between his teeth he held a paper cigar holder in which was one of his long cigars, half smoked. His eyes were fixed straight ahead. He swung his arms as he walked and took no notice of anyone. He did not seem to see the throngs in the street, so intent was his mind on the thing that he was doing. . . . He did not dodge, or walk in and out, or slacken his pace. He simply barged along, as if he had been the only man going down Nassau Street hill past the Sub-treasury. He was the embodiment of power and purpose. Not more than two minutes after he disappeared into his office, the cheering on the floor of the Stock Exchange could be heard out in Broad Street."

NIGHT AFTER NIGHT there had been conferences at the Morgan Library. On Thursday and Friday evenings, the presidents of the banks and trust companies gathered in the lofty East Room, planning the disposition of financial forces for the morrow, while Morgan sat in a red plush armchair by the fire in the West Room, with a *Madonna and Child* by Pinturicchio looking down over his shoulder and Fra Filippo Lippi's altarpiece of Saint Lawrence and saints Cosmo and Damian facing him from the opposite wall. There was a card table before him. Elsewhere in the library the financiers who had become his lieutenants in the struggle against the panic labored at the making of battle plans. Morgan concentrated on the game of solitaire before him, slowly puffing his black cigar as he carefully placed the five of clubs on the two, and the eight on the five, and the jack on the eight. The bankers would work out a scheme, and one of them would cross the marble hallway to the West Room and tell Morgan about it, and he would listen, and say briefly, "No, that won't work."

Another delegate from the East Room would enter and present a new scheme. "No," Morgan would say shortly; and the delegate would retire again, and the game of solitaire would continue under the watchful eyes of the Madonnas and the great ladies of Florence, until at last the conclusion which Morgan could accept had been reached.

At last the week came to an end. The Trust Company of America had not failed; the Stock Exchange had not closed; the decision had been made to put into circulation Clearing House certificates. It looked as if the worst might be over. The newspapers talked as if the panic were a thing of the past. Theodore Roosevelt, who had so often berated "malefactors of wealth," gave out a confident statement in which he praised "those influential and splendid businessmen . . . who have acted with such wisdom and public spirit." Clergymen were asked by a committee of bankers to make reassuring statements to their congregations, following Morgan's advice that "if people will keep their money in the banks, everything will be all right."

But the crisis continued. Still there were runs on banks and trust companies; still there had to be night sessions at the library. And there were two moments of acute danger.

The first came when New York officials approached Morgan to report that the city needed thirty million dollars at once to pay off some short-term obligations that were coming due; they must have an emergency loan lest the city go bankrupt. Morgan took two days to consider the matter, and then acted with his customary boldness. On the afternoon of Tuesday, October 29, the mayor of New York and other city officials came to the library; and Morgan, sitting at his desk in the West Room, wrote out in his flowing script a commitment to buy thirty million dollars' worth of six percent New York City bonds. How his firm could sell those bonds no one at the moment could be sure. But if conditions improved, the rate of interest would be attractive to anyone who had money to spare. Morgan simply took a chance on the coming of more orderly conditions, and by advertising his own confidence saved the credit of the City of New York.

The second crisis came to a head on the following Saturday and Sunday—the second and third of November.

This crisis came about from the fact that a prominent firm of brokers, called Moore & Schley, was in danger of collapse. The fear was that its failure might set off a chain reaction of brokerage failures. The firm had borrowed a lot of money on time loans and it was short of cash with which to meet them.

Now it happened that the firm's head, one Grant B. Schley, was also a member of a syndicate which owned a large majority of the stock of one of the lesser steel companies, known as Tennessee Coal & Iron. The syndicate had bought this stock through Moore & Schley with money largely borrowed through Moore & Schley, which accordingly held a great many of the Tennessee Coal & Iron stock certificates as collateral. Moore & Schley had in turn been borrowing money from various banks, and had used some of these Tennessee Coal & Iron certificates as collateral to secure the loans. And now some of the banks were getting restive; for Tennessee Coal & Iron stock, whatever its normal value might be, was a very inactive security. If a block of it were suddenly thrown on the market during panic times, it might wait long for a purchaser. Meanwhile Moore & Schley desperately needed cash. So somebody—probably Colonel Oliver Payne, who was also a member of the syndicate which owned this Tennessee stock—had a brainstorm.

The Tennessee Coal & Iron Company, he reflected, was a competitor—though a small one—of the United States Steel Corporation. There had been some talk of the Steel Corporation's buying control of Tennessee, though Morgan, when the proposition had been put to him, had turned it down, saying that the price of the Tennessee shares was too high. But perhaps the Steel Corporation would not be wholly uninterested now. And if the Steel Corporation should buy control of Tennessee Coal & Iron by exchanging its bonds for Tennessee stock, the results would be wonderful. Steel Corporation bonds were practically as good as cash. They could be substituted for the Tennessee stock as collateral in the banks. The credit of Moore & Schley would be restored. And, what was more, the rescue of Moore & Schley would have been accomplished without tying up cash for any long period.

On Saturday morning, November 2, Morgan was visited at the library by Lewis Cass Ledyard, who was attorney for

Colonel Payne. Ledyard explained this ingenious scheme to Morgan, who at once embraced it. And once having backed the idea, he drove ahead with it relentlessly, summoning Gary and the finance committee of the Steel Corporation and sweeping them into acceptance of the plan.

On that evening the battle against the panic came to its climax. Morgan had conceived a plan. In the West Room of the library he assembled the presidents of the trust companies once more. In the East Room were the heads of the national banks and other assorted financiers. He, Gary, and a few other men had withdrawn for the occasion into the librarian's office, a small room opposite the entrance. During the evening his plan developed: he would undertake to see that the Steel Corporation bought Tennessee Coal & Iron (obligating his own firm, temporarily, for the twenty-five millions or so that this would require)—thus saving Moore & Schley and removing the immediate pressure of danger from the stock market—*if* the trust companies would raise a further fund of twenty-five million dollars to meet their own emergencies.

The men at this session had been brought together again and again, and had been compelled, against all the dictates of prudence, to subscribe money which they felt their banks could ill spare. Again and again the meetings had lasted till long after midnight. How much longer must this recurring nightmare continue among the rare editions and the gorgeous tapestries and the Renaissance masterpieces?

That evening Benjamin Strong dozed off to sleep on a lounge in the East Room. He had last been to bed on Thursday night. All Friday night he had been reexamining the financial condition of the Trust Company of America. At last he was called to make his report to Morgan; and then, feeling that he might reasonably leave, he went to the front door to go home. It was locked. Morgan had the key in his pocket; this was a conference which no one was allowed to walk out on.

The trust company heads, in the West Room, were reluctant to put up another twenty-five millions. The talk went on and on. At last Morgan walked into the West Room and confronted them. He had with him a document which provided that each trust company would put up its share of the twenty-five million dollars. One of his lawyers read it aloud, then laid it on the table.

"There you are, gentlemen," said Morgan.

No one stepped forward.

Morgan put his hand on the shoulder of Edward King, the dean of the group. "There's the place, King," he said firmly. "And here's the pen." And he put a gold pen in King's hand.

King signed. Then they all signed.

Morgan had carried the day. It was a quarter to five in the morning.

The conferences on the terms of the purchase of Tennessee by the Steel Corporation went on late into Sunday night. Gary refused to consent to a purchase which might make the Steel Corporation subject to government prosecution under the Anti-Trust Act without consulting the President of the United States; so Gary and Frick made a night journey by special train to Washington to talk with President Roosevelt. They met the President Monday morning after breakfast and gave him a quick summary of the situation. Roosevelt said he would interpose no objection. It was not until three or four minutes before ten on Monday morning, November 4, that the Morgan office heard, over a telephone line open to the White House, that the President had said okay, permitting the announcement of the Tennessee deal to be made just as the Stock Exchange opened.

The news had the expected effect. The market rallied.

There would still be runs on banks, minor bank failures, and a short but emphatic slump in American business. But the corner had been turned. Now one could honestly say that the panic was over.

The lesson of the panic of 1907 was clear, though not for some six years was it destined to be embodied in legislation: the United States needed a central banking system, which could build up reserves to be disposed where they were most needed. To the extent that a single man could exercise the functions of a central banking system, Morgan had done this. He had been, as it were, a one-man Federal Reserve Bank.

Not by reason of the wealth of his firm; for though this was great, it could meet only a small fraction of the demands that developed. Not by reason of any special inventiveness on Morgan's part; other men worked up the plans while he sat at his card table. His unique power in the crisis derived partly from the sense in men's minds that if his leadership failed, the whole financial world would go to ruin. It derived partly from his organizing ability; partly from the fact that men trusted him as they would nobody else of comparable authority to work for the general interest; but it derived mostly from his courage. At a time when the almost universal instinct was to pull one's own chestnuts out of the fire, to escape new commitments, he risked everything, again and again.

It is said that one banker told Morgan during the panic, "I am very much disturbed; I am below my legal reserve."

Morgan answered, "You ought to be ashamed of yourself to be anywhere near your legal reserve. What is your reserve for at a time like this except to use?"

Chapter 13

Envoi

AFTER THE PANIC OF 1907, Morgan's absences from business became longer. His annual trips abroad now sometimes extended to six months or more. He liked to be on the move, and would shift back and forth between London, Paris, Aix-les-Bains, Rome, Monte Carlo, or Venice, spending a few days in each place. As always, he enjoyed having a party with him, and the overtones of grandeur still sounded: in Rome he had audiences with the Queen Mother of Italy and with the Pope; in England Queen Alexandra came to Prince's Gate to inspect his art collection. An aging international personage, Morgan liked to surround himself with companions, old or new, familiar or glittering, though often he said little at the gatherings, preferring to smoke and listen and perhaps doze while the others talked; he appreciated the company of Salvatore Cortesi, the Associated Press correspondent in Rome, because Cortesi could drive with him for hours about the streets without saying a word.

If you would see the Morgan of those last years in your mind's eye, picture a somewhat bulky old gentleman, six feet tall, seating himself in an armchair in a Grand Hotel sitting room and pulling toward him a card table on which is a silver box containing two packs of cards. He is rather formally dressed, with a wing collar, ascot tie, and white waistcoat. He sits solidly, his weight forward on his feet, his toes turned out, Chun, his Pekinese dog, curled up beside him. Or picture him in London, wearing a silk hat and a velvet-collared overcoat, entering the Bond Street galleries to inspect an assortment of objects of art, including a famous panel of Flemish tapestry. Morgan looks them over carefully and asks, "How much for the stack?" The dealer names a sum in six figures, to which Morgan replies, "Right," and not only the tapestry but all the other exquisite things are his. Or watch Morgan sitting with Cortesi in the anteroom of the Borgia apartment at the Vatican, waiting for a talk with the Papal Secretary of State, Cardinal Merry del Val. For once Morgan talks volubly, pointing out to Cortesi the masterly handling of light and shade in the frescoes by Pinturicchio. A messenger from the cardinal comes in with apologies for the delay; Morgan sends word that the cardinal must not mind, that he is perfectly happy and only wishes that he had a bed so that he could lie on his back for hours and study the frescoes the better.

At home, in the West Room of the library, Morgan goes over the morning's mail, sorting it into two piles, the letters that must be attended to and those that can wait. Belle da Costa Greene, the devoted young librarian, remonstrates with him at the size of the pile of letters that can wait. He answers that if you leave letters alone long enough, they "die out." After a while he asks Miss Greene to read aloud to him from the Bible, and requests the story of Jonah and the whale. She asks him if he really believes it. He answers that he does; that if the time ever came when he could not believe every word in the Bible, he could believe none of it. . . . At times he sits motionless in the red plush chair while cigar ashes fall on his waistcoat and the cigar goes out; the minutes go by and still he does not move; his eyes are far away as he sits there lost in thought.

"I HAVE LENT MILLIONS TO MEN WHO HADN'T A CENT."

HOW MORGAN WENT THROUGH HIS DAY ON WITNESS STAND

(Special to The World.)
WASHINGTON, Dec. 19.—J. Pierpont Morgan got acquainted with the members of the Money Trust investigating committee this afternoon. He became almost intimate withe Samuel Untermyer, the committee's counsel, whom he had watched suspiciously during the early hours of the examination.

When Mr. Morgan took the stand yesterday he was extremely nervous, and this nervousness was reflected in the attitude of his daughter, Mrs. Herbert Satterlee, and "Jack," as her son sat behind him. When he took the stand this morning it was evident that much of Mr. Morgan's former nervousness had left him. He smiled at the committee and its counsel and signified that he was ready for business.

MR. MORGAN WITH HIS SON AND DAUGHTER; SNAPSHOT TAKEN IN WASHINGTON.

Left to Right—MRS HERBERT SATTERLEE, DAUGHTER of J. P. MORGAN, J. PIERPONT MORGAN and HIS SON, J. P. MORGAN JR. ENTERING the HOUSE OFFICE BUILDING YESTERDAY.

Representative Arsène Pujo of Louisiana, chairman of the House subcommittee that in 1912 investigated money trusts in the U.S. Left, J. P. Morgan testifying before the committee.

In the very last years he would visit the office only to talk with his partners for a few minutes and lunch with them. His son, Jack—J. P. Morgan, Jr.—would one of these days be taking over the senior partnership, with Charles Steele as elder adviser. During these last years, the influence of the firm would become even more pervasive than before, partly as a consequence of Morgan's acknowledged leadership in the panic of 1907.

For a generation Morgan and George F. Baker, the be-whiskered chief of the First National Bank, had been hand in glove. Three Morgan partners sat on the board of the First National, and in enterprise after enterprise the Morgan and Baker banks joined forces. Both concerns had been interested in the Bankers Trust Company, founded in 1903 on the initiative of Henry P. Davison, who was then a vice-president in Baker's bank and later became a Morgan partner. Either or both Morgan and Baker also stood back of the Guaranty Trust Company, the Astor Trust Company, the Liberty National Bank, the Chemical Bank, and the National Bank of Commerce. And after 1907 the cool and silent James Stillman, who as head of the great National City Bank had previously been regarded principally as an ally of Rockefeller's Standard Oil group, drew closer to Morgan. Morgan became a stockholder in the National City Bank, and his son became a director of it.

All in all, one could reasonably say that the Morgan-Baker-Stillman influence was strongly felt in most of the important banks of New York, and from banking it spread into insurance. In 1909, after a series of scandals had rocked the insurance business, Morgan acquired controlling stock in the Equitable Life Insurance Company from Thomas Fortune Ryan. He offered a quarter interest in his investment to Baker and another to Still-man, if at any time they should care to buy these fractions. His object was to put the Equitable, which was a huge purchaser of securities, into "safe hands."

During the Pujo Committee's investigation in 1912, Samuel Untermyer, the committee counsel, questioned Morgan re-lentlessly about the fact that Morgan had paid such a high price for the Equitable stock that it would yield him only a small fraction of one percent on his investment. Why had he been willing to pay so much, Untermyer wanted to know; and why had he wanted to buy control of the Equitable company anyhow?

"Because I thought it was a desirable thing for the situation to do that," said Morgan.

"But that is very general, Mr. Morgan, when you speak of 'the situation.' Was not the stock safe enough in Mr. Ryan's hands?"

"I suppose it was," answered Morgan. "I thought it was greatly improved by being in the hands of myself and these two gentlemen [Baker and Stillman], provided I asked them to do so."

Untermyer persisted with his questions, and in due course Morgan remarked that he had thought the purchase was "good business." The colloquy went on:

UNTERMYER: Where is the good business, then, in buying a security that only pays one-ninth of one percent?
MORGAN: Because I thought it was better there than it was where it was. That is all.
UNTERMYER: Was anything the matter with it in the hands of Mr. Ryan?
MORGAN: Nothing.
UNTERMYER: In what respect would it be better where it is than with him?
MORGAN: That is the way it struck me.

And a little later:

UNTERMYER: Did Mr. Ryan offer this stock to you?
MORGAN: I asked him to sell it to me. . . .
UNTERMYER: What did he say when you told him you would like to have it, and you thought you ought to have it?
MORGAN: He hesitated about it, and finally sold it.

When the Pujo Committee made its report, at the conclusion of its hearings in 1912-13, and proclaimed its discovery of the existence of the "money trust," it was able to produce statistics showing that if you lumped together the Morgan partners and the directors of the First National and National City banks and the Bankers Trust Company and the Guaranty Trust Company, you had a group of men who between them held—

118 directorships in 34 banks and trust companies
30 directorships in 10 insurance companies
105 directorships in 32 transportation companies
63 directorships in 24 producing and trading corporations
25 directorships in 12 public utility corporations

making, in all, 341 directorships in 112 corporations with aggregate resources or capitalization of over twenty-two billion dollars. And of these 341 directorships, the members of the firm of J. P. Morgan & Co. held no less than 72.

According to the Pujo Committee report: "The acts of this inner group . . . have . . . been more destructive of competition than anything accomplished by the trusts, for they strike at the very vitals of potential competition in every industry that is under their protection, a condition which if permitted to continue will render impossible all attempts to restore normal competitive conditions in the industrial world."

But Morgan denied that the firm exercised any controlling authority by means of these directorships. He even went so far as to deny that voting trusts exercised such authority. One case in point was the Southern Railway, in which Morgan, as a member of the voting trust, year after year chose the directors. Untermyer asked him whether he was not in effect dealing with himself when the firm of J. P. Morgan agreed with the officials of the Southern Railway on the prices at which its securities should be issued to the public. "I do not think so," said Morgan. "We do not deal with ourselves."

"Let us see if you do not," persisted Untermyer. "The voting trustees name the board, do they not?"

MORGAN: But when you have elected the board, then the board is independent of the voting trustees.
UNTERMYER: You think, therefore, that where you name a board of directors who remain in existence only a year and you have the power to name another board next year, that this board . . . is in an independent position to deal with your banking house, as would a board named by the stockholders themselves?

MORGAN: I think it would be better.

UNTERMYER: You think it is a great deal better?

MORGAN: Yes, sir.

UNTERMYER: Will you tell us why?

MORGAN: Simply because we select the best people we can find for the positions.

Questioned as to his alleged control of banks, he insisted likewise that the presence of Morgan partners on the boards did not mean control. They were usually in a minority, and in a few banks. "There is no question of control," said he, "unless you have got a majority of the directors . . . in all banks."

He was, of course, overstating a valid point. The House of Morgan exercised a strong and in some matters a determining influence, not only in the councils of many banks but in the affairs of many railroads and industrial corporations. A handful of strongly placed men with similar points of view produced an association of interest that was much too informal to be labeled a "money trust," but that nevertheless was a nucleus of indefinable yet substantial power over a considerable sector of the national economy.

MORGAN'S LAST YEARS brought many discouragements. The concept of social justice which had been making steady headway since the turn of the century had brought with it a popular distrust of great wealth and great economic power. The muckraking journalists and novelists—Ida M. Tarbell with her history of the Standard Oil Company, Lincoln Steffens with his *Shame of the Cities*, Upton Sinclair with his portrayal of the horrors of the meat-packing houses in *The Jungle*—all had dramatized the sins of big business and the influence of money on political life. Reform politicians like Robert La Follette of Wisconsin and Hiram Johnson of California had learned to turn public indignation to practical administrative and legislative use. More and more laws to regulate business were being written. So marked was the steady change in the political climate that, even after the very conservative Taft succeeded Roosevelt in the White House in 1909, the number of prosecu-

TREASURES
FROM THE MORGAN
COLLECTION

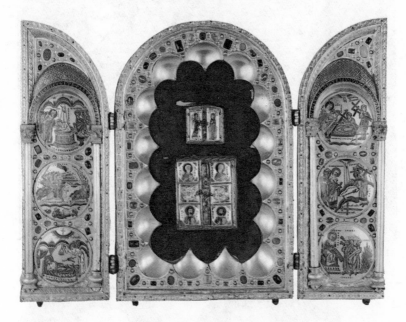

THE STAVELOT TRIPTYCH
A portable altar made about 1150 for the abbot of Stavelot.
The center section contains fragments of
wood and a nail reputed to be from the True Cross.

1.

2.

1.
MADONNA AND CHILD
ENTHRONED
WITH THE SAINTS
by Raphael

2.
Small wedding portraits
of Martin Luther and his wife
by Lucas Cranach the Elder

3.
French pilgrim bottle, about 1585

4.
LADY ELIZABETH DELMÉ
AND HER CHILDREN
by Sir Joshua Reynolds

5.
The star sapphire called
STAR OF INDIA

4.

5.

3.

tions of large companies for restraint of trade increased sharply. The Pujo investigation, shortly after Woodrow Wilson's election in 1912, was but one of many signs that the public at large no longer trusted the men who ran big business.

Morgan could not understand the change. When, in 1911, the federal government brought suit against his own child, the Steel Corporation, under the antitrust laws (a suit which the corporation later won), the news was a body blow. "Well, it has come to this!" he exclaimed sadly to Satterlee, and sat long brooding over this public affront. In April 1912, when the *Titanic*, pride of his International Mercantile Marine, sank with great loss of life, he was appalled that some people were charging that a Morgan-directed policy of economy was reponsible for the disaster. When he was called to Washington in the fall of 1912 to testify before the Clapp Committee on his campaign contributions of earlier years, and then to face the Pujo Committee with its money-trust allegations, his depression deepened.

Shortly after his sessions with the Pujo Committee, though very tired and nervous, he was off once more to Europe and Egypt. Just before his departure Colonel George Harvey, of *Harper's Weekly*, who had for a time been a backer of Woodrow Wilson, came to see Morgan in the library, and in the course of their talk quoted the lines, *"Who never to himself hath said, This is my own, my native land!"*

Morgan sat still for a full half minute, his eyes far away, and then said to Harvey, "When you see Mr. Wilson, tell him from me that if there should ever come a time when he thinks any influence or resources that I have can be used for my country, they are wholly at his disposal." He was thinking, perhaps, of his gold purchase for Grover Cleveland in 1895, and wondering whether ever again his government would call upon him except to answer charges of interference with the public interest.

In Egypt, where his daughter Louisa Satterlee accompanied him, he was in miserable health. He decided to return to more familiar scenes, and got as far as Rome. There he took a turn for the worse. He summoned up strength to go to church on Easter Day; thereafter his strength rapidly deteriorated.

On the evening of March 30, 1913, his mind wandered. Louisa

and her husband—who had hurried abroad in response to an urgent cable—gathered from fragments of his talk that he was back in the old days at Hartford and Vevey. At last they heard him say, "I've got to go up the hill!" He did not speak again; and just after noon the next day he died, at the age of not quite seventy-six.

AFTER MORGAN'S GREAT FUNERAL at St. George's in New York, there were many who said that the Pujo investigation had killed him. Certainly something had gone out of him after those sessions in Washington. Yet it is possible that he had not had long to live in any case. And truly there was drama in his being thus called to account at the very conclusion of his life.

Many of those present on that December day of 1912, listening as Morgan sat in the witness chair at the committee table and submitted hour after hour to interrogation, must have felt that, regardless of his denials, he actually had come to exercise a dangerously extensive authority. Yet even as they felt this, I wonder if some of these listeners did not sense the man's moral weight, and ask themselves to what extent his own rise to power may have illustrated the point he was so vehemently making: that what mattered in any business was the caliber of the men involved.

Over and over he stated this conviction, but never more effectively than in the passage already quoted at the beginning of this book:

"Is not commercial credit based primarily upon money or property?" asked Untermyer.

"No, sir," said Morgan. "The first thing is character."

"Before money or property?"

"Before money or anything else. Money cannot buy it. . . . Because a man I do not trust could not get money from me on all the bonds in Christendom."

ACKNOWLEDGMENTS

The condensations in this volume have been created by The Reader's Digest Association, Inc., and are used by permission of and special arrangement with the publishers and the holders of the respective copyrights.
ABRAHAM LINCOLN: The Prairie Years: copyright © 1925, 1926 by The Pictorial Review Company, © renewed 1953, 1954 by Carl Sandburg, and copyright 1926 by Harcourt Brace Jovanovich, Inc., © renewed 1954 by Carl Sandburg, is reprinted by permission of Harcourt Brace Jovanovich, Inc.
ANNE FRANK: The Diary of a Young Girl: first published in Holland in 1947, copyright © 1952, © renewed 1980 by Otto H. Frank, is reprinted by permission of Doubleday & Company, Inc., and Vallentine, Mitchell & Co. Ltd.
PROPHET IN THE WILDERNESS: The Story of Albert Schweitzer: copyright © 1947 by Hermann Hagedorn, © renewed 1975 by Dorothy Oakley Hagedorn, Dorothea Hagedorn Parfit, and Mary Hagedorn Duvall, is reprinted by permission of The Macmillan Publishing Company. Quotations from Dr. Schweitzer's writings in *Prophet in the Wilderness* are taken from: *On the Edge of the Primeval Forest & More from the Primeval Forest*, copyright © 1931 by The Macmillan Publishing Company, © renewed 1959 by Albert Schweitzer; *Out of My Life and Thought*, copyright © 1933, 1949, © renewed 1961 by Holt, Rinehart and Winston, Inc.; *The Philosophy of Civilization*, published by The Macmillan Publishing Company.
THE GREAT PIERPONT MORGAN: copyright © 1948, 1949 by Frederick Lewis Allen, © renewed 1976, 1977 by Agnes Rogers Allen, is reprinted by permission of Harper & Row, Publishers, Inc.

ILLUSTRATION CREDITS

COVER: top left, Pach Bros./Bettmann Archive; top right, Erica Anderson/The Albert Schweitzer Center, Great Barrington, Massachusetts; bottom left, John Falter; bottom right, Anne Frank Foundation, Amsterdam.
ANNE FRANK: The Diary of a Young Girl: *Pages 280, 283, 291, 292, 303, 307, 316, 323, 332, 345, 384, 389*: Anne Frank Foundation, Amsterdam. *292*: illustration by Frank Crump.
PROPHET IN THE WILDERNESS: The Story of Albert Schweitzer: *Pages 420, 427, 443, 461, 469, 475, 489, 497*: photos by Erica Anderson/The Albert Schweitzer Center, Great Barrington, Massachusetts.
THE GREAT PIERPONT MORGAN: *Page 504:* 1906, by Edward Steichen; photogravure from *Camera Work*; Collection of The Museum of Modern Art, New York, Gift of A. Conger Goodyear. *507:* Pierpont Morgan at Göttingen, 1857; The Pierpont Morgan Library. *518, 540* bottom, *604* center, *630* center, *635:* The Pierpont Morgan Library. *540:* paintings of *Corsair I* and *II* by Ted Lodigensky. *553* top: cartoon, The New York Public Library Picture Collection. *553* lower left corner of game: cartoon of Theodore Roosevelt from *Cartoons Magazine,* published by *Popular Mechanics. 553* bottom: © Ezra Stoller (ESTO); The Pierpont Morgan Library. *575* inset: portrait of Grover Cleveland; photo: Charles Phelps Cushing. *575* bottom: Charles Phelps Cushing. *589* center, left to right: Andrew Carnegie, photo courtesy Carnegie Corporation of New York; John D. Rockefeller, Sr. and Jr., AP/Wide World. *589* bottom: copyright 1899 by J.S. Johnston, N.Y., copied by The Mariners Museum, Newport News, Va. *604* top: painting by Deane Kate. *619:* Wall Street During the Panic, 1907; The Pierpont Morgan Library. *630* bottom left and right: Brown Brothers. *636, 637:* No. 1, The Metropolitan Museum of Art, gift of J. Pierpont Morgan, 1916, (16.30); 2 and 3, The Pierpont Morgan Library; 4, National Gallery of Art, Washington, Andrew W. Mellon Collection; 5, photo courtesy of The American Museum of Natural History.